[Learning and Cognition]

[Learning and Cognition]

The Design of the Mind

MICHAEL E. MARTINEZ

University of California, Irvine

Merrill
Upper Saddle River, New Jersey
Columbus, Ohio

Vice President and Executive Publisher: *Jeffery W. Johnston*
Publisher: *Kevin Davis*
Director of Marketing: *Quinn Perkson*
Editorial Assistant: *Lauren Reinkober*
Marketing Manager: *Krista Clark*
Production Editor: *Gregory Erb*
Editorial Production Service: *Nesbitt Graphics, Inc.*
Composition Buyer: *Linda Cox*
Manufacturing Buyer: *Megan Cochran*
Interior Design: *Nesbitt Graphics, Inc.*
Cover Designer: *Linda Knowles*

Library of Congress Cataloging-in-Publication Data
Martinez, Michael E.
 Learning and cognition: the design of the mind /
Michael E. Martinez.
    p. cm.
 ISBN 0-205-50724-7 (alk. paper)
 1. Learning, Psychology of. 2. Cognition. I. Title.

 BF318.M373 2010
 153--dc22

                    2008047650

This book was set in Minion by Nesbitt Graphics, Inc.. It was printed and bound by Bind-Rite Graphics.
The cover was printed by Phoenix Color Corporation/Hagerstown.

Pearson® is a registered trademark of Pearson plc
Merrill® is a registered trademark of Pearson Education, Inc.

Pearson Education Ltd.   Pearson Education Australia Pty. Limited
Pearson Education Singapore Pte. Ltd.   Pearson Education North Asia Ltd.
Pearson Education Canada, Ltd.   Pearson Educación de Mexico, S.A. de C.V.
Pearson Education—Japan   Pearson Education Malaysia Pte. Ltd.

10 9 8 7 6 5 4 3 2 1

Merrill
is an imprint of

www.pearsonhighered.com

ISBN 13: 978-0-205-50724-5
ISBN 10: 0-205-50724-7

MICHAEL E. MARTINEZ is Professor of Education at the University of California, Irvine. He teaches courses on learning and cognition, and on intelligence, at both undergraduate and graduate levels.

Dr. Martinez received his Ph.D. in educational psychology from Stanford University in 1987. He subsequently joined the research staff of the Educational Testing Service in Princeton, New Jersey, where he developed new forms of computer-based testing for assessment in science, architecture, and engineering. This work resulted in two U.S. patents.

As a faculty member at UC Irvine, Dr. Martinez conducts research primarily on the nature and modifiability of intelligence. He has published in such journals as the *Educational Psychologist* and the *Journal of Educational Measurement*. His publications include the book *Education as the Cultivation of Intelligence*, published in 2000.

Dr. Martinez was awarded a Fulbright Scholarship at the University of the South Pacific in the Fiji Islands (1994–1995). He served as Program Director for the National Science Foundation (2001–2002). His honors include appointments as a College Board Visiting Scholar (2002–2003), a Mellon Visiting Scholar at Columbia University (2003–2004), and the Presidential Commendation for Contributions to Psychology from the American Psychological Association (2003).

BRIEF CONTENTS

CONTENTS

CHAPTER

[**6**] Emotion, Motivation, and Volition   153

PART TWO

DEVELOPING MINDS 191

CHAPTER

[7] Cognitive Development Through the Life Span 191

CHAPTER

[8] The Brain and Cognition   **233**

PART THREE

HOW MINDS DIFFER   272

CHAPTER

[9] Assessment and Individual Differences   272

PREFACE

At times, the horizons of the human intellect seem to stretch on forever. We need all the powers of the human mind if we are to defeat the vicious problems that confront humanity, and to nurture creativity and discovery in the arts, engineering, science, and medicine. Every compelling vision of the future requires capable minds that work together to achieve positive ends.

Fortunately, human cultures have devised programs to promote the mind's rational and creative abilities. Those programs collectively are called *education*, but their manifestations are diverse. Education can take the form of direct personal apprenticeship as practiced from prehistoric times to the present, the dialogic search for fundamental truth that characterized ancient Athens, or the formal curricula that are the mainstays of schools and universities today.

But to recognize diverse forms of education is not to say that they are adequate for the future. Educators and the broader public fully recognize that education must be more effective now than ever before. Today's citizens must be smarter, more knowledgeable, and more creative than previous generations. What will it take to accomplish this? How can education become more effective so that current and future learners will be far more capable than those of the past? A key answer, I believe, is that we need a far greater understanding of the nature and operation of the human mind. After all, if education is intended to develop the mind's capability, then only through a deep understanding of the mind can we chart an optimal course for its development.

For more than a century now, scholars from diverse disciplines have tried to discover the nature of learning, reasoning, problem solving, and intelligence. The cumulative work of theorists and researchers has paid off. Although many mysteries remain, we now know quite a lot about how the mind works. In writing this book, I have tried to organize what we know about the workings of the human mind into a story that is compelling, engaging, and applicable in a multitude of ways.

Writing a book is difficult! Inevitably, it's a massive project that requires a degree of commitment that is easily underestimated at the start. Commitment is required not only of the author, but also from a host of others. Every author knows that writing a book is a collective effort that draws on the generosity, goodwill, and talents of many remarkable people. Special thanks go to Karen Brown, Wayne Brown, Judi Conroy, Janice Hansen, Amy Martinez, Kiely Martinez, Stephanie Martinez, Jamie Stein, Dianna Townsend, Andrea Travisano, Philip Travisano, and Scott Wood. Thank you all!

I also thank reviewers who offered thoughtful comments on my manuscript:

Stacey Duffield, *North Dakota State University*
Linda Metzke, *Lyndon State College*
Ted Miller, *University of Tennessee, Chattanooga*
David Rapp, *Northwestern University*
Mariana Vasilyeva, *Boston College*
Janet Whitley, *Tarleton State University*

Finally, I want to recognize my colleagues, friends, and family members for their substantive contributions to this book as well as their encouragement.

Michael E. Martinez
Irvine, California

[Learning and Cognition]

[1] Introduction

This book is about the human mind. Its purpose is to show how knowledge of the mind's design can lead to improved thinking and learning. This purpose assumes that by understanding the mind we can more effectively guide its development—development that includes the acquisition of knowledge as well as the ability to think well. If this assumption proves to be correct, then we have a promising basis for the improvement of education.

But can the mind really understand itself? The goal of understanding the mind *with the mind* hints of an internal contradiction. Logically, an inquiring mind ought to be in some sense superior to its object of study. Perhaps the mind has met its match in trying to comprehend itself. Indeed, at the end of this book you will see that although we know much about the human mind, much more is not yet understood. Our illumination is real but only partial. The mind remains significantly mysterious.

Four Paradigms

To present a balanced picture of learning and thinking, this book introduces several different theories or paradigms that illuminate the workings of the mind. Somewhat paradoxically, the first paradigm to be considered is **behaviorism** (Chapter 2), which in its strictest form does not consider the mind or mental processes to be legitimate concepts. Instead, behaviorism concentrates on behavior alone. This focus contrasts sharply with the paradigm at the core of this book—that of cognitive theory—which deals directly with thinking. Historically, behaviorism preceded cognitive theory and in some ways gave rise to it. To understand how we have arrived at our current cognitive understanding of the mind, its predecessor must be considered. Behaviorism is important to our inquiry for an additional reason: It has left a deep mark on education and on parenting practices, as well as on how the larger culture thinks about the causes and control of human behavior. Although it has been largely superseded, behaviorism lives on.

The second and central paradigm of this book—**cognitive information-processing theory**—places mental activity at the focus of interest. Drawing on a computer metaphor, the theory examines parallels between the way the human mind processes information and the operation of a digital computer. This paradigm is detailed in Chapter 3, *The Cognitive Architecture*, but it also weaves through most of the other chapters. The comparison of the mind to a computer can carry us quite far. It recognizes that minds, like computers, have different kinds of memory. The computer metaphor also helps to define mental processes in terms of information flow through the system. For example, it presents learning as the formation of an enduring trace in long-term memory.

The cognitive approach is powerful, but in the end it cannot do full justice to exploring what the mind really is or how it works. Other paradigms are necessary. For that reason, Chapter 4, *Theories of Knowledge*, employs multiple disciplinary lenses to secure a more complex understanding of the human mind. The chapter shows that human knowledge has been the subject of inquiry from many different disciplinary angles through the centuries. Beginning with philosophy in ancient times, the nature of knowledge has also been explored by scholars from the fields of semiotics, linguistics, artificial intelligence, and anthropology, as well as psychology. Each discipline gained insights previously uncovered by the other disciplines.

Building on the previous two chapters, Chapter 5, *Complex Cognition*, considers the higher-order mental processes that seem to set humans apart from other species. This chapter shows how the cognitive architecture gives rise to complex forms of thinking, including problem solving and critical thinking. Importantly, the chapter also considers how complex cognition can be promoted as an essential goal of education.

Chapter 6, *Motivation, Volition, and Emotion*, explores how emotional and motivational states can support or inhibit learning, as well as how volition (willful behavior) can sustain learning over the long term. Chapter 7, *Cognitive Development Through the Life Span*, shifts the focus to how cognition changes through maturation over the course of many years. *Development* is the term used for change processes that are clearly part of a child's maturation as well as an adult's intellectual growth, including the transition toward expertise.

Neuroscience, the third major paradigm, is gaining ground as a powerful approach to understanding the human mind and behavior. Chapter 8, *The Brain and Cognition*, shows how research on the brain presents a fascinating picture of biology's effect on cognition and provides insights from brain science that are uniquely important. The study of the brain connects profitably to cognitive theory; a major goal for cognitive neuroscientists is to find connections between thought processes and brain structures. Several important connections—between brain regions and reading skills, for example—have been discovered in recent years.

The fourth major paradigm is **psychometric theory.** Each of us has encountered the psychometric point of view from the earliest days of our school experience. Whenever we take a test and receive a numeric score, the test gains its legitimacy (at least partly) from the psychometric paradigm. We tend to accept that the test score has meaning and that it really indicates how much knowledge or skill we have. These assumptions have amplified importance in today's political climate. The current federal policy for educational reform relies heavily on testing to promote specific goals. As the technical basis for testing, the psychometric paradigm presents the point of view that qualities of the mind can be measured accurately along particular dimensions. The psychometric paradigm is introduced in Chapter 9, *Assessment and Individual Differences*, where some of the most important ideas underlying the measurement of differences among learners will be surveyed. Equally important, we will consider what those individual differences imply for teaching. Chapter 10 explores what is arguably the most studied psychometric quality, *Intelligence*. The chapter presents several competing theories of intelligence and asks to what degree intelligence is fixed or modifiable. We will consider whether the orbit of educational outcomes could widen to include developing a more intelligent mind. Perhaps human intelligence could be cultivated through educational experience.

This book builds upon several distinct theories that have been developed over the course of centuries (in the case of the philosophy of knowledge), decades (in the case of cognitive psychology), and years (in the case of detailed brain imaging). A comprehensive survey of the mind demands attention to several different theories—a multidisciplinary framework is essential. As we deepen our understanding of learning and cognition through these paradigms, we will comprehend more fully how to advance learning and cognition.

Where Does Education Take Place?

Although this book's primary purpose is to illuminate the *nature* of the mind, it also has a practical goal—to guide the *improvement* of the mind. The theories presented here succeed to the degree that readers become more effective thinkers and can help others to use their minds more effectively. This purpose is vital to one of society's most important functions—education. But let's be careful not to assume that we have a good sense of what the word *education* means. In everyday conversation, education is usually equated with schooling or what occurs during prescribed hours in school buildings. This way of thinking about education may be too narrow.

Perhaps we need to think of education, as well as human development in general, more broadly as extending into multiple life contexts, including the home and the larger community (Bronfenbrenner, 1993; Gordon & Bridglall, 2006). Conversations with parents or with peers might well have educational value for the knowledge, beliefs, and ways of thinking that they convey. Similarly, getting involved in community activities, reading independently, and thinking through personal challenges all have potential educational value. The forces that shape the mind's growth—how we learn to think and gain knowledge—exist not only in schools and classrooms but also in multiple contexts. We should therefore regard education as available through many channels of experience.

What Exactly Is Education?

What qualities give experience educational value? To answer that question, consider the insights of John Dewey, the preeminent American philosopher of education. In his landmark book *Experience and Education*, Dewey (1938) saw the potential for any experience to be educational, whether it took place in a school or elsewhere. For Dewey, however, not every experience was educational. To have educational value, an experience had to meet the criterion of **continuity**.

By *continuity*, Dewey referred to the potential of an experience to live on profitably in the future. If knowledge or skill has value only in the school context, then it lacks continuity. It is good only for use in the school and in the present, perhaps only to obtain a good grade. However, when a child gains knowledge or skill that is profitable in the future—and that *lives on* through its usefulness—then that experience is truly educational. The mere acquisition of static knowledge—unchanging facts meant to be dutifully memorized—is unlikely to meet this criterion (Berliner, 2006). Experiences in a school setting might have continuity or they might not. The same is true for experiences outside school. Whether such experiences are educational depend on whether they have value for the future.

What enduring beneficial outcomes can be derived from educational experiences? We might initially consider *conceptual knowledge* to be the primary outcome of education. Knowledge is certainly vital. Chapter 7 describes how expert performance in any field depends on having a very substantial knowledge base. However, knowledge is not the only valuable product of education. Skilled capability, sometimes called *procedural knowledge*, is also valuable. Still other qualities of an educated mind are highly important. One such outcome of education is the ability to *think well*. To think well is not obviously a direct manifestation of knowledge. It is closer to a skill, but even this does not capture fully what is meant by the ability to think well. Proficient thinking is manifest in problem solving, creativity, and critical thinking, as well as in an ability to engage in logical reasoning. All supremely important in the twenty-first century (Bereiter, 2002).

Two broad classes of educational outcome—knowledge and the ability to think well—capture much of what we hope for from educational experiences. They also constitute what an educated mind brings to a complex world. The title of this book expresses these two broad mental capabilities in the words **learning** and **cognition**. Education should promote the acquisition of knowledge (learning), but it should also nurture an ever-increasing ability to think well—clearly, creatively, and productively (cognition). This book is intended to present a clear picture of both learning and cognition, and to show how to advance capability in both.

Valued outcomes of education include more than learning and cognition. Ideally, an educated person would have an ability to experience such feelings as curiosity and wonder, and the capacity to pursue goals purposefully and with perseverance—all topics that are explored in the pages of this text. Desirable educational outcomes are diverse and complex. By considering the nature of the human mind in some detail, we can understand more precisely what those desirable outcomes are and how to promote them.

The Design of the Educational Experience

What teaching methods are most effective? During the last one hundred years or so, researchers in education have tried to answer this question. But over time the focus shifted from the teacher to the student. During the mid-twentieth century, many researchers wanted to know what teachers could do to teach more effectively. They focused largely on teacher *behavior*. In what has been called **process-product research**, the central concern was identifying teaching processes that would produce desirable student products, namely, measurable learning (Gage, 1985). Research on classroom processes was significantly directed toward finding optimal teaching methods. The emphasis sprang naturally from the dominant psychological paradigm of the mid-twentieth century, **behaviorism**. From the perspective of behaviorism, the intended outcomes of learning were straightforward: A student was expected to demonstrate certain specific behaviors. The most important leverage point in changing student behavior was assumed to be *teacher* behavior. Teacher actions were thought to lead reliably to student learning outcomes.

How Do Learners Learn?

Toward the end of the twentieth century, educational research shifted toward the learner as the focus of attention (Calfee, 1981; Lagemann, 2000). The change in focus from teacher to student was a consequence of a more widespread paradigm shift in psychology. During the last third of the twentieth century, American psychology moved away from behaviorism and toward a *cognitive* understanding of human beings. The cognitive perspective recognizes thinking, not exclusively behavior, as essential to understanding human nature, accomplishment, and potential. With cognition now legitimized as a field of inquiry, the complexity of educational outcomes could rise to the complexity of the human mind. As a result, the parameters of education become wildly more challenging. Looking *inside* the mind changed everything.

The cognitive revolution in psychology now informs what teaching, learning, thinking, and education are all about. Desirable educational outcomes are definable in terms of what the learner can think and do, and the range of the learner's possible cognition is astonishingly broad. This does not mean that we can ignore what teachers do and focus exclusively on the student. To the contrary, knowledge of effective education is deeply informed by an appreciation for the complexity of cognition in both the student and the teacher (Shulman, 1986). This appreciation deepens as we recognize that social processes between teachers and students, and among students, further enrich the educational experience.

The Design of the Mind

This book is intended to help you develop a deeper understanding of the human mind through multiple theoretical perspectives. The mind has a design—an architecture— that can account for simple acts of memory as well as for complex cognition, including highly creative acts and leaps of scientific or artistic insight. As we delve into the topics of memory, motivation, development, the brain, and intelligence, our study will illuminate the organization and operation of the mind. The question behind the quest is this: What is the design of the mind, and what does that design imply for education?

By gaining a deeper understanding of the human mind, we can apply that knowledge to make the mind a more capable instrument. At first glance, the book's subtitle, *The Design of the Mind*, might seem to emphasize how the mind works. But consider that the word *design* is both a noun and a verb. The mind *has* a design, but it is possible to consider how a mind might be actively *designed* through education. We can use our knowledge of the mind's design to actively *design* the mind—to nurture its development toward greater knowledge, understanding, insight, creativity, and intelligence. There is hardly a more interesting or worthwhile pursuit.

REFERENCES

Bereiter, C. (2002). *Education and mind in the knowledge age.* Mahwah, NJ: Lawrence Erlbaum Associates.

Berliner, D. C. (2006). Educational psychology: Searching for essence throughout a century of influence. In P. A. Alexander & P. H. Winne (Eds.), *Handbook of educational psychology* (2nd ed., pp. 3–27). Mahwah, NJ: Lawrence Erlbaum Associates.

Bronfenbrenner, U. (1993). The ecology of cognitive development. In R. H. Wozniak & K. W. Fischer (Eds.), *Development in context: Acting and thinking in specific environments* (pp. 3–44). Hillsdale, NJ: Lawrence Erlbaum Associates.

Calfee, R. C. (1981). Cognitive psychology and educational practice. In D. C. Berliner (Ed.), *Review of Research in Education* (pp. 3–73). Washington, DC: American Educational Research Association.

Dewey, J. (1938). *Experience and education.* New York: Macmillan.

Gage, N. (1985). *Hard gains in the soft sciences: The case of pedagogy.* Bloomington, IN: Phi Delta Kappa.

Gordon, E. W., & Bridglall, B. L. (2006). *The affirmative development of academic ability.* Lanham, MD: Rowman and Littlefield.

Lagemann, E. C. (2000). *An elusive science: The troubling history of educational research.* Chicago: University of Chicago Press.

Shulman, L. (1986). Those who understand: Knowledge growth in teaching. *Educational Researcher, 15*(2), 4–14.

CHAPTER

[2]

Behaviorism

One particular theoretical framework predominates in this book—the framework of cognitive psychology. From the cognitive perspective, the human mind is appreciated as a personal entity capable of reasoning, solving problems, and learning complex information. The mind also feels emotions and has intentions; it has goals and plans. Almost every chapter of this book holds to the cognitive point of view because such a framework provides the educator with a rich set of concepts and models that can guide the design of learning experiences.

This chapter, however, begins the study of learning through the framework of behaviorism, the historical precursor of modern cognitive psychology. Many behaviorist ideas have strongly influenced education and continue to be used by teachers to this day. Parenting, as well as education, has also been profoundly influenced by behavioristic principles. Even the daily interactions of adults have been touched by the language and concepts taken directly from behaviorist theory.

Why Study Behavior?

Behaviorism is the study of learning in humans and animals as understood through the analysis of behavior rather than thoughts or feelings. It is forbidden, at least in strict forms of behaviorism, to account for learning (understood by behaviorists as changes in *behavior*) by invoking the mind or mentalistic concepts (Ringen, 1999). Accounts of behavior that invoke the organism's goals, wishes, beliefs, choices, will, or hopes are considered to be outside the explanatory norms of behaviorism.

So what counts as an acceptable explanation of behavior? The behaviorist is interested only in what can be observed directly. Legitimate explanations for behavior are therefore restricted to what can be observed objectively, such as what happens to the organism before or after a particular behavioral act.

Advantages and Disadvantages of Behaviorism

As we approach behaviorism, we need to appreciate its advantages as well as its limitations. One advantage of behaviorism over other approaches to understanding learning can be stated succinctly: By focusing strictly on behavior and on objective explanations for behavior, the methodology of behaviorism appears to be scientific. One potential problem with cognitive explanations of behavior is that such concepts as knowledge, goals, and memory are not directly observable. They must be inferred from what people say and do, leading to subjective and possibly incorrect interpretations. But when the discussion is restricted to what the person or animal actually *does*, agreement is much more likely. The early behaviorists, especially John B. Watson (who we will consider later in this chapter), were acutely aware of the methodological advantages of behaviorism as a scientific approach to understanding humans and animals.

Even though there are distinct advantages to approaching human learning and behavior from the viewpoint of behaviorism, there are also definite disadvantages. Consider what it would be like for a teacher never to use mental language—words such as *remember, think, reason, decide, believe*, and so on. Teachers tend to rely on language that is essentially cognitive. Not only teachers, but also everyday people in everyday situations use the language of the mind. Such language is useful. Moreover, theories that accept mental language and place the mind centrally in accounts of education can enrich the learning process substantially. Throughout this book, we will benefit greatly from cognitive theory as we approach the project of education. Nevertheless, our focus in this chapter is on behaviorism—a more conceptually restricted approach that focuses on what is objectively observable, and on explanations that do not appeal to the mind or to the mind's presumed activity.

Classical Conditioning

The title of this section might provoke two questions: What does *classical* mean, and what does *conditioning* mean? To a behaviorist, **conditioning** is a synonym for *learning*, which, in turn, refers to a change in behavior. This way of defining learning seems narrow, but because behaviorists concentrate on external events (e.g., rewards and punishments), not on internal ideas (e.g., knowledge or intentions), the definition fits. Conditioning, then, refers to an enduring change in behavior that results from events in the organism's environment.

What then is the meaning of *classical* in classical conditioning? To answer, it is important to understand that within behaviorism there are two basic approaches to conditioning: *classical* conditioning and *operant* conditioning. Classical conditioning is primarily associated with the Russian physiologist Ivan Pavlov; operant conditioning is primarily associated with the American psychologist B. F. Skinner. Classical and operant conditioning are quite different, and each is very important. Both are relevant to education.

Ivan Pavlov's Discovery

Let's start our study of behaviorism by considering a major discovery by the Russian scientist, Ivan Pavlov. Psychologists sometimes forget that Pavlov was already a famous scientist before he made any contributions to psychology. He was not merely famous; in 1904 he had won the highest achievement possible in the career of a scientist, the Nobel Prize, for discoveries in the physiology of digestion. Pavlov's later discoveries in behaviorism (1927), and in particular his discovery of classical conditioning, occurred after he had proven himself as an eminent scientist in the field of physiology.

The breakthrough event that prompted the theory of classical conditioning took place in Pavlov's laboratory, where experiments on physiology used dogs as subjects. In the late 1890s, Pavlov's research initially focused on the chemistry of dog saliva. The volume of dog spit was carefully calibrated by precisely marked receptacles. Pavlov's lab apparatus was also designed to deliver precise quantities of food to the dog's mouth through a tube (Figure 2.1).

There was a natural connection between the food delivered to the dog through a tube, and the amount of saliva collected from the dog by a different tube. Now consider parallels when one prompted the other. But something else did surprise Pavlov: The

FIGURE 2.1
Pavlov's Dogs *Even a neutral stimulus could prompt salivation.* [Allyn & Bacon]

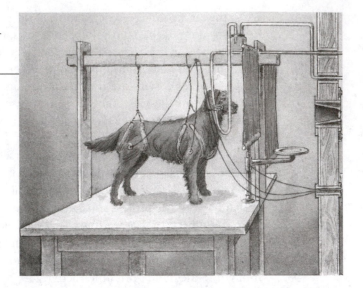

dog sometimes salivated *before* it was given the food. Pavlov wondered what besides food could trigger salivation in the dog. His best guess was that the dog responded to the sound of footsteps of his lab assistant.

Consider what it means for the sound of footsteps to prompt salivation. The sounds of someone walking would not *ordinarily* cause a dog to salivate. At some point, a new connection—footsteps and drooling—had to be *learned*, or in the language of behaviorists, it had to be conditioned. In this example of conditioning (learning) we can easily identify the cause (the sound of footsteps) and the effect (salivation). These are called, respectively, the **stimulus** and **response**. Putting this all together, we can express the connection between stimulus and response as follows:

Footsteps   →   Dog Salivation

(Conditioned Stimulus)   (Conditioned Response)

We know that the connection between food and salivation is quite natural. Saliva is produced in the mouth to aid in the digestion of food. The production of saliva does not need to be learned. So we can say that in the case of food there is an unconditioned stimulus and unconditioned response, denoted as follows:

Food   →   Dog Salivation

(Unconditioned Stimulus)   (Unconditioned Response)

One stimulus-response connection (involving footsteps) is learned, and the second (involving food) is not. One is conditioned; the other is unconditioned.

The conditioned salivation was interesting to Pavlov because it was prompted by a totally neutral stimulus. Nothing about the sound of footsteps should make a human or a dog salivate. The sound of shoes on a floor is *neutral* with regard to saliva production. Pavlov, wondering if other neutral stimuli could evoke a salivation response, found that the sounds of whistles, metronomes, and tuning forks likewise evoked salivation if the sounds regularly preceded the administration of food. At this point in his research, Pavlov was on his way to forming a generalization that *any* neutral stimulus could be made to evoke a natural response through conditioning.

Let's not forget the nature of the response—salivation—is not sophisticated behavior; it's primal. That is why Pavlov called the learned behavior in his studies **conditioned**

reflexes. As behavior, salivation is about as instinctual as it gets. This is key to understanding classical conditioning. It's not about sophisticated behavior. It's about simple, very primitive behavior—and about what causes that behavior. Classical conditioning explains how a neutral (conditioned) stimulus, through learning, can evoke the same response as a natural (unconditioned) stimulus.

One way of thinking about classical conditioning is that it entails *stimulus substitution*, where the conditioned stimulus substitutes for the unconditioned stimulus. For this to happen, the conditioned stimulus must become associated with the unconditioned stimulus—just as footsteps were associated with the dog food. Through research, Pavlov discovered that certain aspects of that association were important. For example, the conditioned stimulus has to occur *before* the unconditioned stimulus, rather than afterward. And the association between the two is strongest if the conditioned stimulus occurs just an instant before the unconditioned stimulus. A separation in time of more than a few seconds weakens the association and produces a weaker response.

Why Is Classical Conditioning Important?

All of this would be pretty uninteresting if the conditioned response was only salivation. But many other forms of primitive behavior are quite important to the survival of both humans and animals. Consider fear, for example. Some kinds of stimuli naturally evoke a fear response. Snakes often evoke fear not only in humans but also in higher primates such as gorillas and chimpanzees. The fear of snakes is apparently unlearned; somehow it's hard-wired into the brains of some species.

Whenever a stimulus causes fear, it produces a physiological state that makes the heart pound faster. Blood is shunted to muscles to get the body ready to move aggressively toward or protectively away from the object of fear. This physiological state is sometimes called the **fight or flight response**. Experiences that naturally evoke fear include loud noises, angry faces, and threatening gestures. These are not neutral stimuli. But classical conditioning teaches that a *neutral* stimulus can evoke the same primitive behavior (such as a fear response) as a *natural* stimulus. In other words, we can learn to fear a neutral stimulus if, through our experiences, that fear has been conditioned over time. This means that negative emotions can, through conditioning, become associated with *any* stimulus. Perhaps you now see how classical conditioning explains how we can acquire strong emotional reactions to objects, events, and people that are initially neutral.

When we speak of primitive behavior, such as salivation, we do not mean *unimportant* behavior. Negative emotional reactions, such as fear or feelings of revulsion, are highly significant. They influence how we live our lives, and in the education arena they influence what and how we learn, as well as the decisions we make along our educational pathways. At issue here are not only behavioral responses that involve negative emotions. Positive emotions, such as interest and feelings of pleasure, are also prompted by certain natural stimuli (such as a teacher's smiling face) and, by extension through conditioning, to all manner of neutral stimuli (such as books and classrooms).

Early Behaviorism in America

Although the Russian scientist Ivan Pavlov played a crucial role in discovering classical conditioning, behaviorism was mainly a phenomenon of American psychology. In fact, behaviorism dominated American psychology for a half-century, from about 1920 to about 1970.

John B. Watson: Psychology as a Science

If any one person is to be credited with launching this era on the North American continent, it is John B. Watson. In a 1913 article entitled "Psychology as the Behaviorist Sees It," Watson argued vigorously that the only appropriate psychology is behaviorism. The basis for this claim is the arguably scientific quality of the behaviorist's methodology and theory. Behaviorists insisted on objective observations and measurement. Their theories, likewise, permitted only concepts that could be directly observable—that is, behavior—and shunned every idea and explanation that could not be observed directly and objectively, including mentalistic concepts. For Watson, these methodological and theoretical restrictions were essential if psychology was to progress as a scientific enterprise.

Watson was also significant for showing how principles of conditioning applied to humans. Ivan Pavlov's earlier work with animals showed that through stimulus association a neutral object could evoke a simple behavior. Watson found that conditioning also applied to people. In his most famous research, Watson conditioned a baby, Little Albert, to fear certain neutral objects. Watson began his experiment by showing that Little Albert had no natural fear of a white rat. When the rat appeared, Little Albert showed interest rather than fear. All that changed when Watson began to pair the appearance of the white rat with loud noises. When the rat appeared, Watson would bang on a loud pipe, causing Little Albert to cry out in fear.

It is easy to predict that the fear reaction prompted by the jarring sound of banging pipes quickly became associated with the white rat. Soon, the appearance of the rat alone, absent loud noises, could evoke a strong fear reaction in Little Albert. In Pavlovian fashion, the role played by the unconditioned stimulus (a loud noise) was taken up by the conditioned stimulus (the rat). Watson's simple conditioning experiment vividly demonstrated behaviorism's significance for understanding human learning and behavior. If fear reactions could be prompted by one neutral object, why not other objects?

Indeed, the next phase of the Little Albert experiment showed that the conditioned response (fear) transferred to other neutral objects—even without additional training. All that was needed was to present stimuli that *looked* something like a white rat. When Watson showed fluffy white toys to Little Albert, the boy displayed the same fear reaction prompted by the white rat. Even a Santa Claus beard made Little Albert cry out in fear. The function of the original conditioned stimulus, the rat, had expanded to other, somewhat similar, stimuli. This expansion beyond the original stimulus, called **stimulus generalization**, is common in behavioristic conditioning. But stimulus generalization extends only so far. If a stimulus is too different from the original, the learned reactions will not be evoked. Presumably, Little Albert would not be afraid of a *red* fluffy toy. This counterpart process is **stimulus discrimination**, in which a person or animal perceives differences between two stimuli such that one evokes a learned response and the other does not.

John Watson was highly impressed with the power he had to shape the behavior patterns of Little Albert and others. To Watson, behaviorism was not simply the proper way to study human behavior, it was also a powerful means to *alter* human behavior. Watson was not thinking here of artificial kinds of conditioning such as the one he set up in his laboratory. He believed that every person is conditioned by the events of a unique life path. From infancy to old age, our behavior is learned through specific experiences, just as Little Albert's was. The insight led Watson to conclude that human behavior is highly malleable—that any baby could be molded into any kind of adult, given the right training. This conviction led Watson (1924, p. 82) to make a stunning claim for which he became famous:

Give me a dozen healthy infants, well-formed, and my own specified world to bring them up in and I'll guarantee to take any one at random and train him to become any type of specialist I might select—doctor, lawyer, artist, merchant-chief, and yes, even beggarman and thief, regardless of his talents, penchants, tendencies, abilities, vocations, and race of his ancestors.

This bold proclamation leaves no question about where Watson stood on the nature/nurture question. Anyone interested in human behavior wants to understand how much of it is dictated by individual biology (nature) and how much is a consequence of the learning that occurs through life experiences (nurture). Watson took a very strong position on this question—he believed that any person could become anything given the right conditions. To John Watson, nurture was radically more potent than nature.

Note an apparent paradox here: The strong role accorded the environment in shaping behavior speaks to human potential. Given the right conditions people could become essentially anything. At the same time, behaviorists denied that anybody has any choice in the matter. Such notions as wishes and intentions are excluded (most of the time) from the lexicon of the behaviorist. There is boundless potential, but no choice. This paradoxical duality (potential without choice) emerges even more explicitly in the theories of Watson's successor, B. F. Skinner. Before considering Skinner's particular contribution to behaviorism, operant conditioning, let's be sure we appreciate the significance of classical conditioning for education.

Classical Conditioning and Education

Classical conditioning shows how a neutral stimulus can evoke a simple behavioral response, including salivation (in the case of Pavlov's dogs), or more significantly, strong emotional reactions, both positive and negative. Emotional reactions are important because they can strongly influence the choices we make and our perseverance in those choices. Using a bit of cognitive language here, emotions can shape our goals and aspirations, our beliefs about what is possible to achieve, and our convictions about what goals are worthy of our sustained efforts. Seen this way, the emotional associations forged by classical conditioning are highly significant for education.

No one doubts that strong emotions are learned in educational settings. Classical conditioning can help us to understand *how* those emotions are learned. Much of the substance of education is relatively neutral in its ability to evoke emotional reactions. A mathematical equation is, by itself, neutral. But through experience, it can evoke interest and anticipation; alternatively, it can evoke anxiety, even fear. Likewise, the first page of a novel can prompt highly positive feelings of anticipation or it can elicit feelings of dread. The world of education is filled with ideas, symbols, objects, and processes that have the potential to evoke strong emotions, which in turn can influence chains of decisions that accumulate to determine educational and career pathways. The course of a life can be channeled through sequences of such decisions.

As educators, we want to encourage positive feelings about learning. Conversely, we want to avoid or reverse negative associations, especially dislike or anxiety. As we think about how emotions originate in learning situations, we should consider the roles of such negative stimuli as anger, shame, and criticism. We can also think of the positive associations of smiles, encouragement, and a friendly and affirming voice. Like Little Albert, each student has the potential to associate strong emotions with new experiences, people, and objects.

The limitations of classical conditioning also must be acknowledged. For example, emotional reactions to specific academic subjects are more complexly determined than is suggested by their simple associations with pleasant or unpleasant experiences. They also involve beliefs about learning and about one's own ability to learn. A more complete account of the emotional aspects of learning seems to require cognitive language. Also—and this is an important limitation—classical conditioning explains only *simple* behavior. But we know that human behavior is complex. To understand and explain *complex* behavior, we need insights from a different form of behaviorism. We need to explore the theory of operant conditioning.

E. L. Thorndike: Instrumental Conditioning

Strictly speaking, E. L. Thorndike used the term *instrumental conditioning* rather than *operant conditioning*, but his research helped launch the operant conditioning paradigm as a new, and very powerful, form of behaviorism. Later, the basic principles of operant conditioning were expanded, sharpened, and popularized by the great behaviorist B. F. Skinner. But Thorndike's contributions were a decisive turning point. Perhaps a little surprisingly, the foundations of operant conditioning were established early in Thorndike's career, as part of his doctoral dissertation.

CAN THE CAT ESCAPE THE PUZZLE BOX? Thorndike's doctoral research employed a device that might seem a little cruel by today's standards, but it gave Thorndike the information he wanted. The device was called a puzzle box, which was a wooden cage in which Thorndike placed a cat. Thorndike was able to observe the cat's behavior through spaces in the walls of the box. The key feature of the puzzle box was a small hatch that allowed the cat to escape. Unfortunately for the cat, the way to open it was not obvious. To open the hatch, the cat had to press an inconspicuous lever inside the cage. Thorndike wanted to know if a cat could escape from the puzzle box by pressing the lever, whether intentionally or accidentally.

When placed inside the puzzle box, the cat exhibited random motions in frantic attempts to get out. Eventually, and without any particular strategy, the cat managed to hit the lever that opened the hatch. But the motion that activated the escape lever was accidental, a result of random behavior. The role of random behavior is important here, as it is in all operant conditioning. Random behavior can sometimes lead to results that are beneficial to the organism. Thorndike pioneered this concept, and later Skinner built an entire theory around it.

Thorndike placed the cat inside the puzzle box repeatedly in order to understand how the cat adapted over time. Would the cat become more efficient in escaping from the puzzle box? Would subsequent escapes require less time? If so, how is that possible given that the initial escape was the result of random behavior? Thorndike indeed found that the cat became more efficient with each subsequent trial. Each escape required less time. Learning was definitely taking place as the cat adapted to the puzzle box, but not immediately through insight into how to escape. The cat's adaptation was gradual. This form of learning seemed unusual, but Thorndike had an explanation.

THE LAW OF EFFECT. Thorndike knew that the adaptation of the cat to the puzzle box was the result of a gradual restriction of behavior. If the cat exhibited a wide range of random behavior initially, the scope of random behavior narrowed over time to actions that were more likely to be followed by a reward—specifically, escaping from the puzzle box. Perhaps only movements at one end of the box were associated with subsequent escape. Likewise, maybe only sideways movements of the paw were often rewarded by freedom. This is not to say that *all* of the repeated random movements were actually effective, but their association with a positive outcome (escape) was enough to encourage their repetition. Note that there is nothing mentalistic about learning here:

The cat never had a singular moment of insight in which it *knew* what to do. Rather, the scope of random behavior was gradually narrowed to behaviors that tended to be followed by a rewarding outcome.

Based on these findings, Thorndike formulated the **Law of Effect**, which specifies that any behavior that is followed by rewards is more likely to be repeated than behavior that is not followed by rewards. The Law is commonsensical and intuitive; it might even seem obvious. But don't forget what the Law explains in the case of the puzzle box; it shows how *random* activity, rather than insightful understanding, can lead to effective behavior. The Law of Effect can explain how a cat can learn to escape from a cage, yet it cannot explain the kind of learning that we are used to attributing to humans—learning that is conscious, insightful, and comprehending. But note a huge explanatory benefit of Thorndike's Law of Effect: It can account for learning (conditioning) of complex behavior in a way that classical conditioning cannot. After all, the behavior of Thorndike's cat was much more than a salivation reflex. Behaviorism now had a way of explaining how complex learning in animals could arise from the consequences of behavior. Soon, but in a different laboratory, the same basic paradigm would be applied to explain complex learning in human beings.

B. F. Skinner: Operant Conditioning

It's no exaggeration to say that B. F. Skinner was the greatest behaviorist of the twentieth century and that he turned the course of psychology in the United States. Even though behaviorism was built on the research and polemical arguments of Watson and Thorndike, Skinner himself was the true flagbearer of behaviorism for half a century. His legacy of influence extends beyond psychology theory to the popular culture; each of us has been affected by the ideas of B. F. Skinner, whether consciously or not.

FIGURE 2.2
B. F. Skinner *He changed the course of American psychology.*
[Copyright by the Archives of the History of American Psychology.]

S-R-R: A DIFFERENT PARADIGM. Skinner's theory followed the same basic pattern of Thorndike's: Animals and human beings could learn complex behavior gradually, as random actions were narrowed to be more and more effective over time. Skinner saw this kind of learning as conditioning, but it was a different kind than the classical conditioning formulated by Pavlov. Skinner called his version of learning **operant conditioning**.

Skinner (1938) formulated the theory of operant conditioning symbolically in a way that made it easy to compare with classical conditioning. Pavlov's theory could be boiled down to two terms, stimulus and response, as follows:

$$\text{Stimulus} \quad \rightarrow \quad \text{Response}$$

In Pavlov's theory, the stimulus changes from the original, unconditioned stimulus to the conditioned stimulus. Still, only two terms were needed to make sense of learning in Pavlov's laboratory.

In Skinner's account of operant conditioning, three terms were needed: stimulus, response, and reinforcement, as follows:

$$\text{Stimulus} \quad \rightarrow \quad \text{Response} \quad \rightarrow \quad \text{Reinforcement}$$

To clarify these terms, we'll use the example of a dog learning to perform a trick, such as rolling over. The situation is simple:

STIMULUS: The dog's owner says, "Roll Over!"

RESPONSE: The dog rolls over.

REINFORCEMENT: The dog gets a treat.

Of course, when a dog learns a trick such as rolling over, the trick is not performed perfectly the very first time. It's learned gradually, in a manner similar to the cat escaping from the puzzle box. Note another similarity between the cat escaping and the dog rolling over: What happens *after* the animal's behavior is crucial. Whether we speak of Thorndike's Law of Effect or Skinner's concept of reinforcement, the *consequences* of performing a particular action are important. This is not the case in classical conditioning where behavior itself is not altered, only the stimulus needed to evoke a certain behavior. Classical conditioning involves learning, but it's a different kind of learning than Thorndike and Skinner were studying.

In Skinner's theory, **reinforcement** is any consequence that leads to the repetition of a behavior. When a dog rolls over, reinforcement is provided in the form of a dog biscuit, or perhaps praising the dog and scratching behind its ears. For Skinner, any specific action that increases the likelihood of a behavior is a **reinforcer**. Reinforcers can be as basic as food or as abstract as money. Social reinforcers such as praise, smiles, and frowns can also be highly effective. Note that a reinforcer is defined by its effects: If a consequence increases the likelihood of a behavior being repeated, then by definition it is a reinforcer. There is a subjective element here: What counts as a reinforcer cannot be specified completely beforehand. It will vary from person to person, and from one animal to another. What works as a reinforcer for one dog will not necessarily work for another; the same is true for people.

SHAPING THROUGH SUCCESSIVE APPROXIMATIONS. When a person or an animal learns a new "trick" through operant conditioning, the new behavior is typically learned gradually (Skinner, 1951). At first, the behavior only approximates the ultimate pattern in a coarse way. Rather than rolling over, the dog might at first lower its body closer to the ground. Over time, the dog might accidentally lower its body so that it *touches* the ground. Because this approximates the intended behavior more closely than before, the trainer of the dog might reward only this new behavior—touching the ground—with a treat. Now, in order to get a treat, merely lowering the body is not good enough; the dog must actually lower its body all the way to the ground.

Eventually, this process can progress toward the target behavior of rolling over. As the animal more closely approximates the complex skill, the criteria for rewarding the dog become stricter. When the dog rolls over for the first time, a new standard has been set. Now it is rewarded by praise or a biscuit only if it completes the trick successfully. This kind of progression is known as **successive approximations**. The terminology makes perfect sense: Over time, behavior evolves gradually toward successively greater approximations of its ideal form. A related term, **shaping**, describes the actions of a trainer or teacher to evoke more effective behavior over time. Behavior is shaped, much as clay is shaped by a sculptor. The behavior is not shaped instantly, but through successive approximations. Shaping is used to train animals to perform complex tricks to the delight of animal trainers and their audiences. Many kinds of animals—dogs, birds, elephants, sea lions, and killer whales, among others—can learn to perform complex behavior on command. Shaping has in fact been practiced since ancient times to domesticate animals for hauling, herding, and hunting (Timberlake, 1999).

FIGURE 2.3
Shamu wows the crowd *Operant conditioning can produce complex behavior in humans and animals.* [Photo courtesy of SeaWorld.]

INTEREST MAGNET 2.1

Teaching Shamu

Principles of behaviorism apply not only to humans, but also to animals (Skinner, 1951). A visit to SeaWorld will give you an impressive demonstration of animal training using operant conditioning techniques. Through the skillful application of reinforcement by animal trainers, the orca or killer whale named Shamu has learned to leap through hoops, balance objects, and carry performers on his back.

Some of the animal's spontaneous behavior—a small leap from the water, for example—resembles what the animal trainer has in mind. If this act is reinforced, such as with a snack of fresh fish, Shamu will be more likely to repeat the small leap in the future. Gradually, the trainer raises expectations—Shamu receives rewards only when he leaps to greater heights than in the past. This method is called shaping or successive approximations. In stages, the rewarded behavior begins to resemble the impressive feats that customers want to see. Not only orcas, but also birds, elephants, dogs and many other kinds of animals can be trained through successive approximations.

How does Shamu learn to leap through hoops and toss human riders high into the air? Through patient application of the techniques of shaping. The whale learns amazing tricks by successive approximations. After being shown a hand signal, Shamu will at times approximate the desired behavior more closely, and at other times less closely. The human trainer carries a bucket of raw fish and judiciously rewards Shamu as his behavior approximates more closely the intended trick. It's important to reinforce behavior immediately. That's why trainers signal desired behavior with a whistle—called a "bridge signal" or secondary reinforcer—which promises that the whale will receive reinforcement in just a few seconds. Desirable behavior is reinforced by the bridge signal; undesirable behavior is not. That's how learning progresses toward a specific behavioral goal.

Stimuli other than hand signals are also used to indicate the desired behavior (SeaWorld, 2002). At SeaWorld, an orca learns to recognize computer-generated sound codes played on a waterproof keyboard. Other sound codes can indicate the name of the orca, the desired behavior, and even how that behavior is to be performed. The sound codes can also serve as bridge signals. Reinforcers other than fish are also used to promote specific behaviors. These are advantageous because the whale might not be hungry during training. Other reinforcers include vigorous touching, squirting with a water hose, or supplying ice to eat and toys to play with. As each animal responds somewhat differently to various behavioral consequences, trainers must learn what works best for each animal.

Training can contribute directly to an animal's health. Shamu can hold still for obtaining blood samples or open his mouth for dental examinations (SeaWorld, 1994). He can even be trained to urinate for analysis on command. These "tricks" help the veterinarians at SeaWorld to monitor the animal's health. Of course, Shamu saves his most impressive tricks for charming the audiences that watch him every day.

Let's return for a moment to Skinner's term, *operant conditioning*. We know that *conditioning* is another word for learning in behaviorist terminology. But what does *operant mean*? An **operant** is a behavior that is generated by the animal, and as I've noted, it has a random element. Remember the cat in Thorndike's puzzle box. Within the scope of a cat's possible behaviors, it expressed or emitted a wide range of activity in its attempt to escape. Only a fraction of those random behaviors, or operants, had any real effect. Thus, the scope of random operants tapered down over time as the cat was conditioned. The same random production of behavior, followed by the reinforcement of a subset of that behavior, can also account for a dog learning to roll over or a killer whale learning to jump through a hoop. Therefore, within Skinner's theory there is a definite role for random behavior as the raw material for eventual complex behavior.

Now consider parallels between two seemingly distant theories, Skinner's theory of operant conditioning and Darwin's theory of natural selection. Both recognize the importance of random variation as the raw material for changes in organisms. For

Darwin, that random variation was genetic. Some subset of random genetic traits are beneficial to organisms as they adapt to their environments. Those traits, and their associated genes, are passed on to subsequent generations. In Skinner's theory, random variation in behavior is displayed. Some of that random behavior—only a subset—is well-suited to the organism's environment and tends to be repeated. Darwin showed how the selection of genes can change organisms from one generation to the next; Skinner showed how the selection of behaviors through reinforcement can shape an organism's subsequent behavior. Normally, the conditioned behavior is not passed on to subsequent generations. There is one major exception to this pattern—human beings. People excel at propagating knowledge from one generation to the next, and education plays a very prominent role in supporting this process.

The parallels between operant conditioning and natural selection hint at the explanatory power of Skinner's theory. After all, if Darwin's theory is so powerful within biology, wouldn't it make sense that a theory with a similar structure could also be quite effective in accounting for human behavior, and for explaining how behavior changes over time? Skinner certainly believed so. Like Darwin, Skinner thought his theory was capable of explaining all the phenomena under its purview. To him, the mechanisms of operant conditioning, such as shaping through successive approximations, are capable of accounting for *all* behavior.

Operant conditioning is far more capable of explaining complex behavior than classical conditioning is. But can it really explain all complex behavior? Think of *everything* that you did today—all the thousands of skilled actions, including reading, writing, note-taking, making phone calls, banking, driving, exercising, dressing, eating, or shopping. Human activity is extremely complex even if we consider only directly observable behavior and momentarily set aside (as Skinner would prefer) such cognitive concepts as thinking, planning, goal setting, and problem solving. According to Skinner's theory, all behavior—everything that you did today, and in fact all your behavior through your entire life—is explainable within the theoretical system of operant conditioning. In other words, all that we do is the product of our reinforcement histories. Some of our past behavior was reinforced, some not, and this long chain of behavior and its consequences produced who we are and what we do today. Once we appreciate this sweeping claim, we understand that operant conditioning was intended to be a *totalizing* theory—one that purports to explain *everything* within its scope of interest.

TEACHING COMPLEX BEHAVIOR. If operant conditioning has the potential to be a totalizing theory to explain human behavior, why not use it also to *control* human behavior? That question certainly did occur to Skinner, who saw no reason not to use behavioristic principles to deliberately control human behavior. If applied carefully and systematically, reinforcement could shape the behavior of individuals in desirable directions. You might suspect, as Skinner did, that this was the basic goal of education anyway. Why not be deliberate about it and use operant conditioning to be still more effective at controlling what people do?

Behavioral modification is the name for any systematic approach to teaching new behavior using the principles of operant conditioning. We have already noted some of the key ideas in behavior modification, including shaping through successive approximations. We also know that reinforcement is important. For Shamu, it's raw fish; for a dog, it's a doggie biscuit. For human beings, money usually works well, but so do dozens of other rewards. Reinforcers, as we know, are defined strictly in terms of their effects—a reinforcer is any consequence to behavior that makes that behavior more likely to recur in the future. What works varies between people and across species.

Shamu is not interested in cash, a dog does not want raw fish, and your next-door neighbor would not be motivated by a doggie biscuit.

Punishment, like reinforcement, is also a significant factor in operant conditioning. If some consequences make particular behavior more likely, then other consequences make certain behavior less likely. If a police officer stops you for speeding, aren't you less likely to drive fast in the future—at least in that vicinity? The theory of operant conditioning recognizes the importance of punishment in learning. Reinforcement and punishment are complementary. One is a green light to continue the behavior; the other is a red light to signal that the behavior must stop. Reinforcement makes the recurrence of behavior more likely; punishment has the opposite effect. **Punishers**, like reinforcers, are always defined by their effects.

Now that we have distinguished between reinforcement and punishment, another dimension to each must be recognized. We can speak of positive and negative reinforcement, as well as positive and negative punishment. Here, the terms *positive* and *negative* do not refer to whether an experience is pleasant or unpleasant. Instead, the terms denote whether a stimulus is being added or removed. **Positive reinforcement** is easy: it's the doggie biscuit a dog gets for rolling over, or the large tip a waiter gets for providing good service. **Negative reinforcement** involves removing an aversive stimulus. When you get into a car, most likely an annoying *ding ding ding* will sound until you latch your seatbelt. Clicking the seatbelt buckle is reinforced by the removal of a stimulus—the irritating sound. More significantly, a prison inmate may have a prison term reduced for good behavior. That, too, is negative reinforcement. But be careful—in everyday speech, the term *negative reinforcement* is often used incorrectly to refer to punishment.

Punishment also has positive and negative varieties. **Positive punishment** is the application of an experience that is typically unpleasant: corporal punishment, an angry voice, or a threatening expression. They are positive, remember, because a stimulus is added. But punishment can also be accomplished by taking something away. Examples of **negative punishment** include the removal of privileges. When a child is prohibited from playing video games, watching television, or spending time with friends, these restrictions typically count as negative punishment. The widely applied techniques of "time out" for children's bad behavior or "grounding" for teenage irresponsibility are also forms of negative punishment.

Reinforcement Schedules

The distinctions made in the previous section—between reinforcement and punishment, and between positive and negative varieties of each—are refinements in understanding how operant conditioning works. But Skinner and other behaviorists went much further in their analyses. They wanted to understand how the timing of reinforcement affects conditioning (Bijou, 1993). For example, in a program of behavior modification, is it best to apply reinforcement after every instance of the desired behavior? Or should reinforcement be occasional rather than given every time? These questions bring us to the topic of **reinforcement schedules**.

Suppose a father wants to apply behavioral modification to teach his daughter to make her bed every day. If the parent is highly motivated and has plenty of cash, he might pay his daughter a dollar each day she makes her bed (to some prescribed standard). When reinforcement is given every time the behavior occurs, the pattern of reinforcement is called **continuous reinforcement**. Continuous reinforcement is the most obvious reinforcement strategy; it's very common, but it is not necessarily the most effective strategy. A father might wish that eventually his daughter will make her bed every day *even in the absence* of a cash reward; that is, one purpose of conditioning might be to reduce dependence on reinforcement over time. If that is the goal, then continuous reinforcement is not the best strategy to adopt.

If continuous reinforcement is not the ideal strategy, what are the alternatives? There are four basic kinds of reinforcement schedules:

- Fixed ratio
- Variable ratio
- Fixed interval
- Variable interval

Fixed ratio schedules involve one reinforcement for every fixed number of displays of behavior. Suppose that father gives his daughter a dollar every *other* day that she makes her bed—or every third day. He can choose the number. If he is consistent in counting the instances of behavior and rewarding the behavior according to some ratio set beforehand—2 to 1, 3 to 1, and so on—then the reinforcement schedule follows a fixed ratio schedule. It is *fixed* because the chosen ratio does not change.

Variable ratio schedules are different in that they involve a random element. Rather than reinforcing behavior after a predictable number of occurrences, reinforcement is applied after a randomly changing number of instances. In the example of a daughter making her bed, she might be rewarded with a dollar after two days of making her bed, or after 4 instances, or 10, then back to 3. The number jumps around and is unpredictable. The daughter knows that she will be rewarded only after she makes her bed, but never knows when that will occur. We will see that this reinforcement schedule, variable ratio, has unusual power for motivating behavior and maintaining habits.

Both fixed interval and variable interval schedules have a time factor, as in time *interval*. With **fixed interval reinforcement schedules**, reinforcement occurs after a predetermined period of time. A weekly paycheck fits this category. If the worker shows up for work and performs effectively, there will be paycheck ready to reward that worker at a predetermined time. With **variable interval schedules**, time is also a factor but the time interval between reinforcement is not fixed. Think about end-of-year pay bonuses. In some companies they are given out only in December, but bonuses might or might not be administered depending on the company's profits. Similarly, quarterly stock dividends reward investors every three months, but they are not guaranteed. After disappointing fiscal quarters the company might not issue dividends to stockholders.

Knowledge of these four reinforcement schedules can be very useful. But above all, we need to appreciate the significance of variable ratio reinforcement. This schedule is more powerful than the others. To understand why, think of what normally happens when a particular behavior is *not* rewarded. If you go to work every day but are not paid, eventually you'll consider not showing up. Similarly, a dog will expect a doggie biscuit now and then if he is to keep performing his tricks. If a month of rolling over produces no treat, he too might take a day off. Without reinforcement, conditioned behavior undergoes **extinction**. The behavior will diminish in regularity and intensity to some pre-conditioning baseline level, or it may stop altogether. No more dog tricks.

There may be times when we want to instill behaviors in others—people or animals—such that the behavior does not require continuous reinforcement. What kind of reinforcement schedule makes a learned behavior most resistant to extinction? The variable ratio schedule.

FIGURE 2.4
The unpredictable rewards of fishing *Variable ratio reinforcement schedules can be highly compelling.* [Photo courtesy of Duane L. Jellison, Registered Master Maine Guide.]

If a child learns that *occasionally* she will be rewarded for making her bed, but cannot predict when that reward will occur, she is most likely to maintain her new behavior for a long time—even in the absence of rewards. There is something about the unpredictability of rewards that makes the activity highly compelling. The power of variable ratio reinforcement is clearly seen in gambling. A gambler never knows when he will hit the jackpot. Even though there may be long runs of bad luck, his fortunes can change in a single card hand or in one roll of the dice. The power of variable ratio jackpots can help explain why gambling behavior persists despite intervals without reinforcement. The ongoing possibility of an imminent reward makes the behavior quite robust, for better or worse. Think about fishing, and you'll see that the reward structure follows much the same pattern—behavior persists through long periods with no tangible payoff.

Variable ratio reinforcement can work well when combined with the initial use of continuous reinforcement. That's because continuous reinforcement is very effective for establishing a new behavior. Once the behavior is established, switching to a variable ratio reinforcement schedule can help make the behavior robust—that is, resistant to extinction in the absence of rewards. Teaming the early use of continuous reinforcement with later use of variable ratio reinforcement is an effective strategy for behavioral modification. It's a contribution from operant conditioning theory that has practical applications.

Behaviorism's Enduring Impact

This book is not really about behaviorism. It focuses more directly on powerful concepts related to human cognition—thinking, reasoning, problem solving, memory, knowledge, beliefs, and many others. Nevertheless, behaviorism offers some really practical strategies, as we have seen. We must also appreciate the profound effects of behaviorism on our culture, especially on how we relate to each other on a human level. Part of living in a culture means that, collectively and as individuals, we try to influence if not control the behavior of other people, perhaps especially children. In our many and varied attempts to influence others' behavior, Skinner's version of behaviorism has had an impact that endures to this day. For example, we see behaviorism's affect on education and parenting techniques. Although not discussed here, behaviorism also strongly influenced the theory and practice of psychotherapy. Still more broadly, the impact of behaviorism was felt in social philosophy, in the way we think about society and culture.

Impact on Education

The strategic use of positive reinforcement is ubiquitous in education. Whenever elementary school teachers draw smiley faces on homework, positive reinforcement is used to encourage the continuation of the behavior. One smiley face or sticker might encourage the child to continue doing homework well and on time. Still more widely used is praise. To smile and say, "Good job, Ryan," is to utter more than a spontaneous commendation. Praise is used to encourage the same behavior in the future. This is not to say that encouraging and positive comments to students are insincere. No doubt they are honestly intended. But teachers intuitively recognize the practical functions of praise—that smiles and commendations can help shape the future behavior of students. Indeed, teachers know that praise is one form of positive reinforcement that can be used to influence children's behavior. Positive reinforcement is the most direct application of operant conditioning to teaching.

Teachers use other principles of operant conditioning besides positive reinforcement. They deliberately *withhold* positive reinforcement in certain situations. When one student displays bad behavior, a teacher might advise the other students, "Just ignore him." Why? Because there is a tacit awareness—an unspoken theory—that the child craves the attention that bad behavior typically provokes. The attention *is* the positive reinforcement. Without reinforcement the behavior will presumably taper off and undergo extinction. The hope is that bad behavior will be extinguished over time, not through active intervention but, counterintuitively, through deliberate *in*action. To ignore misbehavior rather than to confront it directly and forcefully is a break from past traditions of dealing with children when punishment was seen as the obvious response. Skinner himself opposed punishment, partly because he believed that it was

FIGURE 2.5
Stars, stickers, and smiley faces *Teachers use positive reinforcers to shape the future behavior of students.* [Photo by Jamie Stein.]

not as effective as using, or withholding, reinforcement. The shift toward using reinforcement instead of punishment is one of the lasting contributions of operant conditioning theory, though that fact is seldom recognized.

The use and withholding of positive reinforcement are the most common applications of behavioral modification techniques in education, but there are others. Some have faded in popularity over time. In the heyday of behaviorism, Skinner (1958) applied operant conditioning to teaching techniques. The applications extended to so-called **teaching machines**, which were primitive precursors to computer-based learning systems. The instructional strategy was to break down the desired learning goals into discrete units of student behavior. Those units were arranged in an orderly sequence from easiest to most difficult. The teaching machine presented new information and called for responses to ensure that the student was learning. For example, the machine might present a new mathematical procedure followed by a practice problem. The student would write an answer on a roll of paper displayed within a frame. Having given an answer, the student would advance the written response so that it could not be altered. Next, the student would view the correct answer and so received immediate feedback. If the correct answer matched the student's response, that match served as positive reinforcement. The teaching machine would then advance to a more difficult problem.

Although Skinner's teaching machines have long become obsolete, some of the logic of teaching machines has continued to the present. Curricular practices of breaking down learning goals into small units calling for explicit student responses, and then giving feedback on those responses, has continued to the present. This way of organizing instruction has sometimes been transported to a different platform: a modern digital computer. Notwithstanding the rising sophistication of the machine used,

FIGURE 2.6
Skinner's teaching machine *The applications of operant conditioning to education were direct.* [Copyright by the Archives of the History of American Psychology.]

behaviorism has had an enduring legacy in this approach. Whether delivered by machine or not, some forms of instruction break down material (and expected student responses) into very specific and discrete units. The curriculum follows a highly prescribed logic that teachers are expected to follow closely. This form of teaching is known as **programmed instruction**.

Even when instructional sequences are not so strictly prescribed, teachers are sometimes asked to identify goals of learning strictly in terms of what students will be able to *do*. When the goals of learning are expressed solely in terms of objective behavior, the resulting **behavioral objectives** are also a legacy of operant conditioning. Yet another influential movement in education was inspired by behavioristic principles—the approach called **mastery learning**. Promoted by Benjamin Bloom and his collaborators, mastery learning openly acknowledged that students learn at different rates. Mastery learning accommodated these different rates by breaking down the content of teaching into prescribed blocks and allowing students flexibility in the time needed to master a block of instruction. Mastery was operationalized by performance at some pre-established level, such as 80 percent correct on end-of-unit tests. Students would not be allowed to move on to a more advanced topic before mastering the prior unit.

Elements of these varied behavioristic approaches are evident in current educational practices, even though they are not as prominent as they were in the 1960s, 1970s, and 1980s. There is one segment of education, however, in which behaviorist techniques still hold considerable sway. Behavioristic principles continue to be employed broadly in teaching students with developmental delays or behavioral disorders. Effective teaching approaches among these special populations include highly prescribed systems of reinforcement. Sometimes, such tokens as poker chips are given as reinforcement. In this **token economy**, the chips can be exchanged later for toys or treats that are more directly appreciated by students.

Impact on Parenting

Behaviorism has had enduring effects on parenting practices, just as it has on education. Many of the reinforcement techniques adopted by teachers were appropriated by parents. Praising children in order to encourage the repetition of desired behavior has become a normal part of parenting practice. Likewise, many parents deliberately withhold attention for bad behavior—presumably to promote extinction of that behavior for lack of reinforcement. We see a version of this technique in "time out," when children are forced to withdraw from play or social activity for misbehaving. Time out can be seen as the withholding of reinforcement or as negative punishment.

To be clear, the terminology of operant conditioning is not woven into the everyday conversations of parents. Perhaps in years past, parents thought about and spoke of *positive reinforcement* and *conditioning* more frequently than they do now. But even without the behavorist terminology, the use of operant conditioning techniques in current parenting practices affirms that Skinnerian ideas have entered the popular culture. Through theories of operant conditioning, Skinner and other behaviorists have had a lasting influence on the ways in which we try to modify the behavior of other people.

Impact on Social Philosophy

The principles of operant conditioning are so general and powerful that they are highly relevant to questions about how to regulate behavior in societies and cultures.

Philosophers have long speculated about how a civil society is possible, and about the role of government in maintaining the social order and peaceful coexistence. Thomas Hobbes (1651/1963), for example, argued that one legitimate role of government is to stem the rabidly selfish motives of the average human being. Restraint, in Hobbes's theory, is a necessary function of government.

Skinner's theory, by contrast, does not assume that human beings have a greedy or selfish nature. Nor does Skinner's theory assume that people are altruistic. Human behavior is neither basically good nor evil; it is simply the result of past reinforcement or punishment patterns in each person's experience. Random behaviors (operants), allied with the selective force of consequences (reinforcement and punishment), can explain the entire range of human behavior. As John Watson claimed, experience alone is sufficient to transform any newborn infant into a saint or a sociopath.

Reinforcement inevitably shapes the behavior of individuals over time. The pattern applies also to groups of people. Skinner knew that patterns of reinforcement and punishment run through a society or culture, and that these patterns can collectively shift the behavior of those societies. The effects are not always good. Societies may unwittingly reward aggressive acts or punish altruism. Indeed, counterproductive patterns of reinforcement *must* exist; otherwise we would not see violent crime in our society. All behavior, including all destructive behavior, can be fully explained by the patterns of reinforcement and punishment experienced during each person's unique history. Within the confines of operant conditioning theory, there is no other explanation.

Strangely, the implied **determinism** of behaviorism removes blame from the criminal. What choice did he have, really—especially given that *choice itself* is not a reality according to the theory? *Choice* is cognitive talk, which behaviorism rejects. By seeing all present behavior as determined by the consequences of previous behavior, there is no true moral responsibility attendant to self-destructive, antisocial, violent, or traitorous acts. In an odd way, behaviorism is understanding and compassionate in its outlook. The proper response to undesired behavior is to reconfigure the reward structures. A society must replace one form of behavioral modification with another.

If bad behavior is not blamed, neither is good behavior credited. If Jack the Ripper had no choice in the matter, neither did Mother Teresa. Good acts cannot be helped because, once again, behavior is strictly determined by our individual reinforcement histories. Freedom is therefore an illusion. So is virtue, integrity, and dignity. That is why B. F. Skinner (1971) could write a book entitled *Beyond Freedom and Dignity*. Both terms ascribe to humans choice guided by internal values that have moral aspects. To Skinner, this was the wrong way to look at things. Ultimately, the illusions conveyed by such concepts as freedom and dignity, blame and credit, or virtue and vice impede progress toward a better social existence.

Skinner did envision a utopian society in which peaceful coexistence reigned. That society, presented as fiction in Skinner's 1948 novel *Walden Two*, was controlled by an intelligently structured logic of reinforcement. The "right" behaviors were consistently reinforced, producing a community that was cooperative, functional, and peaceful—not to say free, however. Perhaps like any version of a utopian society, the overarching system of behavioral modification running through *Walden Two* is chilling. The reader is struck by the fictitious society's free use of manipulation, the robotic quality of its inhabitants, and the disturbing questions the novel raises about who establishes, maintains, and modifies the reinforcement contingencies that control the behavior of everyone else.

Skinner's version of an ideal society did not attract much serious interest. Perhaps the notion of a world run according to the principles of operant conditioning was not credible to anyone but the most ardent proponents of behaviorism. The social implications of behaviorism were nothing more than a sidelight of Skinner's theory, rather than a centerpiece. Nevertheless, consistency demanded that Skinner assert the implications of his theory for the behavior of entire societies. After all, if freedom is an illusion, then why not control all the contingencies of behavior rather than leave them to chance? In the end, though, maybe it was too much for anyone but academics and intellectuals to believe that freedom and choice are illusions. For the average person, it's hard to accept that we can do without such concepts as plans, beliefs, purposes, goals, wishes, values, and intentions. Can behaviorism really explain everything about human behavior, or are other explanations needed? In time, the totalizing claims of operant conditioning theory were challenged, opening the way for alternative accounts of human behavior and learning. The alternative theories included explanations that acknowledged the role of the human mind, and explored its nature.

Behaviorism Challenged

As the influence of behaviorism grew during the twentieth century, its limitations gradually became apparent. Some of the problems of behaviorism were conceptual and definitional; others were related to inconsistencies between the tenets of behaviorism (in particular, the exclusion of cognition) and what could be observed or inferred from the behavior of animals and humans. Eventually, criticism mounted to the extent that other theoretical approaches, including cognitive approaches, began to rival behaviorism for the dominant position in American psychology.

Circular Definition of Reinforcement

One conceptual problem with behaviorism is the definition of its central concept, *reinforcement*. As noted earlier, reinforcement is defined strictly in terms of its effects: namely, reinforcement is any consequence of behavior that increases the likelihood that the behavior will be repeated in the future. Defining reinforcement in this way makes some sense because what counts as reinforcement for one person (or animal) will not work for another. But there is also a problem created by this definition: It is impossible to test the idea that reinforcement *causes* behavior to be repeated.

The two entities—repeated behavior and reinforcement—are linked by definition. Thus, behaviorism's central declaration that reinforcement leads to the repetition of behavior is not testable. It is not a conclusion; rather, it is an assumption—an assumption, by the way, that can accommodate any evidence because it is not data-dependent. Science relies on the testability of assertions, and the possibility that propositions are falsifiable (capable of being disproved). In the scientific method, ideas are tested against data. Ideas may be vindicated or they may be vitiated; either way, science moves on. The definitional quality of reinforcement does not meet this criterion. Neither does the definition of punishment. Of course, science also relies on assumptions. The question is whether one can accept the definitions of reinforcement and punishment as assumptions rather than as testable claims. For some scholars, acceptance of such crucial circular definitions is asking too much. If so, this counts as one drawback of the operant conditioning form of behaviorism.

Edward Tolman: Rats with Purpose

One research-based finding by a prominent behaviorist proved to be subtly undermining to the overall theory. Experiments in the laboratory of Edward Tolman (1932) suggested that the behavior of rats could not be explained fully by behaviorist principles of stimulus and response. Tolman's research involved studying how rats learn to navigate mazes. The rats in Tolman's laboratory at the University of California, Berkeley, searched for food placed at the end of a path inside the maze. When rats ran the same maze in succession, they became highly efficient. But the rats could also adapt whenever the maze was blocked by choosing an alternative, but still efficient, route. After observing thousands of such maze-running trials, the behaviorist Tolman could not escape a strong impression that the rats navigated the mazes as if they had a "mental map" of the maze structure. Here we must appreciate that a mental map, or knowledge of any sort, is a cognitive concept, not a behaviorist one. So-called radical behaviorists, such as Skinner, would not speak of mental maps or of knowledge, but only of behavior (Ringen, 1999; Skinner, 1990).

Tolman went further. Not only did rats seem to have a mental map of mazes, they also appeared to run the mazes with a sense of purpose. It was as if the rats had a goal, an idea that guided their actions. For this reason, Tolman's ideas are sometimes called **purposive behaviorism** (Innis, 1999). But the term *purposive behaviorism* is an oxymoron: Such notions as goals and purposes were anathema to strict behaviorists, just as references to mental maps and knowledge were forbidden. If these entities existed at all, they were hidden, internal characteristics of the organism, not the sort of strictly observable behavior that Watson and Skinner insisted we confine our discussions to. As early as 1932, Tolman began to question the strict dogma of radical behaviorism with the publication of his book, *Purposive Behavior in Man and Animals*.

Eventually, a new variety of behaviorists began to emerge. These **neobehaviorists** could not accept the stark restriction of their science to observable behavior. Instead, they felt it was necessary to consider the enduring characteristics of the organism. These internal characteristics—whether knowledge, goals, or motivation—influence

FIGURE 2.7
Running mazes *Rats seem to have mental maps and a sense of purpose.* [Courtesy of Cartoon Stock, www.cartoonstock.com]

behavior jointly with the external qualities of the environment. This meant that any science of behavior could not be built around only stimulus and response. A third entity, the *organism*, had to be brought into the conceptual picture. In fact, the basic paradigm of neobehaviorism could be symbolized by placing the organism between stimulus and response, as follows:

Stimulus $\rightarrow$ Organism $\rightarrow$ Response

The new formula showed that a stimulus does not directly produce a response. By inserting the organism between stimulus and response, the paradigm of neobehaviorists explicitly acknowledged the mediating role of the organism in understanding how a stimulus can lead to a behavioral response. The relevant characteristics of the organism included such enduring traits as drive and purpose, as well as the strength of stimulus-response associations, called **habit strength**, caused by variation in reinforcement histories (Hull, 1943; Rashotte & Amsel, 1999). The S-O-R paradigm thereby breached the forbidden territory of the internal characteristics of the organisms—characteristics that were not directly observable but had to be *inferred* from behavior. While neobehaviorists were behaviorists still, their conceptual breakthroughs helped open the way some decades later to the advancement of cognitive theories.

Noam Chomsky: Language Acquisition Device

In time, behaviorism was attacked from yet other quarters. One salvo came from linguistics, and in particular from the linguistic theory of Noam Chomsky. To set the stage, let's recall the strong claims of behaviorism that traced back to John Watson. In Watson's declaration, "Give me a dozen healthy infants . . . ," a strong theoretical position was declared. The position was that all human qualities are learned; every instance of complex behavior is fully a consequence of experience. Skinner sharpened the theory by stating precisely what kinds of experience exert such profound effects: the patterns of reinforcement and punishment that followed the behaviors of the organism. A long track of consequences determines the behavior of every organism. For humans, such behavior includes spoken language.

This is where the linguist Chomsky had a problem with behaviorism. Human beings have such striking facility with language that, to Chomsky, a different conclusion seemed necessary—that humans are biologically programmed to learn language. Especially when considering how rapidly children learn language, some predisposition to learn language must be at work. That's because language acquisition is not merely a matter of learning words. Beyond word knowledge, spoken language requires that the speaker learn rules of language use, called **syntax** or grammar. Chomsky noted, for example, that speakers can easily transform statements into questions, or questions into statements. Such transformations are commonplace, but who is ever taught how to make them? Virtually every speaker uses such transformative grammars without being taught them directly. Instead, speakers infer syntax from the patterns of everyday speech. Mere experience with language prepares humans to acquire not only word knowledge, but also a sense of the underlying logic or deep structure of language. Such abstract understandings are acquired without instruction even by very young children. How is this possible? For Chomsky, it was inconceivable that this ability arises only through the stimulus-response-reinforcement mechanism that Skinner believed to be sufficient. A different conclusion seemed inevitable: Only by carrying such readiness for language *in their brain structure*, and ultimately through genetics as coded in DNA, could such amazing facility with language be displayed with consistency in the human species.

The paradigm wars between Chomsky and Skinner became somewhat personal when Chomsky published a review of Skinner's book *Verbal Behavior*. In the book review, Chomsky (1959) articulated his objections to Skinner's account of "verbal behavior" by citing the contrary evidence described above. Chomsky's strong criticism of behaviorism as an all-encompassing, totalizing theory had a major effect on the field of psychology. Some see Chomsky's review of *Verbal Behavior* as a watershed between the previously dominant American behaviorism and a new era of cognitive psychology. A new consensus was forming; behaviorism could not account for all that was interesting and important about human behavior.

Chomsky's claim that the brain must be pre-wired for language helped to launch a more sweeping movement within psychology. That movement, called **nativism**, recognized that the human brain has some innate knowledge—*unlearned* ways of understanding the world and acting upon it—a product of our DNA-coded biology rather than our experience. Of course, biology must be conjoined with the right sorts of experience for the species' heritage of native knowledge to realize its potential. But complex behavior is not merely a product of simpler behavior followed by consequences. Some pre-programming, Chomsky insisted, must be at work. If nativism holds any degree of truth, then sweeping claims by radical behaviorists (e.g., John Watson) and by "blank slate" philosophical empiricists (e.g., John Locke) must be incorrect.

Albert Bandura: Learning Through Imitation

Still other theorists were questioning the central ideas of behaviorism. One questioned assumption was whether it is always necessary to experience *firsthand* the consequences of behavior. Do we learn only from the consequences of our own actions, or can we learn by observing what happens to other people? To avoid touching a hot stovetop, must we first burn our fingers? A more convenient alternative would be to learn from the mistakes of other people and so avoid their pain. Even better, perhaps we can learn to imitate behaviors that lead to pleasant consequences.

The human capacity for imitation was compelling to psychologist Albert Bandura. He believed that firsthand experiences were not always necessary for learning to occur. He understood that human beings are highly capable of observing the behavior of other people and imitating that behavior—and of *not* imitating behavior that leads to disagreeable consequences. If one person becomes sick after eating leftover soup, there is no reason for others to repeat this mistake. They simply avoid the soup.

The power of learning through observation was a cornerstone in Albert Bandura's **social learning theory**, which recognized the major role of observation and imitation in learning. As such, it challenged the strongly individualistic mechanisms of learning identified by Skinner and other operant conditioning theorists. Even more important, social learning theory required no obvious behavior on the part of the learner. Neither did it require reinforcement and punishment. Somehow, learning can take place without *any* of the elements considered so important by behaviorists. Instead, learning occurred through social observation. For example, Bandura documented social learning in children when those children watched film recordings of other children playing with a doll violently or placidly. Children who watched violent interactions with the doll were more likely later to punch and kick a real doll. Among children, merely *observing* the behavior of other children was enough to influence behavior (Bandura, Ross, & Ross, 1961).

Humans surpass other animals in their ability to learn through imitation. Even primates such as chimpanzees are generally quite poor at imitative learning (Premack &

Premack, 1996). This is not to say that other species do not imitate—they certainly do. But human beings are better at it—more consistent in acquiring knowledge and skill from others, and much more flexible in the range of behaviors that they can imitate. Indeed, the human capacity to learn from the experiences of other people helps to explain the depth and complexity of human culture, which has no rival in the animal world. The efficiency of learning is greatly magnified through social observation. Direct experience is also important, of course, and has an essential role in education. But if all knowledge had to be reconstructed through direct individualistic experience, human culture would probably be forgotten within a single generation.

The imitative processes highlighted in social learning theory strongly suggest that children acquire *knowledge* through observation, and of course knowledge is not an acceptable theoretical concept in Skinner's radical behaviorism. To speak of knowledge is to employ cognitive terminology. Some years later, Bandura added another cognitive concept, self-efficacy beliefs, to advance our understanding of human behavior. **Self-efficacy** refers to a person's sense of his or her own capability—whether or not the person is able to perform specific actions successfully. With this theoretical contribution, Bandura spoke not only of *knowledge* but also of *self-knowledge*, which pushed the theory still deeper into cognitive territory.

From several different directions, Skinner's bold theory of operant conditioning was attacked as either incomplete or incorrect. Chomsky and other nativists declared that human beings had certain capabilities that were inborn rather than learned solely from experience. The exclusive claims that all learning was a product of behavior and its consequences therefore had to be qualified. Another qualification came from Bandura's social learning theory. Especially in humans, learning was not always a product of individual experience. Learning could instead arise from observing the actions of other people, along with the consequences of those actions. Moreover, people act in ways consistent with their beliefs about what they can do. And, as Tolman observed, humans, rats, and other species seemed to act with a sense of purpose. The mighty castle of behaviorism was being shaken down to its foundations. In the castle walls, tiny cracks widened into fissures.

Is There a Downside to Behaviorism?

Theoretical challenges to behaviorism questioned whether learning always occurs through the experiences of reinforcement or punishment. These challenges were directed toward the center of Skinner's behaviorism—how learning actually occurs. But behaviorism was also challenged from yet another quarter—research findings on the practical consequences of operant conditioning. There was no question that behavioral modification worked. Behavior could be altered through the studious application of reinforcement and punishment according to pre-defined reinforcement schedules. But, at least in some cases, behavioral modification led to unanticipated and undesirable consequences.

Undermining Intrinsic Motivation

Typically, positive reinforcement is used to teach new behaviors—actions that would not normally be performed in the absence of reinforcement. But what if those behaviors were already expressed? And what if—to use a *non*-behavioristic concept—people actually *enjoyed* the activity prior to conditioning? What would happen if reinforcement were applied under such conditions? These questions were addressed in a classic experiment by Mark Lepper and his colleagues (Lepper, Greene, & Nisbett, 1973).

To test the idea, the researchers selected an activity that was enjoyable to almost every child: playing with "Magic Markers," felt-tipped pens that draw in a variety of bright colors. The research began by measuring how much time children played with the markers during free-choice periods. Preschool children needed no obvious reinforcement to motivate their play with the markers. They enjoyed playing with Magic Markers for their own sake. The children were **intrinsically motivated**.

After the baseline levels of drawing were measured, children were randomly assigned to one of three conditions. Children in the "expected award" group were promised a "Good Player Award," a badge with ribbons showing the child's name, if they agreed to make drawings for a visitor (the researcher) for about six minutes. These children exhibited interest in the Good Player Award, and each drew with markers to earn the badge. Children in the other two groups were not shown the award, nor were they told that they could earn a badge by playing with the markers. Children in the "unexpected award" condition were later given Good Player Awards even though they had not been shown or promised one beforehand. Children in the third, "no award" group did not know about the Good Player Awards, nor were they ever given one.

Next, in the crucial part of the experiment, the researchers measured how much the children played with the Magic Markers *after* they were no longer associated with a promised reward. One week after children made the drawings, the researchers again observed the children during free-choice activities. Magic Markers and paper were made available to the children; the children could draw with the markers or not, as they preferred. The researchers observed the children through one-way glass so that their play times with the markers could be observed precisely, but the children could not see the researchers. The researchers found that children in both the "no award" and "unexpected award" conditions did not change their overall level of play with the Magic Markers. Their use of the markers neither increased nor decreased from baseline levels.

FIGURE 2.8
Children and Magic Markers *If you reward children for drawing, will their intrinsic motivation be undermined?* [Pearson Education/PH College]

The key finding is that children who had been promised a Good Player Award, and given one, *decreased* their free play with Magic Markers. No longer motivated by the promise of an extrinsic reward, their voluntary level of play dropped below the baseline levels, and to about half the free-time levels of children in the other two groups. Having already earned a Good Player Award, the children were objectively less motivated to play with Magic Markers than they were before the experiment. Children in the second group—those never promised a badge but who were given one anyway—did not differ in their baseline levels of free play with the Magic Markers. Finally, the quality of pictures drawn by the children during the experiments differed among the three groups. Drawings by children in the "expected award" condition were independently judged to be of lower quality than drawings made by children in the other two conditions.

How are these findings to be interpreted? Lepper and his colleagues inferred that the promise of a reward had decreased the intrinsic motivation that children in the first group originally had for playing with Magic Markers. Initially motivated to play with Magic Markers because of the inherent enjoyment they gave, children reinforced to play with the Magic Markers no longer felt as intrinsically motivated. Extrinsic rewards—the Good Player badges—had *undermined* intrinsic interest. As a result, voluntary play with the markers dropped off, and the drawings instrumental to earning the award were poorer in quality than drawings made by children who did not expect an award.

The Negative Effects of Extrinsic Rewards

Around the same time as the Magic Marker experiment, other studies confirmed that extrinsic rewards could undermine initial intrinsic interest in an activity. For example, when adults were paid money for solving a puzzle, their free-time engagement in the puzzle decreased (Deci, 1971). Even token amounts of money were enough to undermine intrinsic interest. This body of research suggests a warning: Extrinsic rewards have the potential to undermine intrinsic motivation.

This conclusion, stated as a possibility rather than a certainty, is highly relevant to education for two reasons. First, operant conditioning is strongly based on the use of extrinsic rewards. Positive reinforcement, as presented by Skinner, is the application of reinforcers that are not directly connected to the intended behavior. The two are distinct, connected only by the reinforcement contingencies set up by the teacher, parent, or animal trainer. Any reinforcer, such as food, money, or a badge, might decrease pre-existing intrinsic motivation for an activity. A second reason to be wary of the use of extrinsic rewards is that intrinsic motivation is universally recognized as an important learning outcome. Virtually every teacher is concerned not simply with teaching particular behaviors, but also is dedicated to increasing students' intrinsic motivation for learning. Intrinsic motivation has the wonderful benefit of sustaining learning long after any particular course has come to an end.

Tangible rewards are much less common in schools than is praise. Is there a worry, then, that the use of praise as a positive reinforcer might undermine intrinsic motivation, just as a badge or money could? The answer is less clear. Among students with lower academic ability, the connection between course grades and praise appears to be positive; however, some research has revealed a slight *negative* correlation between praise and academic achievement among high-ability students (Brophy, 1981). It seems possible that praise could undermine the intrinsic motivation of higher-ability students—but this is speculation. The data only suggest this possibility. Nevertheless, caution is in order: Any extrinsic reward, even praise, has the potential to reduce students' initial intrinsic motivation for an activity, including learning. An undermining effect is not certain, but teachers should keep this possibility in mind when they use reinforcement techniques.

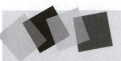

Learning Strategies

This chapter presented an approach to learning that has a distinct theoretical basis: Behaviorism concentrates on observable behavior and how to change the behavior. The two forms of behaviorism, classical and operant conditioning, both have practical applications to teaching and learning. Some of these applications, such as the use of positive reinforcement, have found their way into traditional teaching practices. Beyond positive reinforcement, behaviorism offers several other possible applications to education. This section presents ten strategies to promote learning that build directly on the theory presented in the preceding pages.

1 Avoid associating learning with negative emotions.
Research on classical conditioning shows that neutral objects can evoke strong negative emotions, such as fear. Unfortunately, many students feel negative emotions when dealing with school subjects, books, classrooms, and teachers. Teachers can minimize these negative emotions by trying to avoid inciting feelings of fear, anxiety, or shame among students. Negative emotions may effectively motivate student behavior in the short term, but have counterproductive consequences in the long term. Whenever negative emotions are evoked by school contexts, the result is a very poor context for advancing the goals of learning.

2 Associate learning with positive emotions.
The counterpart to avoiding conditioning of negative emotions is to intentionally associate positive emotions with learning. When a mathematics teacher evokes laughter and smiles, and generates a sense of emotional safety among students, those feelings can become associated, subtly but significantly, with the subject of study. More than one student has been positively influenced by a teacher's affirming personality. Such influences may have been significantly a matter of classical conditioning—the association of positive feelings with neutral objects. The idea is basic, but it is powerful, nonetheless.

3 Use continuous reinforcement to initiate new behavior.
Classical conditioning works well for teaching simple forms of behavior, but for complex learning it's necessary to rely on *operant* conditioning. One principle of operant conditioning is that to establish a new behavior, the most effective approach is to reinforce that behavior every time it occurs. Remember, the organism is inclined to repeat only behaviors that are reinforced. If reinforcement is not applied consistently in the beginning, the child (or the animal) might abandon the newly learned behavior.

4 Tailor reinforcement to the individual.
Skinner defined reinforcement only by its effects—a reinforcer is whatever causes a behavior to be repeated in the future. That same principle applies to differences among people; a reinforcer must be tailored to the preferences of individual students. A hug might be reinforcing to one student but punishing to another. Likewise, public praise might be strongly rewarding to one student, but a major disincentive to another. This complicates the work of a teacher or parent, certainly. But to believe that there is a set category of reinforcers that works for every person every time is simply wrong, and can well be counterproductive.

5 Be careful not to reinforce undesired behavior.
Operant conditioning theorists were well aware that the anger evoked by misbehavior might well be reinforcing to the miscreant student. When a student misbehaves and the teacher's attention shifts immediately to the student ("Stop doing that!"), the student might find the focused attention very rewarding. The teacher thereby mistakes reinforcement (what the student feels) for punishment (what the teacher intends). This simple error is one that most teachers understand very well. We can thank behaviorists for explaining why what seems superficially to be punishment is actually a reward.

6 Reduce reinforcement after the new behavior becomes established.

After a new behavior has been established, a teacher can gradually reduce reinforcement over time. As reinforcement is gradually withdrawn, the new behavior can become self-sustaining, motivated by its own intrinsic rewards. Extrinsic rewards can establish the new competency; but once established, intrinsic rewards can sustain it indefinitely. The progression toward intrinsic motivation for learning is a worthy goal in the value system of every teacher.

7 Switch to random reinforcement to make the new behavior robust.

Continuous reinforcement is effective in establishing a new behavior, such as paying attention to schoolwork. But once a behavior is established with some regularity, the teacher can employ a new strategy. Now, the goal is to strengthen the new behavior so that it does not have to be reinforced every time. For example, a teacher not only wants each learner to pay attention to the task at hand, but also to develop the *habit* of paying attention. The goal is to make the new behavior resistant to extinction so that it will persevere through long periods without reinforcement. To strengthen the new behavior, it's a good idea to switch to a variable ratio schedule of reinforcement—to gradually reduce the frequency of reinforcement and to introduce an element of random timing. Variable ratio schedules can help establish the behaviors as habitual and enduring.

8 Be careful of the undermining effects of extrinsic rewards.

Following the widespread use of behavior modification in education and child-rearing, psychologists found a potentially serious drawback to the use of extrinsic awards—they might undermine intrinsic motivation. Whenever using extrinsic rewards, a teacher should bear in mind this possibility: If a student has an abiding interest in a topic, that interest could actually decrease as a consequence of extrinsic rewards. Course grades, ubiquitous in schools, may well have such undermining effects. Other extrinsic motivators may add to this effect. The undermining potential of reinforcement is not necessarily inevitable—rewards might help to establish a nonexistent behavior. Still, all teachers and parents should be aware of this possible pitfall of operant conditioning.

9 Use unanticipated rewards.

In some experiments on extrinsic rewards, unanticipated awards do not undermine intrinsic motivation. For example, when extrinsic rewards are given as unanticipated surprises for wanted behavior they can help sustain that behavior without subtracting from students' intrinsic interest (Lepper et al., 1973). Skillful teaching might include weaving in unanticipated rewards so that intrinsic enjoyment of the activity can continue and, ideally, build up over time.

10 Use cognitive concepts.

For all the conceptual and practical benefits of behaviorism, the theory has serious limitations for guiding teaching and learning. Any complete account of teaching practice must include such cognitive concepts as reasoning, problem solving, critical thinking, interest, curiosity, and understanding. These concepts are not part of the vocabulary of behaviorism, which concentrates exclusively on observable behavior. Teachers need not—indeed, should not—restrict themselves conceptually in this way. That is why when teachers apply behavioristic principles, it's best not to rely on behaviorism exclusively. Rather than treating behaviorism as a sufficient theory for understanding and influencing all human behavior, a teacher is better advised to be theoretically eclectic, mixing and matching ideas from various theories as they open up possibilities for advancing the goals of education.

These ten strategies show how the principles of behaviorism—both classical and operant conditioning—can advance the goals of teaching and learning. The applications are straightforward and practical, but they are not exhaustive. Like all the principles presented in this book, the ten listed are strategies rather than foolproof rules. Every strategy must be adapted to the characteristics of particular learners and to the unique approach and personality of the teacher. Not all strategies need to be used—perhaps only two or three will work well for any particular teacher and situation. When those strategies are used, they should be applied sensitively and sensibly to the particular mix of learners who, with their teacher, are jointly advancing what their minds can do.

 # Conclusion

This chapter surveys the historical and conceptual high points of behaviorism, from the physiological experiments of Pavlov to the social philosophy of Skinner. In its range of concepts and applications, behaviorism—both classical and operant conditioning—can account for a wide range of human and animal learning. But the kinds of learning accounted for by classical and operant conditioning are different. Classical conditioning can explain how initially neutral stimuli can evoke relatively primitive behavior, including fear reactions. Operant conditioning helps to explain how complex behavior can be learned through a succession of reinforcement and punishment consequences.

Looking back on the history of classical and operant conditioning, we should remember what motivated the restriction of behaviorism to observable phenomena. John Watson articulated the stance most clearly: He believed that psychology could evolve as a scientific field most expeditiously if it confined its range of relevant phenomena to objective behavior. Because such entities as knowledge, goals, beliefs, and intentions are not directly observable, they cannot be reliably studied—or so behaviorists believed.

Eventually, the self-imposed delimitations of behaviorism paid off with theories that illuminated conditions of learning. As we have seen, behaviorism—particularly the principles of operant conditioning—has affected teaching and child-rearing practices in significant and enduring ways. Above all, the legacy of behaviorism is manifest in the deliberate and strategic use of positive reinforcement to encourage the repetition of desired behavior. Positive reinforcement is used routinely by teachers and parents. More obscurely, the use of certain schedules of reinforcement, especially the variable ratio schedule, can make learned behavior robustly resistant to extinction in the absence of rewards.

For all these conceptual and strategic benefits, however, behaviorism does have certain disadvantages. In its application, the use of positive reinforcement can, under some circumstances, undermine pre-existing intrinsic motivation. If students expect their engagement in an activity to be followed by a reward, the students might conclude that they engage in that activity only *because* of the reward—not because they enjoy the activity. This possible effect of positive reinforcement should suggest caution to every teacher and parent who applies techniques of behavioral modification. But there is a more significant downside to strict reliance on behaviorism as a way to understand and influence learning. The language of behaviorism, especially in its original and more radical formulations, excludes the language of cognition.

The exclusion of cognitive concepts from discussions about learning is a huge liability and disadvantage for anyone interested in education. Educators need to consider not only reinforcement contingencies, but also such vital concepts as reasoning, understanding, mental models, problem solving, and critical thinking. Education is enriched by taking such concepts seriously because teachers understand that students have minds, and that students' minds must learn to reason and understand as part of the education process. Moreover, all learners have interests and motives, hopes and fears. A complete theory of learning, as well as a complete theory of effective teaching, needs such powerful ideas at its center.

We can speculate whether or not behaviorism was good for American psychology. Some have argued that its conceptual restrictiveness over a half-century cost psychology dearly (Norman, 1990). Only in the 1960s did cognitive psychology germinate and then flourish among psychologists. Inspired by the metaphor of a digital computer, rigorous models of the human mind began to shed light on the nature of the thinking process, including problem solving. The theoretical payoff was tremendous. We now know much about how the mind works, the nature of knowledge, and the many varieties of complex cognition. Not only has our knowledge of the mind advanced, but we also know better than ever how to promote understanding and complex thought. Our era is perhaps the best yet for teaching and teachers. Today's teachers can profitably apply the legacy of principles derived from behaviorism; but those principles, however useful, are more powerfully complemented by discoveries that emerged from the study of human cognition.

REFERENCES

Bandura, A., Ross, D., & Ross, S. A. (1961). Transmission of aggression through imitation of aggressive models. *Journal of Abnormal and Social Psychology, 63*, 575–582.

Bijou, S. W. (1993). *Behavior analysis of child development* (2nd rev.). Reno, NV: Context Press.

Brophy, J. (1981). Teacher praise: A functional analysis. *Review of Educational Research, 51*(1), 5–32.

Chomsky, N. (1959). A review of B. F. Skinner's "Verbal Behavior." *Language, 35*(1), 26–58.

Deci, E. L. (1971). Effects of externally mediated rewards on intrinsic motivation. *Journal of Personality and Social Psychology, 18*(1), 105–115.

Hobbes, T. (1651/1963). *Leviathan: On the matter, forme, and power of a commonwealth ecclesiasticall and civil.* New York: Collier Books.

Hull, C. (1943). *Principles of behavior.* New York: Appleton-Century-Crofts.

Innis, N. K. (1999). Edward C. Tolman's purposive behaviorism. In W. O'Donohue & R. Kitchener (Eds.), *Handbook of behaviorism* (pp. 97–117). San Diego, CA: Academic Press.

Lepper, M. R., Greene, D., & Nisbett, R. E. (1973). Undermining children's intrinsic interest with extrinsic reward: A test of the "overjustification" hypothesis. *Journal of Personality and Social Psychology, 28*, 129–137.

Norman, D. A. (1990, August 26). The mind exists: Commentary on the death of B. F. Skinner. *Los Angeles Times* (Op-ed page).

Pavlov, I. P. (1927). *Conditioned reflexes.* London: Routledge and Kegan Paul.

Premack, D., & Premack, A. J. (1996). Why animals lack pedagogy and some cultures have more of it than others. In D. R. Olson & N. Torrance (Eds.), *The handbook of education and human development* (pp. 302–323). Oxford: Blackwell.

Rashotte, M. E., & Amsel, A. (1999). Clark L. Hull's behaviorism. In W. O'Donohue & R. Kitchener (Eds.), *Handbook of behaviorism* (pp. 119–158). San Diego, CA: Academic Press.

Ringen, J. (1999). Radical behaviorism: B. F. Skinner's philosophy of science. In W. O'Donohue & R. Kitchener (Eds.), *Handbook of behaviorism* (pp. 159–178). San Diego, CA: Academic Press.

SeaWorld (2002). *SeaWorld/Busch Gardens Animal Information Database.* www.seaworld.org.

SeaWorld (1994). *Training Shamu.* U.S. Kids.

Skinner, B. F. (1938). *The behavior of organisms.* New York: Appleton-Century-Crofts.

Skinner, B. F. (1948). *Walden two.* New York: Macmillan.

Skinner, B. F. (1951). How to teach animals. *Scientific American, 185*(12), 26–29.

Skinner, B. F. (1958). Teaching machines. *Science, 128*, 3330, 969–977.

Skinner, B. F. (1971). *Beyond freedom and dignity.* New York: Knopf.

Skinner, B. F. (1990). Can psychology be a science of mind? *American Psychologist, 45*, 1206–1210.

Timberlake, W. (1999). Biological behaviorism. In W. O'Donohue & R. Kitchener (Eds.), *Handbook of behaviorism* (pp. 243–284). San Diego, CA: Academic Press.

Tolman, E. C. (1932). *Purposive behavior in animals and men.* New York: Century.

Watson, J. B. (1913). Psychology as the behaviorist sees it. *Psychological Review, 20*, 157–177.

Watson, J. B. (1924). *Behaviorism.* New York: Norton.

[3] The Cognitive Architecture

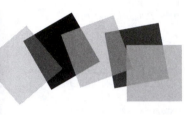

The development of behaviorism, which was crucial to the history of psychology, yielded many insights that have practical value for education. Theories of behaviorism were ultimately recognized to be incomplete, however. When weaknesses began to appear in behaviorism as a totalizing theory, the search was on for an alternative. During that era, **neobehaviorists** concluded that characteristics of the organism must be taken into account to understand behavior. Models based on stimulus and response were not enough. Consequently, the neobehaviorists postulated that a third component—the organism, symbolized by "O"—should be interposed between the stimulus and response. As behaviorism began to loosen its grip on American psychology, the nature of the organism became all-important, eclipsing stimulus-response contingencies as the object of theoretical interest.

At about the same time, digital computers began to attract the interest of universities, businesses, government, and industry. No longer were computers gigantic banks of vacuum-tube electronics and flashing lights that occupied entire buildings. Computers were becoming smaller, cheaper, and more powerful. Even before the advent of personal or desktop computers, their obvious power to store and transform information led naturally to a comparison with the human mind and provided a metaphor for thinking about how the human mind is similarly structured. Against the background of fading confidence in behaviorism and the rising interest in digital computers, a very engaging question began to form: Is the human mind like a computer? This chapter presents the cognitive architecture as derived from such an information-processing view of the human mind.

The Computer Metaphor

The Human Mind Is Like a Computer

MEMORY. The human mind *is* like a computer in several ways. The most obvious similarity is memory. Minds have memory; computers do too. A computer's memory is vital to its power and functionality. The more memory, the better. And we know that computers have different *kinds* of memory. Some computer memory is durable, such as on hard drives; other memory is temporary, such as in RAM (random access memory). Memory of the first kind is safe if you accidentally turn the power switch off; the second kind is not. Humans, too, have more than one kind of memory. The most basic distinction is between short-term memory and long-term memory.

TRANSFORMATION OF INFORMATION. A second similarity between computers and the human mind is that both transform information. The innovation of computers is not that they *store* information—after all, data storage can be accomplished by passive media, such as magnetic tape. The power and potential of computers is in *computation*—the ability to transform information to yield some valuable product. Computers not only can store the numbers 5 and 2, they can add or multiply these two numbers, or compute 5^2 or 2^5. In many kinds of computation, computers are much faster and more accurate than any human being. Of course, minds also transform information. In fact, it's possible to see their transformative function as more impressive than their storage ability. Human minds continuously transform information, in particular by inference—extending what is known to draw new conclusions. The mind is constantly "going beyond the information given." So, we can see that computers and human minds both transform information.

OPEN SYSTEM. A third similarity between computers and human minds is that both are open systems. They interact with realities outside themselves. Both are capable of acquiring information from the outside (input) and of using that information to act on the world in some way (output). To understand the human mind, it is vitally important to appreciate this openness because the mind's larger reality is its surrounding culture—the people, objects, beliefs, and practices that constitute a society's way of surviving and finding meaning.

The Human Mind Is Unlike a Computer

PURPOSE, VALUES, EMOTIONS, PERSONALITY. Computers and human minds are very different in other ways. Many of the qualities that make people distinctively human—their personalities, beliefs, emotions, and life purposes—seem to have no counterpart in computers. These qualities are obvious in people, but it's not at all clear whether computers could *ever* have these qualities.

CONSCIOUSNESS. Another difference between computers and human beings is consciousness—humans have it and computers don't. Once that claim is articulated, though, the follow up question is: What is consciousness? This question could take us very deep into the philosophy of consciousness, but it will suffice to accept the commonsense understanding that consciousness is a self-awareness that we exist, and that we have identities and purposeful agency in the world. No one believes that computers currently have such self-awareness, but this does not mean that consciousness is impossible for computers to achieve. To the contrary, some philosophers and computer scientists believe that computer consciousness is not only possible, but is actually inevitable. Why? Because if consciousness arises from material complexity rather than a nonmaterial soul, then computers must eventually reach a critical point where they, too, become conscious—just as humans have at some point in their evolutionary past. This claim is highly controversial, of course, but it has been expressed.

The articulated differences between human beings and computers are not intended to state for all time how the two will differ. It's possible that computers will become more like humans with time, perhaps even learning to love (a theme of sci fi movies such as *A.I.* and *Bicentennial Man*). The reverse might also be true: that humans will adopt new modes of analytical thinking that are computer-like. For our present purposes we simply need to recognize that a comparison between the human mind and computers can be highly fruitful, but it will necessarily have limitations. The computer can be an illuminating metaphor for the human mind, but every metaphor is limited. The computer metaphor is no exception.

The Sensory Register

Having made a disclaimer about the limitations of a computer metaphor for the human mind, let's now delve into the insights that the metaphor permits. Specifically, let's return to the most obvious similarity between computers and minds—that both have memory. In a computer, the purpose of memory is to hold information. The same is true in the human cognitive system. Information often flows from the outside inward—from the external environment into our conscious awareness. As we follow this outward-to-inward path, we can trace information as it flows among three human memory structures: **the sensory register**, **short-term memory**, and **long-term memory**.

The **sensory register** has special significance because it is the first stop in the mind after information reaches our eyes, ears, fingertips, and other sensory organs. You can gain insight into the special nature of the sensory register by thinking about your own real-life experiences. Imagine that you are on a university campus reading a book. Plenty of people are milling about, talking or walking to their next class. The scene is busy. You look to your left briefly and then look straight ahead again. But something you just saw makes you turn back to the left. What is it? It's that you noticed your friend walking by.

The peculiar thing about this common experience—the "double take"—is that you recognized your friend *after* you looked away. How could that be true? You must have been scanning some brief memory of what your eyes had just taken in. That memory is the **visual sensory register**. The visual scene you took in during your brief glance to the left was detailed, but you can hold this information for only a short period of time. You would not be able to recognize your friend's face in a memory you mentally scan 30 seconds after the fact. So the duration of the sensory register is very brief.

There is a counterpart sensory register for the auditory system. Think of a time when, during a conversation with a friend, your attention drifted momentarily and you missed part of what your friend said. You ask, "What did you say?" Your friend starts to respond, but before she can repeat all her words, you realize that you already know what was spoken—you already know because you replayed the last few seconds of sound in your **auditory sensory register**.

Now let's think about the properties of the sensory register. The duration of the sensory register—whether auditory or visual—is brief (Sperling, 1960). The duration of the visual sensory register is only about half a second. The auditory sensory register lasts a little longer—normally about two seconds.

One unresolved question about the sensory register is whether it is a brain-based memory function, or whether its qualities are instead a function of the sensory organs—namely, our eyes and ears. For example, during a fireworks celebration, a child waves a lit sparkler in the night air. The sparkler creates the sensation of a scintillating trail of light that fades toward the tail. The sparkler trail is one manifestation of the sensory register preserving visual information for a very short period of time. It's unclear, though, whether the briefly preserved information is stored in the retinas of our eyes, or whether it is held in the visual cortex of our brains. This is a theoretical question, one that will presumably be answered by research. The experiential reality of

FIGURE 3.1
Can you see *after* you look away? *You can with the help of the sensory register.* [Photo by Jamie Stein.]

the sensory register is there for us to consider regardless of where in the nervous system that information is stored.

Short-Term Memory/Working Memory

We have seen that the first memory structure, the sensory register, is very volatile—it lasts at most only about two seconds. The human mind would not be very impressive if it depended only on the sensory register. Fortunately, the sensory register interacts with two additional memory structures that compose the cognitive system. You already know the names of these two memories: short-term memory and long-term memory (Atkinson & Shiffrin, 1971). It is these two memory systems that give human cognition its characteristic power of intelligent, rational, and creative thought. First, we will delve into the nature of **short-term memory** (**STM**), also known as working memory.

Properties of Short-Term Memory

What are you thinking about right now? Without a doubt, you are giving full consideration to understanding the human mind. The subject fascinates you. You really *want* to understand short-term memory, and how minds are like computers in some ways and unlike them in others. You also want to know how all this applies to teaching and learning. This *is* what you are thinking about . . . or maybe not.

It *could* be that you are thinking about what's for dinner, or someplace you would rather be, or a special person whose company you would really enjoy right now. *Whatever* you are thinking about, *that* is the content of your short-term memory. We can therefore say that short-term memory is where you hold the content of your current thought. To say it another way: Short-term memory is the cognitive function that corresponds to your awareness. It is the locus of your consciousness.

SMALL CAPACITY. You can appreciate the properties of short-term memory by engaging in a little introspection. To introspect is to "look inward"—to think about how you think. Try this: How many ideas can you consider at one time? Can you think about ten different people all at once? It's unlikely. What about two people at one time? Probably so. Now this difference—two is easy, but ten is impossible—helps bound the capacity of short-term memory. The capacity is somewhere between two and ten.

In 1956, psychologist George Miller narrowed that range in what has become the most famous paper in cognitive psychology: "The Magical Number Seven, Plus or Minus Two." In this paper, Miller "complained" that he was being persecuted by an integer. The number seven kept reappearing in psychological research on memory. The article documented many different experiments in psychology that converged on a general pattern: The human mind can hold only about seven pieces of information at once. The integer seven was important because it helped pin a parameter on human cognition—short-term memory has limited capacity, and that capacity can be stated as precisely as a single integer.

Well, perhaps the number isn't *exactly* seven. Miller admitted wiggle room in the title of his article—plus or minus two. So instead we have a range, between five and nine. Still, the range tells us something very important about human cognition. The capacity of short-term memory is limited to just a few items. We cannot think about a lot of information in any given moment.

SHORT DURATION. If you introspect again, there's something else to discover by considering your conscious thoughts—they are fleeting. Every day our mental awareness is a succession of thousands and thousands of ideas. No idea lasts longer than a few seconds before we move on to others. Any particular idea, such as an arithmetic fact or a person's name, is only briefly the focus of attention—and then it's gone. Ideas are evanescent in our experience, and this temporary quality of ideas presents challenges for learning (to which we'll return). The experience of mental life as a stream of ideas reveals another fact: Although short-term memory is continuously active, the duration of any single idea is short. It is, after all, *short-term* memory.

This quality of short-term memory—its short duration—is not inevitable. It is possible to override the short duration by intense concentration. If I asked you to think about the color orange for the next hour, you might be able to do so. Certainly you could hold the idea in short-term memory for at least several minutes. But the effort and concentration that fixation requires actually reinforces the larger point, which is that in our typical experience ideas in short-term memory have a short duration.

Appreciate this about short-term memory: The two qualities that we can now identify—small capacity and short duration—are really rather significant. What we actively think about is *not much for not long*. That combination imposes major restrictions on the thinking process. The basic architecture of cognition seems to have severe design constraints. When you compare those limitations to the indisputable achievements of the human mind manifest in and through culture, the contrast is striking.

STM Is a Cognitive Workspace

After George Miller pinpointed the capacity of short-term memory (seven plus or minus two), another psychologist, Alan Baddeley, introduced another key idea: The function of short-term memory is not simply storage (1986). In addition, short-term memory is the cognitive resource that is responsible for mental work. Short-term memory not only holds the digits 2 and 7 in conscious awareness; it's also where we compute $2 + 7$, or 2×7, or 7^2, or the decimal value for two-sevenths.

WORKING MEMORY. When Baddeley recognized this second major function of short-term memory, he thought it would be fitting to rename the memory accordingly. He proposed *working memory* instead of short-term memory. The term **working memory** captures everything meant by short-term memory, plus one additional feature—the role of doing work on information. Both terms are acceptable and are used relatively interchangeably, but the term *working memory* implies something slightly different (and something more) than the term *short-term memory*. Working memory conveys short-term information storage plus mental work. These two functions tell us that working memory is the real-time workspace of the mind.

Now we can connect the two functions of working memory—information storage and work—a little more deeply. What is the evidence for claiming that working memory does mental work? One piece of evidence is that the storage capacity of working memory (seven plus or minus two) is affected by whether or not work is done on that information. Imagine that you are given a series of random numbers and you try to remember as many as possible. If you are asked to *do* something with those numbers—say, add them mentally—this will cut into your capacity. Mental work uses some of the capacity of working memory just as information storage uses up capacity. Both are part of the same informational economy of working memory, which is known to be limited. In other words, the two major functions of working memory—storing information and processing that information—share the same limited capacity.

Teaching with Working Memory in Mind

DON'T OVERWHELM STUDENTS' WORKING MEMORY. Can we derive any principles for teaching based on what we know about working memory? Indeed, we can. If we appreciate that working memory has a limited capacity, it becomes necessary not to overwhelm that capacity. If too much information is presented too rapidly, learners will be overwhelmed. Instead of learning and understanding the new concepts, students will lose track of information and become confused. Each teacher needs to appreciate the most important design feature of working memory—that its capacity is limited. Violation of this design feature by presenting too much information too quickly might be the most common pedagogical error of all.

The limited capacity of working memory also has implications for how information should be *structured*. The structural principle derives directly from the recognized capacity parameter of seven, plus or minus two. To state it negatively: It's a bad idea to introduce a topic by saying, "In this lesson, there are ten ideas you should keep in mind." It's better to say, "Four ideas are most important." The difference between four and ten parts is that the first can be accommodated by working memory, and the second cannot. Why should we respect the capacity of working memory in how lessons are structured? Because when learners try to understand the lesson as a whole, it's helpful to see how its major parts relate to each other. A learner can see the overall structure if the number of parts is relatively few—that is, if the basic structure can be accommodated in working memory.

COOPERATE WITH THE DESIGN OF THE MIND. As we have seen, the limited capacity of working memory has implications for teaching. One basic implication is that new information should be paced and structured so that it does not overwhelm the working memory capacity of the learner. When in doubt, slow down and simplify. This instructional principle does not impeach the power of the human intellect. The ability of the human mind to accomplish marvelous feats is beyond question. The mind's productive power is manifest *despite* the striking capacity limitations of its mental workspace— what we call working memory. When we acknowledge this information-processing bottleneck, we respect the design features of the mind. When we cooperate with the mind's design, better thinking and learning follow.

Long-Term Memory

We've been talking about working memory—that function of cognitive awareness and processing with a fairly small capacity. But wait—you know much more than seven pieces of information. In fact, you know more than seven hundred or seven thousand ideas. How much *do* you know? If you were to divide your knowledge into elemental concepts, the number might be closer to seventy thousand or seven hundred thousand. How do we accommodate that fact in our theory of cognition? The answer is simple: **long-term memory (LTM).**

What Do You Know?

You know a *lot*, and your knowledge is of many different kinds. You know many people, and you know *about* many more people, including imaginary ones (e.g., Obi-Wan Kenobi). You also know many places: places you have been (e.g., your hometown), places you probably haven't been (e.g., the Taj Mahal), and places you could never be (e.g., Robert Louis Stevenson's imaginary Treasure Island). You know about many things, both categories of objects (such as *house*) and particular objects (such as *your* house). Beyond people, places, and things, you also know how to do things. You have skills, and those skills are knowledge, too. Your skills include thousands of patterns of learned behavior that extend from everyday actions, like walking and eating, to more specialized skills, such as writing, talking, driving, and shaking hands. Ritualized behavior patterns, such as how to make purchases in a store, are also part of your vast knowledge base. Beyond these, you probably have movie-like memories of your own past experiences. These vivid and dynamic memories are also part of your knowledge base. All are stored in your long-term memory.

One feature of long-term memory should by now be clear: its capacity is enormous. It stores all that you know. For this reason, long-term memory is the warehouse of the mind. Some information in long-term memory might be accessed very infrequently, but it's there nonetheless. The large capacity of long-term memory contrasts sharply with the limited capacity of working memory, as well as the larger, but still quite

FIGURE 3.2
Treasure Island
Long-term memory can hold many kinds of knowledge, including references to imaginary worlds (Courtesy of the Library of Congress)

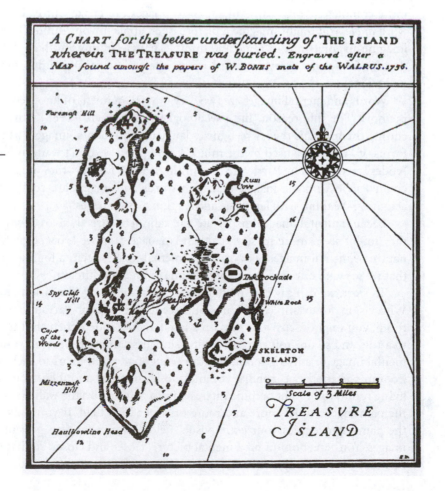

limited, capacity of the sensory register. The three memory structures differ in other ways, too. They differ in duration, for example. Memories in the sensory register are very brief. Ideas in working memory last a little longer, perhaps a minute or so. By contrast, the duration of ideas in long-term memory is long—often very long and possibly even permanent. At least some knowledge stored in long-term memory is recorded for a lifetime.

Multimodal LTM

Now let's look further into the nature of long-term memory. Introspection can help us again. As already noted, long-term memory holds different *kinds* of knowledge.

DUAL CODING THEORY. One very important kind of knowledge is language. Language is not simply a way for people to communicate, it is also an important form of knowledge in its own right. Words help us to understand the world around us because we represent much of what we know in linguistic form. You know many thousands of words. Consider the word *apple*. You recognize the word and can describe what it means. But there is something else—another way of knowing what *apple* means. In your mind you can see an image of an apple. Your mental image might be a shiny green Granny Smith apple or a dark Red Delicious apple. Maybe you can rotate the apple in your mind, or perhaps even slice it mentally.

So here you have two powerful and important kinds of knowledge: words and images. They are quite different, but they work together to make your understanding more complete. Words can evoke images; images can evoke words. Upon reading the word *apple*, you might imagine a picture of an apple in your mind. Or you might first imagine an apple in your mind and think, "That's a Granny Smith apple." Hundreds or thousands of times every day, word-image interactions form an important part of your mental life.

Words and mental images are two very important forms of knowledge in long-term memory. For this reason, the psychologist Allan Paivio (1986) proposed the **dual coding theory**. This theory recognizes language and mental imagery as two dominant forms of knowledge used by the mind. At this point we don't want to say that the two "codes" recognized by Paivio are the *only* knowledge forms—they are not—but we can credit Paivio with the insight that both words and images are central to the mind's activities. We think with language and we think with images.

Because mental images are private and cannot be directly shared with other people, they might seem more mysterious than language. Can we learn something about the nature of mental images? For example, mental images seem a lot like vision—images that we see with our eyes. Are they the same or are they different?

To start, we can say that mental imagery is *something* like vision (Kosslyn, 1980). With vision, for example, you can scan a scene and focus on various objects. In a living room, you might focus your eyes on a lamp, then a couch, then shift to a coffee table, to a rug, and so on. You can carry out a similar scanning process in your mind with a mental image of a living room. You can sequentially shift focus to each object in turn. Zooming is another capability common to both vision and mental imagery. In a real living room, you might become interested in a painting on the wall. As you walk closer, the painting occupies more and more of your visual field. If you walk close enough, the painting occupies your *entire* visual field. Zooming is also possible with mental images. You can zoom in on a mental picture, closer and closer, so that eventually the mental picture fills up your entire mental "screen." These two functions, scanning and zooming, are common to both the visual images we see with our eyes and to the mental images we see inside our heads.

There are differences, however. To illustrate one such difference, close your eyes and imagine a zebra. Can you see the zebra's long neck, mane, legs, and its trademark black-and-white striping? It's an amazing image, even if it is conjured up entirely by your mind.

Now there is one more thing to do: *Count the stripes*. It's unlikely that you can. Why not? Because the stripes in our mental image are not precisely determined as they are on a real zebra. It's as if we have the knowledge that zebras have stripes, and our minds construct them as needed in our mental image. We place the *idea* of stripes on our imaginary zebra at the moment we create the mental image—but the stripes have an abstract quality to them rather than precise physical locations. Mental images often have this indefinite quality. They can be astonishingly vivid, even beautiful, but they do not have the stable precision of the real objects we see with our eyes.

INTEREST MAGNET 3.1

Photographic Memory

People with photographic memory, or *eidetic memory*, have the ability to remember certain kinds of information very accurately and for long periods of time. Eidetic memory is different from a normal memory in that eidetic memory is highly accurate, even years after the memory was formed. Biographies of some highly accomplished people suggest that they may have had eidetic memories. Possible "eidetikers" include the painter Claude Monet, the scientist Jules Henri Poincaré, and the physicist Nikola Tesla. The mathematician John von Neumann was said to be able to recite the content of the page of any book after glancing at it only briefly.

The first detailed study of eidetic memory was conducted by the Russian psychologist Alexander Luria (1968). Luria wrote a short biography of a man named Solomon Shereshevskii, whom he called "S" for the sake of anonymity. As a young man, S was a newspaper reporter who, to his editor's surprise, never took notes on his assignments, yet he could remember information perfectly. S was referred to Luria, a psychologist, to have his memory tested. Luria could present any sequence of information—words or numbers—only once, and S would later remember that information almost perfectly. The length of any sequence did not matter, nor did the elapsed time between initial learning and recall. S's memory for details was nearly perfect. Luria (1968) noted that:

> his memory *had no distinct limits* . . . there was no limit either to the *capacity* of S's memory or to the *durability of the traces he retained*. . . . He had no

difficulty reproducing any lengthy series of words whatever, even though these originally had been presented to him a week, a month, a year, or many years earlier. (pp. 11–12, emphasis in original).

For S, memory was a nonselective collection of concrete particulars—a "junk heap of impressions" (Bruner, 1968, p. viii). Consequently, he had difficulty finding the larger patterns that make sense of commonalities across experience. S's astonishing memory was distinctly low-level, aided by a propensity to form unusual associations. For example, ordinary numbers acquired personalities: The number 7 was a man with a mustache and 8 was a very stout woman.

Uncontrollable elaborations gave S his tremendous ability to remember details, a skill he applied as a professional memory expert later in life. However, this nonselective memory proved confusing and distracting, and sometimes made it difficult for S to understand more abstract meanings. His tested intelligence, in fact, was only average. Luria's study showed that S's ability to remember detail was offset by a deficiency—indeed, a disability—in making sense of his experience. S was an unhappy man; his ability/disability seems to have led to considerable personal turmoil. At the end of his life, he was unable to distinguish recent conversations from those that occurred years earlier, and he was committed to an asylum.

Normal individuals remember selectively from experience. We remember the *meanings* of events in terms of their significance to our lives, values, and goals. Rather than seeing the selective quality of long-term memory as a liability, we should consider the benefits of the selective nature of human memory.

From these observations we can see more clearly how mental imagery works. First, images are a vital part of our mental life as knowledge forms that are distinct from language. Second, mental images are like vision in some ways, but different in others. Teachers can use these facts when planning lessons. For example, teachers might try to help students to form certain mental images. A biology student might benefit from being able to conjure a mental image of a cell with its membrane structure, nucleus, and so on. A more advanced biology student might form mental images of DNA and protein structures in molecular detail. Mental images are a legitimate goal for instruction in many subjects—not only in biology but also in geography, physics, earth science, history, literature, and other domains.

There is one caution, however. Mental imagery as just described is not completely universal. Among blind people, for example, mental imagery is likely to be different than it is among sighted people. But even among people with normal vision, mental imagery may be minimal. A few paragraphs back, I asked you to imagine an apple in your mind. Some people have trouble generating clear and vivid mental images of even common objects (McKelvie, 1995). In fact, some people *never* experience mental pictures. They can't form images of apples and zebras, nor even of people they know and love. They lack the ability to generate mental pictures. There are implications for teaching here: Teachers should bear in mind that mental imagery is an important form of knowledge, and can try to teach students to generate mental images to support learning. But they should also remember that this capability is not completely universal.

OTHER REPRESENTATIONAL MODES. When we speak of mental imagery, there is another fact to bear in mind. We have been speaking of imagery as mental pictures. However, the technical meaning of the term *mental imagery* also includes mental experiences in other sensory modes. This broader meaning of *imagery* includes, for example, the mental experiences of sound, smell, and taste. By extension, we can include imagined kinesthetic experiences—not actual experiences of the material world through the senses, but mental experiences that *seem* real. Putting this all together, you can see that the range of experiences that we call mental imagery closely parallel our sensory experiences in the world. All imagery can be experienced in the moment, but imagery can also be stored in long-term memory and remembered at a later time. And because it can be stored and later retrieved (say, by imagining a familiar face), mental imagery must be considered a major form of knowledge, one that interacts richly with language.

A Fully Cross-Referenced Encyclopedia

There's more to say about long-term memory. One provocative insight by psychologist Herbert Simon (1980) is that long-term memory is a fully cross-referenced encyclopedia. What does that mean? The encyclopedia comparison is easy: Our knowledge in long-term memory is encyclopedic, not that we know *everything*, but rather that we know a lot about many, many different topics. *Cross-referenced* means that everything is interconnected. In some books, an index provides page citations of many different topics—often hundreds or thousands of them. In this book, for example, the index gives you the page references for all the major topics. The index enriches the connectivity of ideas spread throughout the book because it provides the connections—not all of them, but many. Cross-referencing is similar to indexing, but even more convenient. It entails providing the page numbers of other references to the same topic *within* the text rather than in a separate index. As a reader, you can look up the other references directly rather than having to consult an alphabetized index.

IDEAS LINKED BY MEANING. To speak of long-term memory as a *fully* cross-referenced encyclopedia means that *all* mental knowledge is *directly* connectable. There is no need to go to an index—every idea is directly connected to all similar ideas. Take the idea of *music*. When you think of music, you might call to mind your favorite bands or artists. You can think about the history of music through the centuries, the distinctive music of various cultures, the variety of musical instruments, musical notation, music copyrights, jazz, rock, opera, choral music, digitized soundtracks, and so on. In a general book on music, page references to these different topics would be widely scattered. You would have to use an index to make all the connections. In your long-term memory, this is not the case. The connections are immediate and direct. Long-term memory is profusely interconnected, and for this reason one idea can trigger many related ideas. This profuse connectivity is a marvel of human knowledge, and an amazing design feature of long-term memory.

MULTIMEDIA/HYPERMEDIA. In some ways, the special features of long-term memory resemble information presented in electronic form by computers. In the 1980s and 1990s, personal computers began to present information in many different forms—not text only, but also pictures, sound, and video. Over time, these varied forms became more sensibly interconnected. The integration of information in different modes was termed *multimedia*. A parallel development in information technology was the linking of related information. Click on a word or picture, and you could learn more about that particular topic. This direct connectivity of related ideas through mouse clicks was called *hypermedia*.

The modal richness of multimedia and the interconnectivity of hypermedia reached a new plane with the establishment of the Internet. Through search engines and direct links among web pages, it became possible to access an immense body of information created and stored on servers spread around the world. For the first time in history, an inconceivably large body of information was accessible instantaneously. Through its defining properties—multimodality and interconnectivity—the Internet evolved a technology that closely resembled human long-term memory. People approached the Internet with the confidence that they could obtain the information they wanted, much as they would search their own memories for stored knowledge. Of course, the Internet can contain false and misleading information, just as the mind can. In this way also, the mind and the Internet bear a striking resemblance. Like the human mind, the Internet provides direct and virtually instantaneous access to information in multimodal form. Now if the Internet can function as an extension of long-term memory, what does this imply for education?

A Childhood Birthday Party

Often the words and images held in long-term memory have a factual quality that is not directly related to any specific personal experience. But human memory also includes personal experiences from the past. Whenever we mentally travel to the past to relive a personal experience, we use our **episodic memory** (Tulving, 2002). Episodic memory can include mental images that have a dynamic quality such that we experience them much like movies in our head. When we remember events from the past we sometimes "replay" those events as mental cinema.

When I teach on the topic of episodic memory, I ask my students to imagine one of their childhood birthday parties. Who was there? What happened? Did you play games? Did you open presents?

Now at this point in the class, I engage in a little deception. I ask the students NOT to write down what I'm about to say. Then I make the following claim:

The human brain records experience in precise detail. Somewhere in your brain is recorded every event of your life, including a special birthday party from your childhood. If you could access that information, you could relive your birthday party as if you were actually there. You could see the faces and hear the voices of your friends. You could experience again the games you played and the presents you opened. The entire occasion would be preserved perfectly for you to relive just as it originally happened.

Students respond with great interest and with nods. They seem ready to agree that our minds record all past experience, and that these memories could be relived if only they could be accessed. It might take a special machine to probe our brain and to stimulate it appropriately. But it makes sense to students that, given the right electrical stimulation to precise locations in the brain, detailed and accurate memories could be accessed and relived in rich detail.

Next I tell my students to disregard everything I said in the last 60 seconds because none of it is true. I tell them that there is no evidence that their minds have stored accurate and highly detailed memories of their childhood birthday parties, nor of any other event in their lives. They certainly *do* have personal memories that are dynamic and movie-like, but everything we know about episodic memory tells us that these memories are incomplete and often inaccurate. What is actually recorded in memory is subject to personal interpretations, beliefs, and biases.

We can summarize this way: The mind is not a video camera. It does not record experience exactly as it occurs so that it can be played back accurately at some future time. Long-term memory is not a high-fidelity system. Long before the days of CDs and iPods, designers of sound systems created electronic devices that could accurately reproduce recorded music that sounded much like the original performance. Phonographs and tape players that could accurately reproduce the original sound were said to be high-fidelity (highly faithful) systems. Electronics engineers achieved this goal, more

**FIGURE 3.3
A childhood birthday party** *Some episodic memories can seem richly detailed.*

or less, and today's sound systems, even small devices, are widely high-fi. But the human mind—and particularly long-term memory—is not. If we want high-fidelity recordings of experience, it's best to use a video camera.

It can be comical when two people have different memories of what happened during a relatively unimportant event. What's surprising is how strongly each person believes that his or her own version is the right one—even though the two stories are contradictory. Distortions of memory can have serious consequences in the case of legal testimony. When judges and juries try to establish the facts of a case, they often rely on the testimony of eyewitnesses who pledge to be as truthful as they can be. But even a fully cooperative witness can unwittingly "remember" falsely (Loftus, 1996). Two witnesses of the same event can give very different accounts. Discrepancies between eyewitnesses are the result of each trying to reconstruct an event from incomplete or inexact memories. Consequently, there can be as many versions of the truth as there are observers. When the stakes are high—as they often are in courts of law—the frailty of human memory can be a limiting factor in the administration of justice. In

INTEREST MAGNET 3.2

Penfield's Experiments on Memory

Does your brain store a permanent record of your entire life? One of the great neurosurgeons of the twentieth century, Wilder Penfield, once claimed that each of us stores accurate and permanent memories of our experience. As a brain surgeon, Penfield found evidence that led him to this hypothesis—at least initially. In treating patients with epilepsy, Penfield probed areas of the brain's surface, the cerebral cortex, to construct an accurate map of which areas needed to be removed surgically. He applied electrical stimulation to the brain while his patient was consciously sedated and therefore alert. When Penfield stimulated precise locations on the surface of the brain, the patient could describe his or her experience. While probing parts of the brain that controlled sensory or motor functions, the patient sometimes saw lights or heard sounds, or exhibited involuntary muscle movement. None of this was unusual. But when Penfield probed the temporal lobes located on the sides of the brain, the stimulation sometimes led to the vivid recall of detailed personal memories. To Penfield (1958, p. 20), the results "came as a complete surprise."

Some of Penfield's patients heard specific music or the voice of an old friend. After hearing similar reports from a number of his patients, Penfield hypothesized that the patients were reliving memories of events recorded in their brains when those events were first experienced. The memories appeared to be rich in detail. In some patients, re-stimulating the same spot in the brain led to re-experiencing the identical memory. In Penfield's words, stimulation of the cortex "unlocks the experience of bygone days" (p. 34). Penfield summed up his findings this way: "There is within the brain a . . . record of past experience which preserves the individual's current perceptions in astonishing detail" (pp. 34–35).

Penfield's famous experiments had a major effect on beliefs about human memory. The research suggested to psychologists and to the general public that the human brain records experience in complete detail and with perfect accuracy. Among memory experts, however, this view is now widely considered to be a misconception (Loftus, 1996). Far from being complete and accurate, human memory is highly selective and subject to interpretation and distortion. What was wrong with Penfield's original hypothesis? Didn't his research show that the brain records detailed memories of real events? Probably not. Evoked memories were found in only a small percentage of Penfield's patients—by one estimate less than 10 percent. Second, and more crucial, there was no independent confirmation that the recalled memories were accurate accounts. Eventually, Penfield backed down on his claims but never recanted them completely. Nonetheless, the initial hypothesis prompted by the research of Wilder Penfield acquired a life of its own, perpetuating a myth that human memory is complete, detailed, and highly accurate—and that just the right stimulus could potentially bring any memory back to life. A proper understanding of memory requires setting aside that view in favor of a model of memory that is highly selective and filtered through the categories, values, and meanings of each individual mind.

criminal courts, it's possible for perpetrators to go free or innocent defendants to be unjustly punished. The frailties of memory contribute to this imperfect record.

Our understanding of human memory has important pedagogical implications. Let's start with something obvious. It is completely unrealistic to expect students to remember their learning experiences exactly as they occur and in their entirety. Whether students hear a lecture, read a textbook, or engage in a classroom activity, their memories of these learning experiences exhibit the same tendencies toward incompleteness, inaccuracy, and distortion as any other life experience. To see this reality as a fault of students would be totally misguided. Rather than wish that the human cognitive system were like a video camera, teachers and students are wise to capitalize on the characteristic features of memory. If human memory is selective, meaningful, and to a large degree personal, how can this fact be appropriated in teaching and learning?

Summarizing the Cognitive Architecture

Let's step back for a moment to consider the model presented in this chapter. It's a *cognitive* model because it treats cognitive processes—like *thinking, learning, memory, goals, and beliefs*—seriously as objects of study. The focus on mental structures and processes is what distinguishes cognitive theories from earlier behaviorist theories.

But we are building a specific *kind* of cognitive model, namely, an information-processing model. It's an **information-processing model** because it looks to artificial information-processing devices—specifically, computers—as metaphors for how the human mind is structured and how it functions. We have seen, for example, that one similarity between computers and human minds is that both have memories. We have identified three memory structures in the human cognitive system: the sensory register, working memory (also known as short-term memory), and long-term memory. These three memory systems are the foundation of the human cognitive system. Their distinguishing qualities are presented in Table 3.1.

TABLE 3.1   The three memory structures contrast in both capacity and duration.

	Sensory Register	Working Memory	Long-Term Memory
Capacity	Detailed	7 ± 2	Enormous
Duration	Very Short (seconds)	Short (minutes)	Long (years)

In the course of our experience in the world, information first enters our sensory register. Data from our eyes and ears are captured in raw form, largely unprocessed. The sensory register holds detailed information, but only for a narrow slice of time. We impose order on the raw sensation whenever we recognize faces or perceive spoken words, and we hold this processed knowledge in working memory. *Some* of that information is eventually recorded in long-term memory. As depicted in Figure 3.4, the left-to-right order of these three memories makes sense. The sequence from sensory register to working memory to long-term memory is the basic order in which we experience and remember information presented by the environment.

Basic Cognitive Processes

One benefit of an information-processing model of the mind is that cognitive processes can be understood in terms of information flow within the system. To clarify, the three

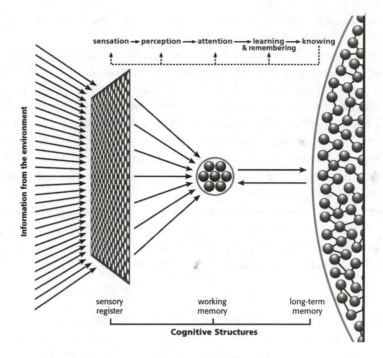

FIGURE 3.4
The information-processing model *It shows that cognitive processes and cognitive structures are part of one system.* [Drawing by Philip Travisano]

memory structures are important not only because they *hold* information, but also because information *flows between* them. Important cognitive processes—sensation, perception, attention, learning, remembering, and knowing—can all be defined and understood in terms of how information flows within the memory system. Figure 3.4 shows how these basic processes relate to the three memory structures in the model.

Cognitive processes have different qualities as information moves through the cognitive system. Here's a capsule summary:

- **Sensation** is the brief recording of environmental stimuli in the sensory register.
- **Perception** is the cognitive act of imposing order on sensory data as it enters working memory.
- **Attention** is holding information in conscious awareness in working memory.
- **Learning** is moving information from temporary working memory to enduring long-term memory.
- **Remembering** is moving information from long-term memory back into working memory.
- **Knowing** is holding knowledge in long-term memory. The dashed feedback loop shows that our knowledge base in long-term memory affects all other cognitive processes. What we know guides and constrains how we think at every step.

The sections that follow explore the deeper meaning and significance of these terms, beginning with sensation. Because the last process, knowing, is so vital to cognition, it is treated separately and in detail in Chapter 4, *Theories of Knowledge*.

Sensation

Psychologists have known for a long time that there is a big difference between the raw data that strikes our senses and the ideas that our minds consider. When raw data impinges on our eyes (as light photons) or ears (as air compression waves), that is what we call *sensation*. The sensory input has no inherent meaning. It requires some degree of intelligence to make sense of the welter of information presented by the environment. Otherwise it is just sensory chaos.

More than a century ago, one of the first American psychologists, William James, described sensation as a newborn baby experiences it. James's famous description is that, for an infant, the world is little more than a "blooming, buzzing confusion" (1890, p. 462). Most of the meaning that a baby will eventually find in the cozy world of home and family awaits the knowledge that language and experience will provide. Even as adults, the blooming, buzzing confusion is what strikes our senses continuously, though we are predisposed to interpret that experience quickly—within seconds.

Within the three-memory cognitive system, **sensation** occurs when data impinges on our senses (eyes and ears, as well as taste buds, fingertips, and so on), and is held briefly in our sensory register. Sensation is what happens when the outside world affects our senses, but *before* that sensory information is interpreted. It is information in a pre-conscious state, just inside the gateway of the body but before that information is recognized and made meaningful by the mind.

Perception

Not all information stays in raw, unprocessed form. We make sense of the information that surrounds and envelopes us by recognizing objects—faces, furniture, trees, buildings, pens, paper, bicycles, basketballs, ice cream cones, and thousands of other material entities that compose the world presented by nature and the culture we dwell in. To recognize those objects in a sea of sensory data, we depend on our minds to segment the visual, auditory, and other sensory fields into meaningful units. Whenever we look at a vague and grainy visual field, perception occurs just at the moment when the meaning of the object becomes apparent. The act of perception is not necessarily accurate. Imagine that while taking a walk you see an enormous dog in the path ahead of you—or for a split second you *think* it's a dog. To your relief, the frightening object was actually a fallen log. Although your misperception was momentary, it may be vivid enough to charge your body with fear-induced adrenaline.

Hearing works the same way. The auditory field must also be segmented into meaningful patterns. When you engage in a conversation, you recognize the individual words spoken by the other person. But the speaker is not uttering discrete bursts of sound (individual words) interspersed by silence. Rather, speech is normally a continuous stream of sound. If you hear individual words, it's your *mind* that is imposing order by perceiving meaningful wholes in the sound stream. Whenever you hear an unfamiliar language, it's more obvious that speech is an unbroken stream of sound. The mind's active role in pattern perception is clearer still when you consider that conversations normally take place in a background of noise. While sitting in a restaurant, for example, you can enjoy a conversation despite the surrounding din of other conversations, music, and the clink and clatter of glassware and dishes.

GESTALT PRINCIPLES OF PERCEPTION. To distinguish a single object from its surroundings is the most basic act of perception. This cognitive act was studied in detail by the **Gestalt** psychologists of the early twentieth century. The Gestalt psychologists wanted to know how the mind actively perceives meaningful patterns. They noted that our senses usually have access to only fragmented or incomplete data, and that the mind must search for patterns in the sensory field in order to understand it. To perceive meaningful patterns, the mind often fills in gaps to perceive a form that is more "whole" than the sensory data initially detected by the eyes and ears. They called this perceived pattern a "Gestalt," which is German for "meaningful whole."

Whenever you see an object, you mentally separate the object from its surroundings. The perceived object is the **figure**; everything else in the visual field is the **ground**. Think about your own vision, and you'll see that separating figure from ground is a constant activity of your mind. Whenever you drive a car, for example, you must constantly perceive individual cars, traffic signs and signals, pedestrians, and lane markers. Your eyes scan continuously to identify new objects in a continuously changing sensory landscape. As your *eyes* scan the visual field, your *mind* actively perceives objects. The ocular and the mental work in tandem, rapidly and efficiently, and ideally without error.

Of course, it's not only while driving that the figure/ground separation is made by a perceiving mind. Perception is ongoing through all of your waking hours. When reading, for example, your eyes see the highly complex visual stimulus of a printed page. The act of reading involves several different cognitive processes, but one of the most basic is confronting the innumerable squiggles of black ink and perceptually isolating individual words (Just & Carpenter, 1980). The perceptual isolation of words is not trivial—in fact, it presents considerable difficulty to many dyslexic readers.

During the act of perception, the mind not only identifies patterns registered by the senses, it also "fills in" missing details to make the patterns intelligible. The simplest possible example, one studied by the Gestalt psychologists, is called the **phi phenomenon**. Imagine two lights arranged one above the other. The lights turn on alternately— top, bottom, top, bottom, and so on. What does the mind see? The most *accurate* perception would be to see two lights blinking in alternating fashion. But the Gestalt psychologists discovered that the mind instead perceives *one* light moving up and down. This is one example of the phi phenomenon.

Why is the phi phenomenon important? Because it tells us that the mind is at work in making even the simplest perceptions meaningful, and it often does so by filling in information that is not present in the stimulus. Let's put it another way: The mind is active in making sense of the world—a philosophy of mind called **constructivism**— and this active role extends *all the way down* to the simplest acts of perception (Bruner, 1957). The Gestalt psychologists realized that the mind is active during the perception of the Gestalt ("meaningful whole"). Patterns in the world are not simply presented to us. Our minds "make" them—at least in part.

One form of the phi phenomenon is at work when you enjoy watching a movie at the cinema. Unlike digital video, film presents a series of static images on the movie screen. It's widely known that the standard presentation rate of 24 frames per second will present to the viewer an illusion of continuous motion. The "smoothing over" function taken up by the mind is all the more remarkable when we consider that the 24 frames flashing on the screen second are not immediately successive, but are separated by very brief periods of darkness.

This is the phi phenomenon applied to a larger and more interesting pattern—the movie screen. Our minds take in successive discrete images interspersed with blackness and perceive a "Gestalt," not a static image but rather a dynamic story that can seem quite lifelike. What a marvel! But is this only about film? Our continuous life experience is also a succession of fragmented images taken in as our eyes scan the visual field in a series of jumps called saccades. Our minds "smooth over" patchwork perceptions so that our visual experience seems continuous and coherent. It's a long way from the elemental phi phenomenon of alternating lights to the daily flow of life experience. But the mind is at work in both, perceiving meaningful patterns in the storm of sensory data, stitching these patterns together and filling in gaps to make a sensible story of human experience.

INTEREST MAGNET 3.3

Subliminal Advertising

The concept of subliminal advertising was born in 1957, when advertising researcher James Vicary conducted an experiment in a movie theatre in Fort Lee, New Jersey. Over a period of six weeks, Vicary flashed messages on the movie screen for very brief periods of time (Moore, 1982). He used two messages:

"Hungry? Eat Popcorn"
"Drink Coca-Cola"

The messages appeared on the movie screen every five seconds, but only for only 1/3000 of a second. To project these messages, Vicary used a device called a tachistoscope. The tachistoscope flashed these two messages on the screen *while* the movies were playing, but the duration of the messages was so short that the audience had no conscious experience of seeing them. They were intended to be *subliminal*, meaning that their viewers were not aware of the flashes or their information content.

Vicary's experiment was conducted in the days when feature movies had a brief intermission halfway through. During intermission, patrons could go to the lobby to buy snacks. The subliminal messages seemed to work. According to Vicary, sales of popcorn and Coca Cola rose dramatically. During the period of his experiment, Coke sales rose 18.1 percent, and popcorn sales rose 57.7 percent. By all appearances, subliminal advertising was a powerful force for product marketing.

Since the time of Vicary's experiment, the possibility of subliminal advertising has been firmly established in the public consciousness. However, Vicary's claims were never published or replicated. In fact, Vicary later recanted his claims, saying that he had fabricated the results. Even without solid evidence to back it up, the idea of subliminal advertising was compelling; it was too good to be false! Soon other writers began to make claims that advertisers deliberately send subliminal messages to influence potential customers. The "theory" of subliminal advertising was brought to the attention of the public in the book entitled *Subliminal Seduction* by Wilson Key (1973). Key claimed that advertisers often used sexual imagery in ads to gain the attention of consumers. By itself, this was a believable, even obvious, claim. The interesting spin revealed in *Subliminal Seduction* was that advertisers sometimes placed erotic imagery in ads that was too subtle to be detected consciously—the pictures were subliminal. Sexual imagery could be hidden within the amorphous shapes and colorations in ice cubes in liquor ads, for example. The messages were said to appeal not to the conscious mind, but rather to the "unconscious." They were intended to reinforce memory for the product. Ideally, for the marketers, this would translate to increased sales.

Whether and how frequently advertisers resort to using subliminal suggestion or subliminal "seduction" is arguable. Subtle and manipulative imagery is undoubtedly used to some degree, but probably much less frequently than proponents of "subliminal seduction" theories claimed. This is not to say that subliminal messages are impossible; psychologists have shown that perception without awareness can occur (Merikle, Smilek, & Eastwood, 2001). As for subliminal advertising, the evidence from research is that sending messages below the threshold of awareness rarely if ever works—and if it does work, its effect is probably quite small (Moore, 1988).

Where in the cognitive system does perception take place? Perception is the reduction of complex sensation to simpler recognizable patterns. This reduction involves the relay of information from the sensory register (which holds raw data) to working memory (which holds just a few meaningful units of information). So these two memory systems are involved in perception. But long-term memory also must be involved. Why? Because the people and objects we recognize are patterns stored in long-term memory. Therefore, we must acknowledge that even in the simple act of perception, all three memory structures work together.

Long-term memory plays an important role in perception through two successive processes. Initially, information from your senses can trigger a concept in long-term memory. For example, you might see a car in the distance that looks something like a Jeep. The shape of the car initiates **bottom-up processing** because *basic sensory information* activates a known concept in long-term memory. The second step is **top-down**

processing. Once you have the concept of a Jeep in mind, you can use your knowledge of the car to form expectations and to look for (or assume) the confirmatory details. This is top-down processing because it proceeds from the *idea* and uses that prior knowledge to fill in missing details in your sensory experience. The two processes work together. Bottom-up processing and top-down processing are jointly involved in just about every instance of perception.

Attention

We've talked about two cognitive processes: sensation and perception. A third cognitive process is **attention**. This process, too, can be defined and interpreted in terms of the basic cognitive system of sensory register, working memory, and long-term memory. *Attention* is the act of holding information in working memory. When we say that a student is paying attention, we mean that he is focusing his working memory on specific information—namely, the information that someone (often the teacher or other adult) wants him to think about. When we say that his attention drifts, we mean that the information content of working memory shifts from one idea to another, and away from the task at hand. Attention deficit disorder similarly can be described as a condition where working memory drifts freely from one thing to another, with the consequence that the attentional focus needed to complete normal tasks, including schoolwork, is disrupted.

Because information in our surroundings is almost always complex, managing one's own attention necessarily involves focusing on certain information and ignoring other information. Several factors influence what we attend to and what we ignore. One factor is the goals we are pursuing. In a classic psychological experiment, participants read a description of a house that had some structural defects, but that also had several valuable objects inside (Pichert & Anderson, 1977). Participants in the experiment were asked to read the house description from either the perspective of a burglar or the perspective of a home buyer. You can probably guess the results. Readers who took the perspective of a burglar paid more attention to the valuable objects in the house, and remembered those. Readers who took the viewpoint of prospective home buyer remembered the structural defects of the house.

Not only goals, but also prior knowledge and interest can determine the focus of attention. If you have no interest in imported sports cars, you will probably ignore the passing Porsche Carrera GT, beyond noting that the car is in an adjacent lane. Likewise while watching a football game, knowledge and interest will strongly guide attention. People who are not familiar with the game do not know where to look in the scramble, or what patterns to recognize. They will find the action on the field not only confusing, but also uninteresting. So knowledge and interest both guide attention, as do the goals we pursue.

The selective nature of attention in a complex sensory field is evident in the **cocktail party phenomenon**. This is the ability to maintain focus on a single conversation in a room where dozens of other conversations are taking place. In a crowded party, the totality of sound is an unintelligible din. Yet, somehow, it is possible to tune in to a single conversation. Unless the background noise is really loud, you find that it's surprisingly easy to carry on a conversation and block out all others. Your mind filters out the irrelevant noise. But what happens when you hear your name spoken nearby in a *different* conversation? Your attention shifts to that other conversation and away from the person speaking directly to you. You might keep nodding and smiling to the person speaking to you, but you no longer hear his or her words. The situation is potentially embarrassing, but you can hardly help shifting your attention. This is another instance where your interests and goals abruptly and irresistibly channel your attention.

With some effort, it might be possible to pay attention to two conversations at once by shifting attention alternately between the two. Everyday activities sometimes require us to allocate attention among multiple stimuli, such as when driving car through thick traffic. The professional activities of air traffic controllers and teachers also require dividing and shifting attention among complex elements of the environment. Attention can also be divided among multiple competing goals, which we call **multitasking**. Although the human cognitive system can distribute attention to multiple stimuli and multiple goals, the distribution of attention has limits. Attention to one goal will eventually detract from performance on another. This constraint on attention simply reflects the limited capacity of working memory.

Consider the party scenario again. If you find that your attention is drawn away— say, when you hear your name mentioned in a nearby conversation—can you force your attention *back* to the person who is speaking to you? Is there a cognitive capability by which you can intentionally control the focus of your attention? Certainly this is possible. Catch the essence here: It is *cognition* (your deliberate will) controlling *cognition* (your attention). Whenever cognition is used to control cognition, that is a form of higher-order thinking called **metacognition**. We will explore the nature of metacognition in depth in Chapter 5. For now we can ask: Would students benefit from having this metacognitive ability? Absolutely. If you were a teacher, you would want your students to have metacognitive control over their own attention, just as you have this control. Whenever you pursue a goal that is important to you, you'll find plenty of distractions along the way. Occasionally, you might want to give attention to some of those distractions—but certainly not all. You want to have some choice about what stays in the focus of your attention, and for how long. Metacognitive control over attention gives you that choice.

Learning

I once had a professor who stated confidently that schools exist for one purpose: learning. You might agree with his conclusion or you might argue with it. Either way, the claim is at least plausible. It's hard to imagine a cognitive process more important than learning. One benefit of the information-processing model is that *learning* too can be defined in terms of information flow within the model. The definition is simple: **Learning** is the recording of information in long-term memory.

Whenever learning is a goal, then a counterpart goal must be to produce some change to long-term memory. If there is no trace of new information in long-term memory, then learning has not occurred. As you read this book, I presume that you want to advance your knowledge about learning and cognition. If so, then some of the ideas presented in this book (ideally the most interesting and important ones) must be recorded in your long-term memory. If you are to be tested on this material, then certainly you'll want to effect changes to your long-term memory prior to the test.

So, is there a problem here? Why not just do what's necessary to record all important information in long-term memory? If only it were that easy! Earlier in this chapter, I asserted that the mind is not a video camera. We do not preserve in memory everything we've ever experienced. Memories of a childhood birthday party are likely to be sketchy at best, and possibly quite wrong. Therefore, learning—a process of enormous importance to education—is problematic in the sense that it is not necessarily easy or obvious how to accomplish it.

Much of what we perceive and attend to is never recorded in long-term memory. As you read this book, you are paying attention to the words and thinking about the ideas behind the words. But not all of the ideas stick. At best, you can hope that a significant fraction of the ideas will be recorded in your long-term memory. The point is that many ideas we consider in the course of every day never make it to long-term memory. Instead, most of our thoughts are ephemeral and evanescent—experienced only once before vanishing forever.

WRITE TIME PARAMETER. What can be done? Is there a way to improve learning? One hint can be found in the relationship between working memory and long-term memory. You want to move information from the former (where it is temporary) to the latter (where it is enduring). How? To answer this question, let's return to our foundational metaphor, the digital computer. When you compose a document on a computer, you should save the document frequently. When you save the file, it is copied or "written" from the temporary memory of the computer (RAM) to the computer's hard drive. The difference between the two forms of storage becomes acutely important if you accidentally turn off the computer. But note one subtle aspect of saving a file to your hard drive—it takes time. Even if saving the file takes only a second or two, some finite time is needed. This is sometimes called the computer's write time, because it's as if the computer is "writing" the document onto your computer's hard drive so that it becomes more permanent.

Human memory also has a write time. Time is needed for temporary information in working memory to be stored more permanently in long-term memory. It does not happen immediately. How much time is required? Much more time than is needed by a computer. To record information in long-term memory takes roughly a minute for a single piece of information.

Almost certainly, you have experienced the effects of this write-time parameter in everyday conversations. What happens when you meet someone for the first time? Often, the first piece of information you share is your name. But there is a problem. Shortly after introductions are made, it's often hard to remember the other person's name, even though you heard it only a moment ago.

The situation is almost hopeless if we are introduced to a *group* of people. We've all participated in meetings where every person says his or her name—as if we could remember them all! (I'm not denying here that there are specially skilled memory experts who can remember lots of names—but this is unusual, which is why it's sensational.) Note, then, this simple fact—even in a social ritual as basic as personal introductions, there is a contradiction. The design of the human mind clashes with an accepted social practice. Could there be similar clashes between the mind's design and the practice of education? Certainly. Such clash patterns re-invoke the central theme of this book: If we understand the design of the mind, then we can tailor educational experience to cooperate with the way the mind works, rather than contradict the cognitive architecture. By so doing we can make learning and thinking processes much more effective.

This does not mean that we always ignore the write time needed for learning. Sometimes we use the fact even if we don't realize it. Consider the following scenario: You are walking across campus when you suddenly realize that you are going to be late for a doctor's appointment. You want to call the doctor's office to say you'll be late. The trouble is that you don't have the doctor's phone number. However, you know someone who does—and you can call that person on your cell phone. But there is another problem: You don't have pen and paper ready to write the phone number down. This is what you do: When your friend tells you the phone number, you intentionally remember that number. How do you do it? By repeating the number over and over until you finish dialing it. Why do you repeat the number over and over in your mind? Because by doing so, you are keeping that phone number alive and active in your working memory. This basic strategy of repetition in order to remember is called **rehearsal**.

Rehearsal is a very common strategy. It's used widely not only to hold on to information temporarily, but also to remember it permanently. Let's say you wanted to commit a fact to memory—perhaps the birthday of a good friend. If you want to memorize that birthday, one possible strategy is rehearsal. Somehow, the simple repetition of information can make the knowledge stick. In our terminology, we can say that rehearsal is one way to move information from (temporary) working memory to (durable) long-term memory. By repeating that information—whether out loud or in your head—you cooperate with the necessary write time for long-term memory.

Rehearsal is not sophisticated; in fact, it's the most basic memory strategy available. Rehearsal is probably used in every human culture, and is practiced even by young children. Interestingly, children are not usually instructed in how to use rehearsal. How do they learn to rehearse as a memory strategy? Perhaps rehearsal is discovered anew by each individual. Or children might observe adults or peers using the strategy, and then imitate them. In either case, rehearsal is not the only memory strategy available, nor is it necessarily the best memory strategy. It is, however, very common and very basic. But let's not forget the central idea here: Rehearsal actively holds ideas in working memory so that they can be recorded in long-term memory—that is, so that those ideas can be *learned*.

There are instructional implications here. Let's put the matter negatively. If a teacher wants an idea to be learned, it would be a mistake to present the idea once, and never mention it again. If an idea is given scant processing time in students' conscious attention (in working memory), then it has little chance of being learned (in long-term memory). To state the principle positively: If a teacher wants an idea to be learned (in long-term memory), then it's good to stay with that idea for several minutes at least—perhaps by exploring that idea from different angles. By keeping the idea active in working memory for longer periods of time, chances are improved that it will make it to the students' long-term memories. It's better still if that idea is revisited several times later in the same class, and again in the future. By returning to an idea, the trace in long-term memory will be made more certain and more durable.

DEPTH OF PROCESSING. There are better ways to learn than simple repetition or rehearsal. Put plainly, learning is more effective if new information is related to what the learner already knows. The more thorough the connections between new knowledge and **prior knowledge**, the better the learning outcome. This idea should be a strong guiding principle for all instructional decisions.

Stark repetition of information (rehearsal) has been contrasted with meaningful learning (through associations with prior knowledge). For those who favor binary categories, these are called **Type I elaboration** and **Type II elaboration** (Craik & Lockhart, 1972). The term **elaboration** means making connections with existing knowledge. In Type I elaboration, the connections to prior knowledge are minimal. By simply repeating a phone number, you are using your prior knowledge of number names, but not much else. You could use Type I elaboration in memorizing a definition in science. For example, you could memorize the following definition of an isotope:

Isotope: One of several varieties of a given element, distinguished from other isotopes of that element by having a unique number of neutrons.

To memorize this definition using Type I elaboration or rehearsal, you could keep repeating the definition over and over. But this approach has a serious drawback: it's possible to memorize this definition and have *no idea* what it means. This is why educators so often speak negatively about rote memorization. There is nothing wrong with deliberate memorization. It does become negative, though, if it substitutes for understanding in the minds of students. Of course, memorization is also negative if a teacher mistakes it for true understanding.

Type II elaboration takes the process of connecting with prior knowledge much further. As new knowledge becomes meaningfully interconnected with what is already known, then **understanding** grows. Those connections are fostered when learners actually process the information to produce something new. When learners integrate the information to form new products—whether sentences, pictures, or equations—the information becomes much more memorable. This finding, called the **generation effect**, strongly indicates that if information is important enough to be learned, it should be used in some meaningful way (Peynircioglu, 1989).

INTEREST MAGNET 3.4

Sleep Learning

The concept of sleep learning was most famously depicted in Aldous Huxley's novel *Brave New World* (1932). In Huxley's frightening portrayal of the future, a Polish boy named Reuben Rabinovich hears radio broadcasts in English while he sleeps. Upon waking, he can recite the broadcast in English, even though he does not understand a word of it.

The possibility of learning during sleep has intrigued psychologists, students, and product marketers ever since. Even today, it is possible to purchase sleep-learning products, such as audio recordings to build vocabulary or to learn a foreign language. The possibility of learning during sleep is attractive because it appears to be effortless and because it capitalizes on what seem to be nonproductive hours of sleep. Sleep learning would appeal to many people if it actually worked—but does it?

The research on sleep learning is equivocal. Early research conducted in the 1950s and 1960s supported some marginal effect for sleep learning (Eich, 1988). When compared to control groups, people exposed to new information during sleep retained some of the information, but only under certain conditions. Specifically, sleep learning worked only when learners were semi-wakeful. The half-awake state was monitored as slow "alpha" brain waves when the learner was just drifting off to sleep or about to wake up. In fact, the stimulus—usually spoken words—would sometimes set off alpha rhythms. A longer duration alpha wave predicted a higher likelihood that the information would be remembered upon waking. This association between learning and semi-wakefulness implied that deep sleep was really not conducive to learning. The theoretical answer seemed to be that sleep learning does not occur, or that its effects are minimal and therefore not very useful. This conclusion contrasted with that of European researchers, who found significant effects for sleep learning. The different conclusions reflected the European researchers' lower concern for theoretical purity and greater interest in practical applications. European researchers in the mid-twentieth century believed that learning can occur during sleep, even if that learning was constrained to the light sleep stage identified by alpha brain waves. The different conclusions drawn by American and European researchers were never really resolved.

These studies investigated sleep *learning*, but there is a further possibility that sleep can be an opportunity for *thinking*. However, the sparse research seems to be even thinner on whether productive thinking can occur during sleep. Some anecdotal reports suggest that logical and creative thinking sometimes happens during sleep. A difficult problem that resists solution during waking hours might continue to press on the mind during sleep, and continued work during sleep could lead to a breakthrough. The most famous example is the dream of the chemist Friedrich August Kekulé, who discovered the structure of the six-carbon molecule called benzene. According to one account, while Kekulé was asleep he dreamed about a snake that swallowed its own tail, forming a circle (Rudofsky & Wotiz, 1988). When he awoke, he realized that the structure of benzene was a ring. To this day, psychological research is divided on the subject of sleep learning. But the idea that we can think productively while sleeping is more widely supported. At least occasionally, these thought processes yield conceptual breakthroughs that have enduring value.

The difference between **superficial learning** and true understanding has become much more important to educators in recent years (Gardner, 1991; Perkins, 1992). This appreciation springs from an awareness that the first (superficial learning) does not always lead to the second (understanding). All learning requires building connections with prior knowledge, but understanding requires much richer and more profuse connections. Understanding is also generative; it entails an ability to extend what is already known to gain new insights, and to find new implications and applications of knowledge (Dewey, 1916). Compared to superficial learning, understanding is more difficult to achieve, but it is also a far more worthy goal of education. Teaching strategies that emphasize interconnectedness of new knowledge with prior knowledge—Type II elaboration—can go a long way toward promoting understanding.

Remembering

We have been examining how the model of human information processing can give precise meanings to cognitive terms that are important in education. *Sensation, perception, attention,* and *learning* can all be defined and understood in terms of how information flows through the cognitive system. There's one term remaining: *remembering.*

Let's start with a simple observation: To learn something is not the same as being able to remember it later. Common experience teaches us that we can know some fact or concept, but can't retrieve that information. This difference—between knowing and remembering—takes on real importance when you are taking a test: You *want* to remember, and you feel certain that you *have* the knowledge, but you just can't retrieve it. More common still is the trouble we sometimes have remembering the name of a fellow student or co-worker. Such experiences can be very embarrassing.

These instances illustrate that remembering information, or what is sometimes called **retrieval**, is a cognitive process that is distinct from learning. The definition of *remembering* in information processing terms is quite straightforward. To remember is to move information from long-term memory (where it is stored) back into working memory (where we consciously think about it). Defined this way, remembering is the inverse of learning:

- **Learning**: Information moves from working memory to long-term memory.
- **Remembering**: Information moves from long-term memory to working memory.

The two processes complement each other. Both are important to education and to the intelligent use of the mind. Both also involve distinct skills that can be taught and learned to make the processes more effective.

Let's recognize another fact related to retrieval: Information in long-term memory is not equally accessible. Some knowledge you know very well—your name, for example. Other information is not as ready at hand. For example, you might have some difficulty remembering the names of the last few vice presidents of the United States. And yet you might feel quite certain that if someone told you the names of the vice presidents you would recognize them.

This difference—the ability to *produce* information from long-term memory without help versus the ability to *recognize* information presented by someone else—is quite important in education. We call the first process **recall**, and the second process **recognition**. Both are forms of retrieval because both involve accessing information from long-term memory and moving that information into working memory so that we can think about it. Recall is harder; recognition is easier. We can *recall* a great deal of information, but we can *recognize* much, much more.

Definite strategies can be employed to make retrieval processes, particularly recall, more likely. The most important of these is the use of **cues**. Cues consist of information that is related to what we are trying to remember—hints or suggestions that can help evoke the knowledge from memory. Think about an actor who momentarily forgets his lines during a live performance. If the play is properly staffed, there will be someone in the wings reading the script along with the actor. If the actor hesitates, the prompter can whisper a few words—called cues—that will help the actor to recall his lines and get back on track.

Cues are widely used to retrieve information from long-term memory. Often teachers will give hints to students to help them remember. These hints are cues, too. Parents will give hints to their young children to help them remember the names of objects or display proper social behavior: "What do you say?" "Thank you!" Sometimes we give cues to ourselves. When we try to remember something, we might think of related knowledge to help prompt recall. For example, as you think of past U.S. vice presidents, you might think of related knowledge, such as the name and political party of the president and the names of the opposing candidates for president and vice president.

The Funnel of Information

As information flows through the human information processing system, there is a pattern to the flow: As information moves from the outside in, less and less of it is used by the cognitive system. It's as if the information is moving through a funnel that becomes progressively narrower.

Decreasing Subsets of Information

We'll consider the narrowing flow of information through four cognitive processes we have already explored: sensation, perception, attention, and learning.

SENSATION. As we have seen, the starting point for cognition is information impinging on our senses from the environment. We call this *sensation*. One fact to appreciate about sensation is that the amount of information striking our senses is enormous. The volume is huge not only in the course of a day, but even during a single second of wakefulness. A fantastically complex pattern of light strikes our retinas, and so becomes available to the visual cortex of the brain. The data flow, or "bandwidth," of the visual system is not unlimited because our retinas and optic nerves can propagate only a finite amount of information each second. But the dynamic capacity for vision is very large, nonetheless. Add to this the data stream that strikes our eardrums in the form of sound waves, patterns of tactile stimulation on our skin, as well as taste, smell, kinesthetic, and balance data. We live inside a sensory storm.

The total sensory apparatus of the human body—all the senses combined—is sometimes called the **sensorium**. The sensorium registers and makes available an enormous amount of information. This information is held very briefly in the first stage of the cognitive system—the sensory register. The sensory register takes in a huge amount of sensory information, but holds on to that information only momentarily and until new sensory information replaces it. Most of the incoming sensory information is lost.

PERCEPTION. We recognize patterns in some of the information held briefly in the sensory register. Our mind works quickly to perceive faces, furniture, plants, books, tools, and so on. These simple acts of pattern detection yield information that is much simpler than the barrage that originally strikes our senses. So, even as information progresses from raw *sensation* to the momentary *perception* of patterns, there is considerable data reduction. The patterns perceived are a subset of the data sensed. Like water moving through a funnel, the data stream becomes narrower as it moves through the cognitive system. The funnel starts out with a wide capacity, but at each stage that funnel becomes more and more constricted.

ATTENTION. Moving further into the funnel of information brings us to *attention*. Attention is the process of holding information in working memory so that we can think about it. Whereas perception is a brief and fleeting engagement of working memory to notice a particular pattern, attention is a more enduring engagement of working memory. But here again we have data reduction. We perceive hundreds of patterns during a single minute, but we can only attend to a fraction of these. Keep in mind that working memory has a capacity of only a few items (7 ± 2 by George Miller's estimate). Therefore, the transition from sensation to perception to attention entails significant data reduction. All along this pathway, the funnel of information tapers down.

LEARNING. In the cognitive model we define learning as moving information from working memory—where we actively think about it—to long-term memory, where information is stored indefinitely. This process, too, is one of data reduction. Only a fraction of the ideas that our minds entertain are ever recorded in long-term memory, and a smaller fraction still is actively recalled later. Several factors affect whether information in working memory is ultimately recorded in long-term memory. One of those factors is the length of time that the ideas are actively attended to in working memory. More time is better, as far as learning is concerned. This is because there is a basic "write time" parameter for long-term memory, just as a computer requires a certain period of time (though much shorter) to save your word processing document to the computer's hard drive. And, unlike a computer, information in long-term memory is not all-or-none, but instead can vary in strength, durability, and ease of recall.

We *learn* only a small fraction of what we *think* about. During learning, as in the prior stages of perception and attention, the bulk of information is lost. Because the funnel of information becomes progressively more restricted, we retain only a tiny fraction of information that originally strikes our senses. Yet as information becomes more restricted in sheer volume, it also becomes more meaningful as it connects to prior knowledge in long-term memory. Our eyes, ears, and fingertips experience a constant blizzard of information, but what is actually *learned* is only a few snowflakes. Ideally, those conceptual snowflakes are good ones—ideas that are interesting, enlightening, and useful in the future. You might think of the function of schooling as arranging the experience of students so that they learn the most valuable and beautiful snowflakes—just a few snowflakes out of the innumerable elements of the data blizzard.

External Memory

There is a fourth kind of memory, which is not actually a memory in the sense of being the property of an individual mind. It's a memory that lies *outside* the brain. The fourth and final type of memory is **external memory** (Newell & Simon, 1972).

Just a moment ago I wrote a note to myself about something I want to accomplish today. I suppose I wrote the note because I was not confident that I would remember otherwise. In fact, I write notes to myself all the time, especially when there is a meeting

I can't afford to miss or a task I must not overlook. Functionally, those notes are a distinct memory system. They contain information that I've generated—but they just happen to exist outside my head and are instead part of my physical environment.

External memory, whether as simple as a shopping list or as extensive as the notes you might take in a class, are often highly functional. To a large degree, external memory can compensate for shortcomings of the human cognitive system—in particular, the points of vulnerability that include whether information is learned, whether that information can be retrieved, and whether learning and later retrieval are complete and accurate. External memory can compensate for the unaided fragility of the human cognitive system. These advantages are why we make "to-do" lists, why courts of law take witness depositions and hire court reporters, why scientists record their raw data, and why anthropologists take field notes of their first-hand observations.

To think of the notes we make to ourselves as a form of memory—external memory—does raise some questions. For example, if someone else writes a note for you (say, a telephone message) does that count as external memory? If so, whose memory? The person who took the phone message or yours? It's not clear, is it? This example raises the profound question of where knowledge is located. Is knowledge in the mind—that is, in the cognitive apparatus supported by the biological brain? I would say, yes. Knowledge *is* in our heads. But is it *only* in our heads? Does knowledge also exist in textbooks, or in the notes you take during a class? What about on the sticky notes stuck to your refrigerator?

Ultimately, we must ask: *Where* is the mind? Traditionally, psychologists have tended to think of the mind and the brain as being roughly parallel—the mind is a property of an individual person, and a function of the physical brain. In recent decades, though, that point of view has been challenged. In many instances, cognition is more adequately thought of as a property of groups of people interacting with the technical features of their environment. One compelling example is the interaction between a pilot and co-pilot, along with their cockpit instrumentation, in landing a commercial airliner (Hutchins, 1995). The pilots must very carefully compute the jet's optimal landing speed based on the airplane's gross weight, wind speed, and settings of the wings' slats and flaps. To set and maintain the approach speed between relatively narrow bands, the pilots rely on data tables, air-speed indicators with adjustable marker "bugs" on the dials, and verbal cross-checking with each other in order to make a safe landing.

Psychologists have had to acknowledge that the activities of individual minds are meaningful only in a larger context of valued cultural activities. There is no mind without culture and no culture without mind. Therefore, the point of view that the mind begins and ends with the individual human brain is either a mistake or a gross oversimplification. The mind might be better seen as centered in the individual human brain, but extending outward in a thousand directions to the network of words, symbols, objects, people, meanings, tools, and practices that compose a culture. It is not easy to think of the mind in these terms, but this more complex understanding of the mind and of knowledge is a more accurate one. And if it is more accurate, it will lead us eventually to more powerful applications, including applications to education.

Chunking and Automaticity

For now, we can set aside the difficult but fascinating questions about the nature of knowledge, and the identity and location of the mind. We will return to these questions in the next chapter on theories of knowledge. Let's instead re-focus on the basic information-processing model. In particular, let's return to a cardinal property of the working memory—the fact that it is constrained to only a few items. The small informational capacity of working memory is a true information-processing bottleneck. This raises the question of how the mind is capable of such fantastic achievements given the restrictions of capacity in working memory. How can we resolve the apparent paradox between the limited information-processing capacity of every human being and the tremendous achievements of human civilizations?

Chunking

The information-processing bottleneck of working memory, though real, is not as debilitating as you might think. To see why, let's return to the claim of George Miller's paper, "The Magical Number Seven, Plus or Minus Two." We need not take the precise value of seven too seriously, but the claim that working memory can handle only a few items at a time still holds. For now, let's accept the number seven as a good approximation of working memory capacity. The question we need to ask is: Seven *what*?

One way to approach the question is to think about the common seven-digit telephone number. If someone tells you a new phone number, you can probably keep that number in mind (in your working memory) indefinitely with a little concentration. Even if you don't have paper and pen to write the number down, you should be able to remember the phone number at least temporarily.

What happens if the number is not seven digits, but ten? In the era of cell phones it's common to give area codes, whereas in earlier times people just assumed a local area code unless told otherwise. These days, ten digits are commonly given rather than seven. Ten digits without any obvious pattern are much harder to remember than seven—hard enough to make the task of holding them in working memory a little dicey.

There's a difference, though, if the area code is familiar. At my university, the area code is 949. If someone uses this familiar code, then (for me) the task of holding the phone number in working memory is easier. The same is true for other area codes I know: 650, 714, 415, and 209. Because they are familiar to me, they are *easier* to hold in working memory than an unfamiliar area code, or any three random digits. The familiar area code is easy to remember because it feels like *one* piece of information rather than *three* separate pieces of information.

This takes us back to our question: The capacity of working memory is approximately seven *what*? The answer to the question involves introducing a new technical term to our discussion—that term is **chunk**. A chunk is a pattern of meaningful information. In the case of area codes, 949 is three chunks to most people in the country, but only one chunk for people who live in or near the 949 area. Its load on working memory is one unit (one chunk) rather than three. This pattern can be extended: On my university campus, the prefix for all phone numbers is 824. That prefix, too, is a single chunk for people who are familiar with it. The structure of a campus phone number is 949-824-XXXX. The area code 949 is one chunk (because it is familiar), and the prefix 824 is one chunk (because it is also familiar) (Calfee, 1981). So the total burden to working memory for those phone numbers with familiar area codes and prefixes is approximately six–two groups of three, plus the four digits at the end. This information can easily be accommodated in working memory, whose capacity is approximately what? That's right, seven *chunks*.

The grouping of information into meaningful units, called **chunking**, works well for all kinds of information, not just phone numbers. The phenomenon was studied among chess experts, for example. For novice chess players, the chessboard can seem complicated, holding as many as 32 pieces in innumerable combinations. But for an experienced chess player, not all chess piece configurations are equally likely. Some configurations are much more probable than others. In fact, some patterns or groupings of chess pieces are quite common, experienced repeatedly over the thousands of games played, watched, or studied by the serious chess player. These familiar patterns on the chessboard—an advancing rank of pawns, a king positioned to "castle," pinning strategies, and so on—become very familiar over time. As these patterns become familiar, they are perceived as single units of meaningful information. They are chunks.

Chunking can make the complex layout of a chess game sufficiently simple that the entire chessboard can be held in the working memory of the expert chess player. This ability permits some experts to play blindfolded because the changing dynamic configuration of the chessboard can be held in mind completely and accurately. The result is that an active chess game, played blindfolded or not, is much simpler for a chess expert than for a novice. Does the working memory of a chess expert have an extra-large capacity? No, both the expert and the novice have a working memory capacity of just a few chunks—but the *nature* of a chunk is different between players at the two levels. The way that a chunk is redefined over time in the mind of an expert provides insight into the nature of expertise, and how a novice develops into an expert. This topic is taken up again in Chapter 7, which focuses on expert-novice differences. In that chapter, we'll again examine expertise in chess and in many other domains.

We can apply the principle of chunking far beyond phone numbers and chess. Think of it this way: In *any* knowledge domain, experience leads to familiarity with recurrent patterns. Those patterns make a complex situation seem much simpler. This process of cognitive simplification holds in thousands of knowledge and skill domains, from school subjects (reading, math, science) to professions (medicine, law), to skilled labor (auto mechanics), to sports (basketball)—and to every performance domain imaginable. Chunking is powerful. It's a form of learning in which complex patterns become familiar and are treated by working memory as single chunks.

FIGURE 3.5
A chessboard *The configuration of chess pieces seems simple to an expert chess player.* [Pearson Education/PH College]

Additionally, familiar knowledge greatly enhances the flow of information between working memory and long-term memory. Among experts, working memory can draw rapidly and easily on knowledge structures in long-term memory (Ericsson & Kintsch, 1995). Consequently, working memory can handle more complexity. The capacity of working memory does not change—it is still constrained. But as the nature of a chunk is redefined for learners in particular domains, the burden for working memory is reduced. Cognitively, this is a huge benefit because the resulting freed-up working memory can be used instead for other purposes, such as planning ahead, anticipating problems, making adjustments, and capitalizing on new opportunities. As a consequence of chunking, cognition can become much more intelligent and creative.

Automaticity

The terminology of chunks and chunking applies largely to factual knowledge. But factual knowledge—sometimes called **declarative knowledge**—is not the only kind (Anderson, 1985). Another important form of knowledge is how to do things, like how to cook an egg or how to ride a bicycle. This is called **procedural knowledge**. We have seen that chunking applies to declarative knowledge. A similar idea applies to procedural knowledge. It's called **automaticity**.

To gain an appreciation for automaticity, think about how you learned to drive a car (if you do drive). At the beginning of your driving experience you had to devote your full attention to driving the car safely. This was hard enough because the information load was almost overwhelming. As a new driver, you did not want to engage in a conversation; even listening to music might have been too much when first learning to drive. Staying safe required all of your working memory.

With time, the cognitive demands of driving changed. Driving became simpler. Steering to keep a car between the lane markers became easier and easier. It became so easy that you did not have to think about it, at least not actively. Other aspects of driving likewise became more automatic with time and experience, such as keeping an appropriate distance between your car and the car ahead of you. The same applied to other driving skills—changing lanes, braking to a smooth stop, and obeying traffic signals. With time, all of these became easy. You developed *automaticity* in your driving skills. Automaticity is the counterpart to the process of chunking declarative knowledge, but it applies to skilled behavior.

As you developed automaticity, the burden to your working memory was reduced. No longer did the demands of driving overwhelm your working memory. Rather than trying to avoid distractions, perhaps you welcomed them. You wanted, perhaps, to engage in conversation during a long road trip, or to listen to music. After all, neither of these seemed to impair your driving performance. Only in the case of a sudden driving hazard would you need to cease conversation so that you could pay full attention to avoiding an accident. Normal driving was easy, maybe so easy that you were tempted to engage in nondriving behaviors, such as using a cell phone, playing percussion on the steering wheel, or eating a burrito—all at high speed. For safety's sake, keep in mind the limits of working memory. Automaticity can work for you and make you a better driver. You can even multi-task under predictable conditions. But if the situation changes abruptly and the car ahead swerves, you'll instantly need all the resources of your working memory to be safe.

Automaticity is highly relevant to academic work, and perhaps to literacy above all (LaBerge & Samuels, 1974). A simple-minded view of literacy might see reading as simply the ability to decode words. However, reading entails far more than translating letters into the strings of distinct sounds (phonemes) that compose spoken words. Reading requires skill in decoding, but decoding must become very efficient so that a reader can devote attention to the meanings behind the words, and how those meanings fit together to permit comprehension. Reading for meaning and comprehension therefore relies on decoding, but also goes far beyond it. Only when decoding reaches a degree of automaticity is skilled reading really possible.

Automaticity applies also to writing—certainly, for example, in the muscle movements that control a pen or that coordinate keystrokes on a computer. As you take notes in class or as you write a letter, you rely on the relatively effortless movements of your fingers. This automaticity allows you to *think* about what you are writing. In mathematics also, basic arithmetic facts and operations should eventually reach the point of automaticity so that working memory can be freed up to engage in more complex and creative work. The larger principle here is that all highly skilled performance depends on the automated performance of lower-level skills.

Automaticity is important, and because of this, every teacher should consider whether building automaticity ought to be *one* goal of student learning. It should never be the exclusive goal because learning should always lead, if possible, to high levels of complex performance in knowledge and skill domains. It makes sense, therefore, to see higher-level skills and lower-level skills as complementary. This complementarity might shed light on what is a perpetual point of contention in educational philosophy and policy. The issue is whether schools should concentrate on basic skills or on higher-level thinking. As we appreciate the capacity limitations of working memory, we can understand that some automaticity of basic skills is a *prerequisite* for higher level thinking. To a certain degree, then, the separation of basic skills and higher-level thinking is a false dichotomy. The two go together. This insight does not erase the controversy completely because educators (and other "stakeholders," such as parents) still need to hammer out specific compromises in the curriculum.

The higher/lower skills controversy illustrates that understanding the design of the human mind does not necessarily lead to definitively "correct" educational decisions. Education is far too complicated for that. As a creative enterprise, education is not amenable to detailed prescription as to how teaching should be carried out. And yet an understanding of how the mind works can illuminate the issues and guide the decisions of educators at all levels—teachers, tutors, principals, and curriculum designers. For example, an educator who understands automaticity may be dedicated to promoting higher-order thinking as a goal of education, but that educator will not want to dismiss attention to basic skills. Likewise, a teacher who is a proponent of basic skills will not necessarily be opposed to higher-order thinking, knowing that one builds on the other.

Laws of Learning

Think back to the basic structure of this chapter, and recall the overall logic: We began with a comparison of the human mind to a digital computer. The computer metaphor, though imperfect, was helpful in distinguishing three memory systems in the human cognitive architecture: the sensory register, short-term (or working) memory, and long-term memory. These three memory structures have different capacities and durations—and correspondingly they have different functions in relating how the human mind stores and transforms information. We examined one conceptual advantage of this triadic memory system—namely, that it can sharpen definitions of cognitive terms that are very important in education. These terms include *sensation*, *perception*, *attention*, *learning*, and *remembering*.

In this section of the chapter, we'll turn our attention to explore a few additional patterns in the operation of the mind. Given that the mind has a design—a particular architecture, if you will—it makes sense that it follows certain patterns in the ways that it works. This section presents some of the best-known of these patterns of operation. Many of the regularities have considerable evidence backing them, having been observed repeatedly over many decades of research. For this reason, this section is called the *Laws of Learning*.

Serial Position Curve

Learning in any field is complex. We might make rapid progress in some aspects of learning a language, for example, but proceed slowly in other aspects. The same holds true for playing a musical instrument, understanding biology, or learning to ski. In this sense, learning is not linear—it can proceed along multiple fronts and at different and varying rates. But there is one sense in which learning is linear, which is that learning takes place within the linear dimension of time. When we read a book or listen to a lecture, the ideas follow sequentially in time. This linear aspect of learning raises a question: How does learning relate to the presentation of ideas in a time sequence?

The most basic answer to this question is depicted in Figure 3.6. In any series of ideas, those presented near the beginning and those near the end are usually the most memorable. The graphical representation of this fact is a U-shaped curve that shows, by extension, that ideas presented near the middle of a series are generally less memorable. This U-shaped curve is called the **serial position curve**.

Particular learning experiences, such as reading a textbook, attending a lecture, or engaging in a multimedia learning experience are often bound by a definable period of time—an hour, perhaps. If so, the serial position curve has something to say about what ideas in a time-bound learning experience will tend to be best remembered. Ideas near the beginning of the lecture or textbook chapter will be somewhat more

**FIGURE 3.6
Serial position
curve** *Learning
improves near the
beginning and end.*
[Adapted from drawing
by Philip Travisano]

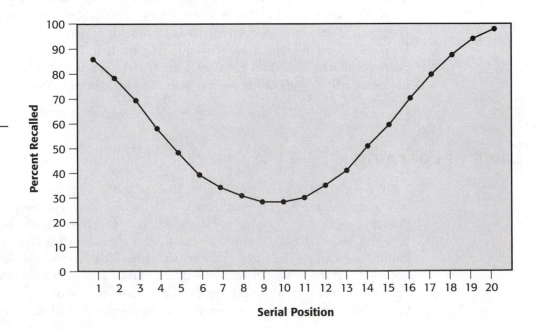

memorable. The boost to ideas presented *first* is called the **primacy effect**. There is a comparable boost to ideas presented near the *end* of any series—the closing words of a lecture or the final paragraph of a chapter, for example—that tends to make these ideas stick in long-term memory. This is called the **recency effect**.

The U-shaped function called the serial position curve obtains its characteristic shape from upward turns on both ends—the primacy and recency effects. What causes these two effects, and the shape of the curve more generally? The answer is that the U-shape results from **interference**. Interference is a familiar phenomenon and common to our experience. Think of a time when you attended a lecture. At first, you follow the sequence of ideas closely. But at a later point in the lecture, new information was presented that seemed confusing and that made you question what you *thought* you understood previously. Interference occurs whenever information X makes learning information Y more difficult.

Interference is always possible during learning. It's something that a learner needs to guard against and that teachers should try to prevent, or at least minimize. You might think about *how* a teacher could reduce potential interference. But for now, let's go back to the serial position curve and see how interference contributes to its shape. The primacy effect shows that information presented first tends to be memorable. When you sit down to study, you usually come to the task fresh. There is no *preceding* information to interfere with learning. Likewise, when you walk into a lecture hall you might have a few minutes before the lecture starts to clear your head. With the primacy effect, there is no immediately prior information to interfere with learning. Because you approach the task fresh, you will be relatively efficient in learning the new material.

A similar explanation applies to the upward turn of the learning curve at the end of a lecture or study session. These final minutes tend to be best remembered. One reason for the boost to learning is that there is no interference from subsequent information. As you walk out of class your mind is free to think about the lecture or discussion. No new information has the potential to compete with the last-presented information. The result is the recency effect.

In contrast to the beginning and end of any learning session, the middle part is the most susceptible to interference. It is *preceded* by information and *followed* by information, so there is the potential for interference from both directions. This combined pattern produces the characteristic dip in learning efficiency in the middle of the serial position curve. We must not think that the serial position curve always applies—it is a tendency, an average over many learning experiences. The curve is a pattern that teachers should understand, and that students too should consider.

The serial position curve is relevant to teaching because it can guide planning for instruction. For example, a teacher could present the most important information near the beginning and end of a lesson. This strategy capitalizes on the primacy and recency effects. Or a teacher can preview important information near the beginning and summarize that information near the end. The strategy conforms to a simple dictum for giving speeches:

- Tell them what you're going to tell them.
- Tell them.
- Tell them what you've told them.

This rhetorical strategy makes sense if you consider the serial position curve.

There are many other applications of the serial position curve. One application is to organize study sessions around breaks. One reason for doing so is to ward off fatigue or exhaustion, sure, but another is to introduce more primacy and recency effects. Each learning session has its own curve—so that after a break you'll experience a learning spike, a new primacy effect.

Consider also how you use the time before and after your study sessions. Sometimes after reading technical material I have a tendency to flip on the radio to catch up on the day's news. This is not good planning. If instead I delay turning on the radio for a few minutes, I can mull over the study material without interference from the news broadcast. Likewise, the period of time just before falling asleep offers a potential recency effect. As you fall asleep, you have no new information to interfere with what you've just learned—except possibly your dreams. But even your dream content might help you process information while sleeping.

The serial position curve, with its primacy and recency effects, is one example of a general pattern of human learning. It can be understood by considering how information is processed within the cognitive system. The serial position curve suggests several teaching applications, as well as several different strategies that can make learning more effective. More generally, it illustrates how understanding the design of the mind and its workings can lead to effective strategies for education.

Encoding Specificity

PHYSICAL CONTEXT. A second general principle of learning goes by the name of **encoding specificity**. Encoding specificity is easiest to explain by example. One vivid example of encoding specificity involves a psychology experiment in which subjects learned lists of unrelated words. Learning word lists is not particularly interesting. The interesting variation in this experiment is that these words were learned in two different conditions—on dry land and underwater (Godden & Baddeley, 1975). Participants in the experiment learned a set of words while wearing scuba diving equipment in each of the two physical contexts. The underwater context for learning was an odd one, but it had a point. It could test the hypothesis that the context for learning (on land or underwater) was associated with the specific material learned in each of these two contexts. If learning *content* is associated with learning *context*, then material learned on land would be best remembered on land and, interestingly, material learned underwater would be best recalled underwater.

For the experiment to work, the psychologists needed to find a way to present word lists in the two contexts. They did this by making audio recordings of the word lists, and then delivering the sound signal to the subjects' jaw bones. The vibrations in the jaw were audible. This apparatus allowed the words to be heard in air or underwater. The recall portion of the experiment, likewise, had to be adapted to work in both contexts. The solution was to have the divers write with wax pencils on submersible tablets, a communication device that is commonly used by scuba divers. The researchers' hypothesis was confirmed. When scuba divers learned a word list on land, they remembered that list best on land. But when a particular word list was learned underwater, the list was remembered best when the divers were back underwater.

Now we can proceed to a definition of encoding specificity. It means that learned (*encoded*) material is linked to (is *specific* to) the context in which it is learned. This linkage of learning to context is interesting in the case of the underwater context—but it also applies to less exotic contexts. For example, given a choice to take a midterm exam on picnic tables outside on a sunny day, students in a chemistry class might prefer to take their examinations in the chemistry classroom. Why? Because according to the encoding specificity principle, knowledge about the context (the classroom in which learning occurred) is linked to the specific content of learning (chemistry).

FIGURE 3.7
**The context of learning
matters** *Encoding specificity means that
the physical or emotional situation is part of
what is learned.* (Photo by Wayne and Karen
Brown, ©2009)

EMOTIONAL CONTEXT. In the examples given above, learning underwater or in a
chemistry classroom, the content of learning is linked to the context of physical location. But that is only one version of encoding specificity. Another version concerns the
emotional state of the learner when learning occurs. The extension here is that the
emotions of the learner at the time of learning are associated with the *content* of learning. Are you happy at the moment? If so, the encoding specificity hypothesis would lead
to a prediction: Your recall for the ideas in this chapter will be best if that particular
emotional state, happiness, is re-created. The same is true for sadness. If emotions and
particular knowledge are linked in long-term memory, then remembering one ought to
help evoke the other.

Psychologist Gordon Bower tested the hypothesis that the encoding specificity
principle extends to emotions. He set up conditions that evoked different emotions
in his subjects and gave them learning tasks while they were experiencing those specific emotions. Bower and his collaborators later re-created those same emotions
(Bower & Cohen, 1982). The important research question was whether experiencing a
certain emotion, such as happiness or sadness, boosted students' memory for knowledge they had learned earlier while feeling that same emotion. The data confirmed
the hypothesis. Emotions were part of what students learned originally—and when
students later experienced those same emotions, their memory for the associated
knowledge was enhanced. This particular form of encoding specificity has been called
mood-congruent processing (Bower & Forgas, 2001).

We should not overestimate the importance of encoding specificity as it pertains to
either physical context or to emotions. The advantage of re-creating the original physical context or emotional context of learning might be quite small. In research terms, we
could say that these effects are statistically significant—they are real and detectable—
but they are not necessarily large. The encoding specificity effect for emotional state, in

particular, is probably rather small. The effect for physical location might be somewhat larger, especially if the two contexts are quite different. Knowledge learned in school might not be easily recalled and utilized outside school settings. The difficulty of transferring knowledge to contexts beyond classrooms is a strong justification for sending students into "real world" situations to learn and to apply their knowledge.

Even if encoding specificity effects are modest, their existence tells us something important about the mind—namely, that it is highly associational. You might associate particular songs with certain emotional memories, for example. Likewise, distinct smells or tastes might evoke specific memories. When you sense these connections, you experience the mind's tendency to associate all kinds of diverse information across sensory modes, often in ways that are unique to the individual person. Learning can be quite idiosyncratic.

Massed and Distributed Practice

Up to this point we have examined, briefly, two laws of learning: the serial position curve and encoding specificity. A third pattern of learning is the law of **massed and distributed practice** (Dempster, 1988). Like the serial position curve, this law is concerned with the relationship between learning and time. The serial position curve deals with the pattern of information learned during a single study session. The law of massed and distributed practice is different in that its focus is on *multiple* study sessions—or more precisely, the advantages of multiple learning sessions compared to a single one.

Massed practice refers to combining all study time into a single session. If you study only on the night before an examination, that is massed practice. **Distributed practice** refers to spreading the learning into numerous sessions. The number of potential study sessions can range from one to a very high number. It's not surprising that learning is more efficient when study time is divided into multiple sessions. In a contest with massed practice, distributed practice wins. But these findings take on more significance when the total study time is held constant. Let's say you can allocate only five hours per week to studying. How would you allocate that time? One possibility, not uncommon, is to save those five hours for the night before an exam. What if, instead, you had spread those five hours over five nights instead of one? The research says that distributed practice will yield the better outcome. Chances are you'll learn more.

If you want to maximize your study efficiency, go with distributed practice. This rule applies whether you are a student planning your own study time, or whether as a teacher you are planning lessons for your students. Given a fixed amount of learning time, the best strategy is to divide it into multiple learning sessions. It's interesting to speculate about *why* distributed practice is generally superior to massed practice. One possible explanation is that each study session leaves an independent learning trace in the brain. That is, study sessions separated by time have somewhat independent memory effects, and these independent traces are superior in the long run to the single trace produced by massed practice.

This superiority of distributed practice over massed practice is an important principle, one that every teacher and student should know. But this principle too has limits. In spreading out five hours of study time, you could reduce those study times to very short intervals that might offer little benefit. Also, some *kinds* of knowledge might be acquired only during an extended learning session. This is one argument behind block scheduling and extended class periods found at some high schools. To plan longer time periods for learning seems sensible. But against this possibility is the backdrop of another principle—the superiority of distributed practice over massed practice—that should be taken into account. This principle, like so many others in learning and cognition, should not be applied blindly, but should inform and guide decisions about how to design learning experiences that are effective and enjoyable.

Learning Strategies

This chapter presents the basic structural layout of the human cognitive system and the consequences of that structure for guiding the flow of information within the system. Examining the cognitive architecture helps us to understand and define important mental processes, including learning. We must now consider more pointedly how knowledge of the cognitive system can help make learning more efficient and effective. To approach this topic, concepts and principles from this chapter will be presented as ten strategies for effective learning.

1 Focus working memory.

Working memory is the gateway to learning. Consequently, learning is most effective when working memory is skillfully directed toward the intended focus of learning. *Attention* and *concentration* are words we use to refer to the control of working memory on the target of learning. Good learners become very skillful at controlling their own working memories. Good teachers, likewise, know how to direct the working memories of the students they teach.

2 "Chunk" information.

Working memory is limited in capacity to only a few pieces of information. We can't think about very many different items at once. There is a consequent need, then, to reduce complexity to just a few elements, and to see how those elements interrelate. The goal, in other words, is to "chunk" the material. The cognitive architecture requires simplicity. Therefore, presented information needs to have a small number of parts *and* clear connections among those parts. This does not mean that knowledge stays simple—almost every subject becomes highly elaborate and complex when studied in depth. But when broken down, simplicity is compatible with the capacity limitations of working memory. The goal of simplicity is a good guide for individual learners, just as it is for teachers who present information to students.

3 Identify the most important ideas.

In almost every learning situation, some ideas are more important than others. Some ideas are so important that, if understood, they can help make sense of an entire field of study. In biology, for example, the concept of natural selection has this organizing function. One important learning skill, therefore, is to find ways to identify the most important ideas. All participants in the learning process have a role to play here. Ideally, writers of books will find ways to communicate to readers which concepts are central. Teachers can convey by language, gesture, and speaking tone which ideas are most important and which are subsidiary. Individual learners, too, need to develop skills in detecting the big ideas. Obviously, note-taking requires skills in prioritizing information because a student cannot write down everything a speaker says, nor would she want to.

4 Seek automaticity for some skills.

It takes time to practice skills to the point of automaticity. There is not enough time to make all skills automatic, but some are worth the effort. The development of skills in basic arithmetic is important because more complex performance builds on automating these more basic processes. In reading also, automaticity is an important educational goal because skillful reading depends on it. It's best for teachers and learners to be explicit about what skills should be developed to the point of automaticity. Remember, automaticity goes beyond correct performance. Automaticity also requires performance that is fluid, efficient, and almost effortless.

5 Divide study time into several sessions.

Research has confirmed the general superiority of distributed practice over massed practice. If you have a fixed study time—X hours—then its best to divide X up into multiple sessions rather than to bunch it up. This requires some discipline and advance planning, but the effort will pay off. Learning is much more effective when it is spread out over time rather than postponed to just before an exam. You'll remember more.

6 Capitalize on primacy and recency effects.
The serial position curve has important practical applications. From the curve, we know that information presented at the beginning or end of any learning session tends to stick best in memory. The upturns at the beginning and end of any series present opportunities for enhanced learning. For teachers, the most important ideas could be prefigured at the start of a lesson and summarized at the end. For students, the recency effect presents an opportunity to leverage learning. One strategy is to reserve a couple of minutes after reading a chapter to mentally review what you've learned. The important point is to extend your study time, if only briefly, to review the most important ideas. By doing so regularly, you can use the recency effect to your advantage.

7 Encode in multiple modes.
One known quality of long-term memory is that it stores information in multiple forms. As recognized in the dual coding theory, two of these forms—language and mental images—are highly important. But there are other knowledge forms as well, such as episodic memory of personal experiences. Talented teachers have long appreciated how important it is to teach their subject in different ways, exposing students to different "modalities" of information. This makes sense given that long-term memory holds information in different forms. Learning that capitalizes on using different modes will help promote understanding. It will also assist learners in recalling information from long-term memory because the different forms of learning present different retrieval pathways.

8 Link to prior knowledge.
New knowledge should connect meaningfully to prior knowledge—to what the learner already knows. Learning virtually always requires such a connection because without it new information would be pure nonsense. But there is considerable variation in the potential depth and richness of interconnections between new knowledge and prior knowledge. When connections are minimal and superficial, we sometimes call the product rote learning. But when connections are rich and the new knowledge integrates with prior knowledge to produce a coherent picture, the result is understanding. One goal for teaching and learning should be to link new knowledge to prior knowledge. Learners should ask: How does this relate to what I already know? Likewise, teachers should continuously seek to connect new information to the knowledge that students bring to the classroom.

9 Learn to self-cue for retrieval.
The cognitive information-processing model tells us that sensation, perception, attention, learning, and retrieval are all distinct processes. They point to different events on the information pathway within the cognitive architecture. We can distinguish, for example, between *learning* and *remembering* (or retrieval) by saying that learning is what happens when we move information from working memory to long-term memory. Retrieval is the reverse: moving learned information from long-term memory back into the conscious awareness of working memory. Both processes are challenges for education in that neither is guaranteed even if we strongly want them to happen. For example, sometimes we know that we know something, but retrieval from long-term memory is hard or seemingly impossible. One important intellectual skill is to provide cues to oneself—to think about related knowledge that can eventually trigger the knowledge that you are searching for in long-term memory.

10 Question what you think you know.
The mind is not a video camera—we do not record experience exactly as it occurs, but rather as we selectively perceive it. Our memories and beliefs about what we have experienced or learned in the past can be incomplete, distorted, or even false—notwithstanding our beliefs about their accuracy! We can be overly confident about what we know, and this misplaced certainty can get in the way of seeking the truth. When we appreciate this hard fact—that what we *think* we know might not be what actually *is*—we can adopt an attitude of suitable humility toward knowledge. Knowledge is provisional and almost always improvable. Such a stance touches on the nature of knowledge and on strategies of higher order cognition, including critical thinking, which are subjects of the next two chapters.

These ten learning strategies are not exhaustive. Many others could be named. But these ten derive most directly from the description of the cognitive architecture that is the centerpiece of this chapter. Even if you agree that these strategies are useful, you might suspect that strategies related to higher-order thinking are not given sufficient attention in this chapter. You are right. Higher-order thinking is of such great importance that it is given separate attention, along with its own list of learning strategies, in Chapter 5.

 Conclusion

This chapter explores the cognitive architecture that is derived from an information-processing view of the human mind. In the 1950s and 1960s, this model was inspired by the then-nascent field of computer science. The digital computer with its multiple memory systems and information flow pathways provided a metaphor for thinking about how the human mind is similarly structured. No metaphor is perfect, and so ultimately we find that the mind is *unlike* a computer in many ways. Still, the metaphor can take us quite far.

We have seen, for example, that the cognitive system is structured around three kinds of memory that have distinct capacities and durations. Those three are the sensory register (with a detailed capacity and very short duration), working memory (with small capacity and short duration), and long-term memory (with huge capacity and very long duration). Information flows between these memory structures and is connected to the "outside" world through the senses. The cognitive system is also connected to nerves and muscles, which permit both speech and motor movements by which we act on our surroundings. Patterns of information that flow within the cognitive architecture help us sharpen definitions of common and important terms describing mental processes. Among those are sensation, perception, attention, learning, and remembering.

One crucial insight into the cognitive system is to realize that it is not like a video camera; it does not record all our experience in high-fidelity form. Rather, it is both selective and interpretive, and often distortive. We should recognize that what we perceive from the environment is only a small subset of the information barrage that strikes our senses. Similarly, what we learn is only a fraction of what we think about, and what we later remember is only a fraction of what we learn. These decreasing subsets are like a funnel that progressively restricts data to smaller yet more meaningful collections of knowledge flowing through the cognitive architecture.

Part of the explanation for why information funnels into smaller subsets is the information-processing bottleneck presented by working memory. Working memory—the memory structure that represents our conscious attention—is surprisingly small in capacity. We can think about only a few things at once. This insight, first formally expressed in 1956 in a paper by George A. Miller, was revolutionary in psychology and, even now, holds implications for teaching. We need to appreciate, though, that there are ways *around* the apparent limitations of a small working memory capacity. Those "ways around" are chunking (for declarative knowledge) and automaticity (for procedural knowledge). Both chunking and automaticity are vital cognitive processes, and both are important as a learner develops higher levels of knowledge and skill. Because they are so important, these two cognitive processes should work into the plans of teachers as they design learning experiences.

Toward the end of the chapter, we saw that the cognitive architecture gives rise to certain regularities, which we can call, loosely, laws of learning. These include the serial position curve, the encoding specificity hypothesis, and the superiority of distributed practice over massed practice. These "laws" can help guide both learning and teaching strategies. Ten possible strategies for teaching and learning formed the final section of this chapter. Together, these ten strategies showed that the basic elements and processes of the cognitive architecture have important implications for teaching and learning. They can be used profitably by teachers as they design instruction and by learners as they regulate their own intellectual development. As we look forward to Chapter 5, which concentrates on higher-order cognition, we will see that this extended exploration of the workings and potential of the human mind yields further insight into how to make learning and cognition more powerful and effective.

REFERENCES

Anderson, J. R. (1985). *Cognitive psychology: And its implications* (2nd ed.). New York: Freeman.

Atkinson, R. C., & Shiffrin, R. M. (1971). The control of short-term memory. *Scientific American, 225*(2), 82–90.

Baddeley, A. (1986). *Working memory*. Oxford: Clarendon.

Bower, G. H., & Cohen, P. R. (1982). Emotional influences on memory and thinking: Data and theory. In S. Fiske & M. Clark (Eds.), *Affect and cognition* (pp. 291–331). Hillsdale, NJ: Lawrence Erlbaum Associates.

Bower, G. H., & Forgas, J. P. (2001). Mood and social memory. In J. P. Forgas (Ed.), *Handbook of affect and social cognition* (pp. 95–120). Mahwah, NJ: Lawrence Erlbaum Associates.

Bruner, J. S. (1957). On perceptual readiness. *Psychological Review, 63*(2), 123–152.

Bruner, J. S. (1968). Foreword. In A. R. Luria, *The mind of a mnemonist*. New York: Basic Books.

Calfee, R. C. (1981). Cognitive psychology and educational practice. In D. C. Berliner (Ed.), *Review of research in education*. Washington, DC: American Educational Research Association.

Craik, F., & Lockhart, R. (1972). Levels of processing: A framework for memory research. *Journal of Verbal Learning & Verbal Behavior, 11*, 671–684.

Dempster, F. N. (1988). The spacing effect: A case study in the failure to apply the results of psychological research. *American Psychologist, 43*(8), 627–634.

Dewey, J. (1916). *Democracy and education*. New York: Harper & Row.

Eich, E. (1988). Learning during sleep. In *Enhancing Human Performance: Background Papers*. Washington, DC: National Academies Press.

Ericsson, K. A., & Kintsch, W. (1995). Long-term working memory. *Psychological Review, 102*(2), 211–245.

Gardner, H. (1991). *The unschooled mind: How children think and how schools should teach*. New York: Basic Books.

Godden, D. R., & Baddeley, A. D. (1975). Context-dependent memory in two natural environments: On land and underwater. *British Journal of Psychology, 66*, 325–331.

Hutchins, E. (1995). How a cockpit remembers its speeds. *Cognitive Science, 19*, 265–288.

Huxley, A. (1932/2005). Brave new world. New York: Harper Perennial.

James, W. (1890). *The principles of psychology*. Boston: Henry Holt.

Just, M. A., & Carpenter, P. A. (1980). A theory of reading: From eye fixations to comprehension. *Psychological Review, 87*, 329–354.

Key, W. B. (1973). *Subliminal seduction*. New York: Signet.

Kosslyn, S. M. (1980). *Image and mind*. Cambridge, MA: Harvard University Press.

LaBerge, D., & Samuels, S. J. (1974). Toward a theory of automatic information processing in reading. *Cognitive Psychology, 6*, 293–323.

Loftus, E. (1996). *Eyewitness testimony*. Cambridge, MA: Harvard University Press.

Luria, A. R. (1968). *The mind of a mnemonist*. New York: Basic Books.

McKelvie, S. J. (1995). The VVIQ as a psychometric test of individual differences in visual imagery vividness: A critical quantitative review and plea for direction. *Journal of Mental Imagery, 19*, 1–106.

Merikle, P. M., Smilek, D., & Eastwood, J. D. (2001). Perception without awareness: Perspectives from cognitive psychology. *Cognition, 79*, 115–134.

Miller, G. A. (1956). The magical number seven, plus or minus two. *Psychological Review, 63*, 81–97.

Moore, T. E. (1982). Subliminal advertising: What you see is what you get. *Journal of Marketing, 46*(2), 38–47.

Moore, T. E. (1988). The case against subliminal manipulation. *Psychology & Marketing, 5*(4), 297–316.

Newell, A., & Simon, H. A. (1972). *Human problem solving*. Englewood Cliffs, NJ: Prentice-Hall.

Paivio, A. (1986). *Mental representations*. New York: Oxford University Press.

Penfield, W. (1958). *The excitable cortex in conscious man*. Springfield, IL: Charles C. Thomas, Publisher.

Perkins, D. N. (1992). *Smart schools: From training memories to educating minds*. New York: The Free Press.

Peynircioglu, Z. F. (1989). The generation effect with pictures and nonsense figures. *Acta Psychologica, 70*, 153–160.

Pichert, J. W., & Anderson, R. C. (1977). Taking different perspectives on a story. *Journal of Educational Psychology, 69*, 309–315.

Rudofsky, S. F., & Wotiz, J. H. (1988). Psychologists and the dream accounts of August Kekulé. *Ambix, 35*(1), 31–38.

Tulving, E. (2002). Episodic memory: From mind to brain. *Annual Review of Psychology, 53*, 1–25.

Simon, H. A. (1980). Problem solving and education. In D. T. Tuma & F. Reif (Eds.), *Problem solving and education: Issues in teaching and research* (pp. 81–96). Hillsdale, NJ: Lawrence Erlbaum Associates.

Sperling, G. (1960). The information available in brief presentation. *Psychological Monographs, 74*, 1–29.

[4] Theories of Knowledge

For thousands of years, the human mind has tried to comprehend itself. Philosophers, along with scholars from other disciplines, have struggled to find answers to these very difficult questions: What is the mind? What is knowledge? Is knowledge the same as reality or are they different? Progress has been made toward formulating satisfying answers to some questions, but answers to other questions have been partial or disputed. Quite often through the centuries, scholars took very different and even opposing views in their attempts to solve the fascinating puzzle of the human mind.

Psychology is not the only discipline to focus on these questions. Indeed, given that psychology originated in the late nineteenth century, it is a relative newcomer. Before the birth of psychology, and to this present day, several different disciplines have focused their distinct spotlights on knowledge to try to understand what it could possibly be.

This chapter examines the contributions of six different disciplines in their approach to understanding knowledge. The contribution of the discipline of psychology, which is central to this book, is considered near the end of the chapter. The six disciplines are the following:

- Philosophy
- Semiotics
- Linguistics
- Artificial intelligence
- Psychology
- Anthropology

Some people extol the benefits of multidisciplinary study. When it comes to understanding knowledge, it truly does help to hear what each of these disciplines has said. The hope is that our understanding of knowledge will be enhanced by their distinct contributions.

Philosophy

Of the disciplines that have tried to understand the nature of knowledge, it makes sense to consider philosophy, the oldest of the disciplines, first. Across the millennia, philosophers have attempted to gain insight into such questions as: What is real? What is knowledge? What is good?

Knowledge and Reality: What's the Connection?

WHAT IS REAL? Let's start with the question of "What is real?" Why should this question pose a problem? Well, for one thing, people from every society understand that appearance and reality are not the same. We can be fooled by visual illusions, for example. Magicians use this vulnerability to entertain us, but illusions are also common in everyday life. For example, we might momentarily mistake a log for an animal, or a shadow might fleetingly look like a lurking person.

Illusions sometimes take on great and lasting importance. For many centuries, the earth was considered to be the center of the universe. The commonsensical geocentric view was believable because the earth was massive, solid, and inhabited by human beings. Lesser spheres—the sun, moon, and planets—seemed to revolve around the earth in predictable paths. This view is completely wrong, as Copernicus taught, but it held sway for most of intellectual history.

The geocentric view of the world is not the only illusion to be widely and commonly accepted. There are many others. Think for a moment about the breakthroughs in science. Many of these involved overturning commonsense "theories" about the way the world works. Illusions are common, which is another way of saying that the mind does not have direct access to reality. What we believe and what is true might not be the same thing; in fact, they could be very different.

ONTOLOGY: THE PHILOSOPHY OF BEING. The question of "What is real?" has particular force in the field of study called **ontology**. Ontology is the branch of philosophy that is centrally concerned with the nature of reality or being. Ontologists want to understand what is real in the universe. This focal question raises subsidiary questions, including, Does God exist? People disagree on the answer to this question, of course, and over the centuries philosophers too have disagreed. Another key ontological question is whether human beings are material in essence, or whether we have souls that exist independently of our bodies. You will see that some ontological questions have direct bearing on the subject of this chapter, the nature of knowledge.

PLATO'S ALLEGORY OF THE CAVE. The branch of philosophy called ontology brings home the point that what we experience directly with our senses and what is considered ultimate reality are not necessarily the same. It could even be claimed that they are usually *not* the same thing. Plato made this point vividly in a story in which prisoners were chained together inside a cave. They were chained in such a way that they could not see outward, but only inward toward the wall of the cave. Their captors built a fire in the cave and used puppets, including shapes of people and animals, to cast shadows on the cave wall. By watching the shadows the prisoners could make guesses about the nature of reality. But what they recognized "as reality [was] nothing more than the shadows of those artificial objects."

There is an interesting twist in Plato's Allegory of the Cave. One of the prisoners was released and entered the real world. Tragically, the sunlight was so intensely bright that it temporarily blinded the man. To examine reality directly was too much—it was painful and overwhelming. Eventually, the man became accustomed to the bright daylight and saw reality more truly. He then understood that "what he had formerly seen was meaningless illusion." For the prisoners in the cave, the best they could hope for was to be clever in interpreting shadows. By necessity, their knowledge was indirect.

EPISTEMOLOGY: HOW WE KNOW WHAT WE KNOW. For us, as for the prisoners in Plato's Allegory of the Cave, how can we know what is real if our knowledge of reality is not direct? The question is so difficult that an entire branch of philosophy, **epistemology**, is dedicated to understanding what knowledge is, and how we know what we know. The two branches of philosophy that are identified here—ontology and epistemology—really do complement each other. If we raise the question, "What is real?" (ontology), then a second question naturally follows: "How can we know?" (epistemology). Ontology and epistemology aren't the only branches of philosophy, but they are the two major branches that have been fairly dominant for more than two thousand years. Many brilliant minds have tried to solve these very tough problems and, unsurprisingly, the problems are still largely unresolved to this day.

Ontology and epistemology connect to education in that one purpose of education is to reveal what is not obvious or apparent. Intellectual insights uncover realities that are often quite different from the way things appear. This is most clear in science, but it's also true of every field, including philosophy. The hard-won insights of geniuses through the centuries are introduced to new generations through education. The mind of the individual student must be similarly engaged. Just as Copernicus could break through to a deeper reality, so can learners be helped to see past the apparent to deeper, more comprehensive truths.

Plato and Aristotle

Returning to the central concern of ontology, we ask, "What is real?" The Allegory of the Cave partially expressed the ideas of one philosopher, Plato, on that subject. Aristotle, a particularly outstanding student in Plato's Academy, had another view. Their two different ontologies are beautifully depicted in a painting called *The School of Athens*, by the Renaissance painter Raphael (Figure 4.1).

FIGURE 4.1
Raphael's *The School of Athens* Plato points upward to emphasize nonmaterial reality; Aristotle gestures downward toward the tangible world.
[Raphael, "The School of Athens." Vatican Museums, Rome, Italy. Scala/Art Resources, NY]

RAPHAEL'S *THE SCHOOL OF ATHENS*. Raphael's painting depicts twenty or so brilliant figures, many of whom are anachronistic because the luminaries painted by Raphael lived in different times and places. Among this assembly of geniuses, two men are central, one young and one old—Aristotle and Plato. Their central placement in the painting is Raphael's way of paying homage to classical Greek thought and to these two philosophers in particular—as if the unfathomable intellectual richness of Western civilization had its origin in these two figures.

There is drama at center stage; the two men, who are in a heated debate, disagree. Plato's finger points upward toward the heavens to indicate his conviction that ultimate reality is nonmaterial. Plato believes that tangible objects are temporary and corruptible, so they cannot possibly be as real as heavenly objects. But young Aristotle cannot accept Plato's ontology. Aristotle's palm is extended downward, toward the earth. Here, says Aristotle, is ultimate reality: It's in the physical world, not in some imaginary nonmaterial forms that reside in another realm.

You might expect that the debates of Plato and Aristotle were resolved long ago, but there are still strong disagreements about ultimate reality. Was Aristotle right? Is the real world completely material? Are such entities as immaterial souls merely fictions? There is still vigorous disagreement in our society about the answers to such questions.

Empiricism and Rationalism

The central drama in epistemology was played out in the era just following the Renaissance. This era, called *the Enlightenment*, placed great emphasis on reason as the key to human progress. It was an era of tremendous optimism: Enlightenment thinkers believed that with sufficient effort the mind could solve any problem. Yet there was considerable disagreement about how the mind actually acquires knowledge. During the Enlightenment, the two leading schools of epistemology were **empiricism** and **rationalism** (Palmer, 1996). These two can be identified approximately with the British Isles (empiricism) and with continental Europe (rationalism).

KNOWLEDGE BEGINS WITH EXPERIENCE. Three prominent intellectuals established the philosophical school of empiricism: John Locke (1632–1704), George Berkeley (1685–1753), and David Hume (1711–1776). Collectively, these three philosophers believed that knowledge begins with the senses. Vision, hearing, taste, touch, and smell—the senses, they reasoned, must be the starting points for knowledge. In *An Essay Concerning Human Understanding*, Locke (1689) wrote that we know with most certainty that which impinges on our senses. We know a candle flame exists when we look directly at it, but we know it with even greater certainty if we touch it. If not directly linked to the senses, knowledge is less certain. This basic empiricist claim is certainly plausible, and in fact the assumptions of empiricists are largely compatible with the assumptions of modern science. Scientists place confidence in data, and data are understood primarily through the senses.

But the empiricists' assumptions were not without problems. For example, the empiricists were aware that the experiences presented by our senses are not identical with reality. Our senses can deceive us. In fact, if our world is known only through our senses, then our senses *define* our world. We become trapped inside our senses! Conclusion: We have no direct access to external reality. Paradoxically, the empiricists connected knowledge to the experience of the senses, which led to the conclusion that we live inside our heads, so to speak. The empiricist epistemology was not entirely satisfactory, arguably raising more questions than it answered.

KNOWLEDGE BEGINS WITH RATIONAL THOUGHT. René Descartes (1596–1650), the French philosopher, understood that our experience of the world and the world itself are not the same. He knew, as did the empiricists, that our senses could deceive us. Therefore, for Descartes, the senses were not to be trusted—or at least not completely. But if the senses could not be trusted, what could be? Descartes had an answer: rational thought.

Depending solely on rational thought was unworkable, however, because even rational thought is not completely trustworthy. It's possible that what we believe is rational actually is not. We might reason badly and so believe ideas that are false without realizing our intellectual missteps. Descartes knew that reasoning could easily go awry, and so he faced a monumental intellectual predicament. He was hungry for truth, yet believed everything that passed for truth was at least tainted with uncertainty and quite possibly untrue. Descartes's problem was severe; his next step was accordingly extreme.

That next step was to doubt everything. He no longer accepted anything that he previously believed as true. If knowledge is interconnected, and every bit of knowledge assumes the truth of other bits, then the whole enterprise was suspect. Solution: hit it with a wrecking ball. That wrecking ball was Descartes's method of **radical doubt**.

Doubting all, where could Descartes begin to find any shred of certain knowledge? Was anything at all certain? Descartes could think of only one fact that was absolutely sure: His own existence. He must exist. Why?—because he was thinking! It was necessary to conclude that he exists. Descartes expressed this inference in the famous proclamation, "Cogito ergo sum" ("I think, therefore, I am" in Latin).

Using this key idea as a starting point, Descartes felt it was possible to build upward. For example, from "cogito" he next concluded that God must exist (which made the theologians happy) and that mathematics exists (which made the scientists happy). By building on these widening foundations, Descartes believed it was possible to place all

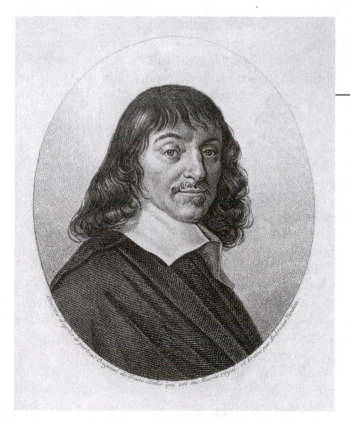

FIGURE 4.2
René Descartes *He doubted everything except his own existence.* (Courtesy of the Library of Congress)

true knowledge on a firm footing. Certain knowledge was possible, but it first required the extreme measure of radical doubt.

Descartes's conclusions have not stood the test of time. Other philosophers have leveled convincing critiques against his arguments. And Descartes is not alone. Part of the story of philosophy, and really of every field of inquiry, is that our best ideas at a particular time are eventually superseded. This fact alone has implications for our view of knowledge. At any moment in time it is provisional, very likely incomplete, and possibly wrong.

But there is something else to be learned from Descartes: a version of his method of radical doubt. Descartes's decision to disbelieve everything was extreme, but if the goal is to be good thinkers, we can adopt his mindset to a limited degree, at least. To be a good thinker means, in part, to test ideas to see if they are worthy of belief. This applies to our own assumptions as well as to claims made by others, whether spoken or in print. When we test ideas by asking, "Does that make sense?" we are thinking critically. Critical thinking is explored more fully in the next chapter, but for now let's recognize that Descartes was good at it. We should all imitate his propensity for critical thinking. Ideally, we can encourage other people to be good critical thinkers, too.

KANT'S ANSWER: THE SYNTHETIC A PRIORI. Besides empiricism (knowledge begins with the senses) and rationalism (knowledge begins with thinking), there is another viewpoint to consider–the theory set forth by the German philosopher Immanuel Kant (1724–1804). Kant is important to this discussion because he understood the strengths and weaknesses of empiricism and rationalism; he thought both were incomplete and that there must be another approach that could help to establish the foundations of knowledge.

To understand Kant's approach it's necessary to introduce some new philosophical terminology. First, there is a distinction between **analytic** and **synthetic statements**. Analytic statements are simply definitional, such as "A circle is round." Nothing new is discovered in saying this because roundness is part of the definition of a circle. A lot of our knowledge is analytic; some things are true by definition. Synthetic knowledge is different. For example, "The earth is round" is not true by definition. It could have been another shape—a cube, for example—but it was eventually discovered to be round. That kind of knowledge—true by discovery, not by definition—is synthetic.

Two more terms are needed: **a priori** and **a posteriori**. These Latin terms mean "before the fact" and "after the fact." A priori refers to knowledge that we can have before discovery. If you love someone, you know it in your heart before you say, "I love you." It's a priori knowledge. But when the person answers, "I love you, too," then you have a posteriori knowledge of that person's love.

It's fairly straightforward to make connections among these four terms. Normally, analytic statements are also a priori. In other words, statements that are true by definition can be stated before our actual experience (such as "A circle is round"). Likewise, synthetic statements are normally a posteriori. Simply put, statements that are not necessarily true by definition are stated only after some experience (such as "The earth is round"). Kant cross-linked these categories by claiming that *some* synthetic knowledge is actually known *before* our experience of it. That is the category of **synthetic a priori** knowledge. Such knowledge includes our understanding that tangible reality is composed of objects that exist in three-dimensional space.

Why all the hubbub? Because to Kant, this philosophical claim bridged the claims of rationalists and empiricists. The empiricists were partly right because sensory experience is important to building knowledge—it can't be done by thinking alone. The only way to possibly make sense of the storm of data impinging on our eyes, ears, and fingertips is to have some knowledge already built into our minds, ready to interpret the information. Synthetic a priori knowledge includes built-in ideas about space, time, and quantity. If our brains are pre-wired with such ideas, then even as infants we have some capability to process our experiences according to those categories. And because we share these basic categories of knowledge, we all interpret the world similarly enough that we can communicate (much of the time, anyway). Just to be clear, these categories are *synthetic* because they did not have to be true (space, time, and quantity did not have to exist) and they are *a priori* because they are known prior to our experience of them. Synthetic a priori.

Kant's complicated philosophy illustrates just how difficult it is to understand the nature of knowledge. As brilliant as Kant was, his ideas have not gone unchallenged. Nevertheless, his concept of synthetic a priori knowledge has implications for current theories of the human mind. Many psychologists and linguists now believe that the mind *does* have some knowledge built in. Infants, for example, show evidence that they expect the world to work in certain ways and are surprised when it doesn't. This hints that babies have some pre-learned, innate knowledge. This orientation to knowledge— that some of it is built-in—is what psychologists call **nativism**. The psychological theory of nativism owes much of its early development to Kant's philosophical theory of synthetic a priori knowledge. In psychology, the influence of nativist thinking extends both to current research on infants and to language learning. And in theories of cognitive development, particularly the theory of Swiss psychologist Jean Piaget (1896–1980), we will see a direct extension of Kant's nativist theory to understanding how logical thinking develops in a child.

Logical Positivism

The philosophies of rationalism and empiricism, as well as Kant's attempt to bridge the two, were attempts to find certain foundations for knowledge. None of these philosophies was completely successful, but the difficulty of building a solid epistemology did not stop other philosophers from trying. A notable effort to build a philosophy with strong epistemological foundations was an intellectual movement in the early twentieth century called **logical positivism**.

The approach of logical positivists was to boil down knowledge into its smallest components. For example, you could say "table flat" or "stove hot" with a high degree of confidence that these declarations expressed something indisputable. Those "atomic facts" give you some idea of the epistemological starting point for logical positivists. Chief among the logical positivists, and the man whose earlier writings inspired logical positivism, was the famed philosopher Ludwig Wittgenstein (1889–1951). To appreciate the origins of logical positivism we must realize that Wittgenstein's major focus in philosophy was logic. Logic deals with necessity, with certain knowledge of a kind similar to statements like "table flat." It makes sense, then, that the epistemology of logical positivists was restricted to the material world as known through the senses, and as expressed in statements that were deemed undeniable. By implication, the concept of God and many other intangible abstractions were excluded from consideration, and their exclusion reveals the ontology of these philosophers. What is real is that which can be sensed directly and stated definitively—nothing more.

THE VIENNA CIRCLE. Wittgenstein, as I said, is credited with inspiring logical positivism. The original logical positivists consisted of only a small group of philosophers, called the Vienna Circle, who met in Vienna, Austria, during the 1920s and 1930s. Wittgenstein was a periodic member of this group. But Wittgenstein's role in the Vienna Circle was interesting because not only did he inspire the philosophy, but he also was a major force in dismantling logical positivism. Thus, it is said that Ludwig Wittgenstein is the only philosopher who can be credited with *starting* and *ending* a philosophical movement.

What changed Wittgenstein's mind? At some point, it became obvious to him that such elemental statements as "table flat" or "stove hot" could not add up to anything resembling the sorts of knowledge people use in their daily lives, or that societies require to function. Such "atomic facts" were verifiable, but they could not serve as a basis for all knowledge. Knowledge in the real world, Wittgenstein eventually concluded, could never be tethered to solid foundations of certainty. This conclusion is very important. If Wittgenstein was right, it implies that the empiricists' attempt to base knowledge on sensory data was doomed. Likewise, Descartes's rationalist quest, beginning with "Cogito, ergo sum," was similarly fated to fail because it too sought certain knowledge in the tangible universe. Stated most generally, the centuries-old project of epistemology, to find the foundations for certain knowledge, suddenly collapsed. With the downfall of logical positivism, the philosopher's perennial hope of certain knowledge was crushed and abandoned.

The Linguistic Turn in Philosophy

If the ambitious hope of finding certain foundations for knowledge was ultimately dashed to the ground, what was the alternative? What possible meaning could epistemology have? Wittgenstein's answer was that knowledge and meaning are inextricably bound to language. Rather than basing knowledge on sense data, Wittgenstein believed that the mental lives of human beings are ultimately a function of the ideas they entertain in their own minds and that are communicated socially. These ideas are understood and shared predominantly in the form of language. If meaning is bound to language, then it is a misguided fantasy to base all knowledge on certain foundations in the tangible world. Instead, it is necessary to explore the implications of a world in which knowledge and language are deeply intertwined.

This conclusion is largely where philosophy lives to this very day. After Wittgenstein, philosophers largely abandoned the long, hard attempt to anchor epistemologies in the physical world or in the powers of the rational mind. Instead, many philosophers focused attention on language: what it is, how it works, what roles it plays. This shift in philosophy is known as the **linguistic turn** (Rorty, 1992).

We live in webs of meaning. This is not to say that the words we use, the claims we make, and the ideas we believe have no connection to the "real world." They certainly do. (Though a very few philosophers might disagree.) Yet the relationship between language and the tangible world is problematic and fails to capture much of the nature of knowledge, belief, and meaning. Language has many functions, not simply to name objects or to state facts, but also to accomplish things in the world (such as "Would you pass the salt?"). Language also carries with it assumptions about norms for behavior and who has power in social relationships. The philosopher Michel Foucault (1926–1984) is known especially for illuminating the role of language in conveying power in the social realm. Consider, for example, the power relations communicated by the words *professor*, *teacher*, and *student*. Such insights about language are further explored later in this chapter under the heading of linguistics.

Semiotics

The trajectory of our discussion has brought us to language, which in turn leads us to the field of **semiotics**. Semiotics is the study of **signs**, which includes language but also any sound, image, or object that conveys meaning. The relative isolation of disciplines means that many scholars, including psychologists and educators, are unaware of the wonderful ideas discovered by semioticians. This ignorance is more characteristic of Americans than of scholars elsewhere in the world. It's a tragedy because semiotics has important things to say to students of the human mind, which includes, of course, teachers.

A good place to start is to recognize two luminaries in the field of semiotics, one from Europe and one from America. The Swiss linguist Ferdinand Saussure started an intellectual revolution when he first taught a course in introductory linguistics in 1909. The American intellect Charles Sanders Peirce launched the American version of semiotics earlier still, starting in the 1860s. One of the greatest American minds, Peirce is barely known, especially (and ironically) in the United States.

Ferdinand Saussure

THE MAN FORCED TO TEACH LINGUISTICS. Sometimes professors are forced to teach courses that they don't particularly want to teach but for which there is a need. In some exceptional cases, this turns out to be a very good idea. Such was the case with Ferdinand Saussure (1857–1913), a linguistics professor at the University of Geneva, Switzerland. The university needed a professor to teach a course in introductory linguistics. Saussure, already a famous linguist, was not exactly enthusiastic about this request, but he decided to make the most of it. He took the teaching assignment as an opportunity to test some ideas that he had been entertaining for the past several years. The beneficiaries of Saussure's speculations were his students who, fortunately for us, took very good notes. The students' notes are relevant because Saussure taught his course in introductory linguistics only three times, and then died. Besides being good note takers, Saussure's students were perceptive in recognizing that they had received an extraordinary intellectual experience. Their notes from Saussure's course became foundational for the field of semiotics (Culler, 1986; Saussure, 1959).

SIGNIFIER/SIGNIFIED. What was so remarkable about Saussure's course? The answer to that question begins with Saussure's insight to look at language in a completely new way. As a linguist, Saussure was trained to study language as it changed over time. You may know, for example, that modern English is very different from English as it was spoken hundreds of years ago in Shakespeare's time, and more different still from when Geoffrey Chaucer wrote *The Canterbury Tales*. Every language is a living system that shifts and evolves over the centuries. Saussure, like other linguists in his day, was an expert in tracing minute changes in languages over long periods of time.

Saussure's first insight was to change the perspective. Rather than ask how language changes over time, he wondered how language functions at any one slice of time—how language works *now*. This led to a very basic question: What is language, anyway, and how does it relate to the thoughts we think? Here, Saussure made a simple, but very important discovery. He noted that the sound of a spoken word and the meaning of the word are two very different things. More than that, the relationship between a word's sound and its meaning is *arbitrary*. The word *dog* makes us think of the idea of a dog, but the word *cat* would work just as well.

Next, Saussure made a general distinction between **signifier** and **signified**. *Signifiers* include spoken words like *dog*. *Signified* refers to what, by convention, that sound stream means—the concept of dog. It's whatever we think of when we hear someone say *dog*. Saussure proposed that *all* language works this way, as pairings of signifier and signified. Taken together, signifier and signified constitute a **sign**. Saussure depicted the structure of a sign with this diagram:

signifier

signified

Signifier and signified go together, like the front and back of a single sheet of paper. But remember, the relationship between the front (signifier) and the back (signified) is arbitrary. They are strictly conventions that are agreed upon (tacitly) by a society. The conventions are extremely functional because they permit communication, but they also have important implications for the way that languages evolve. The pronunciation of spoken words (signifiers) can change because their relationship to signified meaning is arbitrary; Shakespearean English sounded very different from modern English. Similarly, the meaning of a word (the signified) can shift over time; words that have a certain meaning in one era can have very different meanings in another. This formulation helped Saussure to understand how languages change significantly, even radically, over time.

But Saussure went further. He understood that not just language functions this way, but other meaning systems as well. Gestures, for example, as well as facial expressions, traffic signals, and even musical jingles, can signify other meanings. All these are signs. This insight is the basis of semiotics—the system of signs that, by convention, constitute the webs of meaning in any society. Semiotics, therefore, recognizes language as a subset, but a very important subset, of something much bigger.

Why do we need signs, whether linguistic or nonlinguistic? Because, Saussure understood, human societies and civilizations needed ways to communicate elaborate systems of meaning in order to function. This led to yet another insight.

LA LANGUE AND PAROLE. Saussure further distinguished between the system of signs that each of us is born into, and the specific use of signs when we speak. The system of signs—what Saussure called **la langue**—is stable. There's not much that you or I could do to change our language system even if we wanted to do so. The arbitrary relationship between the idea of dog and the word *dog* makes it conceivable that we could call a dog *cat*. In actual practice, though, the word *dog* is accepted by a billion people or so, and anchored to published texts, as well as to recorded speeches, songs, movies, and so on. It would be difficult, verging on impossible, to change the name of four-legged barking canines to *cats*. So the system, called *la langue*, while not stuck, is highly stable.

In contrast to la langue are the specific uses of language that Saussure called **parole**. In actual use, language is very flexible and permits unlimited innovation. Each of us speaks sentences that we have never before heard, and perhaps have never been spoken. I suspect that many of the sentences in this book are unique. We can therefore recognize the stability of the language system (la langue), as well as the freshness and creative potential of specific uses of language (parole). We are surrounded by signs—these are our cultural heritage and the tools we use to survive and thrive within our world. Education and learning can be viewed as induction into the sea of signs (la langue), and nurturance into the skilled and creative use of signs (parole).

Charles Sanders Peirce

Charles Sanders Peirce (1839–1914) was an intellect equal to Saussure who lived slightly earlier in time and hailed from a different continent, North America. Like Saussure, Peirce saw language as a subset of a much larger and more general system. In fact, perhaps because Peirce was a scientist, rather than a linguist like Saussure, he had more success in describing signs that were not language-based. Peirce built large and elaborate taxonomies of such signs that included, for example, animal tracks and smoke signals.

There is another quality to Peirce's theory that sets it apart from Saussure's. Saussure's theory is straightforward in the binary signifier/signified distinction. The two, signifier and signified, jointly compose a sign. It's more complicated for Peirce. His basic model resembles instead a triangle whose parts are *representamen* (a symbol), *object* (a tangible object), and *interpretant* (meaning) (Figure 4.3).

What's new here? To simplify a great deal, Peirce's model introduced the real-world referent of the sign. Let's go back to *dog*. The word *dog* signifies the idea *dog*. Clear enough. But isn't there a real dog somewhere? Often, yes. This is what Peirce wanted to include—the *thing itself*. Together, the word, the idea, and the thing, form a triangle.

Now, whether the *thing itself* should be included as part of the sign has been hotly contested among semioticians, philosophers, and linguists. The issue seems arcane (and is), but it connects to the philosopher's quest for certain knowledge. The question is: Are ideas ultimately connected to tangible objects—or are they largely self-existent, without a necessary relationship to the physical world? Aristotle and Plato differed on the question. Wittgenstein had a change of heart over it. Saussure and Peirce framed their theories differently over it.

Perhaps, as a scientist, Peirce liked to see the connection between a sign and its real-world referent. Saussure, as a linguist, apparently did not feel the need to anchor signs in the tangible world, but instead considered them to be sociocultural units. The modern linguist, Umberto Eco (1976), critiqued the idea that signs should be connected to real-world referents. This of course was a criticism of Peirce's attempt to anchor signs in the tangible. Eco's argument is compelling, although it does raise, again, the implication that our mental worlds are *not* primarily about the physical world around us. If you accept this idea, it holds great importance for understanding how the mind works and how societies function.

INTERPRETANTS. If we set aside one corner of Peirce's triangle as questionable, we can still explore the remaining two. We can find great potential for exploration in one corner especially. That corner is the **interpretant**. The interpretant is rich in importance,

FIGURE 4.3
Peirce's semiotic theory *The meaning of signs has three aspects.* [Adapted from drawing by Philip Travisano.]

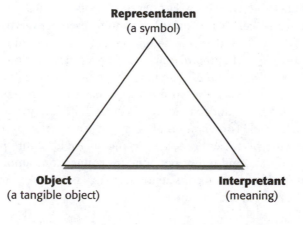

Representamen
(a symbol)

Object
(a tangible object)

Interpretant
(meaning)

even though its meaning was widely misunderstood, even in Peirce's time. People tended to assume that interpretant means interpret*er*, the person who receives and makes sense of the sign. But that is not what Peirce meant. By interpretant, he meant what the sign signifies, the cascade of meanings that a sign presents. When you hear the word *dog*, you might "see" a dog in your mind's eye, and imagine how a dog barks, moves, pants, and so on. This chain reaction of ideas sparked by the word *dog* is the word's interpretant.

Understood this way, Peirce's idea of *interpretant* is comparable to Saussure's notion of *signified*. But the idea of interpretant adds qualities that are helpful. I mentioned that the word *dog* might cause you to imagine what a dog looks like and how a dog barks. In fact, your dog thoughts might extend to include facts about dogs, including different breeds of dogs, famous dogs, dog food, dog care, and so on. Peirce's notion of the interpretant recognized that any sign can trigger a cascade of associations that, like falling dominoes, can go on and on.

An interpretant can be any thought that is triggered, or signified, by a sign (Houser, 1987). A sign might trigger emotions, for example. A dog might elicit delight, as it does for many people, or it might elicit fear, as it does for some. Peirce was clear that a sign's interpretant includes emotions, not just ideas. But actions can also be part of the interpretant. So the sight of a dog might activate motor sequences in nearby humans to stroke the fur on the animal's back. If so, petting motions are part of the interpretant for *dog*. But have I been deceptive here? At first, I was talking about the word *dog*, but then I switched to talking about a real dog. No—both count as signs. In fact, anything can be a sign if it signifies—that is, if it has an interpretant.

You might recognize at this point that there is no necessary stopping point for an interpretant. You might hear the word *dog* or see a real dog. Both are signs that can trigger related ideas, emotions, or actions. This cascade is the interpretant, and it can go on forever. Dogs can make you think about cats, which can make you think about mice, then maybe Disneyland, then American cultural imperialism. Next, you might think about the succession of great civilizations in world history, the pros and cons of representative government, and whether pizza should be government-subsidized. All this from *dog*! In fact, from *dog* you could (conceivably) think all possible thoughts. This potential of signs Peirce called **unlimited semiosis**. Ideas trigger other ideas, ad infinitum.

What's the educational significance of all this? For one thing, Peirce's notion of the interpretant sheds light on the meaning of another word commonly used in education, *understanding*. The word *understanding* is commonly invoked to express what kind of learning schools should produce. Education ought to result in more than rote learning of memorized definitions, something deeper and richer—namely, understanding. But can we say more about what understanding *is*? It helps to think about understanding in terms of interpretants and semiosis (Houser, 1987). Take the word *energy*. Energy is a central concept in science. It's also a word commonly used in everyday speech (as in "I have zero energy today"). A scientific definition for energy would be something like, "The capacity to do work." But this definition is empty unless the interpretant goes further. The word *work* also has an interpretant, which involves moving a force a certain distance. Like *energy and work*, the word *force* also has an interpretant, which must be appreciated for a scientific understanding of energy. The interpretant for energy can branch off to include the conservation of energy, $e = mc^2$, entropy, biological ecosystems, fossil fuels, energy-efficient cars, and on and on. An ideal interpretant for energy would be rich, elaborate, and full of potential for connections among ideas. It would also conform to the interpretants of scientists, though of course scientists' own interpretants would be more extensive still.

Finally, consider the idea of Umberto Eco, that all the signs of a culture together constitute a **semantic universe**. Our culture presents to us a vast number of signs—more than any one person could master in a lifetime. Educators might ask: "What signs must we teach?" and "What interpretants should be developed for those signs?" When posed this way, we see that the mission of education can be expressed in terms of signs. We think in signs. If signs are what the mind knows, then signs are the essence of what each mind must learn. Education involves the acquisition, invention, combination, and skilled use of signs. So it is quite possible to cast the goals and means of education in semiotic terms. This is not to say that we should always invoke semiotics when talking about education, but semiotics can help us see knowledge and education in a fresh way.

Linguistics

What Does Language Do?

SENSE AND REFERENCE. We have seen that the field of semiotics was rooted in linguistics, at least in the case of Saussure's theory. From the point of view of semiotics, language is a kind of sign. It's possible, therefore, to see linguistics as a subset of semiotics, even though semioticians and linguists pursue somewhat different problems and have different research techniques. Nevertheless, there is some overlap of ideas.

One convergence point for linguistics and semiotics is the (by now) familiar question of whether knowledge is anchored in the tangible world or is relatively independent and self-existent. The question harks back to Plato and Aristotle, and to Wittgenstein. It's here in linguistics, as well. The conclusion from the point of view of linguistics is, again, that our knowledge systems are often not tied to tangible realities.

One distinction that helps make this point clear is the difference between **sense** and **reference**. Think of sense as the intellectual meaning of a word; reference is what the word actually indicates in the real world. The words *Statue of Liberty* have a sense. The words commonly express patriotism and freedom, opportunity for immigrants, and American hopes and ideals. But the Statue of Liberty also has reference; there is a real Statue of Liberty located on Liberty Island near Manhattan Island, New York. You can take a ferry from Manhattan's southern tip to Liberty Island. There, you can touch the Statue of Liberty, walk around it, and go inside it. It's a real thing.

So far, this is simple. But if we look further, the sense/reference distinction leads to some puzzling results. For example, linguists note that the word *unicorn* has a definite sense (you know what I mean by *unicorn*, right?), but no one can show you a *unicorn* because none exists. So, for *unicorn*, we have sense but no reference. Likewise for *Frodo* in J. R. R. Tolkien's novel, *Lord of the Rings*. Given the popularity of Peter Jackson's film version of the trilogy, many of us hold Elijah Wood as our mental image of Frodo, but there is no real Frodo and there never has been. *Frodo*, like *unicorn*, has sense but no reference.

None of this would mean much if the sense/reference distinction applied only to fairly tales and fantasy films, but it has relevance also in trying to understand how the world works from a scientific lens. To be clearer, past generations of scientists have introduced ideas that were commonly understood and widely accepted, but had no basis in reality. They had sense, but no reference. Examples include:

- *Ether*: A fictional substance thought to fill the gaps between all solid objects in the universe. We now know that there can be nothing at all (a vacuum) between objects. Ether does not exist.

- *Caloric*: A supposed carrier or heat energy that flows from a hotter object to a colder object. Heat can and does flow, but by such recognized mechanisms as molecular motion or infrared radiation, not caloric.
- *Impetus*: A force carried within objects that keeps them moving for a period of time. There is no such thing as impetus, though it is a common misconception among nonscientists to this very day.

A final example used by linguists presents another interesting twist to the sense/reference distinction and also connects to scientific discovery. It relates to the terms *morning star* and *evening star*. The morning star is the bright object that appears in the eastern sky just before the sun rises. Similarly, the evening star appears in the western sky just after the sun sets. One problem with these descriptions is that the morning star and the evening star are not stars at all, but planets. But far more significant is the fact that the morning star and evening star are not two different objects but are in fact the same. Both are the planet Venus. Venus "precedes" the rising sun at one time in its orbit around the sun. Later in the year, it "follows" the setting sun. But it is the same celestial object. So, in the case of *morning star* and *evening star*, we have two different senses (morning star and evening star), but the same referent (Venus).

The point here is that the sense/reference distinction clarifies that the words we use can have a definite shared sense, but two terms might have the same referent or no referent at all. The connection between our ideas (sense) and tangible world (reference) is not direct or straightforward, but is instead deeply problematic. Another way of saying this is that the naive view of language—that words name things in the material world—is either wrong or grossly oversimplified. Language does much more than simply attach labels to things.

SPEECH ACTS. There is still another way of challenging the function of language as simply naming things in the world. **Speech acts** theory presents the idea that language frequently accomplishes goals that have little or nothing to do with naming things (Austin, 1962). An example is the sentence "I now pronounce you husband and wife." Now you could say there is naming going on here. True. But the more important reality is that the social system has been changed by this pronouncement; a new and important arrangement has been declared centrally through language. Consider also "Your honor, the jury finds the defendant guilty as charged" and "I hereby sentence you to . . ." These declarations carry very important social significance. Collectively, they are called speech acts (Searle, 1969).

Speech acts are ubiquitous in our everyday experience. We agree to certain requests, and in turn make requests of others. We use words to communicate friendliness or hostility. We cheer people up or intentionally irritate them. We accomplish many things through language, and we do it often. Language is a tool we use to achieve our individual or collective goals in a society. Linguists call this the **pragmatic** function of language—the use of language to *do* things. Speech acts, and the pragmatic functions of language more generally, are hugely important. Their importance demonstrates that the naive view of language, that it simply names things, is a narrow view that omits other important functions. Note the general philosophical drift here: Language (and hence knowledge) is significantly a cultural invention for accomplishing human purposes within a society. Language sometimes connects to tangible realities, but at other times signifies things that aren't there. And even when its uses don't relate to the tangible world in any important way, language can accomplish important social goals.

Pre-Wired for Language

Language is rich with potential for accomplishing all manner of things in the world. It's very flexible! That's why it's good that most children learn language easily. One amazing fact about language acquisition is that children are unaccountably good at it. Sure, kids make grammatical errors, which are often cute or funny, but the more important reality is that they acquire the capacity to use language quickly and effectively. Learning to talk includes not only the naming function of language (doggy!) but also the more pragmatic uses of language ("Mommy, could I please . . . ?").

THE LANGUAGE ACQUISITION DEVICE. Language acquisition extends to learning rules for changing sentences. We learn to follow rules of grammar to change statements to questions, and questions to statements, such as "Do I have to?" "Yes, you have to." Changing questions to statements, and vice versa, involves shifts in word order and in the tones used. For questions, voice pitch shifts higher at the end of an utterance— what's called a rising inflection. The rules we use are called **transformational grammars**. But who ever teaches us how to make these changes? Nobody. We pick them up from experience. This is remarkable, so remarkable in fact that one famous linguist, Noam Chomsky, proposed that our brains must be pre-wired to figure out how these transformational grammars work from exposure to language during childhood.

The most significant part of Chomsky's proposal is not that we each acquire transformational grammars, but rather that we come pre-wired to do so. Chomsky is saying that we do not learn language simply from exposure to stimuli (as Skinner would say). Rather, something inside us, something inborn, prepares us to make sense of linguistic stimuli. That internal, brain-based readiness is what Chomsky (1975) called the **language acquisition device**. This proposal is one expression of nativism, the idea that our minds have certain built-in knowledge. We have already seen one example of nativism in the theory of the philosopher Kant in his categories of understanding. We'll see another example in Piaget's theory of cognitive development. In current studies of child development—and particularly cognition in infants—there is now considerable evidence for pre-wired knowledge. It's a safe bet that some version of nativism must be true. Of course, a huge preponderance of what we know is gained through experience. Still, accepting that some human knowledge is pre-wired does have a bearing on how we think of knowledge. Apparently, not all knowledge is learned!

Does Language Make Thought Possible?

We've seen that language is a bit mysterious. Its nature and uses are not as obvious as we might first believe. We can safely reject the view that language functions simply to name physical objects in the world. Language can also refer to things that don't exist as tangible objects. Moreover, language accomplishes purposes in the world through speech acts. But the mystery of language extends further. One powerful hypothesis can be set forth in the form of a question: Does language make thought possible? This idea reverses the way we usually think about language and thought. The normal order is: (1) We think a thought, and then (2) we put that thought into words. But perhaps we could not think that initial thought if we lacked the words to do so. Do we think in words? Or do we *sometimes* use words to think? Or does language present and clarify the concepts that we use when we think?

SAPIR-WHORF HYPOTHESIS. The questions can make your head spin, but they are interesting. Linguists do not necessarily agree on the answers. Some linguists take the point of view that language does in fact shape and constrain thought. This idea is best known as the **Sapir-Whorf hypothesis** (Whorf, 1956). The great anthropologist Franz Boas first pointed out that Eskimos have several different words for snow, including terms for *falling snow, drifting snow, snow bank,* and *snow on the ground* (Boas, 1911). In popular discussions, the numbers of Eskimo words for *snow* has sometimes been inflated to as high as fifty, but the correct number seems to be at least a dozen (Pullum, 1991). The different words available to Eskimos can plausibly help them to think about subtle distinctions in types of snow. If you and I have only a single word, *snow,* then our thinking is thereby limited. In the case of snow, thought seems to depend on language, at least to some extent.

One provocative implication of the Sapir-Whorf hypothesis is that different language systems sometimes divide the world differently. An example is provided by Culler (1986). English has the common words *river* and *stream.* French has two related words, *fleuve* and *rivière.* But the meanings of the French words do not map exactly onto the English words. In English, *river* and *stream* are distinguished by size: rivers are larger, streams are smaller. The French concepts are different. The French word *fleuve* refers to water that flows directly into the sea, whereas *rivières* do not flow into the sea, but rather into *fleuves.* To think using the French words is to entertain somewhat different concepts than those signified by the English words. Generalizing from Culler's example, we can infer that concepts, the ideas that we use to make sense of the world, are guided and constrained by the language system we use. Language has a role in how we see the world—and in how we *don't* see the world.

The Sapir-Whorf hypothesis is probably true only to a limited degree. Linguists who emphasize the brain's native capacity for language see thought as being relatively independent of language (Chomsky, 1975; Pinker, 1995). But many other linguists believe that language at least partially guides and constrains how we think. This function of language shows that the mind exerts forces that bend and shape the realities that we experience. For better or worse, our reality is influenced by language and the concepts that language signifies, not only (as is commonly supposed) by the physical tangible world. These two—the tangible world and our mental concepts—are related, certainly, but they are not equivalent. The mind does more than simply register its physical environment; it provides the categories to do so.

Artificial Intelligence

In the last chapter, we saw that the cognitive revolution overtook behaviorism as a way of understanding the psychology of humans. One impetus for this shift was the development of the computer, which presented a metaphor for how the mind works. This metaphor, though imperfect, proved tremendously helpful in developing theories of cognition.

Besides serving as a metaphor, computers also became a medium for testing ideas about how people think. Given a model of human thought, it was possible to write a computer program that could mimic those same processes. If the model worked—that is, if the computer's processes and conclusions mimicked human thought—then the program constituted a plausible model of what happened in the human mind. Such was the approach taken in the book *Human Problem Solving* by Alan Newell and Herbert Simon (1972). The book was seminal in the field of artificial intelligence, as well as that of cognitive science. It helped reveal how the mind actually does work, and how computers potentially could work.

Production Systems

Computer programs were often written in the form of if-then statements, also called **productions**. Certain programming languages have an if-then logic as their basic pattern. To write any functional program, a computer scientist would have to write many if-then statements.

It's quite possible to model some human behavior and thought in terms of if-then statements. For example, in driving we are given the following rules:

- If red, then stop.

- If green, then go.

There are many other rules used in driving, such as:

- If the pedestrian is in the crosswalk, then stop.

- If two cars arrive at a 90 degree angle in an intersection, then the car on the right goes first.

Not only formal rules or laws, but also motor movements or skills can be modeled as productions. Drinking from a coffee cup is an example. If you were to write a series of if-then statements for drinking from a coffee cup, it would need to be long and elaborate. A series of productions, necessary for modeling complex thought or behavior, is a **production system** (Anderson, 1996). Production systems can be used as a general format for modeling thought and behavior. Conveniently, it's a form of modeling that can be applied to both humans and computers.

Complex production systems have sometimes been used to control robots. Building robots to exhibit complex behavior is a tough challenge. Even getting robots to interact skillfully with material objects can be very difficult. To some degree, the limitations of robots exemplify just how hard it is to build an intelligent machine. Many observers feel that progress on artificial intelligence during the past 50 years has been disappointing. The rather slow progress of artificial intelligence also suggests another conclusion: The intelligent human mind is fantastically complex and more than a little mysterious.

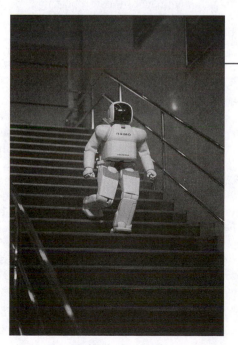

FIGURE 4.4

Robot *Some robots can mimic human qualities.*

[Photo courtesy of Honda Motor Co., Ltd.]

The invention of production systems was a tremendous step forward for cognitive science and for artificial intelligence. There is, however, one strange quality to production systems that might make you think about their connection to the behaviorist theories they were overtaking. I think you'll see a lot of similarity between the old-style *stimulus-response* architecture for modeling behavior and the *if-then* production systems for modeling thought. Are production systems essentially just stimulus-response pairs that are *inside* the organism? Possibly. But aren't behaviorism and cognitive psychology competing paradigms? Yes they are, but it helps to remember that thousands of behaviorists were "converted" to a cognitive perspective. To use a theoretical tool from the old paradigm to build a new one is understandable and, ultimately, helpful.

Another distinction should be introduced at this point. Production systems obviously pertain to knowledge about how to do something. Not all knowledge works this

INTEREST MAGNET 4.1

Kasparov versus Deep Blue

Who is better at chess: The world's best human chess player, or a powerful computer designed to search thousands of potential moves before making the optimal choice? For many decades, there was no question that the best human player could defeat the best chess-playing computer. All of that changed, however, in May of 1997. During that month, an IBM-designed supercomputer, Deep Blue, defeated the world's highest-ranking chess master, Gary Kasparov. The defeat of Kasparov in a six-game match was the culmination of the long development of chess-playing computer programs, both Deep Blue and its predecessors, with such oddball names as Chaos, Cray Blitz, Chiptest, and Deep Thought. Kasparov's defeat was a stunning victory for Deep Blue's designers. More significantly, it was a milestone in the history of artificial intelligence (A.I.).

Gary Kasparov had previously defeated Deep Thought, the predecessor of Deep Blue, in a two-game match played in 1989, winning $10,000 for his efforts. Kasparov also defeated Deep Blue in 1996 (Newborn, 1997). It was in the following year, 1997, that Kasparov lost to Deep Blue. The match was controversial: Kasparov made uncharacteristic errors. Even so, the computer's victory over the world's best chess player signaled something new: In a complex game long associated with the power of human intellect, the world could no longer conclude that humans would always have the upper hand. Artificial intelligence had come a long way since computers were first programmed to play games following World War II. Just after the war, the ingenious British mathematician, Alan Turing, adapted code-breaking programs to play chess. By 1951, Turing pitted his chess-playing program against a human. Turing's program lost.

The power of computers to defeat the best human players in games of intellect varies by the specific game. In checkers, for example, a computer will normally win; in poker, skilled humans are much better than computers. The difference in who wins depends on the kind of computation required to play the game successfully. In checkers, winning hinges largely on the ability to make rapid computations of the most promising moves. Checkers is quite amenable to the kind of exhaustive "brute-force" searching that computers excel in. Poker, on the other hand, involves far more possible patterns. Moreover, a poker player must also infer missing information—most importantly, the cards held by the opposing player. In such missing-information situations, humans have the advantage because of their superior ability to conduct pattern-matching (Ginsberg, 1998).

These computational differences say a lot about how humans and computers think differently. Whereas humans excel at pattern-matching, computers are good at exhaustive computation when all relevant information is known. A.I. researchers see these human-computer differences as making for a happy marriage where one can learn from the other. When the backgammon program TD-Gammon learned to defeat the best human players, it displayed innovative moves that were studied and later imitated by the humans (Tesauro, 2002). This finding affirms a general conclusion from the history of A.I. research: Humans and computers have complementary skills that "permit problems to be solved that neither could have figured out alone." That, says one A.I. researcher, is "exceptionally good news for all of us, carbon and silicon alike" (Ginsburg, 1998, p. 89).

way. Much of what we know can be stated as facts, or what philosophers call propositions (statements that are claims). This dichotomy is a handy one. The terms typically used for these two kinds of knowledge are **declarative knowledge** (for propositions, or knowing *that*) and **procedural knowledge** (for skills, or knowing *how*). This distinction was actually introduced by the philosopher Gilbert Ryle in 1949, but it has been used by psychologists, computer programmers, educators, and neuroscientists. Interestingly, knowledge of one kind does not automatically translate to another. Test this by your own experience: Isn't it sometimes hard to explain in words how you carry out a specific skill?

Psychology

It may seem strange to introduce a psychological perspective on knowledge at this point in this chapter because this book is dominated by a psychological point of view. But the inclusion is justified: Psychology is a discipline in its own right and has made distinct contributions to theories of knowledge, complementing insights from the other disciplines.

Concept Formation

A good starting point for approaching knowledge according to psychologists is the concept of . . . **concept**. A concept is typically what we mean by any word we say. For example, what exactly do you mean when you say the word *bird*? Well, it's difficult to give a precise definition for what a bird is. Can we define the concept of *bird* by its features? To a degree we can, but we also find that many bird-like features are not absolutely necessary for category membership. Most birds fly, but not all. Feathers? Yes, but the feathers of some birds are so tiny that they look nothing at all like feathers, but rather like fur (as in penguins). Consequently, it's easy for children and possible for adults to misclassify a bird. Misclassification is not an issue if we gaze upon a robin or a sparrow, but it does become more likely when we consider an ostrich, a penguin, or a bat. In teaching concepts, then, psychologists have found that it helps to present different examples—the more the better. Borderline cases, such as penguins and ostriches, are valuable because they can help the learner see just how far the concept extends, and that there are exceptions to typical features. Counterexamples, such as bats, can teach learners that some creatures seem a lot like birds, but in fact are not.

One function of science is to increase precision in the ways we describe the natural world. Everyday language involves concepts that are not sharply definable, but rather fuzzy (Rosch, 1977). Reasoning about such **fuzzy sets** may require a **fuzzy logic** that allows for degrees of truth or partial category membership (Zadeh, 1965). Can you say truthfully that the earth is round? The earth is very nearly spherical, but not precisely so. Scientific literacy partly entails becoming more precise about categories that define the natural world, such as through quantification (hot and cold are measured as temperature) and through clarifying the defining features of concepts. Think about the concept *fish*—biology helps us understand why sharks *are*, but dolphins are not.

It's not just learners' concepts that adjust over time, but also concepts as understood by experts. As an example, take the word *continent*. For centuries, the word *continent* was understood by the common person and by the scientist alike to refer to the fixed landmasses of the earth. It was not until the mid-twentieth century that geologists began to accept the unlikely hypothesis that the continents move. Now geologists know that continents are enormous landmasses that rest on plates of rock, which in turn float on the molten rock beneath. Those massive plates are in constant motion. We are all adrift on rock boats that float on an ocean of liquid rock. This theory, called the theory of plate tectonics, has completely revolutionized geology. The word *continent* accordingly has a different meaning than it once had. The larger point here is that concepts change for experts just as they do for novices.

Let's remember the philosophical point that the categories represented by concepts are often not perfectly fitted to physical realities. Our knowledge about the world is significantly a product of the human mind's constructive efforts to find order in the world and to share that order with other people. This point of view has been called the **social construction of knowledge**. As functional as our concepts and categories are, they are not the same as the physical things that compose our world. In yet another way, this principle dashes any hope that **naive realism**, the view that knowledge is a straightforward internalization of the material world, could possibly be correct.

SUPERORDINATE AND SUBORDINATE CONCEPTS. To be meaningful, concepts must be related to other concepts. Often these relationships connect **superordinate** and **subordinate** concepts. In the case of the words *planet* and *Mars*, *planet* is the superordinate (higher, more general) concept and *Mars* is the subordinate (lower, more specific) one. Likewise *animal* and *dog* are superordinate and subordinate concepts, respectively. Much of our conceptual knowledge is organized this way, but not all of it, so we don't want to take this idea too far. Also, the relationships linking superordinate and subordinate concepts are of at least two different types. We can think of *car* and *Ford*, whose link expresses the relationship "type of." We can think of *car* and *engine*, which have a "part of" relationship. These are two kinds of superordinate-subordinate relationships. Finally, note that most dictionary definitions make use of superordinate-subordinate concepts. For example, we can define *shovel* as a tool used to dig.

CONCEPT MAPS. Whenever concepts are related to other concepts, it's possible to show that relationship in a diagram. Taking the words *car* and *Ford* and *Mustang*, for example, we can show the relationship as:

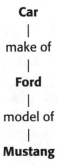

Car
|
make of
|
Ford
|
model of
|
Mustang

This pattern can be extended indefinitely to include other makes of car. For example:

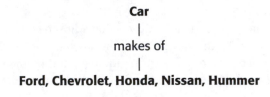

Car
|
makes of
|
Ford, Chevrolet, Honda, Nissan, Hummer

We could be more sophisticated by depicting how these brands cluster by manufacturer (General Motors) or by country of origin. We could include exotic cars or models no longer in production. In other words, our diagram of car makes and models could become very elaborate. But notice something else: Whether the diagram is simple or complicated depends on the knowledge of the person drawing. A more knowledgeable person could draw a more elaborate map. Moreover, a diagram could contain errors, and such errors would reveal faults in the knowledge of the person who drew the diagram. The drawing would expose errors that another, more knowledgeable person, could then correct.

These diagrams are known as **concept maps**. They are tools to express and understand what a person knows (Novak, 1998; Novak & Gowin, 1984). Concept maps are not the only way to express knowledge. We could ask a person to write a few paragraphs on a particular topic, or we could have a conversation with the person. These, too, could reveal what a person knows. But concept maps have advantages, such as the clear identification of key ideas and a low reliance on language if that distracts from a pure appraisal of knowledge. Concept maps have been used extensively in science education, but they could be used in just about any field. Consider them to be part of the teacher's toolkit for assessing what students know.

Schema Theory

Our discussion of concept maps leads naturally to another topic—one that has great importance in our quest to understand the nature of knowledge. Here, I refer to the idea of **schema**. Schema is the name given to clusters of related knowledge. In information-processing terms, long-term memory is organized into schemas. For example, each of us has a *car* schema. We know certain things about cars, and that knowledge is in our car schema. Likewise, we have schemas for dogs, birds, planets, geology, and thousands of other topics. In other words, our knowledge is not composed of individual discrete bits. Rather, knowledge is organized into clusters that compose our understanding of any concept or object. These knowledge clusters are schemas.

It's important here to say that concept maps and schemas are not the same. To put it simply: A concept map is a tool, a device typically drawn on paper to show what a person knows or believes. A schema is not an external tool, but is an abstraction of what we know internally—of how we store (or represent) knowledge. At the end of a day you might place your concept map in the paper shredder, but you would continue to carry your schema in your mind—though if you had learned something your schema would be different from what it was earlier that day.

THANKSGIVING SCHEMA. Let's take another example of schema because there are thousands to choose from. To illustrate what a schema is, consider what the word *Thanksgiving* means to you. It might conjure up such ideas as turkey, cranberry sauce, relatives, and televised football. Thanksgiving might remind you of Pilgrims and Native Americans, or your childhood, or cold weather and pumpkin pie. No doubt, most of you have a well-developed schema for Thanksgiving. Perhaps not all of you, though. If you were born outside North America you might not be able to relate to Thanksgiving. Even if you were born in the United States or Canada, your Thanksgiving schema might be very different from the one I have suggested.

DOG SCHEMA. Let's go back to *dog*. Dog schemas reinforce the previous point—that schemas vary widely among individuals—even sharper. For some of us, our *dog* schema is very basic. As I wrote the previous sentence in a public patio, a large dog walked behind me. What kind of dog? I wish I could tell you—all I can say is that it was big (and fortunately on a leash). So, perhaps to the disappointment of you dog people out there, my dog schema is not very impressive.

But many people know a *lot* about dogs. They can easily distinguish subtleties of breed, and have the confidence and motivation to ask about the breed of a dog if they don't know. They might be familiar with dog pedigree, dog nutrition, nuances of dog health and disease, temperaments, quarantines, shots, surgical ear enhancements, dog show protocol, and so on. Some people really are dog people. Not only do they have a great deal of interest and experience in the subject, their dog schemas are extensive, elaborate, detailed, and accurate. My point is that although we undoubtedly share much schema knowledge (in our common understanding of Thanksgiving, for example), we vary widely in other schema knowledge not just about dogs but also about many, many other topics.

SCRIPTS. The examples of Thanksgiving and dogs are largely about *factual* knowledge. But there is a kind of schema that guides our *actions* in familiar situations. That procedure-oriented schema is called a **script**. For example, most of us have a well-developed script that we employ whenever we visit a restaurant. Familiar elements of the script include:

- Check the menu for entrees and prices.
- Check to see if there is a wait and, if so, how long.
- Wait to be seated.
- Your host says, "Your server will be right with you."
- Your waiter says, "Hi, my name is Justin and I'll be your server. Can I get you started with something to drink?"

The restaurant schema makes the process of dining predicable. It's negotiated with little trouble because the script for restaurants is fairly standard across the U.S. Even when there are variations, the restaurant script can be adapted to greasy-spoon diners or elegant five-star establishments. You probably can think of other schemas that take the form of scripts, including scripts for buying food in a grocery store or shopping for clothes in a department store.

NODE-LINK STRUCTURES. As we think of schemas, it's worthwhile to consider yet another related idea. I refer here to **node-link structures**, which also go by the name of **semantic networks** (Collins & Quillian, 1969). To get an idea of what a node-link structure is, think of concept maps. We looked at concept maps for cars. Bear in mind that concept maps are external expressions of knowledge, one of several ways that we can communicate what we know. When we speak of semantic networks, though, please recognize that these represent knowledge in long-term memory. We've already seen one way to model knowledge, in the if-then structures of production systems. Node-link structures of knowledge are another way to model knowledge in long-term memory.

Node link structures are pretty simple in design. The nodes are concepts, and the links are relationships. Let's consider Thanksgiving again. In a Thanksgiving node-link structure, the nodes include turkey, relatives, and football. A very simple structure might look like this:

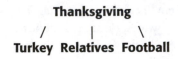

We won't label the connecting links, but you can probably think of labels that would fit.

So what's the advantage of thinking about knowledge as node-link structures? First, it conforms to our intuition that all ideas are connected to other ideas. You might even say that every idea is related to every other idea, if only distantly.

To understand the advantages of node-link structures, let's add another element. Imagine that energy flows through the network. That energy would be related to whether the node is active in your thoughts. So, if you think about *Thanksgiving,* then the Thanksgiving node is activated. That activation can then proceed to flow through related links, and activation might spread to the node corresponding to *turkey.* If the activation for *turkey* is high enough, you will consciously think of turkey. In just this way, thinking about Thanksgiving can lead to thinking about turkey and other ideas related to Thanksgiving. That's how node-link structures work: Activation spreading from node to node.

We can generalize this **spreading activation model** to any other schema modeled as a node-link structure (Collins & Loftus, 1975). Think about any idea, and related ideas also come to mind. Activation flows from the original node to related nodes. From there, activation can spread to yet other, more distant nodes. So our thoughts might travel a fair distance from idea to idea, but always through a pathway of ideas that are related in some way. Your daydreams probably work this way. You start thinking about idea Q, then move on from there to ideas R, S, T, U, and V. Then you wonder: "What does V have to do with Q?" But when you retrace your ideation you realize that there is a chain connecting the first and the last. We can make sense of this mental walkabout with the spreading activation model. Something similar happens in conversations. You ask: "How did we get to *that* topic?" There is a logic to your conversational pathway, though it may be a contorted logic.

Still other mental experiences make sense when interpreted through a spreading activation model. One such experience is the **tip of the tongue phenomenon**. Example: I'm thinking of the song, "Pretty Woman," but can't remember the name of the artist who sang it. You can't remember either. Yet both of us feel that we *should* know—indeed, that we *do* know but just can remember. I say, "Wait, I almost have it." I can feel the name of the singer perched at the threshold of my awareness, but then it slips away. It's a little frustrating. Then the thought returns, stronger this time, and I say the name aloud. You say, "Right!" We have just experienced the tip of the tongue phenomenon. We know that we know, and can feel the desired knowledge just at the edge of our awareness, but it's not quite retrievable. In our spreading activation model, we would say that the name of the musician was activated, but not quite to the threshold needed to bring it to conscious awareness.

It's a funny idea, the notion that concepts can be partially activated but not quite enough to bring them to our awareness. Psychologists have known about this reality for a long time. They call it **priming**. In one kind of psychology experiment, people are given a series of words and non-words. They are asked to distinguish the two. It's an easy task, so if you are the respondent the psychologist expects you to be right 100 percent of the time, or close to it. Accuracy is not an issue. Instead, the dependent variable is reaction time. How long does it take you to answer correctly? If the word is *apple*, you will say it's a real word. But it helps if previous words are also names of fruit. If previous words are *orange*, *banana*, and *pear*, then your reaction time for *apple* will be speeded up. *Apple* was primed by the other fruit names.

Priming can be helpful in real-life communication. If you and I converse about any topic—cars, sports, food, music, movies, politics, or religion—then ideas related to the topic schema will be primed. We can move around easily within a schema, understanding each other with little difficulty (we hope). We bring new ideas to mind and express some of them. In education, too, we can use priming. One teaching technique, popularized by David Ausubel, is to use **advance organizers**. Advance organizers are previews of the day's activities or concepts. The preview helps pre-organize the experience in everyone's mind, but it also primes related knowledge.

SCHEMAS AS INTERPRETIVE FRAMEWORKS. Let's recognize another function of schemas: They help us to interpret our experience. Oddly, as they help us interpret our experience, they also can distort it. Schemas therefore serve as filters by which we make sense of experience. To the extent that schemas differ from person to person, people might interpret the same event very differently. This effect takes on real significance when eyewitnesses to the same crime remember it differently. The possibility of distortion is greater still when cultural differences factor in. The strong influence of culture on schemas was first described by Frederick Bartlett in the 1930s.

In his book *Remembering* (1932), Bartlett reported results from his experiments on memory. The stimulus he chose was crucial: It was a story told by Native Americans recalling the legend of warfare between neighboring tribes. The story, which follows, is called *The War of the Ghosts*:

> One night two young men from Egulac went down to the river to hunt seals and while they were there it became foggy and calm. Then they heard war-cries, and they thought: "Maybe this is a war-party." They escaped to the shore, and hid behind a log. Now canoes came up, and they heard the noise of paddles, and saw one canoe coming up to them. There were five men in the canoe, and they said:
>
> "What do you think? We wish to take you along. We are going up the river to make war on the people."
>
> One of the young men said, "I have no arrows."
>
> "Arrows are in the canoe," they said.
>
> "I will not go along. I might be killed. My relatives do not know where I have gone. But you," he said, turning to the other, "may go with them."
>
> So one of the young men went, but the other returned home.
>
> And the warriors went on up the river to a town on the other side of Kalama. The people came down to the water and they began to fight, and many were killed. But presently the young man heard one of the warriors say, "Quick, let us go home: that Indian has been hit." Now he thought: "Oh, they are ghosts." He did not feel sick, but they said he had been shot.
>
> So the canoes went back to Egulac and the young man went ashore to his house and made a fire. And he told everybody and said: "Behold I accompanied the ghosts, and we went to fight. Many of our fellows were killed, and many of those who attacked us were killed. They said I was hit, and I did not feel sick."
>
> He told it all, and then he became quiet. When the sun rose he fell down. Something black came out of his mouth. His face became contorted. The people jumped up and cried.
>
> He was dead.

The War of the Ghosts is different in logic, sequence, and tone from the stories that most of us find familiar. It does not conform to our idea, or *schema*, for what a story is.

Bartlett asked his subjects, Britons in the 1930s, to read *The War of the Ghosts* and to remember as much as they could, as accurately as they could. The deviation of *The War of the Ghosts* from a "normal" story schema was at least as marked for Bartlett's subjects as it is for us. Can you guess what happened? Bartlett's subjects were not very good at remembering the story. They left out some stated events and inserted others that did not belong. But more important was that the omissions and insertions made *The War of the Ghosts* more similar to the plots that were familiar to readers. In other words, the story was distorted in its remembering so that it resembled the story schemas known by the British readers.

Bartlett's study of memory is important because it introduced the concept of *schema* to psychology. It showed that a schema not only organizes information, it also functions to interpret and later retrieve information. Knowledge is not a direct translation of external reality into mental representations. They are different realms—with correspondences, certainly—but different realms nonetheless. Bartlett's studies, and many others that followed in subsequent decades, helped psychologists to realize that schemas have an interpretive function. We see the world through our schemas.

The notion that schemas are interpretive grids is shown vividly and charmingly in the children's book called *Fish is Fish*, by Leo Lionni (1974) (Figure 4.5). In the story, a fish wants to learn about the world outside the pond. He befriends a tadpole who, later, as a frog, explores the world of land creatures and then returns to the pond. The frog tells of a fabulous world of people, cows, birds, and much more. But in the fish's mind

FIGURE 4.5
Fish is Fish (Leo Lionni) *Humans also interpret new information through existing schemas.*
[Used by permission of Random House Children's Books, a division of Random House, Inc. and Nora Lionni.]

(and in the book's illustrations), each of these fantastic creatures is really a modified fish. He imagines a man as a fish who wears clothes and walks on fins; a cow is a fish with horns and udders. The fish cannot understand the world apart from what he already knows. So too with humans.

SCHEMA CHANGE. Up to this point, you might gather that schemas are fixed knowledge structures that morph our experiences to make them conform. Our subjective experience often conforms to schemas, true, but schemas can also conform to our experiences. Thankfully, schemas can and do change. In fact, schema change is a major function of education. We know, for example, that learning involves adding knowledge to schemas. Every day our schemas are modified as they grow fuller and more detailed. But schemas change in other ways besides through the simple addition of knowledge (Murphy & Mason, 2006).

One model recognizes three kinds of schema change: accretion, tuning, and restructuring (Norman & Rumelhart, 1975; Vosniadou & Brewer, 1987). **Accretion** is the additive change we've just recognized. The addition of new information to our knowledge structures is one common and important kind of schema change. It may be the most common kind of change. If our basic knowledge structures are incomplete, then accretion is what's needed. But sometimes our ideas are not quite right. They need correction. That's where **tuning** comes in. For most of my life, I have known that Pluto is the outermost of nine planets in the solar system—or so I was taught and I believed. Now, the status of Pluto is not so certain, and neither am I so certain! Apparently, Pluto might *not* be a planet, after all. Or, if it is a planet, it might not be the outermost one in our solar system. In 2002, a planetlike object larger than Pluto was discovered. Variously called *Quaoar* or *Xena*, it orbits the sun far beyond Pluto's orbit, and it has its own moon. Consequently, I have to adjust my knowledge about the planets. This correction of understanding is tuning. Schema tuning is common in our experience, particularly if we are open-minded and continually seek to test and improve our understanding.

A third kind of schema change is more significant and substantial than the other two. It's schema **restructuring**. This is a major overhaul of schema—a complete rethinking of the order and logic of beliefs and understanding. Perhaps the most straightforward illustration would be religious conversion, which re-orders a person's ontology of the universe. You can imagine other intellectual "conversions" of one sort or another. In studying history, for example, a student might have an insight that the dichotomization of "good guys" and "bad guys" is not as convincing as it once was. The commonly accepted moral imperatives of history may become more gray than black and white, and the inevitability of certain outcomes (e.g., American independence, the preservation of the Union) may start to seem less certain. History *could* have turned out differently. Likewise in science (evolution of species), art (cubism), literature (stream of consciousness), and social relations ("My parents aren't perfect."), major revisions of knowledge are part of the individual learner's cognitive development.

TEACHING AS SCHEMA-BUILDING. Schemas and schema change tie deeply into the purpose of education. You can see learning as schema change, for example. And teaching? Well, teaching can be described as arranging the experiences of learners so that schema change occurs—not just any schema change, but change in good directions: toward knowledge structures that are more complete, accurate, and open. Sometimes we hear that the goal of education is *understanding*. Can we understand *understanding* in terms of schema change? Why not? Let's say that understanding is the kind of rich, developed knowledge and capability that conforms to well-developed schemas. Mature schemas likely have gone through various change processes that include accretion, tuning, and restructuring. Because teachers are very often involved in this process, teachers are schema-builders. Or if schemas are faulty, teachers are sometimes "schema-busters." Ideally, the skilled teacher shapes learner's schemas—artfully, effectively, and masterfully—toward something better.

How do we achieve schemas that conform to real understanding? Here, we can learn from an idea of David Perkins (1992). In his **realm theory**, Perkins has said that we can become so familiar with a body of knowledge that we can feel at home in it. Just as we come to "know our way around" our own neighborhoods, so we can know knowledge as familiar territory. When we feel at home in a physical space, we can navigate routes that we've never taken before. Spontaneity is possible. We feel confident that we can traverse new paths and arrive where we intend. So it is with knowledge. It can become so familiar, so navigable, that it becomes our personal realm. Largely, this familiarity and comfort comes from thinking about, through, and with that knowledge. "Understanding," says Perkins, "comes on the coattails of thinking." If understanding is a major goal of education, then thinking is an excellent way to get there.

Mental Images

What is knowledge? It's easy, perhaps, to see knowledge as equivalent to concepts, and concepts as equivalent to word meanings. Knowledge and language are indeed closely related. But the mind knows far more than words and word meanings. Minds think also in mental images that are like seeing pictures in "the mind's eye." We saw in the last chapter that much of our knowledge in long-term memory is stored as mental pictures. So important is imagery to the way we think, that the term **dual coding theory** has been used to recognize that both words *and* images are primary to our mental life. We store knowledge and think in other ways than these two, but languages and mental imagery are both extremely important.

When I say *mental imagery*, you're likely to think about static images. For example, you might think of the face of someone you know. Perhaps the image looks like a photograph in your mind. But it's possible to imagine the person moving. You might know the distinctive ways in which the person walks, reaches, stands, and gestures. You can imagine that person in motion. So mental images can be dynamic, not simply static. Not just people, though—you can probably picture all sorts of objects in motion. Try to imagine, for example, a bicycle. Now imagine the pedals turning, the chain moving over the gears, and the wheels spinning. That special kind of dynamic imagery is called a **mental model**.

The term *mental model* is a little tricky because sometimes it's used more generally and casually to mean *any* knowledge structure, much like we use the word *schema*. In this book, though, we'll use a more precise definition. *Mental model* here refers specifically to dynamic mental imagery. Defined this way, mental models can have special importance in thinking and learning. Consider, again, the solar system. Your understanding of the solar system might include a mental model of a central sun and the various planets revolving around it. Can you "see" the mental image? Some planets are very large; others are comparatively small. Some are near the sun; others are fantastically distant. Some planets have moons, which in turn revolve around the planets. Maybe you can imagine the moons, too, as moving pieces in your dynamic mental model.

You might expect that the mental model of a planetary astronomer would be much more elaborate than the average person's. It could include planetary spin, an asteroid

FIGURE 4.6
Two balls on a flat-track (A) and a V-track (B) *Which ball finishes first?* [Adapted from Dufresne, Mestre, Thaden-Koch, Gerace, & Leonard, 2005. Drawing by Philip Travisano. Reprinted by permission of Information Age Publishing.]

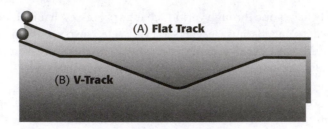

belt, and comets, as well as satellites and space debris. Imagine what happens when the astronomer considers a question about the solar system. Say that the question involves sending a probe into space. The question might be something like: Would it be possible to launch a space probe that could "fly by" several of the planets, taking pictures and collecting data? This would be possible only if several planets were aligned. To answer the question, the astronomer might imagine the solar system and the planets in their current configuration. Knowing the relative speeds of the planets, the astronomer might mentally press "play" and watch how the planets revolve and realign. By "running" the mental model, the astronomer might be able to say whether and when a multi-planet "fly by" is possible.

This example shows that mental models, especially those that display cause-and-effect patterns, can be useful as **runnable mental models** for making predictions and reasoning through problems. Car or bicycle mechanics might employ mental imagery to diagnose a problem or to test the feasibility of design changes. Runnable mental models have general utility in scientific thinking and scientific expertise. Because of this, the purposeful development of runnable mental models should be a deliberate goal of science teachers and science curriculum designers.

There's no reason to assume that all mental models are correct, however. We might very well have a *faulty* mental model, which could lead us to make *incorrect* predictions. This possibility has been shown vividly by the physicist and educator, Jose Mestre. He and his collaborators present the scenario shown in Figure 4.6 (Mestre, Thaden-Koch, Dufresne, & Gerace, 2004). Two metal balls start at the same time down two different tracks, a "flat track" and a "V-track." The question they pose is simple: Which ball finishes first? Surprisingly, scientists and laypeople alike are predictably poor at answering the question correctly. Most run their own mental models and "see" (in their minds) the two balls "racing" along the two tracks. But they do not converge on the right answer with any reliability.

Jose Mestre's experiments reveal just one instance of a much larger phenomenon: misconceptions. Researchers have discovered that misconceptions in science are common. That discovery has implications for education—both in the appraisal of its past success and in the design of future science curricula.

Misconceptions and Naive Theories

When I was in eighth grade, my friend Chris proposed an outrageous idea. He held up a quarter and a dime and told me, confidently, that if he dropped both at the same time they would hit the ground together. I knew this was completely preposterous. The quarter must fall faster because it is heavier. Gravity pulls harder on heavier objects, and that's why they fall faster than lighter objects. Chris foolishly offered to put a dollar bet on his prediction. For me, this was easy money.

I lost. The quarter and dime hit the ground together. At the moment of impact I found my commonsense notion so completely defeated that, intellectually, I crossed a threshold. I knew then, and still know, how wrong I can be even when my ideas seem absolutely certain. Have you had the same thought? I *feel* right, but I *could* be wrong.

In science education, the misconceptions movement reached its high point in the early 1990s. The occasion was the release of an educational film called *A Private Universe*. In a mere 18 minutes of video, *A Private Universe* presents the reality and educational importance of science misconceptions so strikingly that it often has a lasting effect on viewers, whether or not they teach science.

A Private Universe begins with footage from a graduation ceremony at Harvard University. Distinguished faculty and students file past the camera in splendid academic regalia. It's a proud occasion for an eminent university. The camera then focuses on just a few faculty and students. A question is posed: Can you explain the cause of the seasons? On camera, new graduates and professors give explanations with confidence

INTEREST MAGNET 4.2

Newton's Misconceptions

Isaac Newton (1642–1727) was possibly the greatest scientific mind of all time. Newton is famous for his discoveries of the fundamental laws of motion, the decomposition of white light into colors, and the invention of calculus. But Newton was not immune to scientific misconceptions. For most of his life, he believed in centrifugal force, the misconception that objects moving in a curved path are pulled outward. Think of how it feels when a car turns a corner sharply. Centrifugal force is a fiction, however, because in reality passengers inside a turning car are not pulled outward; they are pulled *inward* toward the center of the circle.

One purpose of science education is to help students abandon seductive but false concepts like centrifugal force. But the idea of centrifugal force was difficult for Newton himself to reject. In fact, he may never have abandoned the idea completely. Scattered references to centrifugal force can be found in Newton's writings even to the very end of his life (Steinberg, Brown, & Clement, 1990). In explaining the motion of planets, for example, Newton proposed that planetary orbits around the sun were maintained by a balance between inward pull (gravity) and outward pull (centrifugal force).

Centrifugal force was described by Newton as the planets' "endeavors of receding from the sun" (Westfall, 1980, p. 152). He held this belief at least until 1679, when he received a letter from fellow scientist Robert Hooke in which Hooke suggested there are not two forces, but only one—gravity. He explained that planets are deflected from their straight-line paths by the pull of gravity (Steinberg, Brown, & Clement, 1990). To Newton, Hooke's explanation seemed believable, and in fact later proved to be correct, but it took hold in Newton's mind only gradually.

Rejecting centrifugal force was one challenge; understanding gravity was another. According to the well-known myth, Isaac Newton suddenly understood gravity while sitting under an apple tree and fortuitously seeing an apple fall to the ground. Whether or not Newton was inspired by a falling apple, he brilliantly understood the terrestrial reality of falling objects as applying to moons and planets. Gravity was finally known to be a universal principle that applied equally to apples, moons, and planets—across distances both tiny and astronomical. But Newton's acceptance of gravity as the deflecting agent of planetary motion was not immediate, just as his dismissal of the need for a counterbalancing "centrifugal" force did not occur in a single moment, but only gradually over a period of years (Steinberg et al., 1990).

Newton's biographers have documented that the scientist's intellectual advances were often followed by relapses. Eventually, the powerful ideas of inertia and gravity triumphed both in Newton's thinking and in his writing (Steinberg et al., 1990). The extension to science education is immediate: When teachers ask students to understand inertia or other elementary principles of physics, the expectation is to achieve something that was difficult even for Isaac Newton himself. Newton's Laws are elementary only in that they are foundational, not that they are easy.

and eloquence—and those explanations are utterly wrong. The second part of the video shifts to a local high school. It shows that misconceptions about basic scientific concepts, including what causes a lunar eclipse, are common among high school students, even the most talented ones. Moreover, the misconceptions persist despite instruction on the very same science topics. What's even more telling is that the high school science teacher, clearly talented and dedicated, expresses surprise and disbelief when shown evidence that her best students just don't get it. It's never stated directly, but is implied throughout: The nation's best students can obtain all the accolades of academic success and yet, somehow, harbor deep misconceptions about science.

The research literature on misconceptions would have been significant even if it applied only to learning science. What gave it greater force was further research showing that misconceptions were common in other domains also. In mathematics especially, but also in history and art, misconceptions were discovered among even successful students. Blame for this apparently widespread phenomenon could not be fairly placed on the shoulders of students or teachers. A somewhat ominous conclusion appeared to be inevitable: The problem of widespread and fundamental misconceptions in multiple subject domains was clearly a *systemic* problem, heretofore unacknowledged. There was something in the nature of schooling that allowed (or worse, encouraged) misconceptions. That alarming conclusion led Howard Gardner and others to call this research stream "the disaster studies."

It wasn't long before the nature and seriousness of misconceptions began to be rethought. In particular, some researchers thought they could see a silver lining in this dark cloud. What could possibly be the good news? Just this: Students displayed a predilection toward sense-making, a wish to explain. Even if they offered the wrong explanation, it was an explanation still. The impulse to make ideas sensible was surely good, wasn't it? Another phrase appeared: **naive theories**. This term recognized that sometimes misconceptions form semi-coherent systems of explanation. Students can fabricate their own theories, albeit naive ones. The impulse to seek coherence in one's explanations presented the possibility of an important, and possibly underutilized, resource among learners (Smith, diSessa, & Roschelle, 1993).

The research literature on misconceptions seemed ripe for application to education. But the theoretical breakthrough of finding widespread and serious misconceptions yielded no clear and simple instructional prescription. There are reasons for this. One is that misconceptions, particularly in math but also in science, are often unstable. Math students might use an erroneous procedure on one occasion but not on another. Likewise, science misconceptions are not always consistently expressed. Complicating matters further, identified misconceptions are likely to be idiosyncratic: Different students hold different misconceptions. Although some misconceptions might be fairly common, others are unique to individual learners, which makes specific teaching strategies difficult to prescribe.

Given the difficulties of pinpointing stable misconceptions, it's unclear what to do about them. Consider two basic strategies: One is to confront the student directly with his or her false beliefs; the other is to ignore the specifics of the misconception, recognize that correct principles or theories were not really learned initially, and simply reteach. There are good reasons backing each strategy. For the first, direct confrontation of false beliefs with first-hand evidence of their unworkability might cause students to face the inadequacy of their misconceptions and open up to better ideas. On the other hand, lingering on faulty ideas could potentially deepen the memory traces of those ideas, making them more robust. That's why a counterstrategy is simple re-teaching. The research has produced no clear evidence that one or another of these strategies is more effective. The best strategy will, for now, be a matter for teachers to decide based on their own professional convictions and intuitions, and their best hypothesis about what the individual student needs.

Episodic Memory

By now it should be clear that we can identify several different kinds of knowledge. A starting point is the basic distinction between **declarative knowledge** (knowing *that*) and **procedural knowledge** (knowing *how*), presented earlier. But this distinction, however important and illuminating, was only a starting point. We also needed to consider mental images—pictures that we see in our minds. Yet mental imagery is not unitary: some mental images are static (like photographs) and others are dynamic (like movies).

How many different forms of knowledge are there? No one seems able to say for sure. For our purposes, we don't need a definitive list. As we identify and characterize other knowledge forms, we will gain a more accurate sense of the nature, or natures, of knowledge. This understanding, in turn, will help us to develop better and more complete goals for teaching and learning, and more effective strategies for reaching those goals.

Besides the forms of knowledge that we have already considered, there is another that has great importance in human experience—**episodic memory**. Think of an episode from a television program. You might be able to recall the story in your mind so vividly that it's a little like seeing the program on a TV screen. Can you "play back" experiences from your own life as if they were movie segments? If so, you are experiencing episodic memory.

Episodic memory is an important kind of memory that we experience often, probably daily. The idea of episodic memory was most famously advocated by the psychologist Endel Tulving (1983). Tulving described episodic memory as a uniquely human capability. Tulving certainly understood that animals learn, but in his view animal learning consists of associations that are not specific memory events. A dog "knows" it will be punished for digging up the garden, but probably has no specific memory of being scolded last week for digging up the turnips. Humans clearly *do* have such memories. Does episodic memory have advantages for knowledge acquisition? Does our ability to remember past experiences prepare us for future experiences?

Perhaps there is a connection between episodic memory and human culture. Might it support the storytelling and myth-building that have been so central to civilizations throughout history? Still more speculatively, could episodic memory be the basis of a more fundamental human capability—the ability to imagine? Episodic memory might help us to envision future possibilities, including opportunities for success or hints of danger. Such imaginings could be tremendously instrumental in setting near- and long-term goals, and in forming plans to achieve them. Long-term planning might rely on our ability to imagine the future in a way that parallels episodic memory for past events.

Tacit Knowledge

As we move deeper into exploring the nature of knowledge, we must accept that the subject is much more complicated than we first thought. The distinction between **tacit knowledge** and **explicit knowledge** takes this inevitable conclusion further still. The kind of knowledge that we can talk about is explicit knowledge: If we know it and can communicate it, then it's explicit. For most of us, explicit knowledge *is* knowledge. Is there another kind? Could we have knowledge that we can't communicate and possibly don't even realize that we have?

There is indeed a huge category of such unspoken and unspeakable knowledge. We "know" things that guide our everyday actions, attitudes, and assumptions. Skilled behavior is a good example. Can you say precisely how you sign your name? Even as I type these words I realize that my fingers are moving over the keyboard without seeming to be directly controlled by individual finger presses. I think of a word and my fingers take over. Somehow, between intending to type a sequence of words and the words appearing, my brain makes countless connections of which I am not aware. And it's not about typing only. Driving, walking, giving handshakes, and interacting socially, as well as writing and speaking conventions are often employed without conscious realization. We know a great deal, but can communicate only a fraction of that functional knowledge. The rest lies hidden beneath the level of our conscious awareness. This is tacit or "quiet" knowledge.

Tacit knowledge presents a challenge for education: If it's important, how can we teach it? Teaching and learning in schools concentrates forcefully on explicit knowledge, and for good reason. Explicit knowledge is highly amenable to schooling because it can be stated outright in symbolic form, mostly in words. Also, it's relatively easy to determine if explicit knowledge has been learned—simply administer a test. But tacit knowledge by its very nature is hard to describe, hard to teach, and hard to test. Yet if it's an important element of a complete education, then we must find a way.

There is another reason why tacit knowledge might be neglected in education. That reason is connected to a deeply held but misleading assumption about the mind. Carl Bereiter (2002) has identified the culprit as the **container model of the mind**. According to Bereiter, our most common metaphor for the mind is a container. That container holds objects (knowledge) that are acquired from the outside (through learning). While this model can be helpful, it sometimes prevents us from appreciating forms of knowledge that are not explicitly stateable. Tacit knowledge does not fit the model well, and so it can easily be overlooked in teaching and learning.

One problem is: If we do not fully accept the container model of the mind, what's the alternative? In common computer systems, the container model seems to hold up pretty well. Devices inside digital computers, whether in memory or on storage media, do hold content—namely, data and programs. It's easy to imagine the mind working in much the same way. But there is a kind of computer that has a very different architecture, and Bereiter sees this computer architecture as offering a new way of thinking about knowledge. Bereiter refers to a kind of computer known as a **parallel data processor**, also known as a **neural network**.

Neural networks operate in a manner that is completely different from normal computing. Our familiar desktop and laptop computers are all von Neumann machines. They do computation serially, one step at a time, on data structures that are discrete: represented as some unique combination of binary (0 or 1) codes at the most basic level. With a **von Neumann machine**, you can always say precisely what content a computer holds and where in memory it is located. Like a word on a page, each idea is either present or absent, and if present you can say exactly where it is.

Inside a neural network, information is not locatable to only a single spot in the computer. Instead, what that computer "knows" is spread or "smeared" across an assemblage of hardware (Tank & Hopfield, 1987). Neural networks can perform such **pattern recognition** functions as identifying fingerprints. It works this way: Neural

FIGURE 4.7
A Neural Network
*Knowledge is spread
through the system.*
[Adapted from drawing
by Philip Travisano.]

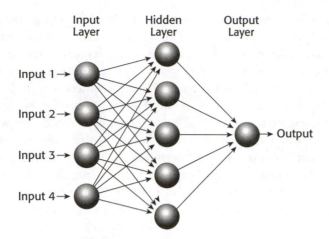

networks have input data (the fingerprints) and output data (the identities of people). Both sets of data go into the network. Connecting the two are "hidden units," which are pieces of hardware that can take on variable (rather than binary) values, and that also influence nearby hidden units positively (by exciting them) or negatively (by inhibiting them). These hidden units adjust and influence each other so that, eventually, they come to "connect" the inputs and outputs. If the network recognizes a fingerprint pattern as belonging to Al Capone, it's the hidden units that are making the connection. Just as in a human brain, that specific "knowledge" is not in any single location—it's spread throughout the system. The architecture of hidden units operating in parallel, influencing one another through patterns of excitation and inhibition, also resembles the ways that neurons operate in the brain.

Why is this so important? It's important because, for Bereiter, neural networks present an alternative metaphor for mental computation. Unlike a von Neumann machine, neural networks can have knowledge without specifiable content. You can't say exactly what's in the neural network, but you *can* say that it performs intelligently. Similarly, a human being might perform intelligently, though it might be hard to say exactly what knowledge underlies the intelligent behavior. Bereiter proposes that neural network models of computing can open our thinking to a wholly different model of the mind, one that does not necessarily involve containment. If we accept this, then our educational goals could likewise expand to include goals that do not reduce neatly to the acquisition of specific mental content. That's a liberating possibility.

Anthropology

Situated Cognition

Just as neural networks can help us to see knowledge from a new angle, so can perspectives achieved through a deep study of knowledge in culture. Here, we benefit from the perspective of the anthropologist. As we consider culture, and the role that knowledge plays in the functioning of culture, our minds can open to yet another challenge to the psychological view that knowledge is content held by specific minds.

The perspective we'll examine is **situated cognition**. Situated cognition advances the idea that our knowledge is not simply a matter of mental content but lives in (or is constituted by) the goals, practices, people, language, and tools in a culture. Like Bereiter's metaphor or neural networks, the situated view of cognition rejects the container model. Knowledge is not about, or not *only* about, what's in the minds of individual people. Instead, knowledge is a property of the whole system of cultural practice.

Situated cognition theory is best illustrated by specific research that gave rise to the theory. We'll take a couple of examples. In a seminal study, Barbara Rogoff observed dairy workers in their daily activities of filling containers with milk cartons. Rogoff (1990) noted that mathematical computation was necessary for the workers to do their jobs well. To calculate how much milk a container could hold, and whether the containers could be lifted, the dairy workers invented mental shortcuts that proved quite handy to support their estimates and decisions. But their mathematical shortcuts were nothing like school mathematics. They were tailored entirely to the microcosm of the dairy and to the work that needed to be done there. The dairy workers were knowledgeable, but their knowledge was bound to their specific work and to the tools at their disposal.

A second example of situated cognition is based on research by Geoffrey Saxe (1988; 1991). Saxe studied Brazilian street vendors—children who bought candy at wholesale from suppliers and sold it on the street for profit. To be successful, the children needed functional mathematical competence in order to provide change, to offer volume discounts, and to take into account high rates of currency inflation. Because many of the children had minimal or no school-based instruction in mathematics, their calculations were almost always performed without reference to numerals, place values, or the sort of paper-and-pencil arithmetic taught in classrooms. Rather, their math was bound to the particulars of the local currency, the Brazilian *cruzieros*, and especially to the values marked by the color of bills and the portraits depicted on them. Nonetheless, the street vendors were highly skilled in both arithmetic and ratio comparisons of monetary value. In fact, candy-sellers were more skillful than nonsellers in calculations that dealt with currency, but their knowledge was almost entirely bound to the cultural practice of selling candy on the streets. Saxe did find some limited influence of street-selling mathematics on school-like math problems that he devised: Young candy-sellers (second graders) used regrouping strategies more effectively than peers who were not street vendors. Likewise, formal arithmetic was sometimes used by vendors who attended school to make sales calculations. Although there was some influence of school-based mathematics on out-of-school math, and vice versa, the two forms of mathematical competence were largely situated in one context or the other.

How much of our everyday knowledge is situated? Possibly a *lot* of it. Situated cognition theory therefore challenges the very way we conceive of knowledge, and consequently the way we teach and learn in schools. In schools, we favor knowledge that is general and that works in many different situations. We also think of knowledge as, ideally, transferable across different contexts rather than bound to specific situations. But if this view is wrong, then our basic assumptions about knowledge, and hence teaching, are unfounded.

Let's consider math again. It's easy to think of the mathematics used by a commercial painter as being closely linked to his work. A painter needs to estimate the amount of paint needed to cover a house. This requires quick calculations of wall area. Total area, divided by the coverage per gallon of paint, gives the amount of paint needed. Multiply this by the cost of paint per gallon. Add labor costs, and so on. All of this must be done quickly and efficiently, particularly if estimates for painting jobs are offered free to prospective customers. In the situated cognition perspective, the mathematics of house painting are bound to the specifics of paint cans, tape measures, tarps, and ladders. We can easily believe that such knowledge is situated.

Now consider the middle school student. This student might learn to calculate the area of a rectangle, knowledge that ought to apply to estimating the amount of paint needed to paint a bedroom. If the student wants to paint his room on the weekend, can he perform the needed calculations? Can he estimate the area of wall space in his bedroom, and from that area determine how much paint he will need? Maybe not. Maybe this student performs well in math class, but has difficulty using the same taught and tested concepts on the weekend to paint his room. If so, then his math knowledge too is situated, not in contexts of paint estimation or street vending, but in the specific cultural practice of learning mathematics in schools.

Transfer

The theory of situated knowledge can help us to understand **transfer**. Transfer is a major concept in theories of learning and cognition. How important is transfer? To answer, I'll respond by recounting a short conversation I had many years ago.

Early in my graduate student career, I posed a question to a more advanced student—a question perhaps only a neophyte graduate student would pose. It was: "What is the ultimate goal of education?" She took the question seriously, but she did not deliberate long, nor did she give an extended response. Her answer was given in a single word: "Transfer."

It's not that I necessarily believe that transfer is the undisputed ultimate goal of education. What has stayed with me, though, is its believability as an answer to my question. Transfer is so important that it arguably *is* the ultimate goal of education. And even if it is only *arguably* so, then it must be very important. To make this case more plausible to you, the reader, I'll need first to define transfer. I'll define it as follows: Transfer is the application of knowledge learned in one context to a different context.

Consider again the student learning to calculate the area of a rectangle in mathematics class. Imagine again that on Saturday that same student cannot apply this knowledge to calculating the amount of paint needed to paint his bedroom. The problem is not that the student lacks the math skills. More likely, it would simply not occur to the student to use the formula for area to estimate the amount of paint needed. Knowledge that you hope would cross from one context to the other—from the classroom to the home—does not transfer. Mathematical knowledge is confined to the classroom—perhaps it is *situated* in the classroom. What use is it, then?

Another student might be very successful in a French class. The student performs well enough on speaking exercises and on writing assignments to earn an "A" grade in French. Based partly on this student's success, her family takes a vacation to Montréal during the summer. Both this student and her parents believe that this will be a great opportunity to practice speaking French in a Francophone community. But, to everyone's surprise and disappointment, the student finds that she can't speak French for any real effect. Beyond *bonjour* and *merci*, the academic success that she had in her French studies does not pay off in Montréal. Transfer has failed.

Extrapolate this to all classroom learning. Imagine the dire scenario where no knowledge acquired in the classroom has meaning or significance outside the classroom. Without transfer, the exercise of education would be totally sealed off and self-referential. The world of schools would function autonomously from the "real world." Grades and textbooks and lectures and papers would support the classroom agenda, but not worthwhile activities outside the school grounds. This scenario has been feared by many educators, even if its realization is partial, not total. Alfred North Whitehead

(1929) spoke of the possibility of **inert knowledge** that has no usefulness outside getting good grades in schools. The American philosopher John Dewey based much of the progressive school movement on improving the organic connection between school activities and the larger community. Dewey and Whitehead both understood that transfer is essential to education, but that transfer is certainly not guaranteed to happen.

Psychologists, also, have been concerned about transfer. Their concerns have centered more on whether transfer occurs and, if so, how commonly and under what conditions. Their questions are theoretical. We can summarize the longstanding position of psychologists on transfer as follows: Transfer does not occur readily, even when you think it should. One piece of evidence leading to this conclusion is research on the **mental discipline hypothesis**. The central idea of mental discipline is that we can exercise our minds in one subject, and the knowledge gained will help us in another, distantly related subject. In the early 1900s, educators commonly believed that the study of Latin would make students generally smarter, and so Latin would have carryover effects in the study of many other disciplines: mathematics, literature, history, and so on. Even today, there are undoubtedly many people who believe that the pursuit of some cognitively challenging activities—chess or mathematics, even Latin—exercise the mind in a generic way that will spill over to other pursuits. This believable hypothesis can, of course, be put to the test.

The hypothesis was indeed tested long ago by one of the first educational psychologists, E. L. Thorndike (1924). Thorndike contrasted students who studied Latin with those who did not. Did students who studied Latin perform better in other subjects? Thorndike found that they did not, even when controlling for initial academic differences among students. Thorndike's research findings put the mental discipline hypothesis under a cloud of doubt, one that remains hovering to this day. It's not to say that Thorndike's experiment defeated the mental discipline hypothesis for all time. Maybe Latin and chess actually *do* sometimes convey a general effect. But Thorndike's results have caused most psychologists to believe that such effects are unlikely. Cross-disciplinary transfer in the form of mental discipline appeared to be an interesting idea with little or no data to support it.

Psychologists have found many other instances in which transfer does not occur, even in conditions where most people would predict it should happen. A famous example (famous among psychologists, at least) is the Gick and Holyoak (1983) study of transfer in problem solving. An initial scenario is presented:

> A fortress surrounded by a moat is connected to land by numerous narrow bridges. An attacking army successfully captures the fortress by sending only a few soldiers across each bridge, converging upon it simultaneously.

Now a second scenario is given, one whose solution can take advantage of information in the first scenario. Here's the second problem:

> A patient has a cancerous tumor. Beams of radiation will destroy the tumor, but in high doses will also destroy healthy tissue surrounding the tumor. How can you use radiation to safely eradicate the tumor?

The key question is: Can a learner apply the solution of the first problem (attacking the castle) to solving the second problem (attacking the tumor)? The basic answer is no: Very few participants were able to make the connection between the first problem and the second. Even though the two problems and their solutions are structurally identical, or isomorphic, transfer did not occur. Dramatic failures of transfer in this research and in other studies have caused psychologists to question seriously the frequency with which transfer does occur. Transfer appears to be rare; perhaps the human mind is poorly prepared to transfer knowledge.

WHEN TRANSFER DOES OCCUR. Are we being too pessimistic about transfer? Probably so. There are reasons to believe that transfer does happen. Still, the forgoing examples tell us that simple beliefs about the ease of transfer are incorrect. So what's the positive news about transfer?

There is a logical argument that transfer is not only common, it is ubiquitous and continuous. Consider that, every day, we face situations that are new. In large ways or small, the problems and tasks that we face today differ from those we have encountered before. How are we able to manage today's demands? Only by marshalling the knowledge, skills, and thinking abilities that we acquired in the past. For the sake of survival and success, transfer must occur. It may not occur with the regularity and certainty that we would wish, but it does happen.

Not only performance, but also learning, requires transfer. Almost always, learning requires a connection between new knowledge and what is already known. Seen this way, every instance of learning is also an instance of transfer because it requires the application of existing knowledge to the acquisition of new knowledge. Transfer, therefore, does happen. But, as educators, we must be careful to heed the lessons of research, which tells us that transfer is not necessarily easy or dependable. There is a risk that the learning that occurs in schools will apply to schoolwork only.

TYPES OF TRANSFER. Our discussion of transfer must extend beyond whether or not it happens. Research has shown that there are different kinds of transfer, and these varieties avail themselves to somewhat different teaching strategies. Let's first distinguish between **positive transfer** and **negative transfer**. To this point, we've been talking about positive transfer—when learning in one area helps us in a different area. Sometimes, though, knowledge gained in one skill or knowledge area can hurt our performance in another area. Let's say that you are a racquetball player, and a good one. Now a friend invites you to play tennis. Will your racquetball skills be a help or a hindrance? Perhaps a little of each. But if we are talking about negative transfer, we are considering the negative influence of racquetball on tennis. It's possible that you'll use your fine wrist snap from racquetball on the tennis court. That's not a good idea, but it may be a difficult habit to break. Negative transfer, in this case, implies that you would be a better tennis player if you had never taken up racquetball.

This racquetball/tennis example seems to give negative transfer limited scope and applicability, but that's not necessarily the case. Lots of different experiences might have undesirable effects on later learning. Whether that previous learning is primarily knowledge or skills or beliefs or attitudes, it's common for prior knowledge to interfere with new learning. These are instances of negative transfer. Of course, there are also countless instances where prior learning assists us in further learning. Indeed, teachers depend on this latter fact, but need to be aware of the former.

Another distinction is between **near transfer** and **far transfer**. The difference is easily intuited. Near transfer occurs whenever we apply knowledge to situations that are similar to the original learning context. Say that your driving experience is limited to a small car with an automatic transmission. You would probably have little difficulty driving a different small car with an automatic transmission. Your driving skills would transfer. But if you drove a much bigger car or a truck, then transfer would be more difficult. This is far transfer. If you are asked to drive a moving van, it's quite possible that you could handle this, but probably with more difficulty. If the moving van required you to shift gears, this could prove to be a real challenge—possibly one beyond your reach. Again, this represents far transfer (or a failure of far transfer).

If a teacher wants to encourage transfer, there are straightforward applications from theory. Obviously, near transfer is easier than far transfer. If a teacher wants to encourage far transfer—if she wants knowledge to "travel well" to diverse contexts and problems—then it's sensible to start with near transfer tasks. The teacher can then extend the application range to situations that are more and more unlike the original learning context. The order is: near transfer first, then far transfer.

Still another distinction that can be helpful in teaching is **vertical transfer** and **horizontal transfer**. Up to this point the focus has been on horizontal transfer— transfer *across* situations. But there is also vertical transfer, which is transfer *within* a situation or problem. Vertical transfer occurs whenever complex skills are taught by first providing instruction in their component subskills. For example, a swimming instructor teaching the breaststroke might have children practice the arm motions and leg motions separately. Once these independent motions are learned, they can be integrated into a coordinated swimming stroke. When combined, the subskills transfer vertically into the more complex performance of the breaststroke. Vertical transfer refers to the way that component subskills combine into more complex performances. This approach to teaching and learning is very common not only in sports but also in academic pursuits.

Finally, here is a newer conceptualization of transfer that is fresh and provocative. Remember that all occasions of learning can be seen as instances of transfer. Why? Because in order to learn we rely on intellectual resources we've acquired in the past. Our current knowledge is the basis and means by which we learn new knowledge. So it must be said that learning involves transfer. This idea has been extended by John Bransford and Dan Schwartz (1999) to redefine transfer. The proposal is not to replace historical definitions of transfer, but to add to them in this way: Transfer can be defined as the advantage to learning that comes from prior learning. To take an example, imagine that you have studied Spanish in high school. If you visited Japan, would your knowledge of Spanish help you? No, there would be no transfer. But suppose you were then inspired to study Japanese. The question changes: Would your prior study of Spanish help you to learn Japanese faster and better than you would have if you had not studied Spanish? If so, then the previous study of Spanish transfers. It does not transfer in the classic sense of immediate performance. But it does transfer in the Bransford and Schwartz sense of increased quality and efficiency of learning.

Defining transfer as an effect on future learning might make you think that transfer is not as limited in scope as psychologists have long believed. Could the study of Latin or chess transfer widely? Probably not in the traditional sense of immediate performance on far transfer tasks. But maybe our experiences do build skills, attitudes, preferences, and habits that serve us well in diverse pursuits. Perhaps as learners we can "learn to learn"—a mindset that does indeed travel well, ideally for a lifetime across pursuits that vary widely. To develop such a mindset is an excellent goal for a teacher: both for herself and for her students.

Learning Strategies

In this chapter, the multidisciplinary survey of theories of knowledge enlarges our view by showing how the topic has been approached over many centuries. The overview also has practical applications; theories of knowledge can suggest strategies for teaching and learning. The ten strategies presented below collectively draw from the disciplines of philosophy, semiotics, linguistics, artificial intelligence, psychology, and anthropology.

1 Look for evidence, but remember that the senses can deceive.
The empiricists knew that sensory data from the material world is a very good basis for making knowledge claims. But our senses are not perfect, and neither are the interpretations we place on sensory data. We can become overly confident in what we think the evidence means. Learners need to search for evidence, but also be mindful that the meaning of data is virtually never self-explanatory nor above errors of interpretation.

2 Question your beliefs.
Descartes took skepticism to an extreme form by employing his method of radical doubt. Good critical thinkers don't need to go as far as Descartes, but they should imitate him in questioning even cherished beliefs, "safe" assumptions, and seemingly obvious inferences. By placing an appropriate level of confidence in beliefs and being open to contrary evidence, we adopt an epistemological stance that will serve us well in building sound knowledge.

3 Encourage semiosis.
The founder of American semiotics, Charles Sanders Peirce, proposed that all knowledge is interconnected through chains of signification. One sign prompts other signs, and those trigger still others—a process that Peirce called semiosis. The prized educational outcome of understanding can be expressed in terms of semiosis—by the ways in which any idea can prompt a rich cascade of others.

4 Be a "schemabuilder."
Most educators can appropriate the notion of schema from psychology in their own teaching practice. The idea of schema is that knowledge in any area is organized, and that the organization of knowledge changes over time as learning proceeds. Schema change can mean the accretion of new information, tuning to correct or refine ideas, and restructuring as knowledge is overhauled. Teaching and learning can be understood in terms of "schemabuilding."

5 Build mental models.
Mental models are knowledge representations in the form of dynamic images. Mental models are particularly good for representing the operation of physical systems, such as the ever-changing arrangement of planets in the solar system or the way that a bicycle gearing system turns the back wheel. In science and technology especially, teachers can help their students to build mental models that complement knowledge represented in language and symbols.

6 Consider the power of language to shape thought.
As we look back on the history of philosophy, we see that the quest to build certain foundations of knowledge was not successful. For the past century, philosophers and linguists have understood that knowledge is structured more around language than it is on the tangible world. This makes knowledge seem less grounded, but it also opens a window into the deep significance and flexibility of language. For a complete view of human cognition, we must appreciate the power of language to mold the ways in which we understand and interpret our world.

7 Search for misconceptions.
A realistic view of knowledge acquisition appreciates that learning is not simply the addition of more and more correct knowledge. Often what we learn is faulty, naive, or misleading in some way. We develop misconceptions about the world and about the subjects we study. Instruction must take into account that students develop misconceptions prior to and during the course of instruction. Teachers must strategically decide how best to deal with misconceptions given the particulars of the subject, the student, and the situation.

8 Develop tacit knowledge.
Much of what we know is not easily translated into words, but is nonetheless an important part of growing expertise in any area. Tacit knowledge is by nature much harder to teach and assess than explicit knowledge. Even so, every teacher must

recognize and value tacit knowledge as one aspect of what students need to learn.

9 Develop situated knowledge.
One easily overlooked feature of knowledge is that it is deeply woven into the fabric of our experience, and so relates meaningfully to particular tools and social practices. The discovery that knowledge is by nature "situated" presents direct implications for teaching. For knowledge to be maximally useful it should be related meaningfully to real-world situations.

10 Encourage positive transfer.
Transfer is a vital aspect of high-quality learning, but it is not easily achieved. Psychological research supports the suspicion that transfer often fails when by any reasonable expectation it should succeed. Transfer must therefore be pursued as an important learning goal in its own right. To achieve this goal, teachers will need to present knowledge as useful in multiple contexts rather than in a single, abstracted form.

The nature of knowledge is not easy to grasp, and building high-quality knowledge is not easy to achieve. The ten strategies present insights and applications offered by a multidisciplinary understanding of what knowledge is and how it is built. A comprehensive view can help us to develop the sort of rich, integrated knowledge that defines what it means to understand. In this book, we give more attention to cognitive psychology than to other disciplines, but we must remember that psychology has no monopoly on theories of the mind and its functions. Various other disciplines, in combination, present a fuller and richer picture of learning and cognition than can be obtained from a single disciplinary perspective.

 **Conclusion**

This chapter explores two major themes. The first is that the study of learning and cognition—the subject of this text—requires specific attention to the nature of knowledge. It is not enough to consider only memory structures or cognitive processes, such as reasoning and inference. Knowledge itself must be understood. But this is no easy task: Even defining the word *knowledge* is difficult. Still, the intellectual reward is worth the effort. While seeking to deepen our understanding of learning and cognition, we must also try to comprehend what knowledge is and how it is acquired.

The second major theme of this chapter is that our understanding of *knowledge* should not be illuminated by psychology alone. Rather, several disciplines have shone bright lights on knowledge by trying to understand what it is. This chapter is rightly multidisciplinary—not because of some vague notion that multidisciplinarity is a good idea, but with the awareness that our subject (knowledge) has historically been pursued by great minds whose intellectual homes were in different disciplines. The timeline of this multidisciplinary inquiry is long, extending back to the ancient Greek philosophers. Intellectual activity in the other disciplines reaches back several centuries to the post-Renaissance Enlightenment. As students of the mind, of learning, and of education, we must understand and appreciate these developments.

Is there a single sweeping conclusion that we can draw from our survey? Perhaps this: We can safely reject one view of knowledge, which is that of naive realism. This view says that knowledge is a straightforward translation of what is in the tangible world into the mind. From this point of view, knowledge is unproblematic. What we know is simply what is out there to be observed, and learning is a process of acquiring more of it. Given everything presented in this chapter, I hope you'll agree that this point of view is completely untenable. Still, I suspect that such a perspective is not uncommon. If naive realism is a distortion of the nature of knowledge (and it is), then it is not a friend of the educator or the student of the human mind.

If not naive realism, then what? We can't yet give a definite answer because there is not one to be had. But we can, with confidence, assert the following:

- Knowledge is not limited to, and does not fully capture, tangible reality. We can entertain many ideas that have no physical reference. Much of our mental life and communication concerns things that have no tangible substance.

- Knowledge shapes our perceptions. We interpret our experience in terms of the categories we already know and beliefs we hold.

- Knowledge comes in many forms, including words and images (both static and dynamic).

- Explicit declarative knowledge is not the only kind. We also have tacit knowledge that does not conform well to assumptions and expectations common in teaching and learning.

- Knowledge is a product of culture. It is constituted significantly in the situated practices of a culture that involve other people, tools, and traditions.

There is much, much more, of course. But, looking back, these points give a sense of the complexity of the subject of knowledge. We should not be troubled by the open-endedness of our inquiry, or by the fact that not all our questions have been answered. Open-endedness is not a quality of this chapter only, but of the entire subject of learning and cognition. The human mind is complicated! In our lifetimes and in our work, we should adopt the perspective that the subject will not be neatly laid out and dissected, with all mysteries dissipated through scholarship and research. Instead, let's reside in the middle space, acknowledging that we know a lot already, but also appreciating that many questions still endure. What we know can guide our practice as educators, and what we don't yet know can make us suitably humble about our assumptions and decisions. This halfway state can also help us to anticipate future discoveries: We can confidently believe that in the years ahead, more insights into the human mind will be revealed. Anticipation and openness can characterize both the field of study and the mind of the educator.

REFERENCES

Anderson, J. R. (1996). A simple theory of complex cognition. *American Psychologist, 51*(4), 355–365.

Austin, J. L. (1962). *How to do things with words.* Cambridge: Cambridge University Press.

Bartlett, F. C. (1967 [1932]). *Remembering.* Cambridge: Cambridge University Press.

Bereiter, C. (2002). *Education and mind in the knowledge age.* Mahwah, NJ: Lawrence Erlbaum Associates.

Boas, F. (1911). Introduction to *The handbook of North American Indians, Vol. 1, Bureau of American Ethnology Bulletin* 40, Part 1. Washington, DC: Smithsonian Institution. Reprinted by Georgetown University Press (1963) and by University of Nebraska Press (1966).

Bransford, J. D., & Schwartz, D. (1999). Rethinking transfer. A simple proposal with multiple implications. *Review of Research in Education, 24,* 61–100.

Chomsky, N. (1975). *Reflections of language.* New York: Pantheon.

Collins, A. M., & Loftus, E. F. (1975). A spreading activation theory of semantic processing. *Psychological Review, 82,* 407–428.

Collins, A. M., & Quillian, M. R. (1969). Retrieval time from long-term memory. *Journal of Verbal Learning and Verbal Behavior, 8,* 240–247.

Culler, J. (1986). *Ferdinand de Saussure.* Ithaca, NY: Cornell University Press.

Dufresne, R., Mestre, J., Thaden-Koch, T., Gerace, W., & Leonard, W. (2005). Knowledge representation and coordination in the transfer process. In J. Mestre (Ed.), *Transfer of learning from a modern multidisciplinary perspective* (pp. 155–215). Greenwich, CT: Information Age Publishing.

Eco, U. (1976). *A theory of semiotics.* Bloomington, IN: Indiana University Press.

Gick, M. L., & Holyoak, K. J. (1983). Schema induction and analogical transfer. *Cognitive Psychology, 15*(1), 1–38.

Ginsberg, M. L. (1998). Computers, games, and the real world. *Scientific American, 9*(4), 84–89.

Houser, N. (1987). Toward a Peircean semiotic theory of learning. *The American Journal of Semiotics, 5*(2), 251–274.

Lionni, L. (1974). *Fish is fish.* New York: Random House.

Locke, J. (1689/1965). *An essay concerning human understanding.* New York: Macmillan.

Mestre, J., Thaden-Koch, T., Dufresne, R., & Gerace, W. (2004). The dependence of knowledge deployment on context among physics novices. In E. Redish & M. Vicentini (Eds.), *Proceedings of the international school of physics "Enrico Fermi," Course CLVI, Research on Physics Education* (pp. 367–408). Amsterdam: IOS Press.

Murphy, P. K., & Mason, L. (2006). Changing knowledge and beliefs. In P. A. Alexander & P. H. Winne (Eds.), *Handbook of educational psychology* (2nd ed.)(pp. 305–324). Mahwah, NJ: Lawrence Erlbaum Associates.

Newborn, M. (1997). *Kasparov versus Deep Blue: Computer chess comes of age.* New York: Springer.

Newell, A., & Simon, H. A. (1972). *Human problem solving.* Englewood Cliffs, NJ: Prentice-Hall.

Norman, D. A., & Rumelhart, D. E. (1975). *Explorations in cognition.* San Francisco: Freeman.

Novak, J. D. (1998). *Learning, creating, and using knowledge: Concept maps as facilitative tools in schools and corporations.* Mahwah, NJ: Lawrence Erlbaum Associates.

Novak, J. D., & Gowin, D. B. (1984). *Learning how to learn.* New York: Cambridge University Press.

Palmer, D. (1996). *Does the center hold? An introduction to Western philosophy.* Mountain View, CA: Mayfield Publishing Company.

Perkins, D. N. (1992). *Smart schools: Better thinking and learning for every child.* New York: The Free Press.

Pinker, S. (1995). *The language instinct.* New York: Perennial (HarperCollins).

Pullum, G. K. (1991). *The great Eskimo vocabulary hoax and other irreverent essays on the study of language.* Chicago: University of Chicago Press.

Rogoff, B. (1990). *Apprenticeship in thinking. Cognitive development in social context.* New York: Oxford University Press.

Rorty, R. M. (1992). *The linguistic turn: Essays in philosophical method*. Chicago: University of Chicago Press.

Rosch, E. H. (1977). Human categorization. In N. Warren (Ed.), *Advances in cross-cultural psychology* (Vol. 1). San Diego, CA: Academic Press.

Ryle, G. (1949). *The concept of mind*. London: Hutchinson.

Saussure, F. de (1959). *Course in general linguistics* (Edited by C. Bally & A. Sechehaye; Translated by W. Baskin). New York: McGraw-Hill.

Saxe, G. B. (1988). Candy selling and math learning. *Educational Researcher*, August–September, 14–21.

Saxe, G. B. (1991). *Culture and cognitive development: Studies in mathematical understanding*. Hillsdale, NJ: Lawrence Erlbaum Associates.

Searle, J. R. (1969). *Speech acts: An essay in the philosophy of language*. Cambridge: Cambridge University Press.

Smith, J. P., diSessa, A. A., & Roschelle, J. (1993). Misconceptions reconceived: A constructive analysis of knowledge in transition. *The Journal of the Learning Sciences, 3*(2), 115–163.

Steinberg, M. S., Brown, D. E., & Clement, J. (1990). Genius is not immune to persistent misconceptions: Conceptual difficulties impeding Isaac Newton and contemporary physics students. *International Journal of Science Education, 12,* 265–273.

Tank, D. W., & Hopfield, J. J. (1987). Collective computation in neuronlike circuits. *Scientific American, 257*(6), 104–114.

Tesauro, G. (2002). Programming backgammon using self-teaching neural nets. *Artificial Intelligence, 132,* 181–199.

Thorndike, E. L. (1924). Mental discipline in high school studies. *Journal of Educational Psychology, 15,* 1–22.

Tulving, E. (1983). *Elements of episodic memory*. Oxford: Clarendon Press.

Vosniadou, S., & Brewer, W. F. (1987). Theories of knowledge restructuring in development. *Review of Educational Research, 57,* 51–67.

Westfall, R. S. (1980). *Never at rest: A biography of Isaac Newton*. New York: Cambridge University Press.

Whitehead, A. N. (1929). *The aims of education*. New York: Macmillan.

Whorf, B. L. (1956). *Language, thought, and reality: Selected writings of Benjamin Lee Whorf*. (J. B. Carroll, Ed.). Cambridge, MA: MIT Press.

Zadeh, L. (1965). Fuzzy sets. *Information and Control, 8,* 338–353.

[5] Complex Cognition

Throughout the millennia, the human capacity for complex thought has always been important. It has been a seedbed for the origin of cultures and for their propagation from one generation to the next. Now, in the twenty-first century, complex cognition is more than important—it's indispensable. Sweeping changes in modern economies have been marked by a shift in the nature of work from mechanical production to the use, transformation, and dissemination of information. People work with their *minds* more than ever. Work, and therefore the generation of economic wealth, is significantly cognitive.

Consequently, the importance of complex cognition as an educational goal has never been greater. Whether widely recognized or taken for granted, the propagation and modification of culture is a vital purpose served by education, as is preparation for economic viability. More abstractly, education cultivates the power of intellect to sustain and improve who humans are and what they do. Education is largely about nurturing complex cognition.

Complex cognition is different from straightforward, simple, linear thinking. It is often multifaceted, evaluative, and open-ended. Although it makes sense to refer to complex cognition as a broad category of intellectual expression, in reality it has several distinct subdivisions, four of which will be explored in this chapter:

- Problem solving
- Critical thinking
- Inferential reasoning
- Creative thinking

Although discrete, these four categories do share some common features. Most important, all four are supported by a fifth form of complex cognition: **metacognition**. Because of its centrality, metacognition is our entry point for understanding complex cognition.

Metacognition

A single cognitive process that binds together all of complex cognition, metacognition is commonly defined as "thinking about thinking." Whenever we think about our own thought process, we are engaged in metacognition. For example, whenever you realize you don't understand a few pages from a book that you have read, that awareness—that you don't understand—is a form of metacognition. This example suggests a somewhat more precise definition of metacognition: the monitoring and control of thought. An active and effective mental life relies on metacognitive ability. Its development, therefore, is an educational imperative.

Metacognition and Metamemory

Metacognition is such a powerful idea that you would think it has a long history, but in fact it does not. The concept was first proposed around 1978, and then gained popularity as a cognitive construct through the 1980s and 1990s (Brown, 1978; Flavell, 1979). The first research on metacognition was applied to memory. This variety of metacognition, called **metamemory**, refers to how accurately we appraise what we know and what we don't know.

For example, if you are asked to name the planets in our solar system, you might *say* that you can name them but be unable to do so. Or, you could say that you *can't* name the planets, but you really can. So, independent of your knowledge of the planet names is your *accuracy in appraising* your own knowledge.

There is evidence that good metamemory is an important quality for a learner. A student's ability to appraise his or her own knowledge state accurately is correlated to superior learning outcomes (Tobias & Everson, 1996). Accurate metamemory is positively related to more effective learning. This positive correlation does not by itself show that metamemory contributes directly to better learning outcomes, but the connection is certainly plausible. It's easy to think of pitfalls faced by a student who thinks he understands topic X, but really does not. Likewise, the student who underestimates her knowledge of topic Y might miss opportunities by electing not to take advanced courses in the subject. Accurate metamemory is clearly a desirable quality for all learners.

Metacognition and Learning

It is critical that students know how to think metacognitively, especially whenever they encounter new information. The student who is metacognitive during reading monitors comprehension continuously, always asking the question, Do I understand? If the answer is *no*, the student can choose to reread the last paragraph, page, or chapter. Alternatively, he can opt to read on, hoping that the meaning will become clear in the next few pages. Metacognitive awareness of a lack of comprehension gives the student a vital choice of what to do next.

The same advantage of strategic choice applies to the student in a classroom. If a teacher presents a lesson that the student does not understand, then metacognitive ability will allow the student to realize that he does not understand, and to do something about it. Metacognition involves monitoring (Do I understand?) and control ("Could you explain that again?"). The metacognitive functions of monitoring comprehension and strategically correcting lapses in comprehension can apply to any learning or communicative activity: discussions among peers, tutoring sessions, computer-based instruction, media news reports, controversial claims and counterclaims in philosophy, religion, and politics.

Conversely, a student who lacks metacognitive awareness is greatly disadvantaged. Failing to understand challenging text, the student might simply read on, with no awareness that his comprehension has faltered—no awareness of the choices he has. It's possible for a person to read many pages from a book and never realize that he does not understand. Similarly, a student might take notes during a lecture, watch a demonstration, or participate in classroom instruction, yet not register his *lack* of comprehension. In fact, the state of noncomprehension might feel normal to the student. Where the lack of comprehension begins to feel normal, the student will not *do* anything to correct it, such as attempting to reread or to ask for help, because there is no sensed need to understand the material.

The failure to register a lack of comprehension during reading applies not only to children and to unsuccessful students. It's somewhat common even among ostensibly successful college students. In one study, passages of text were written to contain internal contradictions. After reading these passages, students were asked whether they understood them. Many responded *yes*, which is impossible if we believe that text with internal contradictions cannot truly be comprehended. The unwarranted confidence that these students understood what they had read was called the **illusion of knowing** (Glenberg & Epstein, 1985). How common is this illusion? It's probably very common.

Usually, metacognition is assumed to be quite conscious and deliberate, but this need not be so. For example, some students may become so practiced at monitoring new information that they react rapidly when hearing a contradiction voiced by their teacher. Such students might speak up or immediately raise their hands to point out the contradiction. In this instance, catching an error seems more habitual than premeditated. Metacognitive monitoring is therefore not always deliberate and controlled; rather, it can become an ingrained habit of mind. This possibility has implications for teaching. A teacher might want her students not only to develop metacognitive skills, but beyond that to acquire the routine practice, or habit, of metacognition.

Metacognition and Action

Metacognitive monitoring and control applies not only to information, but also to action. For example, as you pursue an important goal, you might come to realize that your strategy is not working. When you realize that your approach is ineffective, you can choose to pursue a different action that has a chance of leading to success. But not everyone can shift strategies well or consistently. Often, people will pursue a chosen strategy long after it has been proven to be ineffective. For example, a homeowner might decide to fix a leaky faucet himself rather than call a plumber. The handyman might make the problem much worse, but have trouble realizing and then admitting that the faucet repair is beyond his skill level.

In everyday life, metacognition is not only relevant to deciding whether actions are *effective*, but also to whether they are *efficient*. You might be effective in painting a room with a one-inch paintbrush, but you will certainly not be efficient. You are being metacognitive when you realize that painting with a small brush is wasting your time, and then switch to a larger brush. But in some cases a person might continue to paint with a one-inch brush until the job is done. The continuation of action despite its ineffectiveness or inefficiency is sometimes called **perseveration**.

In academic tasks, metacognitive awareness lets you know when your strategy needs to change. A student attempting to solve a math problem might get stuck and realize that a change in tactics is warranted. Likewise, when trying to write a poem, editorial, or research paper, a student may feel blocked from writing progress and need a fresh approach. All goal-directed activity, including schoolwork, benefits from periodic appraisal. The relevant question is: Is this working? If the answer is *no*, then a change is called for. Metacognition applies equally to ideas and actions; it is the ability to appraise the quality of both and to take corrective action when it is warranted.

Metacognition and Group Work

Metacognition applies not only to individuals but also to groups. A possible benefit of working together in a group is that one person might be metacognitive even if the others are not. Let's face it: as individuals, we are not consistently good thinkers. We may try to be rational, but our rationality has limits. The rationality of each person is a **bounded rationality**, as Herbert Simon (1969, p. 190) put it. He described bounded rationality as what we can expect from humans when "the complexity of the environment is immensely greater than the computational powers of the [mind]." We do not always detect errors or inefficiencies, nor do we always see opportunities as they arise or pitfalls in the road ahead. But in collaborative situations, other people might come through for us even if our own cognitive performance falls short of the mark.

The result of effective collaboration is that the cognitive performance of a group as a whole can exceed the level achieved by its participants as individuals. The possibility is captured in the homespun phrase "two heads are better than one." We can understand *why* the phrase rings true if we consider bounded rationality. Of course, it's not inevitable that groups produce good intellectual work. Groups can get off course and collectively become blinded to what is obvious (as in "groupthink") or yield rationality to a demagogue (resulting in cults or dictatorships). At their best, though, groups can be highly effective cognitive units whether in business (Japanese quality circles), in science (the lab), or in government (democracy) (Dunbar, 1995).

Metacognition as a Goal for Teaching and Learning

Metacognition is all about the monitoring and control of thought. And because the quality of human cognition is variable (e.g., we sometimes think well; we sometimes think poorly), then monitoring and control is essential to every thinking person. In the pages ahead we will see how metacognition applies to specific kinds of complex cognition, including problem solving and critical thinking.

Metacognition needs to be on the mind of every educator. In planning instruction, teachers should aim for their students to grow in their metacognitive ability; students also should aspire to become more effective metacognitive thinkers as part of their own intellectual and professional development (Lin, Schwartz, & Hatano, 2005).

Problem Solving

Problem solving, so important to what humans do and who humans are, may be our defining quality. Because of its supreme importance, it is critical to consider how education can improve students' ability to solve problems.

A definition of **problem solving** that works well and that conforms to the ways that it has been studied in research and applied to education is the following: Problem solving is the pursuit of a goal when the path to that goal is uncertain (Martinez, 1998; Mayer & Wittrock, 2006).

Whenever you try to accomplish something, but don't know exactly how to do it, you are engaged in problem solving. That's why people describe problem solving more colloquially as *what you do when you don't know what you're doing.* Every day we pursue goals that have no obvious formula, no obvious pathway from A to B. And even though the pathway is unclear, we often have confidence that we will reach our goal anyway. Starting at A, we believe that somehow we will arrive at B. After all, we have solved problems many times in the past, so we expect similar success in the future.

Whenever you engage in problem solving, you are attempting something new. For this reason, success cannot be guaranteed. In just this way, problem solving is distinct from following an algorithm—a set of rules that will produce success every time. If you are following a "recipe," you are not solving a problem. This is not to disparage algorithms; we depend on set procedures every day in our routine activities, such as getting dressed in the morning. Many life goals, however, cannot be achieved by following a set of rules; they are more open-ended and complex; they are *problems*. And here, the word *problem* does not necessarily mean something negative, as it does in everyday conversation. A problem is simply a goal whose attainment is not straightforward. Many problems are *good* problems because they help us advance toward ends that we value.

Examples of Problem Solving

APOLLO 13. Sometimes problem solving can be a matter of life and death. Such was the case in 1970, when the Apollo 13 space mission encountered a series of breakdowns and mishaps during its planned mission to the moon. Inside the spacecraft, three astronauts struggled against time to fix serious problems that threatened not only their mission but also their very lives. One of the more dire problems was the failure of the air filtration system. Compounding the crisis, when the astronauts attempted to repair the system, one of the filters broke. As a result, the carbon dioxide breathed out by the astronauts began to accumulate inside the rocket. Everyone understood the implications: When CO_2 reaches a certain level of toxicity, it is lethal.

The Apollo 13 saga was conveyed to audiences in the 1995 movie of the same name. In one sequence, NASA engineers were briefed on the conditions faced by the astronauts, including their desperate need for a replacement air filter. Because there was no back-up filter onboard the spacecraft, the NASA engineers needed to find a way for the astronauts to assemble a new and functional filter using only materials and tools available to them in the spacecraft. In a scene that epitomizes problem solving, the head engineer presented the problem: "We gotta find a way to make this . . . fit into the hole for this . . . usin' nothin' but that."

The NASA engineers were engaged in serious problem solving, obviously, but in the end they needed to convert their process into an algorithm that the Apollo astronauts could follow to build the replacement air filter. The result was success. Onboard the spacecraft, the astronauts followed the steps formulated by the NASA engineers to build a functional air filter. Within a few minutes, carbon dioxide levels began to nudge downward, making the air breathable again. Other serious problems that threatened the Apollo 13 mission, in turn, were also solved—seemingly against all odds. Within days, Apollo 13 returned to earth having rounded the moon but never landing. No lives were lost.

EVERYDAY PROBLEM SOLVING. Very few problem-solving activities involve such riveting, life-and-death dramas. Everyday problem solving, although quite mundane, is also important. Problem solving in daily life could involve, for example:

- How to make an edible dinner from the few items in your refrigerator.
- How to dress for an important interview when all your laundry is dirty.
- How to make and keep a friend.
- How to become more successful in your profession.

Tying shoelaces, however, is not an example of everyday problem solving because it involves following a set procedure that guarantees success—in other words, an algorithm. When you decide to tie your shoes, there is no doubt about the outcome: Your shoes will be tied. Success is not so certain when little children try to tie their shoes, however. Because they may not always follow a set procedure, and they are uncertain of the outcome, children learning to tie shoelaces *can* be problem solving.

The shoelaces example illustrates that problem solving for one person is not necessarily problem solving for another. Some people have no clue as to how to cook an omelet, whereas others can make one while half-asleep. It's a matter of problem solving for the first person, but it's algorithmic for the second. The same principle applies to fixing a car, installing computer software, assembling a bicycle, doing taxes, cutting hair, or delivering a baby. For many people, these activities are fairly routine and so do not normally involve problem solving. In fact, we often pay highly-trained professionals to perform what is for them a routine algorithm so that we don't have to engage in problem solving with its attendant risks of something going wrong.

Navigating a Problem Space

Think of problem solving as moving through a hypothetical space from a starting point to the intended goal (Newell & Simon, 1972). The conceptual terrain is something like a map, but without a prescribed route. The starting point includes all the initial conditions we face. If it's dinnertime, the initial conditions might be, for example, *no money* and *only moldy cheese* in the refrigerator. The goal state is to eat an edible dinner. Between the initial state and the goal state is the **problem space**—all the possible options that could take you from your initial state to the goal state. Within the problem space you can take certain actions (permitted moves) but not others (illegal moves). In the "finding dinner" problem, you might appeal to a friend to feed you (a permitted move) but you would not steal french fries from a child (an illegal move).

Imagine a corresponding problem space for a game of chess. The initial state is the chessboard before anyone moves a piece. The goal state for each player is to conquer the king of the opposing player. Thus, the initial state is a particular board layout, but the goal state of taking the other person's king could happen in many different ways. The problem space is highly complex, consisting of all possible moves and piece configurations during the course of a chess match.

Note that in both examples, procuring dinner and winning a chess match, problem solving is fairly open-ended; there are numerous possible pathways through the problem space. There is almost always more than one way to accomplish a goal—more than one way to traverse the problem space to take yourself from where you *are* to where you *want to be*. We see this open-endedness manifest in the choices that people make in daily life. Often people pursue similar goals but go about achieving them in very different ways. Educators understand this; sometimes teachers will encourage students to explore different pathways to accomplish a goal, implicitly encouraging them to engage in problem solving.

Not all pathways through a problem space will result in success, and not all paths that lead to the desired end-state will be efficient. Efficiency is therefore not guaranteed in problem solving. Even when a valued goal is achieved, there could well be mistakes, missteps, and counterproductive actions. In some ways, then, problem solving is risky. The potential for missteps and the possibility of failure present challenges for the individual and for the group—particularly if there are expectations that problem solutions should be straightforward and error-free. Problem solving has, for these reasons, sometimes been compared to traveling through a maze. Some routes will take you to the goal, but others—even those that look promising—may take you too far afield or leave you in a blind alley.

Heuristics

There is no set procedure for problem solving; if there were (such as an algorithm), then the activity would not be problem solving. But if there is no set procedure, what guides the problem-solving process? Problem solving relies on **heuristics**, which are rules of thumb that increase the likelihood of success but don't guarantee it. Consider the most basic heuristic: **trial and error**. When you enter an unfamiliar room, sometimes you want to turn on a particular lamp. The trouble is that the light switches on the wall don't tell you which one connects to the lamp in the corner. If there are two rocker switches, then within two moves you ought to get the desired result. This is trial and error at its best because the number of possible moves is highly restricted. Two on-off switches present only four combinations. The cost of an error is very low—the loss of only a split second of time. Other kinds of problem solving, such as surgery, do not lend themselves to trial and error. For more complex problems, other heuristics are needed.

General Heuristics

A good problem solver has several different heuristics at his or her disposal. General heuristics apply to many different kinds of problems and include means-ends analysis, working backward, and working forward.

MEANS-ENDS ANALYSIS. Taking an action that will reduce the distance between the current state and the goal state—or **means-ends analysis**—is the most common general heuristic. Note that the objective is not to *solve* the problem in a single step, nor even to integrate that step into a coherent plan. The immediate goal is much more modest than that; it is simply to *make progress toward* the goal.

Means-ends analysis is not guaranteed to succeed. The incremental step you take might seem to bring you closer to your goal, but sometimes it will turn out to be counterproductive. Still, means-ends analysis is a good heuristic if it results in true progress most of the time. Intuitively, we recognize that some kinds of problem solving are too complex for us to plan our way through from beginning to end. We need to content ourselves with incremental progress—with doing the next thing that will bring us closer to the goal that we desire. Think of the college freshman arriving at the dorms for orientation. The grand goal—a bachelor's degree—is too much to take in when the more immediate needs are to figure out how to register for classes and how to do laundry.

WORKING BACKWARD. By considering what we ultimately want to achieve, and then asking, "What would be the step just prior to that?" we are using the **working backward heuristic**. This sequence involves repeatedly working backwards from distant goals to more proximal goals that we can act on. Building a house works this way. First, a design is selected. Then, based on the architectural plans, subcontracts are arranged to prepare the foundation, frame the house, and install plumbing and electricity. Subcontractors, in turn, know what materials they need, and make arrangements accordingly. The house design is the ultimate goal that drives all the other constituent activities. The key is to break the problem down by moving from distant goals to more immediate ones, and then to take action on the more immediate goals. Career aspirations can be guided by a working backward heuristic. For a person who someday wants to become president of the United States, the step just prior to the presidency might be state governor, and before that, city mayor or movie star.

The working backward heuristic is similar to a design process called **reverse engineering**. Sometimes engineers want to understand how a competitor's product is designed and how it works so that they can replicate it or build a better product. Reverse engineering starts with the final product, and then asks what manufacturing steps went into making it. It involves taking something apart in order to put it back together again.

WORKING FORWARD. In applying the **working forward heuristic**, a problem solver recognizes the look and feel of the problem and knows what to do next. This is what an expert does. Through exposure to thousands of problems in a particular field, an expert comes to recognize familiar problems. A family doctor might be presented with a set of symptoms in a patient and think, "This pattern looks familiar. I think I know what diagnostic tests to run." Likewise, car mechanics, movie directors, artists, and teachers all recognize familiar problem situations in their domains. If the current conditions look familiar, those conditions generate a strong sense of what to do next. Problem solving, in this way, works forward from present conditions to ultimate solutions.

SUBGOALING. All of these heuristics, in one way or another, involve breaking down a larger problem into smaller subproblems. This process is sometimes called **subgoaling**. It's as if the grand problem by itself is simply too daunting to take on. For the sake of cognitive simplicity, it must be broken down into problems that are more manageable. Sometimes, even those subproblems must be broken down further into still smaller subproblems. Eventually, by breaking down large problems into smaller pieces, they become tractable in the sense that they can suggest specific action. Inasmuch as problem solving is guided by ultimate goal states, those large goals can be broken down into smaller, more manageable subgoals.

Domain-Specific Heuristics

Unlike general heuristics, in which rules of thumb are applied to many different kinds of problems (from making dinner to becoming President), domain-specific heuristics have strong applicability within particular knowledge and skill domains (Mayer & Wittrock, 2006).

MATHEMATICS. Mathematics is not primarily concerned with such activities as computing percentages or long division. Authentic mathematics more truly involves trying to accomplish a goal with a set of conceptual or procedural tools, but without a predetermined pathway. In other words, most of real mathematics is problem solving, not algorithmic computation.

Over the centuries, mathematicians have developed a set of informal heuristics that can assist their own problem-solving pursuits. One heuristic is to draw a diagram of the problem. If the mathematician is having trouble making progress in the medium of mathematical symbols, then sometimes drawing a graphic depiction of the problem can lead to an insight that advances the problem-solving process. A number of heuristics specific to mathematics have been developed. However, they were not explicitly formulated until the mathematician Polya (1957) described them in his book *How to Solve It*.

Besides the heuristic of drawing a picture, Polya recognized several other heuristics that he saw as an important part of a mathematician's knowledge and skill base. They include:

- Try to think of a related problem.
- Separate the parts of the problem.
- Try to solve part of the problem.
- Check each step of the solution.

Several of Polya's heuristics are general enough to apply not only to mathematics, but also to other domains. When applied to mathematics problems, the heuristics are valuable for the professional mathematician as well as for the student of mathematics. Taking up this idea several decades after Polya, mathematics education professor Alan Schoenfeld (1992) taught heuristics to students to guide them during mathematical problem solving. Schoenfeld found that as the students acquired a working knowledge of domain-specific problem-solving heuristics, their performance improved substantially. They became better mathematicians as a result of their greater knowledge of heuristics, and their ability to apply those heuristics to mathematical problem solving.

WRITING. Domain-specific heuristics are valuable for problem solving in many activities other than mathematics, such as writing. There is no formula for how a writer goes about producing an excellent product, whether a novel, short story, essay, scientific paper, or newspaper editorial. Always, though, writers engage their specific form of problem solving with specific rules of thumb or heuristics, such as the following:

- *Write about what you know.* It seems pointless to try to write with conviction or interest if you are writing on a topic that you know little about.

- *Be organized.* Write from a plan about how the ideas should be structured.

- *Be clear.* Make your ideas as transparent as possible. Try not to be vague or excessively wordy.

Over time, with practice and coaching, the writer incorporates these domain-specific heuristics (as well as others) into his or her writing habits. These heuristics help to form that writer's particular writing style.

WHEN EXPERTS SOLVE PROBLEMS. Expertise is relevant to education in part because the expert presents a kind of idealized goal for learners to achieve. In some ways, it determines the direction of the learners' development—toward that idealized goal of expert status.

Think about expertise as it relates to problem solving. When experts solve problems, they often use heuristics that are tailored to their areas of expertise: domain-specific heuristics. Do experts ever use general heuristics? They must do so when faced with a problem that is novel to them. Sometimes even experts confront problems—whether by choice or not—that are far beyond their previous experience. Such was the case in the design of the Sydney Opera House. In terms of aesthetics and structural design, it was unique and completely unprecedented. How did the Danish architect Jørn Utzon go about specifying such an innovative design so that it could actually be built? No doubt the project required a lot of domain knowledge and domain-specific heuristics to solve the design problems. But certainly it also involved general problem-solving heuristics for some of its more far-reaching elements, especially its bold, shell-shaped rooflines. Other great innovations—heart transplants and hybrid engines—emerge in the same way.

Experts depend enormously on their vast knowledge base to do what they do. Extensive knowledge largely defines who an expert is. And yet we know that experts often take on challenges that extend beyond their current knowledge and prior experience. When experts solve problems, their domain knowledge interacts with their problem-solving skills (including heuristics) in a powerful way. Let's not minimize either domain knowledge or problem-solving skills in understanding what an expert does. For Herbert Simon, these are "the two blades of scissors." Neither is particularly impressive by itself, but in combination they are amazingly versatile and effective.

FIGURE 5.2

The Sydney Opera House. *With this design, architect Jørn Utzon displayed exquisite problem-solving ability.* [Copyright 2009 by Wayne and Karen Brown.]

Problem Solving and Emotions

One very human aspect of problem solving—the implications of problem solving on emotions—deserves attention. Problem solving can evoke strong feelings, and these emotions can threaten the problem-solving process. The problem solver often does not know what to do next, and may be well aware of the possibility of failure. Because of the uncertainties attendant to all problem-solving behavior, certain emotions—disorientation, confusion, and anxiety—might stand in the way of success (Wertime, 1979).

THE DISCOMFORT OF UNCERTAINTY. The prospect of failure can be highly threatening. We all want to convey competence to other people. Whenever there is a possibility of feeling incompetent or foolish, our sense of self-worth is threatened (Covington, 1984). If each of us wants to preserve our sense of self-worth, and problem solving by its nature involves uncertainty—then the two might be in conflict. In fact, some people actively try to avoid situations that evoke feelings of uncertainty. For many, the act of problem solving is highly threatening. They would prefer to follow a set procedure. Here, then, is another challenge for the teacher: If the goal is to encourage problem solving among students, how can that be accomplished given the possibility of ego threat?

PROBLEM SOLVING AND THE CULTURE OF SCHOOLING. The emotional threat to students posed by problem solving might be aggravated by the typical values and expectations found in schools. Clearly, traditional school processes implicitly value error-free performance and confidence of success. These expectations run counter to everything we know about problem solving. Confidence is not warranted if it means blind faith that one is taking the right path. Instead, problem solving requires being open to the possibility that a different path might be better. The value of error-free performance is also misplaced because, in almost every case, problem solving entails missteps and setbacks. We must remember that problem solving, by its very nature, involves error and uncertainty. Whenever educators see these as faults or weaknesses, problem solving will be thwarted, and the learning process will be reduced to the memorization of pre-formed knowledge and algorithmic skills.

The point is to convey that *it's all right* to have feelings of uncertainty because those feelings are part of problem solving. But how often is the opposite communicated to students? Are students told implicitly that errors are always bad? Do students and teachers feel embarrassed when they are not sure of what to do next? Does uncertainty suggest a lack of ability or low intelligence? Teachers, principals, and all education leaders can play a role in shifting the values and expectations in schools to be more consistent with the nature of problem solving. Errors and uncertainty do not signify that something is wrong. On the contrary, they may well be evidence that problem solvers are hard at work.

Problem Solving and Human Purpose

As we engage in routine tasks in our everyday lives, we rely on habits and regimens that are simple and dependable, and do not constitute problem solving *per se*. But the things we care most about do seem to be problems in the sense that they have no obvious solution. These worthy problems include:

- Being successful at work.
- Being a good parent.
- Being a good spouse.

- Becoming an educated person.
- Being a good friend.

There is no formula for accomplishing these goals. Even if they are reduced to more concrete objectives, the subgoals still require problem solving. Remember the original definition of problem solving: the pursuit of a goal (which often involves the things we care about the most) when the path to that goal is uncertain. To reach our most valued goals in life, and to be successful people, we need to engage in problem solving. We need to teach our students to be problem solvers so that they, too, can reach for the kind of life they most hope for.

Earlier, we noted that a problem space consists of an initial state, a goal state, and a set of legal moves. But sometimes the ultimate goal is fuzzy. We might have only a vague idea of what we want to achieve. A thick haze might also obscure our "initial conditions" and "legal moves"—these, too, might be hard to define precisely. In other words, some worthwhile problems are **ill-structured problems** (Simon, 1973). Ill-structured problems require the problem solver to sharpen and clarify goals, and to select and modify strategies, as problem solving proceeds. This kind of problem solving is more demanding than well-structured and pre-defined conventional problems. This brings us to the topic of problem finding.

If the many worthwhile goals of our lives significantly involve problem-solving activities, there is a question of what goals to pursue. Which of the innumerable problems that we *could* pursue are worthy of our time, attention, and sustained effort? If we can attempt to solve only a limited number of problems, which problems are best to tackle? In a free society, each of us engages in the task of **problem finding** (Arlin, 1989; Mackworth, 1965). Problem finding is a counterpart to problem solving that entails imagining potential problems, and determining which problems are worthy of our efforts. We cannot solve every problem—not even every worthwhile problem—so we must choose. The term *problem finding* suggests opportunities, which in turn suggests something good. Earlier we noted that the use of the word *problem* in everyday conversation carries a definite negative connotation—as in, "You think *you* have problems. Let me tell you about *mine*." When we use the word *problem* in the context of problem solving or problem finding, the word indicates a goal whose attainment is not guaranteed. A problem in this sense might be negative (such as environmental pollution), but it might well be positive (such as an opportunity for career advancement).

Here's one more thought about problem solving as it pertains to professionalism. People sometimes disagree about whether teaching is a profession or not (Ornstein & Levine, 2003). Teaching is unequivocally a profession precisely because it involves problem solving in every aspect. Other professions—medicine and law, for example—are essentially problem-solving activities. True, they draw on an extensive base of knowledge and skill, but these need to be applied insightfully, not formulaically, with every patient or client. Likewise, teaching well is never accomplished by following a formula. It's never a recipe. A teacher, rather, has a problem to solve—how to advance learning and thinking among her students. Therefore, to be an excellent teacher is to be a problem solver, and to be a problem solver is to be a professional.

Critical Thinking

Problem solving is not the only form of complex cognition. There are many others. But of all the ways in which we engage our minds, perhaps there is only one other kind of complex thinking that rises in importance to the level of problem solving: **critical thinking**.

Testing the Quality of Ideas

There are differences between problem solving and critical thinking. Most fundamentally, problem solving focuses on choosing a course of action to achieve a goal. It involves making decisions about *what to do*. Critical thinking, on the other hand, is about evaluating ideas for their quality. Suppose you read a newspaper editorial that takes a position different from the one you hold. To be a good thinker, you need to ask: Does this make sense? Is there evidence for what this person is saying? Is the argument rational and logical? Whenever you ask such questions, you are thinking critically.

So roughly, problem solving and critical thinking can be characterized by the questions they pose:

- Problem solving: What to do?
- Critical thinking: What is true?

These two can overlap: Effective problem solving might well entail critical thinking. We need to understand in order to act. Or as part of critical thinking we might need to go searching for evidence, a form of problem solving. So these two—problem solving and critical thinking—work together in an organic way. They involve other kinds of complex cognition that we will consider in the pages ahead. Even if these forms of complex cognition often weave together, they are still distinguishable. By understanding the nature of each, we can improve our own thinking skills and help others, including students, to do the same.

Ask: Does This Make Sense?

Let's now move to a definition of critical thinking: *Critical thinking is the evaluation of ideas for their quality, especially in judging whether they make sense.* In trying to distinguish between problem solving and critical thinking, I suggested that critical thinking is largely connected to the question: What is true? But that's not entirely correct. In many cases we can't know confidently what is true about a given claim. Sometimes the claim is not even really about what is true—as in an editorial—but rather about what the facts mean. That's why critical thinking is more directly about whether ideas make sense—whether the ideas hold together in a way that makes them believable.

Undoubtedly the process of finding out whether or not ideas makes sense is complex and somewhat personal, but we can hold up certain criteria that work well—criteria that have long been used by philosophers (and perhaps unwittingly, by yourself). Two important criteria are coherence and correspondence.

Coherence is whether ideas are internally consistent rather than contradictory. Normally we expect coherence from other people. If we perceive a lack of coherence, it's unlikely that we will be persuaded to their point of view. If they can't keep their story straight, why would we believe them? Such was the situation faced by Alice in Lewis Carroll's *Alice's Adventures in Wonderland* (1865). Even though we are entertained by Alice's intolerably confusing situation, perhaps we feel a little sorry for her for having to endure the perpetual *lack* of coherence provoked by the Cheshire Cat, the Mad Hatter, and the Queen of Hearts.

Correspondence is about data. Do the claims have data backing them? Is there a correspondence between what is claimed and the available facts? If someone claims that smoking is good for your health, you will likely want that claim backed up by

evidence of some sort. Likewise for the innumerable other claims you hear or read about: A critical thinker looks for data to back up claims. Evidence is important—it might not always be available and it will rarely be definitive. But even if evidence is lacking, the claim need not necessarily be rejected. It may be *entertained* as a *possibility*, rather than accepted fully.

Calibrating the Quality of Knowledge

The notion that we can entertain ideas without fully accepting or rejecting them tells us something about knowledge. Much of what we "know" is provisional. How much of our knowledge do we really believe is completely and unequivocally true? Probably very little. What, then, does our knowledge consist of? If you think about it, most of our knowledge consists of beliefs that we hold with varying degrees of confidence. Some ideas we believe very strongly (Mom loves me); others have some evidence in their favor, but are not at all certain (coffee, chocolate, and red wine are all health-promoting); still others might be unlikely, but not impossible (there are intelligent extraterrestrials).

The realization that ideas vary in quality is one consequence of the **constructivist** view of knowledge. If we accept that knowledge is not some sort of direct readout from experience in the world (see **naive realism** in Chapter 4), then the knowledge we construct is related to the world but it is not identical to it. We may hold beliefs that are inaccurate or incomplete. Truth, then, is not a ripe peach ready to be plucked from a tree. It must be constructed, critiqued, and—ideally—improved over time. The quest of science is fully consistent with this view. The driving objective is to continually test theories, to find their inadequacies, and then to build better theories. The hoped-for result is progressively deeper insight into how nature operates. In the social sciences the goal is much the same—to build better theories about how human beings think and behave. A similar progressive direction toward better ideas is the ideal goal of learning in individuals, too. Critical thinking can advance this goal because, as we test and revise ideas, they can become more accurate, more insightful, and more explanatory.

Such a view of knowledge ought to result in certain attitudes and beliefs. If what we believe so confidently could well be wrong, then the appropriate attitude ought to be humility about what we *think* we know. Humility is just what the philosopher Socrates wanted from his students in ancient Greece. Often, when educators think of Socrates, the "Socratic Method" of teaching comes to mind. The Socratic Method involves teaching by asking a series of questions. By posing questions to young philosophers, Socrates was able to evoke what they knew about a topic—such as justice, love, or virtue (Palmer, 2001). Inevitably, the dialogues resulted in much greater clarity about what was known and what was unknown.

Typically, the young philosophers approached the master, Socrates, fully confident that they understood the topic under consideration. Socrates responded with feigned delight—finally, he exclaimed, he found a young student who was truly wise! Then, gingerly, Socrates would ask a simple question to probe the student's understanding. When the young philosopher could not answer, this revealed a tiny gap in his presumed edifice of understanding. Socrates would follow this question with other innocent-sounding questions, which resulted eventually in the young philosopher's admission that he really knew nothing at all about justice, love, or virtue. In some cases, the truth was devastating: The young philosopher was reduced to tears as he faced the depths of his own ignorance. That was precisely the outcome Socrates wanted. Now, Socrates would declare, both he and the young philosopher could proceed together toward understanding. The prerequisite for pursuing knowledge was an admission that they really did not understand.

FIGURE 5.4

Socrates. *He was masterful at cultivating critical thinking among his pupils.* [Nick Nicholls/The British Museum]

Socrates was a critical thinker *par excellence*. He knew how much he did not know. In fact, Socrates declared that he was the most ignorant man in Athens. In his favor, he said, was that at least he *knew* that he was the most ignorant man in Athens, and this self-knowledge must be good for something.

Many other philosophers through the ages pondered the nature of knowledge, as Socrates did. They wanted to understand *how we know what we know*—a branch of philosophy called **epistemology**. As described in Chapter 4, Socrates, like many other philosophers, wanted a strong epistemology—a way of establishing knowledge that would result in a high degree of confidence in beliefs. In the case of Socrates and many others, this project required deep questioning of assumptions, which sometimes led to despair that certain knowledge could ever be attained. The eminent French philosopher René Descartes took a very strong position on the certainty of knowledge. Descartes (1641) began a major philosophical project by doubting *everything*. Descartes's method, which he called **radical doubt**, is a bit extreme. But for those interested in advancing critical thinking, a certain degree of doubt is appropriate. Doubt can lead to a deeper questioning of claims and beliefs, and this stance toward knowledge is what critical thinking is all about.

Without a doubt, part of the agenda of advancing complex cognition is to cultivate critical thinking. A good thinker will never hold all that he believes with absolute confidence. Instead, a good thinker will know how much confidence to place in a particular claim or belief. The knowledge we hold is distributed across a range of believability, based on evidence and coherence. To hold beliefs with graded confidence as to their validity is difficult. It takes more intellectual work than simply believing or disbelieving, but it is consistent with what we know about both knowledge and good thinking. Philosophers have exercised critical thinking for many centuries. Critical thinking is good for us, too. In an era when we are bombarded with truth claims, it's more important than ever that we, and our students, practice critical thinking as a way of life.

Inferential Reasoning

One broad and important category of complex cognition is inferential reasoning. The term is based on the word **inference**, which is the cognitive act of "going beyond the information given" to draw a new conclusion; using the available data, X, to generate a conclusion, Y (Bruner, 1973).

Our minds are so completely dedicated to inference that our many daily inferential acts go largely unnoticed. For example, we have expectations about how people will behave and we act accordingly. We do not know for certain that our best friend will not lace our meal with arsenic, but based on our previous experience and what we believe about the feelings and commitments of friends, we trust most people not to harm us intentionally. These assumptions and the inferences that result (e.g., the food is safe to eat) work well *most* of the time.

In addition to the everyday assumptions we make about the regularity of people's behavior, we also "read into" variations in their behavior. For example, you can infer that Nancy is in a bad mood today because of her facial expression and her curt replies to your questions. It's not certain that she is in a bad mood, but your conclusion is a reasonable inference based on what you can observe. We often engage is this kind of reasoning; inference is a continuous reality of our mental lives. We constantly form beliefs that go beyond what we can observe directly. So common is the mental act of inference that the human mind has sometimes been called an *inference engine*.

Of course, just because inference is common to our mental experience doesn't mean that it is always right. Whenever we infer, we can err. Have you ever angered someone because that person misinterpreted what you said? You *meant* one thing, but the other person *thought* you meant something else. The other person inferred your meaning—incorrectly, as it turned out. Such "misunderstandings" are really just one form of inference gone wrong. Unfortunately, unwarranted inferences about what other people think or believe is probably a major source of interpersonal strife and emotional turmoil. When judging other people's beliefs and intentions, it's easy to get it wrong without realizing it.

Inductive Reasoning

Let's now delve into the two basic kinds of inference: inductive reasoning and deductive reasoning (Nickerson, 1986). Think of these as going in opposite directions. **Inductive reasoning** is moving upward from specific facts and experiences to a broader generalization. Let's say that you independently meet several Canadians during the course of a year. Each of them is kind, thoughtful, and friendly. You feel confident that you could ask each person for help, and the Canadian goodwill would come through for you. Now you start to form an opinion: Canadian people are really nice. Of course, you don't think that this applies to every single Canadian, but as a generalization (which is what inductive reasoning produces) it works pretty well.

We use inductive reasoning whenever we form a generalization from limited data. When you think about it, limited data is usually all we have. We almost never have all the facts. Consequently, whenever we induce larger patterns of meaning and significance, we do so from limited information. This is how science proceeds. Think of Charles Darwin's voyage aboard the *Beagle* (Gould, 1992). Working alone, Darwin could only collect a limited amount of data on species variation among the birds of the Galapagos Islands. Darwin observed that even among the remote islands of the Galapagos, birds varied significantly according to the ecological niche they occupied. Their beaks were adapted accordingly—some long, some short, some curved. Based on these limited data, Darwin was able to formulate a far-reaching generalization that could account for these facts: Birds vary naturally, and the ones with characteristics suited to their local environments are better able to survive and reproduce. This was inductive reasoning of a very high order. It produced a single powerful generalization that could account for, and make sense of, innumerable and diverse facts. It applied not only to birds, but also to every single life form, not only in the Galapagos Islands, but also around the world. For biology, the value of this breakthrough was incalculable.

As the example of Charles Darwin demonstrates, inductive reasoning is an important part of scientific reasoning. A scientist gathers data to try to find a more general pattern; that pattern might place a large number of individual observations into a simpler, more general statement, model, theory, or equation. It's all about seeking simplicity—identifying the larger pattern. Grand simplifications in the history of science have been tremendously powerful: Pasteur's germ theory of disease, Copernicus' heliocentric model of the solar system, and Newton's Laws of Motion. All are grand examples of inductive reasoning that moved from specific observations to large, powerful, and enduring truths.

Here is an example of inductive reasoning that is not so grand: Near your apartment there are two Thai restaurants, one of which you've visited at least ten times because the food has been very good. You have visited the other Thai restaurant twice; you don't remember the first visit, but the second was not a pleasant experience. Based on this experience, you engaged in a little inductive reasoning and came to a more general conclusion: One Thai restaurant is really good; the other is not. However, you could be wrong about the second Thai restaurant because you have only one reliable data point—your last meal there.

It is important to remember that inductive reasoning can go wrong. The history of science is not a straight arrow of progress from one brilliant insight to another. Over the centuries, scientists (previously called *natural philosophers*) sometimes generated theories that were completely bogus. One famous example in biology is Lamarckism, which is the belief that acquired characteristics can be inherited. The theory held that as giraffes stretched their necks to reach the high leaves in acacia trees, their necks would grow in response. Subsequent generations of giraffes would have long necks as a result. This example is not isolated—strange theories also emerged in other branches of science. In everyday life, we sometimes form opinions that are quite wrong—that is, unsubstantiated by data. Prejudices about this or that group of people are egregious examples of inductive reasoning gone tragically awry. Superstitions and paranoias further illustrate the vulnerability of inference to error.

Even though it can go wrong, inductive reasoning is an incredibly productive intellectual tool. All of science is based on inductive reasoning, and refinements of inductive reasoning are part of the scientific method. Inductive reasoning is also woven into the fabric of our mental experience in everyday life. For these reasons, helping students to become good inductive reasoners is an important goal of education. Students should search the general rule—the overall explanatory pattern—but should also be careful

FIGURE 5.5
Inductive Reasoning Gone Awry.
Lamarck's theory that the long neck of a giraffe is acquired by repeated reaching toward higher branches shows how inductive reasoning can go awry. [DK]

before placing full confidence in that generalization. Remember, one limitation of our humanity is that we do not have access to all available data. Our knowledge, beliefs, and expectations must be based on partial information. Therefore, inductive generalizations are always suspect, at least to some degree.

INSIGHT. In the everyday language about thinking, **insight** and discovery have rather direct associations with inductive reasoning. Consider insight to be a special kind of inductive reasoning in which a meaningful pattern emerges very quickly. One minute we can't see the logic or order of a situation; the next minute everything becomes perfectly clear. The pieces fit together instantly to form something that makes sense—this is the sudden experience of insight.

Insight does not necessarily occur in the time span we would wish, however. Being in a hurry or stepping up effort does not necessarily increase the likelihood of experiencing insight. These apparent paradoxes interested the German Gestalt psychologists of the early twentieth century. One of the psychologists in this group, Wolfgang Kohler, studied insight in a chimpanzee called Sultan. Kohler concluded that Sultan was able to find nonobvious solutions to obtain his goal, which was often a bunch of bananas. For example, Sultan could stack boxes to reach a banana cluster hanging from the ceiling in his cage.

In humans, we know that the singular moment of insight is often part of an extended process. One classic model recognizes four stages: preparation, incubation, illumination, and verification (Wallas, 1926). The stage of *preparation* recognizes that the chances for insight occurring are more favorable when a person has the necessary background knowledge. Certainly, Charles Darwin's training as a naturalist provided the mental preparation that would later make his insight a penetrating one. The second stage is incubation. The word *incubation* brings to mind a bird egg under a warm light (or under a warm hen) until the time is just right for the egg to hatch. Incubation can't be rushed. Sometimes insight requires relaxation and disengagement from the problem for a while. The potential of incubation is expressed in the "bed-bath-bus phenomenon," which playfully claims that great insights often occur when their discoverers are taking it easy, through such activities as lying in bed, soaking in a bathtub, or riding on a city bus. The third stage is *illumination*—the instant "aha" when the insight crystallizes in the mind. Finally, there is *verification*, when the flash of insight that initially seems so right is put to a rigorous test.

DISCOVERY. The process of discovery, like that of insight, proceeds from specific data to a larger, more explanatory pattern. **Discovery** refers to the act of attaining new knowledge about the world—especially the natural world. It may be sudden (involving insight), or it may be extended over a long period of time. Although the process of discovery seems highly mysterious to many people, Herbert Simon instead saw it as rather straightforward and easily comprehensible. Simply stated, discovery is a matter of pattern recognition. The crucial factor in Simon's model of discovery is the preparatory knowledge that allows the discovery to be made once the discoverable pattern presents itself.

The concept of discovery can guide approaches to teaching, particularly in science education. Discovery teaching is an alternative to teacher-centered didactic instruction. Rather than students being told directly about key ideas in science, they "discover" those concepts from data, typically through some sort of lab activity. **Discovery learning**, then, is the application of inductive reasoning to a theory of instruction, wherein the chief goal is to have the student infer larger explanatory principles from direct experience and analysis of data gathered first-hand. While discovery learning is attractive in concept, insufficient guidance by a teacher can sometimes lead to poor learning outcomes (Kirschner, Sweller, & Clark, 2006).

Deductive Reasoning

Remember that inferential reasoning is of two basic types: inductive and deductive. In the last few sections, we have been considering inductive reasoning, which is an upward generalization from particular data to more general patterns, principles, truths, laws, and theories. Now we'll consider the counterpart of inductive reasoning, which is deductive reasoning. Deductive reasoning is inference that proceeds downward from generalizations, theories, and principles to specific predictions or applications. If you know you are lactose intolerant, then you can predict that you will have severe stomach pains if you eat a slice of cheese pizza. That's deduction—general to specific. But how do you come to know that you are lactose intolerant? A few instances of upset stomach after consuming dairy products leads to a general conclusion: I'm lactose intolerant! That's induction.

In everyday thinking, inductive and deductive reasoning complement each other. If we can form a generalization (through induction), that generalization allows us to make predictions and so guides our choices (through deduction). The processes of induction and deduction, as forms of inferential reasoning, are deeply woven into the fabric of our mental lives. We continually look for order in our world, and then on the basis of the order we find, we make decisions and take actions. Induction and deduction are component processes of an intelligent mind, and in combination they are very powerful. This is not to say that they will never lead us astray. As you already know, whenever we infer (go beyond the data given), we can err. But even when we accept this possibility, we can be sure that induction and deduction are power tools in our cognitive toolbox.

Deductive reasoning has been the subject of considerable study by logicians. In fact, the most basic reasoning form in logic, the **syllogism**, is a form of deductive reasoning. A simple syllogism includes two premises, such as:

- All men are mortal.

- Socrates is a man.

    The two premises lead naturally to a conclusion:

- Socrates is mortal.

Note that the classical syllogism has an if–then structure. The premises are "if" statements; the conclusion is a "then" statement. For logicians, the truth status of the premises is not important. They can be complete nonsense. What matters to a logician is the validity of the reasoning process, in particular the validity of conclusions drawn from premises, even if the premises are not strictly true.

If-then deductive reasoning can be much more difficult than the *Socrates is mortal* example. The potential difficulty of deductive reasoning is illustrated in the Wason card task (Wason & Johnson-Laird, 1972). The layout of the task is simple, consisting of four cards. Each card is printed with a letter or number on both the front and reverse sides, as follows:

E   K   4   7

The task is to test the following rule:
If the card has a vowel on one side, it has an even number on the other side.

The challenge is to turn over only the minimum number of cards necessary to test the rule. Which cards would you need to turn over?

It seems necessary to turn over the E card. If the rule is true, then the flip side of the E card will have an even number. If you see an odd number, the rule is false.

On the other hand, it seems *un*necessary to turn over the K card. After all, the rule says nothing about consonants. So the K card could have anything on the other side, and the rule would not be contradicted.

Two cards remain: Which should be turned over? Here's where most people go astray. Only one of the cards, 4 or 7, can detect a contradiction in the rule. Which one is it? Most people choose to turn over the 4 card, perhaps seeking to confirm the rule by looking for a vowel. But what if the 4 card has a consonant on the other side? Again, the rule says nothing about consonants, so the 4 card cannot prove or disprove the rule.

Instead the 7 card must be turned over. That's because if the 7 has a vowel on the other side, the rule is contradicted. Summarizing, then, only the E card and the 7 card have the potential to contradict the rule, and therefore to prove it untrue.

Based on this task, we might be tempted to use inductive reasoning to form a generalization, such as: Humans are bad at deductive reasoning. This generalization would not be entirely wrong. But to gain a better hold on why the Wason task is so difficult, let's consider what happens when the same basic problem is presented in a slightly different form (Wason & Shapiro, 1971).

| Manchester | Sheffield | Train | Car |

Now let's test a new rule: *Every time I go to Manchester I travel by train.*

Which cards would you turn over to test the rule? You would turn over the Manchester card, certainly. You would not need to turn over the Sheffield card. To disconfirm the hypothesis, you would need to check the other side of only one other card. Which one? It's the Car card. If it says Manchester on the other side, the rule does not hold up. Now the interesting result of this variation on the Wason card task is that most people are successful at it.

Because performance on the Wason task improves dramatically when it is cloaked in an everyday context that people can relate to, we must modify our initial generalization. It seems that, in general, people are not very good at *decontextualized* deductive reasoning—the kind that logicians study. But people are generally fairly successful—or at least much more so—when deductive reasoning is contextualized in everyday problems and situations. This finding would give people who hold to the **situated cognition** view (that knowledge is inextricably embedded in a cultural matrix) a reason to say: "See, I told you so."

To recap, we have been speaking about inferential reasoning as one important category of complex cognition (along with problem solving, critical thinking, and others). Inferential reasoning is what we do when we "go beyond the information given"— when we form a conclusion based on partial information. And let's face it: we almost always have only partial information. We have recognized two forms of inferential reasoning: inductive and deductive. Inductive reasoning moves from specific facts to general conclusions, which can be as vaunted as a scientific theory or as mundane as whether a restaurant serves good food. Deductive reasoning works the other way, from the general to the specific. Once we understand something, then we can draw specific conclusions about what to believe or how to act. In combination, inductive and deductive reasoning constitute a vital sector of complex cognition.

Creativity

To round out the discussion of the three categories of complex cognition (problem solving, critical thinking, and inferential reasoning), let's consider a fourth form of cognition: creativity. Creativity has a unique way of enhancing human experience in both the life of the creative person and the lives of others. Creativity is human thought at its best.

Creativity can be difficult to understand because it seems to be even more complex than the other forms of cognition we have considered. Creativity is slippery—it's hard to pin down and define. Worse still, trying to be precise about what creative thinking is can sometimes distort the phenomenon. For example, some approaches to creativity have concentrated on **divergent production**. This refers to thinking about the uses of objects or the connections between ideas in ways that extend beyond, or even violate, their traditional associations. Creativity certainly can involve the generation of unconventional ideas. But by itself, this realization does not take us very far. Divergent thinking—the ability to generate new ideas—is only one of several processes that contribute to creativity (Lubart, 1994). Divergent thinking is not equivalent to creativity. At best, it is one element of the creative process.

Another approach to creativity is an attempt to concentrate on the created product. This approach recognizes that the most valued expressions of creativity in our society are those that result in some socially valued product. By definition, then, the nature of creativity will vary widely from field to field. What is the meaning of creativity when the word is applied to cooking, car design, surgery, poetry, architecture, music, or teaching? Once we acknowledge that creativity is linked to specific domains of creative behavior, then it seems harder to find the unifying processes that bind these together. Creativity then begins to resemble a syndrome with various manifestations that have a certain family resemblance, rather than a fundamental unity (Mumford & Gustafson, 1988). Are certain people highly creative in a general way, or is creativity always bounded by specific knowledge and skill domains? Our best evidence suggests that the truth is somewhere in the middle: Creativity is neither totally specific to particular fields, nor is it completely general. In other words, people who display creativity in one field are somewhat more likely to be creative in another field, but only moderately so.

Background knowledge is key to creativity. Significant creative thought almost always requires extensive background knowledge (Nickerson, 1999). Here we see a parallel to problem solving: By itself, problem solving skill is of limited value, but when it is combined with a significant knowledge base, the result can be truly remarkable. The same seems to apply to creativity. When a creative mind is also a knowledgeable mind, wonderful things can happen.

Still, knowledge is not enough. Even if a person acquires extensive background knowledge, creative products are not guaranteed. Creativity implies something more—seeing old ideas in new ways, combining ideas that are ordinarily kept separate, inventing something that evokes surprise. Personality characteristics come into play; creative people tend to have unusual perseverance, an openness to new experience, and a high tolerance for ambiguity (Lubart, 1994). The environment also matters; some conditions encourage experimentation, free-thinking, and the generation of possibilities. Creativity theories affirm that social environments—either school or workplace—can promote idea generation or suppress it, support cognitive autonomy or squeeze it out. Much as different social environments encourage problem solving or critical thinking, some actively cultivate the open-minded thinking that creativity requires.

Let's be careful in our assumptions about which practices encourage creativity and which do not (Nickerson, 1999). Brainstorming, for example, is a group process that is supposed to generate lots of creative ideas, often with the goal of solving a particular problem. The traditional ground rule of brainstorming is that negative comments are not allowed. Criticism is banned in order to get all participants to think freely and to express ideas openly, no matter how wacky those ideas are. The presumption is that the lack of censorship will result in a pool of ideas that ranges widely, with some likelihood that at least a few good ideas will be contained in the mix. Later, the sifting process winnows out the weaker ideas from the more promising ones.

Unfortunately, only minimal evidence suggests that brainstorming really works. The quality of ideas resulting from the group processes are often no better than the

INTEREST MAGNET 5.1

Synesthesia: The Color of Music

Starting in the late 1800s, psychologists began to study the strange phenomenon of people who experience sounds as colors or shapes as tastes. These experiences are called synesthesia, and people who have these experiences are synesthetes. Synesthesia involves blending two or more senses that are normally distinct.

More than 100 forms of synesthesia have been documented. In the most common form—grapheme-color synesthesia—letters of the alphabet appear to have particular colors. For example, the letter "A" commonly appears to be red or has a red outline around it. Certain letter sequences can evoke the sensation of a rainbow of color. Letters can change colors even as one letter is transformed into another. For example, when writer Patricia Lynne Duffy (2001) was sixteen years old, she recalled what happened when years earlier she learned how to change a "P" into an "R."

> I realized that to make an R all I had to do was first write a P and then draw a line down from its loop. And I was so surprised that I could turn a yellow letter into an orange letter just by adding a line (p. 1).

Duffy's father reacted with astonishment. Until then, Duffy had just assumed that everyone experienced letters of the alphabet and numerals as having distinct colors.

One fascinating form of synesthesia is music-color synesthesia, in which music evokes different color sensations depending on the pitch, timbre, or key. Synesthetes who report music-color correspondences often see colors streaming through their field of view as they listen to music. Colors elicited by music tend to be idiosyncratic, but in general, higher-pitched notes are more brightly colored. One very rare form of synesthesia is lexical-gustatory synesthesia in which different sounds evoke different taste sensations. One synesthete reported that the phoneme /k/ evokes the taste of an egg.

The reality of synesthesia is well documented. People with synesthesia show a very high reliability of reported experience (Ramachandran & Hubbard, 2003). For example, evoked colors are highly consistent even if testing is separated by long periods of time. Moreover, neuroimaging shows that patterns of brain activation differ between synesthetes and non-synesthetes. Grapheme-color synesthesia, for example, shows up in brain images as activation of the brain's color-processing regions. These areas do not "light up" in normal individuals.

No one knows for sure what causes synesthesia, although one theory is that it is caused by neuronal cross-wiring. Brain regions that process color are anatomically close to brain regions that process written symbols; neurons connecting the color and symbol functions may literally be "crossed." An alternative explanation is that neurotransmitters that control brain inhibitory processes may not work as effectively in synesthetes, causing brain activation to spill over to adjacent areas.

Synesthesia is rare; only about one person in 200 has the condition. Although the underlying neurology of synesthesia is abnormal, the condition seems not to be highly associated with psychopathology. In fact, the experience of synesthesia is most often reported as neutral or pleasant and may even have cognitive benefits. Research suggests that synesthesia can lead to enhanced memory or creativity, for example. It might also stimulate creativity by suggesting cross-sensory metaphors to express meaning in writing, painting, or music.

ideas of people working individually and separately. Brainstorming might be fun, and so might have value for building morale or team spirit, but as a mechanism for generating good ideas, it is no panacea. So, although we can use brainstorming as a group process in our lives and work, it might be wise to reserve judgment about the power of brainstorming to generate really creative ideas.

The cautions raised about brainstorming do not reduce the importance of attempting to enhance creativity. Just as education seeks to cultivate students' abilities to solve problems, to think critically, and to reason well, education should also cultivate students' ability to be creative. Our collective knowledge of creativity and how to improve it is not as developed as we would hope, despite considerable focused research over the decades. If we are honest, we will admit that creativity is a very difficult subject—but this admission in no way reduces its importance (Nickerson, 1999). What do we know about creativity? Let's remember that creative acts involve the application of knowledge in new and valuable ways. Teachers can advance creativity by appreciating the role of knowledge in the creative act, and also by setting conditions that accept and encourage free thinking in the use of that knowledge. Innovative ideas should be valued, but they should also be tested for their quality in the hope that some, perhaps a small percentage, will be both novel and excellent.

The Nature of Higher-Order Thought

Let's now consider broadly what the different kinds of complex cognition have in common. We have looked at four categories of complex cognition: problem solving, critical thinking, inferential reasoning, and creativity. Is there a thread that binds these together? They do indeed have some qualities in common. We noted at the start of this chapter that metacognition is manifest wherever we find complex cognition. But there is something else: Whenever we deal with complex cognition, our ideas can vary widely in quality. It's not that every idea is simply true or false. Rather, because ideas are human constructions, they can range through a spectrum of quality from brilliantly insightful to humdrum, worthless, or just plain wrong.

If ideas vary in quality, then part of the job of engaging in complex cognition is evaluating ideas for their quality. For problem solving, what matters is the soundness of the tactics used and the worthiness of the problem. For critical thinking, it's whether the ideas as presented make sense. For inferential reasoning, the key concern is whether the reasoning processes that lead to particular conclusions are sound. For creativity, it's whether the creative product is an intellectual breakthrough that is functional and, possibly, aesthetically satisfying.

The Pinnacle of Bloom's Taxonomy

Decades ago, the educational psychologist Benjamin Bloom (1956) proposed a simple way to categorize thinking processes. He articulated six types of thinking processes arranged in order from the most basic to the most advanced: knowledge, comprehension, application, analysis, synthesis, and evaluation. The model, shown in Figure 5.6, has become famously known as Bloom's Taxonomy for the Cognitive Domain (Bloom, 1956; Anderson & Krathwohl, 2001).

At the pinnacle of Bloom's Taxonomy is the cognitive process of *evaluation*. Why did Bloom choose evaluation as the highest of all cognitive processes? If ideas vary in quality, then to evaluate ideas is to confront that reality directly. The person who evalu-

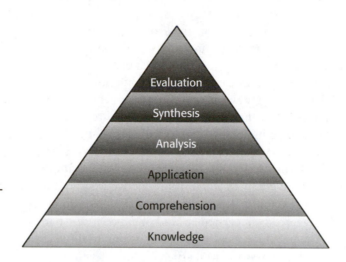

ates is the one who continually tests ideas for their soundness, workability, defensibility, power, insight, subtlety, and novelty—for their potential to construct or subvert beliefs, to reconcile or to inflame conflicts, to build knowledge edifices or to kick down the foundations of what we think we know. As one manifestation of metacognition, evaluation is crucial to the pursuit of good ideas and sound plans. Adept thinkers know that knowledge-building is a human enterprise, so declared truth is never definitive, never beyond doubt, and never perfect. We evaluate so that we can test and, if possible, improve what we know. This is the essence of complex cognition: forever evaluating and evolving ideas toward something better.

Habits of Mind

If there is something that binds together all of complex cognition, it's the practice of testing ideas for their quality. Some people continually monitor ideas for their quality; these people are good thinkers by habit and therefore good role models. How is it possible to establish higher-order thinking as a habit—to build metacognition into our mental software as a "background application" that runs continuously?

Through the decades, education scholars and psychologists have not only proposed that higher-order thought can be practiced habitually, but also advocated the establishment of such habits among learners as a worthy goal of education. For John Dewey (1933), the American philosopher of education, a supremely desirable goal of education was to teach learners to be reflective thinkers. In Dewey's theory, reflectivity has a strong conceptual resemblance to both metacognition and evaluation. **Reflection** is the act of considering deeply the ideas that one engages, the evidence for those ideas, and their implications. Rather than passively accepting what one reads or hears, the reflective thinker weighs new ideas, appraises them, and gauges them accordingly.

A contemporary and more psychological ideal was proposed by psychologist Ellen Langer (1997), who made a case that people often act in ways that show **mindlessness**. Even in everyday tasks, people behave in ridiculously foolish ways, presumably acting out social scripts about what they were "supposed" to do, even though these acts are sometimes absurd. An example of mindlessness is a sales clerk who ran a credit card through for a purchase. The customer had failed to sign the back of the credit card, though. When the clerk pointed this out, the customer promptly signed the back of the credit card. Now satisfied, the sales clerk compared the signatures on the back of the credit card and on the sales slip to be sure they matched. It seems comical when we consider a single instance, and we might shake our heads in wonderment. Langer's point, though, is that *all* of us tend to be mindless—and not infrequently.

The alternative, Langer suggests, is that each of us can be more effective at displaying **mindfulness** (and minimizing mindlessness) in our everyday lives. We can learn to be better thinkers by asking whether our ideas or actions are working, whether they make sense, and whether they connect to what we already know and to the available evidence. What does mindfulness require? In answering this question, the ideas of David Perkins and his colleagues are relevant (Perkins, Jay, & Tishman, 1993). Perkins has distinguished thinking skills from **thinking dispositions**, wherein the latter includes not only the *ability* to think in productive ways, but also an active *tendency* to think well. For example, Perkins described the disposition to think clearly. This disposition is triggered by a particular kind of experience—namely, inexact, fuzzy, or unclear ideas. The person with a thinking disposition to think clearly will take steps to reduce intellectual fuzziness and to sharpen ideas.

Finally, consider an idea proposed by psychologist Jonathan Baron (1985)— **search**—that refers to the amount of time (and therefore the level of cognitive engage-

INTEREST MAGNET 5.2

When Cognition Fails Tragically

On December 29, 1972, Eastern Airlines flight 401 flew directly into the Florida Everglades, killing 100 of the 176 passengers and crew on board. The only mechanical malfunction of the aircraft was the failure of a cockpit light to illuminate, indicating that the plane's nose gear was down. But that light failure was not the cause of the crash. Rather, the plane's pilot and crew became so pre-occupied with the failure of the light to illuminate that they did not notice that the jet's autopilot program had somehow disengaged. The airplane slowly descended until it was less than 1000 feet from the ground. An air traffic controller radioed the plane to ask "how things were coming along," but by that time it was too late. The plane had hit the ground because nobody was flying the aircraft. The crash of flight 401 is an extreme example of how a cognitive error can result in horrible tragedy. The human mind is prone to making mistakes. Without checks, controls, and feedback loops, a small cognitive error can result in disaster.

Cognitive errors can lead to disastrous outcomes not only in the operation of complex machinery such as a jet airplane, but also through engineering design flaws. Errors in design can pose huge threats to human safety, whether through collapsing buildings or bridges, factory explosions or fires, toxic leaks, or malfunctions of cars, trains, and airplanes. All of us must trust cars and elevators not to fail us when we use them. But perhaps somewhere in our consciousness we understand that machines are not infallible. One expert on disasters remarked, "Machines going crazy are among the few things left in this civilized planet that can still inspire deep dread" (Chiles, 2001).

Whereas errors in engineering design appear to be comparatively rare, medical errors are not. Medical errors vividly demonstrate the disastrous effects of human fallibility. In surgery, documented errors include removing the wrong kidney, operating on the incorrect side of the brain, and amputating the wrong foot. Doctors have performed surgery on the wrong patient, administered the wrong gas (nitrous oxide instead of oxygen), and given the wrong drug or the wrong dosage. Lab errors can result in the wrong diagnosis, or the right diagnosis for the wrong person.

Cognitive errors also have tragic consequences in other domains. DNA analysis has clearly shown that many inmates convicted of violent crimes were in fact innocent, and these prisoners are now being exonerated. The exonerations prove that a legal system can produce a high number of wrongful convictions even when those convictions are made on the strict evidentiary basis of "beyond a reasonable doubt." Errors may be attributable to the tactical errors of lawyers, judges, or juries. Perhaps more likely, the trial process relies on the fallible cognition of all participating minds. All these examples—in transportation, medicine, and law—illustrate the disastrous effects of cognitive errors and, conversely, the high value we must place on thinking well.

ment) given to any idea or decision. Have you noticed that some people take a *long* time to decide what to order at a restaurant? They want to give some thought to their selection, but they prolong *search* a little longer than average, sometimes too long. In general terms, it's possible to spend too much time making a decision or, alternatively, too little time on everyday decisions. Think of buying clothes: A person can walk into a clothing department and select a shirt within 30 seconds; another person might take 3 hours to decide between two shirts. Neither extreme is ideal.

It is possible to err by searching (mentally investing) too little or too much, which is where Baron's provocative hypothesis comes in. Baron argues that human cognition is biased in one direction. In other words, one error is much more common than the other. Which one is it: Too much search or too little? The general bias of human cognition, according to Baron, is toward *too little* search. If Baron is right, we humans tend to think about things not quite long enough; we terminate *search* a little too early. The implication is that if we were able, through education or will, to extend our average thought processes just a bit, we would generate better decisions and have better-founded beliefs. Our knowledge and action would be of higher quality as a result, and the goal of advancing complex cognition would be served. Can you think of applications to teaching others? To your own thinking?

All the habits of mind we have considered—reflection, mindfulness, thinking dispositions, and search—are applicable across the various forms of complex cognition. These habits can make us more effective as we engage in problem solving, critical thinking, inductive reasoning, and creative expression. Habits of mind are about how consistently—how *habitually*—we use the intellectual resources at our disposal. Here is yet another application to teaching and learning: Education entails, in part, the development of good habits of mind.

The Social Origins of Complex Cognition

Although not infallible, the amazing reach and flexibility of higher-order cognition is awesome. Where does in complex cognition come from? One possible answer seems unlikely—that the capacity for higher-order thought is pre-programmed into our brains, hard-wired because it is coded directly by our DNA. Although we can acknowledge that *some* human knowledge is likely to be "native" (facial recognition, for example), this does not seem to be a satisfactory explanation for higher-order cognition. Of course, at some level our DNA must make complex cognition possible by coding for the appropriate brain structures, such as a large cerebral cortex. But the ability to engage in complex thought is instead learned from experience rather than being coded directly by our genes. The most likely source of this essential experience is human culture. Culture is that complex web of meanings in which we live, passed on from one generation to the next, stable but never static.

This is where the forceful and convincing ideas of the Russian psychologist Lev Vygotsky (1986/1934) enter. Vygotsky, a brilliant intellect in the era of revolutionary Russia, introduced many important ideas for the educator, one of which relates directly to the origins of higher-order thinking. Vygotsky proposed that higher-order thinking originates in a person's social environment—that it comes from other people.

To understand this idea, consider the example of a child who is seated in the back seat of the family car, listening to his parents trying to make a decision together. In the front seats, Mom and Dad are disagreeing about whether or not to take the kids to the zoo.

FIGURE 5.7
Lev Vygotsky. *He connected the social and the psychological realms through language and showed how both realms support higher-order thinking.* [Archives of the History of American Psychology.]

"We should go," says one parent. "I know it's raining, but the kids won't even notice."

"But we'll notice," says the other parent. "We aren't dressed appropriately, and we'll be miserable if we go now. And if we're miserable, then the kids will be too."

"I don't think they will be," rejoins the first parent. "And besides, we made a promise to them."

The child listening to this conversation might be highly interested in the outcome of the discussion and might even join in the conversation. However, the part of the conversation that seems most useful for future thinking is the actual structure of the argumentation. Point-counterpoint; pro-con; yes-no; for-against. It's the structure of a debate that deals with a complex situation by trying to characterize the important considerations and how they play off each other. Included in the debate are helpful word-concepts, such as *because*, and the *if-then* structure. By eavesdropping on a minor family disagreement, the child has an opportunity to hear higher-order cognition as it applies to real-life problems. The higher-order cognition is expressed in *spoken* language as part of a *social* process.

Now a second process brilliantly identified by Vygotsky ensues: transforming the social discourse to the psychology of individual mental processes. The child seated in the back of the family car will eventually face situations where the best decision is not obvious. Imagine this train of thought in the child's mind:

Should I do my homework now, or should I play video games first? If I do my homework first, Mom will be happy. But I'm tired of thinking about schoolwork, and I need a break. If I have fun for a while, then I'll have more energy to do my homework.

A silent discourse unfolds in the child's mind that is directed toward making a good decision. The thinking process resembles the yes-no, pro-con structure of a debate between his parents overheard some time ago. The difference now is that the "debate" takes place inside the child's mind. It was appropriated from the sociocultural realm into the psychological. In the process, it transformed from audible language to private thought.

Play out this scenario a thousand times and in a thousand variations, and you'll have some idea of the power of Vygotsky's insight. He perceived that all of us (not just children) learn to think complexly from other people in our social environment. Higher-order thought is initially social and later becomes psychological. Through engagement with other people in our culture, we learn to form strategies, to project consequences, to search for reasons, to detect contradictions and inconsistencies, and to explore promising new ideas. This is what Vygotsky meant when he spoke of the social origins of higher order thought. The idea has monumental importance for education; it might even be the most important idea in this entire book.

We must not think that the pattern of influence flows in one direction only, from social to psychological. Once a person has internalized an ability to engage in complex cognition, that ability becomes shareable in the social space. Others, in turn, can benefit. There is a reverberation here between the social and the psychological, with enrichment flowing in both directions. There is also a wonderful alternation of language and thought—one audible and one silent. Think of how these processes replicate in societies everywhere and every day, and their power becomes obvious. Now let's ask: Granting the importance of these Vygotskyian processes, are they being used optimally in education?

Cognitive Modeling

For a teacher, the most direct application of Vygotsky's theory of complex cognition is the use of the technique called **cognitive modeling**, in which she vocalizes her thought processes so that students can hear them. Let's say that the teacher approaches a math word problem written out on the classroom whiteboard. The teacher looks at the problem and says:

> Let me see. Well, first I have to be sure I know the goal. What am I trying to solve? Okay, the goal is stated right here. But how can I get there? What information is relevant? I'm a little confused just for a moment—but now I see. This piece of information is crucial. Now it's beginning to connect.

The multiple benefits to the children in the classroom listening to the teacher's audible reasoning include the students inferring that the teacher's solution of the word problem is not some sort of magical wizardry, or the application of brilliance to simplicity. The teacher, like the student, can be momentarily uncertain about what to do, or temporarily unclear about what information is relevant and what is not. These insights are crucial for students because they can proceed with problem solving knowing that their momentary uncertainties are a normal part of the process.

By using cognitive modeling, a teacher can help to create the right emotional climate for problem solving by demonstrating to students that she—the teacher—feels the same kinds of uncertainty whenever she engages in problem solving. The teacher models, in her soliloquy, how to cope with uncertainties and setbacks. These are not occasions for self-doubt or frustration. Instead, impediments to problem solving can be "talked through" so that they do not take an emotional toll. A math teacher confronting a difficult problem can say, "Well, I'm not immediately sure how to proceed. Let's see, what do I know and what do I want to find out? Okay, take it slowly." By using language of this sort—that is, by speaking her own thoughts aloud—the teacher communicates to students that even experts experience uncertainty during problem solving. Uncertainty is not a cause for panic and alarm. The good problem solver has the self-management skills needed to take care of worry, discouragement, and potential threats to feelings of self-worth. By verbalizing these self-management techniques, a teacher can convey to students that expertise is not equivalent to always knowing what to do next.

Of course, cognitive modeling is a little risky in that it reveals a teacher's human limitations. The teacher as all-knowing authority is unmasked. The teacher is revealed, more truthfully, as a fellow learner and problem solver, which may be unacceptable to the teacher or to the students, or awkward when the teacher is eclipsed by a fast-thinking student. Even with ego threats and challenges to stereotypes of what a teacher is, however, cognitive modeling is a potent tool for teaching students how to engage in complex, higher-order cognition. It also flows quite directly from Vygotsky's theory.

Cognitive modeling is a great tool for teachers to use; it can also be used by students to vocalize their cognitions and so put their ideas into the public sphere for other students to consider and appropriate for their own thinking. Whenever individual students express their best thinking to a group of fellow students, the group is enriched. This is possibly the best justification for group processes in education. Educators are often enthusiastic about getting students to work collaboratively, but the justification is often vague or lacking. Vygotsky's theory, however, provides a good rationale for group processes in education. This is not to say that group process will always be effective. They can easily go off course and be quite ineffective or even a complete waste of time. But when collaborative learning works well, it can be extremely beneficial to thinking and learning.

Finally, it is important to remember that Vygotsky's theory of complex cognition using cognitive modeling is relevant to your own intellectual development. If you participate in conversations, discussions, and debates with people who are intellectually engaged, you can learn from them, and they can learn from you. The transactive nature of the social and the psychological, the linguistic and the cognitive, works not only in the family car or in the math classroom; it is good whenever people gather to debate, discuss, create, and solve problems.

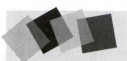

Learning Strategies

This chapter was designed to clarify the nature and types of complex cognition. It presents several categories of complex cognition and describes the mental processes that make each category distinct. Along the way, we found that the conceptual presentation of these different kinds of cognition has implications for teaching and learning. Here, then, are ten learning strategies that apply theories of complex cognition directly and specifically to education.

1 Make higher-order thinking an explicit goal.
Open discussion about complex cognition can improve the chances of making real progress toward improved thinking. If a teacher wants to improve her students' ability to engage in complex cognition, it makes sense to recognize that goal explicitly and to talk about it. The improvement of problem-solving skills or critical thinking capability could be included among the goals for a science or English course, or in the goals for an entire school.

2 Create an atmosphere conducive to problem solving.
Problem solving, by its very nature, often involves inefficient pathways in moving toward the eventual goal. The problem-solving pathway is likely to be marked by errors and setbacks, and by considerable uncertainty along the way. Such characteristics may conflict with traditional classroom or workroom expectations, such as the belief that people should act with certainty, and that performance should be error-free. If teachers want to promote problem solving, they need to create a classroom atmosphere that recognizes errors and uncertainties as inevitable accoutrements of problem solving. Values must shift accordingly.

3 Practice cognitive modeling.
Vygotsky's insight that higher-order thinking proceeds from the social to the psychological presents many applications to education, one of which is the teaching technique called *cognitive modeling*. This is the rather straightforward practice of a teacher speaking her thoughts aloud as she engages a problem or thinks critically about a claim or a writing sample. Students can then appropriate the cognitive tools that the teacher used to engage the problem, such as how to stay focused and how to manage uncertainty, setbacks, or lack of confidence. Teachers should look for oppor-

tunities to use cognitive modeling, and build such occasions directly into their lesson plans.

4 Align assessment to learning goals.
During the past few decades, considerable advances have been made on theories of assessment. Recent educational reforms have built directly on the strong connection between assessment and learning. The implication is that advancement of any goal of education, including complex cognition, is unlikely unless assessment supports that goal. Therefore, complex cognition should be built into each assessment. It need not dominate, but there should be some expectation for problem solving or critical thinking on every teacher-made test or more formal assessment.

5 Present all knowledge as improvable.
One idea that unifies the various forms of complex cognition is that all knowledge is improvable. No statement, law, theory, claim, or finding is established for all time as definitive truth. All can be superseded by a more correct or more encompassing knowledge claim. It's the nature of knowledge; the construction of knowledge—whether in an individual mind or in collective communities—is a human enterprise. The human capacity for complex thought is impressive, but not perfect. For students, one key insight is to see the continuity between the improvability of their own knowledge and the improvability of shared knowledge, such as what they read in textbooks. These are two versions of the same process.

6 Teach students to calibrate their beliefs.
Essential to the process of becoming a really good thinker is learning how to place the right level of confidence in one's own beliefs. The coarsest judgment, requiring zero critical thought, is the know-it-all attitude of 100 percent confidence that whatever you believe is true beyond doubt. The person who thinks this way is un-teachable and, to his peril, stuck in the unlearning state guaranteed by this inability to calibrate. If we are intellectually careful and honest, we will see that we hold thousands of beliefs—some nearly certain, others with moderate backing and justification, and still others that are mere possibilities. Students must learn how to calibrate their knowledge accordingly. Practice in doing so may

result in a revelation—possibly threatening, possibly liberating—that much of what we *think* we know is quite open to questioning and revision.

7   As a teacher, express uncertainty.

It does a student little good if his or her teacher conveys the image of the always-right authority on every subject. If, instead, the teacher admits (directly through words or indirectly through action) to not always having an immediate correct answer, then the student sees that the teacher is a learner too. Many teachers know how important it is to convey this truth and weave this stance directly into the way they teach. To admit that very capable people don't always know can free the mind of the student. Socrates understood this, and lived by it.

8   Teach heuristics.

Keep in mind the guiding force that heuristics can apply to problem solving. As rules of thumb, heuristics never guarantee success, but they can make reaching the problem-solving goal more likely. More often still, heuristics can advance progress toward subgoals—smaller subproblems that must be engaged as part of solving a larger problem. Teachers should be prepared to teach general heuristics, such as means-ends analysis and working backward, but should also be aware that many heuristics are domain-specific, applying to the particular subject being taught and learned. Many teachers have discovered that personal heuristics also help considerably—and these, too, can be taught to learners.

9   Use writing as a springboard for critical thinking.

When exercising critical thinking in a detailed, extended manner, it often helps to focus on a piece of writing. Written documents have a unique ability to develop reasoning in much greater depth than spoken discourse does. This does not mean that ideas in writing are always backed by good thinking. In writing, specific claims can be justified well or poorly. Chains of reasoning are sometimes well articulated and sometimes badly integrated. The stability of text over time, the option to reread, and the affordance that many people can pore over the same document and share insights makes writing an ideal object of critical thought.

10   Model the rewards of cognition.

For all the attention we give to the nature of higher order cognition, and to fostering the ability to think well, we must not forget the rewards that it offers. Indeed, if it were not for the fact that complex cognition has compelling rewards—think of how good it feels to solve a difficult problem—we might feel little incentive to strive for excellence as thinkers. For many people, the difficulty of complex cognition might outweigh the mental rewards of occasional success. Here, the teacher can help by communicating the emotional payoff of complex cognition, by describing how wonderful it feels to think well. Then this sociocultural reality might too be learned, in Vygotskian fashion, by younger learners.

These ten strategies are only a sampling of possible applications of the concepts of this chapter to teaching designs and decisions. Here, as elsewhere in this book, specific applications to teaching and learning are never formulas to be applied indiscriminately. Teaching, after all, is problem solving. If we place powerful ideas at the center of our study of human learning and cognition, then applications can emanate in a thousand directions.

 ## Conclusion

This chapter presented an overview of complex cognition. When we speak of complex cognition, we are not talking about mere learning—the incorporation of information into long-term memory—though certainly learning is part of the process. Rather, we refer more directly to our ability to apprehend complex ideas, to test them, and to improve them. That is why metacognition—the monitoring and control of thought—is placed at the center of our study of complex cognition.

Metacognition is a binding force across all forms of complex cognition. We can be metacognitive about the ideas we entertain and the actions we take. For both, we can appraise their quality: Are the ideas sound? Are the actions effective? Metacognition, in turn, applies to the four major categories of complex cognition discussed in this chapter:

- Problem solving

- Critical thinking

- Inferential reasoning

- Creativity

Of these four categories, the first two are especially important: problem solving and critical thinking. Both cover broad spectra of the ways in which we use our minds. Problem solving is the pursuit of a goal when the path to that goal is uncertain. Critical thinking is the evaluation of ideas for their quality, especially in judging whether they make sense. The first is primarily about action, the second about ideas. Of course, these distinctions are not exclusive. The wall between these categories of mental activity is permeable—one involves the other. Inevitably, problem solving calls upon the ability to think critically, and vice versa.

There are other instructive connections between problem solving and critical thinking. Above all, both exhibit the fact that ideas and plans, as constructions of the human mind, do not exist in a pure state of fixed correctness. Rather, human knowledge is, as a rule, imperfectly evidenced, articulated, and formulated. All knowledge is a work in progress—and this holds whether we talk about the knowledge state of an individual or the collective theoretical commitments of experts. Both forms of knowledge are dynamic. They change and, ideally, improve over time. As for instructional applications, teachers who convey that knowledge is partial and improvable are likely to encourage complex cognition. To the degree that teachers accept errors and uncertainty as inevitable in the pursuit of good thinking, they help foster attitudes among learners that favor the development of complex cognition.

Commitment to the open-endedness of knowledge applies also to the other two categories of complex cognition we have studied: inferential reasoning and creative thinking. These, too, involve moving into the intellectual unknown. Inferential reasoning builds from what we know toward something new—it means going beyond the information given. There are two main kinds of inferential reasoning—inductive (building generalizations from particulars) and deductive (applying generalizations to particulars). A fourth category of cognition, creative thinking, involves finding connections that lie outside conventional uses and interpretations, and designing products that are both novel and valuable.

Further insight into complex cognition can be gained by Lev Vygotsky's powerful idea that higher-order thinking originates in a person's social environment—in the interpersonal interaction between people as they disagree, debate, collaborate, cross-pollinate, and in general press one another toward better ideas. Vygotsky saw that individuals can internalize the forms of audible conversations so that these become part of the individual psychological apparatus. The direction is outside to inside, social to psychological. Vygotsky's idea has unlimited applications to the design of educative experience.

With recent advances in theories of cognition, the potential is greater than ever for the educator to advance the ability of students to think well. It's a goal that can weave through everything a teacher does, and can inspire a teacher toward self-improvement as a thinker. In fact, that's the best way to proceed: teacher and student advancing together. Both are students, really, honing their knowledge and ability to think well in every way possible.

References

Anderson, L. W., & Krathwohl, D. R. (Eds.). (2001). *A taxonomy of learning, teaching, and assessment: A revision of Bloom's taxonomy of educational objectives.* New York: Longman.

Arlin, P. K. (1989). The problem of the problem. In J. D. Sinnott (Ed.), *Everyday problem solving: Theory and applications* (pp. 229–237). New York: Praeger.

Baron, J. (1985). *Rationality and intelligence.* New York: Cambridge University Press.

Bloom, B. S. (1956). *Taxonomy of educational objectives, handbook I: The cognitive domain.* New York: David McKay Co., Inc.

Brown, A. L. (1978). Knowing when, where, and how to remember: A problem of metacognition. In R. Glaser (Ed.), *Advances in instructional psychology: Vol. 1* (pp. 77–165). Hillsdale, NJ: Lawrence Erlbaum Associates.

Bruner, J. (1973). *Going beyond the information given.* New York: Norton.

Chiles, J. R. (2001). *Inviting disaster*. New York: HarperBusiness.

Carroll, L. (1865). *Alice's adventures in Wonderland*. Wordsworth Classics.

Covington, M. (1984). The motive for self-worth. *Research on Motivation in Education, 1*, 77–113, Orlando, FL: Academic Press.

Descartes, R. (1641). *Meditations on first philosophy*. Cambridge, England: Cambridge University Press.

Dewey, J. (1933). *How we think*. New York: D. C. Heath.

Duffy, P. L. (2001). *Blue cats and chartreuse kittens*. New York: W. H. Freeman.

Dunbar, K. (1995). How scientists really reason: Scientific reasoning in real-world laboratories. In R. J. Sternberg & J. E. Davidson (Eds.), *The nature of insight* (pp. 366–395). Cambridge, MA: MIT Press.

Flavell, J. H. (1979). Metacognition and cognitive monitoring: A new area of cognitive-developmental inquiry. *American Psychologist, 34*, 906–911.

Glenberg, A. M., & Epstein, W. (1985). Calibration of comprehension. *Journal of Experimental Psychology: Learning, Memory, and Cognition, 11*, 702–718.

Gould, S. J. (1992). *Ever since Darwin: Reflections on natural history*. New York: W. W. Norton.

Kirshner, P. A., Sweller, J., & Clark, R. E. (2006). Why minimal guidance during instruction does not work: An analysis of the failure of constructivist, discovery, problem-based, experiential, and inquiry-based teaching. *Educational Psychologist, 41*(2), 75–86.

Langer, E. J. (1997). *The power of mindful learning*. Reading, MA: Addison-Wesley.

Lin, X., Schwartz, D. L., & Hatano, G. (2005). Toward teachers' adaptive metacognition. *Educational Psychologist, 40*(4), 245–255.

Lubart, T. I. (1994). Creativity. In R. J. Sternberg (Ed.), *Thinking and problem solving* (pp. 289–332). San Diego, CA: Academic Press.

Mackworth, N. H. (1965). Originality. *American Psychologist, 20*, 51–66.

Martinez, M. E. (1998). What is problem solving? *Phi Delta Kappan, 79*, 605–609.

Mayer, R. E., & Wittrock, M. C. (2006). Problem solving. In P. A. Alexander & P. H. Winne (Eds.), *Handbook of educational psychology* (2nd ed.) (pp. 287–303). Mahwah, NJ: Lawrence Erlbaum Associates.

Mumford, M. D., & Gustafson, S. B. (1988). Creativity syndrome: Integration, application, and innovation. *Psychological Bulletin, 103*(1), 27–43.

Newell, A, & Simon, H. A. (1972). *Human problem solving*. Englewood Cliffs, NJ: Prentice-Hall.

Nickerson, R. S. (1986). *Reflections on reasoning*. Hillsdale, NJ: Lawrence Erlbaum Associates.

Nickerson, R. S. (1999). Enhancing creativity. In R. S. Sternberg (Ed.), *Handbook of creativity* (pp. 392–430). New York: Cambridge University Press.

Ornstein, A. C., & Levine, D. U. (2003). *Foundations of education* (8th ed.). Boston: Houghton Mifflin.

Palmer, D. (2001). *Looking at philosophy: The unbearable heaviness of philosophy made lighter* (3rd ed.). Boston: McGraw-Hill.

Perkins, D. N., Jay, E., & Tishman, S. (1993). Beyond abilities: A dispositional theory of thinking. *Merrill-Palmer Quarterly, 39*(1), 1–21.

Polya, G. (1957). *How to solve it: A new aspect of mathematical method* (2nd ed.). Princeton, NJ: Princeton University Press.

Ramachandran, V. S., & Hubbard, E. M. (2003). Hearing colors, tasting shapes. *Scientific American, 288*(5), 52–59.

Schoenfeld, A. H. (1992). Learning to think mathematically: Problem solving, metacognition, and sense making in mathematics. In D. A. Grouws (Ed.), *Handbook of research on mathematics teaching and learning: A project of the National Council of Teachers of Mathematics*. New York: Macmillan.

Simon, H. A. (1969). *The sciences of the artificial*. Cambridge, MA: MIT Press.

Simon, H. A. (1973). The structure of ill structured problems. *Artificial Intelligence, 4*, 181–201.

Tobias, S., & Everson, H. T. (1996). *Assessing metacognitive knowledge monitoring*. College Board Report No. 96-1. New York: College Board.

Vygotsky, L. S. (1986/1934). *Thought and language* (A Kozulin, Ed. and Trans.). Cambridge, MA: MIT Press.

Wallas, G. (1926). *The art of thought*. New York: Harcourt Brace Jovanovich.

Wason, P. C., & Johnson-Laird, P. N. (1972). *Psychology of reasoning: Structure and content*. Cambridge, MA: Harvard University Press.

Wason, P. C., & Shapiro, S. (1971). Natural and contrived experience in a reasoning problem. *Quarterly Journal of Experimental Psychology, 23*, 63–71.

Wertime, R. (1979). Students, problems, and "courage spans." In J. Lochhead and J. Clement (Eds.), *Cognitive process instruction: Research on teaching thinking skills* (pp. 191–198). Philadelphia, PA: The Franklin Institute Press.

[6] Emotion, Motivation, and Volition

We saw in previous chapters that cognitive psychology offers insights into learning and teaching that go far beyond what strict behaviorism offers. Cognitive information processing theory, in particular, offers a window into reasoning, knowledge, understanding, problem solving, and other capabilities and qualities of the mind central to education. These complex processes can be understood in terms of the flow of information among memory structures—the sensory register, working memory, and long-term memory.

The computer metaphor is highly instructive for understanding human cognition. But, like all metaphors, it has limitations. The logical calculating aspect of the human mind can most easily be accommodated by the computer metaphor. The more "human" aspects of thinking are not as easily understood within the information-processing paradigm. Three of those qualities—emotion, motivation, and volition (or will)—are the focus of this chapter.

We will consider aspects of the mind that experience and express "hot cognitions"—those that extend beyond cool, dispassionate rationality. Emotions, motivation, and volition are deeply entwined with thinking and learning, often propelling intellectual growth and sometimes standing in the way of it. Hot cognitions are far too important to ignore.

The Trilogy of Mind: Cognition, Affect, and Conation

How can we best divide the many different expressions of the human mind? Which categories do justice to its analytical properties—the ones that conform best to the computer metaphor—along with hot cognitions? One taxonomy, elegant in its simplicity, was proposed by the psychologist and historian Ernest Hilgard (1980). Hilgard showed that scholars from ancient times to the present understood the human psyche as a **trilogy of mind** composed of cognition, affect, and conation. **Cognition**, which is rational thought scrubbed free of complicating emotions, wishes, or will, has been the focus of the previous chapters in this book. **Affect** is roughly equivalent to emotion, and includes temporary feeling states as well as more enduring moods. The third component of Hilgard's trilogy is **conation**, which refers to purposeful striving toward valued goals (Snow, Corno, & Jackson, 1996).

INTEREST MAGNET 6.1

Can Computers Have Emotions?

The connection between computers and emotions has a long history, dating back to the founding of artificial intelligence (AI). As the early AI researchers began to design systems that could mimic intelligence, some also aspired to design computer programs that could make computer behavior similar to, or even indistinguishable from, human behavior. The famous Turing test, proposed by the legendary mathematician Alan Turing, is that computers would be intelligent when a human observer could not distinguish computer behavior from human behavior. Satisfaction of the Turing test implied that the computer would have the capacity for emotions, or at least the capability of mimicking emotions.

One of the earliest AI programs, called ELIZA, indirectly challenged the Turing test. It was designed to provide counseling to people seeking psychological therapy. ELIZA provided this "service" by imitating such rudimentary active listening strategies as restating a "client's" claim. Of course, ELIZA did not have emotions, nor did it even mimic human emotions very well, but for AI researchers it was the first step down the long and difficult road to equipping computers with affective sensibilities.

Why even try to build computer programs with emotions? One possible benefit is that a computer with emotional capability can, in some form, interact more effectively with a human user. For example, a computer-based tutor that can read a learner's emotions—whether interest, boredom, or anxiety—can adjust its teaching strategy accordingly (Picard, 1997). Reading emotions is possible if the computer is equipped to analyze the learners' facial expressions, for example. There is also an advantage if the intelligent tutor can mimic interest, such as delight at a correct response. But that means that a computer must produce voice inflections or on-screen facial expressions that are credible displays of the target emotion. Done well, the capability to project emotion could help to motivate the learner. Realistic emotional interpretations and expressions could also help to enhance the pleasure of electronic games, "digital pets," and computer-mediated selection of entertainment media such as music or movies.

Picard (1995) argued that emotions play a necessary role in rational thinking and decision making. If this is so, then the ability to read emotions is not incidental to intelligent reasoning and action, but is instead a vital component of intelligence. Computers might not reach their potential as aids to human needs and aspirations unless they are equipped with sensitivity to human emotions, or perhaps the ability to have and express emotions.

Can a computer really *have* emotions or must it merely *mimic* emotions? Research might not answer this question, but philosophy can try to address it. Or, undeterred by reality, fiction writers can explore the implications of computers that have their own emotions—usually emotions that have a runaway quality. In the short story collection *I, Robot*, Isaac Asimov (1950) depicted a future in which robots had genuine personalities and eventually rebelled against their human makers. A more disastrous scenario was painted by mathematician and sci-fi writer Vernor Vinge (1993), who predicted that eventually the collective intelligence of machines will cross over into self-aware consciousness. At that point—which he called *technological singularity*—computers will no longer accept their second-class status.

Hilgard's model divides conation into two subprocesses: **motivation** and **volition**. Motivation includes all processes that precede a decision to pursue a particular goal; volition refers to all processes that follow a decision and guide action toward a particular goal. We may be *motivated* by hunger to make a sandwich, but may or may not decide to make it. Once we decide to make a sandwich, *volitional* processes take over as we select ingredients and order the steps necessary to achieve the goal.

Although Hilgard's trilogy of mind model helps disentangle the different forms of thought engaged by the human mind, it would be a mistake to consider these processes as completely distinct. At any time, the mind might simultaneously engage "cool" analytic cognitions as well as the "hot" cognitions of emotions, purposeful planning, and striving toward goals. The entire trilogy of mind participates interactively during nearly all mental activity, including learning and thinking. As we delve into each of these complex aspects of the mind, we will find applications that support the purposes of education.

Emotions

Learning Emotions

Emotions are highly relevant to learning because long-term memory stores not only factual information but also emotional associations that connect to what we know (Bower & Forgas, 2001). Sometimes these associations are so strong that when we think about a specific person, event, or idea, that memory elicits powerful feelings that are just as salient as the memory's factual content. Emotions can, in turn, strengthen initial learning. Research has shown that when new information evokes emotions, that information is much more likely to be remembered. Emotions have this effect for at least two reasons: First, emotions have the power to focus attention, which is a prerequisite for learning; second, emotional experiences tend to be recalled at a later time, leading to rehearsal and therefore a stronger memory trace (Bower, 1994; Bower & Forgas, 2001). Many teachers intuitively understand the role of emotions in learning, and strive to infuse their teaching with emotional value—to get students excited. When teaching stirs emotions, learners pay more attention and better connect new information with what they already know. Positive emotions in particular help students form associations with prior knowledge, contributing to deep understanding rather than superficial learning (Bower, 1994).

It is easy to name many different emotions, dozens perhaps. You can feel anxious, excited, curious, ashamed, proud, angry, or elated. Not surprisingly, psychologists have tried to organize emotions into frameworks. One of the best-known taxonomies of emotion was advanced by Robert Plutchik (1980; 2001). The model, displayed in Figure 6.1, shows eight basic emotions at the central core, with opposites arranged as pairs (e.g., ecstasy and grief, or rage and terror). Plutchik's model illustrates the

FIGURE 6.1
Plutchik's Model of Emotions.
In this highly structured model, emotions are shown to vary in pleasantness and intensity.
[Reprinted by permission of Annette de Ferrarri.]

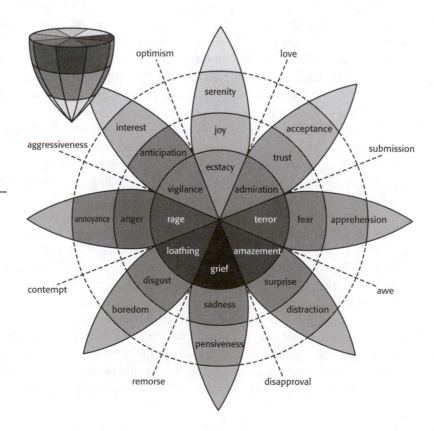

different intensity of emotions by presenting basic and more intense emotions at the core and placing less intense and subtler versions of emotions on the periphery. The model also shows that some emotions are combinations of others. Specifically, emotions listed in the open spaces, between the "flower petals," are combinations of the two adjacent emotions.

Although the order and symmetry of Plutchik's model is attractive, emotions may not be as neatly organized as the model suggests. Other psychologists have offered somewhat different taxonomies of basic emotions (Ortony & Turner, 1990). Some of the recognized categories—anger, joy, fear, sadness, and surprise—correspond closely to the core emotions listed in Plutchik's model, but others are different. A model by Parrot (2001) makes more modest claims about the logical structure of emotions. Instead of presenting a faceted framework, Parrot advanced six primary emotions— love, joy, surprise, anger, sadness, and fear. Each of the six primary emotions branches off into secondary emotions, forming a tree structure. The secondary emotions in turn subdivide into a large number of tertiary emotions. The emotions listed as tertiary are typically quite precise and subtle compared to the raw and undifferentiated quality of the primary emotions.

The psychology of emotions is not yet a settled matter, but several patterns can be affirmed. For example, the number of distinguishable human emotions is quite high, yet there seems to be a rather small set of basic or primary emotions, such as fear, anger, desire, sadness, and joy (Panksepp, 1994). These basic emotions are related to others, often by subtlety of feeling or cause (e.g., guilt versus shame, or pity versus sympathy). Moreover, emotions can be arranged along a positive-negative dimension. Some emotions are clearly pleasant (e.g., happiness) and others unpleasant (e.g., anger). A basic positive-negative dimension seems to hold up as a sensible way to organize emotions (Watson & Clark, 1994).

The positive-negative axis of emotions suggests a direct educational application: to encourage positive emotions toward learning. Educators want their students to enjoy learning and to feel drawn to the subject of study, whether it is literature, physics, computer science, architecture, ancient history, art, or any other domain. If teachers derive satisfaction from advancing their own knowledge and are passionate about their fields of study, they will want their students to experience the same emotions. But as teachers know all too well, attempts to instill positive emotions toward learning are not guaranteed to work. Often, just the opposite occurs; many students develop anxiety, fear, or other negative feelings toward school subjects. Even more worrisome, students sometimes generalize those negative feelings to the entire school experience. Surely, cultivating positive emotions among learners and curtailing the formation of negative emotions is one of the greatest challenges every educator faces.

Asking a teacher to instill positive feelings about learning is a tall order. We experience particular emotions for any number of reasons, some of which are quite accidental. Early in this book we saw that classical conditioning is a very elemental process that can associate strong emotions to new stimuli. The mechanism of classical conditioning is simple—it involves the pairing of two stimuli. One stimulus, the unconditioned stimulus, naturally evokes a particular feeling or physiological response. An angry face or a loud disapproving voice is enough to elicit negative emotions in most children, for example. If that natural stimulus is paired with a neutral stimulus, then the neutral stimulus can prompt the same emotion. For Pavlov's dogs, the neutral stimulus was a bell. For students in the classroom, stimuli that are themselves neutral—books, pencils, and math equations—can acquire positive or negative valences over time. The simple pairing of stimuli can account for some learning of emotional associations.

Positive emotions obviously serve educational ends in a variety of ways. A prime example is the delight we feel when we have an intellectual breakthrough. Whenever we have a flash of insight into a difficult problem, we are likely to feel a rush of satisfaction. Likewise, when we hear and comprehend a clear explanation of a difficult concept, we experience the positive feelings that accompany understanding. For more experienced and successful learners, the *anticipation* of emotional satisfaction that accompanies understanding can sustain their focus. Effective learners look forward to the cognitive breakthrough and persevere to experience its emotional rewards. The implications for teaching are direct: Along with imparting knowledge, teachers can help students to anticipate the deep emotional rewards that accompany intellectual activity, including mastery of difficult but powerful ideas.

Of course, the task of the educator is much more complicated than trying to instill positive emotions and minimize negative emotions. Even "negative" emotions can have potential educational value. What happens, for example, when we read a passage of text that lacks clarity? Perhaps we feel vaguely irritated because it seems fuzzy or ambiguous. We might experience the same feelings when listening to an explanation of a new concept or an illogical rationale for an important decision. This emotional reaction is valuable if it prompts us to ask questions, to develop alternative opinions, and to seek ideas from new sources. In other words, even superficially negative emotions can sometimes lead to improved cognition.

Emotional associations that advance thinking and learning cannot be taught directly. You can't *make* someone feel a prescribed emotion. Still, nothing prohibits a teacher from modeling the emotional rewards of intellectual gains—of curiosities satisfied and insights gained. This does not mean the teacher must put on an act—just the opposite, really. To model the full range of emotional rewards of thinking and learning means to let students into the teacher's private mental world. The teacher can openly convey what he or she is feeling. When the teacher "thinks aloud" through the steps of an intellectual process, she demonstrates cognitive modeling, which can include expressing emotions through voice and gesture.

By communicating the full range of her emotions, a teacher imparts not only the subject matter, but also something of herself. This aspect of teaching—of teaching *oneself* to students—is easily overlooked and infrequently discussed as a vital element of the teaching profession. The opportunity was nicely summed up in the pithy advice of mathematics educator Liping Ma: "Do not forget yourself as a teacher of yourself" (Herrera, 2002). What does it mean for a teacher to teach something of herself to students? For virtually every teacher, it means sharing not only knowledge and skill, but also a deep appreciation, even love, for the subject of study. The intense and enduring enjoyment of literature, mathematics, science, or history is part of what a dedicated teacher can instill in her students.

Intrinsic Motivation

Intrinsic motivation refers to the emotional associations that lead a person to engage in an activity for its own sake, rather than for rewards that lie outside the activity. Any recreational activity that is enjoyable by itself, that you engage in freely without needing compensation or recognition, can be said to be intrinsically motivated. Reading a novel, watching a movie, and spending time with friends can all be enjoyable in themselves. Although placing intrinsic motivation under the heading of emotions might seem odd, intrinsic motivation largely refers to positive feelings toward an activity or the anticipation of positive feelings, which in turn motivate engagement in the activity.

Most educators deeply wish for their students to develop and maintain an intrinsic motivation to learn. Intrinsic motivation easily qualifies as one of the most important goals of education, and for good reasons. Intrinsic motivation is positively correlated with both academic achievement and perceptions of academic competence (Gottfried, 1985). One of the best indications that a teacher has been successful is when a student develops an ongoing interest in the subject of study, such as when a student adopts her English teacher's passion for literature or her biology teacher's love of science. Teachers often hope to spark a deep interest among at least some students—an interest that will continue for the long term, perhaps even affecting a student's course of study and choice of a career.

Unfortunately, available data tell us that intrinsic motivation is not commonly developed as a product of educational experience. Susan Harter (1982) found that intrinsic motivation trended strongly downward as students progressed through the school years. Cross-sectional data showed that for every year that passed between grades 3 and 8, average student intrinsic motivation decreased substantially (Figure 6.2). Intrinsic motivation was replaced with **extrinsic motivation**; in place of curiosity and interest, students were increasingly motivated by the extrinsic incentives of teacher approval and grades (Harter, 1982). This lamentable pattern, which every teacher must confront at some level, indicates a very real risk that, with every passing year, the average student will become less interested in school and less motivated by the **intrinsic rewards** of learning. Teachers must somehow prevent this downward slide and, if possible, reverse it.

The decline of intrinsic motivation during the elementary school years is possibly caused by the widening use of **extrinsic rewards** in schools. Though extrinsic rewards can be effective motivators, they can also erode pre-existing intrinsic motivation. Unlike rats running through a laboratory maze, children have the capacity to wonder *why* their behavior was rewarded. Children can perceive not only the informational aspect of reward ("I am successful"), but also a controlling aspect ("I

FIGURE 6.2
Decline of Intrinsic Motivation.
With each passing grade, students become less motivated by their own curiosity and interest. [Adapted from Harter (1982), Reprinted by permission of Elsevier Global Rights Department].

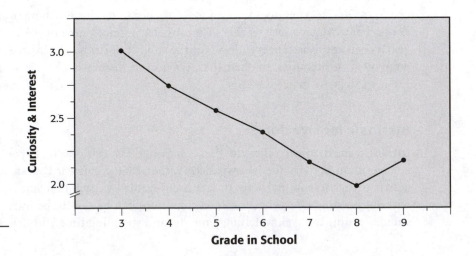

am being manipulated") (Deci, 1985). They can also contemplate their own motives for striving to achieve. Extrinsic rewards alone may be sufficient to rationalize to a student *why* he studies. If so, there is no need to appeal to intrinsic motives; the student's own behavior is **overjustified** by the system of extrinsic rewards.

The system of extrinsic rewards that so pervades education is perhaps necessary and is arguably effective. Gold stars, candy, and smiley faces for reinforcement of desired behavior are ubiquitous. Among older students in the upper grades, in high school, and at the university, test scores and course grades provide frequent feedback to students. Parents, teachers, and fellow students react to these scores and grades, and convey (sometimes intense) social approval or disapproval. The system comes with a cost: Students might feel that the pressure to earn high grades overwhelms any budding interest in a subject of study.

On the other hand, extrinsic rewards are not always counterproductive. Research has shown that praise by itself does not necessarily detract from intrinsic motivation. In fact, extrinsic rewards seem to have an undermining effect only if they are given to students completing a task without regard to the quality of the work (Cameron & Pierce, 1994). Rewards linked to the quality of performance can provide valuable feedback to students and generate beliefs about personal competence where none existed initially. As a precursor to self-confidence, extrinsic rewards might pave the way for intrinsic interest to grow at a later point in the learner's development. Moreover, the typical decline of intrinsic motivation during the school years can arise from factors that have little to do with the system of extrinsic rewards that pervades schooling. The subject matter under study can be difficult and confusing. Complex and abstract knowledge domains, especially those studied in high school, are potentially alienating (Gardner, 1991). To nurture and protect intrinsic motivation among learners is no easy accomplishment. Whenever students pursue a deep understanding of any complex subject or skill, the pathway is almost always fraught with impediments and rife with challenges to self-esteem.

Teachers rightly want to instill intrinsic motivation in their students because they know about the potential intellectual rewards for thinking and learning. Yet another good reason for wanting to develop intrinsic motivation is that positive feelings toward a knowledge domain can influence future decisions to pursue study in that area. The continued willingness of students to learn as evidenced by the choices they make has been called **continuing motivation** (Maehr, 1976). At some point in the education of every student, there comes a time when a choice is offered to continue toward more advanced study or to stop. For some students, this choice is offered during the final years of high school when students choose elective courses. Options open further during college when students choose a major and, after graduation, a career. Continuing motivation is powerful because it encompasses decisions that affect the course of a life and career. This is why Martin Maehr (1976, p. 444) speculated that "continuing motivation may well be *the* critical outcome of any learning experience."

There are additional reasons for cultivating intrinsic motivation as a key outcome of education. Intrinsic motivation is associated with high levels of performance and creativity (Amabile, Hill, Hennessey, & Tighe, 1994) as well as deeper processing of information and greater conceptual understanding (Vansteenkiste, Lens, & Deci, 2006). There seems to be a natural connection between the enjoyment of an activity and highly skilled performance in that activity. Stated differently, excellence and enjoyment coexist and are mutually reinforcing. This connection was explored by the psychologist Mihaly Csikszentmihalyi in his concept of *flow*.

Flow

Most people intuitively understand the concept of flow because they have experienced it personally. Have you ever been so engrossed in a project that you lost track of time? Have you become so completely absorbed by your activity that it becomes, for a while, your entire world? Everything else drops away as your attention focuses like a spotlight on what you must do next. Subjective feelings of intense concentration on a focal activity can be highly pleasurable and even addictive. Csikszentmihalyi (1975) called this zen-like state of consciousness **flow**.

Csikszentmihalyi studied flow states experienced by rock climbers and surgeons, as well as specialists in other areas. He found that the experience of flow was one factor that kept experts highly engaged in their professional or recreational pursuits. He also discovered that flow was associated with particular qualities of activity. In *Beyond Boredom and Anxiety*, Csikszentmihalyi postulated that flow is experienced whenever there is a good match between the difficulty of the task and the ability of the performer. If the task is too easy, boredom sets in; if it is too hard, the performer will become anxious. Either way, enjoyment will diminish. Flow results from an optimal level of challenge. When there is a good match between task difficulty and ability level, boredom and anxiety are equally avoided. Motivation and interest are engaged, and performance is at its peak when ability is stretched without being overwhelmed. That ideal fit produces flow—a psychological state that is highly compelling both intellectually and emotionally.

If you have experienced flow, then you know that such a state of mind is one of the major emotional rewards of intellectual activity. There are good reasons to cultivate the

FIGURE 6.3
Rock Climber in the Flow. *Intense concentration on a challenging activity where the difficulty of the task matches the level of ability can create flow—a zen-like state of consciousness.* [DK]

ability to experience flow among learners. If each student could experience flow, either regularly or just occasionally, one consequence might be a more widespread intellectual engagement and academic success. Greater numbers of students might engage in serious and sustained pursuit of knowledge and understanding. Perhaps the ability to experience flow should be considered an essential goal of education.

Motivation Theories Based on Global Motives

Theories of human motivation are quite varied in scope and perspective. Some focus on specific ways that people tend to interpret events, or the manner in which they judge their behavior in specific contexts and domains. This section examines theories that account for behavior in terms of broad or global factors. These theories present activity as a consequence of general motives that have a wide influence across the gamut of human behavior.

Physiological Theories

Why human beings do what they do is not at all easy to account for. Nonetheless, there is a basic theory that can explain *some* aspects of human motivation as well as the motivation of animal behavior. That simple account is the **drive theory** of motivation. Drive theory, most famously advocated by the psychologist Clark Hull (1943), specifies that behavior is, at its root, motivated by physiological needs. Drives for food, sex, and sleep are primary examples of physiological demands that motivate behavior. In drive theory, behavior is motivated by a need to reduce "tissue deficits," which is another way of saying that action is motivated by the physiological demands that press insistently on the organism.

The **arousal theory** of motivation is a second but related theory that focuses on the organism's degree of physiological arousal. In this context, *arousal* refers to an organism's level of physiological activity as indexed by heart and breathing rates. An organism, human or animal, in a low state of arousal would be relaxed or asleep; in a high state of arousal, the organism would be agitated and nervous, perhaps afraid or angry, and ready for action. As we have just seen, drive theory implies that behavior is directed toward meeting physiological needs, and presumably toward satiation and a relaxed state—in other words, toward *low* arousal. But is low arousal best? In a theory advocated by Yerkes and Dodson in 1908, optimal performance is associated with *moderate* states of arousal. For any given activity, performance will suffer if arousal is too low or too high. At moderate levels of arousal, performance will tend to be optimized.

The principle of optimal arousal was captured in the **Yerkes-Dodson Law** about a century ago. On a graph, the law takes the form of an inverted U, with the horizontal axis on the graph indicating physiological arousal, and the vertical axis indicating performance level. The peak represents optimal performance. The Yerkes-Dodson Law seems to hold up as a general principle, but it does vary somewhat depending on a person's level of skill. For experts, the curve will tend to shift to the right, meaning that performance will be best at somewhat higher states of arousal.

Consider what can happen on a basketball court toward the end of a close game. In the final seconds, a foul is committed that puts a player on the free throw line. The game's outcome will be decided by whether the player can make the shot. In this situation, tremendous psychological pressure as well as the noise of the crowd can detract

FIGURE 6.4
Yerkes-Dodson
Inverted-U Curve.
Performance is optimal at moderate states of physiological arousal—neither too relaxed nor too agitated.

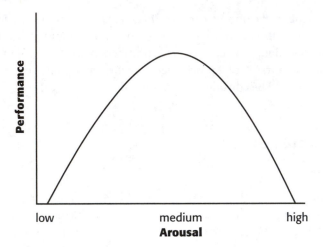

from the shooting ability of a less-experienced player. For a professional basketball player, however, skill and concentration might be sharpened by the higher state of arousal prompted by the stressful situation. Likewise, an expert chef might work very efficiently under high-pressure conditions. Under those same conditions, a novice chef might make mistakes if the arousal produced by high demands becomes overwhelming. The inverted U holds for chefs, basketball players, and all skilled performers, but its peak shifts to the right as novices transition toward expertise.

Curiosity

Jerome Bruner (1966) proposed that among the most basic of all motives is the "will to learn." Bruner noted that this basic human desire, in turn, is strongly motivated by curiosity. When we consider curiosity as a primary motivator of learning, we enter the realm of the cognitive. Drive theory can be construed in completely behavioral terms, and arousal is purely biological. Neither evokes or needs the mind. Curiosity, by contrast, arises from a discrepancy between what learners expect and what they observe. It is fundamentally cognitive.

Infants and young children are drawn to vivid and changing stimuli. They are attracted to new and varied shapes, patterns, colors, and movement. Much infant behavior, in fact, has the effect of causing greater sensory experience. Sensory exploration, in turn, appears to be essential for normal intellectual development (Bruner, 1966). As a child matures, his curiosity changes form. Among older children, curiosity is evoked by complex and incongruous patterns, not only by novelty and vividness. By the early school grades, children are drawn to pictures and stories that have incongruous and surprising elements (Berlyne & Frommer, 1966).

What is the function of curiosity in learning? Above all, curiosity reflects a desire to improve the cognitive organization of ideas (Malone, 1981). The mind is constantly engaged in reconciling new experiences with prior knowledge. In Piaget's theory of cognitive development, for example, cognitive disequilibrium occurs whenever new information cannot be incorporated into existing cognitive structures. The perceiver is motivated to reduce the discrepancy. This process, which Piaget called **accommodation**, advances mental development. As learning proceeds, cognitive structures become more complete and coherent—and more consistent with external realities. Curiosity can prompt and motivate cognitive change in these directions.

Competence Motivation

Drive theory and arousal theory are somewhat contradictory. Drive theory specifies that behavior is an attempt to *reduce* drives. The motive is to satisfy the physiological needs of the body and to make them "go away," at least temporarily. The theory of optimal arousal as formulated by Yerkes and Dodson specifies that lower is not necessarily better. Instead, the organism performs optimally when experiencing a moderate physiological state, one better understood as homeostasis or dynamic balance rather than drive reduction.

Evidence that behavior is not always directed toward drive reduction can be seen even in laboratory mice. In contradiction to Hull's drive theory, mice whose biological needs are satisfied engage in exploratory behavior. Why do they explore? Certainly not to *reduce* any drive, but rather to *raise* physiological or neural activity to a higher, more optimal level. From an evolutionary perspective, it's easy to think of reasons why exploratory behavior would be adaptive and lead to a higher chance of survival in the long run. The important point to note is that exploration of the environment cannot be explained solely by appealing to Hull's drive theory; it must be explained in some other way.

The exploratory behavior of mice seems to have a direct parallel in human behavior. Human beings like to understand their environment and exert some control over it. The idea was formulated in Robert White's (1959) theory of **competence motivation**, which recognized that a basic human motive is to demonstrate control. Drive theories were unable to explain the gamut of human and animal behavior, especially the tendency to explore. Exploratory behavior, as it turns out, is not always in the service of reducing "tissue deficits." To the contrary, exploration often leads to *increases* in arousal, rather than to reductions as drive theory would predict. The self-reinforcing quality of exploratory behavior—exploration prompts *more* exploration—was antithetical to drive theory. This contradiction led White to propose competence as a need in its own right, independent of basic physiological needs.

Much human behavior can be accounted for by the need to exhibit competence. It is possible that, beyond survival needs, a person's primary motivation is to be effective in exerting control over life events and circumstances (deCharms, 1976). The need to be causal reflects perhaps the most basic adaptive response to the environment, helping to ensure immediate survival and longer-term prospects for a thriving existence.

Achievement Motivation

Competence motivation is highly relevant to students' engagement in school activities. The need to exhibit competence can be harnessed to help students advance toward greater knowledge and skill. Of course, students vary considerably in the need to be competent in school settings. Personality theories can help to account for these differences. According to one theory, people differ in a global personality dimension called **achievement motivation** (McClelland, 1961) or **need for achievement** (Atkinson, 1958). For a person to be successful, talent is not enough; there must also be a desire to *use* that talent to become successful. This enduring desire, the need for achievement, helps translate high ability into success (Simonton, 1984).

In *The Achieving Society*, McClelland (1961) described the need for achievement as a deep commitment to standards of excellence. Within any group, some individuals will exhibit a strong need to achieve and others will show comparatively little need for personal achievement. There will be individual variation, with most people displaying moderate levels of achievement motivation. According to McClelland's theory, whole societies and cultures also differ in achievement motivation. He wondered why fifteenth-century Florence experienced such a profusion of talent and concluded that the artists and intellectuals of Florence—Michelangelo, Leonardo da Vinci, and Galileo, among many others—were driven by a high level of achievement motivation that inspired an outpouring of creative achievement during the Italian Renaissance. Societies can differ with respect to the need for achievement, and those levels can change over time. Achievement motivation is therefore a dynamic quality that fluctuates with a society's core beliefs and values.

Soon after achievement motivation was postulated as a global personality trait, one assessment process became favored for measuring a person's need for achievement. That test is the Thematic Apperception Test (TAT) (Murray, 1943). The TAT is a **projective test** of personality. Unlike tests that are common in academic settings, there are no correct or incorrect answers; instead, responses are highly subjective. Projective tests present ambiguous stimuli, such as pictures, and ask the examinee to say what each stimulus means to him or her. The open-ended interpretation that the examinee "projects" onto the ambiguous picture gives important information to the examiner. To the degree that subjects identify achievement-related themes in the TAT pictures, they are judged to have a high need for achievement. As more achievement-related themes are projected onto the pictures, the examinee's overall score on the need for achievement goes up.

The Thematic Apperception Test and the personality trait known as the *need for achievement* are not often employed in educational contexts. Neither the theory nor the assessment is in vogue to the degree that they were in decades past. Part of the reason for the decline in popularity of the TAT and other projective tests is that their generated scores are necessarily somewhat subjective. A score may vary depending on who administers the test, therefore lowering the test's reliability. Nonetheless, the theory of achievement motivation tells us something important about why student behavior varies greatly in academic contexts: Success in schools and other learning environments can be understood partly as arising from differences in this personality dimension. For whatever reason—perhaps a combination of genetic predisposition and environmental experience—people differ in their need to achieve.

A more recently identified personality dimension, called the **need for cognition**, also recognizes individual differences that are strongly related to thinking and learning. The need for cognition refers to the variation among people in their tendency to engage in and enjoy cognition (Cacioppo, Petty, Feinstein, & Jarvis, 1996). People who are on the low end of the need for cognition are cognitive "misers." They minimize efforts to understand information and solve problems, tending instead to rely on the opinions and solutions generated by other people. In contrast, those with a high need for cognition have a strong personal desire to exercise their minds—they have an "endless intellectual curiosity" that compels them to raise questions and seek answers for themselves (p. 247). If we want to understand why there is significant variation in academic achievement, then we can look to the personality dimensions of need for achievement and need for cognition for two promising explanations.

Expectancy-Value Theories

As a personality trait, the need for achievement is not particularly cognitive in its theoretical conceptualization. Other approaches to motivation are much more cognitive in orientation. One such approach, **expectancy-value theory** (Fishbein & Ajzen, 1974), is cognitive in that it speculates on the kind of mental calculation a person makes when facing decisions, and on the nature of information that feeds into those calculations. The very name of expectancy-value theory indicates the two kinds of information that enter into decisions: *expectancy* refers to the likelihood that a particular choice will result in a particular outcome; *value* is the perceived benefit of that outcome.

Decision-making can be quite complicated, of course. Any point of decision might present several options from which to choose. Each of those options will lead to consequences, but those consequences are not necessarily predictable in advance. Perhaps the best a person can do is estimate the probability of each outcome (its expectancy) and how good or bad that outcome would be (its value). Should you ask your friend on a date? Certainly, there is positive value if the invitation is accepted, and negative value if it is rejected. What is the probability of each response? Let's say it's 50/50. In your rough mental calculation you might decide that the pleasure of an acceptance has twice the value as the pain of rejection. Now you know what to do: The rational decision is to ask the person out because the expectancy-value of that decision pathway is highest (even if it is highly subjective, approximate, and intuitive, rather than calculated).

The decision calculus becomes more complicated if you have several different options. When a high school student faces the prospect of finding a date as the prom approaches, he or she may be lucky to have several options (or unfortunate to have to face them). A student might consider the expectancy-value of asking each, and weigh these against the option of not going to the prom at all. Any student would approach the question of prom dates rationally, right? Well, perhaps not. But even if expectancy-value theory only *approximates* the way we make decisions *some* of the time, it has value for interpreting the choices that students make in their academic pursuits. A student can choose to try hard or to slack off, to enroll in an advanced course or to avoid further study, to ask for help or to go it alone. If equipped with the intellectual tools for rational decision making, students will experience greater success in the long run.

Expectancy-value theory recognizes not only the positive value of success but also the negative value of failure. Both enter into the calculus that has the potential to guide decision-making. We differ in our feelings about success, as we have seen in the theory of achievement motivation. Some people have a much stronger personality-driven need to achieve than do others. Expectancy-value theory recognizes that people differ also in their reactions to the prospect of value. Some people have a great aversion to negative consequences—a paralyzing **fear of failure**. For other people, though, the prospect of failure is not debilitating—it may even be energizing as a necessary component of challenge.

Maslow's Hierarchy of Needs

Expectancy-value theory led us to consider that decision making is guided not only by the chances of success and failure, but also by the value of those consequences. How is value decided? Is it entirely subjective, or are there commonalities across people about the value of particular outcomes? Certainly, value is predictable to a degree. A person whose car has broken down in the desert will be extremely thirsty after a few hours of wandering on foot. To a very thirsty person, thoughts of anything but a drink of water are rather insignificant. The same could be said for a starving person; food assumes very high importance. Basic biological needs can be highly compelling, as Hull recognized in his drive theory—but they don't tell the whole story.

FIGURE 6.5
Maslow's Hierarchy
of Needs. *The
ordered needs range
from basic survival
requirements to the
pinnacle of
fulfillment, self-
actualization.*
[Adapted from Maslow,
1987. Electronically
reproduced by per-
mission of Pearson
Education, Inc.]

Human beings have many other needs besides those that are essentially biological. For example, we have needs for safety and the respect of other people. We also have a need to control our environment and our circumstances as proposed in the theory of competence motivation. When we consider this spectrum of needs, the picture of human motivation starts to look highly complex. Is there a way to simplify things—to lend order to the array of motives that prompt human behavior? One highly influential attempt to organize human motives into a comprehensible schema was made by the psychologist Abraham Maslow (1968). Maslow proposed that certain needs—namely, physiological needs—are fundamental. If those needs are not met, then they automatically assume priority in guiding behavior. But if basic physiological needs are satisfied, then other needs come to the fore. Those needs are presented in the diagram of Maslow's hierarchy (Fig. 6.5).

Maslow's hierarchy shows that the most basic needs are biological. Above those are safety needs. Next in order of priority is belongingness, which refers to the pervasive human need for social connection, for affection, and for love. Still higher up in the hierarchy is self-esteem. If these more basic needs are met, then the need for self-esteem rises in importance. The need for self-esteem probably motivates a significant degree of effort in academic and career success. But if a learner's more basic needs are not met, then activities motivated by self-esteem needs will not be important. This alone says much about the probable impact of poverty on learning. If a child is hungry, in danger, or unloved, then the self-esteem needs that drive a good portion of achievement in academic settings will simply not be relevant.

Maslow was intensely interested in the need placed at the top of his hierarchy—the need for **self-actualization**. The concept of self-actualization is by itself a major contribution of Maslow's theory. Self-actualization refers to the rare instance in which a person reaches his or her highest potential as a human being. When circumstances coincide to produce a person who possesses self-insight, wisdom, intelligence, and the capacity for love—in a combination that is unique to that individual—self-actualization has been achieved. The self-actualized person has become that best possible "version" of himself or herself. By Maslow's reckoning, very few people become self-actualized, but the potential and driving need is within each one of us. The hierarchy specifies that the quest for self-actualization usually builds on the satisfaction of more basic needs.

Self-actualization is the centerpiece of Maslow's theory. In fact, Maslow envisioned a branch of psychology that was directed toward helping people reach their highest potential. He saw psychology as overly focused on understanding and treating people with psychological disturbances—neuroses and psychoses. This was certainly the focus of Freud in his psychodynamic theory of mental illness. The alternative proposed by Maslow was to study psychologically *healthy* people, to understand them, and to apply that knowledge so that others could more fully realize their potential for growth, psychological health, and fulfillment. This orientation to psychology was shared by many other psychologists in the 1960s and 1970s, including Carl Rogers and Rollo May. Collectively, these scholars formed **humanistic psychology**, a branch of research and practice that has diminished in popularity since its heyday, but still has adherents among psychotherapists. The contemporary branch of scholarship known as **positive psychology** is similarly concerned with advancing the theory and achievement of health, well-being, success, and happiness (Bornstein, Davidson, Keyes, & Moore, 2003).

In significant ways, educators can sympathize with the tenets and motives of humanistic psychology. Educators want their students to reach toward their highest potential, even if few will actually achieve that exalted state. Teachers might not use the term *self-actualization,* but many teachers pride themselves in having a role in shaping students' lives toward greater fulfillment, maturity, and productivity. Effective teachers see that potential within each child, and try to awaken each student to his or her unique talents and gifts. Like Abraham Maslow, they realize that unfulfilled basic needs—the need for food, safety, belongingness, and self-esteem—can block students from reaching their potential. But when basic needs are met and with the right opportunities to learn and grow, students can move toward something higher.

Motivation Theories Based on Beliefs About Events

The desire to become self-actualized seems compatible with the larger goals of education. But self-actualization is possible only if a person senses a certain degree of control over the events of her life. After all, how is it possible to grow intellectually and to become successful if there is not some feeling of control? And yet, people differ significantly in the actual degree of control they have over the events of their lives, and in the degree of control they *think* they have over their lives. The theories presented in this section focus on how people differ in interpreting life events, especially experiences of success or failure.

Locus of Control

Psychologist Julian Rotter (1966) proposed that there are two contrasting explanatory styles for interpreting who or what controls a person's life. Some people have an internal **locus of control**. Whatever events transpire—good or bad—they see themselves as responsible. They are willing to take credit for success and assume responsibility for failure. Essentially, they see themselves as exercising control over whatever happens to them. Naturally, they interpret events consistently with this belief. Other people, by contrast, see themselves as *being controlled* by their circumstances. People with this explanatory style have an external locus of control. Whether they experience success or failure, they see external circumstances as responsible for the outcome.

Internal locus and external locus are associated with the parallel terms **origin** and **pawn** (deCharms, 1976). Think of a fairy tale prince on a quest to slay the dragon and rescue the princess locked in a tower. The prince presumably sees himself as an origin because he believes that the outcome of his quest depends on his courage and skill. He has an internal locus of control. The stereotypical princess, meanwhile, waits patiently to be rescued. Like a pawn on a chessboard, she is a pawn to the stronger forces that envelop her. Having an external locus of control, the princess can only hope that the events of her life will work out favorably.

These contrasting explanatory styles are certainly extreme. But in more moderate forms, these two ways of interpreting who or what has control over life events answer a question faced by real people, not fairy tale characters. Children and adults alike often gravitate toward an internal locus of control or external locus of control. Those who see themselves as pawns are quick to blame others for failure. "It's not my fault," they say, because in their own minds they are not in control. Passive by nature or by habit, they have difficulty in setting ambitious goals. Rather than work to create their own reality, their lives "happen" to them. People with an internal locus, however, see life events as emanating from the choices they make. Perhaps overly willing to accept blame for setbacks and failures, they are also more confident of their ability to direct their life path in productive directions. They are convinced that if they can imagine an exciting goal, they will have the personal resources to reach it.

In the continuum between internal and external locus of control, some people think they are capable of just about anything they set their mind to—and perhaps they are. But there are also those who are radically passive toward the circumstances of their lives. These are victims of what has been called **learned helplessness** (Seligman, 1975; Garber & Seligman, 1980). A student who fits this description feels that there is nothing he can do to become successful. The condition is *learned* in that it arises from the repetitive failure of effort to lead to a good outcome. The student might try repeatedly to earn high grades and to please the teacher—all to no avail. Repetitive failure leads to an obvious conclusion: "Nothing I do can produce the outcome I desire." Perhaps at home, also, repeated attempts to please his parents are ineffectual. For the person experiencing learned helplessness, there is a complete disconnection between personal initiative and desired outcomes. The strategy that makes the most sense is simply to stop trying.

Learned helplessness is devastating to the education process. Students who experience feelings of helplessness may find emotional protection in the armor of withdrawal. Laziness, irresponsibility, truancy, and uncooperativeness all protect "helpless" students from the risk of failure and its consequences, although not from other sanctions. Slow learners, students with learning disabilities, and special education students are all vulnerable to learned helplessness. An alert teacher is mindful of signs of learned helplessness, including passivity and deep discouragement, and will take steps to prevent a further slide into withdrawal.

Teachers' leadership styles can influence how students perceive the causal force of their own actions. Ideally, teachers will steer students away from an external locus of control and toward an internal locus. They want students to know that they can exercise control over the events of their lives, particularly in school. A teacher who monitors her students too closely may hinder the development of an internal locus of control. Under close surveillance, students have little opportunity to develop an internal locus.

When students are granted some autonomy, however, they are likely to perceive their actions as arising from within—from the force of their own decisions. There is an additional benefit to giving choice to students: Choice, or even the illusion of choice, is intrinsically motivating (Deci, 1975).

When a teacher nudges students toward a sense of control—toward an internal locus—the teacher advances the causes of learning and intellectual growth. Students' interpretive frameworks can shift accordingly. If a test result is disappointing, a student might consider that he could have studied harder or prepared more fully. The locus is *within*. Likewise, when he experiences success he will not pass it off as a fluke or the result of luck, but rather as a sign that he is able.

Attribution Theory

Theories subsequent to Rotter's locus of control theory expanded on the notion that people have different characteristic explanations for the events of their lives. **Attribution theory** focuses on the explanations people give for success and failure experiences

INTEREST MAGNET 6.2

Helpless Fish

Imagine a scenario in which a person or an animal faces a highly unpleasant situation. There may be a way to escape physical or psychological pain but, strangely, the organism does not try to do so. What explains such passivity? Perhaps previous attempts to escape unpleasant stimuli did not bring relief, so the person or animal does not attempt to escape suffering.

This passivity in the face of pain is the hallmark of the dire psychological condition known as *learned helplessness*. The study of learned helplessness originated in experiments with dogs who were given brief but inescapable electrical shocks (Maier, Seligman, & Solomon, 1969). Later, the dogs did not try to escape the shocks even though they could have done so easily by leaping over a low barrier. After conducting research on dogs, psychologists found that learned helplessness also occurs in people, not as the result of experimental manipulations, but through the difficult circumstances of life.

Early research also led to the discovery that learned helplessness could occur in animals as uncomplicated as the common goldfish. Researchers first needed to know whether goldfish could learn to escape an electric shock (Frumkin & Brookshire, 1969). To teach this behavior, the researchers relied on classical conditioning. A few seconds after a light was turned on in the fish tank, part of the tank was electrified. Through trial and error, the fish learned that by swimming to the other end of the tank they could avoid the electric shock that followed the light. Those fish were not helpless—they "knew" how to escape suffering.

However, certain kinds of experiences interfered with the ability of the goldfish to learn the escape behavior (Padilla, 1973). In one experiment, untrained fish were placed into a tank that did not allow escape. The tank had a clear barrier that prevented the fish from swimming to the safe portion of the tank. When the clear barrier was later removed, allowing the fish to escape the shock, they were poor performers. They were no longer effective at learning to avoid the shock even though avoidance was as simple as swimming to the other end of the tank. Here was proof that learned helplessness could be acquired by fish, just as it could be acquired by dogs.

Interestingly, even when the goldfish were previously trained to avoid the shock, they subsequently became passive when they later faced a series of unavoidable shocks. When a goldfish learns that an unpleasant situation cannot be avoided, this creates an enduring disposition of passivity. Even when it becomes possible to control events, the organism does not take advantage of the opportunity. Like goldfish, people also can acquire learned helplessness. If there is no felt connection between actions and outcomes, initiative can shut down. When repeated efforts have no effect, a person may eventually stop trying. Humans become helpless not because they run out of options, but because they have learned, tragically, that their efforts to achieve success or to avoid pain have had no effect.

(Weiner, 1985). Those explanations are *attributions* because they *attribute* the event to this or that cause. Building directly on locus of control theory, one dimension of attribution is *locus*. The locus can be internal, with such attributions as ability (or lack thereof) and effort (or lack thereof). Internal attributions may be controllable or not, which leads to a second dimension, *controllability*. Effort is controllable, but ability usually is not. Many external attributions (e.g., "the test was hard" or "the teacher was unfair") are likewise uncontrollable. Another uncontrollable attribution is luck. A person might say, "I was lucky" or "I was unlucky." But is luck a stable trait, or does it come and go? A person might believe "I'm a lucky person," in which case luck is stable; alternatively, a person might claim that "I just happened to be lucky on that particular occasion," revealing a belief that luck is unstable. This attribution points to a third dimension of attributions: *stability*.

Attribution theory therefore recognizes three dimensions along which explanations can be categorized: locus, controllability, and stability. Each of these three dimensions crosses the other two in a 2 by 2 by 2 matrix, creating eight possible combinations. People tend to develop characteristic patterns of attributions, habitually seeing the events of their lives as a result of luck, ability, effort, and so on. Not all attribution patterns are equally conducive to success in academic settings, or to progress in developing academic ability over time. Consider the statement, "I'm not good at math," an attribution all too frequently spoken or believed, perhaps especially by girls. The attributions are not necessarily backed by evidence. Sometimes students claim to lack ability in mathematics despite good scores on exams and on achievement tests. Attributions are sometimes socialized as elements of gender roles. For example, in 1991, the notorious Teen Talk Barbie doll complained: "Math is hard!"

What attributions are most conducive to learning and to academic success? The answer is equivocal. Ability attributions can be helpful if they reflect beliefs about high ability rather than low ability. Attributions of high ability have a potential downside, however. A person who relies on ability might be reluctant to apply effort and extend perseverance over time because high effort is actually counterevidence to high ability attributions. People who believe they are highly able might be reluctant to try hard. Considering the three dimensions, the best attributions are those that have an internal locus, are controllable, and are stable over time. One attribution fits these categories best—effort.

Effort is arguably the most desirable attribution. It works for success ("I succeeded because I worked hard") and for failure ("I was disappointed in my performance because I did not try hard enough"). Effort is universally adaptive because if a person has experienced success, that person will continue to apply effort in the future. If there has been a failure or setback, there is recourse to trying again and trying harder. Too few students see their success and failure efforts as a consequence of level of effort. In the United States, especially, students are prone to interpret their academic successes as a consequence of high ability. Japanese students, by contrast, are more likely to attribute their success to effort (Holloway, 1988). Effort attributions, in turn, lead to greater applications of effort over time. Could this be one reason that Japanese students routinely outperform American students in international studies of mathematics learning?

Knowing what attributions are most conducive to learning and academic success is useful knowledge for teachers. Teachers are likely to hear a variety of explanations for students' performance:

- The test was too hard.

- I got lucky this time.

- I'm not good at this.
- I'm stupid.
- The teacher doesn't like me.
- I studied really hard this time.
- I wasn't prepared for this test.

Of these explanations, teachers should encourage only the last two, which appeal to effort as the cause of success or failure. To a disappointed student, a teacher can suggest, "Well maybe you should study harder next time." The teacher's suggestion is premised on an assumption that level of effort is a legitimate explanation for the student's performance. A student who prefers a different attribution may not like the suggestion. After all, it places responsibility back on the student and implies that hard work lies ahead. In the long run, though, a teacher does the student a favor by encouraging effort attributions. Of course, ability also enters into explanations for success and failure. But ability can be seen as either fixed or changeable, as we will see later in this chapter. If intellectual ability is changeable, then it can be improved through exercising effort toward its advancement.

Motivation Theories Based on Beliefs About Self

Cognitive Dissonance Theory

Motivation theories vary quite a bit, shifting focus from personal values to explanations for success and failure. Another possible focus for motivation theories is beliefs about oneself (Schunk & Zimmerman, 2006). Cognitive dissonance theory is premised on the idea that people wish for consistency between what they believe (or say they believe) and what they do. If the two are inconsistent, the conflict produces an unsettled feeling of tension.

Whenever beliefs and behavior are contradictory, **cognitive dissonance** can result. The word *dissonance* means "an unharmonious clash." Think of the irritating sound of musical instruments that are out of tune—that's musical dissonance. Cognitive dissonance refers to the unharmonious clash of our ideas with our experience, especially our own behavior. To reduce cognitive dissonance requires a change in either beliefs or behavior so that the two become mutually consistent and harmonious (Festinger, 1962). Sometimes people change their behavior to match their beliefs; in fact, doing so is often presented as a moral imperative because we are supposed to "practice what we preach." An alternative, and a more theoretically interesting possibility, is that we sometimes change what we believe to match what we do. This second possibility is what makes cognitive dissonance theory particularly interesting as well as potentially useful.

Imagine you are given a choice between two equally attractive alternatives. Despite the difficulty of choosing between the two, you later interpret the choice you made as obviously the better one. In other words, your beliefs changed to match and to justify, or rationalize, the choice you made. A more sinister example is that the cognitive dissonance engendered by lying can be reduced either by admitting the lie (changing behavior) or by coming to believe that the lie is true (changing beliefs). It may be easier to believe that we were telling the truth all along than to admit dishonesty, even if reducing cognitive dissonance requires blatant self-deception.

One conclusion we could draw from cognitive dissonance research and theory is that human beings are not truly rational. Instead, we are *rationalizing* beings. That a thought process is coherent and backed by evidence seems to be less imperative than making it *seem* justified. This may seem like a pessimistic conclusion; nonetheless, there is potential here for positive application. A student may firmly believe, "I don't like science." But what happens if by the skills of a talented teacher the student finds himself fascinated during science class? Such an emotion is inconsistent with the declaration, "I don't like science." For the sake of cognitive consistency (and to reduce cognitive dissonance) the student might conclude instead, "Well, maybe I do like science after all." Another student may strongly believe that he hates to read. But when persuaded or forced to read a novel, he might become captivated by the story and have a desire to read other novels (Duchein & Mealey, 1993). For the sake of consistency, he might revise his beliefs to conclude that, in some cases at least, he actually enjoys reading. In these roundabout ways, new behavior can lead to new beliefs, and those new beliefs can be liberating.

Self-Worth Theory

Beliefs about self can include convictions about likes and dislikes, as we have seen in cognitive dissonance theory. Beliefs can also focus on oneself as a person of worth and dignity. In fact, it's possible to construe much of human behavior as directed toward protecting self-worth. We act in ways that elevate other people's opinions of us, or that shield us from low opinions. This strong motive is the focus of **self-worth theory**. Self-worth theory is quite powerful in explaining the choices we make (Covington, 1984). We want to be seen as able, as competent. The desire to enhance feelings of self-worth leads us to select and pursue goals and activities that will likely result in success. We avoid other goals and activities if they are likely to expose our inabilities and so threaten self-worth.

Strategies chosen to avoid threats to self-worth can be serious impediments to learning and personal growth. For example, in order to protect self-worth, two possible strategies are to choose unrealistically difficult goals or ridiculously easy goals. Why would opposite strategies support the same goal of protecting self-worth? Both do so because neither reveals any information about our true ability. If a student enrolls in a very difficult course without sufficient background, nobody is surprised if that student fails. What could anyone expect given that the course is so hard? Likewise, a student might choose unreasonably easy goals, goals that are far below his or her level of competence. We might regard low aspirations as a waste of ability and potential, but for a person who chooses the easy path that choice could be a way of protecting self-worth. Guaranteed success eliminates the possibility of failure and yields no information about one's true ability, which might be precisely the point.

A similar purpose is served by the various excuses, disclaimers, or provisos that we all make from time to time. A student about to take an important test may say to his fellow students, "I didn't study at all for this test!" This statement is strategic if the goal is to protect a sense of self-worth. After all, if the student does poorly, the outcome is completely understandable. On the other hand, if the student does well he can be credited with an impressive achievement. Perhaps his peers will conclude that the student is highly intelligent for having done so well without having studied. By disclaiming having studied at all, the student can only win. Poor performance is excusable and high performance is impressive—either way, self-worth is preserved. Sometimes on the basketball court I hear my fellow players make similar disclaimers before the game begins. A favorite strategy is to say something like, "I haven't picked up a basketball in two years." By this simple declaration a player's self-worth is effectively insured against later damage. If he plays poorly, we all understand why; if he plays well, we will be in awe—or so he might hope.

A similar purpose is served when a student claims a lack of effort. If he says, "I didn't try at all," the opinions of others are hedged in his favor. Strategies gauged to protect self-worth may have social utility, but they are not necessarily good for education or learning. A student might claim not to have studied for an examination in order to protect self-worth. Another student might claim a lack of effort for a school project or a homework assignment. Low effort signals to everyone that the work product contains little information about the students' true ability. Yet another student might dismiss the importance of an assignment or the educational enterprise altogether. To disengage from the norms and expectations of school, as in learned helplessness, is one way to protect self-worth against injury or attack.

Classrooms are places where feelings of self-worth are always vulnerable to some degree. Feedback about performance and social comparisons about ability are highly salient in the life of a student. Teachers can amplify or attenuate these realities, and should do so, but to remove them altogether is probably impossible and to deny them outright is counterproductive. Teachers should try to understand the importance of self-worth and the strategies that students use to protect those feelings. In making pedagogical choices, teachers can also try to protect those vulnerabilities while curtailing the counterproductive strategies that students sometimes adopt.

Entity and Incremental Theories

As students develop belief systems about themselves and their experiences, they also develop personal theories about the nature of intellectual abilities. These personal theories can differ dramatically from one student to another. According to the model proposed by Dweck and Leggett (1988), students view their intellectual abilities in one of two ways. Some students see their abilities as essentially fixed. They hold an **entity theory** of ability. Intelligence is believed to be present to a greater or lesser degree, and is highly stable through life. No amount of effort can raise ability, and disuse cannot erode it. In the entity view, ability is preset and unalterable.

Students who hold an **incremental theory** of ability see things very differently. To these students, intellectual abilities, including intelligence, are not fixed but instead are modifiable through experience and effort. If a student views his ability as low, this is not a cause for resignation or passivity. Rather, the student can try to increase his or her ability over time. Just because the learner sees his present ability, say, in mathematics or music, as low does not mean it must stay low. Mathematical or musical ability, like the ability to write well or to be knowledgeable in a field of study, can be learned. Ability, to a large extent, is modifiable. Students who perceive ability this way—as alterable through experience—have an advantage over students who see ability as static. For educational purposes, the incremental view of ability is preferable to the entity view.

Perhaps you have detected some overlap between Dweck and Leggett's entity/incremental model of ability and Weiner's attribution theory that we considered earlier. Incremental beliefs align well with effort attributions; entity beliefs align with ability attributions. Successful students are more likely to make effort attributions to explain their academic achievement. They see their immediate performance as a product of effort, and are likely see their intellectual ability as changeable over time. In a later chapter, we will see that the development of expertise is strikingly consistent with entity theories of ability. With focused effort applied over a long timeline, the expert becomes extraordinarily capable.

Self-Efficacy Theory

Among the various belief systems that guide human behavior, self-efficacy beliefs are among the most important. In Albert Bandura's theory, **self-efficacy** beliefs are estimates that people make about their ability to perform specific actions. Self-efficacy refers to the self-assessment of one's ability to perform specific tasks in specific situations. It is a major construct in social science, one that is highly relevant to educators.

Self-efficacy is different from self-esteem, which is concerned with generalized feelings about personal worth. Self-efficacy also differs from self-concept, which is comparatively broad in referring to beliefs about oneself along a wide range of concerns. Self-efficacy is specific. We might hold a high self-concept of ourselves as good students, but our self-efficacy beliefs would depend on the specific academic area. For example, we might have high self-efficacy beliefs about our ability to do well in mathematics or music, but low self-efficacy in creative writing or debate. In athletic domains, self-efficacy would vary by the specific sport. Although Lance Armstrong proved that he was a champion cyclist, he freely admitted that he had poor hand-eye coordination. He had high self-efficacy as cyclist, but neither his self-efficacy nor his skill extended to athletic performance generally. Like Lance Armstrong, we can differentiate the skill areas we excel in from those we don't.

We all have some sense of what we do well and what we do poorly. Each of us has self-efficacy beliefs about dozens or hundreds of specific performance domains. Those beliefs are not necessarily accurate. Self-efficacy is not the same as ability; what we believe about our ability might not be true. Moreover, beliefs about what we can do can have real effects on performance. Self-imposed mental limitations are well known in the world of competitive sports. American weight lifters, for example, have encountered barriers to progress at certain poundages, whereas European lifters have experienced mental barriers at round numbers of kilograms (Mahoney, 1979). In track events, the four-minute mile was long considered to be unattainable until Oxford medical student Roger Bannister broke that temporal threshold in 1954. Only a month later, Australian runner John Landy beat Bannister's time by a full two seconds. Thereafter, many other world-class distance runners ran sub-four-minute miles.

If self-efficacy is not identical with true ability, is that a problem? Should we strive for accuracy in our self-efficacy beliefs? Maybe not. It is not at all clear that having a completely accurate sense of self-efficacy is ideal. Research has shown, for example, that psychologically healthy people have slightly exaggerated self-efficacy beliefs when judging their social skills and their degree of control in a situation (Bandura, 1986). Strangely, depressed people often have a *more accurate* sense of their social skills and causal control.

Self-deception is not always helpful, of course. In the many cases where self-efficacy differs from true ability, such beliefs are not only inaccurate, they are also self-limiting. Fortunately, self-efficacy is modifiable—a fact that teachers and parents can use to help the developing learner. Modifiability is important because self-efficacy beliefs have real-world consequences on the choices we make and on our development as learners. Self-efficacy influences goal selection, for example. If we believe that we have the ability to achieve a goal, the pursuit of that goal becomes an option. Conversely, if we believe that we lack the necessary ability (whether we actually do or not) then we are not likely to pursue that particular goal. To the extent that personal success arises from the sequence of goal choices we make, self-efficacy will decisively influence our life paths. Self-efficacy influences not only our choice of goals, but also the level of effort we are

FIGURE 6.6
Roger Bannister
Breaks the Four-
Minute Mile. *Once
Bannister crossed
the mental barrier,
many others were
able to do the
same.* [Keystone/
Getty Images.]

willing to devote to pursuing them. An abiding belief that we are capable of success in a given context will lead us to exert effort toward attaining that goal. High perceptions of self-efficacy can help us persist when we face tough challenges (Bandura, 1982). Choice of goals, level of effort, and perseverance are all important consequences of self-efficacy beliefs.

FOUR INFLUENCES ON SELF-EFFICACY. Because self-efficacy is so crucial in the developing learner, we must try to understand the forces that shape beliefs about what we can do. Bandura (1986) noted four sources of information that form self-efficacy beliefs. One very important source of information—the most important, in fact—is *enactive attainments*. Enactive attainments refer to actual personal accomplishments. Beliefs about what we *can* achieve in the future are clearly influenced by what we have *already* achieved in the past. That is why one way to influence self-efficacy is to point out a person's previous accomplishments, to remind the person of what he or she has already done. Bandura found that some patients recovering from heart attacks were reluctant to exercise because they feared they were incapable of sustained physical effort. When these patients agreed to try exercising on a treadmill, they learned that they were far more capable of vigorous exercise than they first believed. Their self-efficacy beliefs were raised by their own successful performance, and so they were more likely to exercise again in the future.

Strangely, people are not always convinced of their ability by their own past performance attainments. A person's self-efficacy beliefs can be higher or lower than their true ability. Some students have an inflated sense of their own talents. Others underestimate what they can do despite evidence of competence, perhaps because their performance conflicts with what they believe about themselves. In educational settings, this biased pattern of interpretation can have serious consequences if a student continues to believe, falsely, that he is incapable. A student might be convinced that he has little mathematical ability despite evidence to the contrary, such as high test scores. So even though actual performance attainments are quite important as sources of information about self-efficacy beliefs, they do not guarantee that subsequent beliefs will be accurate or beneficial.

Fortunately, several other sources of information also feed into self-efficacy beliefs. A second source is *vicarious experience*. This refers to our ability to form beliefs *vicariously*, that is, indirectly by observing the experience of other people. A student who doubts her ability might observe the choices and performances of a similar peer and think, "If she can do it, then so can I." In effect, the peer models successful performance. Modeling is an important mode of learning in Bandura's social cognitive theory. Recall that Bandura proposed, contrary to the tenets of behaviorism, that we need not experience reinforcement directly in order to learn. Instead, we can observe what happens to other people as a consequence of their actions. A similar principle applies to self-efficacy beliefs—we can learn about our own abilities by observing what other people can do. When students choose ambitious and capable peers as models for their own behavior, they will enlarge their visions about what they are capable of doing.

A third source of information influencing self-efficacy is *verbal persuasion*. At one time or another, all of us have been encouraged by the affirmations of a respected teacher, relative, or other esteemed adult. We were told to expect more of ourselves, to set our sights higher than we had in the past. That respected person perceived the latent potential within us and helped us to see our own unrecognized possibilities. This kind of influence—what Bandura called verbal persuasion—illustrates the power of teachers to influence the course of students' lives. Many aspiring teachers choose to enter the teaching profession in part because they want to influence students positively during the course of a teaching career.

Of course, verbal persuasion can exert negative as well as positive effects. A discouraging statement from a teacher or parent, even a peer, can have devastating long-term consequences. One careless remark can cast enduring doubts about what a student is capable of achieving. Parents and teachers need to guard against excessively negative statements to students—statements that can deflate their sense of self-efficacy over the long term. Responsible adults must recognize the power of their words to influence young learners. They can use that power to do tremendous good by speaking honestly and positively about students' abilities to learn and to achieve.

In the context of discussing verbal persuasion, we will now consider a very important and related topic—teacher expectations. Teacher expectations do indeed influence student achievement (Brophy, 1983). Highly effective teachers—those who regularly elicit strong gains in student achievement—believe that their students are capable of learning, and that they, as teachers, are capable of teaching them effectively (Brophy, 2006). The largest expectation effects are found among "proactive" teachers who form their own expectations about students' capabilities without being overly swayed by prior achievement, diagnostic labels, or the opinions of students' former teachers. Proactive teachers see their responsibility as actively transforming the students' capabilities rather than simply accommodating to what those students have accomplished in the past. They are willing to adapt their instructional techniques to achieve these goals. If one teaching approach or curriculum does not work, they will try alternatives (Brophy, 2006). Typically, teacher expectation effects explain about 5 to 10 percent of the variance in student achievement during a single school year. During a single year, such an effect size is not huge, but over multiple years it can amount to a very appreciable influence on students' learning.

Building on these research findings, some professional development programs for teachers have spotlighted teacher expectations as being critically important for determining the academic success of students. In years past, vaunted claims were made that teacher expectations could influence even the measured intelligence of students. In one famous experiment, teachers' expectations for their students were manipulated to determine whether those expectations later affected the children's IQ levels (Rosenthal & Jacobsen, 1968). Teachers in an elementary school were the given names of a few students who were expected to make great intellectual progress ("bloomers") during the school year in comparison to their peers. But selection of the "bloomers" was completely random and had nothing to do with their actual IQ scores. The point was to test the influence of teachers' *beliefs* on changes in the children's measured IQ. The researchers reported that the IQ scores of the "bloomers" had increased by the end of the school year. These students seemed to benefit from teachers' positive beliefs and responded with measurably higher IQ scores. Teachers' beliefs were said to result in a **self-fulfilling prophecy** (Merton, 1948).

Can the beliefs and expectations of teachers really have such powerful effects on children's IQ scores? Subsequent analysis cast doubt on the reported findings and conclusions. One problem was that the IQ test used in the study had technical inadequacies, making the data questionable. When teacher expectation effects were found, they were statistically significant only in first and second grades, not in higher grade levels (Wineburg, 1987). Later attempts to replicate the experiment showed only weak effects or no effects at all. Unfortunately, the limitations of the original research were largely ignored in the popular press. The idea of a self-fulfilling prophecy seemed to resonate with the commonsense expectations of the public—namely, that teachers' beliefs, positive or negative, are potent forces in shaping the intellectual growth of students. The data did not support this belief as it pertains to IQ scores, or did so only weakly.

Bandura recognized a fourth source of information that influences self-efficacy beliefs: *physiological state*. Think about how the body responds to a difficult task. Whenever we face a tough challenge, we might become quite nervous. The body inevitably responds. If the heart beats faster and respiration rate increases, this physiological response may raise doubts about our ability to be successful. In this way, high physiological arousal can signal low ability, and therefore low self-efficacy. On the other hand, a low heart rate and a calm state can signal that a person is capable, implying high self-efficacy. Of course, a teacher does not have direct knowledge of a learner's heart rate, but does have some control over the emotional tone of the classroom, and so can indirectly influence a student's physiological state.

These four sources of information—enactive attainments, vicarious experience, verbal persuasion, and physiological state—are crucially important because they influ-

FIGURE 6.7
Bandura's Triadic Reciprocality Model. *Behavior influences (and is influenced by) the external environment as well as by the internal characteristics of the person, including beliefs. [Adapted from Bandura, 1986. Reproduced by permission of Pearson Education, Inc.]*

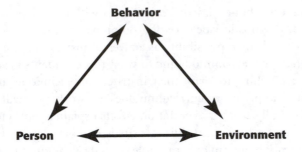

ence self-efficacy, and self-efficacy directly affects performance. Many studies have shown that enhanced self-efficacy can lead to measurable improvements in performance, including performance in academic settings. When teachers help students to develop beliefs about their competence in mathematics, for example, students will learn math more effectively and be more likely to pursue the study of mathematics with confidence. Self-efficacy beliefs organize and influence all stages of performance, including goal selection, persistence, and the interpretation of success outcomes. Beliefs affect behavior.

TRIADIC RECIPROCALITY. Bandura recognized the reciprocal influence of beliefs and behavior as part of a more general model of behavior that he called **triadic reciprocality**. The model specifies three components: the person, the environment, and behavior (Figure 6.7). Two of these—the environment and behavior—were commonly acknowledged by behaviorists as important. The third component, the person, includes all the ways that people differ, including self-efficacy beliefs. The triadic reciprocality model postulates that among the three (triadic) components, each influences the other two (reciprocality).

As we have discussed, self-efficacy is not simply a product of behavior (behavior→person); self-efficacy beliefs can also influence behavior directly (person→behavior). This aspect of triadic reciprocality—that beliefs can influence behavior—implies that high self-efficacy should be an important goal of education. If this is so, then self-efficacy should be regarded as an important focus for teaching. Among the many worthwhile goals that teachers can have for students, the elevation of self-efficacy is among the most important. As teachers take steps to build students' self-efficacy beliefs—whether through enactive attainments, vicarious experience, verbal persuasion, or physiological state—those beliefs will help students to become more effective learners. In the long run, healthy self-efficacy beliefs are essential to every student's success.

Goals

As every teacher knows, motivation varies tremendously from student to student. One point of variation is found in the goals students set for themselves. Even when students share the general goal of being successful in school, the standards by which they judge their success can vary greatly. For example, students can adopt different thresholds of evidence to decide whether or not they are succeeding. To some degree this is appropriate: Whether performance is "good" or "poor" may well be subjective. What a professional athlete defines as impressive athletic performance will probably differ from the average person's definition.

In the same way, success in school can be judged in more than one way. Here, a simple binary distinction is helpful: Progress can be judged against one's own past performance or against the performance of other people. These two ways of judging success have profoundly different implications for how students view themselves and the task at hand.

Task versus Ego Involvement

John Nicholls (1984) proposed two basic ways that students can evaluate their own competence: **task involvement** and **ego involvement**. Although Nicholls presented these dichotomously, they are more accurately viewed as endpoints on a continuum. People are said to be ego-involved if they judge their competence by comparing their own performance to the performance of others. Rather than focusing on the task, their attention is directed toward social comparison. To feel competent under these conditions, a student must perform at least as well as others, and with equal or less effort. Ego-involvement can be induced when tasks are presented as tests of valued skills, such as intelligence. Competition and the presence of an audience can also induce ego involvement.

In Nicholls' theory, people are task-involved if they use their own past performance, rather than the performance of others, as the basis for judging competence. A student who is task-involved is satisfied to know that he is making intellectual progress—that he understands more than he did yesterday or a week ago. The task-involved student is not concerned with his standing relative to peers. Instead, attention is focused on the task at hand. Task involvement has important benefits. Nicholls (1979) found that students who are task-involved are more likely to be intrinsically motivated. Moreover, Nicholls speculated that outstanding creative achievements are more often made by people who are task-involved rather than ego-involved.

In schools, each student's performance is most often evaluated by how it compares to the performance of others. These are conditions that foster ego-involvement. One serious drawback of social comparison is that individuals might be afraid to attempt a task if it could reveal low ability relative to others. Fortunately, teachers can create conditions that are conducive to task-involvement. The most important role for the teacher in this regard is to de-emphasize social comparison as the basis for students' self-evaluation. Teachers can focus on mastery rather than on normative comparisons—on what the student *can do*, rather than on how the student *compares to others*. Teachers can also exercise caution in using competition as a pedagogical device. Finally, a teacher can judiciously choose challenging tasks for students, activities that are neither too easy nor too difficult. Challenging tasks, those that require and will probably yield to high effort, are most likely to generate task-involvement (Nicholls, 1984). Other conditions conducive to task-involvement are the reduction of stress and the reduced salience of extrinsic incentives. All these conditions are to some degree under the control of the teacher.

The distinction between task-involvement and ego-involvement is important and useful. A parallel distinction to that drawn by Nicholls was the identification of learning goals and performance goals among students (Elliott & Dweck, 1988). **Learning goals** are organized around increasing personal competence. **Performance goals** are geared toward gaining the positive judgments of other people. Between these two types of goals, learning goals are the most conducive to school success. For students who struggle with school tasks, learning goals are less likely to lead to discouragement and strategy deterioration.

Goal Properties

Goal-setting is deeply woven into the fabric of human cognition. Starting at age two and a half, children start to form connections between their actions and outcomes that are not physically present (Klossek, Russell, & Dickinson, 2008). Their behavior thereby acquires an instrumental quality that extends their control beyond the immediate environment. Goal-directed behavior is strongly adaptive and indispensable to intelligent thought and action. Goals help to organize behavior and resources toward achieving valued outcomes. The formation and pursuit of goals contributes significantly to success in schools, on the job, and in virtually every context of life. Some goals are preferable to others in maximizing the probability of success. Researchers have found that specific properties of goals bear strongly on the likelihood of those goals being reached, as well as on the level of satisfaction or frustration that accompanies the pursuit of goals.

PROXIMAL AND SPECIFIC GOALS. Goals differ in their operational timeline: whether they are near-term or long-range. On a practical level, near-term **proximal goals** are more likely to be reached than are long-term distal goals (Locke, Shaw, Saari, & Latham, 1981). When students approach tasks that are large and cumbersome—a science project, for example—proximal goals can guide and motivate practical action (Bandura, 1982). Proximal goals can also lead to perceptions of competence and to increased intrinsic motivation. We might wisely set far-off and ambitious **distal goals**, but it is the nearer-term goals—those we will try to accomplish this month, this week, or even today—that are more likely to bring us concretely toward our desired ends. Proximal goals have a further advantage over far-off distal goals: They are correlated with a sense of well-being (Emmons, 1999).

Goals also differ in degree of specificity. **Specific goals** are precisely stated and afford clear criteria to judge whether or not they have been achieved. At a more general level are **abstract goals**, or "goals for goals." Those higher-level goals determine whether or not lesser goals serve valued ends (Haslam & Baron, 1994). One abstract goal might be to become a highly educated person. This general goal can guide the selection and pursuit of more specific goals, such as reading more books or pursuing a master's degree. Typically, proximal goals are also specific goals. Ideally, the specific and proximal goals that guide and motivate our daily behavior are consistent with the longer-range and more abstract goals that define our values and most cherished hopes. A rational goal structure can be judged for its "co-satisfiability"—the degree to which it balances short-term impulses and long-term satisfaction (Bronowski, 1973). Haslam and Baron (1994, p. 44) described goal coherence as consisting of "an integrated vision of the good life as an extended unity in time."

CHALLENGE. Goals have their most positive effects on interest and intrinsic motivation when they are challenging—that is, when they are closely matched to ability. In one research study, elementary school children were asked to choose among classification tasks that varied in difficulty. The children tended to select tasks that were just a little beyond their present abilities and reported those tasks as most interesting

(Danner & Lonkey, 1981). The challenging tasks had high information value. The children implicitly sought accurate information about their abilities, a strategy that is opposite to strategies that *conceal* information about ability in order to protect feelings of self-worth.

TIME MANAGEMENT. One important aspect of goal-directed behavior is the management of goals within the constraints of time. Britton and Tesser (1991) investigated whether college students' ability to manage their time well predicted their grades. The researchers found that two dimensions of time management—short-range planning and time attitudes—predicted total college grades even better than SAT scores. *Short-range planning* included such practices as setting goals for each day and creating a schedule of activities. *Time attitudes* measured whether students felt in control of their time, such as by prioritizing their goals and avoiding unprofitable activities. SAT scores, which are specifically designed to predict college grades, correlated with the students' college grade-point average (GPA) at $r = .20$. The predictive validity of the time management dimensions was higher, with *short-range planning* correlating with GPA at $r = .25$ and *time attitudes* correlating with GPA at $r = .39$. The time-management aspects of goal setting may have more to do with real-world attainment, including academic success, than we usually appreciate.

COOPERATIVE, COMPETITIVE, AND INDIVIDUALISTIC GOALS. Another dimension of goals is whether their pursuit depends on cooperation, competition, or individual effort. All three goal structures are familiar elements of school life. Researchers have long been interested in which provides the greatest educational benefit. The question is complicated by the fact that cooperation and competition can co-exist, as in the kind of inter-group competition common in team sports. On balance, the research evidence points to the overall superiority of cooperation to both competitive and individualistic goal structures in promoting educational achievement (Johnson, Maruyama, Johnson, Nelson, & Skon, 1981).

Slavin (1980) described specific teaching strategies as **cooperative learning** in which students work in small groups and receive rewards based on group performance rather than individual effort. He found several benefits to cooperative learning, including enhanced group cohesiveness and positive race relations. In most cases, cooperative learning also produced advantages in academic achievement over traditional teaching methods. Slavin found no cases in which cooperative learning produced a disadvantage in learning outcomes. Cooperative goal structures have also been found to be superior to competitive and individualistic goal structures in promoting problem-solving (Johnson, Johnson, & Stanne, 1985).

Goal-setting and goal-directed behavior are important components of an intelligent, successful life. In contrast to biological evolution, which is not goal directed but instead arises from random genetic mutations, the human mind can imagine what possible states of affairs are desirable, and then think and act to achieve those imagined states. The ability to formulate and pursue goals is an important product of education. As we seek to elevate our own intelligent functioning and that of others, we can promote specific and proximal goals as a means to progress toward longer-term aspirations and a greater sense of fulfillment. We can ask our students (and challenge ourselves) to imagine and express those goals, both in speech and in writing, and then stay true to plans to make them reality. To accomplish valued goals through determined pursuit requires sustained volitional control, a topic we consider next under the banner of self-regulation.

Self-Regulation

Volition

When Hilgard proposed the trilogy of mind model, he chose the term *conation* to refer to goal-driven, purposeful activity. He then divided conation into two subprocesses, motivation and volition. This second distinction sharpens the conceptual landscape considerably. **Motivation** refers to all factors that lead up to a decision about a course of action. **Volition** refers to all of the processes that maintain goal-focused behavior once the goal is adopted. The first is *pre-decisional* analysis; the second is *post-decisional* self-regulation (Corno, 1993). The crucial dividing point is the decision to act. The forces that feed into the decision are motivational. After a decision is made to act, the processes that sustain focus toward achieving the selected goal are volitional.

In **action control theory**, psychologists Heinz Heckhausen and Julius Kuhl (1985) suggested an image of how motivation and volition relate sequentially. They took the historical metaphor of Julius Caesar's military campaign in 49 B.C. While in northern Italy, Caesar was warned by the Roman Senate to resign command of his army. He could have complied with the Senate's orders by turning back early in his march toward Rome. But the leader reached a critical point at the Rubicon River. When Caesar crossed the Rubicon River, he committed himself to challenging the leadership of Rome and to sparking a civil war. Crossing the Rubicon was the decisive point, the point of no return, when turning back became inconceivable or nearly so. In these metaphorical terms, Heckhausen and Kuhl cast the point of decision as "crossing the Rubicon" in all goal-directed behavior (Corno, 1993). The Rubicon of decision-making divides motivation from volition.

Both processes, motivation and volition, are vital to successful action. Both can also go awry, leading to ineffective behavior. To illustrate, let us say a student has been

FIGURE 6.8
Caesar Crossed the Rubicon River. *The phrase, "crossing the Rubicon," refers to the decisive moment when motivation culminates in a volitional decision to act.* [Rodney Shackell/DK]

assigned to write a term paper that is due on Monday. It's Friday night, and there is just enough time over the weekend to write a paper that will earn a grade of B. The paper will require some background research, an outline, and many hours of writing and rewriting. The student is motivated to write the paper, but faces some distractions, including the options of going to the beach or attending a concert. His motivation to write the term paper competes with other attractive possibilities.

Just after dinner on Friday night, the student makes a decision to set aside all distractions and to dedicate the weekend to writing the term paper. Once the student decides to write the paper, volitional processes take over. These include decisions about what subgoals must be pursued, and how to arrange those activities over a workable timeline. For example, the student might decide to complete an outline on Friday evening, to produce a good draft by the end of the day on Saturday, and to have a polished paper by Sunday night. Of course, the decision to pursue a goal does not guarantee that the goal will be achieved. Setbacks and distractions can litter the pathway of good intentions. Subgoals that initially seemed reasonable can turn out to be overly ambitious. Unplanned events,

INTEREST MAGNET 6.3

Is Hypnosis Real?

"You are feeling sleepy, very sleepy. When I snap my fingers, you will believe you are a chicken." So goes the cliché of hypnosis. Is it hocus-pocus fakery or a genuine form of mind control? Neither one, actually. Hypnosis is a state of consciousness induced to make a person more receptive to suggestion. Uses of hypnotism range from entertainment (e.g., getting people to act like chickens) to treatment of chronic pain. The exact nature of hypnosis has been highly controversial, however. One extreme interpretation is that hypnosis does not really exist as a psychological phenomenon, but simply involves role-playing on the part of the hypnotized person. The other extreme view is that hypnosis is a form of "mind control" that can compel a person to do something against his or her will. Neither interpretation is consistent with the evidence.

Most psychologists now accept the reality of a hypnotic state and agree on its usefulness, but still disagree on its nature. Although different theories have been advanced to account for hypnotism, most explanations accept that the hypnotized person is in a highly relaxed state. A hypnotist almost always tries to induce this state by instructing a person to close his eyes, and by suggesting that the person is becoming more relaxed and his limbs are becoming "heavy." Physiological changes attest to the authenticity of the hypnotic state. For example, hypnotism is associated with reduced sensitivity to pain. In some people, the pupils become less reactive to light and therefore do not constrict as readily as they would in a normal state. Brain researchers have documented a shift in brain waves toward alpha rhythms, EEG signals that are midway between alert states ("beta") and sleep states ("delta").

A highly relaxed brain state makes some people much more open to suggestion (Nash, 2001). A suggestion during the hypnotic state might prompt unusual behavior for the sake of entertainment, a practice called stage hypnosis. However, hypnosis can also be applied to pursue an important outcome, such as weight loss, cessation of smoking, reduction of chronic pain, and other important goals. Hypnotism has long been used by some dentists as a pain-management strategy for patients, and was employed by medical doctors before the development of reliable anesthetics. One use of hypnotism that is much more controversial and fraught with danger is "memory recovery." This involves use of hypnosis to recall memories—often traumatic memories from childhood. Research has shown that such memories can feel true even if they are false. Because hypnosis places the person in a relaxed state, even a false memory can be "remembered" without much effort. The person can mistake ease of recall for the truth of the memory (Nash, 2001).

Nevertheless, hypnosis is now widely acknowledged to be useful. Hypnotism is used in the treatment of certain disease conditions, such as asthma. It can also add value to psychotherapy, improving the effectiveness of treatment. Moreover, growing evidence from brain scans shows that the hypnotized brain exhibits different patterns of activation than a non-hypnotized brain. The hypnotic state is real, not magical, and it can be useful as well as entertaining.

such as a phone call from a family member or a surprise visit from a friend, can throw a plan off course. Volitional processes keep us on track despite impediments to progress. Some of us are better than others at dealing with distractions and difficulties. Just as we differ in the motivational forces that lead to goal-setting, so we also differ in volitional skills that keep us focused on achieving our chosen goals.

In reality, then, making a decision to pursue a particular goal does not guarantee that we will maintain that commitment over time. A decision to write a term paper over the weekend can be derailed by distractions, fatigue, or even forgetfulness. We all face impediments to the volitional decisions we make. We also differ in our ability to "protect" our own volitional intentions from disruption. Perhaps you know iron-willed, highly focused people who pursue their goals relentlessly. You might know other people who are comparatively poor at following through on their commitments. They are easily distracted; perhaps they even wish for distractions so that they have an excuse to abandon their plans. These individuals are poor at protecting their volitions. They may have their motivational priorities in order and dependably choose worthwhile goals, but are weak at follow-through. From these hypothetical examples you can see value in equipping students not only to be focused motivationally, but also skilled volitionally. Each of us needs the ability to protect our intentions so that we can stay focused, even if we sometimes deviate from a preset plan.

Volitional control, like any form of self-regulation, can improve with practice. Students can employ volitional control strategies when facing social distractions or self-doubt (Corno, 1993). For example, a student might reward herself with relaxation or recreation after completing her math homework. Self-rewards often entail the **delay of gratification**, which in itself may be crucial for success in schools and elsewhere. Children vary significantly in their ability to delay gratification. Psychologist Walter Mischel showed four-year-old children a marshmallow and then offered a choice: Each child could eat one marshmallow immediately or have two after the psychologist returned to the room about 15 minutes later (Mischel, Shoda, & Rodriguez, 1989). Mischel found that children who opted to wait for two marshmallows—those who could delay gratification—were more likely to be successful students as teenagers. They had higher SAT scores, were more goal-focused, and had a greater capacity to cope with stress.

Volitional control strategies include the ability to manage such intrusive emotions as frustration and boredom. A larger set of **self-regulation strategies** have been recognized as strong predictors of academic success (Pintrich, 2000; Zimmerman & Pons, 1986). These strategies include goal-setting, planning, seeking information, monitoring progress, and structuring the environment to reduce distractions. Strategies that protect volitional commitments can be seen as "meta" functions alongside metacognition. Just as higher-order cognition employs metacognitive functioning, so too it relies on metavolitional processes. In Vygotskian fashion, students can focus on and protect their volitional intentions by observing the same skilled process in others, including the teacher. In group processes also, students can learn from others how to stay focused on the task at hand, monitor progress toward goals, and persist through difficulties and setbacks.

Volitional control is important to effective intellectual activity. Intelligent problem solving requires breaking down a complex problem into multiple subgoals and pursuing each in a sensible order, without losing track of any. For some people, the volitional drive to achieve chosen goals is so intense that their determination almost defies belief. Yet exceptional perseverance through setbacks can lead to eventual vindication. Unusual grit through a gauntlet of rejections can become legendary. The novelist Stephen King is rumored, early in his career, to have driven a spike through his many rejection letters from potential publishers and displayed the sheaf near his typewriter.

In cases where dogged perseverance pays off, it looks like virtue; in other cases, though, it can appear delusional. Does extraordinary success require a degree of volitional intensity that seems imbalanced or even pathological? Possibly. But extreme volition can also be counterproductive in everyday situations. After all, intelligence requires not only the ability be focused on goals, but also the sense to disengage from strategies when they are not working. For lower-ability learners, this disengagement can be challenging as those students sometimes persist long after their strategies have proven to be ineffective (Corno, 1993).

Volitional control is not only important for success, it is also necessary for developing the high levels of skill that constitute expert performance. In the next chapter on cognitive development, we will see that expertise is achieved only after many years of dedicated engagement in a field. World-class performance requires a degree of focus and self-discipline that is unusual in the general population. In the development of expertise, volitional control over thought, action, and effort are indispensable.

New Directions

Perhaps by its very nature, rational cognitive activity is simpler and easier to understand than are human feelings, motives, and intentions. Theories of hot cognition—of emotion, motivation, and volition—are certainly complex. Every valuable framework presented in this chapter, such as self-efficacy theory or attribution theory, seems to capture a slice of what is important. None of the frameworks seems to be a candidate for a grand theory that can bring order to the many different aspects of motives, feelings, and intentionality.

One possible direction for developing a more comprehensive theory is to combine constructs from different models to present a fuller picture of the feeling, striving person. For example, aptitudes can be considered in combined pairs. Such **aptitude complexes** combine two or more motivational traits, or they may combine a motivational trait with a cognitive dimension, such as intelligence (Snow, 1992). The hope is that with a more complete description of the student by trait pairs or higher-order complexes, more precise recommendations can be made about suitable instructional approaches.

Motivation theory is also finding expression in teaching practices. Historically, the impetus for child-centered teaching approaches has been partly to give the individual child choice over activities, as well as choice within activities. The assumption is that self-direction is more motivating than teacher-centered and highly prescriptive instruction. Similar benefits might apply to learning that is mediated by computer technologies. Computer-based learning environments can offer a high degree of sensory interest (through captivating audio and video) as well as adapt to the child's pace of learning. Opportunities for social interaction over computer networks offer additional motivational benefits alongside cognitive advantages (Wigfield, Eccles, Schiefele, Roeser, & Davis-Kean, 2006).

The advancement of motivation theory is important because motivation touches such vital practical concerns. Much of the disparate achievement in education is the inevitable result of differences in motivation for learning. Nicholls (1979) proposed that schools could work toward equality of optimum motivation—the ideal that *all* students ought to have the motivational resources to be successful learners. The goal of **motivational equity** can be seen as a natural complement to the broader ideal of equity in educational achievement and is arguably a necessary condition for greater parity in educational outcomes.

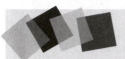

Learning Strategies

The theories presented in this chapter lend themselves to practical application. Widespread negative feelings toward school, for example, sharpen the imperative to use our current understanding to reverse the pattern. Our growing knowledge of "hot cognitions" can help make the experience of learners more enjoyable and more positively directed toward goals that will lead to long-term success.

The strategies presented below are a sampling of the many potential applications of motivation theory to educational practice. Only a subset will be relevant to any single context, and then only by tailoring the strategy to particular characteristics of the students. Whenever an educator applies a general theoretical principle, it is wisely done with a clinical eye, one that appreciates the unique considerations that each instance requires.

1 Develop positive emotional associations. The human mind is associative, a truth both behavioral and cognitive psychologists appreciate. Unpleasant negative emotions frequently become associated with the objects and contexts of education, including books, desks, classrooms, and teachers. Good teachers find ways to infuse students' experience with positive feelings that can become generalized to learning.

2 Present the right conditions for flow. One manifestation of positive emotion is the state of high attentional focus called *flow*. When the demands of an activity are closely matched to the ability of a person, that task can be completely absorbing—so much so that the person can lose track of time and the larger context. Teachers may experience flow states while teaching; they might also try to encourage the conditions that will help their students to feel flow as they go about their work.

3 Encourage effort attributions. Not all attributions are equally beneficial. Ideally, students develop attributional styles that emphasize an internal locus. Among attributions with an internal locus, *effort* attributions are probably best. When students see their successes as the product of effort applied over time, they know how to proceed

when faced with a new challenge. They also have an optimistic recourse if they experience failure. An effort attribution means that it's time to try again, and possibly harder.

4 Watch for evidence of learned helplessness. Whenever a student concludes that there is no connection between effort and outcomes, education has effectively ended. Slow learners and students with disabilities are particularly vulnerable to discouragement and to simply giving up. Teachers must be alert to impending frustration and do whatever they can to avert learned helplessness. They must try to ensure that effort does not cease, and that every student experiences some success.

5 Build self-efficacy through verbal persuasion. Self-efficacy beliefs are constructed through several sources of information. One of the most important is verbal persuasion. A respected peer or adult can communicate to a student that he or she is able to rise to the challenge. A teacher has substantial power to do good by helping students recognize their ability to succeed when that ability is allied with steady effort.

6 Encourage incremental theories of ability. Many students develop "entity" theories, which portray abilities as predetermined and fixed. A much better stance is to see abilities as changeable or improvable over time. This is the "incremental" view of ability. Those who see ability as improvable will have options open for them. Even if students presently lack ability in a domain, that lack is not necessarily permanent. Students with an incremental view see ability as potentially improvable with effort.

7 Develop task-involvement in students. Students judge their success according to different criteria. One standard for judging success is comparison with other students; in this case the student is ego-involved. Ego-involvement is not as adaptive in the long run as task-involvement. Teachers can encourage task-involvement, where the basis for judging competence is students' gains compared to their own past performance. Social comparison can be toned down or minimized.

8 Teach students to protect volitional intentions.

Every successful person knows how to make good decisions, and how to follow through after those decisions have been made. Follow-through requires the protection of volitional intentions from competing goals, distraction, fatigue, and discouragement. Through cognitive modeling, encouragement, and reminders, teachers can help instill volitional control skills in their students.

9 Develop students' perseverance.

Many people who eventually achieve success and acclaim do so through unusual perseverance. The capacity for high volitional control is tremendously valuable. Teachers understand that great achievements are never easy. One vital educational goal for all students should be to develop the ability to persist through difficulty in order to achieve valued and challenging goals.

10 Set specific and proximal goals.

Ultimate goals provide overall direction to life's decisions, but near-term and precisely stated goals are those most likely to lead to measurable progress and to well-being. Teachers and students alike need to develop habits of setting specific and proximal goals. These goal structures lead to higher levels of satisfaction, and they contribute directly to an intelligent life.

These ten strategies show that theories of emotion, motivation, and volition lend themselves to direct application in educational settings. To the degree that teachers can help students develop positive feelings toward learning, as well as positive beliefs about themselves as learners, important goals of education will be advanced. The strategies apply not only to teachers' instructional decisions, but also to how teachers view their own professional skills and growth. The best schools are filled with positive and highly motivated students and teachers.

 ## Conclusion

Ernest Hilgard's model of the trilogy of mind explicitly acknowledged that mental activity was not a simple matter of cool rationality. This was a necessary corrective to the simplistic assumptions of information-processing theory. Cognitive science, itself a reaction to the anti-mentalist zeal of radical behaviorists, was largely centered on understanding "cool" cognitions by looking to its favorite metaphor, the digital computer. Unfortunately, it left precious little room for purposeful striving. Bruner (1990) lamented the early omission of will and emotion from information-processing psychology:

> With the mind equated to [a computer] program, what should the status of mental states be—old fashioned mental states identifiable not by their programmatic characteristics in a computational system but by their subjective making? There could be no place for "mind" in such a system—"mind" in the sense of intentional states like believing, desiring, intending, grasping a meaning. (pp. 8, 9)

The computer metaphor is a wonderful heuristic for research, an excellent entry-point into the otherwise bewildering complexity of the mind and mental processes. But taken too seriously it turns the human mind into a "living machine," a grotesque depiction that humanistic psychologists, among others, detested (May, 1969). Unlike machine computation, human thought is imbued with emotions, wishes, and intentions.

Hilgard proposed a trilogy of mind composed of cognition (rational thought), affect (emotional thought), and conation (purposeful thought). Hilgard also subdivided conation into motivation (forces that feed into decisions) and volition (forces that control thought and behavior after decisions). We have followed Hilgard's typology in exploring "hot" cognitions by considering, in turn, emotion, motivation, and volition. All three are vital to the mission of education; each is within the orbit of educational concerns.

Even with helpful guidance from Hilgard's typology, the subject of this chapter is complex. Its inherent complexity is partly related to distinctively cognitive aspects of the mind. People have belief systems about what they can do (self-efficacy), about their own abilities (entity and incremental abilities), about the probable payoff from courses of action (expectancy-value theories), and about what constitutes success (ego- versus task-involvement). The power of belief is manifest negatively as learned helplessness and positively as unusual perseverance toward high achievement. Indeed, knowledge that belief systems are *learnable* makes these subjects even more complex, but also potentially alterable.

Theories of hot cognition—emotion, motivation, and volition—must be considered an unfinished project. Cognitive analysis of "cool" cognition has led to great advances in organizing the vast array of cognitive abilities and uncovering their mechanisms. Perhaps information-processing psychologists began with the computer metaphor intuitively realizing that the problem of understanding rational thought was more tractable than comprehending human feelings, drive, and will. Progress toward the identification of psychological constructs

dealing with emotion, motivation, and will have been slower and more difficult. Yet for all the remaining work to be done, there is a greater recognition than ever that an understanding of the complete range of mental functions is necessary not only to a complete science of mind, but also for the extension and improvement of human functioning.

For now we have to content ourselves with theories that are not neatly integrated, but nonetheless hold important applications to teaching and learning. Building on our best theories, we can employ strategies to help students understand that they are capable of experiencing success—or, if they lack ability, that it can develop over time. We can help students to enjoy learning, and when learning becomes difficult, to persist. With guidance from theories of emotion, motivation, and volition, we have strategies to shape the feelings and belief systems that help students advance toward their highest potential as learners.

References

Amabile, T. M., Hill, K. G., Hennessey, B. A., & Tighe, E. M. (1994). The work performance inventory: Assessing intrinsic and extrinsic motivational orientations. *Journal of Personality and Social Psychology, 66*(3), 950–967.

Asimov I. (1950). *I, Robot*. New York: Gnome Press.

Atkinson, J. W. (1958). *Motives in fantasy, action, and society*. Princeton, NJ: Van Nostrand.

Bandura, A. (1982). Self-efficacy mechanism in human agency. *American Psychologist, 2*, 122–147.

Bandura, A. (1986). *Social foundations of thought and action: A social cognitive theory*. Upper Saddle River, NJ: Prentice Hall.

Berlyne, D. E., & Frommer, F. D. (1966). Some determinants of the incidence and content of children's questions. *Child Development, 37*, 177–189.

Bornstein, M. H., Davidson, L., Keyes, C. L. M., & Moore, K. A. (Eds.)(2003). *Well-being: Positive development across the life course*. Mahwah, NJ: Lawrence Erlbaum Associates.

Bower, G. H. (1994). Some relations between emotions and memory. In P. Ekman & R. J. Davidson (Eds.), *The nature of emotions: Fundamental questions* (pp. 303–305). New York: Oxford University Press.

Bower, G. H., & Forgas, J. P. (2001). Mood and social memory. In J. P. Forgas (Ed.), *Handbook of affect and social cognition* (pp. 95–120). Mahwah, NJ: Lawrence Erlbaum Associates.

Britton, B. K., & Tesser, A. (1991). Effects of time management practices on college grades. *Journal of Educational Psychology, 83*(3), 405–410.

Bronowski, J. (1973). *The ascent of man*. Boston: Little, Brown, & Company.

Brophy, J. E. (1983). Research on the self-fulfilling prophecy and teacher expectations. *Journal of Educational Psychology, 73*, 631–661.

Brophy, J. E. (2006). Observational research on genetic aspects of classroom learning. In P. A. Alexander & P. H. Winne (Eds.),

Handbook of educational psychology (2nd ed.)(pp. 755–780). Mahwah, NJ: Lawrence Erlbaum Associates.

Bruner, J. S. (1966). *Toward a theory of instruction*. Cambridge: Harvard University Press.

Bruner, J. S. (1990). *Acts of meaning*. Cambridge, MA: Harvard University Press.

Cacioppo, J. T., Petty, R. E., Feinstein, J. A., & Jarvis, W. B. G. (1996). Dispositional differences in cognitive motivation: The life and times of individuals varying in need for cognition. *Psychological Bulletin, 119*(2), 197–253.

Cameron, J., & Pierce, W. D. (1994). Reinforcement, reward, and intrinsic motivation: A meta-analysis. *Review of Educational Research, 64*(3), 363–443.

Corno, L., (1993). The best-laid plans: Modern conceptions of volition and educational research. *Educational Researcher, 22*(2), 14–22.

Covington, M. V. (1984). The self-worth theory of achievement motivation: Findings and implications. *The Elementary School Journal, 85*(1) 5–20.

Csikszentmihalyi, M. (1975). *Beyond boredom and anxiety*. Hoboken, NJ: Jossey-Bass.

Danner, F. W., & Lonkey, E. (1981). A cognitive-developmental approach to the effects of rewards on intrinsic motivation. *Child Development, 52*, 1043–1052.

deCharms, R. (1976). *Enhancing motivation*. New York: Irvington.

Deci, E. L. (1975). *Intrinsic motivation*. New York: Plenum.

Duchein, M. A., & Mealey, D. L. (1993). Remembrance of books past . . . long past: Glimpses into aliteracy. *Reading Research and Instruction, 33*, 13–28.

Dweck, C. S., & Leggett, E. L. (1988). A social-cognitive approach to motivation and achievement: *Journal of Personality and Social Psychology, 54*, 5–12.

Elliot, E. S., & Dweck, C. S. (1988). Goals: An approach to motivation and achievement. *Journal of Personality and Social Psychology, 54*(1), 5–12.

Emmons, R. A. (1999). *The psychology of ultimate concerns.* New York: The Guilford Press.

Festinger, L. (1962). Cognitive dissonance. *Scientific American, 207,* 93–102.

Fishbein, M., & Ajzen, I. (1974). Attitudes towards objects as predictors of single and multiple behavioural criteria. *Psychological Review, 81(1),* 29–74.

Frumkin, K., & Brookshire, K. H. (1969). Conditioned fear training and later avoidance learning in the goldfish. *Psychonomic Science, 16(3),* 159–160.

Garber, J., & Seligman, M. E. P. (Eds.)(1980). *Human helplessness: Theory and applications.* New York: Academic Press.

Gardner, H. (1991). *The unschooled mind.* New York: Basic Books.

Gottfried, A. E. (1985). Academic intrinsic motivation in elementary and junior high school students. *Journal of Educational Psychology, 77,* 631–645.

Harter, S. (1982). A developmental perspective on some parameters of self-regulation in children. In P. Karoly & F. H. Kanfer (Eds.), *Self-management and behavior change: From theory to practice* (pp. 165–204). New York: Pergamon Press.

Haslam, N., & Baron, J. (1994). Intelligence, personality, and prudence. In R. J. Sternberg & P. Ruzgis (Eds.), *Intelligence and personality* (pp. 32–58). New York: Cambridge University Press.

Heckhausen, H., & Kuhl, J. (1985). From wishes to action: The dead ends and short cuts on the long way to action. In M. Frese & J. Sabini (Eds.), *Goal directed behavior: The concept of action in psychology* (pp. 134–160). Hillsdale, NJ: Lawrence Erlbaum Associates.

Herrera, T. (2002). An interview with Liping Ma: Do not forget yourself as a teacher of yourself. *ENC Focus, 9(3),* 16–20.

Hilgard, E. R. (1980). The trilogy of mind: Cognition, affection, and conation. *Journal of the History of the Behavioral Sciences, 16,* 107–117.

Holloway, S. D. (1988). Concepts of ability and effort in Japan and the United States. *Review of Educational Research, 58(3),* 327–345.

Hull, C. L. (1943). *Principles of behavior.* New York: Appleton-Century.

Johnson, D. W., Maruyama, G., Johnson, R., Nelson, D., & Skon, L. (1981). Effects of cooperative, competitive, and individualistic goal structures on achievement: A meta-analysis. *Psychological Bulletin, 89,* 47–62.

Johnson, R. T., Johnson, R. W., & Stanne, M. B. (1985). Effects of cooperative, competitive, and individualistic goal structures on computer-assisted instruction. *Journal of Educational Psychology, 77,* 668–677.

Klossek, U. M. H., Russell, J., & Dickinson, A. (2008). The control of instrumental action following outcome devaluation in young children aged between 1 and 4 yrs. *Journal of Experimental Psychology: General, 137(1),* 39–51.

Locke, E. A., Shaw, K. N., Saari, L. M., & Latham, G. P. (1981). Goal setting and task performance. *Psychological Bulletin, 90,* 125–152.

Maehr, M. L. (1976). Continuing motivation: An analysis of a seldom considered educational outcome. *Review of Educational Research, 46,* 443–462.

Mahoney, M. j. (1979). Cognitive skills and athletic performance. In P. C. Kendall & S. D. Hollon (Eds.), *Cognitive-behavioral interventions,* (pp. 423–443). New York: Academic Press.

Maier, S. F., Seligman, M. E. P., & Solomon, R. L. (1969). Pavlovian fear conditioning and learned helplessness. In B. A. Campbell & R. M. Church (Eds.), *Punishment and aversive behavior* (pp. 299–342). New York: Appleton-Century-Crofts.

Malone, T. W. (1981). Toward a theory of intrinsically motivating instruction. *Cognitive Science, 4,* 333–369.

Maslow, A. H. (1968). *Toward a psychology of being* (2nd ed.). New York: Van Nostrand Reinhold.

May, R. (1969). *Love and will.* New York: Delta.

McClelland, D. C. (1961). *The achieving society.* Princeton, NJ: Van Nostrand.

Merton, R. K. (1948). The self-fulfilling prophecy. *Antioch Review, 8,* 193–210.

Mischel, W., Shoda, Y., & Rodriguez, M. L. (1989). Delay of gratification in children. *Science, 244,* 933–938.

Murray, H. A., (1943). *The Thematic Apperception Test.* Cambridge, MA: Harvard University Press.

Nash, M. R. (2001). The truth and the hype of hypnosis. *Scientific American, 285,* 46–55.

Nicholls, J. G. (1979). Quality and equality in intellectual development: The role of motivation in education. *American Psychologist, 34,* 1071–1084.

Nicholls, J. G. (1984). Conceptions of ability and academic motivation. In R. Ames & C. Ames (Eds.), *Research on motivation in education: Vol. 1. Student motivation* (pp. 39–73). Orlando, FL: Academic Press.

Ortony, A., & Turner, T. J. (1990). What's basic about basic emotions? *Psychological Review, 97,* 315–331.

Padilla, A. M. (1973). Effects of prior and interpolated shock exposures on subsequent avoidance learning by goldfish. *Psychological Reports, 32,* 451–456.

Panksepp, J. (1994). The basics of basic emotion. In P. Ekman & R. J. Davidson (Eds.), *The nature of emotions: Fundamental questions* (pp. 20–24). New York: Oxford University Press.

Parrot, W. (2001). *Emotions in social psychology.* Philadelphia: Psychology Press.

Picard, R. W. (1995). *Affective computing.* MIT Media Laboratory Perceptual Computing Section Technical Report No. 321.

Picard, R. W. (1997). *Affective computing.* Cambridge: MIT Press.

Pintrich, P. R. (2000). The role of goal orientation in self-regulated learning. In M. Boekaerts, P. R. Pintrinch, & M. Zeidner (Eds.), *Handbook of self-regulation* (pp. 451–502). San Diego, CA: Academic Press.

Plutchik, R. (1980). A general psychoevolutionary theory of emotion. In R. Plutchik & H. Kellerman (Eds.), *Emotion, theory, research, and experience: Volume 1: Theories of emotion* (pp. 3–33). New York: Academic Press.

Plutchik, R. (2001). The nature of emotions. *American Scientist, 89,* 344–350.

Rosenthal, R., & Jacobsen, L. (1968). *Pygmalion in the classroom: Teacher expectation and pupils' intellectual development.* New York: Holt, Rinehart & Winston.

Rotter, J. B. (1966). Generalized expectancies for internal versus external control of reinforcement, *Psychological Monographs, 80,* (1, Whole No. 609).

Schunk, D. H., & Zimmerman, B. J. (2006). Competence and control beliefs: Distinguishing the means and ends. In P. A. Alexander & P. H. Winne (Eds.), *Handbook of educational psychology* (2nd ed.)(pp. 349–367). Mahwah, NJ: Lawrence Erlbaum Associates.

Seligman, M. E. P. (1975). *Helplessness.* San Francisco: W. H. Freeman.

Simonton, D. K. (1984). *Genius, creativity, and leadership.* Cambridge, MA: Harvard University Press.

Slavin, R. E. (1980). Cooperative learning. *Review of Educational Research, 50,* 315–342.

Snow, R. E. (1992). Aptitude theory: Yesterday, today, and tomorrow. *Educational Psychologist, 27(1),* 5–32.

Snow, R. E., Corno, L. & Jackson, D. III (1996). Individual differences in affective and conative functions. In D. C. Berliner & R.

Calfee (Eds.), *Handbook of educational psychology* (pp. 243–310). New York: Macmillan.

Vansteenkiste, M., Lens, W., & Deci, E. L. (2006). Intrinsic versus extrinsic goal contents in self-determination theory: Another look at the quality of academic motivation. *Educational Psychologist, 41*(1), 19–31.

Vinge, V. (1993). *The coming technological singularity: How to survive in the post-human era.* http://www-rohan.sdsu.edu/faculty/vinge/misc/singularity.html.

Watson, D., & Clark, L. A. (1994). Emotions, moods, traits, and temperaments: Conceptual distinctions and empirical findings. In P. Ekman & R. J. Davidson (Eds.), *The nature of emotions: Fundamental questions* (pp. 89–93). New York: Oxford University Press.

Weiner, B. W. (1985). An attributional theory of achievement motivation and emotion. *Psychological Review, 92*, 548–573.

White, R. W. (1959). Motivation reconsidered: The concept of competence. *Psychological Review, 66*, 297–333.

Wigfield, A., Eccles, J. S., Schiefele, U., Roeser, R. W., & Davis-Kean, P. (2006). Development of achievement motivation. In W. Damon & R. M. Lerner (Eds.), *Handbook of child psychology* (6th ed., Vol. 3)(pp. 933–1002). Hoboken, NJ: John Wiley and Sons.

Wineburg, S. (1987). Does research count in the lives of behavioral scientists? *Educational Researcher, 16*(9), 42–44.

Yerkes, R. M., & Dodson, J. D. (1908). The relation of strength of stimulus to rapidity of habit formation. *Journal of Comparative Neurology of Physiology, 18*, 459–482.

Zimmerman, B. J., & Pons, M. M. (1986). Development of a structured interview for assessing student use of self-regulated learning strategies. *American Educational Research Journal, 23*(4), 614–628.

CHAPTER

[7]

Cognitive Development Through the Life Span

Alongside the numerous more-or-less immediate changes that constitute learning, there are also long-term developmental changes whose time course is measured in years rather than in seconds or minutes. Of course, the two interact: The kinds of learning that are possible at any life stage are determined largely by the developmental state of the person. Schools and curricula are organized accordingly. We have differing expectations for students depending on whether they are six or sixteen. Our expectations are adjusted to children's normal capabilities for learning and behavior.

Educators need to understand cognitive development so that they can organize their teaching efforts wisely. Development normally figures prominently in lesson planning. For example, teachers often consider developmental readiness: whether a child is able to learn a new skill or concept. If the child is not developmentally ready, then it will be pointless to try to teach that new curricular element. The child might even be harmed in the attempt because the resulting frustration can have negative emotional consequences, possibly complicating attempts to re-introduce the concept or skill at a later point in time. In fundamental ways, learning and development are strongly interacting concepts, and both are central to the educational enterprise.

What Is Development?

In contrast to the compressed timeline for learning, the time parameters for development are measured in months (for infants), years (for children), and even decades (for adults). These longer time spans present noticeable, even obvious, changes in the developing person. The changes are partly intellectual in nature—which is the focus here— but they are not only intellectual. Human development proceeds along several dimensions, including physical development, social development, emotional development, and moral development. Along each dimension, development is manifested as changing capabilities, thinking, appearance, and behavior.

Development irrevocably moves a person toward becoming something new and leaves a permanent mark. Most of the time we see development as a positive force, adding new capabilities and potential, but development can also subtract capability and potential from a life. Among the elderly, most noticeably, there is often a decline in physical capability and, in some cases, in mental agility and effectiveness.

The forces that impel development often have a biological aspect driven by genetic necessity. Brain maturation, for example, is significantly attributable to changes programmed into the human genotype. Normal brain development produces the ability to use language and abstract thought. The genetic predisposition to develop greater cognitive sophistication depends on the right sorts of experience, certainly, but the positive effects of such experience also rely on a biologically driven readiness that gradually unfolds. No newborn infant is capable of abstract reasoning (biological maturation is important) and no child learns to read without at least some instruction (focused experience is important).

For the educator, development is a crucial dimension of human variation. Implicitly at least, instruction is designed around assumptions about development. Teachers know that it would be foolish to disregard readiness in setting goals for their students and in making plans for teaching. If development is a guiding consideration for educational decision-making, then we must deepen our understanding of development. This task is complicated by the fact that genetically driven processes interact with specific experience. Nature and nurture both exert important effects, and it is impossible to say which has primacy.

Historical Views

Human cognitive development has such obvious theoretical and social importance that it has been the subject of inquiry, speculation, and theorizing for many centuries. We begin our study by considering some of the older, but still influential, theories of human development.

ROUSSEAU. The ideas of Jean-Jacques Rousseau (1712–1778) are a fitting entry point into human development, particularly into development of the child. Rousseau, a Swiss philosopher, is rightly considered the first European scholar to develop an articulated theory of the developing child. His theory had an enormous influence on the formation of educational institutions and on teaching methods for more than 200 years. Rousseau's central dilemma of development was how to reconcile the moral purity of the child with the obvious corruption of adult society. To Rousseau, it was obvious that the young child had strong moral qualities of curiosity, courage, and spirit. Somehow in the course of life, the child's beauty of spirit was crushed and corrupted. What went wrong?

If there is a corrupting influence during the process of individual change over the years, there was a ready explanation that had been widely accepted for centuries. The child was corrupted from within by original sin, a propensity for evil that was an unfortunate consequence of being human. To avoid being defiled by sin was a major life task, one that Christianity was intended to inform and assist. But the potential for personal ruination was something that each individual carried inside. Rousseau rejected this answer in favor of another, quite different explanation. He believed instead that the innocent and noble state of the child was corrupted by the surrounding society. In a European society, the authoritarian structures of institutions, including schools, drove out the child's inherent goodness, and eventually remade the child in the form of its own insipid and warped mold.

Rousseau's prescription for this dire state view of the human condition was to preserve as completely as possible the original nature of the child. This meant easing the repressive forces exerted by society and its institutions, including schools. In the place of repression, the child needed freedom—freedom to explore, to play, to ask, to experiment, to *be*. With sufficient freedom, Rousseau believed, the child could retain his original state of nobility—he could be a **noble savage**. When society was structured to preserve the child's inner and original goodness, all of humanity would benefit.

Rousseau's radical reframing of human nature, and of the proper societal response, may seem far-fetched and esoteric. As a philosophy, Rousseau's theory probably would have been ignored by all but the French-speaking intellectual elite. But in practice Rousseau's ideas were tremendously influential in framing a strong curricular and pedagogical focus for education. Loosely, the educational orientation can be described as **child-centered**, which contrasts sharply with traditional **teacher-centered** approaches. In the most extreme version of teacher-centered education, the teacher has absolute authority, perhaps backed by the threat of corporal punishment. Student activities are regimented; obedience and order are strictly enforced. Discussion, creative expression, and group work are viewed as dangerous and shunned because of the possibility that they would lead to dissention and chaos.

CHILD-CENTERED EDUCATION. Nowadays, many educators support a child-centered approach to teaching. A child-centered philosophical orientation distrusts the repressive tactics of schools and other social institutions and sees these as contrary to the best interests of the student. Within this orientation, the most desirable teaching strategies give the child some freedom to explore, choose activities, pursue interests, and interact freely with adults and peers. Rousseau's theory supplied a moral and philosophical rationale for child-centered education.

Child-centered education and child rearing have appeared in many forms since the time of Rousseau. Most famously, the great Italian educator and physician Maria Montessori strongly promoted a child-centered philosophical orientation in the preschool child's experience. Montessori preschools all over the world stay true to this philosophy in that they maintain a high priority on giving the individual child freedom to play and, with freedom, the opportunity to learn most felicitously.

A child-centered philosophical orientation also led the German educator, Friedrich Froëbel, to establish the original kindergarten or "child's garden" as vital preparation for formal education. Before being cast into the staid and strict environment of an elementary school, the child could benefit from a gentle transition from the protective home environment. Froëbel's philosophy and the kindergarten movement spread around the world. In the United States, *Kindergarten* is regarded as a normal introduction of the 5-year-old child to the world of formal education. Its basic structure and purpose were presented by Froëbel more than a century ago, and its more abstract philosophical basis was advanced by Rousseau a century before that.

PROGRESSIVE EDUCATION. Child-centered philosophies of education have had some influence on elementary and secondary education, but they have been much more widely influential in preschool or kindergarten education. In the upper grades, the relative preferability of child-centered and traditional teacher-centered approaches has been much more a matter of debate. Over the decades, one approach or the other has gained favor by educators or by those who have the political power to set education policy. During the early twentieth century, the **progressive movement** in American education spawned experimentation in student-centered, activity-oriented curricula and pedagogy. In the United States, the intellectual force behind progressive education was the great American educator and philosopher, John Dewey. In Britain, a more radical form of progressive education was advanced by the Scottish educator, A. S. Neill (1960). In Neill's famous alternative school, Summerhill, attendance at classes was completely optional. Traditional authority structures were subverted as students were given authority to make important decisions. For example, disciplinary actions against students were the prerogative of a student-run tribunal.

FIGURE 7.1
Summerhill *In this famous progressive school, class attendance was optional.*

Progressive education, with its emphasis on the needs and interests of the developing child, seems to have a permanent place in educational philosophy and practice. Over the decades, progressive orientations have competed with traditional approaches for control over educational curricula. When we speak of the pendulum swinging in educational policy, we often refer to the tension between progressivism and traditionalism. To some degree, these basic orientations to education arise from differing conceptualizations of the child. Though many luminaries have guided our thinking about these vital issues, we can credit Jean Jacques Rousseau with framing the intellectual space in such as way as to present us with vital choices.

Perspectives on Development

NATURE VERSUS NURTURE. Both progressive and traditional education address the dynamic forces within and outside the child—forces that shape the child's developing character and mind. Similar dynamic tensions reappear in every theory that seeks to understand human nature, and especially in theories of human development. The central forces are most often described as nature and nurture. Does either nature or nurture predominate in developing human capability, or do they jointly and equally contribute to the formation of the individual person?

Among the theoretical perspectives that emphasize forces within the individual, **behavioral genetics** explicitly characterizes and quantifies the contribution of genetic heritability to personal traits. Traits that are highly susceptible to genetic influence include the psychological qualities of intelligence, personality, and psychopathology. Behavioral geneticists quantify the genetic influence by comparing family members—parent with child, sibling with sibling, and so on—with known degrees of genetic relatedness. As a broad generalization, behavioral geneticists have found that genes (nature) and environment (nurture) make roughly equal contributions to explaining the variation of psychological traits in the population. The ways we think are partly given, partly gained.

Nativism, another perspective that recognizes inborn qualities that contribute to cognitive functioning, theorizes that the brain is prewired to perform certain cognitive

INTEREST MAGNET 7.1

Feral Children

According to ancient Roman legend, two boys, Romulus and Remus, were raised by a wolf. Roman coins depict the two brothers suckling their wolf-mother. Tragically, the boys eventually became enemies. Romulus killed Remus, and the city of Rome was named after him. Modern-day myths also feature children raised by wild animals. These include Tarzan of the Apes, the character of Edgar Rice Burrows' novels, and Mowgli, the wolf-child character of Rudyard Kipling.

These stories and legends appear to be nothing more than pure fantasy. But is this the case? The available evidence suggests that, in very rare instances, children have spent part of their lives living alone in the wild. These are referred to as *feral* children—a comparison to undomesticated animals, such as feral cats. About a hundred or so cases of feral children have been alleged through history. No doubt some of those cases are fabrications, but others seem to be authentic. Among the most famous is the appearance of Victor of Aveyron. In 1797, Victor was seen living alone, wild and naked, in the woods of Aveyron, France. Although the boy was caught, he escaped and three years later was finally recaptured. Victor was later adopted by Dr. Jean-Marc Itard, physician and educator of the deaf.

Victor could not speak or be controlled. However, Dr. Itard believed that he could teach Victor the skills necessary to be integrated into French society, such as how to speak, eat with utensils, and give and receive affection. Itard's attitude toward Victor was different from the era's prevailing treatment of the disabled, which typically meant isolation from the rest of society. Dr. Itard was optimistic that with the right experiences Victor could acquire the skills of a normal boy, including the use of language. Itard was partially successful: Victor made progress but never fully reached normal levels of development. Some see Itard's attempts to teach the "Wild Boy" of Aveyron as the beginning of special education.

Rudyard Kipling's story of the boy Mowgli being raised by wolves may have a factual counterpart. In 1920, Christian missionary J. A. L. Singh and his wife ran an orphanage south of Calcutta, India (Newton, 2002). Exploring the jungle at night, Singh and a group of men saw a wolf accompanied by her wolf cubs. Two of the "cubs" had human faces—girls with matted hair who ran on all fours. After the wolves retreated into their den, Rev. Singh and his men dug into the hillside. When the excavators encountered the mother wolf, she ferociously defended the cubs (including the girls). The men shot the mother wolf and retrieved the two girls, presumably sisters, who were later named Kamala and Amala. Rev. Singh brought the girls back to his orphanage. Kamala (about 8 years old) and Amala (about 1½ years old) staunchly resisted attempts to integrate them with other children in the orphanage. Little Amala died a year later of illness; Kamala lived eight years in the orphanage before she, too, became ill and died.

Through the centuries, reports have claimed that feral children have been raised variously by sheep, wolves, bears, dogs, monkeys, and chimpanzees (Newton, 2002). These extraordinary accounts hint that the limits of human adaptability, and perhaps nonhuman skill and compassion, may differ from what we typically assume.

tasks. Native behavioral capabilities are obvious in animals, who often exhibit sophisticated behavior without prior exposure to models. Horses can walk within minutes of being born; certain species of birds display their characteristic birdsong even if they are *never* exposed to examples from other birds. Humans, too, have native capabilities. The best-known nativist claims were articulated by Noam Chomsky, who argued persuasively that human beings are innately wired to learn and use spoken language. Chomsky's argument is not that language is already stored in the brain at birth, but rather that the child's brain is predisposed to acquire language through exposure to its language-using culture.

In recent decades, research has shown that infants have far more unlearned capabilities than was previously assumed. Such capabilities include judgments about numerosity; newborns can discriminate between two objects and three objects during the first week of life (Antell & Keating, 1983). Infants also have expectations about how physical objects interact in the environment (e.g., they collide rather than pass through each other). Indeed, when babies are shown images of impossible events, such as solid objects passing through each other, they exhibit surprise by looking at the objects longer than expected. Surprise, in turn, implies that expectations have been violated. A persuasive argument can be made that infants lack sufficient experience to form those expectations. Instead, their expectations about the physical world are, at least in part, hard-wired—biologically built into the brain as species knowledge that is propagated genetically rather than learned experientially (Spelke & Kinzler, 2007).

If expectations about the physical world constitute knowledge, then babies can be said to have knowledge that is inborn. Innate knowledge is presumably stored in brain areas dedicated to specific information processing functions, such as understanding and predicting how physical objects interact. Karmiloff-Smith (1992) proposed that **modular brain functions**—those dedicated to specific kinds of information processing—direct attention and guide the behavior of the infant and young child. Strict nativism may neglect some aspects of the developing mind—it tends to downplay the flexibility of human cognition, its sensitivity to experience, and its openness to self-reflection. Even so, nativism spotlights an important and surprising truth: Some knowledge is unlearned. *Unlearned knowledge* may seem like a contradiction in terms, an oxymoronic impossibility, yet we have evidence that at least *some* of what we know is inborn.

SOCIOECONOMIC INFLUENCES. Among the theoretical perspectives that highlight forces external to the individual are sociological models that show a connection between socioeconomic status and child development. **Socioeconomic status (SES)** refers to the social class of a family. Social class categories most frequently divide families into wealthy, middle-class, working class, and poor. Socioeconomic status, or social class, is a complex construct, but it has been operationalized in fairly simple terms as a combination of family income and parent education, sometimes with the addition of occupational prestige. Sociologists have found that SES predicts many important social and psychological outcomes. For our purposes, we can acknowledge the strong connection among SES, cognitive abilities, and academic achievement. SES predicts not only measurable cognitive abilities, such as intelligence and verbal ability; it also predicts school learning, including such highly valued outcomes as reading comprehension and mathematics achievement.

Of course, it is one thing to acknowledge a statistical correlation between two variables, such as SES and cognitive outcomes, and quite another to interpret that correlation. What specific aspects of SES contribute positively to the developing intellectual capabilities of the child? Certainly, family income does not *directly* help a child to become a better reader. What then are the proximal causes of cognitive growth and success in learning? Several possibilities can be cited. Perhaps most straightforward is that wealth can guarantee a level of medical care and nutrition that will contribute to the child's health. Sufficient income will also make it easier for a family to acquire material resources that can help spur the child's developing intellect: interesting toys, books, computers and software, for example. More complex and elusive are explanations that relate social class differences to child-rearing practices, including differences in linguistic patterns between parents and children, and to peer influences (Harris, 1995). There is also the possibility of differing compatibility between school life and family life. Some scholars have noted that the values and practices of formal education conform more closely to middle-class culture than to the cultural patterns of poor families.

CONTINUITY VERSUS DISCONTINUITY. Many changes during childhood can be described without much trouble, but some aspects of child development are deeply puzzling. For example, it is hard to say whether change occurs in discrete **stages** or whether it is basically continuous. Certainly there are singular milestones in human development—the onset of puberty, for example. But other important changes seem much more gradual: The child's evolving capability to deal with abstractions is hard to pin down to a specific point in time. Perhaps the casual observation that child development occurs in stages is an imagined projection onto a process that in reality is smoothly incremental. Nevertheless, in trying to understand the nature of cognitive development and to present an orderly model of change, psychologists have often seen change as occurring in definite stages.

Cognitive Development: Jean Piaget

Among theories of *cognitive* development, the stage theory advanced by the great Swiss psychologist, Jean Piaget, stands above all others in influence and importance. As we approach Piaget's theory, it's helpful to bear in mind that it places emphasis on forces *internal* to the developing child. While Piaget thought the external environment was important, he regarded the child's internal predispositions as crucial. Piaget believed that the only way to make sense of the marvelous intellectual capacity of human minds was to appreciate the nature of those internal forces. Perhaps Piaget concentrated on internal mechanisms of development because his disciplinary training was in biology. After all, the early- to mid-twentieth century was a time of great ferment among biologists, with the discovery of DNA presenting a mechanism to explain not only how species change over time, but also how a single organism can develop in an orderly fashion from a single cell to a highly complex plant or animal.

A mature plant grows from a seed according to an internal "plan" encoded in the seed's genetic material. The seed germinates and becomes a tiny seedling; leaves unfold, permitting life-sustaining photosynthesis. With sunlight, air, and soil nutrients, the plant eventually develops flowers, seeds of its own, and fruit that enable its own reproduction. Biological unfolding was, for Piaget, a powerful metaphor for human development. Like a plant seed, the individual child has potentials and propensities hidden within. Piaget wanted to understand the nature of those internal propensities, the conditions necessary to activate the mechanisms of cognitive growth, and the manifestations of development over time as distinct stages.

Basic Processes

No matter how remarkable genetic mechanisms are for guiding and constraining the biological unfolding of developing organisms, the growth of plants and animals can occur only within a range of prescribed conditions. Sometimes these conditions are quite specific and unusual. One rather extreme example is the knobcone pine tree (*Pinus attenuata*), which produces seeds so durable that they can only germinate after a fire on the forest floor. Heat from the fire opens the seed clusters of the fallen cone and allows the seeds to drop onto the soil. The perpetuation of the knobcone pine species depends completely on fire! So, too, the development of the human mind depends on exposure to the right kinds of conditions. Just what *kinds* of conditions and *when* they are needed constitute crucial knowledge for the educator.

For Piaget, the most important experiences for promoting cognitive development are those that create psychological tension between beliefs and experience. Much of the time, our experience matches our beliefs—and the world seems sensible. But inevitably

FIGURE 7.2
The Knobcone Pine Needs Fire to Survive *Similarly, the developing human mind has its own contextual requirements.*

we encounter experiences that lie beyond, and clash with, our previous understanding. For a child especially, the newness of everyday experience provides many instances that prior knowledge cannot interpret or explain. That mismatch—between prior knowledge and current experience—is a powerful engine for cognitive advancement.

Now let's put labels on these processes. In everyday situations where our current knowledge is an adequate basis for interpreting our experience, and for acting intelligently in our world, **assimilation** occurs. We easily *assimilate* our experience into our knowledge or belief system. The two are compatible, and everything seems to make sense. But in the numerous cases where there is a clash between our expectations and what we actually experience, the mismatch prompts a change in knowledge, beliefs, and actions. When the mind changes to conform to new experience, **accommodation** occurs. We *accommodate* our mental structures and habits to the new information. The mind responds to experience, therefore, either by assimilating (taking in) experience or by accommodating (changing) in response to it.

Assimilation and accommodation are both crucial to the developing mind, but one is more important than the other for prompting learning and cognitive growth. Accommodation has greater power to push the individual mind forward. When there is a conflict between the expectations that derive from current knowledge and actual experience, the mismatch prompts a sense of unsettledness or **disequilibrium** in the mind of the individual. Similar in a way to the disequilibrium you might feel when getting off a wild carnival ride, new experiences can be dizzying and disorienting, but possibly also quite thrilling. To Piaget, the mind has a tremendously adaptive tendency to regain its "balance" by accommodating to the new information. The mind's tendency is toward **equilibration**, toward regaining the mental balance or homeostasis that will result in a harmonious relationship between our knowledge and the world as we experience it.

The process of accommodation in response to disequilibrium puts the learner in an active position of trying to make sense of the world. This is the way Piaget saw the learner. Through a combination of assimilation and accommodation, equilibrium is restored and cognitive development is advanced. This does not mean that the child's attempts to reconcile experience to his or her knowledge are always successful. In fact, children often generate explanations that are oversimplified or incorrect, but those provisional explanations (which normally mature in later years) are honest attempts to understand. The child's work to make sense of the world is a manifestation of **constructivism**. From the constructivist point of view, the learner is active in making

FIGURE 7.3
Jean Piaget *The Swiss psychologist had an enormous influence on our conceptualization of the child.* [Copyright by the Archives of the History of American Psychology.]

sense of the world. We rightly view Jean Piaget as a constructivist, and possibly the most important originator of psychological constructivism.

Piagetian Stages

As children mature, they become more adult-like in their capacity to understand and to reason. In Piaget's theory, cognitive development produces differences among children at different ages—and not simply differences in *degree* but also in *kind*. Children become not only progressively better thinkers, but different *kinds* of thinkers. Piaget believed he could distinguish stages marked by abilities and inabilities that are common to all children within each stage. He identified four such stages: sensorimotor, pre-operational, concrete operational, and formal operational. Let's explore them.

SENSORIMOTOR STAGE (0 TO 2 YEARS). Piaget's first stage of cognitive development is the **sensorimotor stage**. "Sensory" indicates the importance of the senses—sight, smell, touch, and so on—to the infant's growing understanding of the world. The word "motor" signals that the infant learns largely through muscle movements that result in the manipulation of objects, crawling, and walking. A baby's attraction to brightly-colored and shiny objects, and the strong wish to touch and manipulate those objects, shows how important the immediate sensory environment is to the newborn baby and the toddler. For a very young child, understanding is rooted in present action.

Another key feature of the sensorimotor stage is that the child lacks an understanding of **object permanence**. Because the child's reality is so strongly tied to the here and now, the child may not realize that an object hidden from view continues to exist. Instead, it's "out of sight, out of mind." A baby might become fascinated by your keys, but if you hide them behind your back, the child will lose interest and shift focus to something else in the immediate environment. The lack of object permanence shows how apt the name *sensorimotor* is for this stage. The child's world is the tangible present. And even though language use becomes manifest during this period, its use is strongly oriented to sensory experience rather than to abstractions.

PREOPERATIONAL STAGE (2 TO 7 YEARS). The **preoperational stage** is marked by the child's increasing independence from here-and-now reality. Object permanence has been mastered; the child now understands that if you place a toy in the closet, *it still exists*. The increasing independence from material reality is manifest most noticeably in the skilled use of language. The young child normally develops language skills to name things, to make requests, and in general to navigate the social and cultural environment. Language also presents an opportunity to explore abstract concepts. The child, for example, begins to have a concept of justice along with concerns about what is "fair" or "not fair." Initial skill in the interpretation and manipulation of symbols is manifest in the child's initiation into reading and writing.

Nevertheless, the pre-operational child has significant cognitive limitations. Even though object permanence has been mastered, the child still manifests a view of reality that is strongly guided, even constrained, by the child's own point of view. This limitation is manifest in the child's **egocentrism**. To appreciate egocentrism in the Piagetian sense, imagine that you and a friend are both looking at the same object, a chair. Each of you views the chair from a distinct vantage point—you are looking at the chair straight on, but your friend sees the chair from the side. Obviously, the chair *looks* different from these two perspectives. The relevant questions are: Can you draw what the chair looks like to your friend? And can your friend draw the chair as you see it? If the answers to both questions are *yes*, then you and your friend are no longer egocentric— at least by one measure.

Egocentrism is manifest not only in a child's visual point of view, but also in his or her ethical and moral reasoning (Kohlberg, Levine, & Hewer, 1983; Piaget, 1977). In preschool, Jack might grab a toy from Andy. We might ask Jack, "How would *you* feel if Andy took the toy away from you?" But Jack might have *no idea* how Andy felt, so how could he possibly imagine the emotions that arise from being fleeced of a favorite toy? He is egocentric in that he cannot take Andy's point of view to interpret injustice and the emotions that arise from being treated unfairly. The child is not being intentionally cruel; rather, he is having trouble with the complex cognitive act of taking the other person's point of view.

Another key limitation besides egocentrism marks the preoperational stage. Again, the name of the stage describes its psychological nature. *Preoperational* means that the child cannot carry out operations. But what are operations? Here we must appreciate that the term has an important specific meaning within the Piagetian theoretical framework. One meaning of *operation* in everyday usage is a manipulative activity that changes the world around us. In a loose way, such activities include making a meal, responding to e-mails, and driving to work. These are operations—all involve making changes in the external world, changes guided by a valued goal.

So, too, in Piagetian theory, an **operation** is a physical change in the environment. Think of pouring water from one container to another. If the two containers are different in shape, the water may look as if it changed in volume, but in reality the volume has remained the same even though the appearance changed—it has been conserved. The understanding that some qualities of a changing substance remain the same through many physical transformations is called **conservation**. How do you know that the volume has stayed the same? Perhaps you have memorized the fact that a change in appearance does not imply the volume has actually changed. For an educated adult, the constancy of volume despite apparent changes in shape is a known fact, even common sense. But there is another way that you can know that the volume has not changed despite appearances: You can *mentally* reverse the procedure and, *in your mind*, pour the water back into the first container. In fact, you can mentally perform this sequence, this operation, over and over again without any trouble. Through the **reversibility** of this mental experiment you can know that, as the water changes form, it keeps the same volume.

The ability to *conserve* the volume of water as it undergoes changes in form depends on the ability to carry out mental operations that are reversible. A child at the preoperational stage lacks the ability to carry out reversible operations, and so has difficulty conserving. The water experiment shows this, but so can this experiment with beans: Place a pile of beans in front of child and then spread those beans over the tabletop. The child is likely to believe that there are *more* beans if they have been spread out over the surface. The child cannot conserve the number of beans, partly because there is an inability to mentally reverse the bean spreading and then mentally gather them back into a pile. For children who are able to imagine the operation of spreading or gathering beans, it's easy to understand that the number of beans does not change despite appearances. Conservation despite change is beyond the child's mental grasp.

CONCRETE OPERATIONAL STAGE (7 TO 11 YEARS). When a child enters the **concrete operational stage**, a new of level of sophisticated thinking becomes possible. The child can separate dimensions of stability during change, therefore permitting conservation. Why is the ability to conserve so important? For one thing, the world around us constantly undergoes change, but every change process also involves some continuity. To structure experience, the child must understand what actually does change and what remains the same. The ability to perceive the difference is a key achievement of cognitive development (Gibson, 1969).

This stability-change distinction is manifest in classification tasks, which require recognizing similarities and differences—how people, objects, and events are similar and how they differ. Accurate understanding requires making distinctions simultaneously along multiple dimensions. Classifying objects can be as simple as recognizing that wooden blocks differ in shape and in color, and that they can be grouped according to either or both characteristics. Classifying people is far more complicated, and a fair understanding of human beings means appreciating that they differ along many dimensions. Children in the concrete operational stage learn to make classifications along multiple dimensions and so make increasingly precise distinctions.

The newfound abilities of the concrete operational thinker are also manifest in a growing capacity to **decentrate**, to adopt multiple perspectives in making judgments. Young children sometimes strongly associate a person's age with height, for example—not an unreasonable approximation. I once overheard a child exclaim, "How old is he?!" when he saw an unusually tall man in his 20s. Decentration is a widening of the cognitive field of view to consider multiple factors when making judgments, rather than just one. Decentration also indicates an ability to adopt the perspectives of other people. This opens the child's mind to wonder about the opinions of others. The preadolescent can become highly sensitive to the opinions of peers, or even to *possible* opinions. Excessive efforts to gain peer approval are therefore interpretable in the Piagetian theoretical framework as one manifestation of concrete operational thought.

Concrete operational thinking allows the child to comprehend that physical qualities, such as the volume of water or the number of beans, remain constant despite superficial changes in appearance. The ability to separate dimensions of similarity and difference contributes to the ability to classify objects. Ordering objects—or **seriation**—along a single dimension, such as size, height, or weight, is also easily accomplished. However, the limitations of the concrete operational child are suggested by the word *concrete*. Whereas the child gains facility with understanding and ordering the physical world, the same degree of sophistication for abstract concepts is largely out of reach. Comprehending hypothetical assumptions or causation is difficult; combining the two to think about testing scientific hypotheses is almost impossible. The ability to think about abstractions, consider causal influences, and reason scientifically is characteristic of the fourth and final Piagetian stage, formal operations.

FORMAL OPERATIONAL STAGE (11 YEARS TO ADULT). Given time, the opportunity to learn, and biological maturity, most children eventually develop a high degree of facility in mentally manipulating abstract concepts, just as earlier they had learned to think in a facile way about concrete objects. The ability to deal with abstractions coincides with entry into the **formal operational stage**, the highest level of cognitive development postulated by Piaget. In the formal operational stage, the child, adolescent, or adult can think flexibly about abstract concepts. This ability permits complex classification as well as thinking about multiple causal forces. An individual at the formal operational stage can also engage in hypothetical, "what if?" thinking.

As Piaget appreciated so deeply, understanding the natural world entails not only learning about science concepts and their interconnections, but also learning about the nature of scientific knowledge and how it is acquired. Accordingly, formal operational thinking is partly identified with scientific reasoning—in particular, the ability to infer causal relations through systematic manipulation of variables. At the heart of scientific reasoning is a certain logic—not the standard deductive logic that proceeds from premises to conclusions, but rather a combinatorial logic manifest as the systematic isolation and control of variables (Inhelder & Piaget, 1958). The child is able to form and systematically test multiple competing hypotheses during the formal operational stage. Thus, **scientific reasoning** arises from formal operational thinking with a degree of sophistication and authenticity that was not possible in earlier stages.

For Piaget and like-minded developmental psychologists, one task that illustrates, as well as tests, scientific reasoning is the balance beam task. The task involves a beam balanced on a fulcrum. Weights of differing size can be placed on the beam at various distances from the fulcrum like a miniature see-saw, as shown in Figure 7.4. The task is to make predictions about whether the beam will balance or whether it will tip one way or the other. Some versions of the task are easy. For example, if two objects of differing weight are each placed the same distance from the fulcrum, then obviously the heavier weight will indicate the direction of tipping. Or if the weights are equal, the weight further from the fulcrum indicates which way the apparatus will tip. But there are many combinations that are not easy to predict—combinations in which the weight differences are combined with distance differences. What happens, for example, when heavy and light weights are used, but the lighter weight is place further from the fulcrum? In this case, the combination of weight and distance must be jointly considered. Moreover, weight and distance differences might be subtle, making prediction difficult. Fortunately, the requirement to consider offsetting influences is not an impediment for the formal operational thinker. Facility in just such combinatorial abstractions is a defining quality of formal operations.

FIGURE 7.4
**The Balance Beam
Problem** *The
effects of weight and
distance are easy to
predict in isolation,
but their combina-
tion can be tricky.*
[Drawing by Yukari
Okamoto.]

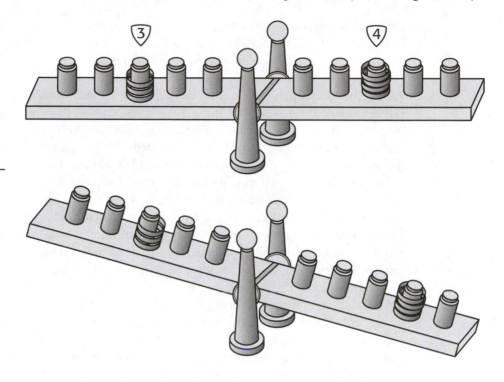

In the Piagetian framework, formal operational thinking is crucial to engaging complex subject matter, most obviously in mathematics and science (Gardner, 1983). Formal operations permit thinking about multiple causal influences and their precise
interactions, and facilitate proportional reasoning. Reasoning about proportions, often
expressed as ratios, is central to algebraic thinking and is ubiquitous in science. There are
serious implications if a learner does not reach the stage of formal operations. Some
adults never acquire the mental skills that are the hallmarks of formal operations—
abstract thinking, hypothetical reasoning, and comprehension of logical combinations
(Karplus, Pulos, & Stage, 1983). If formal operational thinking is a prerequisite to entry
into advanced study in science and mathematics, as well as other complex domains, then
the non-universal attainment of formal operations means that a segment of the population is cognitively barred from advanced study in these fields, and perhaps from holding
jobs that are most economically rewarded in the information age (Reich, 1992).

The Challenge to Piaget

Jean Piaget's theory of cognitive development stages was a monumental achievement
and a tremendous contribution to twentieth-century psychology. Nevertheless, all theoretical advances are subject to testing, critique, and, indeed, attack from other quarters. Competition among ideas helps to ensure that the theories psychologists construct
are of high quality. It is not surprising, therefore, that the ideas of Jean Piaget were
spared no criticism. And when put to the test, some of the central proposals of Piagetian theory did not hold up to scrutiny.

Starting in the 1970s, the initial enthusiasm for Piaget's ideas began to wane, especially among American psychologists. Research data did not always confirm the generalizations about cognitive development that the Swiss psychologist tried to communicate
to the world. Most problematic for Piaget's theory were data that contradicted his
claim that the child's exhibited competences were guided by a central logic core. Numerous exceptions were found to Piaget's proposal that a child's mental state is expressed

consistently across tasks. Sometimes young children reasoned in ways that were characteristic of adolescents or adults on some tasks, but performed in childlike ways on other tasks. This is the phenomenon of asynchrony or **decalage**.

Of all the evidence brought against the claims of Piaget's theory, the discovery of widespread decalage was the most damaging. But there were other objections to Piaget's theory. Performance on any task was quite sensitive to a child's level of knowledge or experience in a domain. Children might develop precocious knowledge about dinosaurs or astronomy, for example. Equipped with substantial content knowledge, children could deal with related abstractions and complexity in a manner that seemed adult-like. Moreover, performance on tasks responded to instruction—much more so than Piaget's theory predicted. Remember, the stage theory advanced by Piaget saw cognitive development as emanating from *internal* structures that are domain-general, and therefore applicable no matter what the content. The new evidence challenging this theoretical position was that intellectual performance was significantly affected by *external* factors, including instruction, and could be quite domain-specific.

Yet another objection was raised: Piaget's stage theory seemed overly built around modes of thought that are logical, mathematical, and scientific (Gardner, 1983). All of us are guided by our own backgrounds and assumptions, and Piaget was no exception. As we have noted, Piaget was a biologist by training. There is no mistaking that he viewed the developing child as growing in proficiency by making inferences about the environment—categorizing, quantifying, and separating cause from coincidence— much like a scientist. We should not be surprised, then, if *formal operational* thinking bears a strong likeness to *scientific* thinking. Piaget saw the child as a budding scientist who is eager to understand the world, and who builds a repertoire of competencies that assist this quest for understanding (Tweney, 1998). This association, narrow as it is, can be viewed as a limitation of the theory.

Certainly, human cognition cannot be *equated* to scientific thinking—the human mind does much more than think in a hypothesis-testing, logic-finding mode. Hypothesis testing is scientific reasoning only in a narrow sense. The combinatorial logic of formal operations is one kind of scientific reasoning (Kuhn, Amsel, & O'Loughlin, 1988). Now if combinatorial logic is inadequate to serve as a general model for scientific reasoning, it fails more seriously as a model for complex and abstract reasoning in nonscientific domains. Eventually, Piaget realized this. Toward the end of his career, he expressed doubt about whether formal logic could serve as a unifying mechanism across broad classes of mental activity (Kuhn, Amsel, & O'Loughlin, 1988).

Despite these substantive critiques, a great deal of Piaget's theory remains valid. Above all, Piaget sensitized psychologists to the crucial fact that the cognitive life of the child is not a scaled-down version of the mental life of an adult. The child's ways of thinking are fundamentally different from those of an adult. Moreover, Piaget helped psychologists to see that there are predictable sequences of cognitive development within domains. These ordinal progressions are not necessarily universal across domains, nor are they strictly tied to chronological age, but they are discernable patterns through the years. These patterns are worthy of study for the insights they allow into human cognition, and for their potential value to education.

Neo-Piagetian Theories

Empirical data contradicting Piaget's theory raised the possibility that cognitive development was really a process of smooth continuity rather than a succession of discontinuous stages. The new evidence led some developmental psychologists to abandon

Piaget altogether. Other psychologists, such as Case (1991), Fischer (1980), Halford (1993), and Karmiloff-Smith (1992), advanced theories that rejected the all-embracing logic of Piaget's theory, but that retained a stage-like progression in modeling the intellectual advancement of the child. The theories that built on, rather than abandoned, Piaget's ideas are called **neo-Piagetian theories**.

Neo-Piagetian theorists took the objections to Piaget's theory seriously. They recognized the reality and importance of decalage—that the cognitive performance of a child depends significantly on his or her background knowledge. Research showed that instruction and experience mattered to a degree that was unanticipated by Piaget. These findings had to be incorporated into the new theories. Many neo-Piagetian theories also imported findings from cognitive science, such as the relationship of task performance to the child's expanding working memory capacity (Halford, Wilson, & Phillips, 1998).

Robbie Case's Neo-Piagetian Theory

The work of Robbie Case (1991) is an excellent example of neo-Piagetian theorizing in that it responds to the evidence against a general stage model, but retains the quality of rising competence that Piaget's theory so clearly articulates. As the child matures, the direction of cognitive development is toward increasing sophistication, complexity, and effectiveness. Case's challenge was to characterize more accurately the nature of this progression.

Case's first strategy was to acknowledge that intellectual development could not be fairly described as an across-the-board, domain-general trajectory as Piaget hypothesized. That claim, clearly, was unsupportable. But Case also thought it was an error to think of all intellectual development as radically domain-dependent, as if the sophistication of mental processes was entirely linked to specific knowledge rather than being a function of maturation. Children differed by age—infants, preschoolers, school-age children, and adolescents thought and reasoned in ways characteristic of their own age group. Case's solution was to take the middle ground, proposing that developmental progressions were linearly ordered within broad domains. He called those domains **central conceptual structures**. Examples of these domains include *number* and *causality*, so they are quite broad. Case carefully balanced two competing truths: Children could vary in their sophistication from one structure to another (Piaget was partly wrong), but within each conceptual structure, cognitive development proceeds in an orderly sequence toward greater sophistication and competence (Piaget was partly right).

Case's second strategy was to acknowledge the burgeoning research from cognitive information-processing theory and integrate the new insights into his theory. Two aspects of cognitive theory were especially important: the constraints of working memory capacity and the liberation of those constraints by automaticity. Information-processing psychologists had built a strong case that performance on any task was constrained by the amount of information that could be actively attended and processed in working memory. There was also widespread agreement that working memory capacity increased as a function of age. Generally, a young child can entertain and coordinate fewer ideas than an older child, who in turn has a smaller working memory capacity than an adult. Clearly, working memory is one piece of the puzzle of how children's thinking develops over time.

But the constraints of working memory are not inviolate. As we saw in Chapter 3, automaticity interacts with working memory capacity. With focused experience, knowledge and skill that are originally complex become perceptually simpler and so tax working memory less. Case integrated both working memory constraints and automaticity into his theory. By integrating these two elements, and by concentrating on orderly development within broad domains, Case advanced a theory that, like Piaget's, was organized by stages. Case identified four stages: sensorimotor, interrelational, dimensional, and vectorial. In structure, these strongly resemble Piagetian stages. But there is an important difference: Cognitive growth within stages is limited by how many task elements can be considered by working memory.

Case's theory portrays cognitive development as a process of coordinating skilled behavior, or schemes, that operate independently at first but that eventually become integrated. With experience and consequent automaticity, task elements become consolidated and therefore informationally simpler. More complexity can be tolerated and performance becomes increasingly sophisticated. At the end of each stage, the consolidated (or chunked) proficiencies become the individual elements of the next stage, and the process repeats.

Let's take an example from the sensorimotor stage. In learning to reach for an object, an infant integrates two muscular control skills: visual and motor. Initially, these are separate skill sets or "schemes." At substage 1, there is only limited coordination between the two. The child can visually focus on a toy and manipulate it. At substage 2, the infant can perform a reversible action, such as reaching, but not in a coordinated way. At substage 3, there is a smooth and reversible coordination of the two systems, visual and motor, that were initially distinct. The child can give visual attention to different aspects of the toy and perform reversible actions, such as grasping and releasing, smoothly and at will.

The dimensional stage offers another example. At this stage, rising competence is more mental than physical in character. In the balance beam task, weights are placed on each arm of the beam. At substage 0, a child can say which way the balance beam will tip only when one side is obviously heavier than the other. At substage 1, the child can count the number of weights on the left and right sides of the beam and compare the totals, thus integrating the physical system with an abstract counting system. At substage 2, the child can take into account weights being different distances from the fulcrum, and can count the number of pegs to decide which way the balance will tip. At substage 3, the child can make accurate predictions even when weights are different distances from the fulcrum and have different masses. At this stage, the physical system and the abstract counting system are fully integrated in making predictions.

In Case's neo-Piagetian theory, performance on any cognitive task is a function of information-processing constraints, but those constraints are not biologically fixed. Automaticity gained through experience decreases the burden to working memory and facilitates the consolidation and coordination of "schemes." In this way, the growth of intellectual competence retains a Piagetian quality of ordinal progression that can be subdivided into stages and substages, as Figure 7.5 illustrates. The staircase metaphor that was so convincingly advanced by Piaget was retained by Case. But in Case's theory, there is not a single staircase, but rather multiple staircases that lead to different "rooms" of competence, rooms that corresponded to different broad domains—number, causality, and so on—which Case called central conceptual structures.

Jerome Bruner's Theory

Whereas Piaget presented development as a stage-like progression through increasing levels of abstraction and complexity, the American psychologist Jerome Bruner proposed a theory less distinguished by stages of rising abstraction than by modes of

FIGURE 7.5
Robbie Case's
Neo-Piagetian
Theory *Case kept*
Piaget's staircase
metaphor but applied it
to narrower domains.
[From Case (1991), Re-
printed by permission of
Copyright Clearance Cen-
ter, Inc. on behalf of
Lawrence Erlbaum, Inc.]

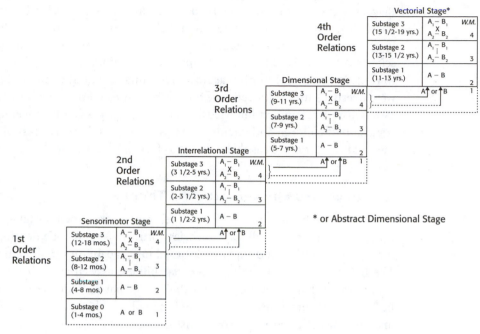

knowledge representation. Bruner (1964) recognized three modes as important to cognitive development: enactive, iconic, and symbolic. *Enactive* representation refers to knowledge as the movement of muscles to manipulate objects. Enactive representation corresponds largely to Piaget's sensorimotor stage; it conforms to the way infants represent the world almost exclusively. Unlike Piaget's stage theory, however, Bruner's theory does not present this first stage as being superseded by another, more advanced way of thinking. Instead, enactive representation is *supplemented*, not supplanted, by other representational modes.

The second representational form is *iconic*. Here, the child recognizes images as conveying meaning. Whether such images are the repeated appearance of actual objects—houses, people, animals, plants, and cars—or stylized drawings or photographs, the child learns to build understanding around interpretable visual experience. By understanding of the world through interpretable images, the child supplements enactive representation to gain a richer understanding of the surrounding environment.

The third representational form is *symbolic*. In the experience of the child, symbolic representation is first expressed as spoken language. Later, written language and other symbol systems—mathematical and perhaps musical—add to the richness and utility of symbolic representation. Symbol systems are not simply a means of interpreting experience, but equally a means of communication and expression. Through the power of symbolic representation, a child can transcend the limits of the here-and-now inherent in enactive representation and, to a lesser degree, in iconic representation. Bruner's three representational forms—enactive, iconic, and symbolic—are successive layers that expand the worldview of the growing intellect. Each stage adds to, rather than replaces, the understandings afforded by prior representational modes.

Because Bruner focused less on abstraction than did Piaget, Bruner's theory does not make such strong predictions that some forms of cognition are beyond the reach of young children. Educators guided by Piagetian thinking are aware of the risks of presenting abstract content prematurely to young learners. Educators with a more Brunerian orientation are less worried about a child's lack of "readiness." In the early 1960s, at a time when English-speaking educators and psychologists were becoming aware of

Piaget's ideas, Jerome Bruner (1960, p. 33) hypothesized in his book, *The Process of Education*, that "any subject can be taught effectively in some intellectually honest form to any child at any stage of development." Bruner was writing specifically to science educators and to scientists, but the wider implications of his theoretical claim were clear: Strict prohibitions against presenting advanced content to the young mind were overly cautious. Indeed, as evidence accumulated over the next two decades, the assumed restrictions on knowledge and thought processes that seemed to define the cognition of children and infants were less severe than initially presumed. The mind of the child was far more capable than it was formerly credited to be.

Kieran Egan's Epistemological Theory

The three theories of cognitive development examined so far—those of Piaget, Case, and Bruner—are all stage theories (Bruner's less so); the developing child gains through maturation and experience broad new capabilities in a predictable sequence. The theories characterize those new capabilities, as well as their underlying mechanisms, somewhat differently. A fourth theory, that of Canadian philosopher Kieran Egan, similarly proposes a sequence of broad phases that characterize the child's evolving thinking as developing through distinctive forms. Egan is concerned primarily with the child's developing **epistemology**—how the child knows what he knows. Egan (1996) proposed five stages: somatic, mythic, romantic, philosophical, and ironic. These five stages characterize both the developing mind and the sequence of dominant epistemologies in the history of Western culture.

As recognized by Piaget and other stage theorists, the infant's preliminary understanding of the world is strongly bound to bodily, or somatic, experience. Egan's *somatic* stage is roughly equivalent to Piaget's sensorimotor stage and Bruner's enactive representation. Early in the child's experience, patterns in the environment that are most engaging are those that involve vivid contrasts of color and shape. The second stage, *mythic*, presents the child as comprehending the world through stories. Narratives provide the child with such categorical opposites as good and evil, and these help to structure the child's growing comprehension and worldview.

Egan's portrayal of the third stage, *romantic*, shows how his theory diverges from previous ways of interpreting the child's growing understanding of the world. In romantic understanding, the child is fascinated by contrasting extremes and unusual combinations. Superlatives of all kinds—the unusual feats and features that qualify for the *Guinness Book of World Records*, for example—are highly interesting. It's as if the child needs to test the limits of standard categories to understand them more deeply. Interest in the limits of categories extends to violations of those categories, as exemplified by the talking animals in cartoons and superheroes' ability to fly.

The fourth stage in Egan's theory is the *philosophical* stage. Now the child is ready to find overarching patterns of meaning in his or her experience. Forming generalizations about the way the world works and about the child's own identity presents a huge intellectual task. The desire to find broader patterns of significance and meaning might well extend to the natural world and to social, political, and religious experience. Abstract and theoretical modes of inquiry required by the natural and social sciences are now within the orbit of the child's capabilities. Inductive inference—reasoning from specific data to general principles—also rises in importance within the child's cognitive toolkit.

The fifth and final stage identified by Egan is the *ironic* stage. This stage recognizes fundamentally that the generalizations yielded by philosophical thinking do not always hold up. Neat philosophical assumptions break down in unexpected ways: Villains are

FIGURE 7.6
A Fascination with
Extremes *A child at the*
romantic stage of Egan's
theory is fascinated by
extremes of all kinds, as if
he or she is testing and
understanding the limits of
standard categories.
[Corbis/Bettman]

not always thoroughly evil and heroes have feet of clay; democracy can be tragically unfair; authority figures tell lies; belief systems that once seemed airtight now appear to have troubling gaps and inconsistencies. The quest for overarching understanding now seems to be an impossible task. The wild complexity of the world can be unsettling, disturbing, and even disillusioning, but in the ironic stage this reality is accepted as the true order of things. A new contentedness, rooted in acceptance rather than cynicism, emerges as the most apt response to a puzzling, ironic world.

Kieran Egan's theory of cognitive development lacks the detailed articulation of Jean Piaget's monumental theory. Nevertheless, his theory is remarkable for its creative divergence from its psychological predecessors. The stages Egan describes capture aspects of the child's growing understanding of the world using concepts that are quite different from the perhaps hyper-logical, overly psychologized models presented by others. Starting from the discipline of philosophy, Egan offers the educator an alternative way of conceptualizing the child's cognitive development.

Vygotskyan Theory

There was a time in the education of teachers when the name Jean Piaget dominated the theoretical basis of instruction. If there was a single theory worth knowing and paying attention to when making curricular and pedagogical decisions, it was Piaget's. But sometime during the 1980s and 1990s, the theory of Jean Piaget began to slip from its status as the pre-eminent theoretical influence on education. In its place were the "new" teachings of a then-obscure Russian psychologist who lived in the early twentieth century, Lev Vygotsky.

Part of the reason for the decline of Piagetian ideas and the ascendance of Vygotsky's theory was the barrage of empirical and theoretical challenges to Piaget (reviewed earlier in this chapter). Empirical counterevidence to a monolithic stage theory as well as the rise of information-processing cognitive psychology made Piaget's ideas less believable and less relevant, at least in their original form. More important than these factors, however, was a rising awareness that the dominant theories of cognitive development and education paid insufficient attention to *social* aspects of learning and development. The new information-processing theory as well as its predecessor, Skinnerian behaviorism, emphasized individual psychology to the neglect of social processes. Much the same criticism can be made of Piaget's stage theory of cognitive development.

Vygotsky's (1978) theory filled the gap beautifully. Not only did it acknowledge both individual and group processes, it also wove them together into a coherent conceptual system. Social and psychological processes were equally important, mutually influential, and understandable in a way that made their application to education fairly direct. Vygotsky's ideas illuminated the growth of the human mind and moved educational thought into new territory. The central ideas of the theory have proved to be widely applicable to educational processes. Indeed, many decades after the formulation of Vygotsky's theory, the implications for educational practice are still being worked out.

Lev Vygotsky's theory is a rich, complex body of thought backed by his own experiments as well as the research of others. By necessity, we can examine only the high points of Vygotskyan thought, just as we could consider only the essential aspects of Piagetian theory. Fortunately, the basic concepts driving Vygotsky's theory can be described fairly economically. One has already been noted: Vygotsky attended to both individual psychology and to social processes, treating them as equally important and interwoven. A second conceptual basis is directly linked to the first: Vygotsky saw a vital role for social influences that originate outside the individual learner—in particular, the people and culture in which the individual mind lives and grows. By acknowledging the influence of forces external to the developing mind, Vygotsky's theory contrasts sharply with the internal processes so strongly emphasized by Piaget. To be fair, Piaget did not deny the influence of social processes, but his theory clearly stressed the unfolding *internal* logical structures of the child's mind.

Consistent with the emphasis on social influences, Vygotsky recognized the tremendous power of language to shape cognition and cognitive development. He perceived a direct connection between language and thought—indeed, the title of one collection of his writings is *Language and Thought* (1986). He did not see the two as equivalent but appreciated the dynamic link between them. That connection is obvious in interpersonal communication through speech and writing; but in Vygotsky's view, language also plays a strong role in individual psychology. We *think*, at least in part, using language. In two fundamental ways—social communication as well as individual psychology—language and thought are deeply intertwined.

If we boil down Vygotsky's many important ideas to the essentials, we can identify two concepts as both central to Vygotsky's theory and consequential for education. One of those concepts is the zone of proximal development; the other is the internalization of higher order thought.

The Zone of Proximal Development

In the traditions of both education and psychology, we are used to measuring competence of an individual by what that person can do acting alone, unassisted. School-based tests of learning are almost always presented as tasks for individual students. The **zone of proximal development (ZPD)** model challenges that conceptualization. It recognizes that individuals often exhibit higher levels of skill through the assistance, encouragement, and coaching of other people. Social influences interact with psychological capability and elevate performance to a more advanced level. We can therefore define the zone of proximal development as the difference between the competence of a person acting alone and what that person can achieve with the assistance of others.

A learner's zone of proximal development is a place of tremendous pedagogical potential. Essentially, the zone bounds the space for potential learning at any moment in time. Increases in competence can be achieved when tasks and supports are within the zone of proximal development. For example, a teacher might present tasks that are slightly beyond the skill level of a child acting without assistance. If the difficulty level is selected judiciously, then the child will be able to succeed in the challenging task with only minimal assistance. After prompting a child to higher levels of competence, the teacher can gradually remove helps and hints as they become unnecessary. The skilled assistance lent by teachers, parents, or other skilled adults is sometimes called **scaffolding**—although that term is not properly Vygotsky's but rather Bruner's.

Whether familiar with Vygotsky's theory or not, a skillful teacher intuitively presents instruction so that the challenge level is compatible with the learners' zone of proximal development. It would be a waste of time to present tasks that are beneath the competence of students. If expectations are too low, then tasks are below the child's zone. At the other extreme, it is pointless for teachers to present tasks that are far beyond the capabilities of students even if they are given strong support. In mathematics, a student learns arithmetic first, then algebra, then calculus. A different order makes no sense. To present tasks that are far beyond what a child can achieve produces only confusion and frustration. These expectations lie beyond the zone. But within upper and lower bounds—within the zone of proximal development—a teacher can find the cognitive territory in which the student can learn profitably. Inside the ZPD, the teacher can masterfully and sensitively scaffold the learner toward greater understanding and skill. Both social and psychological processes come into play and raise the learner to new heights of proficiency.

The Internalization of Higher-Order Thought

The second major idea that emerges from Lev Vygotsky's theory is an explanation for the origin of higher-order cognition. Vygotsky saw higher-order thinking as arising distinctly from the social environment. This hypothesis was introduced earlier in this book in Chapter 5, *Complex Cognition,* along with an example of children listening to their parents debating the pros and cons of going to the zoo in bad weather. Taking different positions, the parents discuss why going to the zoo was a good idea or why it was a poor plan. The child, by listening to this conversation, is able to internalize the debate in his own decision-making. To weigh ideas for and against, to compare options alongside competing values, promises, uncertainties, and hopes—all these considerations feed into making good decisions. The child can appropriate the wealth of thinking tools in his social environment by incorporating them into his own cognitive skill set. Those tools can later be re-used in other situations that require good problem-solving and critical-thinking skills.

Higher-order thinking skills acquired in a social situation can be re-used in a different group setting, but—and this is a key component of Vygotsky's theory—they can also be used by the individual person thinking alone. In other words, forms of cognition originally presented to the individual learner as *social* processes can become internalized and so take on *psychological* value. For example, the child, or any learner, can use the pro-con debate structure to think through the best possible decision using entirely silent thought processes. Initially the learner might actually verbalize his thinking so that it is audible. Gradually, the individual's spoken chain of reasoning becomes silent, internal cognition. Vygotsky called this sequence—the sequence from (1) social discourse to (2) individual thought spoken aloud to (3) unvocalized thought—**going underground**.

Once a new cognitive process is acquired socially and becomes individually psychological, there is no reason why the process cannot be reversed. Individual thinkers in a group setting can use their learned cognitive skills privately or interpersonally. In groups, thinking skills become available in the vocalized social space and can be internalized by other learners, who can then appropriate them into their own cognitive toolkits. The dynamic dialectic between the social reality and the psychological realm is a breakthrough concept in Vygotsky's theory, one that is highly illuminating as to the nature and origin of cognition, and highly applicable to education. Vygotsky's theory tells us that the growth of cognitive proficiency involves appropriating the intellectual wealth from the social and cultural space. This fantastic insight highlights the power of group processes to advance educational aims. It also clarifies one of the ways that a teacher can advance the thinking of her students—namely, by making her own cognitive skills more observable to students.

Reciprocal Teaching

Various teaching techniques are motivated by a desire to capitalize on the intellectual wealth inherent in groups for the benefit of all participants. Prominent among those techniques is the **reciprocal teaching method**, advanced by Brown and Palincsar (1989) specifically as a way to improve reading comprehension. Using this process, a small group of students and a teacher study a common text. To a significant degree the roles of teacher and student are minimized. The teacher assumes the role of participant and each student has occasion to lead the group. Thus, the roles of teacher and student are to some degree interchangeable, which explains the *reciprocal* in reciprocal teaching.

Reciprocal teaching further involves a division of responsibilities and role-taking. While the role of "teacher" can rotate among participants, other circulating roles focus on one group process or another to summarize, critique, and keep the group focused. The assignment of roles within the group can help to ensure that a variety of perspectives are taken in understanding a text, in forming consensus, and in recording gains in comprehension. Reciprocal teaching is deliberately built around Vygotskyan theory to improve thinking by leveraging the cognitive wealth that resides in groups—resources that surpass the intellectual capability of any single individual.

Language Development

In the development of a child, the cognitive skill that accelerates most obviously is the use of language. Within a few short years, a normally developing child acquires enough skill to understand much of any conversation, and to use language to make his or her wishes, wants, and needs known. The preschooler can use language to ask questions, to present reasons, and to express emotions. Language is a major conduit by which the child becomes socialized into the local community and culture. The skilled use of language is extremely powerful, perhaps without equal as a device that advances cognitive development.

Language has several manifestations. As a basic distinction, language has productive and receptive aspects. Language can be generated through speech (productive) or comprehended by listening (receptive). The receptive and productive aspects of spoken language are normal elements of every human community with one exception, the deaf community, whose members instead use sign language for interpersonal communication. But there is another side of language use that may or may not be present in a community—*written* language. Text is not a necessary element of human culture. The human species had long existed with no written text, only spoken language. Even during the past century, great segments of the world population could not read or write. But both writing and reading are now essential to any acceptable definition of education. Education must include instruction in the skilled use of written language—in other words, literacy.

Written language, like spoken language, includes receptive and productive aspects. The literate person can both read (receptively) and write (productively). Thus we can make a four-part division: Language can be found in both spoken and written forms, and each of these can be subdivided into productive and receptive aspects. Education properly entails advancement in all four forms of language use.

Listening and Speaking

At the most elementary level, listening comprehension involves the perception of individual sound elements—the phonemes of speech. Of course, language operates at levels beyond the identification of individual speech sounds. Listening and speaking involve skill in syntactical aspects of speech that indicate verb tense, pronoun reference, and so on. At a more abstract level, the pragmatic aspect of language use allows a speaker to accomplish goals in the world—to ask for information, make requests, clarify ideas, and express feelings. Proficiency in these different layers of language use is never acquired passively. All language development, from elemental to highly complex, involves the child's active participation in linguistic activities, most often as participants in social interactions.

Listening comprehension begins with **parsing**. To parse is to divide and connect a continuous sound stream into a meaningful organization of words, phrases, and large units of discourse. Listening comprehension also involves becoming familiar with discourse forms such as story schemas (Thorndyke, 1977). Through exposure to a variety of stories, children learn to form expectations about the plot of a new story, and those expectations aid comprehension. The form of stories can differ widely from culture to culture, a pattern explored by Sir Frederic Bartlett (1932) in his pioneering work on narrative schemas (see Chapter 4). Extensive experience with story schemas is an important aspect of early literacy. In time, the child learns other forms of discourse, including the presentation of factual information in expository form, and that growing familiarity also aids linguistic comprehension.

Reading

Reading is complex. It involves the coordination of both basic-level reading processes and higher-order comprehension activities. The most important basic reading process is **decoding**, in which written letters, vowels and consonants, are translated into their respective sounds. Decoding may seem straightforward and the most easily accomplished of all reading skills, but several considerations can complicate skilled decoding. One factor is the collection of irregularities found in written English. Many letters, especially vowels, can stand for several distinct sounds.

A second complicating factor is a common *inability* to distinguish individual phonemes—to hear them in speech as isolated sounds, and to retain an awareness of their temporal order. Learning to decode assumes the reader has the ability to hear the individual phonemes of the spoken word, but the ability to hear distinct sounds and sound sequences is often imperfectly developed among readers. **Dyslexia** is a learning disability that involves particular difficulty in processing written language, even though the dyslexic person's intelligence falls within the normal range. Dyslexia greatly complicates the tasks of learning to read and becoming a highly proficient reader.

At a higher level of organization, reading involves the analysis of word meaning. Word comprehension has both morphemic and semantic aspects. Morphemic qualities of reading include recognizing written words as holistic units rather than as mere sequences of letters. Indeed, skilled reading eventually requires a shift from decoding letters to the recognition of words as whole units. In skilled reading, word and word parts such as prefixes *(re-, in-, anti-,)* and suffixes *(-s, -er, est-, -able)* are the basic units of cognitive processing, rather than individual letters. These **morphemes** must be quickly recognized and interpreted as conveying meaning. This rapid recognition of words and word parts is an essential component of reading skill.

Of course, reading assumes that the printed word will have personal meaning to the reader—this is the semantic aspect of comprehension. Skilled decoding is pointless if the identified words have no semantic significance. Reading comprehension, therefore, relies on knowledge of word meanings. Word knowledge is strongly supported by exposure to printed materials, because written language is a much richer source of diverse vocabulary than is either spoken language or television (Cunningham & Stanovich, 1998). Here we find huge differences among learners. Children whose reading proficiency is at the 90th percentile read, on average, almost two million words each year independent of schoolwork. Those at the 10th percentile read a mere 8,000 words outside school.

Skilled reading entails comprehension. Perhaps it is more accurate to say that skilled reading *is* comprehension. Comprehension is the ability to find the overall structure of ideas presented in the written text and to separate main ideas from subsidiary ones. The skilled reader can find the main driving idea, or the "gist" of the text, and express it succinctly as a summary. The interpretive aspects of reading—such as the critical appraisal of ideas—exist at still higher levels; here, reading comprehension also includes making inferences about unstated but important ideas and assumptions, testing implications, and finding gaps and flaws in reasoning. So literacy extends far beyond the ability to decode; it is more accurately defined as the ability to engage in higher-level text comprehension. That, after all, is the degree of reading skill required in a complex, information-rich society.

The proper way to teach reading has been a matter of bitter debate among educators for at least a century. Historically, the debate has contrasted two different approaches: whole-word instruction and phonics. The **whole-word method** concentrates on words as the units of learning. Reading primers that use recurrent vocabulary (e.g., "see Spot run") teach words as familiar units that can be memorized and mixed as elements of a story. The whole-word method has been contrasted with **phonics**, an approach that emphasizes teaching letter-sound correspondences. The rationale for phonics is that English is a phonetic language, and that skilled reading requires understanding the **alphabetic principle**—that letters map onto sounds—even though the mapping is not simply one to one (Snow, Burns, & Griffin, 1998).

In recent years, the terms of the debate have shifted. Those favoring a holistic approach began to advocate the **whole-language method**. The whole-language method assumes that learning to read should be a natural process in which children are immersed in literature and writing. As cultural activities that can be highly motivating, reading and writing can make literacy development fun. The hope is that immersion into written language is sufficient to build reading skills, much as immersion into spoken language is sufficient to teach children how to talk. Advocates of whole-language instruction have felt that phonics, in contrast, is artificial and potentially dull, and can turn off budding readers to the joys of literature. Some proponents of the whole-language approach have explicitly rejected the direct teaching of letter-sound correspondences.

Research has informed the debate. Accumulating research on reading has affirmed the vital importance of alphabetic decoding. One strand of research makes it quite clear that poor readers often have difficulty at the level of decoding; the essential problem is inadequate **phonemic awareness** (Paris, Morrison, & Miller, 2006). Phonemic awareness is the understanding that spoken words can be broken down into their constituent sounds (phonemes) and, conversely, that a series of phonemes can be blended together to form a meaningful word. A child needs to know that the word *cat* can be divided into its constituent sounds, and that the sounds of *c*, *a*, and *t*, when blended together, form *cat*. Researchers now know that poor readers often have inadequate phonemic awareness, and that specific training can produce gains in phonemic awareness, which in turn leads to improved decoding fluency. The goal is for decoding to reach the level of **automaticity** so that the limited cognitive resources of working memory can be spent on higher-level activities, notably comprehension.

Obviously, skilled readers must do much more than decode fluidly. Nevertheless, the need for skilled decoding never goes away. Every reader encounters unfamiliar words that must be decoded letter by letter. Unfortunately, the skilled application of decoding is not guaranteed using the whole-language method. Almost all students, especially those from lower socioeconomic backgrounds, benefit from direct instruction in phonics. This does not mean that phonics needs to be the sole approach to teaching reading—only that it should be one component of reading instruction. Indeed, there is some evidence that a combination of phonics and whole-language instruction, sometimes called **balanced literacy**, is a more effective way of teaching reading than either approach by itself (Alvermann, Fitzgerald, & Simpson, 2006; Pressley, 2002; Rayner, Foorman, Perfetti, Pesetsky, & Seidenberg, 2002).

Writing

Writing is widely considered to be an essential component of literacy and a key goal of education. Writing also has great importance in the pursuit of higher education, and is crucial to the skilled performance of every worker in an information economy. How can instruction that leads to high levels of writing proficiency be carried out most effectively? The answer depends partly on understanding the collection of skills that constitute good writing.

The skills that constitute writing ability have been understood in part through studying expert writers (Hayes, 1996; Hayes & Flower, 1980). For example, researchers have determined that expert writers both generate more ideas and revise their writing more extensively than do novice writers. Contrary to a reasonable assumption that expert writers produce high-quality text on the first draft, they behave as if their best written products are achievable only through extensive re-writing. The practical importance that experts place on revision coincides with their initial high production of ideas. Not all ideas generated by an author are worth keeping. The process of revising text into a high-quality product requires expert writers to be selective about ideas, retaining some and excising others.

INTEREST MAGNET 7.2

Speed Reading

The great philosopher John Stuart Mill was said to be able to read as rapidly as he could turn the pages of a book. Wouldn't you like to have that ability? The possibility of rapid reading with high comprehension has long been fascinating and highly desirable. With speed reading skills, a student could use study time efficiently. For those wanting to expand their knowledge base, the possibility of reading several books a day—and being able to remember the information presented in those books—is very exciting. For book lovers and for everyone who loves to learn, speed reading almost seems too good to be true.

Speed reading techniques based on research by the U.S. Air Force were first developed in the 1940s. The Air Force found that a device called a tachistoscope could present visual information extremely briefly—for less than 1/100 of a second. The early military experiments started a trend. In the 1950s, a schoolteacher named Evelyn Wood developed the most well-known training program in speed reading. The technique relied on pacing the reader's eyes by moving the hand over a page of text steadily. Ambitious pacing, whether by hand, fingertip, or a computer display guide, is a common speed reading technique. Another common method is reducing subvocalization, the "voice inside the head" that corresponds to the spoken word. Subvocalization might include minor mouth movements that coincide with mental processing of text.

Research has shown that maximum reading speeds are rather modest compared to the claims of speed readers. The average reading rate for college seniors is about 300 words per minute, with the very fastest (the top 1 percent) readers able to read about 500 words per minute with good comprehension (Carver, 1990). Companies that market speed reading products or training programs claim that speed readers can read more than 1000 words per minute with high comprehension. Those claims have turned out to be false. Speed reading inevitably results in superficial processing of text—skimming or scanning—which in turn produces decreased comprehension (Cunningham, Stanovich, & Wilson, 1990). Even self-proclaimed speed reading experts have demonstrated poor reading comprehension. Worse still, speed readers may not even realize that their comprehension is poor. Superficial processing of text may compromise a reader's ability to separate crucial information from information that is less important.

What then does speed reading offer? Speed reading is essentially a technique for skimming—rapidly sampling text to search for specific information or to gain a general sense of the subject. There is no question that skimming is an important reading skill for some purposes, but it is not a substitute for reading with comprehension. Indeed, good reading comprehension may require that a reader *slow down*, especially if the material is complex or if the reader wants to retain the information (Carver, 1990). Knowing whether reading rates need to speed up or slow down requires metacognitive judgment—the kind of cognitive self-awareness and executive control that training in speed reading might undermine rather than enhance.

Expert writers also produce text that has greater cohesion than text written by novices. This is largely a product of extensive planning (Graham, 2006). Experts pay strict attention to the structure and sequence of ideas. One sentence follows sensibly from another, pronoun referents are clear, and transitions make connections easy to follow. Fortunately, the skills needed to write effectively can be taught as strategies, and instruction in such strategies has been shown to be effective. With practice in these key strategies, students can become more effective writers.

Development Toward Expertise

This chapter concerns human development, particularly cognitive development. Historically, research on cognitive development has focused on children and adolescents. Although there has been some research on cognitive development among adults, some of it conceptualized in Piagetian terms as post–formal operational thinking, much of the work has been preliminary (Alexander & Langer, 1990, King & Kitchner, 2004). One branch of research, however, directly addresses an important form of cognitive development that occurs during adulthood: the developmental trajectory of the transition from novice to expert.

Our knowledge-based society requires experts—people who perform very competently in a defined field. More than ever before, the economy rewards workers who are highly knowledgeable and intellectually skilled. Every segment of society needs experts: companies, educational and research institutions, hospitals, and governments. The blazing speed of innovation and the expansion of international trade and competition make expertise essential for economic survival and prosperity.

The Nature of Expertise

Psychologists have conceptualized the growth toward expertise as a trajectory from novice to expert status. The trajectory is a long one, spanning many years. The transition from novice to expert resembles the developmental trajectories identified in Piagetian and neo-Piagetian theories. There are differences, however, between the growing competence of a child and the growth toward expertise in an adult. One difference is that transitions in children are often more conspicuous as changes in behavior. The path from novice status to expertise is more gradual, but eventually produces large changes in manifest competence.

What does an expert do differently than a novice, and how can we discover those differences? Like children, experts may not be able to explain how they do what they do—they simply do it. Their knowledge is often **tacit**—inexplicit in their own thinking and therefore hard to describe. The researcher must find ways to probe the differences with a hope that the resulting knowledge will be useful in helping novices transition toward expertise.

The Expert's Knowledge Base

Of the many qualities that differentiate novices from experts, one trait rises above all others in importance: the enormous fund of knowledge that experts possess. Herbert Simon has estimated that expertise in any field requires a mental store of approximately 50,000 pieces of information (50,000 chunks). The expert not only knows where to look for the needed information, but also has much of that information immediately accessible in long-term memory.

Access to a huge array of familiar patterns helps the expert to deal effectively with complex problems without being overwhelmed by excessive information. Because an expert's knowledge is chunked, an expert can actively process more information than a novice can. It's not that an expert has a larger working memory capacity. If experienced patterns are meaningless, such as when chess pieces are placed unsystematically on a chessboard, an expert will have no greater capacity to remember than a novice. The relevance of *meaningful* patterns to expert performance was discovered by de Groot (1965) in a study of chess masters and novices. De Groot tested experts and novices for their ability to remember a variety of chess configurations. When chess pieces were placed in patterns encountered in real chess games, the experts could remember the layout of the chessboard very accurately, whereas novices could remember the locations of only a few pieces. But the story changed dramatically when de Groot presented the experts and novices with another task—chess pieces placed *randomly* on the chessboard. Now the differences between experts and novices narrowed considerably: No longer did the chess masters have a significant advantage over novices. With the pieces placed randomly on the chessboard, the experts could no longer "chunk" the board to reduce its complexity to simpler configurations. Experts, like novices, could remember only a few chess pieces.

De Groot's experiment proved that novices and experts do not differ in working memory capacity. Both are highly constrained to process only a small number of chunks at any one time. But what constitutes a chunk is different for the expert and the novice. A vast array of highly chunked knowledge is a main ingredient in every field of expertise. In medicine, familiar chunks include knowledge of disease syndromes, symptom patterns, pharmaceuticals, and diagnostic and treatment procedures. Because the expert has access to a vast knowledge base of relevant chunks, the immediate information-processing capacity of the expert is expanded. Just as the expert has chunked a huge array of knowledge, much of the expert's procedural skill is practiced to the point of automaticity. Chunking and automaticity both contribute powerfully to expertise.

How Experts Solve Problems

Experts are distinguished not only by their extensive knowledge base, but also by their approaches to problem solving. They differ from novices, for example, in the strategies or heuristics they apply during problem solving.

WORKING FORWARD HEURISTIC. Experts tend to let the given conditions of the problem drive their problem solution forward. Because many problem situations look familiar, they often know how to proceed. A doctor might think, "This set of symptoms looks familiar—I think I know what to do next." Likewise, a car mechanic might perceive a familiar pattern in the sound of an engine and have ideas about what diagnostic tests to run. This is **working forward heuristic**; the context presents clues to the expert about what to do next.

The working forwards heuristic is driven by the knowledge and experience an expert brings to bear on a problem. A veteran mathematics teacher might know exactly how to begin to solve a new math problem because that problem is like others he or she has solved in the past. Novices lack extensive experience, and so they are forced to use the comparatively weaker **working backward heuristic** of considering the ultimate goal and generating strategies that are likely to move toward that goal. Not knowing how to proceed initially, a math student might have to set subgoals that lead partway toward a solution. And under certain conditions, experts act like novices: When experts face problems that are very unfamiliar, they too tend to adopt a working backwards strategy (Larkin, McDermott, Simon, & Simon, 1980).

PROBLEM REPRESENTATION. Besides applying particular heuristics during problem solving, experts tend to think of a problem in somewhat different terms than do novices. Experts mentally *represent* problems differently. Expert-novice differences in problem representation became clear in a classic psychology experiment that involved sorting physics problems. Physicists and physics students were asked to classify problems taken from introductory college physics texts (Chi, Feltovich, & Glaser, 1981). The problems were written on 3 by 5 cards that the participants sorted into piles based on similarities in how the problems would be solved. Novices in this study were undergraduates who had just completed a semester course on the physics of motion; experts were advanced Ph.D. students in physics.

The main finding from the study was that novices used the **surface features** of problems as the basis for classification. Surface features included the particular objects

FIGURE 7.7
Classification
of Physics
Problems *Experts
and novices sort
problems differently.*
[From Chi, Feltovich, &
Glaser, 1981, and Halli-
day & Resnick (1974)]

Problem A

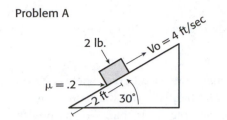

Problem B

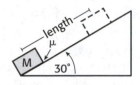

Problem C

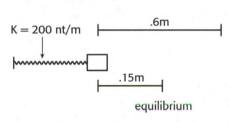

**Novices' Explanations for Their
Similarity Groupings**

Novice 1: "These deal with the blocks on
an *incline plane*"

Novice 5: "*Inclined plane* problems,
coefficient of *friction*"

Novice 6: "Blocks on *inclined planes*
with *angles*"

**Experts' Explanations for Their
Similarity Groupings**

Expert 2: "*Conservation of Energy*"

Expert 3: "*Work-Energy Theorem.*
They are all straight-forward
problems."

Expert 4: "These can be done from energy
considerations. Either you should
know the *Principle of Conservation
of Energy*, or work is lost
somewhere."

mentioned in the problem description—pulleys, springs, and inclined planes—as
well as particular terms, such as *friction*, used in the problem statement. Experts, however, classified problems according to the **deep structure** of domain principles, such as
Newton's Second Law. It was as if the experts could see past the specifics of the problem
to the deeper reality of domain principles. By avoiding the distractions presented by
pulleys or inclined planes, they could detect the concepts and laws of physics that led
more directly to an efficient solution of the problem.

Figure 7.7 illustrates the pattern. Seven out of eight novices grouped problems A
and B together, with the justification that both problems deal with inclined planes.
By contrast, six of the eight experts grouped problems A and C together because both
deal with conservation of energy, even though their surface characteristics differ. Not
only the sorting behavior, but even the basic categories used by experts and novices differed dramatically. The classification strategies employed by experts and novices
showed only minimal overlap: only 5 out of the 20 categories were shared by experts
and novices. On the basis of these differences in sorting behavior, Chi and colleagues
(Chi, Feltovich, & Glaser, 1981) inferred that expert knowledge is organized by *deep
structure* rather than *surface features*. Chi also studied the thought processes of senior
undergraduates majoring in physics, a group whose competence was midway between
experts and novices. These students tended to use both deep structure and surface

characteristics of problems in their classification. This finding suggested a developmental sequence in which novices gradually release their dependence on the surface features of problems and slowly restructure their knowledge by the principles of the discipline.

ALLOCATION OF TIME. Another strategic difference between experts and novices in problem solving behavior is how they allocate their time. In the Chi experiment, experts actually took *longer* to sort the cards than did the novices. On average, the experts took 18 minutes to sort 24 problems, whereas the novices took only about 12 minutes. This difference conforms to the findings of other investigators: Experts tend to invest considerable time and effort to represent a problem mentally prior to solving it. Although experts may solve problems more quickly than novices, they spend a greater *proportion* of the time thinking about the problem before actually trying to solve it. Novices tend to act more impulsively—they jump in and try different approaches, hoping that one action or another will spur progress toward the goal. This strategy difference suggests an application for teachers: They can coach students to spend relatively more time *thinking* about a problem before actually attempting to solve it. Time spent developing a workable problem representation is one mark of an expert. Novices can emulate this behavior as they move toward expertise.

The Timeline for Expertise

An expert does not accumulate his or her base of knowledge quickly. Time is needed—a lot of time. The acquisition of expert knowledge and skill requires an investment on the order of ten years of concentrated study and practice. Herbert Simon (1980, p. 82) noted that "there is no such thing as expertness without knowledge—extensive and accessible knowledge. [In chess, for example], no one, no matter how intelligent, skilled in problem solving, or talented becomes an expert with less than ten years of exposure to the task environment of chess." More generally, Simon (1991, p. 36) claimed that "the level of world-class expert is never achieved with less than 10 years of intensive, round-the-clock effort." This time parameter has been called the **ten-year rule** (Ross, 2006).

To explain why an expert's knowledge base takes so long to acquire, consider the relatively slow and inefficient "write time" characteristic of human cognition along with the sheer immensity of information needed for expert reasoning. Each chunk requires time to assimilate and retain, and the process is far from 100 percent efficient. Multiply the two factors together—chunks and time per chunk—and the result is that the acquisition of expertise is time-intensive, requiring an effort of about ten years' duration. And a decade of concentrated study, according to Herbert Simon, is typical for the attainment of the highest academic degree, the doctorate. Within any field, we cannot expect a person to display high levels of proficiency without the intensive and extensive experience that produces highly chunked knowledge and automated skill. The phenomenon is universal: it holds for geniuses, whiz-kids, mavens, wizards, and gurus alike. Being very good at anything takes a long time.

We should not assume that a time investment of a decade will *guarantee* expertise. Here, the qualifier *necessary but not sufficient* applies. Knowledge is necessary for expertise, but expert performance may well require other ingredients, including immersion into the social community of experts along with its values, customs, and standards. Expertise entails several qualities that can be defined in cognitive terms, but expertise is not simply cognitive; it is also social and cultural. Nevertheless, the ten-year rule is a good guide for aspiring experts, including experts in education. For novice teachers, the goal to become truly excellent cannot be achieved in a year or two. Only through the intense pursuit of teaching excellence over a decade or so can a teacher reach his or her professional potential.

Bloom's Studies of Talent

Some of the research that illuminates the nature and development of expertise in adults also applies to understanding talent development in children and adolescents. Children and teenagers can develop high levels of proficiency in many performance domains—music, mathematics, and athletics, for example. In some cases, such as Olympic sports, their levels of expertise can reach world-class status. Even when children do not reach performance levels that are truly world class, they can exhibit very high levels of proficiency, such as in chess or music, that stand far above the typical performance of peers. Such children are called **prodigies**.

Benjamin Bloom, famous for Bloom's taxonomy and his theory of mastery learning, also made substantial contributions to the study of talent development in youth. Bloom (1985) found that children developed very high levels of talent through a combination of special circumstances. Above all, talent was developed only after investment of enormous amounts of time (Sosniak, 1985). Very often, children began involvement in a talent domain with little thought, either by themselves or by their parents, that it would be pursued seriously. After initial engagement in an activity that showed that the

FIGURE 7.8
Talent Development in Children *Benjamin Bloom found that exceptional talent in swimming and other domains is developed through the dedication of extraordinary time and effort.* [Pearson Education/ PH College]

child had high aptitude in the domain, the child shifted to a more able teacher or coach. More distinguished teachers in turn raised expectations, holding the child to ever-higher standards of performance and to dedicated practice that extended to several hours each day. At this point, the parents' involvement became atypical, requiring a substantial investment of time driving the child to lessons or attending competitions.

Bloom concluded that several factors coincided for high levels of talent development in children. First, there had to be an aptitude in the performance domain. Second, a large time investment, amounting to several hours each day over many years, was a necessary element of talent development. The child's ability to engage in consistent and extended practice required particular personality dispositions more than it hinged on raw talent. The dedication typically extended to the parents, or even to the entire family (Sloane, 1985). It was unusual, for example, for parents to devote the same level of dedication to more than one child. Talent development therefore became a family project in which everyone made sacrifices. Extreme dedication became even more obvious when a child reached a level of national or world-class ability. In such instances, the family often perceived a need to find the best coaches available, which sometimes meant relocating to a different area of the country so that the child could enter the tutelage of the very best instructors.

Deliberate Practice

The research literature explains how an expert's vast reservoir of knowledge and skill accumulates over time. Across all fields, the development of expertise requires habits of dedicated **deliberate practice** sustained over years (Ericsson, 1996). Deliberate practice is defined as a daily regimen of intense activity designed expressly for improving knowledge and skill in the target domain. Practice sessions provide **feedback** through expert coaches, internalized standards of excellence, or textbooks and strategy guides (Schraw, 2006). Deliberate practice is so demanding of focused concentration and effort that aspirants can engage in it only for a few hours each day, typically ranging from a minimum of two hours to a maximum of five. Those hours are dedicated to skill building. Less demanding but still relevant activities, such as "jam sessions" with other musicians, can fill in several additional hours each day.

Ericsson (1996) found that deliberate practice is essential to the development of expertise. All experts engage in daily focused efforts to extend their ability in the performance domains. Not only is deliberate practice necessary, it also differentiates more talented experts from less talented ones. Ericsson asked musicians to inventory their practice habits starting when they first took up their musical instrument. The musicians estimated the number of hours they practiced each day extending back many years. Ericsson corroborated those estimates by contacting family members and asking for their independent estimates of the musicians' practice times. With confidence that the estimates were sufficiently accurate, Ericsson then compared the total amount of practice time with the current proficiency levels of musicians. He found a good fit. In fact, the total number of lifetime hours invested in deliberate practice differentiated levels of talent *even among* the elite musicians.

What does the combined research on expertise tell us? Can we form any sort of generalization? Decades of research on expertise lead to this broad conclusion: In the achievement of expertise we find a very significant role for experience. Herbert Simon estimated that expertise requires an enormous fund of knowledge, which he estimated at 50,000 chunks, developed over ten years of full-time pursuit. Ericsson found that deliberate practice—the sustainable regimen of focused daily effort to improve skill—

defines the lifestyle of expert musicians and athletes. Expertise requires dedicated and focused effort applied over many years. These combined findings present a very interesting possibility: The level of talent in a society may be less a function of genetic predispositions than it is a product of societal support for developing the habits necessary to achieve very high levels of proficiency.

We tend to think of extreme talent as being mysterious, an expression of an inexplicable gift. Without denying that inborn differences contribute to outstanding talent, we sometimes find that highly talented performers ascribe their achievements to dedicated practice. Wayne Gretzky, widely regarded as the greatest ice hockey player of all time, insisted that his prodigious talent was the result of practice. Sports writer Peter Gzowski (1981) notes:

> What we take to be creative genius is in fact a reaction to a situation that [Gretzky] stored in his brain as deeply and firmly as his own telephone number. When I put this possibility to him, he agreed. "Absolutely," he said. "That's a hundred per cent right. It's all practice. . . . Nine out of ten people think it's instinct, and it isn't."
> (pp. 188, 189)

Now we can connect what we know about expertise to broader research on human learning. We know, for example, that time and learning are directly related. Learners differ, however, in the steepness of the learning curve: Some learn faster than others. But for both faster and slower learners, the relationship between time and learning is positive. More invested time will inevitably yield greater knowledge and skill. What then determines how much time and effort will be devoted to the development of talent? Here, motivational and volitional factors must enter—the "hot cognitions" that are the subject of Chapter 6, *Motivation, Volition, and Emotion.* Learning over shorter time spans—intervals of weeks or months typical of school curricula—deeply depend on motivational and volitional factors. When it comes to outstanding levels of talent developed over *years*, motivation and volition are more important still. Besides personal factors, opportunity and social support must be in place, a fact most obvious in Bloom's studies of talent development in children. One of the many ways that teachers can positively affect the lives of students is to help provide the support and encouragement that students will need to develop this level of dedication.

Beyond Expertise

Two Kinds of Experts

Are all experts alike, or does one expert differ from another in important ways? Perhaps one difference is obvious: Some experts are highly creative and others are not. One kind of expert is a mold-breaker who thinks and acts in ways altogether different from the expert who performs with great technical skill but with little flair. In *Surpassing Ourselves,* Bereiter and Scardamalia (1993) differentiated between these two types of experts, calling them *innovators* and *technicians.* The innovator is the creative expert; the technician is the expert who performs at a very high level of competence, but without generating anything particularly new. Perhaps the word *technician* does not quite capture the impressive achievement of this brand of expert. We might say that this expert is a virtuoso, able to display amazing levels of technical competence, but without being truly innovative.

Bereiter and Scardamalia called the kind of expertise displayed by the innovator **adaptive expertise**. This version of expertise tends toward new ways of seeing things and doing things. In Chapter 10, we will see that intelligence has both crystallized and fluid aspects. Crystallized intelligence corresponds roughly to knowledge, whereas fluid intelligence entails the ability to think flexibly about how to solve problems. Adaptive experts think fluidly about their work, and that fluid thinking is vitally important. More than ever, rapid cycles of innovation in technology and in research require fluid and flexible thinking. In the development of hybrid vehicles, Toyota engineers outpaced engineers at Ford in working out the technological challenges that made gasoline-electric vehicles feasible for mass production. The conceptual challenges of reconfiguring car engines to a new and workable design forced Ford to delay production of hybrid vehicles, resulting in a loss of potential sales. Innovation allied with technical competence is vital to economic viability and to individual and collective success in just about every field of pursuit. Could education be designed to contribute more dependably and powerfully to both aspects of expertise?

Eminence

Dean Simonton's (1996) studies of eminence in a variety of fields, including science, further sharpen our knowledge of conditions that lead to high levels of professional achievement. Among the more surprising of Simonton's findings is that high levels of professional recognition, or eminence, are strongly a function of overall productivity. This contrasts with a more intuitive belief that highly acclaimed scholars receive recognition for every work that they produce. That is not the overall pattern. Instead, Simonton found that the probability of producing a highly recognized work product, such as an influential research article, is roughly the same for all contributors, whether eminent or not. This is what Simonton called the **equal-odds principle**. What distinguishes highly eminent scholars is the overall *volume* of works they produce. By sheer dint of productivity, those who reach professional eminence stack the odds in their favor of producing another masterpiece.

The equal-odds principle and the predictive value of overall productivity to eminence jointly illuminate the mechanisms of professional success. Besides this important finding, Simonton discovered other interesting patterns related to eminence. For example, the chances of achieving high levels of recognition in a field are associated with life span. Specifically, eminence tends to be associated with either an early death or a long life. Another finding, which might not have much value for career planning but is interesting nonetheless, is that eminence is mildly associated with emotional instability. Although genius is not inevitably tied to "madness," there is in fact a higher incidence of mental turmoil and pathology among great achievers. No one really knows why. Perhaps high achievers are aided by a capacity for long periods of working alone or have lower-than-average needs for social approval. Simonton emphasized that *angst* is not a prerequisite for exceptionally high achievement—plenty of outstanding achievers are well-adjusted. But it is wrong to think that there is no relationship at all between mental instability and eminence.

Genius

This discussion leads us now to the topic of **genius**. Does the word have meaning and significance in our pursuit of understanding the human mind? Let us first define a genius as one who makes outstanding contributions to a field, and by doing so leaves a permanent mark on that field (Simonton, 1984). We can think of genius as an extreme form of adaptive expertise. A genius is one who *generates*—who adds new, important, and valued ideas or products. The word *genius* is therefore virtually never a fitting label for a child, even one with a very high IQ. Instead, genius could be regarded as an extension of the novice-expert trajectory, building on expertise but then transcending it. Genius requires understanding and using the conventions of a field without being bound by those conventions (Ericsson & Charness, 1994). Genius is manifest in the presentation of something novel, a transcendent product that is also an enduring contribution to the field. Beethoven introduced classical musicians to the soaring emotionality of romantic compositions, and a new musical era began. In architecture, Jørn Utzon's design of the Sydney Opera House was an aesthetic achievement that had no precedent.

The overall drift of the discussion has been to demystify expertise and eminence. In the case of genius, there is good reason for trying to do so. The word *genius*, besides its etymological associations with *generate* is also related to the word *genie*, suggesting a supernatural and therefore inscrutably mysterious explanation for extreme levels

INTEREST MAGNET 7.3

Genius and Madness

Is there any truth to the superstition that genius is akin to madness? The stereotypes of the mad scientist, the detached artistic primadonna, and the tormented writer come easily to mind. It is tempting to assume that the association of genius with psychological turmoil or maladjustment might be just another popular myth about how the human mind operates. This appears not to be the case, however. Psychologists who have studied the question do not dismiss the idea that there is a connection between high creativity or genius, and madness. Psychologist Dean Simonton has gone so far as to say that "this linkage between creative expertise and psychopathology has substantial empirical and theoretical support" (1996, p. 245).

To determine why there might be a connection between genius and madness, consider first that genius is marked by an ability to generate lots of ideas. Some innovative ideas may seem extreme or impossible; to entertain and develop those ideas may require the ability to suspend disbelief. Knowledge must be profusely interconnected so that the creative mind can produce unusual *combinations* of ideas. To build profuse knowledge in the talent domain might require that the creative mind focus effort obsessively, even to the point of neglecting responsibilities and relationships. Moreover, ideas generated by the creative person might well be rejected by mainstream thinkers. To survive intellectually, the innovator might need to weather blistering criticism. Creative accomplishment might therefore be facilitated by a highly unusual personality that includes traits that verge on mental instability. Any of

these qualities, when taken to an extreme, could be evidence of psychosis (Jensen, 1996). A truly psychotic mind, however, would probably be too disabling to permit the original contributions to science and culture that are properly called *genius*.

Many highly creative people do exhibit a tendency toward extreme behavior and ideation. Though rarely psychotic, they frequently display a personality trait known as *psychoticism*. This trait can be manifest as being aloof, antisocial, callous, or even cruel. Detachment from other people may reveal an inability to form meaningful and nurturing social relationships. An individual with higher degrees of psychoticism also typically suffers from depression. According to one expert, "severe depression has been linked time and again with creative performance in poetry writing, and other artistic pursuits" (Eysenck, 1998, p. 164).

Some creative luminaries are strongly identified with unhappy or unstable personalities. The painter Vincent Van Gogh is emblematic of the tormented genius, as is the American writer Edgar Allen Poe. Perhaps equally often, the unpleasant or troubled personal qualities of highly accomplished people are concealed by their friends and family members, even posthumously. Yet extreme personality characteristics that trend toward psychosis without quite reaching that dysfunctional extreme might actually have a *causal* role in stimulating highly creatively accomplishments (Eysenck, 1998). Some unstable personality qualities increase the probability of creative accomplishment—again up to a point. An association between "madness" and highly creative accomplishment—creative genius—seems to be one "myth" that actually has some evidence to back it up.

of skill and knowledge. Making talent less mysterious is important to the work of the educator. Although educators can admit to inborn differences in temperament and talent in learners, they are professionally dedicated to leveraging the *experiential* aspects of development, to pushing the education factor in the equation for success just as far as it will go. Teachers cannot change the DNA of the individual learner; instead, they work exclusively in the medium of experience. They are designers of experiences that draw the learner toward deeper understanding, greater capability, and higher fulfillment of their potential (Dewey, 1938).

Studies that have tried to demystify genius have, like research on expertise, looked for explanations that relate to experience and to habits that extend over time. Studies of genius have found that beyond a certain threshold of intelligence, a universal characteristic of eminent people is their unrelenting devotion to their work (Ochse, 1990). This devotion is driven by a singular commitment to excellence and a belief in one's capacity to achieve it. Devotion can be so extreme that it becomes obsessive. In the book *Genius Explained*, Howe (1999) presented case studies of Wolfgang Amadeus Mozart and the Brontë sisters, exemplars of creative genius that few would challenge. In the case of Mozart, Howe traced the highly unusual childhood of young Wolfgang and his father, a man obsessed with transforming his cooperative son into a child wonder. Herr Mozart's strategy was to immerse Wolfgang in musical practice and performance for several hours every day, beginning around age four. As an adolescent, Wolfgang toured the courts of Europe with his father and his sister, also a musical prodigy. Obviously, Wolfgang was temperamentally and intellectually predisposed to musical performance and composition to a degree that is extremely rare. But Howe showed that potent forces in the development of Mozart's extreme talent included the obsessive quality of his father's vision for his son and daughter, and the highly unusual life that Wolfgang lived almost from infancy.

A similar story applies to the famed Brontë sisters of English literature. As children, they and their less-recognized brother worked incessantly at writing stories for their own entertainment. Over the years, and often for several hours each day, they wrote stories, and read and critiqued each other's work. Howe shows that the Brontës' initial work products were unremarkable, much as Mozart's early musical compositions were

FIGURE 7.9
The Brontë Siblings *The famous literary sisters—Charlotte, Emily, and Anne—and their brother Branwell practiced the craft of writing obsessively over many years.* [The Bronte Family (engraving) Bronte, Patrick Branwell (1817–1848) (after)/Private Collection,/The Bridgeman Art Library]

A FAMILY GROUP BY BRANWELL BRONTË

undistinguished. But through an extensive investment of effort applied over many years, the writings of the Brontës matured, as did Mozart's musical compositions. But note something interesting here—levels of quality that could be called *expert* or *world-class* were not attained by Mozart or the Brontës until their late teens, at which time they had been engaged in their creative enterprises for a decade or more.

Like the Mozarts and the Brontës in earlier times, the Polgár sisters are contemporary examples of the power of experience to hone high levels of talent. László Polgár, a Hungarian educator, trained his three daughters in chess by having them practice as much as six hours per day. The three daughters became highly accomplished in chess, one an international master and the other two grandmasters. Judit, the youngest daughter, was ranked fourteenth in the world at the age of 30. The Polgárs are yet further evidence of the power of experience to generate expertise. The universal requirement is very intense, very focused experience—and lots of it. Even in cases where talent levels are fearsome, the ten-year rule formulated by Herbert Simon seems to hold up as

INTEREST MAGNET 7.4

Child Prodigies

Prodigies are children who demonstrate exceptional levels of talent, usually by the age of ten or twelve. Quite often, the display of talent is so striking that it seems inborn—the child is said to be "gifted." This may be true, but talent development is also the result of highly dedicated practice, which requires intense and sustained motivation.

The strong motivation to improve is what Ellen Winner (1996) called a "rage to master." Winner cited the case of Jacob, who first heard heavy metal music when he was four years old. When he heard the music, Jacob begged his parents for music lessons so that he could learn to play the guitar. Jacob implored his parents for two years before they finally relented, bought him a guitar, and hired a music teacher. After the first half-hour lesson, Jacob refused to leave. After the second lesson, Jacob's teacher called him a prodigy, expressing wonder that he could master complex arrangements so effortlessly. Later, after Jacob and his father passed a group of street musicians, Jacob asked if he could try the electric guitar. Jacob astonished the bystanders, who commented that he must be the reincarnation of Jimi Hendrix.

Precocious children sometimes emerge from unlikely circumstances. Such was the case with Vietnamese chess champion Nguyen Ngoc Truong Son (Marshall, 2003). When Son was three years old, he used to watch his mother and father play chess in the family's ramshackle house in Vietnam's Mekong Delta. Son's parents' chessboard was fashioned from a piece of plywood with the board pattern drawn with a marking pen. Son pestered his parents to let him play. To his parents' surprise, Son already knew how to set up the chessboard and, through observing his parents play, knew the rules of the game. Within a month, he was easily defeating his parents. He began competing in national tournaments at age 4, and he was winning them by age 7. By the time he was 12, Son became Vietnam's youngest national chess champion.

Are prodigies the product of nature or nurture, or some combination of both? In some cases, nurture plays an obviously important role: Child prodigies are sometimes subjected to rigid training programs conceived by parents to turn their children into "geniuses." This was true of John Stuart Mill, whose father, James Mill, isolated him from peers for fear that other children would interfere with his son's education. John Stuart Mill's intellectual advancement was indeed prodigious, and he developed into an eminent philosopher.

The childhood isolation and intense training of John Stuart Mill is an example of raising "hothouse children"—kids whose parents deliberately expose them to extraordinary conditions designed to be super-enriching. Whether such abnormal experiences can result in happy, well-adjusted children is a matter of debate (Radford, 1990). Certainly, such a program makes unusual demands on both children and parents. But even in less drastic forms, prodigies often rely on the dedication of parents—a strong nurture component seems necessary. But an intense internal drive, the mysterious "rage to master," also seems to be a necessary component of talent development. When a strong internal drive (nature) meets with an opportunity to learn (nurture), amazing levels of talent can develop.

a rough guide for the order of investment necessary for achieving expertise, including expertise in its most rarefied form, creative genius.

Educating for Expertise

The achievements of a Wolfgang Mozart, Charlotte Brontë, and Jørn Utzon are worthy of great admiration for their singular beauty and insight. We rightly celebrate the amazing skill of the expert and, even more so, the marvelous breakthroughs of the creative genius. But we are not helped by assuming that expertise and genius are utterly mysterious. If we are motivated to understand the workings of the human mind and to assist its development through education, then we must try to understand the experiential factors that contribute to the highest levels of skill and achievement. This stance seems to minimize individual differences in talent, but how much evidence do we have that inborn differences can really explain expertise? After studying specific cases of extraordinarily high talent, one writer concluded that "belief in the importance of talent, strongest perhaps among the experts themselves and their trainers, is strangely lacking in hard evidence to substantiate it" (Ross, 2006, p. 70).

Even if we take a very optimistic view of the role of experience and dedication in the development of expertise, it is probably unreasonable to believe that *any* person can become highly skilled in *any* field. Some people might train for thousands of hours and remain unremarkable in their skill levels. Yet if individual inborn differences are highly relevant, the educator must work with those initial differences to help each person reach more of his or her inborn potential. As educators understand very well, differences in native talent do not inevitably dictate success outcomes. Often, it is learners who have the will to pursue study over the long haul who eventually surpass those who are merely talented.

To a significant degree, expertise can be taught. Enough is known about expertise to be much more effective in the preparation of highly competent people. Educational leaders might well consider how to develop the skills of learners through deliberate practice over a period of many years. When students understand the requirements of expertise, many will be willing to invest the extensive time and intensive effort needed to become highly skilled. Genius builds on expertise, so experiences that contribute to expertise seem likely to contribute indirectly to the creative accomplishments that become enduring cultural achievements. Finally, teachers, parents, and communities must value original thinking and creative efforts at whatever level they occur, whether from the novice, aspiring expert, or potential creative genius.

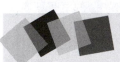

Learning Strategies

Developmental psychologists, as well as their intellectual predecessors in philosophy, have long found practical value in gaining a deeper understanding of the child. The philosopher Rousseau shifted the course of educational practice through his insight that the child needs and deserves freedom to develop. Progressive educational philosophies, methods, and institutions looked to Rousseau and to subsequent reformers, including Montessori and Froëbel, for guidance in how to offer educational experiences that are centered on the child.

This chapter examines the traditional subject of cognitive development during childhood, as well as expertise, eminence, and creative genius—expressions of development that are most often attained, if at all, during adulthood. In this section, we re-examine conceptual insights on cognitive development through the lifespan as they apply to practical strategies for teaching and learning.

1 Appreciate the importance of freedom and exploration in education.

The early philosophers and reformers of education proclaimed that societal institutions, including schools, did not allow children sufficient freedom to explore. They believed that by giving greater respect to the child's needs and interests, children would grow unimpeded toward their inborn potential. This philosophy grounded progressive education, and is worthy of consideration by every teacher and parent.

2 Respect the cognitive limitations of young children.

Of the many conceptual insights of developmental psychologists, the most important by far is the knowledge that, intellectually and in other ways, children are not miniature versions of adults. A child progresses through cognitive sequences that differ in *kind*, not only in *degree*. This idea was the cornerstone of Piaget's life work and is an insight that no educator can afford to ignore.

3 Do not think of a child's cognitive stage as being absolute.

We know enough about the research of Piaget's successors to realize that the sequence of cognitive stages each child traverses is not as absolute and ordered as Piaget believed. Children vary in the ages at which they can engage abstract ideas, and their readiness for abstraction and complexity is partly a function of their knowledge and previous experience in a domain. The relevance of experience to a child's growing intellectual competence gives a teacher more pedagogical freedom than Piaget's theory implied.

4 Present advanced content in an intellectually honest form.

In a challenge to overly cautious warnings to delay the presentation of complex ideas to children, Bruner offered that any complex idea could be taught to a child in some form that was intellectually honest. Conceivably, any complex idea could be communicated simply but without distortion. This was a working assumption more than a research conclusion, but the possibility it articulated gave considerable respect to the child's intellect and extended a challenge to the skilled teacher.

5 Teach through a variety of representational forms.

Good teachers know that presenting ideas in a variety of ways can make instruction more effective and more interesting, as well as better able to reach a variety of learners. There is not one single framework for understanding representational forms. Bruner suggested the accumulation of enactive, iconic, and symbolic representations. Egan's philosophically oriented scheme presents another possibility. These and other frameworks can help a teacher to present ideas in a variety of ways.

6 Teach reading and writing as sets of complex skills.

No goal is more important in education than literacy. But learning to read and write well can be difficult. Advanced performance, such as reading comprehension and critical reading, relies on the automation of such basic skills as decoding and word recognition. Especially when working with struggling readers, teachers should attend to both the automation of lower-level skills and to the development of higher-order cognition.

7 Treat nativism as a conceptual ally.

The nativist's insight—that the human brain has inborn modules that support higher-order cognition—can give the educator confidence that children have a biological readiness, a predisposition, to learn. The acquisition of spoken language is a prime example. Growing evidence shows that there are also brain-based capacities sensitive to quantity, and that these modules can be a foundation for building mathematical competence. The discovery that these inborn capabilities are constituent to the human brain should give teachers confidence that even students who struggle have the necessary "wiring" to extend their understanding of the world through language and mathematics.

8 Cultivate the ability to engage in deliberate practice.

Among the various practical strategies that help to build expertise, none is more important than developing a regimen of focused practice. A long timeline of dedicated practice, extending over a decade or more, is a prerequisite of expertise. Any child or adult who wishes to become an expert should understand that expertise is not born of sheer talent, but is significantly a product of dedication and perseverance. Educational systems could more effectively teach students the habits needed to build extensive knowledge and skill through deliberate practice.

9 Build toward expertise in your own professional pursuits.

How long does it take for a teacher to attain the highest levels of skill that qualify as expert, even world class? We now know from the research literature on expertise that it is unrealistic for a beginning teacher to attain very high levels of pedagogical skill in just a year or two. More likely, a teacher will not reach his or her professional potential until a decade or more of dedication to teaching excellence. This expectation and its implications should be conveyed to every aspiring teacher.

10 Cultivate and celebrate creative genius.

Genius is rare, yet historical studies have shown that creative flourishing can wax or wane in a culture. Modern renaissances are possible, and with them the innovative excellence that characterize genius. On what does genius depend? One factor is the foundation of expertise in a society, which in turn is partly a function of educational systems. Another factor, harder to define and harder still to cultivate, is creative innovation. In small but important ways, every teacher can encourage both expertise and creative thought.

 ## Conclusion

This chapter traces our growing understanding of how the individual mind develops over time. Although the mind of the child is of particular interest, a life span perspective allows us to also consider development toward expertise and creative genius. Cognitive development is emphasized; social, physical, and moral development, de-emphasized, though these too are important aspects of how humans change through the life span. The various dimensions of development, especially cognitive development, are clearly relevant to the design of education.

Social philosophies emerging from Europe during the Enlightenment, especially the philosophy of Jean-Jacques Rousseau, emphasized the repressive nature of society and its institutions, and the essential goodness of the child. The implications for education and child-rearing were clear—the child's interests were best served by allowing the child more freedom to explore. Rousseau's central idea was developed practically by subsequent education reformers. These reformers included American philosopher John Dewey, the great proponent of progressive education.

Twentieth-century theories of cognitive development were dominated by the research and writings of the Swiss psychologist, Jean Piaget. Piaget taught that the emergence of intellectual competence in the child was not a simple linear extrapolation from childhood through adulthood, but rather that the child thinks in ways that differ from an adult. Piaget proposed a theory of cognitive stages spanning from birth to late adolescence. His theory was highly influential in education because it helped teachers consider a child's readiness to engage in complex and abstract subject matter. Subsequent researchers challenged Piaget's conclusions by showing that the stage progression was not always even across fields. Sometimes, even young children could engage in quite sophisticated thinking.

Neo-Piagetian theories integrated findings from cognitive psychology, recognizing, for example, that cognition is limited by working memory capacity. This capacity limitation can be finessed by automaticity of skills. In valued academic skills, reading in particular, automaticity is necessary for reaching high levels of performance. Other cognitive-developmental perspectives, including nativism and the sociocultural theory of Lev Vygotsky, painted a more complete picture of the forces that shape the development of the child. These theoretical perspectives also held relevance for conceptualizing new educational practices, such as collaborative learning and reciprocal teaching.

Finally, the analysis of cognitive development extends to the development of expertise. Cognitive research helped to make expertise less mysterious, showing that the expert relies on a massive knowledge base acquired over a long period of time—often a decade or more. The development of expertise is assisted by regimens of practice that extend to several hours a day. Creative genius builds on expertise by transcending existing ideas and practices, and generating a product that has enduring value.

The theoretical panorama of cognitive development presents a hopeful picture for education. It tells us that internal qualities of the human mind, presumably driven by brain mechanisms, lead dependably to the ability to use spoken language, to engage in abstract thought, and to learn from highly developed cultural systems. Other research reveals the power of experience to accelerate cognitive development and to raise competence to very high levels. By both predisposition and sensitivity to experience, the human mind is primed to benefit from the opportunities presented by a society—educational opportunities that can elevate learners toward their highest potential.

References

Alexander, C. N., & Langer, E. J. (1990). *Higher stages of human development.* New York: Oxford University Press.

Alvermann, D. E., Fitzgerald, J., & Simpson, M. (2006). Teaching and learning in reading. In P. A. Alexander & P. H. Winne (Eds.), *Handbook of educational psychology* (2nd ed.)(pp. 427–455). Mahwah, NJ: Lawrence Erlbaum Associates.

Antell, S. E., & Keating, D. P. (1983). Perception of numerical invariance in neonates. *Child Development, 54,* 695–701.

Bartlett, F. C. (1967 [1932]). *Remembering.* Cambridge: Cambridge University Press.

Bereiter, B., & Scardamalia, M. (1993). *Surpassing ourselves.* Peru, IL: Open Court.

Bloom, B. S. (1985). Generalizations about talent development. In B. S. Bloom (Ed.), *Developing talent in young people* (pp. 507–549). New York: Ballantine.

Brown, A. L., & Palincsar, A. S. (1989). Guided, cooperative learning and individual knowledge acquisition. In L. B. Resnick (Ed.), *Knowing, learning, and instruction: Essays in honor of Robert Glaser* (pp. 393–451). Hillsdale, NJ: Lawrence Erlbaum Associates.

Bruner, J. S. (1960). *The process of education.* New York: Vintage.

Bruner, J. S. (1964). The course of cognitive growth. *American Psychologist, 19,* 1–15.

Carver, R. P. (1990). *Reading rate: A review of research and theory.* San Diego, CA: Academic Press.

Case, R. (1991). *The mind's staircase: Exploring the conceptual underpinnings of children's thought and knowledge.* Hillsdale, NJ: Lawrence Erlbaum Associates.

Chi, M. T. H., Feltovich, P. J., & Glaser, R. (1981). Categorization and representation of physics problems by experts and novices. *Cognitive Science, 5,* 121–152.

Cunningham, A. E., & Stanovich, K. E. (1998). What reading does for the mind. *American Educator, 22*(1 & 2), 8–15.

Cunningham, A. E., Stanovich, K. E., & Wilson, M. R. (1990). Cognitive variation in adult students differing in reading ability. In T. H. Carr & B. A. Levy (Eds.), *Reading and its development: Component skills approaches* (pp. 129–159). New York: Academic Press.

de Groot, A. (1965). *Thought and choice in chess.* The Hague: Mouton.

Dewey, J. (1938). *Experience and education.* New York: Macmillan.

Egan, K. (1996). The development of understanding. In D. R. Olson & N. Torrance (Eds.), *The handbook of education and human development: New models of learning, teaching, and schooling* (pp. 514–533). Malden, MA: Blackwell.

Ericsson, K. A. (1996). The acquisition of expert performance: And introduction to some of the issues. In K. A. Ericsson (Ed.), *The road to excellence: The acquisition of expert performance in the arts and sciences, sports, and games* (pp. 1–50). Mahwah, NJ: Lawrence Erlbaum Associates.

Ericsson, K. A, & Charness, N. (1994). Expert performance: Its structure and acquisition. *American Psychologist, 49,* 725–747.

Eysenck, H. J. (1998). *Intelligence: A new look.* New Brunswick, NJ: Transaction Publishers.

Fischer, K. (1980). A theory of cognitive development: The control and construction of hierarchies of skills. *Psychological Review, 87,* 477–531.

Gardner, H. (1983). *Frames of mind.* New York: Basic Books.

Gibson, E. J. (1969). *Principles of perceptual learning and development.* New York: Appleton-Century-Crofts.

Graham, S. (2006). Writing. In P. A. Alexander & P. H. Winne (Eds.), *Handbook of educational psychology* (2nd ed.)(pp. 457–478). Mahwah, NJ: Lawrence Erlbaum Associates.

Gzowski, P. (1981). *The game of our lives.* Toronto: McClelland and Stewart.

Halford, G. S. (1993). *Children's understanding: The development of mental models.* Hillsdale, NJ: Lawrence Erlbaum Associates.

Halford, G. S., Wilson, W. H., & Phillips, S. (1998). Processing capacity defined by relational complexity: Implications for comparative, developmental, and cognitive psychology. *Behavioral and Brain Sciences, 21,* 803–865.

Harris, J. R. (1995). Where is the child's environment? A group socialization theory of development. *Psychological Review, 102*(3), 458–489.

Hayes, J. (1996). A new framework for understanding cognition and affect in writing. In M. Levy & S. Randell (Eds.), *The science of writing: Theories, methods, individual differences, and applications* (pp. 1–27). Mahwah, NJ: Lawrence Erlbaum Associates.

Hayes, J., & Flower, L. (1980). Identifying the organization of writing processes. In L. Gregg & E. Steinberg (Eds.), *Cognitive processes in writing* (pp. 3–30). Hillsdale, NJ: Lawrence Erlbaum Associates.

Howe, M. J. A. (1999). *Genius explained.* New York: Cambridge University Press.

Inhelder, B., & Piaget, J. (1958). *The growth of logical thinking from childhood to adolescence.* New York: Basic Books.

Jensen, A. R. (1996). Giftedness and genius: Crucial differences. In C. P. Benbow & D. Lubinski (Eds.), *Intellectual talent: Psychometric and social issues* (pp. 393–411). Baltimore, MD: Johns Hopkins University Press.

Karmiloff-Smith, A. (1992). *Beyond modularity: A developmental perspective on cognitive science.* Cambridge, MA: MIT Press.

Karplus, R., Pulos, S., & Stage, E. K. (1983). Proportional reasoning in early adolescents. In R. Lesh & M. Landau (Eds.), *Acquisition of mathematics concepts and principles* (pp. 45–90). Orlando, FL: Academic Press.

King, P. M., & Kitchener, K. S. (2004). Reflective judgment: Theory and research on the development of epistemic assumptions through adulthood. *Educational Psychologist, 39*(1), 5–18.

Kohlberg, L., Levine, C., & Hewer, A., (1983). *Moral stages: A current formulation and a response to critics.* New York: Karger.

Kuhn, D., Amsel, E., & O'Loughlin, M. (1988). *The development of scientific thinking skills.* San Diego, CA: Academic Press.

Larkin, J., McDermott, J., Simon, D. P., & Simon, H. A. (1980). Expert and novice performance in solving physics problems. *Science, 208,* 1335–1342.

Marshall, A. (2003). Small wonders. *Time (Asia), 161(7).*

Neill, A. S. (1960). *Summerhill: A radical approach to child rearing.* New York: Hart Publishing Company.

Newton, M. (2002). *Savage boys and wild girls: A history of feral children.* London: Faber and Faber.

Ochse, R. (1990). *Before the gates of excellence: The determinants of creative genius.* Cambridge, England: Cambridge University Press.

Paris, S. G., Morrison, F. J., & Miller, K. F. (2006). Academic pathways from preschool through elementary school. In P. A. Alexander & P. H. Winne (Eds.), *Handbook of educational psychology* (2nd ed.)(pp. 61–85*).* Mahwah, NJ: Lawrence Erlbaum Associates.

Piaget, J. (1977). *The moral judgment of the child.* New York: Penguin.

Pressley, M. (2002). *Reading instruction that works: The case for balanced teaching* (2nd ed.). New York: The Guilford Press.

Radford, J. (1990). *Child prodigies and exceptional early achievers.* New York: The Free Press.

Rayner, K., Foorman, B. R., Perfetti, C. A., Pesetsky, D., & Seidenberg, M. S. (2002). How should reading be taught? *Scientific American,* March, 85–91.

Reich, R. (1992). *The work of nations.* New York: Vintage.

Ross, P. E. (2006). The expert mind. *Scientific American, 295*(2), 64–71.

Schraw, G. (2006). Knowledge: Structures and processes. In P. A. Alexander & P. H. Winne (Eds.), *Handbook of educational psychology* (2nd ed.)(pp. 245–263). Mahwah, NJ: Lawrence Erlbaum Associates.

Simon, H. A. (1980). Problem solving and education. In D. T. Tuma & F. Reif (Eds.), *Problem solving and education: Issues in teaching and research* (pp. 81–96). Hillsdale, NJ: Lawrence Erlbaum Associates.

Simon, H. A. (1991, Fall). The cat that curiosity couldn't kill. *Carnegie Mellon Magazine,* pp. 35–36.

Simonton, D. K. (1984). *Genius, creativity, and leadership.* Cambridge, MA: Harvard University Press.

Simonton, D. K. (1996). Creative expertise: A life-span developmental perspective. In K. A. Ericsson (Ed.), *The road to excellence: The acquisition of expert performance in the arts and sciences, sports, and games* (pp. 227–253). Mahwah, NJ: Lawrence Erlbaum Associates.

Sloane, K. D. (1985). Home influences on talent development. In B. S. Bloom (Ed.), *Developing talent in young people* (pp. 439–476). New York: Ballantine.

Snow, C. E., Burns, M. S., & Griffin, P. (1998). *Preventing reading difficulties in young children.* Washington, DC: National Academy Press.

Sosniak, L. A. (1985). A long-term commitment to learning. In B. S. Bloom (Ed.), *Developing talent in young people* (pp. 477–506). New York: Ballantine.

Spelke, E. S., & Kinzler, K. D. (2007). Core knowledge. *Developmental Science, 10*(1), 89–96.

Thorndyke, P. W. (1977). Cognitive structures in comprehension and memory of narrative discourse, *Cognitive Psychology, 9,* 77–110.

Tweney, R. D. (1998). Toward a cognitive psychology of science: Recent research and its implications. *Current Directions in Psychological Science, 7,* 150–154.

Vygotsky, L. S. (1978). *Mind in society.* Cambridge, MA: Harvard University Press.

Vygotsky, L. S. (1986). *Language and thought.* Cambridge, MA: MIT Press.

Winner, E. (1996). The rage to master: The decisive role of talent in the visual arts. In K. A. Ericsson (Ed.), *The road to excellence: The acquisition of expert performance in the arts and sciences, sports, and games* (pp. 271–301). Mahwah, NJ: Lawrence Erlbaum Associates.

[8] The Brain and Cognition

Previous chapters reviewed the nature of the mind—its memory structures and representational forms, as well as its capacity for complex cognition. Conspicuously absent up to this point has been any exploration of the role of the brain in making cognition possible. This chapter begins that exploration. The objective is to extend our understanding of how the mind is related to the brain, and how the mind-brain association can advance our practical agenda—the improvement of learning and cognition through education.

To pursue the mind-brain connection is a daunting task. One reason for the difficulty is that both cognitive science and neuroscience are young fields of study. Although both fields have intellectual precursors that extend back 100 years or more, only within the past few decades have both fields gained real analytic power and a rapidly accumulating knowledge base. The frontier quality of research on the mind and brain attracts a large number of young scholars to these fields and to their vibrant intersection, cognitive neuroscience.

Mind and Brain

Let's begin with the obvious: The mind and brain are not the same. The brain is a biological organ located within the skull. The mind, by contrast, is an abstraction. We could say that the mind *is* what the brain *does*, and that seems at least superficially correct. The mind is not directly observable but is understood only by its effects. The mind's activity is manifest as behavior, much as the capacity to walk is a function of the legs, or reaching is a function of the arms and hands. But the mind is more than this— it is also structural (we can identify parts), experiential (we are conscious), and intelligent (we can think, reason, solve problems, and create). Defining the mind only as what the brain does is intolerably simplistic—it leaves out too much.

As understood through the lens of information processing theory, the mind is an abstract model. The abstraction is *related* to its ultimate biological manifestation but does not necessarily exhibit one-to-one correspondence. In this chapter, we assign importance both to the abstraction of the mind and to the biological substrate of the mind—the human brain. The mind depends on the brain and, as we shall see, the development of the brain also depends on the mind and its activity. The two are beautifully interdependent and transactive.

The Philosopher's Dilemma

To philosophers who have struggled for centuries to understand the nature of the mind, one problem seemed especially difficult: How can the mind's operation—perceived subjectively as consciousness—possibly be explained in terms of a purely material reality? The question assumes philosophical **monism**—a philosophy of being that asserts that there is only one kind of reality: the material world. If the real world is entirely material—a stance that most modern philosophers accept—how is this ontology capable of explaining the subjective experience of the mind? If there is only a material universe, then what is the meaning of the word *mind*?

The philosopher René Descartes understood the dilemma very well. Unlike modern philosophers, he was not committed to the view that the entire universe is one substance, the material. Rather, he took the view that alongside the material was a nonmaterial reality of the human soul, the mind, and God—entities that many people believe are real and important but not dependent on the material universe. This common ontology, that reality is both material and nonmaterial, is philosophical **dualism**. Although philosophical dualism remains popular as a personal worldview, it is quite unpopular among contemporary philosophers for several reasons. Since the time of the medieval scholar William of Ockham, Western intellectuals, and especially scientists, have preferred *parsimonious* explanations, explanatory accounts that are as simple as possible. If a simple explanation can take the place of a more complex one, then the simpler one is preferred. That general rule is called **Ockham's razor**. The math is simple: Monism (1) is more parsimonious than dualism (2).

A second reason for preferring monism is the problem of how to describe the connection between material and nonmaterial realities. If we assume the brain is material (which it is) and the mind is nonmaterial (which it conceivably could be), then how do the two relate in any functional way? What "bridge" connects the two realms? Specifying that connection in any rational way is tremendously difficult. This puzzle has been called the **mind-body problem**—historically considered an unsolvable riddle by philosophers. Descartes was well aware of the mind-body problem; undaunted, he proposed a famous, or rather infamous, solution. In *The Treatise of Man*, published in 1664, Descartes (2003) suggested that the mind and the body are bridged at one particular anatomical location, the pineal gland.

FIGURE 8.1

The Pineal Gland *Descartes hypothesized that it is the seat of the soul; in reality, it secretes the hormone melatonin that controls sleep-wake cycles.*

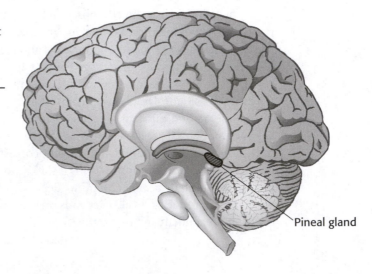

Pineal gland

The pineal gland is a real brain organ, now known to release the hormone melatonin, which controls the sleep-wake cycle. Perhaps Descartes proposed the pineal gland as the bridge connecting the material and nonmaterial worlds because it lies exactly on the brain's midline, rather than appearing in symmetrical pairs. But the pineal gland hypothesis has long been regarded as nonsense. Descartes' odd solution to the mind-body problem did not help the cause of philosophical dualism. Nevertheless, the alternative that the mind is a straightforward manifestation of biological processes is not completely satisfactory. The most interesting manifestations of the mind, including subjective consciousness, still beg to be explained. Philosophers have continued to work toward a sensible explanation of how consciousness can arise strictly from the material (Dennett, 1991). By setting aside one puzzle (the mind-body problem), we are instead forced to face another set of puzzles (consciousness, intelligence, and creativity arising from a material brain).

The Limitations of Reductionism

The quest to understand how the mind and brain relate is profoundly difficult. One paradigm, the cognitive theory emphasized in this book, largely sets aside the mind-body problem. The paradigm grants legitimacy to the mind on its own terms without appealing to philosophical dualism. Within a monistic (matter-only) framework, the mind can be studied as the manifestation of brain activity, but without insisting on explanations at the level of molecules and their interactions. This stance amounts to a rejection of pure **reductionism**.

Like Ockham's razor, reductionism is a knowledge-building heuristic profitably employed by scientists. The assumption is that as analysis moves toward simpler, more atomistic levels, more fundamental and satisfactory explanations emerge. Reductionism has been an effective guide for building scientific theories that later had tremendous practical payoffs. For example, Pasteur's discovery of infectious microorganisms was a huge step toward instituting antiseptic practices that curtailed ravaging epidemics. Later, explanations at the level of molecules led to precisely designed pharmaceuticals that were highly effective in combating disease. Similarly, the Green Revolution in agriculture multiplied crop yields per acre by recognizing the molecular mechanisms of plant growth, greatly reducing hunger and malnutrition around the world. These examples illustrate the power of reductionism to build theories that lead ultimately to highly effective applications.

Reductionism is an important strategy for understanding some aspects of the mind and its operation. As we shall see, memory mechanisms are being studied at the level of individual nerve cells, called **neurons**, and molecular changes within those cells (Kandel, 2006a). But can all mental processes be boiled down to simple molecular mechanisms? Can consciousness, or intelligence, or creativity be reduced to atoms and their interactions? Perhaps the mind has essential qualities that cannot be reduced to simpler elements without sweeping those very defining qualities aside. Although the mind's activities may *arise* from biological processes that are fundamentally material, the mind may have certain **emergent** qualities that cannot be explained (or that simply disappear) when reductionism is the sole strategy for trying to gain insight into complex phenomena.

One famous cognitive neuroscientist, Roger Sperry (1995), argued strenuously that the mind is an emergent phenomenon that cannot be understood through a strictly reductionist approach. Sperry proposed that the cognitive paradigm accepts the mind on its own terms as distinct from, though interfused with, the brain. If this is so, Sperry maintained, then the cognitive revolution of the last century was a true paradigm shift because it recognized the inadequacy of reductionism that had dominated scientific inquiry for 200 years (Kuhn, 1962). In the cognitive paradigm, cognition includes *irreducible* patterns of functioning, such as consciousness and personal agency, or will. "Subjective agency," noted Sperry, "may thus be viewed as a special instance of top-down control, a special case of emergent causality" (p. 42).

Granting that the mind is real and important does not mean rejecting material reductionism but rather recognizing its limitations. Within the framework of cognitive psychology, emergent qualities of mind such as thought, will, emotions, and values are not written off as **epiphenomena**—as mere byproducts of a more fundamental and real process. Rather, the most interesting manifestations of the mind have explanatory value even if they cannot be fully accounted for by more elementary phenomena.

Although the cognitive paradigm rightly studies the mind on its own terms, this does not mean that scholars should give up on seeking connections between the mind and the brain. The vibrant field of cognitive neuroscience grants legitimacy to both cognitive phenomena and neural mechanisms. Cognitive neuroscientists examine correspondences between the mind and the brain, and search for functional mechanisms that can account for cognitive changes, especially learning. Through a variety of analytical techniques, the field has made steady progress toward elucidating the connections between the biological brain and the information-processing mind.

Brain Anatomy and Function

Finding the correspondences between the mind and the brain begins with an understanding of brain morphology, a general mapping of brain anatomy and function, to which we now turn.

Brain Anatomy

The brain, which has been called the most complex entity in the universe, is composed of about a trillion neurons, a number far greater than the entire population of the earth. But that is only the beginning; what makes the brain fantastically complex is the enormous number of *interconnections*, or **synapses**, between neurons. With each nerve cell branching to form about 1000 synapses, and each branch connecting with other neurons, the number of synapses in the cerebral cortex alone reaches an unfathomable quadrillion. Neuroscientists are beginning to understand some of the mechanisms that lead to the formation of synapses. Unlike the circuitry of a computer chip, however, the patterns of connection between one particular neuron with another in the brain are largely unknown. In fact, the functional nature of neuronal branching and interconnection is a massive intellectual puzzle. In addition, neuronal interconnections change constantly, especially during development, as new connections are formed and old ones are modified or eliminated.

THE BRAINSTEM, CEREBELLUM, AND CEREBRAL CORTEX. The brain's anatomy consists of a hindbrain, midbrain, and forebrain. The midbrain (not considered in this discussion) and parts of the forebrain are hidden deep within the brain. Shown in Figure 8.2 are the cerebral cortex—the largest structure of the forebrain—and two components of the hindbrain, the brainstem and the cerebellum. Think of the **brainstem** as something like the stem of a plant—functionally it is critical to sustain life, but it does not really express the plant's

FIGURE 8.2
The Brain
Brainstem, cerebellum, and cerebral cortex.

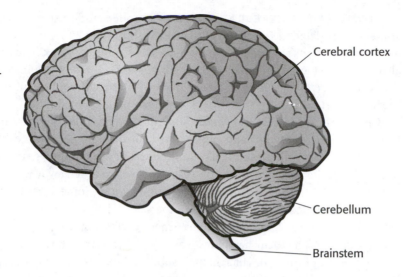

Cerebral cortex

Cerebellum

Brainstem

beauty or distinctiveness. The brainstem connects directly to the bundle of nerves called the **spinal cord**, which runs directly in front of the spine. The spinal cord relays sensory information to the brain; it also relays brain signals that control muscles. The brainstem itself regulates basic survival functions. It controls breathing and heart rates, and modulates sleep and alertness states. Of the three components of the brain, the brainstem is the most primitive—the part that keeps animals alive. For this reason it is sometimes called the reptilian brain, again reflecting its role in controlling primitive functions. Other brain components build on this biological foundation.

The **cerebellum**, the second component of the hindbrain, is located at the back of the head, set low on the skull. Its primary functions are balance and coordination. Everyday locomotion—walking, running, and climbing stairs—relies on a functional cerebellum. Less prosaically, the amazing dexterity of bonobos, a kind of ape similar to a chimpanzee, demonstrates the marvel of a high-functioning cerebellum. Swinging from branch to branch, the bonobo's elegant coordination displays both economy of motion and effortless play. We see examples of exquisite cerebellar functioning in people, too. Think of a tango dancer, an Olympic figure skater, or a freestyle snowboarder. In hundreds of ways, human beings elevate cerebellar functioning to the status of art.

The **cerebral cortex** or, more simply, the cortex, is responsible for the qualities that distinguish human beings. Much of what you would see, were you to look at a real human brain, is cerebral cortex; the brainstem would be hidden inside; and the cerebellum would be exposed only at the back of the brain. The function of the cerebral cortex can be gathered from the word *cerebral*, meaning *intelligent*. The cerebral cortex is the anatomical origin of the mind's higher-order functions—reasoning, intelligence, creativity, and problem-solving—as well as the coordination of sensory input and motor control that helps us relate skillfully to our environments.

Greatly simplified, that is the brain's basic layout: the brainstem supplies basic life support; the cerebellum conveys balance and coordination; and the cerebral cortex enables reasoning and cognition. But, of course, that is just the beginning—especially if we want to understand the higher-order functions of the cerebral cortex. To gain further insight into how the brain makes cognition possible, we must go deeper by degrees into understanding the functioning of the brain, with a special focus on the cerebral cortex.

ANATOMY OF THE CEREBRAL CORTEX. To understand the cerebral cortex we must appreciate its detailed structure. The cortex is thin (only 2 to 4 millimeters thick), but to the naked eye, its ridges, folds, and grooves look quite complex. The cerebral cortex is also complex at a microscopic level, where it is the site of a large number of neuronal connections. As we try to understand higher-order cognition, we must recognize the special importance of this thin outer layer of the brain.

Clues to how the cerebral cortex functions are provided by the superficially contorted anatomy of its folds and ridges. These, unsurprisingly, have technical names. A groove is a **sulcus** (plural, **sulci**); a prominence is a **gyrus** (plural, **gyri**). The cortex is so folded that more than two-thirds of its surface area is tucked away within the sulci. The bumps and folds vary according to the individual: Some brains are much more anatomically folded and grooved than others, and the precise locations of those folds and grooves also vary. These differences make each brain unique, just as every fingerprint is unique. The focus here, however, is on the commonalities between brains. The location of the grooves, or sulci, help us subdivide the cerebral cortex into four distinct **lobes** that have identifiable functions. The four lobes are the frontal, parietal, temporal, and occipital lobes, shown in Figure 8.3.

Let's first consider the **frontal lobe**. Of the four lobes, the frontal lobe is the most distinguishing for complex cognition. The frontal lobe lies in front of the central sulcus and extends to the very front of the brain. The most forward section, called the **pre-frontal cortex**, lies just behind the forehead. This is the part of the brain most associated with higher-order functioning. Complex cognitive functions, including attentional control, planning, decision making, goal-setting, strategic reasoning, and self-monitoring are all accomplished by the pre-frontal cortex. When we think of higher-order functions, especially metacognitive control, we should remember that these qualities of human intelligence are associated most directly with a specific brain location, the pre-frontal cortex.

Just behind the frontal cortex is the **central sulcus**, the prominent groove that runs crosswise along the top of the brain, stretching almost from ear to ear. The central sulcus is what divides the frontal lobe from the **parietal lobe**. The frontal lobe lies in

FIGURE 8.3
Four Lobes of the Cerebral Cortex
The four distinct lobes—frontal, parietal, temporal, and occipital—have different functions but work in a coordinated way.

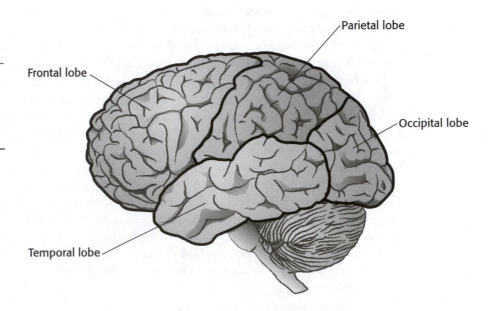

Parietal lobe

Frontal lobe

Occipital lobe

Temporal lobe

front of the central sulcus; the parietal lobe is set behind the central sulcus and extends backward over the crown of the head. The coordination of sensory information and motor control originates along the central sulcus. Sensory input—including touch, temperature, body position, and pain—is processed in the **somatosensory cortex,** which is located at the front edge of the parietal lobe; motor control is processed in the **primary motor cortex,** which is located at the rear edge of the frontal lobe. Moreover, there is a logical mapping of specific sensory input and motor control along the central sulcus, which is depicted in the so-called homunculus (Latin for "little man"), a grotesque fantasy image that vividly displays how the sensory and motor areas are arranged on each side of the central sulcus (Figure 8.4).

The anatomical proximity of the somatosensory cortex and the primary motor cortex is highly functional. Sensation and motor control need to be precisely coordinated. Consider the precise articulation of touch and finger movement needed to play a piano, knit a sweater, or manipulate a paintbrush. Sensory processing and muscular control are not accomplished *only* along the central sulcus, however. We have noted, for example, that the cerebellum is responsible for balance and coordination. Likewise, other brain areas also process sensory input. But the association areas along the central sulcus are especially important to processing and coordinating sensory and motor information.

The **temporal lobe** sits along both sides of the brain, just below the **lateral sulcus** (or lateral fissure). The temporal lobe is best known for its role in processing complex auditory information, especially language. The left temporal lobe, in particular, is crucial both to the interpretation of speech and to speech production. The association

FIGURE 8.4
The Cortical Homunculus *The neurosurgeon Wilder Penfield created this interesting and instructive diagram to display how the somatosensory cortex (right diagrams) and the primary motor cortex (left diagrams) are arranged on each side of the central sulcus.*
[Allyn & Bacon]

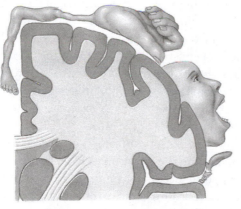
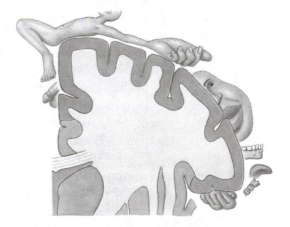
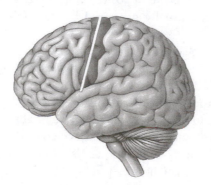
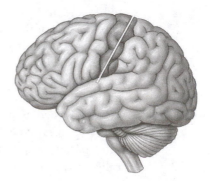

between the left side of the brain and the processing of spoken language was one of the first discoveries of functional associations between specific cognitive functions and brain anatomy.

A fourth lobe of the cerebral cortex, the **occipital lobe**, is set at the back of the brain, just above the cerebellum. The occipital lobe is best known for its role in processing visual information, and for that reason it is known also as the **visual cortex**. The visual cortex is well developed in human beings and in other primates, such as apes and monkeys. Compared to nonprimate species that often have more developed senses of hearing and smell, primates rely on a finely tuned visual system.

Much of the cerebral cortex does not have a specifically defined function. Instead, a large percentage of the brain, including the cortex, integrates information from various specific brain regions. This tells us that human cognition relies not only on dedicated processing, such as of visual or auditory information or of motor control, but also on functional connections between one area and another. Nondedicated brain regions, which are common in the cortex and elsewhere, are called **association areas**.

Lateralization

Even at a fairly gross level, the anatomy of the brain exhibits important functional distinctions. We noted the simple division of the brain into the brainstem, the cerebellum, and the cerebral cortex. The cerebral cortex can in turn be subdivided into four lobes—frontal, parietal, temporal, and occipital—each of which has distinct functions. Beyond these important divisions, the brain also exhibits an obvious anatomical symmetry along its midline. The brain is divided into two symmetrical parts, called the right and left **hemispheres**, which look something like two halves of a shelled walnut.

The most interesting feature of the right and left hemispheres is that each plays a somewhat distinct role, the clearest difference being that each hemisphere controls the opposite, or **contralateral**, side of the body. Movement of the right hand is accomplished by brain activity in the left hemisphere; movement of the left hand is controlled by the right hemisphere. All motor control works according to this crossover logic. This pattern is manifested most clearly in the case of brain injury that affects only one side of the brain. For example, if a brain stroke results in paralysis to the right side of the body, it is known to originate in the left side of the brain.

Not only motor control, but also sensory information is largely processed by the contralateral side of the brain. Input to the left visual field is shunted by nerve bundles to the right hemisphere; the opposite occurs for input to the right visual field. In the case of hearing, sound directed toward each ear is transduced and sent both to the brain hemisphere on the same (ipsilateral) and opposite (contralateral) side, but most of the interpretation takes place in the opposite hemisphere. To summarize, sensory input and motoric control are usually processed by the brain hemisphere on the *opposite* side of the body.

More interesting still than the crossover functions of sensory processing and motor control is that the right and left hemispheres have somewhat different *cognitive* functions (Reuter-Lorenz & Miller, 1998). Two generalizations can be made. The first relates to the *kind* of information processed preferentially by each hemisphere. In general, the left hemisphere is specialized to process language, and the right hemisphere is specialized to process spatial information. A second functional division describes the *way* that information is processed. The left hemisphere tends to process information analytically—to see the parts of a pattern and how they fit together. The right hemisphere tends to process information holistically—to see the overall pattern. To summarize: the left hemisphere is oriented to language and to analytical thought; the right hemisphere is relatively specialized to process spatial information and holistic thought.

These generalizations are interesting, but come with important qualifications. The different hemispheric functions are averages, not inevitabilities. For one thing, the generalizations are qualified by handedness. As a rule, they work for people who are right-handed. For about 40 percent of left-handed people, language is processed in the right hemisphere. Even among right-handers, the right-left associations do not always hold up: About ten percent of right-handers do not have language functions in the left hemisphere.

A second qualification of the hemispheric specialization is that the functions are a partial, not absolute, division of labor. There is a clear anatomical reason for this qualification: The right and left hemispheres are connected by a nerve bundle, the **corpus**

INTEREST MAGNET 8.1

What Causes Handedness?

Every human society consists of a mixture of right-handers and left-handers. Right-handed people, of course, are much more common. Only about 10 to 12 percent of people are left-handed. Nevertheless, the prevalence of right-handers has been shown to be characteristic of human civilizations throughout history as evidenced by ancient art. Animals, too, have individual preferences for a right or left paw, hoof, or claw, but these preferences tend to be roughly 50-50 in the animal kingdom.

The origin and cognitive significance of human handedness remains largely mysterious (Wolman, 2005). Handedness is partly genetic, but not completely so. Even if both parents are left-handed, their child has only about a 25 percent chance of being left-handed. The likelihood of being left-handed is increased, but obviously not determined. Some environmental influence on handedness is also likely. For reasons that are not fully known, left-handers are much more common in the mentally retarded population. One possible explanation is that perinatal brain damage might be a common cause for both. However, it is also true that "lefties" are more commonly represented among highly creative people, suggesting advantageous cognitive qualities.

In one-on-one sports and in combat, left-handers often have an advantage. There is a statistical explanation for this fact: Right-handers typically face other right-handers in competition, but face left-handers only rarely. Left-handers typically face right-handers, however, and so are practiced in doing so. The comparative advantage of left-handers in combat has led to speculation that the level of violence in a society is correlated with the preva-

lence of left-handers. This connection is controversial, but there is at least suggestive evidence of an association between the two.

A new theory of "mixed-handedness" has recently gained some acceptance. The theory argues that left- and right-handedness is not an either-or distinction. Instead, there are degrees of handedness—some people are *strongly* left- or right-handed, whereas many others are *mixed*-handed and so use both right and left hands for tasks, with perhaps a preference for one. People who can use either hand with equal facility—ambidextrous people—are rare. But so are people who are strongly left-handed or right-handed. The theory further hypothesizes that mixed-handed people tend to have a larger corpus callosum, the nerve bundle that connects the left and right hemispheres of the brain. A larger corpus callosum would improve communication between the right and left hemispheres, possibly aiding memory. Perhaps this is why typical brain hemispheric functions don't hold up well among left-handed people. In right-handers, language functions are almost always concentrated in the left hemisphere; in left-handers, though, language can be associated with either hemisphere, or with both.

Societies through the centuries have often had strong negative associations with left-handedness. The word *sinister*, for example, is derived from the Latin word *sinistra*, meaning *left*. The French word *gauche*, which English speakers sometimes borrow to mean *clumsy*, is also the word for *left*. *Adroit*, which means *skillful*, derives from the French word *droit*, which means *right*. But these etymological insults are undeserved: left-handed people have distinctive qualities that enrich culture, and so right-handed people should think twice before calling a lefty "gauche."

callosum, that runs like a sheet underneath the two hemispheres. The corpus callosum ensures that information is communicated between the two hemispheres. Fortunately, we can think both linguistically *and* spatially, both analytically *and* holistically. Ideally, our cognition in these different modes is highly coordinated. The corpus callosum helps to make that coordination possible.

In special cases, however, the corpus callosum is not intact. Such is true of epilepsy patients who are treated surgically by severing the corpus callosum, effectively isolating brain activity in the right and left hemispheres. In these patients, sensory information still projects to the contralateral side, but that information is not communicated between hemispheres. Starting in the 1960s, experiments on these so-called **split-brain** patients contributed enormously to our understanding of the relative specialization of the right and left hemispheres. The results of these early experiments, conducted by Roger Sperry and Michael Gazzaniga, ranged from highly interesting to bizarre.

Severing the corpus callosum led to the functional isolation of each cerebral hemisphere (Milner, Taylor, & Sperry, 1968). As a result, the language function of the left hemisphere became more obvious. Among split-brain patients, for example, objects seen only in the right visual field could easily be named because the image projected to the language centers of the left hemisphere. But objects seen only in the left visual field could not be named by the "mute" right hemisphere. Even though these objects could be manipulated skillfully with the right hemisphere (via the left hand), the right hemisphere could not name them. The severed corpus callosum prevented the information from crossing from the right hemisphere to the language centers in the left. The left hemisphere had linguistic knowledge of the objects that the right hemisphere lacked. The same pattern applied to objects touched by the hand. Objects manipulated by the right hand (and left hemisphere) could be named, but those manipulated by the left hand (and right hemisphere) could not.

More complex tasks yielded stronger—and stranger—results. For example, subjects were sometimes given contradictory instructions in the left and right ears. An instruction to the left ear might be, "Pick up the paper clip," but in the right ear the subject might hear, "Pick up the eraser." The instruction to pick up the paper clip projected to the right hemisphere, which in turn would control the left hand to pick up the paper clip. However, the subject would often misname the object, calling it an *eraser*, because "eraser" was projected to the language centers in the left hemisphere. In one case, the right and left hemispheres even had different career goals. A 15-year-old boy was asked, separately in the left and right ears, what sort of job he would pick. In this boy, both the left and right hemispheres had the ability to produce speech. His left hemisphere answered "draftsman," but his right hemisphere responded "automobile racer" (Gazzaniga, 1980).

Even more astonishing, the left hemisphere sometimes misinterpreted actions carried out by the right hemisphere. In one case, the right hemisphere was given the command "rub," causing the subject to rub the back of his head. When asked to interpret this action, the left hemisphere responded "itch." This reaction suggested that the left hemisphere interpreted the activity of the independent right hemisphere and imposed meaning on it—namely, that the rubbing action was in response to an itch (it was not.) Gazzaniga (1980) linked this finding to cognitive dissonance theory, which recognizes a human propensity to reconcile beliefs with actions by first "observing" ourselves and then making sense of our behavior *after* it occurs.

Gazzaniga's research vividly demonstrates that, in split-brain patients, the left and right hemispheres can have different knowledge and goals. These findings present a provocative possibility for understanding the average person with an intact brain. Perhaps "the person or self is not a unified psychological entity" (p. 233). Instead, the mind may be better described as "an arrangement of mental systems, each with its own values and responses." The brain's language centers may have a powerful role in providing the "glue" that allows the federated mind to function as a unified system. The brain component that coordinates language also monitors, controls, and inhibits somewhat autonomous activity in other brain regions. The language centers might therefore help to regulate the "impulses of the many selves that dwell inside us" and bind them together into a unity of the conscious self (p. 233).

Through research on hemispheric specialization, the quest to map cognitive function to brain location was advanced, and the workings of the brain became fractionally less mysterious as a result. But there is a danger here: It is easy to overgeneralize and overextend these interesting findings. It is possible, for example, to state the functions of the right and left hemispheres in absolute terms—to believe that the division of labor is strict rather than shared and partial.

A still more serious error is to assume that the right-brain/left-brain discoveries are a legitimate basis for classifying people into **right-brain thinkers** and **left-brain thinkers**. It may seem like a simple inference to conclude that the brain research provides a scientific basis for distinguishing between classes of people who prefer to think analytically (left-brain, detail-oriented) from those who prefer to think holistically (right-brain, big picture). But there are serious problems with such an easy division. One problem is the assumption that people can be divided into two camps reliably on a sound cognitive and psychometric basis. A second difficulty is showing that, even if such a distinction could validly identify two kinds of people, such a division would map onto differences in hemispheric activity. Would "right-brain" people really show more neural activity in their right hemisphere than "left-brain" people? Such evidence was certainly not available when widely popular theories of right-brain and left-brain thinking entered the popular culture and the informal theories of some educators. Nor does current research warrant a two-category distinction between "right-brain" and "left-brain" learners.

Here we must recognize a pervasive risk of applying brain research to education. Historically, there has been a tendency to overgeneralize and overextend research on the brain to support educational beliefs and practices. The applications of brain research to education have sometimes gone far beyond what science actually supported, and consequently the findings were distorted and misapplied. For example, research that revealed hemispheric specialization told us something important about the brain, but the misapplications that followed should remind us not to overextend brain research findings and apply them prematurely to educational practice. This does not mean that we should ignore exciting discoveries on brain function—for brain research is now at a stage when it really does illuminate our study of mind and education. It does mean, however, that in the pursuit of understanding the brain-mind mystery, we need to be cautious as we move forward.

Brain Modularity

So far in this chapter we have found that brain function maps to brain anatomy in rather general terms. We have considered the special roles of the brainstem, the cerebellum, and the cerebral cortex. We also noted that the four lobes of the cerebral cortex have identifiable differences in function. In the last section, we found that the left and right cerebral hemispheres support somewhat different forms of cognition. In this section, we will continue to identify associations between particular functions and specific brain regions. Correspondences between brain function and anatomy reflect one overarching truth about the brain's organization: It is modular. The mapping of brain structure to function is a basic activity of neuroscience, one that originated from the early days of the study of the brain centuries ago, and that continues apace today with the use of modern brain imaging technologies.

Some of the earliest discoveries about brain function related language capabilities to specific brain regions. We noted that language is associated with the brain's left hemisphere while recognizing that this generalization does not always hold up, especially in left-handed people. This caveat aside, two regions are crucial for language processing: Broca's area and Wernicke's area, shown in Figure 8.5.

Broca's area, located in the posterior portion of the left frontal lobe, permits the articulation of spoken words. Damage to Broca's area disrupts a person's ability to speak, resulting in a disability called **aphasia**. A French neurologist, Marc Dax, first discovered the connection between speech and the left hemisphere in 1836. Ultimately, the identified brain area was named for Pierre Paul Broca, a French physician, who rediscovered the correspondence in 1861. Like Dax, Broca observed that people who suffered brain damage to the area lost the ability to speak.

Localized brain damage in the left temporal lobe produces a different compromise of cognitive function. As the German neurologist Karl Wernicke discovered in 1874, damage to what has come to be known as **Wernicke's area** destroys the ability to comprehend language and to produce *coherent* speech. People who suffer damage to Wernicke's area can speak sequences of words with a natural rhythm and normal-sounding syntax, but their sentences are gibberish—they do not make any sense. Thus, the left hemisphere has two vital language centers: One regulates the ability to articulate spoken words (Broca's area) and the other controls the ability to comprehend and produce meaningful speech (Wernicke's area). Not surprisingly, those two regions are connected by a large bundle of nerve fibers, together forming a "language loop."

GARDNER'S MULTIPLE-INTELLIGENCES THEORY. The isolation of function from localized brain damage played an important role in Howard Gardner's theory of multiple intelligences, set forth in his 1983 book, *Frames of Mind*. Gardner's book became highly influential in educational circles because it challenged the reigning paradigm of a single dominant general intelligence. As an alternative, Gardner proposed that the

FIGURE 8.5
Broca's Area and
Wernicke's Area *Two
regions of the temporal
lobe regulate both the
ability to articulate
spoken words (Broca's
area) and the ability to
make those words
meaningful (Wernicke's
area).*

Broca's Area   Wernicke's Area

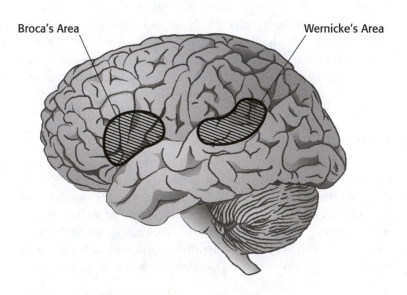

mind has several identifiable "intelligences" that operate relatively independently. Gardner's theory will be taken up in more detail in the chapter on human intelligence. For our present purposes, we will consider Gardner's insightful application of brain research to justify his theory of multiple intelligences. Gardner marshaled evidence from brain damage to show that each of the proposed "intelligences" corresponds to a specific brain area.

Gardner argued that each semi-autonomous intelligence is independent by virtue of its anatomical and functional isolation. Clinical evidence for this isolation was that localized damage to one area of the brain would disrupt its special function, but not the functioning of other intelligences. This was the criterion of selective impairment, one of several that Gardner applied when constructing, explaining, and justifying his theory. For example, linguistic intelligence was disrupted by damage to the left temporal lobe, a functional association that we have already seen is connected to Broca's and Wernicke's areas. Something of a counterpart to natural language is found in the right hemisphere where musical intelligence is focused in the right frontal and temporal lobes. Damage to the left hemisphere can produce aphasia; damage to the right can produce **amusia**, an inability to discriminate tones or to appreciate music. Just as Gardner found brain regions that corresponded to linguistic intelligence and musical intelligence, so he was able to cite clinical evidence to support many of the proposed intelligences.

THE CASE OF PHINEAS GAGE. The criterion of selective impairment that Howard Gardner used to build his theory of multiple intelligences had actually been applied much earlier in understanding the specific effects of localized brain damage. One famous case study on the effects of localized brain damage was the story of Phineas Gage (Macmillan, 1986). Gage, a 25-year-old railway worker, was responsible for setting off explosives that were necessary for laying railroad track in rural Vermont. At 4:30 p.m. on September 13, 1848, Gage was packing down an explosive powder with a metal tamping bar when the powder accidentally ignited, launching the tamping bar at

FIGURE 8.6
Phineas Gage *The case of the 25-year-old railway worker who survived a serious brain injury established that the frontal lobes are essential to cognitive and emotional self-regulation.*
[Courtesy of the National Library of Medicine]

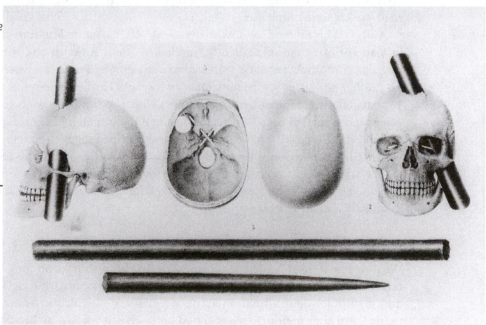

FIGURE 8.7
Working Memory and Brodmann Area 46 *Active processing of information relies on the region of the prefrontal lobe, known as Brodmann area 46.*

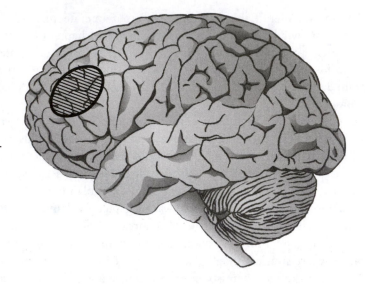

high speed. The bar struck Gage on his left cheek just above the jaw, passed behind his left eye, and exited the top of his skull. The bar landed on the ground 100 feet away. In a mere instant, Gage's left frontal lobe was completely penetrated by the projectile. Remarkably, Gage not only survived the accident—he could walk and talk later that same day.

Within just a few months, Gage returned to his work on the railway. But something had changed—whereas before the accident Gage was an amiable man, after the accident he often became irascible and angry. He used harsh language, something utterly uncharacteristic of his personality prior to the explosion. Phineas Gage also became less capable of controlling his emotions. The self-regulatory capabilities that we ascribe to the frontal cortex, including the functions of inhibition, were seriously compromised. Gage could no longer exert control over his own behavior as he did prior to the accident. To Gage's fellow-workers, he was no longer the same man. His days as a railroad worker were numbered.

Gage left his railroad job and briefly joined P. T. Barnum's Museum in New York as a human curiosity. He subsequently traveled to South America and worked driving a stagecoach in Chile. Later, Gage moved to old-west San Francisco, where he lived with his mother and sister for the remainder of his days. He died of severe seizures in 1860, 11 years after the railroad accident. From a clinical point of view, the case of Phineas Gage was important because it established that the frontal lobes are essential to cognitive and emotional self-regulation. The case also helped shape the larger debate around whether brain function is localized or diffused across the brain. The consequences of Gage's brain injury were taken as evidence for the localization of function. As such, it informed the long controversy among neuroscientists about whether brain function is essentially local or global.

Mapping Memory to Brain Structures

We now know from neuroscience research that both short- and long-term memory relate to specific brain areas. Working memory, the cognitive function of holding and manipulating information actively, is associated with the frontal lobe. In particular, working memory is associated with what is known as **Brodmann area 46,**

FIGURE 8.8
Long-term
Memory *The hip-*
pocampus is crucial
for the formation of
enduring memories.

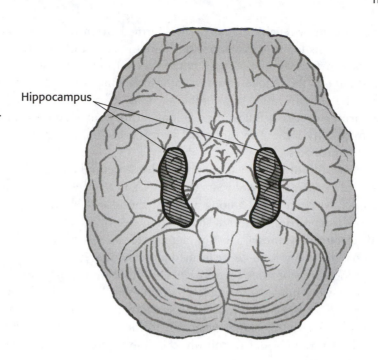

Hippocampus

shown in Figure 8.7. Long-term memory has a counterpart in the functions of the **hippocampus**, a small pair of structures situated deep within the brain. (Figure 8.8).

The function of the hippocampus was discovered partly through evidence of amnesic patients who lost the ability to form new and enduring memories. Such was true of a patient known as H. M., now regarded as the most famous case in the history of neuroscience. In an attempt to relieve severe epilepsy, H. M. underwent surgery to remove most of his hippocampus. After the surgery, his ability to learn was severely compromised. Memories from before the surgery—of particular people, events, and locations—were largely intact. Although H. M. could interact with other people in a manner that seemed almost normal, he was incapable of forming new memories. In other words, H. M.'s *working* memory functioned, but he was unable to form new *long-term* memories. One consequence was that the neuroscientists who worked with H. M. had to reintroduce themselves at every meeting, even if they had been working with H. M. for years. Moreover, H. M.'s caretaker tried to preserve the layout of his house as much as possible over the years following the surgery. Any change in the house's layout or the placement of objects would cause confusion because of H. M.'s inability to learn.

Further research showed that H. M.'s inability to learn had to be qualified. Certainly, he was unable to learn *one kind* of knowledge, namely, declarative knowledge—the kind expressible in words. When taught a new skill involving procedural knowledge, however, H. M. was able to make progress. Over the course of several weeks, H. M. practiced mirror drawing—copying shapes, such as a star, by looking at their images in a mirror. H. M. had no experiential memory for practicing the task, yet the quality of his drawings improved over time. H. M. was definitely learning—otherwise, how could his drawings improve?—but it was a kind of learning for which he had no awareness. The ability to learn procedural skill was spared despite the partial removal of H. M.'s hippocampus.

H. M.'s condition revealed yet another fascinating pattern: Among his memories formed prior to surgery, his more *remote* memories were more stable than were recent memories. Something in the processing of those older memories led to their being stronger and more reliable than memories formed just prior to the removal of his hippocampus. This led to speculation that initial long-term learning involves the hippocampus in *fast* processes. These processes conform to the way that we normally think about our ability to learn a new name or fact in a matter of a minute or two. But this may be only the initial stage in the way long-term memories are formed. At least *some* learning processes follow a much longer time course. Brain structures may continue to modify long after the initial learning occurs, becoming more stable and robust in the process.

Some aspects of memory therefore involve structural changes in the cerebral cortex over the course of several years (Squire & Kandel, 1999). Evidence for these slow processes have been found among patients who receive electroconvulsive therapy to treat severe depression. Research showed that electric shock therapy commonly produced **retrograde amnesia**, a loss of memory for past events. But the therapy had *less* effect on older memories—those formed more than three years prior to the therapy—than on memories of more recent events. In other words, memory traces older than three years were not as susceptible to destruction by electric shock therapy. Some brain process or processes continued to strengthen these older memories even two or three years after the memories were first formed. These slow processes of memory consolidation could be one reason why the time course for building expertise extends over many years.

Brain Plasticity and Redundancy

Direct correspondences between anatomy and function present just one side of brain organization. The other side—a competing truth—is that the brain exhibits flexibility. Consequently, particular brain functions are not irrevocably assigned to one specific location. This is clear in case studies of patients recovering from serious brain trauma. Even in cases when large sections of the brain are damaged or surgically removed, there is often surprisingly little deterioration of cognitive function. More telling still, cognitive functions can be relearned, and relearning requires that the brain flexibly adapt by shifting the functions previously associated with damaged areas to new areas of the brain.

The remapping of brain function can follow an accident or brain injury, but it can also be the result of more felicitous adaptive processes. For example, the brain region that controls finger dexterity in the left hand is normally restricted to well-defined regions of the somatosensory cortex. For professional violinists, dexterity of the fingers of the left hand assumes special importance. The brain adapts to the demands by dedicating relatively more neurons to finger control. Scans of brain activation among violinists show that significantly greater areas of brain are devoted to controlling the fingers of the left hand (Elbert et al., 1995). No such enlargement was found in the brain regions that control the right hand (used for bowing) or among nonviolinists. The expansion of brain regions dedicated to greater finger speed, dexterity, and control is highly adaptive up to a point. The spreading of control to larger brain regions for each finger can lead to overlap and, ultimately, to a loss of control—a disorder called focal dystonia. A similar phenomenon has been found among Braille readers who over time can lose the ability to distinguish which fingers have touched the Braille markings (Hamilton & Pascual-Leone, 1998; Sterr et al., 1998).

The brain can adapt to specific occupational demands that are more cognitive in nature than they are motor. Such is the case among licensed taxi drivers in London. To be licensed, prospective taxi drivers need to demonstrate near-perfect comprehension of London street names and locations. London does not follow a grid plan as do many other major cities. Deviation from a grid plan means that efficient driving in London involves a highly accurate understanding of the spatial locations of street addresses, and of how to navigate efficiently from one location to another through nonlinear routes. The possibility of road closures and traffic jams means that an efficient taxi driver must be aware of alternative routes, and how traffic patterns along those routes can fluctuate during the day. For these reasons, spatial cognition is a dominant mode of reasoning among taxi drivers. They exercise intensive spatial reasoning during every working day, and indeed must display considerable ability to understand city-level spatial information even before beginning their careers.

Mappings of neural activity in the brains of 16 London taxi drivers showed that the posterior hippocampus, which supports two-dimensional spatial cognition, occupied a greater area than it did in a control group (Maguire et al., 2000). The posterior hippocampus was largest in taxi drivers with more than 40 years experience. The finding implies that the increased demand for spatial cognition led to the growth of brain areas dedicated to navigation, which in turn implies that some brain tissue normally serving other cognitive functions was reassigned to the function of spatial cognition. As in the case of violinists, we find that professional experience can shape the function of brain tissue. To a significant degree, the functions served by specific brain areas respond to the real demands placed on the brain.

Summarizing, then, two complementary patterns are discernible: (1) Brain anatomy maps to specific, definable cognitive functions, and (2) the brain can *deviate* from that normal mapping in response to particular cognitive demands. The first is an instance of biology dictating cognition; the second is cognition having a degree of influence on biology. The influence is bidirectional. Models that emphasize one-way influence from biology to cognitive function oversimplify and distort the truth. In important ways, the brain defines and enables a span of human cognition, but the brain is also marvelously adaptive, responding structurally to the functional demands placed on it. The brain shapes the mind, and the mind shapes the brain.

Brain Circuits

By appreciating how the brain responds to the cognitive demands of violinists and taxi drivers, we can put to rest the misconception that brain anatomy dictates cognitive function in a straightforward fashion. But then what is the relationship between anatomy and function? The classic debate among neuroscientists centered on two competing positions: the **globalist hypothesis** and the **localist hypothesis**. Globalists believed that the brain as a whole participated in cognition; localists promoted the idea that cognition was identifiable with specific brain areas.

The Russian scientist Alexander Luria proposed a third alternative that combines elements of the first two, yet is conceptually distinct. Luria advanced the idea that complex brain functions involve coordination among several brain areas, whereas simple cognitive functions are controlled locally in specific brain locations. Luria's hypothesis has turned out to be basically correct. In general, higher cognitive functions are served not by single locations in the brain, but instead by combinations of brain sites that work in coordination. These multiple sites, commonly referred to as **neural circuits**, act in concert to produce complex cognitive performance. As a rule, complex cognition is the product of activity in neural circuits rather than the isolated activity of single brain locations.

Neuroimaging technologies that reveal circuit-like patterns of activation tell us something about the nature of the cognitive process being imaged. For example, when various brain areas are activated and the functions of those separate areas are known, the image pattern provides evidence of what component cognitive functions are utilized. Solving a math problem might activate a brain region associated with visualization, suggesting that the problem solving entails forming mental images. The frontal cortex might also be activated, suggesting that the math problem is calling upon certain executive functions, such as planning and monitoring. In just this way, data from brain imaging can suggest or confirm presumed cognitive processes underlying complex intellectual activity. Differences between one person and another can reveal characteristic styles of cognition. Changes in one person over time can show how learning and development influence patterns of cognitive activity and modifications in brain circuitry used during complex cognitive performance.

A recent surge in the precision of brain imaging technologies that map brain activity to cognitive functions has opened new research vistas for brain scientists and bolstered the emergent field of cognitive neuroscience. Several brain-imaging technologies are available, each with its own affordances and limitations. No imaging procedure is superior to others in every respect.

The two most commonly used brain imaging technologies are PET and fMRI. **PET (positron emission tomography) scans** require the injection of a small dose of a radioactive glucose tracer. The glucose is taken up by brain cells, just as normal glucose is used to support metabolism. As a rule, the more active a cell, the more glucose is taken up. During any cognitive activity, some neural circuits will be relatively more active and others less active. That difference is expressed metabolically as an increase in the uptake of radioactive glucose by the more active circuits. Like all radioactive compounds, radioactive glucose is unstable and decays. An unstable fluorine atom in the tracer glucose releases a positively charged electron, called a positron. By recording the emission of positrons across the brain, the resulting image indirectly displays differential glucose uptake, which in turn reflects heightened local activity.

PET scans are excellent for projecting high-resolution images that show precisely which brain regions are most metabolically active. However, the uptake of glucose is not a rapid process. Differential rates of neural metabolism may be subtle, and so detecting differences between more active and less active brain regions typically requires several minutes. During that time, local differences in positron emission rates show which brain circuits are exhibiting heightened activity. PET scans are therefore best suited to cognitive activities that extend over many minutes and that are more or less continuous (such as reading a story), rather than tasks in which cognitive activity is fleeting or in flux (such as solving a verbal analogy).

The other commonly used brain imaging technology, **fMRI (functional magnetic resonance imaging)**, produces images that have a much higher *temporal* resolution, which allows for detection of rapid or transient changes that occur in narrow time intervals. fMRI takes advantage of the fact that the brain shunts blood flow to active areas. When a brain region is activated by specific cognitive demands, blood vessels dilate to produce an increase in cerebral blood flow. This increase allows local neurons to consume more oxygen and boost metabolism. In the locally active region, blood vessels have a higher concentration of the blood's oxygen-carrying molecule, hemoglobin. Not only is more hemoglobin present, there is also a shift toward a higher ratio of *deoxygenated* hemoglobin compared to oxygenated hemoglobin because the active neurons extract oxygen from the blood. fMRI technology is designed to detect subtle changes both in the *amount* of hemoglobin and in the *ratio* of oxygenated and deoxygenated hemoglobin.

To produce an fMRI image, the person is placed inside a large, very strong magnet. The magnet affects the body's protons, causing them to align like tiny bar magnets. The alignment is then briefly disturbed by a pulse of radio waves. When the protons realign under the influence of the magnetic field, they emit radio waves that can be detected by the machinery. The fMRI technology is precisely attuned to measure changes in the levels and forms of hemoglobin that signal changes in blood flow and metabolism. As noted, the imaging technology is capable of recording changes to blood flow patterns that occur over just a few seconds. However, fMRI has relatively poor spatial resolution; mapping activity down to the grain size of about a cubic millimeter—still fairly coarse. It cannot provide the finely detailed images that are possible with PET scans. But if the cognitive activity is fleeting or changes rapidly, fMRI scans may be the best technique to show which brain regions are responding.

To map a specific cognitive activity to its supporting brain regions, cognitive neuroscientists must select the optimal brain-imaging technology—PET, fMRI, and others—as well as carefully elicit the cognitive processes of interest. When done well, this matching results in images that offer a window into how the brain responds to a variety of important cognitive processes. These forms of cognition include those that are highly valued in education, such as mathematical reasoning and reading.

Mathematical Reasoning

Images of brain activation show that the way the brain responds to a math problem depends on the kind of problem. In other words, mathematical reasoning activates different brain regions in response to different types of mathematical activity. *Calculation* activates areas associated with language, whereas *estimation and comparison* activate brain areas associated with spatial representation (Dehaene, Spelke, Pinel, Stanescu, & Tsivkin, 1999). These different patterns of activation are evident in PET scan images. In one experiment, subjects were told two digits and asked either to multiply the two digits (calculation) or to say which of the two digits was larger (comparison)(Dehaene, 1997). The research question was whether these two tasks, comparison and calculation, activated different portions of the brain. The PET images showed that the tasks indeed activated two different brain circuits (Figures 8.9 and 8.10).

The PET scans showed that *calculation* activated speech centers in the left hemisphere, probably because multiplication tasks are often understood in verbal terms. *Comparison* tasks activated more of the right hemisphere, probably because numeric

FIGURE 8.9
Areas of Cortex Activated During Numeric Comparison *The non-linguistic right hemisphere is especially active.* [From Dehaene, 1996, Reprinted by permission of MIT Press Journals.]

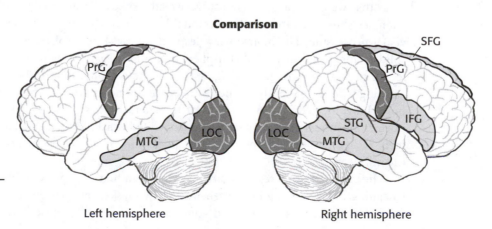

Comparison

Left hemisphere   Right hemisphere

FIGURE 8.10
Areas of Cortex
Activated During
Multiplication *Left
hemisphere speech
centers are acti-
vated.* [From Dehaene,
1996, Reprinted by per-
mission of MIT Press
Journals.]

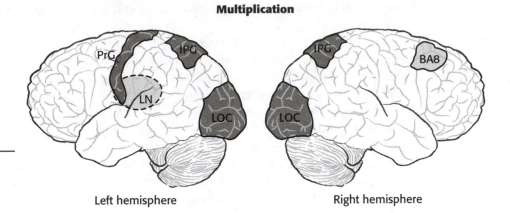

comparison is essentially a nonlinguistic activity that occurs even in pre-lingual children and in animals. Infants' ability to make simple quantitative comparisons is
believed to arise from inborn brain modules dedicated to numerosity.

Some activated brain regions were common to both tasks. For example, the most
posterior portion of the brain, the occipital cortex, was activated during both comparison and calculation. The occipital cortex supports visual information. A broad conclusion can be drawn from these results: Brain activation stimulated by arithmetic is "not
associated with a single calculation center" in the brain (Dehaene, 1997, p. 221).

Language Processing

Cognitive neuroscientists have studied the brain regions activated by language processing during reading. Reading is a cognitively complex activity, involving a combination of three code levels: visual (the printed word), phonological (the spoken
representation of the word), and semantic (the meaning of the word). Cognition
during reading was therefore believed to require the coordination of "circuits" of
activity identified with different brain sites. Brain imaging studies tested whether
this hypothesized mapping of activities to different brain regions could be substan-
tiated by data.

Pioneering work by Michael Posner and his colleagues (1988) demonstrated that
different codes or levels of language processing indeed activated different brain regions.
Figure 8.11 shows the composite results from PET scans. The triangles indicate brain
areas that were activated when a subject read a series of unrelated words silently. The
triangles show activation in the occipital lobe, the region of the brain that conducts
visual processing. The hollow triangles indicate right hemisphere activation, and the
solid triangle indicates left hemisphere activation. Passive silent reading was largely
localized to the visual processing system in the occipital lobe in both hemispheres.
Reading word lists silently did not activate the sound-processing areas in the left temporal lobe, located just to the right of the lateral sulcus (groove). This finding supported one model of reading in which the printed word is directly analyzed in its visual
form rather than being translated into a phonological equivalent that is "heard" inside
the mind.

The circle and squares show areas of the brain that were activated by the semantic
(meaningful) processing of written words. Two tasks were presented. The first asked
subjects to *generate* a use for each noun. For example, if "hammer" were presented, a

FIGURE 8.11
PET Scan Activation During Reading *Passive reading (triangles) and reading for meaning (circle and squares) activated different brain regions. Solid shapes indicate left hemisphere activation; hollow shapes show right hemisphere activation.* [From Posner et al., 1988 Reprinted by permission from AAAS.]

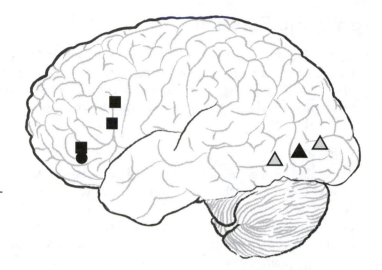

correct response would be "pound." The squares show the brain regions activated by the *generate* task. The second task was a *monitor* task. In this task, subjects were presented with a series of animal names. They were asked to count, mentally, the number of dangerous animals. The circle shows a brain region activated by the *monitor* task. Clearly, the *generate* and *monitor* tasks both involved understanding the meaning of the words—they required semantic processing. Semantic processing activated brain regions different from those activated by passive reading of word lists. Specifically, brain activity shifted substantially to the frontal lobe. Moreover, brain activity was concentrated in the left hemisphere as indicated by solid (rather than hollow) circles and squares.

The general conclusion is identical to that drawn from brain images during mathematical reasoning—namely, that there is not a single brain center for each form of complex cognition. An activity as simple as word recognition requires the orchestration of several brain centers. The distributed quality of brain activation is therefore a major discovery from brain imaging studies. Dehaene noted that "ten or twenty cerebral areas are activated when a subject reads words, ponders over their meaning, imagines a scene, or performs a calculation" (Dehaene, 1997, p. 217). Thinking is a distributed activity that cannot be accomplished by a single brain cell or a single cerebral area, but rather by a circuit.

Brain imaging technologies are tremendously important to cognitive neuroscientists. Their essential benefit can be expressed rather simply: Brain imaging helps neuroscientists to map cognitive functioning to specific brain anatomy. Imaging reveals differences or changes in cell activity measured as glucose uptake or blood flow. Associations between cognition and the brain can be discovered by using differential metabolism as the connecting variable. The result has been tremendous progress in advancing our understanding of neural circuitry. Yet mappings made possible by these brain imaging technologies can only tell us so much; they amount to a high-tech cartography by which cognition can be overlaid onto anatomy. Many important mysteries on the mind-brain association are not at all illuminated by brain imaging technologies. Among the most important, brain images say nothing about the specific mechanisms by which individual brain cells support learning, how those neurons change over short and long time intervals, and how they connect to form the circuits that underlie specific cognitive functions.

Neuroanatomy and Plasticity

Up to this point we have explored aspects of the human brain at the relatively "macro" level of visible or potentially visible structures. Now we need to examine the operation of the brain at a "micro" level—at the level of neurons, the connections between neurons, and neurochemical processes associated with neuronal activity.

Neurons

The brain is composed of individual cells, called **neurons**. How are we to think about neurons? Remember that in speaking of brain regions activated by complex cognitive activity, we use the word *circuits*. The term *brain circuit* recalls an old-fashioned electrical circuit composed of batteries, light bulbs, switches, resistors, and wires. In electrical circuits, wires carry electricity that can light a bulb or energize an appliance. As a first approximation, we can think of neurons as serving the function of wires in electronics: Neurons carry signals much as a wire carries a signal. Neurons have other important functions that make them different from a metallic wire, but as a starting point we can think about their common functions.

We must also appreciate that neurons are **cells**. A basic course in biology teaches us that cells are the fundamental building blocks of nearly all life forms—animals, plants, and microbes. A single human body is composed of trillions of cells, each of which is a tiny membrane-wrapped sack of fluid, microscopic structures called organelles, and a genetic blueprint coded in DNA. Most cells have the ability to replicate, and almost all have the ability to serve specialized functions. Beginning with an identical genetic potential, cells in the human body differentiate into thousands of cell types, including heart cells, muscle cells, red and white blood cells, and, importantly, neurons. Even with their distinct and vital function, neurons share properties with all other body cells— they have DNA, membranes, and the capacity for metabolic activity.

NEURON STRUCTURE. The control center of any cell is its nucleus. In a neuron, the nucleus holds the cell's DNA, which regulates all cell functions, including replication. The nucleus is contained in the region of the neuron called the **cell body** or **soma** (Figure 8.12). Like all cells, neurons have distinguishing features that assist their special functions (Society for Neuroscience, 2002), the most obvious being its form and structure. Many neurons are very long, which enables them to function as wire-like relays. Neurons can stretch up to several feet in length, as in the case of neurons that extend from the base of the spine to the toes. The part of the neuron that extends over a long distance is the cable-like tube called an **axon**. The axon is the part of the neuron that functions most like a wire—it carries a signal from one location to another. Signaling has obvious importance in the body (e.g., to control hand movement) and in the brain (e.g., to send information from the eyes to the visual cortex). Relaying information from one location to another is a major function of the nervous system. Neurons are adapted to carry out this function through signals carried along the axon.

The length of axons is one distinguishing feature of their typical shape; a second characteristic quality is *branching*. Many types of neurons branch profusely, much as a tree branches. Borrowing the metaphor of a branching tree, the branching structures of neurons are called **dendrites** (from *dendros*, the Latin word for *tree*). This branching shape hints of a second vital function of neurons—not only do neurons relay signals like wires, they also intricately connect to other neurons. Dendrites are a physical manifestation of neuronal potential for interconnectivity. In their interconnectivity, neu-

FIGURE 8.12
A Neuron
A schematic illustration—there is plenty of variation between actual neurons.

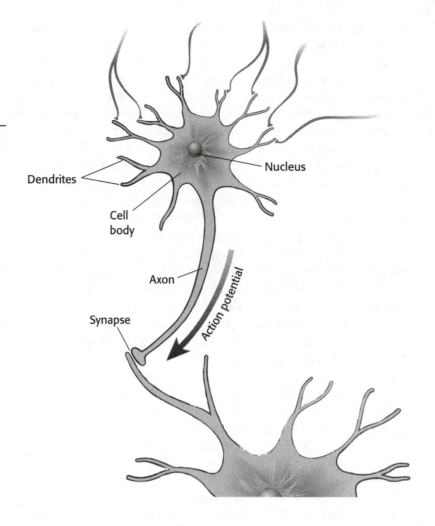

Dendrites

Nucleus

Cell body

Axon

Action potential

Synapse

rons are again like electrical systems (albeit complex ones), but in degree of branching they exceed even the most elaborate electronics.

ACTION POTENTIALS. Each neuron's branching system of dendrites receives electrical signals from other neurons. If the input to the dendrites is sufficient, the neuron will fire. The resulting electrical signal, called an **action potential** or **spike**, will travel down the axon, in one direction only—away from the cell body and along the length of the axon. Within a fraction of a second, the action potential reaches the end of the axon, which in turn often splits into numerous terminal fibers. The terminal fibers may connect to one or more other neurons, or possibly to a muscle cell. Tiny knob-like structures at the ends of the fibers, called **terminal boutons** (the French word for *buttons*), release chemicals, called **neurotransmitters**, which can cause the next neuron to fire.

The action potential that travels down the axon is not a purely electrical signal. It is actually electrochemical because it involves the movement of charged molecules, called **ions**, into and out of the membrane of the axon. Normally, a resting neuron maintains a low internal concentration of positively charged sodium atoms. This inside-outside *chemical* difference across the membrane also creates a *charge* difference, with the outside having a positive charge (sodium is Na^+) and the inside a relatively negative charge.

A charge difference means that there is a tiny negative voltage difference—an electro-hemical gradient—between the inside and outside of the membrane.

Because sodium is more concentrated outside the axon, it will have a tendency to enter the neuron. Sodium pumps continually expel sodium to keep the concentration of sodium ions low inside the neuron. But an excitatory stimulus applied to the neuron opens up channels in the membrane to allow some sodium ions inside. The influx of sodium causes a slight reduction in voltage, called depolarization, which opens up additional sodium channels. The result is a positive feedback cycle, which, if strong enough, can open up large numbers of sodium channels leading to massive depolarization in the neuron. This is what happens when the neuron "fires." The depolarization spreads down the axon. The mechanism of the action potential is therefore a spreading depolarization caused by a rapid influx of sodium.

The depolarization of a neuron is extremely rapid, occurring within a fraction of a second. After depolarizing, the neuron must re-establish the membrane voltage so that the cell is ready for another action potential. This is accomplished by the outward flow of potassium ions. Therefore, **depolarization** is caused primarily by the influx of sodium ions, and **repolarization** is caused by the outflow of potassium ions. Many cycles of depolarization and repolarization can occur within in a single second, which means that a neuron can fire repeatedly in rapid succession. The propagation of an action potential down an axon is also extremely fast. When a finger touches a hot stove-top, the signal travels up the arm to the spinal cord and then back down the arm to acti-vate muscles that will retract the hand. Clearly, the rapid conduction of nerve signals can be a matter of life and death. One other structural feature of neurons influences the speed of action potentials: the degree of fatty insulation on the axon. Axons are often coated with a fatty substance called **myelin**. The fatty insulation speeds up the signal; the more heavily coated an axon is in myelin, the faster a signal will travel down the length of the neuron.

Neurons have help from other cells in the brain—an enormous number of support cells called **glial cells**. In fact, about 90 percent of the cells in the brain are glial cells. These accomplish several important functions, including formation of the myelin sheath, removal of dead tissue, and support of signaling chemicals called neurotransmitters.

Neurons, then, are the basic functional elements of the nervous system, which includes the brain as well as the spinal cord and the peripheral nerves that extend throughout the body. They are essentially cells that are adapted to carrying and storing information. We have concentrated thus far on their properties for carrying signals as the rough equivalent of wires in electrical systems. This is a good metaphor because neurons do indeed carry signals as action potentials down the length of their axons. But signal transmission is not the only function of neurons. They also *store* information. And, in fact, the mechanisms by which neurons store information—by which they *learn*—is one of the most interesting functions of the nervous system, as well as one of the most difficult to understand.

NEURONAL FUNCTION. A normal human brain, vast in its store of knowledge, con-trols a complex repertoire of behavior. The intricacy of the human central nervous system must rise to the level of complexity of human knowledge and behavior. It does so in part by sheer numbers: The human brain is composed of about a trillion (10^{12}) neurons. Compare this number to the population of the earth, about 8 bil-lion, and we see immediately that the brain population (in neurons) far exceeds the earth's population (in people). To reach such a high number of brain cells, the devel-oping child generates neurons profusely, on a scale that is hardly conceivable. The

INTEREST MAGNET 8.2

Einstein's Brain

Within hours of Albert Einstein's death in 1955, his brain was surgically removed, placed in a glass jar, and preserved with formalin. Einstein's autopsy, which included the removal and preservation of his brain, was conducted by a Princeton, New Jersey, hospital pathologist named Thomas Harvey. Harvey claimed, but could not prove, that Einstein's family had given him permission to take the brain (Abraham, 2001). When Princeton University asked Harvey to turn over Einstein's brain, he refused to do so. He was seemingly determined to keep the brain for himself.

The location of Einstein's brain was the secret of a small group of people, including Thomas Harvey, for the next two decades. That changed in 1978 when journalist Steven Levy (1978, 1999) tracked down Harvey in Wichita, Kansas. After much cajoling, Harvey "sighed deeply and pulled from a cardboard box two glass jars with the sectioned pieces of Einstein's brain." Levy's magazine article led neuroscientists to ask for samples of Einstein's brain to analyze the tissue. They wanted to determine if Einstein's prodigious intellect was correlated to any identifiable feature of brain anatomy. One of the first scientists to receive a sample of Einstein's brain tissue was U. C. Berkeley neuroanatomist Marian Diamond. Comparing Einstein's brain to the brains of eleven deceased males, Diamond found that the brain tissue had about 73 percent more glial cells than the average brain (Diamond, Scheibel, Murphy, & Harvey, 1985). The high density of glial cells, which are responsible for support and maintenance of neurons, suggested that Einstein's brain was "well fed." Not all scientists have agreed with Diamond's conclusions, however. Hines (1998) pointed out that the average age of the comparison subjects was 64 years; Einstein was 76 when he died.

Another research team, which included Thomas Harvey, compared Einstein's prefrontal cortex with the brains of five other males (Anderson & Harvey, 1996). The prefrontal cortex is the region most often associated with higher brain functions, including metacognition. The researchers compared "columns" of cerebral cortex 1 mm^2 in cross-sectional area. Their main finding was that the total number of neurons in the cortex columns did not differ between Einstein's brain and the others. However, because Einstein's cortex was relatively thin and so had less overall volume, his brain had the highest *density* of neurons. This high density may have been important. The authors speculated that "an increase in neuronal density might be advantageous in decreasing interneuronal conduction time" (p. 163).

In terms of visible structure, Einstein's brain at first seemed to be of average size and structure. Thomas Harvey, the Princeton pathologist, was convinced that Einstein's brain was completely normal when Levy first contacted him in 1978. More recently, however, Harvey's photos of the intact brain have been re-examined. Now it appears that Einstein's brain was in some ways unusual (Levy, 1999). For example, the brain had a particularly large inferior parietal lobe, a region that underlies mathematical cognition as well as mental imagery. This is interesting because by Einstein's own account many of his own insights into physics, including the special theory of relativity, were initially inspired by thinking with mental images rather than with mathematical abstractions. An enlarged inferior parietal lobe may have helped Einstein to integrate mathematical and mental imagery. He famously used mental imagery to imagine how a light beam would appear if he were traveling alongside the beam at the same speed (Einstein, 1979). His insight—that it would appear to be moving rather than static—helped prepare Einstein to develop the special theory of relativity.

rate of formation of new neurons, called **neurogenesis**, can rise as high as 100,000 per second, prenatally. That's equivalent to the population of a medium-sized city every second. Later we will see that not only neurogenesis, but also the rate of formation of neuronal interconnections, called synapses, is also inconceivably rapid in infants.

Neuron formation is most rapid prenatally and in infants. After infancy, the number of neurons is relatively constant throughout life (Terry et al., 1987). This stability led some brain scientists to infer that adults lose the ability to generate new brain neurons. Children were warned against reckless behavior for the reason that once a brain cell dies, it cannot be replaced. That conventional wisdom has turned out to be incorrect:

The human brain is now known to be capable of neurogenesis, at least in the hippocampus, through adult life and even among the elderly (Eriksson et al., 1998).

The complex behavior and intricate knowledge that springs from the human mind is accounted for partly by the huge numbers of neurons that compose the brain. Added complexity is achieved by variety in *types* of neurons. For simplicity, we can recognize three kinds of neurons. To illustrate, consider again what happens if someone accidentally touches a hot stove. Receptor cells in the hand activate **sensory neurons**. Those sensory nerves carry the signals toward the **central nervous system (CNS)**, composed of both the brain and spinal cord. When the CNS processes the information, as in the case of the hot stove, it activates **motor neurons** to contract the appropriate muscles to pull the hand away. Motor neurons act on the external world based on information provided by sensory neurons. Ideally, the two work together so that motor activity is coordinated intelligently with sensory information. Whenever you encounter a dangerous stimulus, such as a hot stove, the sensory signal can be processed in the spinal cord *without* having to register first in the brain. The sensory neuron brings the signal to the spinal cord. The spinal cord, composed of **interneurons** that connect input and output, activate the appropriate motor neurons to remove the hand. That three-neuron relay—from sensory neuron to interneuron to motor neuron—is called a **reflex arc**. It has the advantage of prompting adaptive and possibly life-saving behavior without having to involve conscious decision-making via the brain. Subsequently, of course, the signal reaches the brain, registers pain, and makes us consider appropriate first aid for burns. But the great advantage of the reflex arc is that it allows the hand to be pulled away *before* the initiation of what we would normally call "thinking."

As noted, the cells composing the spinal cord are interneurons. The neurons that form the brain are also interneurons, whose function is the intelligent coordination of information about the world (gathered via sensory neurons) and action in the world (expressed via motor neurons). Brain interneurons can accomplish this intelligent coordination in a sophisticated manner, unlike the more primitive interneurons of the spinal cord.

Synapses and Neurotransmitters

To understand how neurons communicate, it is important to realize that, structurally, neurons don't actually touch. Instead, between any two communicating neurons there is a tiny gap. That gap, called a **synapse**, is the space between the terminal bouton of one neuron and the dendrite of another. The number of synapses in the brain is immense. Each neuron typically connects to hundreds of other neurons, which means that each neuron can form *thousands* of synapses. While we might find the number of brain neurons to be staggering (about a trillion, or 10^{12}), the number of synapses in a single human brain is greater by a factor of about 1,000, totaling about a quadrillion (1,000,000,000,000,000, or 10^{15}) synapses in adulthood. The dazzling intricacy of the resulting structure, the web of interconnection among the neurons, prompts some neuroscientists to say that the human brain is the most complex object in the universe. Strictly speaking, this claim may not be provable, but the fact that no one disputes this characterization testifies to the unmatched complexity of the brain. The supreme complexity clarifies why understanding the brain has been an arduous and extended pursuit, and why we can anticipate that gains in understanding brain function will continue for many years.

Within any single neuron, information is propagated as a basic binary signal—on or off—that travels along the length of an axon. An action potential is an all-or-none event. But communication between neurons has an entirely different logic. Rather than being all-or-none, the signal crossing from one neuron to another is a graded event. The signal can range from weak to strong. This is because the mechanism of communication across synapses also differs. Rather than being carried by a massive influx of ions, the signal between neurons is chemical in that it corresponds to the release of tiny molecules called **neurotransmitters**. Neurotransmitters are released from the terminal boutons of one neuron, cross the synapse, and are taken up by the dendrites of a second neuron.

The neurotransmitters that diffuse across synapses can be excitatory or inhibitory. Excitatory neurotransmitters increase the likelihood of an action potential in the next neuron in the chain, allowing the signal to propagate effectively. Inhibitory neurotransmitters make an action potential less likely, which can prevent a signal from accidentally affecting nearby neurons. Imagine, then, two neurons connected by a single synapse. The action potential in the **presynaptic neuron** travels down the length of the axon to the tiny knob-like structure called a terminal bouton. Boutons normally form synapses with the dendrites of other neurons, but can also form synapses with the soma or the axon of another neuron. When the action potential reaches the bouton, it causes the release of neurotransmitters into the synapse. Those neurotransmitters then diffuse across the gap to the postsynaptic neuron and bind to specific receptors in its membrane. If enough excitatory neurotransmitters bind to receptors on the **postsynaptic neuron**, it will fire. The particular level, timing, and mix of neurotransmitters (excitatory or inhibitory) determines whether the postsynaptic neuron will reach the threshold of excitation needed to set off a new action potential. Within a fraction of a second, the released neurotransmitters are pumped back into the presynaptic neuron. The terminal boutons have chemical pumps that reabsorb the released neurotransmitters so that they do not "flood" the synapse and overstimulate the postsynaptic cell. This enables the postsynaptic neuron to reset so that it can fire again with the arrival of a new action potential.

The discovery of neurotransmitters greatly complicated the scientific understanding of brain functioning. No longer could neurons be viewed as the straightforward biological counterparts of wires in electronic gadgets. Communication between one

FIGURE 8.13

A Synapse *Tiny chemicals, called neurotransmitters, diffuse from the terminal bouton across the synapse or gap, and are taken up by the dendrites of a second neuron.*

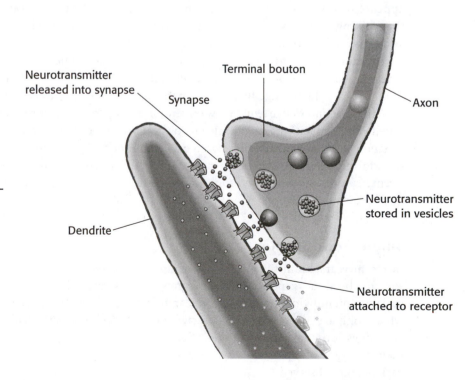

Neurotransmitter released into synapse

Terminal bouton

Synapse

Axon

Neurotransmitter stored in vesicles

Dendrite

Neurotransmitter attached to receptor

neuron and another is now known to be mediated by fast-acting chemicals, which vary in structure and properties. Of the dozens of different kinds of neurotransmitters, we will briefly consider two, **dopamine** and **serotonin**.

Serotonin regulates memory, emotions, wakefulness, sleep, temperature, and blood pressure. Low levels of serotonin are associated with depression, anxiety, migraine, and bipolar disorder. A serotonin reuptake inhibitor (commonly known as the drug Prozac) inhibits presynaptic pumps from reabsorbing the neurotransmitter. As a result, it increases the length of time that serotonin remains in the synaptic cleft, and therefore its likelihood of binding to the postsynaptic neuron. The drug called "ecstasy" is thought to cause a release of serotonin, which results in feelings of well-being, comfort and, in high doses, feelings of empathy. Serotonin receptors are also implicated in the mechanisms of other drugs, including LSD and psilocybin, the chemical agent responsible for the psychoactive properties of psychedelic mushrooms.

Among its many functions, dopamine regulates the brain's ability to exercise motor control. Dopamine deficits can cause Parkinson's disease, a condition that reduces a person's ability to control muscle movement. Dopamine deficits in the prefrontal cortex are also likely to contribute to attention deficit disorder (ADD) and to schizophrenia. As brain reward mechanisms, dopamine-producing neurons may emit a "teaching signal" for learning new behavior. Dopaminergic receptors control the reward mechanism for such experiences as gambling wins and insight (the "aha" phenomenon). Dopamine-sensitive neurons also control the "pleasure system" in the brain, mediating the enjoyment that leads to the repetition of behavior. Dopamine is released by such experiences as food and sex, as well as neutral stimuli that become associated with primary reinforcers. Cocaine blocks the reuptake of dopamine, leaving the neurotransmitter in the synapse longer than it normally would be. Dopamine also seems to have a role in reward anticipation, and may figure more prominently in motivating behavior than in rewarding it. Dopamine neurons fire especially strongly when rewards are greater than expected, thus having a teaching role in motivating future behavior. In this way, dopamine appears to influence the anticipation of pleasure—to control "wanting" more so than "liking." Low levels of dopamine also appear to reduce levels of social pleasure and thus are linked to social withdrawal.

In addition, serotonin and dopamine may regulate different types of memory (Kandel, 2006b). In studies of animals, serotonin seems to support "implicit" memory— those forms of knowledge that control habitual behavior, such as eating. Synapses that store implicit knowledge tend to rely on serotonin. Dopamine, on the other hand, is associated with "explicit" memory, which involves learning the characteristics of a particular situation, such as remembering *not* to eat certain foods. In humans, we sometimes call these forms of learning declarative and procedural knowledge. The point here is that different neurotransmitters—serotonin and dopamine among them—sometimes modulate distinct forms of learning.

Single Gene Studies

In recent years, brain scientists have begun to understand associations between neuron function and genetics. The emerging genetics research examines the effects of variation on individual genes. This research differs from studies in behavioral genetics, which compares the behavioral characteristics of people with known degrees of genetic relatedness on *all* genes. In studies of single gene expression, people are classified by their genotype of a particular gene on a specific chromosome, and the effects of that variation are observed.

Any single gene can have several variants or **alleles**. One gene that has been associated with deterioration of brain function related to aging is APOE (Espeseth et al., 2006). The APOE gene produces a protein that carries lipids to form new synapses. This gene has three alleles, one of which (APOE-∈4) is associated with **Alzheimer's disease**, a degenerative condition that leads to the progressive deterioration of brain neurons. The disease is manifest in steady declines in memory formation and retrieval, and eventually the inability to administer self-care and to recognize one's own family members. Its physical manifestation is the accumulation of fibrous plaques in the brain that disrupt the normal function of neurons. Although Alzheimer's disease cannot yet be cured, drug treatments can slow the progress of the disease.

Compared to other APOE alleles, the APOE-∈4 allele seems to be inefficient in repairing neurons if the brain is somehow injured. People with the APOE-∈4 allele are therefore more susceptible to reduced cognitive functioning, including compromised working memory capacity, in middle age. The effects of the APOE-∈4 allele are most serious in individuals with two copies of the allele. Fifty percent of these people develop Alzheimer's disease.

This section is not meant to suggest that cognitive variation is well understood at the level of specific gene variation. The intent is more modest—to show that bridges are now beginning to connect cognition to the function of genes. In some cases, measurable cognitive variation can be linked to a specific gene on a specific chromosome, and indeed to particular alleles of a gene. Those genes, in turn, may differ only by the minor substitution of a few molecules on a long chain of DNA. That such a tiny variation can be pinpointed and linked to measurable differences in cognitive performance is remarkable.

Brain Development

Brain changes associated with learning and development are strongly bound to the formation of connections between brain cells in synapses. Indeed, the structural changes at the level of synapses are crucial for learning, cognition, and cognitive development. The human brain is distinguished by having an enormous number of synapses. But, surprisingly, the number of synapses in the human brain reaches a maximum at about age three (Huttenlocher, 2002).

Blooming and Pruning

During the first three years of life, a child's brain undergoes a massive proliferation of synapses. This process is called **synaptogenesis**, or more colloquially, **blooming**. The result of blooming is that young children have many more brain synapses than adults have—more, in fact, than they need. The overabundance of synapses at age three is followed by a long-term reduction in the number of brain synapses—a process called **pruning**. Synaptic blooming and pruning are sequential processes, each of which is a normal mechanism of cognitive development.

Why should an overproduction of synapses be followed by a reduction? One way to think about the value of blooming and pruning is that the brain adapts over time to its specific cultural context. The brain of the infant is ready to adapt to any human culture. However, the features of any particular cultural context imply that some neural pathways are more important than others. One way the brain adapts is by strengthening certain neural pathways and allowing others to weaken. An illustration can be taken from language. Languages differ considerably in the sounds and sound combinations that are employed—sounds used routinely in one language are not used at all in another. Indeed, immersion into a culture's language typically results in an *inability* to produce or even hear certain sounds. If the brain does not need to detect particular sounds, then neurons and synapses that would be dedicated to detection and production of those sounds might be pruned back in favor of other, more culturally relevant, synapses.

Both synapse formation and synapse reduction are mechanisms of learning. When an image is sculpted from clay, the sculpture takes its form as clay is added to some areas and removed from others. In any medium, structure can be advanced by both addition and subtraction. In just this way, learning involves the addition of new synapses through the life span, but subtraction of synapses is also an important mechanism for advancing brain structure. The disuse of synapses leads to their resorption (Huttenlocher, 2002). Synaptic pruning extends at least into adolescence. In the prefrontal cortex, for example, synaptic density decreases steadily from the age of 3 to about 15, after which it remains fairly constant.

Brain Development and Experience

Synaptic blooming and pruning are two processes that illustrate how brain structure is shaped by both biological and experiential forces—by nature and nurture. The characteristic direction of change, called development, involves a complex interplay of nature and nurture (Nelson, 1999). The role of experience during brain development takes two basic forms. In **experience-expectant development**, experiences that are typical of a species stimulate the overproduction of synapses (blooming) and guide their selective elimination (pruning) (Greenough & Black, 1992). In contrast, **experience-dependent development** results in brain changes, including the formation of new synapses, that are keyed to the particular experiences of the individual organism. Specific experience gives rise to the particular synaptic structure of the organism, and leads to abilities that are not necessarily common to the species.

Experience-expectant development is especially relevant early in life, up to and including adolescence. This form of development occurs in any normal environment. Vision perception, for example, will develop in animals in any of a normal range of habitats. Likewise, speech will normally develop in any child within a broad range of social experiences. Extreme environments may interfere with experience-expectant development. Severe malnutrition and exposure to disease and toxins can interfere with normal development.

Extreme deprivation can also disrupt normal brain development (Davis, 1947). Such was the case with Genie, a girl who was socially isolated by her parents until she was rescued at age 13. Often strapped to a potty chair during the day and confined to a sleeping bag at night, Genie's rescue brought her into daily contact with a team of doctors and scholars who wanted to help Genie as well as to study the consequences of her isolation. Genie was eager to learn and eventually developed an expanded vocabulary, but never acquired the ability to speak fluent, complex sentences. Interestingly, her spatial abilities were excellent. A brain scan revealed a highly active right hemisphere and a subactive left hemisphere. The case of Genie is a sad illustration of how a lack of normal experience can frustrate experience-expectant human development.

Experience-dependent development, which operates through the life span, results in learning specialized skills of a particular culture. Every able-bodied child learns to walk, but only a few learn to dance the tango. Reading and writing are also experience-dependent: They will not develop in the absence of specific experiences that are designed to teach the requisite skills. Minimally sufficient environmental support seems to permit normal development of the experience-expectant type (Wachs, 2000). But *optimal* development may well depend on experiences that are not typical of the species. Schools exist in part to ensure the continuity of knowledge and skills that are essential to the culture and the success of individuals within that culture. Many of those skills would not develop solely through the less formal, everyday interactions that compose community life.

Brain Mechanisms for Learning

One crucial question for neuroscience is: How does the brain make learning possible? What are the brain changes that actually correspond to learning? For example, when you meet a person for the first time and you learn a name and a face, how is that information recorded in your brain's structure? Presumably this new knowledge changes the brain in some way, even if only minutely. That hypothetical change has a name—it was dubbed the **engram** by the famous neuroanatomist, Karl Lashley. The word *engram*, it should be stressed, is not by itself a physical property of the brain, but rather an abstract concept that calls for a physical mechanism. That is why Lashley (1929) could write about "the search for the engram." The engram was a logical necessity that begged for a physical explanation. In 1950, toward the end of his career, Lashley concluded that a mechanism for learning was probably not discoverable through research. Lashley was overly pessimistic: To a large degree, the mechanisms for specific memory traces have been elucidated, but the search is far from over.

When Lashley searched for the brain mechanisms of learning, he established an important fact: Acquired knowledge rarely or never could be identified with a specific location in the brain. This was certainly true for rat brains. Lashley trained rats to run mazes efficiently and later surgically removed various sections of the rat brains. He found that even when he removed large sections of their cerebral cortex, the rats still remembered how to run the maze. Declines in maze performance were correlated with the *amount* of area removed, but not with the specific *location* (Squire & Kandel, 1999). In humans also, specific knowledge is virtually never localizable to a specific neuron. Hypothetically, a bump on the head might mean that you lose a neuron, but you are not likely to forget your grandmother as a result. Knowledge of your grandmother is still stored in your brain, but is not dependent on a single neuron. In ways that are still not completely understood, knowledge is distributed widely over the brain. Your knowledge is stored and is accessible through a multiplicity of neurons and their interconnections. This distributed quality of knowledge holds not only for specific information but, as brain imaging studies show, it also holds for cognitive processes such as reading and mathematical reasoning.

Experience and Synaptic Formation

Research has shown unequivocally that learning produces brain changes at the level of synapses. The effects of learning on synapses first became evident in animal studies that contrasted rats raised in two different environments. Greenough (1976) placed rats in two conditions: One was the standard laboratory condition of living alone or in pairs in a barren cage; the second condition was a more complex and stimulating environment that encouraged rats to explore and play. The complex environment was changed daily, allowing the rats to explore a new set of play conditions.

Later the two groups of rats were tested on a learning task. The rats raised in the complex environment learned more quickly and made fewer errors, suggesting that they were "smarter" than the rats raised in more impoverished environments. The smart rats also developed more complex synaptic structures in their brains, with 20 to 25 percent more synapses per neuron in their visual cortex (Turner & Greenough,

1985). The neurons also exhibited more profuse branching and had a richer supply of blood vessels. The conclusion was clear: Learning through enriched environments changed the actual structure of the rats' brains at the level of neurons and synapses.

Synapse formation in humans is also a mechanism for learning, although the formation of new synapses is offset by the loss of pre-existing synapses, because the number of synapses in the human brain is relatively constant through adult life (Huttenlocher, 2002). Still, the generalization holds: Whenever learning occurs, synapses change. Learning changes synapses in two basic ways (Kandel, 2006b): The first involves temporary improvement in the efficiency of communication across existing synapses. This kind of change, called **short-term potentiation**, works by altering the release of neurotransmitters or sensitivity to neurotransmitters in the synapse. A second, more structural change involves durable strengthening of existing synapses or the formation of new synapses, called **long-term potentiation**. This form of learning requires the synthesis of new proteins to increase the number or strength of synaptic connections between neurons.

Synapse formation may well follow a connectionist mechanism (Huttenlocher, 2002). In connectionist models, the initial formation of synapses is random. Subsequent environmental stimuli strengthen synapses consistent with the stimuli and lead to the resorption of synapses that are inconsistent with environmental stimulation. Through feedback loops, the initially random connections become tuned. This pattern, manifest as the increased connectivity of two neurons that interact over time, is the central feature of the theory of the Canadian neuropsychologist Donald Hebb (1949). Paraphrased, the **Hebbian model** is that *neurons that fire together, wire together*. Computer architectures designed as neural networks have demonstrated that such a progression from initially random connections to tuned connections can result in intelligent machine functioning, even though this architecture is completely different from a standard serial computation that relies on a computer program. Connectionist computer models therefore present a plausible mechanism for how large masses of synapses can collectively acquire tuned functionality over time.

Learning and Brain Efficiency

As learning and development progress, the brain finds ways to become more efficient. We have seen one manifestation of efficiency from a cognitive perspective—chunking and automaticity lighten the load on working memory. As a consequence, performance in any domain can become easier and more sophisticated. Brain research has revealed brain mechanisms that support increased automaticity. As skill levels increase with experience, images of brain activity show a characteristic pattern: Areas of activity tend to shift toward the posterior portions of the brain. Simultaneously, activity within the frontal cortex becomes less diffuse and more anatomically focused. The apparent explanation is that, with increasing automaticity of skill, less executive control is required by the frontal cortex (Rivera, Reiss, Eckert, & Menon, 2005). Other brain lobes—parietal, temporal, and occipital—can begin to carry out the skilled activity with less direct executive effort. The shifting of brain activity away from the frontal cortex, called **posteriorization**, is a biological manifestation of increasing skill in the novice-expert progression.

Another change that accompanies rising expertise is that brain activity supporting particular cognitive functions becomes more metabolically efficient over time. Metabolic efficiency increases as competencies reach high levels in the transition from novice to expert state. This pattern was first detected when Haier and colleagues (1988) used PET scans to study brain activity as subjects solved problems on Raven's Matrices, a test of nonverbal intelligence. They found that *higher* scores on Raven's Matrices were associated with *lower* rates of glucose utilization in the brain. In other words, higher performing subjects had more efficient brain metabolism. These mechanisms—posteriorization and increased metabolic efficiency—display the brain counterparts to the cognitive process of automaticity that characterizes the transition toward expertise. The transition is marked not only by advancing knowledge and skill, but also by dramatic and enduring changes to the brain.

Exercise and Nutrition

The brain is a physical structure, so it makes sense that brain health and function are consequences not only of abstract information flow, but also of exercise, nutrition, and protection from mechanical and chemical injury. Like every organ in the body, the brain is responsive to biological nurturance and protection. Consequently, each person can make decisions that will promote the health of the brain and enhance and protect its functioning in the short- and long-term.

Exercise

Exercise has surprisingly important positive effects on brain functioning. Undoubtedly, ongoing engagement in cognitive activity maintains the brain's ability to support cognition. Recent research suggests that physical exercise may be even more important to protecting brain functioning (Kramer, Bherer, Colcombe, Dong, & Greenough, 2004). Aerobic fitness counteracts the normal brain deterioration that occurs with age. Researchers have found strong correspondences between aerobic fitness and the preservation of brain tissue density among adults age 55 and older (Colcombe et al., 2003).

Exercise contributes to brain health and efficiency through at least two mechanisms. First, exercise improves brain vascularization. The brain is highly dependent on access to nutrients and consumes much more energy than average cells in the body. Proliferation of blood vessels triggered by exercise can help to ensure that the brain receives a sufficient supply of blood, and therefore of glucose and other important nutrients.

A second mechanism by which exercise can enhance brain function is by releasing locally acting hormones called **neurotrophins**. Neurotrophins induce the proliferation of neurons as well as stimulate vascularization. Over the course of a lifespan, neurotrophin levels in the human brain tend to drop significantly. Fortunately, levels of neurotrophins can be altered by specific activities and lifestyle choices (Cotman & Neeper, 1996). Neurotrophins are released through cognitive activity, which is one way that cognitive engagement can help to keep brain circuits functioning proficiently. Exercise also stimulates the release of neurotrophins that can promote neuron development and the formation of synapses (Cotman & Neeper, 1996).

The relationship of exercise to brain health, functioning, and preservation suggest a rather direct connection between school learning goals and habits of exercise. Longitudinal research shows at least a moderate relationship between attitudes toward exercise developed during childhood and fitness during adulthood (Thompson, Humbert, & Mirwald, 2003). Physical fitness appears to be much more important to cognitive development than was typically appreciated. The data affirm what we ought to know from common sense: A healthy body promotes a healthy mind.

Nutrition

Good nutrition contributes to optimal brain and cognitive functioning. Ideally, every child would have regular and nutritious meals to promote their physical, social, and intellectual development. Unfortunately, about ten percent of U.S. households lack dependable access to nutritionally adequate and safe foods. The affected children suffer a range of negative consequences, including poorer social skills and lower-than-expected academic achievement in comparison to their peers who have adequate and nutritious diets (Jyoti, Frongillo, & Jones, 2005).

Let's look at how nutrients directly support brain development. One important component of brain tissue is the class of fats known as poly-unsaturated fatty acids, which includes omega-3 and omega-6 fats. These fats are somewhat delicate in being prone to spoilage through oxidation and tend not to be found in processed foods. Omega-3 fats are abundant in cold-water fish, however, which is one reason that salmon is commonly regarded as highly nutritious. Omega-3 and omega-6 fats are also found in fresh fruits and vegetables. Importantly, they are also found in breast milk but are sometimes missing from baby formula. The absence of omega-3 fats from infant formula may explain the cognitive advantage associated with breastfeeding (Horwood & Fergusson, 1998).

The body requires many essential nutrients in addition to essential fats, including vitamins and minerals. In developing countries, especially, iodine deficiency has negatively affected the brain development of millions of children (Kretchmer, Beard, & Carlson, 1996). Iron deficiency is also a common problem worldwide and is associated with adverse affects on children's cognitive performance. Some researchers have linked vitamin and mineral supplementation to improved academic achievement, especially among students who had a measurable nutrient deficiency.

Glucose, the main fuel for brain activity, is also highly important for cognitive functioning (Donohoe & Benton, 2000). Variation in levels of blood glucose has surprisingly potent effects on mental activity. Thinking and learning depend squarely on having an adequate fuel supply. The connection between blood glucose and cognitive performance affirms the importance of regular meals for thinking and learning in schools. Children who skip breakfast may well suffer diminished cognitive efficiency, especially on memory tasks (Pollitt & Mathews, 1998). They are also more likely to have poorer school attendance than children who regularly eat breakfast. Inadequately nourished children suffer debilitating consequences in their immediate ability to learn and, more seriously, in their long-term cognitive development.

Overextending Brain Research

Research on the brain is increasingly relevant to understanding thinking and learning, and to educational practice. But there are good reasons to be cautious in applying brain research to education. Scientific findings about the brain can easily be overextrapolated and, in the process, distorted (Fischer et al., 2007). Psychologist John Bruer (1997) documented several misapplications of brain research to education. He noted, for example, the unwarranted inferences from discoveries about the lateralization of brain function. From the original research on the specialization of the right and left hemispheres, there arose theories of learner "types" in which students were classified as "right-brained" or "left-brained." Presumably, students would learn more effectively if instruction were tailored to their cognitive preferences. But such theories were advanced with little or no data to back them up. To Bruer, the direct application of brain research to education is often a stretch—a "bridge too far."

Bruer also cited the discovery of **critical periods** as an example of research that has been overextended. Research on animals found that brain development included "windows" that required exposure to certain kinds of environmental stimuli. For example, a monkey deprived of exposure to light in one eye will have a reduced ability to develop vision later in that same eye. The general principle seemed to be that all brains go through periods in which exposure to particular classes of stimuli are essential for normal development. If the critical period is missed, then the brain could never recover fully from the missed opportunity.

The concept of critical periods seemed to apply naturally to human learning and to cognitive development. In humans, however, there is virtually no unequivocal span of development that, like a window, opens and shuts discretely. Only one cognitive capability may have a critical period, and that is capacity for learning language with native-like proficiency. The ability to hear and reproduce the characteristic sounds of a language—to speak without an accent—normally requires exposure to that language during childhood. But even the capacity for producing native-like speech is not necessarily bound to learning during childhood (McCandliss, Fiez, Protopapas, & Conway, 2002). The absence of clear-cut, now-or-never critical periods of brain development implies that a more fitting term for the concept applied to humans is *sensitive periods*. The term conveys that learning particular skills is best matched to particular periods of brain development. But if that period is missed it does not mean that there is no chance for recovery.

INTEREST MAGNET 8.3

Do You Use Only 10 Percent of Your Brain?

One of the most widespread and enduring myths about brain function is that we use only 10 percent of our brain's capacity. This claim implies that 90 percent of the brain is unused and presumably holds tremendous potential for much greater intelligence and creativity.

The ten percent claim is widely regarded by neuroscientists as a myth, but where did it come from? A few scholars have tried to identify the origin of the ten-percent myth (Beyerstein, 1999). The belief can be traced back to a statement by William James, the great nineteenth-century psychologist. James wrote popular articles in which he expressed a belief that people "make use of only a small part of our mental and physical resources." James's belief was later reinterpreted in 1936, when Lowell Thomas cited James as saying "the average man develops only ten percent of his latent mental ability" (p. 11). Thomas wrote this in the preface to *How to Win Friends and Influence People* by Dale Carnegie (1936). William James's identification with the 10 percent figure gave the claim instant credibility. The 10 percent claim has also been attributed to Albert Einstein, although there is no evidence that he ever said anything on the topic. The idea that we use only 10 percent of our brains seems to be a myth that "insinuated itself into our cultural storehouse of 'truths' through mere repetition" (Beyerstein, 1999, p. 5). It sounds plausible, and so has been widely propagated and widely believed.

Another source of the ten percent myth lies closer to brain science. Early research on the brain identified vast regions whose specific functions could not be identified. These were initially called "silent areas." Now, neuroscientists call these brain regions association areas, which recognizes their function as integrating information from various parts of the brain. The earlier term, *silent area*, probably led to an assumption that much of the brain was dormant and therefore untapped. Now we know that association areas, like brain regions linked to sensory functions and motor control, play important roles. Indeed, a large area of consistent neural inactivity would be evidence of pathology.

Finally, the ten percent myth might also have been inspired by the research of the famed neuroscientist, Karl Lashley. Lashley (1929) discovered that the brain has considerable plasticity and redundancy of function, and can sometimes function surprisingly well despite damage. The adaptability of the brain, both in response to physical trauma and to specialized demands such as musical performance, is a well-documented capability of the brain. Perhaps the brain's plasticity has been confused for untapped capacity. But the remarkable plasticity of the brain does not suggest that large regions are unused. In contrast to the ten percent myth, a more accurate statement is that skillful thinkers use the entirety of their brains to conduct their lives in ways that are rational and intelligent.

To Bruer, the application of brain research to educational decisions, including instructional strategies and curricular design, is fraught with the possibility of error. By examining the record of extending brain research to education, Bruer could identify several instances of misapplication, where the basic science was distorted and the educational prescriptions were unfounded. Bruer questioned whether the *direct* application of brain research to education was a wise strategy. He suggested that a safer way to connect brain research to education is to interpose a middle discipline of cognitive science. By inserting the connecting discipline of cognitive psychology—the base discipline of this book—it is possible to provide a more cautious and coherent interpretation of how findings from neuroscience can inform the design of education.

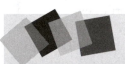

Learning Strategies

In this chapter we have considered the organization of the brain at macro and micro levels. At the macro level, we saw that the anatomical organization of the brain corresponds to identifiable brain functions. This principle operates at the level of brain lobes, as well as between the left and right hemispheres. More localized brain regions, such as the language regions of the left hemisphere, likewise serve essential and rather specialized functions. We also noted important processes at the micro level of brain function, especially the growth of synapses as a function of learning and the counterpart role of neurotransmitters in the synapses for determining whether a neuron will fire. Other molecular signals, called neurotrophins, encourage neuronal growth and synapse formation.

The discoveries surveyed in this chapter lead to implications for teaching and learning. Here, those implications are formulated as ten strategies that build upon our current understanding of the brain.

1 Give the mind cognitive simulation.
An extensive base of research has shown that synaptic growth in animals is a function of the complexity of environments in which they are raised. Sensory and social complexity promote neuronal complexity. Parents and teachers naturally appreciate the importance of a stimulating environment to a child's developing mind. Interesting and cognitively stimulating environments lead to the kinds of synaptic connections that will support advanced cognition as the child grows.

2 Have confidence in the brain's dedicated modules.
The human brain, as well as the brains of many animals, has a built-in capacity for understanding numeric concepts. Judgments of numerosity are precise for small quantities, and for larger quantities judgments of relative size can be accurately formed. Knowing that the brain has built-in modules for numerosity, the educator can teach with the confidence that the brain has a natural propensity to understand quantity. Mathematics teaching and learning can build on this foundational ability.

3 Develop brain efficiency.
Brain research has confirmed the reality and importance of cognitive automaticity. As the brain becomes more practiced at a skill, brain activation shifts away from the frontal lobe toward the posterior regions, a process called posteriorization. The metabolic activity of brain regions also declines, suggesting more efficient processing. These two changes, posteriorization and greater metabolic efficiency, are biological counterparts to the cognitive process of automatization. For the educator, these findings reinforce the importance of automaticity for complex thinking.

4 Appreciate the brain's ability to reorganize.
Research on those who develop specialized skill—violinists and taxi drivers, for example—shows that the brain is highly adaptable. Brain regions that support the specialized activity can expand to co-opt

adjacent brain regions. This adaptive response to real-life demands shows that, although the brain has a typical organization, that layout is flexible. Brains adapt to the demands we place on them, and that adaptation can support high levels of skill. This can give us confidence that as the brain is exposed to new challenges and demands, it will reorganize accordingly.

5 Remember that mechanisms of brain learning extend over years.

From experience we know that learning can occur over a time span of minutes, days, and weeks. Common learning experiences—meeting new people, reading newspapers, and attending lectures—lead to increased knowledge. Besides these shorter-term experiences, some learning processes extend over time periods of years. Studies of retrograde amnesia show that the most robust memories are more distal in time. This research suggests that certain brain processes continue to consolidate learning for several years after the knowledge is first acquired. We can appreciate that long-term immersion in a field of study has a learning counterpart in slow processes of brain adaptation. This time course also corresponds to our understanding of the time requirements for building expertise.

6 Exercise the frontal lobe.

The cognitive structure of the mind includes the executive functions of monitoring and control, a class of mental activities that we collectively refer to as metacognition. In terms of brain anatomy, executive functions are centered in the frontal cortex. The cross-mapping from cognitive category to anatomical counterpart means that educators can have confidence in the reality and importance of executive functions and can deliberately cultivate metacognitive functions in learners.

7 Ensure adequate essential fats.

Naturally enough, the mind's capacity to process information rests on the physical integrity of the biological brain. To function well, the brain requires the right sorts of molecular building blocks. This fact highlights the importance of nutrition to brain function. Of the many nutrients required by a brain, one class may be especially important: essential fats. Poly-unsaturated fatty acids, which include omega-3 and omega-6 fats, are rather delicate molecules that are found more often in natural foods rather than in processed foods. Perhaps the broad mission of education should include more careful attention to nutrition.

8 Promote exercise to improve brain function.

No one is surprised to learn that there is a connection between exercise and brain function. What does seem surprising is how strong that connection is. Research on animals has shown that exercise leads to increased vascularization of brains as well as to increased neuronal growth. Exercise stimulates the production of locally acting hormones called neurotrophins, which in turn stimulate the formation of new synapses. Exercise is known to be so important to brain function that among the elderly it may eclipse heightened cognitive engagement in its ability to preserve cognitive function.

9 Ensure adequate glucose.

The brain is hungry for fuel. Its primary fuel, glucose, is consumed at a high rate by an active brain. To a surprising degree, the level of available glucose in the brain has positive effects on cognitive performance. An adequate glucose supply can help the brain to do its work better, and more effective cognition is the result. The application is direct: Intense thinking must be supported by regular meals. For school children, ensuring adequate nutrition is essential to optimal learning.

10 Be wary of claims for brain-based education.

In an understandable zeal to apply brain research to student learning, some educators have overextended findings from neuroscience. Discoveries about hemispheric laterality and critical periods, for example, have sometimes been applied prematurely to educational problems. Educators should look to brain research for how it can inform the design of education, but should also exercise caution so that brain science is not distorted in the process.

Even while exercising caution not to overextend findings from brain research, we find it is possible to connect brain science and educational practice. Those profitable connections are certain to increase in the years ahead. During the careers of practicing and prospective educators, we will see many more important and exciting applications of neuroscience to education.

 **Conclusion**

The study of the human brain over the past few centuries has led to a deeper understanding of how the brain is organized, and how that organization supports the cognitive functions that are essential to intelligent thought. One entry point into understanding brain function is to examine its basic anatomy. The brain is organized into lobes and hemispheres. Its more basic functions include biological support for breathing and blood circulation, the capacity to process information from the senses, and the ability to control motor movement. But the human brain also permits higher-order cognition, which is largely associated with a thin layer of neurons in its outer surface—the cerebral cortex. The cerebral cortex, and especially its highly developed frontal lobe, conveys an amazing capacity for abstract thinking, complex cognition, elaborate planning, and problem solving. Normal human development and the ambitious enterprise of education rely significantly on the cerebral cortex and its frontal lobes.

The brain can be understood not only at the macro level of lobes and hemispheres, but also at the micro level of neurons, synapses, and neurotransmitters. At the micro level, specialized cells called neurons function something like wires in electrical systems by carrying signals and making connections. Each of the trillion or so neurons in the brain makes many thousands of connections, called synapses, raising the aggregate complexity of the brain to an inconceivable degree. Synapses, in turn, are complex structures whose function depends on neurotransmitters, chemicals that diffuse across the tiny synaptic gap to excite or inhibit activation of an adjacent neuron. Given these discoveries, the claim that the human brain is the most complex system in the universe, although unproven, seems believable.

This chapter affirms that brain research has important applications to education and has provided confirming evidence for the concepts and distinctions derived first from cognitive research. For example, the processes of automaticity and the executive functions of metacognition have measurable counterparts in brain anatomy and physiology. The human brain also evidences specialized functions, including an innate capacity for numerosity that supports central purposes of school learning, such as mathematical literacy. Moreover, the brain is structurally adaptive to specialized demands. It reorganizes its functions to support the requirements placed upon it, in some cases expanding those functions into adjacent brain regions. Brain plasticity also includes structural changes that occur over a period of years—a slower learning process that may contribute to expertise. Finally, habits of exercise and nutrition have measurable and surprisingly strong effects on brain and cognitive function.

The field of brain research is fascinating. We now know quite a bit about brain function and can identify important connections to our understanding of the mind in cognitive terms, as well as applications to teaching and learning. Perhaps more obvious than what we *do* know is that the brain yet harbors many deep mysteries. Future discoveries of brain research will sharpen our understanding of the structure and function of the human mind. Inevitably, a deeper understanding of the mind and the brain will convey powerful conceptual tools for more effective teaching and learning.

References

Abraham, C. (2001). *Possessing genius: The bizarre odyssey of Einstein's brain.* New York: St. Martin's Press.

Anderson, B., & Harvey, T. (1996). Alterations in cortical thickness and neuronal density in the frontal cortex of Albert Einstein. *Neuroscience Letters, 210,* 161–165.

Beyerstein, B. L. (1999). Whence cometh the myth that we only use 10% of our brains. In S. Della Sala (Ed.), *Mind myths: Exploring popular assumptions about the mind and brain* (pp. 3–24). New York: John Wiley & Sons.

Bruer, J. T. (1997). Education and the brain: A bridge too far. *Educational Researcher, 26,* 4–16.

Carnegie, D. (1936). *How to win friends and influence people.* New York: Simon and Schuster.

Colcombe, S. J., Erickson, K. I., Raz, N., Webb, A. G., Cohen, N. J., McAuley, E., & Kramer, A. F. (2003). Aerobic fitness reduces brain tissue loss in aging humans. *Journal of Gerontology, 58A*(2), 176–180.

Cotman, C. W., & Neeper, S. (1996). Activity-dependent plasticity and the aging brain. In E. L. Schneider & J. W. Rowe (Eds.), *Handbook of the biology of aging* (4th ed., pp. 283–299). San Diego, CA: Academic Press.

Davis, K. (1947). Final note on a case of extreme isolation. *American Journal of Sociology, 52*(5) 432–437.

Dehaene, S. (1997). *The number sense: How the mind creates mathematics.* New York: Oxford University Press.

Dehaene, S., Spelke, E., Pinel, P., Stanescu, S., & Tsivkin, S., (1999). Sources of mathematical thinking: Behavioral and brain-imaging evidence. *Science, 284,* 970–974.

Dennett, D. (1991). *Consciousness explained.* Boston: Little, Brown, and Company.

Descartes, R. (2003). *Treatise of man.* Amherst, NY: Prometheus Books.

Diamond, M. C., Scheibel, A. B., Murphy, G. M, & Harvey, T. (1985). On the brain of a scientist: Albert Einstein. *Experimental Neurology, 88,* 198–204.

Donohoe, R. T., & Benton, D. (2000). Glucose tolerance predicts memory and cognition. *Physiology and Behavior, 71,* 395–401.

Einstein, A. (1979). *Autobiographical notes.* Open Court Publishing.

Elbert, T., Pantev, C., Wienbruch, C., Hoke, M., Rockstoh, B., & Taub, E. (1995). Increased use of the left hand in string players associated with increased cortical representation of the fingers. *Science, 220,* 21–23.

Eriksson, P. S., Perfilieva, E., Björk-Eriksson, T., Alborn, A.-M., Nordborg, C., Peterson, D. A., & Gage, F. H. (1998). Neurogenesis in the adult human hippocampus. *Nature Medicine, 4,* 1313–1317.

Espeseth, T., Greenwood, P. M., Reinvang, I., Fjell, A. M., Walhovd, K. B., Westlye, L. T., Wehling, E., Lundervold, A., Rootwelt, H., & Parasuraman, R. (2006). Interactive effects of APOE and CHRNA4 on attention and white matter volume in healthy middle-age and older adults. *Cognitive, Affective, & Behavioral Neuroscience, 6*(1), 31–43.

Fischer, K. W., Daniel, D. B., Immordino-Yang, M. H., Stern, E., Battro, A., & Koizumi, H. (2007). Why mind, brain, and education? Why now? *Mind, Brain, & Education, 1*(1), 1–2.

Gardner, H. (1983). *Frames of mind: The theory of multiple intelligences.* New York: Basic Books.

Gazzaniga, M. S. (1980). *Psychology.* San Francisco: Harper & Row.

Greenough, W. T. (1976). Enduring brain effects of differential experience and training. In M. R. Rosenzweig & E. L. Bennett (Eds.), *Neural mechanisms of learning and memory* (pp. 255–278). Cambridge, MA: MIT Press.

Greenough, W. T., & Black, J. E. (1992). Induction of brain structure by experience: Substrates for cognitive development. In M. R. Gunnar & C. A. Nelson (Eds.), *Developmental behavior and neuroscience: The Minnesota symposia on child psychology* (pp. 155–200). Hillsdale, NJ: Lawrence Erlbaum Associates.

Haier, R. J., Siegel, B. V., Nuechterlein, K. H. Hazlett, E., Wu, J. C., Paek, J., Browning, H. L., & Buchsbaum, M. S. (1988). Cortical glucose metabolic rate correlates of abstract reasoning and attention studies with positron emission tomography. *Intelligence, 12,* 199–217.

Hamilton, R. H., & Pascual-Leone, A. (1998). Cortical plasticity associated with Braille learning. *Trends in Cognitive Sciences, 2*(5), 168–174.

Hebb, D. O. (1949). *The organization of behavior: A neuropsychological theory.* New York: Wiley.

Hines, T. (1998). Further on Einstein's brain. *Experimental Neurology, 150,* 343–344.

Horwood, L. J., & Fergusson, D. M. (1998). Breastfeeding and later cognitive and academic outcomes. *Pediatrics, 101*(1), 1–7.

Huttenlocher, P. R. (2002). *Neural plasticity.* Cambridge, MA: Harvard University Press.

Jyoti, D. F., Frongillo, E. A., & Jones, S. J. (2005). Food insecurity affects children's academic performance, weight gain, and social skills. *The Journal of Nutrition, 135,* 2831–2839.

Kandel, E. R. (2006a). *In search of memory: The emergence of a new science of mind.* New York: W. W. Norton & Company.

Kandel, E. R. (2006b). Learning to find your way. *Natural History, 115*(2), 32–38.

Kramer, A. F., Bherer, B., Colcombe, S. J., Dong, W., & Greenough, W. T. (2004). Environmental influences on cognitive and brain plasticity during aging. *Journal of Gerontology, 59A*(9), 940–957.

Kretchmer, N., Beard, J. L., & Carlson, S. (1996). The role of nutrition in the development of normal cognition. *American Journal of Clinical Nutrition, 63,* 997S–1001S.

Kuhn, T. S. (1962). *The structure of scientific revolutions.* Chicago: University of Chicago Press.

Lashley, K. (1929). In search of the engram. In physiological mechanisms and animal behavior. *Symposium of the society for experimental biology, no. 4.* New York: Academic Press.

Levy, S. (1978, August). My search for Einstein's brain. *The New Jersey Monthly,* p. 43.

Levy, S. (1999, June 28) The roots of genius: The odd history of a famous old brain. *Newsweek, June 28,* p. 32.

Macmillan, M. B. (1986). A wonderful journey through skull and brains: The travels of Mr. Gage's tamping iron. *Brain and Cognition, 5,* 67–107.

Maguire, E. A., Gadian, D. G., Johnsrude, I. S., Good, C. D., Ashburner, J., Frackowiak, R. S. J., & Frith, C. D. (2000). Navigation-related structural change in the hippocampi of taxi drivers. *Proceedings of the National Academy of Sciences, 97*(8), 398–403.

McCandliss, B. D., Fiez, J. A., Protopapas, A., & Conway, M. (2002). Success and failure in teaching the [r]-[l] contrast to Japanese adults: Tests of a Hebbian model of plasticity and stabilization in spoken language perception. *Cognitive, Affective, and Behavioral Neuroscience, 2*(2), 89–108.

Milner, B., Taylor, L., & Sperry, R. W. (1968). Lateralized suppression of dichotically presented digits after commissural section in man. *Science, 161,* 184–186.

Nelson, C. A. (1999). Neural plasticity and human development. *Current Directions in Psychological Science, 8,* 42–45.

Pollitt, E., & Mathews, R. (1998). Breakfast and cognition: An integrative summary. *American Journal of Clinical Nutrition, 68,* 804S–813S.

Posner, M. I., Peterson, S. E., Fox, P. T., & Raichle, M. E. (1988). Localization of cognitive operations in the human brain. *Science, 240,* 1627–1631.

Reuter-Lorenz, P. A., & Miller, A. C. (1998). The cognitive neuroscience of human laterality: Lessons from the bisected brain. *Current Directions in Psychological Science, 7*(1), 15–20.

Rivera, S. M., Reiss, A. L., Eckert, M. A., & Menon, V. (2005). Developmental changes in mental arithmetic: Evidence for increased functional specialization in the left inferior parietal cortex. *Cerebral Cortex, 15,* 1779–1790.

Society for Neuroscience (2002). *Brain facts: A primer on the brain and nervous system.* Washington, DC: Author.

Sperry, R. W. (1995). The impact and promise of the cognitive revolution. In R. L. Solso & D. W. Massaro (Eds.), *The science of the mind: 2001 and beyond* (pp. 35–49). New York: Oxford University Press.

Squire, L. R., & Kandel, E. R. (1999). *Memory: From mind to molecules.* New York: Scientific American Library.

Sterr, A., Müller, M. M., Elbert, T., Rockstroh, B., Pantev C., & Taub, E. (1998). Perceptual correlates of changes in cortical representation of finders in blind multifinger Braille readers. *The Journal of Neuroscience, 18*(11), 4417–4423.

Terry, R. D., DeTeresa, R., & Hansen, L. (1987). Neocortical cell counts in normal human adult aging. *Annals of Neurobiology, 21,* 530–537.

Thompson, A. M., Humbert, M. L., & Mirwald, R. L. (2003). A longitudinal study of the impact of childhood and adolescent physical activity experiences on adult physical activity perceptions and behaviors. *Qualitative Health Research, 13*(3), 358–377.

Turner, A. M., & Greenough, W. (1985). Differential rearing effects on rat visual cortex synapses. I. Synaptic and neuronal density and synapses per neuron. *Brain Research, 329,* 195–203.

Wachs, T. D. (2000). *Necessary but not sufficient: The respective roles of single and multiple influences on individual development.* Washington, DC: American Psychological Association.

Wolman, D. (2005). On the other hand. *New Scientist,* November, 36–39.

[9] Assessment and Individual Differences

Sometime during the elementary school years, or perhaps even earlier, a child takes a test for the first time. The child responds to set questions, and those responses are compared against a standard of quality (often right or wrong). Appraisals of response quality are then compressed into a single number. That one number, the test score, has significance that can seem almost magical because it is assumed to say something important about the child. The claims implicit in the number are not simple and straightforward, like the measurement of shoe size. Inferences from a test score are far broader because they reference the child's knowledge or capability in vast, complex knowledge and ability domains. The test score can be compared to the scores of other children, and those comparisons are widely believed to translate to true, meaningful, and precise differences.

An entire industry—the testing industry—has been built around this astonishing set of assumptions. The assumptions that underlie testing are so distinctive that they really constitute a theory of mind—a paradigm that stands alongside the cognitive paradigm as a major conceptual system. That paradigm is sometimes called the **psychometric model**. At root, it assumes that complex personal traits, including knowledge and cognitive abilities, can be measured in a way that parallels the measurement of physical qualities, such as weight and distance.

In education, the assumption that complex cognitive traits can be measured accurately and meaningfully is rarely questioned. The psychometric model is so pervasive that it may be hard to imagine what formal education would be like if it did not exist. Moreover, the psychometric model has tremendous power to influence life decisions. Decisions to classify children as gifted, learning disabled, or emotionally disturbed are all based significantly on test scores. Admissions tests for college and professional schools can turn a life course one way or another. Both academic and career successes hinge significantly on a string of test performances that build directly on the assumptions and methodologies of the psychometric model.

Testing is gaining importance in the world of education. Throughout the United States, public school systems are conducting reforms that are guided, if not driven, by assessment-based accountability policies. Test results are often assumed to be the most direct means by which stakeholders—parents and community members—can judge the effectiveness of the public education they support with their tax dollars. The rising importance of test scores places assessment in a new light.

Tests are more than passive measures of knowledge; they can embody, by design or default, what is important in education. Tests communicate to students the standards, scales, and competencies by which they will be judged. In this role, testing can assume tremendous power to shape the course of individual lives and institutions. This prominent role of testing raises a fundamental question: Does testing serve to advance the goals of teaching and learning, or does it lead to outcomes that run counter to the purposes of education? The answer to that vital question depends on the way test scores are used, as well as on specific qualities of the test.

To understand how tests influence education, the first part of the chapter considers the two most important qualities of a test—reliability and validity. Reliability refers to a test's ability to produce a consistent score. Validity refers to the *meaning* of that score—whether the score really does justice to the measured trait. We will see that test validity is crucial in determining whether tests influence the educational process for good or for harm. Although reliability and validity are foundational, they are only two of a large body of ideas that gives coherence to the psychometric approach. Later sections of the chapter present other powerful concepts that are widely used in both standardized testing and classroom-level assessment.

The purpose of this chapter is not only to understand the measurement of student differences, but also to apply that understanding to improve teaching and learning. Toward the end of the chapter, we will explore what the measurement of learner differences implies for instruction and sharpen a very important intuition—that different learners learn best under different conditions. Taken together, the ideas presented here clarify how the psychometric paradigm has the potential to work either for or against the most important values of education. Ideally, educators will use this knowledge to avoid some of the pitfalls of testing and, instead, use the psychometric paradigm to optimize learning for all students.

Reliability

We begin with a key concept in test theory: reliability. In essence, the **reliability** of a test is the replicability of the score it yields. To illustrate, imagine a badly designed measuring tape made of rubber. A stretchy measuring instrument has a basic problem: It will not give consistent results from one occasion to another; it is fundamentally unreliable. Note that the tape's unreliability is not simply a consequence of using it on multiple occasions. Even if the measuring tape is used only once, unreliability is inherent to the stretchy measuring tape because even a one-time measurement is not to be trusted. All measurements yielded by this instrument are unreliable.

The issue of reliability also arises in sports. In track events, for example, race times are more accurate if several timers use stopwatches. Stopwatches, like tests, can be used unreliably. However, in timing races, the unreliability is less a function of the watch than of the person holding the stopwatch. Variable reaction times, as well as inconsistencies in judging when the start gun was fired or when the finish line was crossed, all contribute to variation in judgments between race officials. Such inconsistency is at the heart of measurement unreliability. Test quality depends on minimizing such inconsistency.

True Scores and Observed Scores

Perfect reliability is impossible. Every test measures its intended construct only approximately. Imperfections creep into all attempts at measurement and make all tests less than perfectly reliable. The combined effect of various contributors to unreliability is called **measurement error**. One effect of measurement error is that you can never

FIGURE 9.1

A Test Result *We now know the observed score, but what is the true score?* [Photo by Jamie Stein]

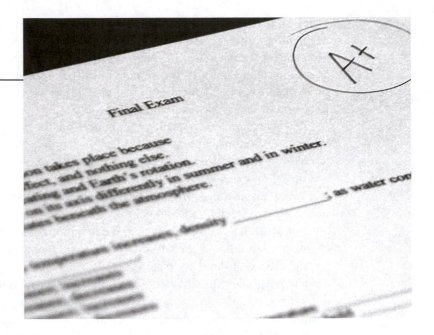

know for sure what a person's **true score** really is. The true score is what a perfect test would measure if such a test existed. In a perfect world, there would be only true scores, but in the *real* world there are only **observed scores**—the scores that are derived from real tests and reported back to students, parents, and teachers. Any college applicant may take the SAT or ACT test several times and get somewhat different scores on each occasion because each test result is simply an observed score.

The three values discussed here—true score, observed score, and measurement error—are all related in a precise way. For any test result, the difference between the true score and the observed score *is* the measurement error. Expressed as an equation, the relationship is the following:

Observed Score = True Score ± Measurement Error

The observed score indicates only *approximately* what the true score is. Moreover, you can never say whether an observed score will be higher or lower than the true score (which is why the equation has a plus/minus, ±, sign). In theory, 50 percent of observed scores will be higher than the true score, and 50 percent will be lower. How can you get a good idea of what the true score is? The only way to do so is to take a test repeatedly. In fact, the best way is to take the test, as well as other tests of the same construct, an *infinite* number of times. Suppose a college applicant took the SAT test an infinite number of times. In that impossible situation, the true score could be determined with absolute certainty. It would simply be the average, or mean, of an infinite number of observed scores.

Taking the SAT an infinite number of times would produce a distribution of scores for each person (Figure 9.2). We have said that the mean of that distribution is the true score. Scattered about the mean are the observed scores. Measurement error is what produces this scatter because measurement error is unpredictable in both size and direction. There is, however, a way to calibrate the magnitude of measurement error and therefore estimate its influence. Although on any single occasion measurement error is unpredictable, the symmetry of the distribution tells us that, in aggregate, measurement error has predictable effects. In particular, the **standard error of measurement** tells us how much of a difference there is likely to be between a true score and an observed score. The standard error of measurement is the *standard deviation* of observed scores around the true score. The term *standard deviation* is defined more precisely later in this chapter, but for now, think of standard deviation as the average degree of data spread around a mathematical mean. For the sake of test reliability, we want the standard error of measurement to be as small as possible. A high-quality test will minimize the standard error, even if it cannot eliminate it completely.

Confidence Intervals

Now that the single test score has been established as an observed score rather than a true score, the question remains: how *close* is the observed score to the true score? This is where that standard error of measurement can help. The logic of this maneuver is simple. It can be interpreted from Figure 9.2 that the observed scores will be within the standard error of the true score a certain percentage of the time (68 percent). The reverse is also true: The true score will be within the standard error of any observed score a known percentage of the time (68 percent).

To illustrate, say that an observed score on a test is 42 and the standard error is 5. If you add and subtract 5 from 42, you find that the true score is probably between the values of 37 and 47. That score range, 37 to 47, is called a **confidence interval**. It indicates that the true score will be within the confidence interval with a known level of probability, namely, 68 percent. To know the range of the true score with more confidence, extend the confidence interval to two standard errors of measurement. Now add and subtract a score of 10, giving a confidence interval of 32 to 52. This is a wide range, but by using two standard errors to form the confidence intervals, the true score will fall within that range 96 percent of the time. Confidence intervals specify a range within which the true score lies, and they do so with a specific probability.

Number of Items

Test questions, along with every individual task that asks for a response, are known as **test items**. They vary in quality—any given item might or might not offer good information about the trait being measured. In larger numbers, however, the test items collectively give more accurate information than a single test item. This is why it is advantageous to have several timers holding stopwatches at a track event; the more important the race, the more timers and stopwatches we want. Many observations are desirable for just about any judgment we make; more observations mean our judgments become more reliable.

Clearly, high reliability is desirable. The simplest way to boost the reliability of a test is to increase the number of test questions. To understand this pattern, consider what would happen if a professor distributed a major test with only two **multiple-choice**

FIGURE 9.2
Standard Error of Measurement *The distribution of observed scores can help us determine the probable range (confidence interval) of the true score. With a standard error of 5, the confidence interval for test score A (42) is 37 to 47.*

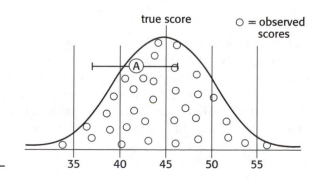

questions. Most students would judge the test unfairly short. If for any reason they happen to respond incorrectly to one question, their performance is only 50 percent, which might be a poor estimate of their actual knowledge. There would be fewer protests if the exam consisted of ten questions and perhaps none at all if the test had 20 or 30 multiple-choice questions. Somehow, students have a sense that somewhat longer tests will more accurately appraise their true level of understanding. This generalization has limits, of course: A test with 1000 items will introduce other factors, such as fatigue or exhaustion, which could undermine reliability. But, within reason, a larger number of test items makes a test more reliable. Fortunately, test length is a design parameter that teachers can often control when constructing their own unit tests.

The advantages offered by tests with a large number of test items seem to argue for the benefits of traditional multiple-choice test questions, and for other test items that require only short, **discrete** responses. The responses are called *discrete* because they do not involve lengthy arguments or explanations; they are short responses that are usually judged right or wrong. Besides multiple-choice items, discrete item formats include true-false items, matching tasks, and fill-in or completion items. In the U.S., multiple-choice questions are a dominant form of discrete item formats. As noted, one advantage of discrete item formats is their brevity, which means that many items can be included in a normal-length test, boosting its reliability.

A second advantage of discrete items is that scoring them is usually quite objective; they do not require the subjective interpretation needed for scoring an essay, for example. For this reason, multiple-choice items and other discrete item formats are sometimes called **objective items**. The items involve some subjectivity in the choice of content and the format of the item, but scoring itself is straightforward. Objective scoring helps to minimize one potential source of score unreliability—*scoring* unreliability. Stated the other way around, discrete items, such as the multiple-choice format, typically have high **scoring reliability**, which in turn contributes to the reliability of a test score.

Traditional testing, particularly testing that uses multiple-choice items exclusively, has been criticized for some good reasons. But traditional multiple-choice testing does have advantages. Many discrete observations, in the form of a large number of items, add to the reliability of whatever the test measures. Whereas traditional discrete item tests tend to have high reliability, tests that involve complex responses may have lower reliability because these tests typically entail fewer observations. Also, because scoring of complex responses is often subjective, achieving high rates of scoring reliability is difficult. But even if complex responses have disadvantages with respect to reliability, they can provide a richer and more complete picture of the measured trait. Another way of saying this is that complex responses can help to increase a test's **validity**.

Validity

Validity is the second cardinal virtue of a test. Validity is concerned with the meaning of what is measured. A completely valid test measures fully and accurately what it is intended to measure. A totally valid test is fiction, however. Validity, like reliability, is always a matter of degree. One major objective in the design of any test is to maximize its validity. The inferences that we draw from a test, and the fairness of those inferences for making important decisions, depend heavily on reliability and validity (Messick, 1995).

What Does the Score Mean?

CONSTRUCT VALIDITY. Validity is chiefly concerned with whether a test measures what it is intended to measure. One test might be considered a measure of reading comprehension, another of science knowledge, and still another of intelligence. These traits are intangibles, however—abstractions that are presumed to be enduring properties of people. They are all **constructs**, which play a prominent role in psychology and education. In fact, most of the abstractions presented in this book are constructs. Constructs are often quantifiable by degree. This makes it possible to associate a number with a person and believe that person has some "amount" of the trait that is more or less accurately reflected by that number. This is **construct validity**—the degree to which a test really does measure the construct it is said to measure.

Not every named construct is a real construct. We could invent a name for a construct such as "aesthetic intelligence," but there may be little or no evidence that such a trait really exists. Nevertheless, many psychological constructs do have considerable evidence both for their reality and importance. Moreover, theories built around, say, reading comprehension or intelligence present a basis for measuring those traits by tests. This points to an important consideration—the theory of any psychological construct is always a work in progress. As we achieve a deeper understanding of any construct, we can appreciate that the construct itself is in flux. Ideally, tests designed to measure a particular construct are revised over time to reflect current theory. For example, as the theory of reading processes improve, so can tests of reading proficiency. At any point in time, a test has high construct validity to the extent that it conforms to our best theories of that construct.

Construct validity does have a slippery quality—it is always partial and in flux. Every construct changes as our understanding improves through research, but in addition, every construct is embedded in a larger and more stable theoretical system, which links every construct to many others. For example, a test of reading proficiency would connect to such other constructs as phonemic awareness and word knowledge. Construct validity depends, therefore, not only on understanding the construct of interest, but also on knowing how that construct relates to a larger universe of constructs. At its core, then, construct validity is highly articulated to a theoretical system that includes not only the measured construct, but also other related constructs.

CONCURRENT AND PREDICTIVE VALIDITY. Construct validity is especially important because it serves as a kind of umbrella over all other forms of test validity (Cronbach & Meehl, 1955). Another important kind of test validity, **concurrent validity**, is evidence that a test measures a distinct construct within a theoretical system. Normally a new test is expected to correlate positively and strongly with other tests of the same or similar constructs, and mildly or not at all with tests of unrelated constructs. Consider what happens when a newly constructed test of mathematics achievement is introduced when other widely accepted math tests already exist. How does the new test relate to existing tests? Does the new test correlate positively with other math tests? If there is a high degree of correlation among the tests, then the new test has some support for its concurrent validity.

A complementary question is whether the new test correlates at low levels with tests that are intended to measure *different* constructs. For example, if the new mathematics test correlates more strongly with a reading test than with another well-regarded mathematics test, there may be a concern that the new test is not measuring the intended construct. The evidence does not support the new test's concurrent validity.

By comparing correlations of tests with tests of other constructs, both similar and different, test designers can look for evidence that the new test is tapping into the intended construct within a larger theoretical system. Patterns of correlation can support claims that the test is measuring what it is supposed to measure and therefore support claims about construct validity.

A related form of validity, **predictive validity**, is basic to test design and to the intended functions of a test. Many tests are intended to *predict*. When Alfred Binet designed the first intelligence test, for example, the primary purpose of that test was to predict students' success or failure in school. College admissions tests similarly are intended to predict college-level academic success. Whether such tests as the SAT actually do predict college success is crucial—if data do not support claims of some predictive power, then the test lacks predictive validity. Without evidence of predictive validity, the utility and fairness of a test's use can be challenged. Note one other implication: Lack of evidence for predictive validity undermines claims for construct validity. The empirical evidence for or against predictive validity can support or erode claims for construct validity—that the test is a valid measure of the intended construct.

The Limitations of Assessment

No test has perfect reliability or validity; consequently, an important goal for test designers, whether professional test designers or classroom teachers, is to raise validity and reliability as high as is feasible. The professional test designer can use technical tools to help provide this assurance of quality. Reliability and, to some extent, validity, can be quantified for prospective test users to help convince them that the tests are of high quality and worthy of their intended uses. A classroom teacher is not likely to have these technical tools at her disposal for designing unit tests, but she can nonetheless be aware of the importance of validity and reliability. This awareness can influence the design of homegrown tests to help make them more accurate and meaningful.

CONSTRUCT UNDER-REPRESENTATION. Of the two cardinal properties of tests—reliability and validity—achieving high validity is the greater challenge because it can be undermined in several different ways. Perhaps the most pernicious impediment to validity is **construct under-representation** (Messick, 1995). Construct under-representation means that a test falls short of representing all that is intended by the construct. For example, mathematics achievement might be understood to mean not only the capability to set up equations and to do computation accurately, but also a deeper intuitive understanding of mathematics, including number sense and the ability to estimate. Mathematics achievement might also entail the ability to think flexibly and creatively, to use mathematics to explore "what-if" scenarios, not merely to solve analytical problems. Expanded notions of mathematical ability are commendable and are rightly considered as goals of teaching and learning. But it is difficult to design, build, administer, and score tests that actually tap into these diverse aspects of mathematical proficiency. Often a test will fall short of the more expansive construct it is intended to measure. When this happens, the test exhibits construct under-representation.

Construct under-representation is a potential worry for virtually every measured construct. The constructs of reading proficiency, writing ability, science understanding, and knowledge of world history might all be quite broad. Curricular goals might include the ability to think critically and flexibly, to gather and synthesize evidence, to pose and solve problems, and to seek alternative explanations. Can a test really tap into every valued aspect of learning in a domain? Perhaps, but building such a test is not easy. Any given test is likely to underrepresent the construct to some degree, and sometimes it will do so by a wide margin. The potential for construct underrepresentation applies not only to tests of school achievement, but also to tests of cognitive ability, including intelligence.

Construct under-representation becomes more obvious as our ideas about what constitutes the construct develop over time. As worthwhile goals for instruction in reading, mathematics, science, and other subjects expand to include higher-level cognition and critical thinking, the potential deficiencies of tests become plainer. This fact illustrates the dynamic relationship between a test and its underlying construct. Linear measurement with an ordinary ruler is simple because distance is uncomplicated (setting aside Einstein's theory of curved space). By contrast, theories of cognitive understanding and proficiency in any ability or achievement domain are highly complex. As a rule, tests lag behind our best understandings of the constructs they represent.

CONSTRUCT OVER-REPRESENTATION. Up to this point, the focus has been on the inability of most tests to tap fully into their referent construct (construct under-representation). Now consider a complementary deficiency that can also undermine the quality of a test. That is the quality of **construct over-representation**. This problem is manifest whenever a test measures something *other than* the construct that it is intended to measure. A common example is a test that requires an essay response. Suppose the test is meant to measure understanding of science concepts *independent of* writing ability. If responses are written as essays, then the scores might be partly a reflection of science understanding, but also partly a measure of writing ability.

Some students can take advantage of their writing talent so that they can compensate for suboptimal conceptual understanding. There is nothing wrong with a test tapping partly into writing ability because the ability to communicate in writing might be part of what is intended to be taught and learned, and therefore should be tested. But if measurement of writing ability is *not* part of what is intended, then the test result might mask deficiencies in conceptual understanding, falsely suggesting that the examinee knows more than he really does. When this happens, the construct of science understanding is overrepresented because it contains elements of incidental, rather than central, personal traits. This unintended aspect of measurement is called **measurement contamination**.

Measurement contamination can arise from sources other than a valued skill like writing. For example, performance on some kinds of tests might rely on specialized skills whose value is largely restricted to test taking. The multiple-choice item format illustrates that, to some degree, success on multiple-choice questions benefits from specific strategies that help the examinee to narrow down the list of presented options. Consider the following analogy question:

DOCTOR: PATIENT (A) pilot: airplane (B) lawyer: client (C) painter: brush (D) jockey: horse (E) parent: child

Suppose you can't say immediately what the correct response is. What do you do? You could try to eliminate a few of the presented options to improve your chances. You might reason that, superficially, (A) pilot: airplane and (C) painter: brush seem implausible because they name inanimate objects. Likewise, you could set aside (D) as being unlikely. Now you are down to two options, (B) and (E). Using what is known as a **response-elimination strategy**, you have set aside three response options as being implausible. Even if the remaining two options seem equally attractive, there is now a 50 percent chance of selecting the correct response by chance. What contributed to those favorable odds? Your skill in using the response elimination strategy.

The response elimination strategy is a form of **testwiseness**. Skills that are specific to test taking can contribute to a student's score. In one provocative study, students were able to answer multiple-choice reading comprehensions without actually reading the passages on which the questions were based (Powers & Leung, 1995). The questions were similar to those found on the verbal section of the SAT. One common strategy was to select the response that seemed most consistent with the question. Students' ability to choose the correct answers was positively correlated to their actual SAT verbal scores. Whenever testwiseness contributes to a score, then the test itself has measured, at least to some degree, testwiseness. Here, again, is an example of measurement contamination. The intended construct has been *over*-represented because it has been supplemented by individual variation that is not part of what was intended by the measurement. Such contamination, whether minimal or large, is a threat to validity and so should be mitigated by those who design and administer tests.

Construct-irrelevant factors can creep into measurement in still other ways. The individual trait called **test anxiety** can be highly debilitating to test performance. Sometimes test anxiety is a reflection of worry over poor preparation for a test. In other cases, test anxiety is an enduring personal trait that seems to manifest itself in every testing situation, whether a student is well prepared or not. For students who are test-anxious as an enduring trait, test scores will be lower by some degree *because* of test anxiety. What is measured in the test score is partly the intended cognitive construct, but also partly test anxiety. Test anxiety can contaminate the score.

MEASUREMENT VARIANCE. Variation in test scores among examinees can be expressed quantitatively. Remember that *variation* is what we are interested in whenever we talk about measurement. If there is no variation, then there is really no point to measurement. Runners are timed in track events only because they arrive at different times. Individual variation is the basic fact that the psychometric paradigm builds on and tries to capture precisely. Numerical precision can be obtained because variation among people can be translated to a quantity called **variance**.

In any data set, variance is computed by first calculating the mean and then determining how far each data point departs from the mean. Each deviation is squared, and the squared deviations are summed. The total is divided by the number of data points minus one (n–1). The formula for variance is:

$$S^2 = \frac{\sum (X - \overline{X})^2}{n - 1}$$

S^2 is variance
$\sum$ means sum, or add together
X is a single data point's value
$\overline{X}$ bar is the mean
n is the number of data points

One interesting property of variance is that it can be divided arithmetically in order to understand what factors contribute to it. One example of dividing variance is splitting measured intelligence (IQ) into nature and nurture. The next chapter, which focuses on intelligence, demonstrates that behavioral geneticists have developed techniques to divide overall IQ variance into the proportion controlled by genetics (nature) and the proportion controlled by the environment (nurture). Without such techniques, questions about how much nature and nurture contribute to intelligence would be a matter of speculation.

Variance among people is infinite because they differ in an unlimited number of ways. If we have good measures of those dimensions of variation, then *each* dimension has variance that can be divided up. This book concentrates on such dimensions as learning and cognitive abilities, but there are many other dimensions, including the physical dimensions of height, weight, health, and life span. People also differ on personality dimensions such as shyness and aggressiveness, as well as measures of mental health. The world around us presents a huge amount of variance to be explained. Quantitatively, this problem can be expressed in terms of a fairly simple statistic—namely, variance.

Let's return to reliability and validity and see how it is possible to divide the variance of test scores. For any single test, the total variance of scores can be divided into contributing sources of variance. If we focus on test reliability, it is possible to say how much test score variance will reflect reliable measurement of some trait and how much will be measurement error. Variance can also help us to understand a test's validity. In the case of construct overrepresentation or contamination, we can say how much of the test score reflects some trait that is not part of the intended construct. For example, we might suspect that an essay exam in history is partly measuring writing ability. It is possible to administer a "purer" test of writing ability and then statistically estimate how much writing ability is affecting scores on the history essay exam. That can give us an estimate of **construct-irrelevant variance**.

Every test is contaminated to some degree by construct-irrelevant variance. Some sources of construct-irrelevant variance include artificial skills associated with the specific test format, such as the response elimination strategy used in multiple-choice testing. Ideally, the influence of this rather artificial strategy is small, but if it affects test scores, then at minimum it is a bit unfair to those less skilled in the strategy. As we have seen, writing ability can also compromise the meaning of a test score. Both testing formats—multiple-choice tests and essay tests—are potentially contaminated by measurement variation that is specific to the form of testing rather than the construct. The contribution of format-specific skill to test scores is called **method variance**.

Fortunately, something surprisingly simple can be done to reduce method variance: use *more than one* testing format. By using a combination of different testing formats—not just essay or not just multiple-choice—the method variance of one format will be diluted by the method variance of another. By using a combination of testing approaches, test scores are less likely to reflect a single source of unwanted variance. The practical application is direct: Test designers should focus on a full representation of the central construct, and then vary the method by which the construct is measured to dilute method variance.

Construct Validation: An Ongoing Research Project

As the most general form of test validity, construct validity is the degree to which a test measures its intended construct. One problem with this formulation is that our knowledge of any construct can change over time. The meaning of reading comprehension, mathematics proficiency, or intelligence transforms as the construct becomes better understood through research. Construct validity is therefore a moving target, shifting and adapting as our best understanding of the construct evolves. Because of this, construct validity is not a test quality that can be settled permanently.

A second way that claims about construct validity must be considered temporary and provisional is that establishing construct validity is always a matter of degree. To make claims about construct validity requires that an investigator set forth evidence that a test really does measure the intended construct. We have considered two basic forms of validity evidence: concurrent validity and predictive validity. Concurrent validity asks how scores from a new test relate to other measures of the same or different constructs. Ideally, the trait should correlate with some tests positively, some negatively, and others not at all. Predictive validity is shown by whether a measured trait can predict certain outcome variables. For example, an intelligence test normally would predict school success to some extent.

Evidence for a test's validity is important, but by nature it is always incomplete—a work in progress. Therefore, test validation is an ongoing research project that is never quite finished—not a task that can be completed once and for all. Test validity is established as a matter of degree through evidence rather than through definitive proof.

How Tests Influence Learning

Washback Effects

Tests are normally considered independent measures of something important about the individual. In the purest and perhaps somewhat most naive version of the way tests are supposed to work, they simply measure the trait without actually affecting the trait itself. In some instances, however, the act of measuring the trait can affect the trait's presumed value.

Consider the case of a child who wants to stay home from school and so feigns illness. The concerned parent might want to know if the child has a fever and therefore takes his temperature. This drama is depicted in the movie *E.T.—The Extraterrestrial*. Elliot, a boy who has befriended the alien E.T., is desperate to stay home from school so that he can take care of the alien hidden in his bedroom closet. While Elliot's mother is not looking, Elliot removes the thermometer from his mouth, holds it close to a light bulb for a few seconds, and then places it back into his mouth. The temperature nudges upward, enough to convince his mother that he has a fever. Elliot's mother trusts in the validity of the temperature reading, but that validity is compromised by the application of an external heat source. What motivates the utilization of artificial heat are the thermometer's anticipated consequences for Elliot.

School-based testing can have effects that are something like the thermometer example from *E.T.* If the consequences of any particular test are minimal, then there is little reason to manipulate the test results. But when the consequences of test scores are important—when the tests are **high-stakes tests**—then the incentive for high scores can lead to actions that artificially raise the scores and compromise their meaning. The anticipation of test consequences can feed back to influence the processes of learning and teaching that lead up to the test. These have been called **washback effects** (Anderson & Wall, 1993; Messick, 1996b).

Washback effects are potentially very important and can be either positive or negative (Cheng, Watanabe, & Curtis, 2004). One basic washback effect is **teaching to the test**. In an era when high test scores are consequential for school funding, and when teachers feel pressured to boost test scores, teachers will sometimes adjust their teaching and the curriculum to the content and format of the test. Indeed, greater conformance of teaching to test content may well be an explicit goal. The trouble with this approach is that no test is a perfect instrument; no test fully captures the range of knowledge, skill, and ability that is widely valued. More seriously, traditional tests tend to focus on discrete, factual information. Teaching to the test can therefore lead to an overemphasis on forms of learning that the test measures best. This sometimes implies a corresponding underemphasis of complex cognition. A second risk of washback effects is that they can taint inferences that are drawn from test results. We saw this in the example of Elliot's thermometer, but it is also true of high-stakes tests. Test scores are no longer meaningful in the same way that they were before the stakes were raised.

The wide-scale use of standardized tests for school accountability can compromise test score meaning. If the response is teaching to the test, then test scores can rise without comparable increases in underlying knowledge and skill. If so, teaching to the test might produce early gains that are at least partly artificial. Authentic gains in knowledge and understanding may be much harder to obtain. When tests are used for accountability, test scores often rise for a few years and then level off. These increases may reflect real gains by students in the valued skills and knowledge—that is certainly the hope. Another possibility, however, is that teachers and students are merely gaining familiarity with the test content and format.

The questionability of reported test score gains was widely publicized during the 1980s. At that time, John Cannell (1988) discovered that a majority of states reported that their students were scoring above the national average—a mathematical impossibility. This effect was dubbed the Lake Wobegon Effect, a term taken from Garrison Keillor's fictitious Lake Wobegon, "where all children are above average." Cannell's report created a media stir and was an embarrassment for the reporting states. But it was also an important wake-up call to the risks inherent in high-stakes assessment, not only the dishonest manipulation of data, but also the potential for self-deception about what rising test scores actually mean. Current federal policies reward or sanction schools largely on the basis of standardized test scores. On the eve of the current policy era, inaugurated by the passage of the No Child Left Behind Act of 2002, psychometrician Robert Linn (2000, p. 12) sounded a warning: "the Lake Wobegon effect may be largely forgotten; it is not necessarily gone."

Measurement Driven Instruction

The use of test scores to influence teaching and learning can be quite deliberate. When testing is openly recognized as a major driving force in educational processes, it conforms to a model known as **measurement-driven instruction**. Here, washback effects of testing are not accidental or incidental—they are intentional. Teaching and learning are understood to derive from the anticipation of tests, as well as the known aspects of what will be tested and how. Used in this way, tests can be a powerful lever for educational reform (Popham, 1987).

An important form of measurement-driven instruction, **minimal competency testing**, is intended to guarantee that students have at least basic skills, especially in literacy and numeracy. Most recently, minimal competency tests have been used as a screen to assure that high school graduates have learned basic skills. Given the opportunity to take the tests more than once, specific results can provide diagnostic feedback, which can be used to re-teach skills that are not yet mastered.

For better or worse, the role that testing can play in steering the process of education has prompted a reconsideration of what validity means. One proposal is that validity considerations ought to include the larger *effects* of testing (Messick, 1995). **Consequential validity** recognizes that part of the meaning of a test is the effect that it has on learning and, indirectly, on the social repercussions of test use (Frederiksen & Collins, 1989). For example, the social consequences of testing might include differential results by race or ethnic group, advantaging some and disadvantaging others. The introduction of a high school competency exam might result in greater numbers of low-SES or minority students failing to graduate from high school. This social implication would be considered one manifestation of test validity. Test selection and test use should always entail consideration of validity—the meaning of a test score. Consequential validity directs attention to the aspect of validity that includes the effects of test use.

Inferences from Scores Tainted

Let's examine how high-stakes testing can distort the interpretation of test scores and, in the process, have possible negative effects on teaching and learning. Testing tends to concentrate on discrete forms of thinking—on expressions of knowledge and skill in bits and pieces rather than in integrated form (Frederiksen, 1984; Martinez, 1999). The tendency of tests to focus on discrete knowledge becomes a serious weakness when combined with another limitation: Every test is limited in length. Normally, a test cannot ask every possible question to determine an examinee's knowledge and skill. Instead, tests *sample* from a larger domain of proficiencies. The assumption is that performance on a sample of items would reflect hypothetical performance on a larger set of proficiencies. To make this assumption credible, one important goal in test construction is careful **sampling** of that larger set of knowledge and skill. The problem is that some valued outcomes might be very difficult to measure. In other words, the sampled knowledge on the actual test and the larger hypothetical set of valued performances would be correlated, but not perfectly so.

Inferences from testing are therefore something like taking measurements on the visible part of an iceberg. Sailing in the north Atlantic, a ship's captain might really care about the entire iceberg, but getting detailed and accurate information about the submerged part is too difficult and impractical. He must be content, therefore, to make inferences about the hidden part of the iceberg from what is visible. In a similar fashion, a test score represents just a fraction of what we really want to know—how an individual rates on a construct that we care about. Only a limited number of observations are available—normally, responses to test items—but if all goes well, then inferences about the examinee are reasonably accurate estimates of the larger construct. Our confidence in this inference is conditioned by the test's reliability and validity.

The situation changes, however, when the stakes are raised. First, the specific content and format of testing assume the role of educational goal, and begin to shape instruction directly. In this more influential role, the test becomes a lever to move the educational system. This process is prone to fail, however, because the kinds of tasks used in most tests—those that are inexpensive to administer and easy to grade—are not designed to embody all that is meant by a high-quality education. Instruction guided by traditional tests can sometimes lead to the degradation of teaching. Moreover, the assumption that testing samples knowledge and skill from a larger and more valued domain of learning starts to break down. The visible part of the iceberg—the observable test score—no longer provides accurate information about what lies below the surface. Scores are no longer reliable indicators of a more extensive and significant educational achievement. Test scores lose their meanings, and inferences drawn from them may well be invalid.

What is the best way to respond to this dilemma? One simple approach is to reduce the extent of testing in schools. Another strategy is to construct tests that are more worthy of the importance placed on them, such that "teaching to the test" means focusing on exactly the kind of knowledge and skills that are valued. This is more easily said than accomplished, but the notion that tests could be worthy models for instruction has inspired considerable efforts to improve the quality of tests. Rather than consisting solely of discrete items that correlate loosely with a larger set of educational goals, newer forms of testing are meant to reflect more faithfully the knowledge and skills that are most valued as learning outcomes. These newer forms of testing do not simply reveal the tip of the iceberg that is a basis for extrapolation; instead, they are intended to represent the *entire* iceberg—to reflect the full range of proficiencies that are prized as learning outcomes.

Performance Assessment

What if tests could truly reflect the full range of valued outcomes for education? If that condition were met, then there would be no reason *not* to use tests as models for what should be learned and as metrics for whether educational processes were succeeding. Tests could help guide instruction so that teaching would link directly to the performances appraised by tests. Moreover, test results could be used diagnostically because specific performances by students would precisely indicate which knowledge and skills were mastered and which were not.

No test fulfills all these desirable functions. In the past few decades, however, there have been widespread efforts to construct new forms of tests that overcome some of the limitations of traditional testing. Broader functions of tests, such as asking for complex responses and providing diagnostic information, are often collectively referred to as **assessment**. In one important version of the new assessments, students actively demonstrate their proficiency through some sort of constructive activity, such as by designing and carrying out a science experiment. These tests are collectively referred to as **performance assessments**. Performance assessments are intended to have educational value such that "teaching to the test" is likely to lead to deep understanding and skill. Students may well learn a great deal while participating in the assessments. As embodiments of educational goals, performance assessments are more worthy of the time and attention of teachers and students than are less carefully constructed assessments.

Several different terms have been used to describe emerging forms of assessment. Besides performance assessment, these include alternative assessment and authentic assessment. All these terms have a family resemblance in that they refer to tasks that are both complex and significant in their own right. In principle, they have educational value. The assessments often require the *production* of responses by students. Rather than simply reacting to a stimulus on a page or computer screen, perhaps by filling in a bubble, students design, create, or otherwise construct a response. The thought processes elicited by the assessment are meant to be more complex than those evoked by more traditional forms of testing. Moreover, because the tasks correspond to meaningful instructional activities, such assessment has instructional value. Assessment might have real-world applications, which would warrant the name **authentic assessment**. Authentic assessment leads to products and outcomes that have intrinsic value. For example, students might launch a campaign to preserve a nearby open space from overuse or littering. Alternatively, students might design a useful artifact, such as a piece of furniture. Practicality and value are important features of authentic assessment.

At first glance, performance assessments seem like a tremendous improvement over the traditional, discrete item formats that have dominated traditional testing. But performance assessments have some drawbacks that should be considered. For example, scores from performance assessments tend to be less reliable than scores from discrete item tests. One reason for this is that scores from performance assessments are based often on fewer observations, as well as less reliable scoring of those observations.

Additionally, scoring performance assessments is likely to involve some degree of subjective judgment. Essays, for example, normally require human graders, although testing companies have increasingly supplemented human scoring with computer algorithms for grading essays. The automated grading process can search text for syntax that indicates complex arguments, and does so very rapidly (Burstein, Kukich, Wolff, Lu, & Chodorow, 2001). With human graders, scoring is time-consuming. Graders for large-scale examinations need to be trained and are normally paid for their time. In comparison to discrete tasks, complex performance tasks are usually more expensive to construct and administer. These practical considerations influence not only the cost, but also the issue of whether such forms of testing are even possible. Cost considerations become pressing or even prohibitive when applied on a large scale, such as in statewide or nationally representative assessments. On the positive side, the training and grading processes can be professionally rewarding. When teachers develop and apply scoring guides together, the need for reliable scoring necessitates agreement on criteria for separating levels of performance from poor to superior. The experience can provide a shared sense of goals and camaraderie, as well as a deeper shared sense of what counts as excellent performance in the subject area.

Classroom Assessment

Everyday Assumptions of Testing

One important insight for teachers is to see that the psychometric paradigm—that complex human traits can be quantified— applies to classroom tests as much as it does to large-scale standardized testing. When a teacher administers a unit test or simply a quiz, the results are normally reported back to students as a numeric score. The score is believed to be meaningful; a higher value implies, in some vaguely defined way, greater knowledge or skill. This interpretation assumes an ordinal mapping between the numeric value of test scores and the underlying mental quality—the construct that is of interest. The rationale for that mapping, however, is usually taken for granted; we make the inference without much thought, seeing past the magnitude of the test score to what it is presumed to mean.

The traditional psychometric model makes strong assumptions about the way mental qualities are structured. Specifically, it assumes that the measured mental construct is unidimensional. If we think about a complex skill, such as reading, we might imagine that different learners vary in their mastery of component subskills. But if an overall reading score is reported, that variation is set aside for a simpler model that assumes that all skills of interest cluster together around and along the measured dimension. To be fair, some psychometric tests determine if test performances are sufficiently unidimensional to warrant the practice of aggregating test performance into a single number. The psychometrician is motivated to find evidence to assume unidimensionality because it is a major simplifying assumption for mental measurement.

Enough is known about human cognition to understand that what the mind does is complex and dynamic. The measurement of cognition on predetermined scales should be seen as a somewhat peculiar convenience of the psychometric model, rather than a fundamental truth about the nature of the human mind. Remember that the mind constructs knowledge. What it knows cannot be captured fully by a series of responses to pre-established questions. The psychometric model, as remarkable and powerful as it is, can take us only so far in characterizing the mind. Tests can be greatly convenient as practical tools and can even lend insight into the nature of the mind. We must remember, however, their simplifying assumptions and not confuse the story they tell with the vastly more complex realities of the mind—realities to which no single paradigm can do justice.

Designing Tests

A sense of what is important, made explicit in educational goals and objectives, affects both assessment and instruction. This logic—from explicit goals to assessment and instruction—is strongly emphasized in measurement-driven instruction and in test-based accountability practices. If tests are to reflect significant goals of education, then the origins of those goals should be very clear. Ideally, approved content standards are generated through a careful consensus process by organizations of professional educators or by state-level curriculum committees. The standards can then guide the construction of assessment materials. The resulting tests can have a powerful effect on what is taught and learned, especially when test scores have important consequences. The specific knowledge measured by a test is not the only important quality of test design, however. Different types of tests promote different kinds of thinking. The cognitions elicited by a test are partly a function of specific assessment formats, such as multiple-choice questions or items that call for student-generated constructed responses. Still another factor in test design is how the tests are scored. The scoring guide used to evaluate responses—often called a **rubric** when the responses are complex—also shapes the quality of student thinking demanded by the test.

MULTIPLE-CHOICE QUESTIONS. Multiple-choice questions are usually designed and presented as discrete test items. Discrete items carry the odd assumption that a brief response is not embedded in a larger task. Each test question stands on its own. In fact, modern test theory is often founded on the assumption of **local independence**, which means that each test item is independent of all others. Exposure to one test item should not help or hinder performance on another item. Perfect achievement of local independence may be difficult. Most tests meet this assumption only approximately, and some item formats, such as matching terms to definitions, violate it openly. Still, this common presumption from test theory—that each item stands on its own, functionally independent of all others—reveals something important about the ideology of testing: Discrete bits of knowledge, held and expressed in isolation from others, together give insight into the mind of a learner. Such a way of thinking about knowledge could be acceptable to a behaviorist, but it does not conform to the way most educators think about either knowledge or the learner.

Multiple-choice item formats face three major criticisms. The first is that multiple-choice and other discrete item formats seem to assume the particulate view of knowledge. As a rule, educators do not view knowledge as a collection of independent bits of information, nor do they want to promote this kind of learning when they teach. The assumptions about knowledge that seem to undergird the use of multiple-choice items grate against a more organic view of knowledge that educators hold. A second criticism is that multiple-choice items are susceptible to format-specific testwiseness strategies, such as the response-elimination strategy described earlier. A third and quite serious criticism is that multiple-choice questions require only low-level thinking. There is some truth to this view; although it is possible for multiple-choice questions to elicit complex cognition, in practice multiple-choice items often do call for rather low-level cognition (Frederiksen, 1984; Martinez, 1999).

Although multiple-choice and other discrete item formats can be justifiably criticized, they do have significant advantages. They offer obvious practical features for administering to large numbers of examinees. In one common format, examinees "bubble in" an oval on a response sheet, which is later read by an optical scanner that can detect the presence or absence of responses made with a pencil lead. Optical scanning permits highly accurate and rapid scoring, efficient reporting of scores, and cost-effectiveness. Scoring unreliability is also minimized. These conveniences mean that the number of test items can be higher than it would be for a test composed of more extended responses, boosting overall reliability. These *psychometric* advantages are added to the more obvious *practical* ones. In summary, although discrete items, most notably multiple-choice, are favored targets for criticism (much of it valid), their real advantages can make them a legitimate choice in many learning environments.

CONSTRUCTED RESPONSE ITEMS. For the sake of simplicity, test item formats can be divided into two basic kinds: multiple-choice and constructed response. The term **constructed response** refers to a wide range of test item formats in which the examinee *generates* information as opposed to simply *selecting* a response from a list, as in multiple-choice questions. Of course, this characterization oversimplifies because it is quite possible for a multiple-choice item to require mental response generation so that the correct response can be selected.

The range of constructed response items is extraordinarily wide. Simple constructed responses include defining a word or, simpler still, recalling a word given its definition. Constructed responses can also be elaborate and complex, however. Examples of complex constructed responses include extended writing and artistic creation. These responses can elicit such psychological processes as problem solving and critical thinking. The possibility of eliciting complex cognition is one of the primary advantages of constructed responses. Compared to multiple-choice questions, constructed response items more often require the production of a valued complex response. They also more consistently require complex mental activity in order to generate the response. If there is any causal influence from the test back to processes of learning or teaching, then the higher demands of constructed response testing seem to be beneficial to educational processes.

Psychometric considerations are important when thinking about constructed response items. By their nature, constructed response questions usually require more time per item. The inevitable result is that the test elicits fewer responses overall from the examinee, leading to lower measured reliability. Fewer responses mean less complete sampling from the referent domain. For any single examinee, there is a question of whether the score is a fair and reliable estimate of what the examinee knows. Therefore, whereas constructed response items and especially performance assessment more clearly promote complex cognition and valued behavior, they also present challenges that prevent them from being an obvious substitute for multiple-choice items.

To summarize, both discrete and complex constructed response items have advantages and disadvantages. Neither is superior to the other in every circumstance and for all considerations. Sometimes, one format is clearly advantageous given the goals of assessment. Open-ended responses seem clearly the best way of assessing writing ability, for example; discrete items might be appropriate for testing students' mastery of a wide range of content or skill. On other occasions, the most prudent approach to the design of assessments might be to strike a balance between the two formats, while trying to bring out the best features of each. Discrete items, for example, should be designed to stimulate complex thinking rather than rely on simple recognition. Whenever possible, constructed response items should be paired with well thought-out scoring guides or rubrics (discussed below). As students learn to anticipate tests that elicit complex cognition, their implicit expectations will shape what they learn and how they think.

SCORING RUBRICS. One practical and important tool for administering constructed response items is a scoring guide, commonly known as a **scoring rubric**. A scoring rubric communicates the valued characteristics of a response and permits reliable scoring. Scoring rubrics can also focus the efforts of both students and teachers, especially when scoring criteria are "transparent," that is, readily available before a test is given. A good rubric states what constitutes excellent work and presents to students and teachers in explicit terms what is often concealed or assumed in traditional testing. Rubrics should therefore be as clear and unambiguous as possible.

Holistic scoring of complex responses involves separating performances into levels with descriptions for each level. The number of levels is typically small—somewhere between four and seven. Descriptions of each level provide a way to interpret scores. A student who receives a grade of "5" on an essay can refer to the rubric's description of a "5" and have some idea of the strengths and weaknesses of his essay, and how his writing could improve to make it more consistent with qualities of higher-rated essays. **Analytical scoring** involves evaluating responses on a more detailed basis. For example, analytical scoring might entail scoring an essay on three separate dimensions: the coherence of the argument, writing style, and the mechanics of grammar and spelling. The score for each separate dimension then could be combined to yield an overall rating.

Formative Assessment

In general, testing provides information about how well students have achieved desired educational outcomes, especially valued knowledge and skills. Traditional tests provide this information as a summary of what students have learned. The summary is retrospective in that it looks back toward what has already been achieved. Traditional tests estimate what a student has learned and, indirectly, the success of teachers and schools in fostering academic achievement. Such uses of tests are called **summative assessment** because they *summarize* the effects of a past educational experience. Because they are retrospective, they are not particularly useful for guiding teaching and learning during the course of instruction (Popham, 2003).

In contrast to summative assessment, tests and other less formal feedback methods can be used to provide information to teachers and students during the flow of teaching and learning. This version of student evaluation, called **formative assessment**, is designed to guide the efficient and effective match of ongoing teaching and learning experiences. For example, formative assessment can help teachers to realize that students are having difficulty with particular concepts or that students have already mastered the intended ideas and are ready to move on. It can also inform teachers whether particular students or groups of students are having difficulty and need extra help.

Formative assessment is a highly effective but underutilized method of improving learning outcomes. Black and Wiliam (1998) found that teaching programs that emphasize formative assessment commonly improve learning with an effect size of 0.4 to 0.7 over teaching that does not emphasize formative assessment. In this analysis, formative assessment was embedded in teaching rather than standing apart from instruction. Because formative assessment promotes student learning rather than simply evaluating its products, it is also called **assessment for learning** (Chappuls & Stiggins, 2002).

Formative assessment can be carried out in several different ways (Black, Harrison, Lee, Marshall, & Wiliam, 2004). One highly effective method is posing questions during instruction. Students' responses, or lack of responses, can provide immediate feedback to both the teacher and students about the students' level of comprehension. On pretests, unit tests, or classroom assignments, teachers engage in formative assessment by providing written comments on the students' work rather than merely assigning a letter grade or numeric score. Formative assessment can also include students' **self-assessment**, in which a learner appraises his or her own success in learning and adjusts accordingly. Self-assessment is metacognitive in nature. A related practice, **peer assessment**, involves students evaluating the work of their peers, providing feedback about the quality of work and how it can be improved.

Standardized Testing

The term **standardized testing** normally refers to the way a traditional summative test is administered. When a standardized test is given, the conditions are kept as uniform as possible to permit comparisons among scores. Instructions to examinees are prescribed and the time allocated for the exam is fixed. The goal is to present examinees with conditions that vary as little as possible from one person to another so that test scores reflect differences only in the targeted proficiency, not in the testing conditions. But while the term *standardized* refers directly to the conditions of testing, it also implies standard methods of analyzing the test data. Indeed, much of the "technology" of test score analysis and reporting arises directly from student performance on standardized tests. In standardized testing, we often find the most precise forms of the psychometric paradigm.

The most basic measure of test performance for an individual examinee is the person's **raw score**. The raw score is simply the point value of a particular examinee on a particular test. Raw scores are a common and acceptable way to summarize performance on both classroom-level tests and standardized tests. But by itself, a raw score does not provide information about how a particular score compares to the scores of other examinees. Without additional information, there is no way to know whether a particular raw score is about average, slightly above or below, or extreme in one way or another. In standardized tests, which commonly report test scores of many thousands of examinees, raw scores are usually converted to numeric values that are much more informative. This conversion is a **standard score**. Before describing standard scores, we will first consider the normal distribution, which is the conceptual basis for standard scores.

The Normal Distribution

There is a ready method to report test scores that compare a particular score to the scores of other examinees. The method capitalizes on the well-known **normal distribution** or **normal curve**. The curve, shown in Figure 9.3, has a bell shape that is familiar to most readers. The curve is derived from a mathematically determined equation, and so is quite precise in shape. But its meaning can be expressed in terms that are qualitative and quite intuitive. The curve arises from a recurring pattern in nature. Many measurable features of the natural world—such as the height and weight of people, as well as various facets of nature, such as air or water temperature—tend to cluster around average values. Extreme values exist, but they tend to be rare. These two patterns—common average values and rare extreme values—converge naturally in the normal distribution. The mathematical precision of the normal curve may not perfectly represent the true distribution of natural variation, but it is a very good approximation for thousands of hypothetical distributions. The normal distribution also characterizes natural variation in mental traits, just as it captures the variation found in the physical qualities of nature.

The normal curve is marked off in segments that, like the curve itself, are mathematically defined. The simplest mark along the curve is the **mean**, the mathematical average

FIGURE 9.3
The Normal
Curve *Average*
values are common;
extreme values are
rare.

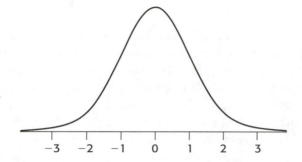

of all measured values. Because the displayed curve is symmetrical, the mean corresponds precisely to the peak of the normal curve. It is the value that is most frequent, also known as the **mode** of the distribution. The mean and the mode can be different, however, when distributions are not symmetrical. Other divisions along the normal curve are crucial because they tell us how far a particular value or score deviates from the average. These other positions are shown as **standard deviations** from the mean. The curve in Figure 9.3 shows markings at one, two, and three standard deviations above the mean and, correspondingly, at one, two, and three standard deviations below the mean.

What is a standard deviation? The easiest comparison is to think about it as an *average* deviation. If you know the average height of men, you might want to know: *How much taller* is a *tall* man from a man of average height? The standard deviation can give you a reasonable answer to that question. The standard deviation is determined by calculating how far all the data points deviate from the computed mean. Knowing the heights of every man in a large group, you could subtract the mean (the average) from each of those values. Those differences are deviations; you are interested in the typical deviation—or what is known as the *standard* deviation.

It might seem that the way to compute the standard deviation is simply to take the mathematical mean of the deviations, but the best way is a little more complicated than that. It involves squaring each of the deviations, adding up the squares, dividing by the number of data points minus one, and taking the square root of everything. The formula looks like this:

$$S = \sqrt{\frac{\sum_{i=1}^{n}(X_i - \overline{X})^2}{n-1}}$$

$\overline{X}$ is the mean,
i is the index, or counter, for data points 1, 2, 3, etc.
n is the total number of data points
X_i represents a data point

The formula for the standard deviation looks a lot like the formula for **variance** presented earlier. The difference is that the standard deviation includes a square root function. The relationship between the two is simple: Standard deviation is the square root of variance. We can expect a lot from this formula. The segmentation of the bell curve should divide it into intervals that are consistent across many different data sets. The formula for standard deviation accomplishes this function well, and so it is widely used. In fact, the mean and the standard deviation are the building blocks for understanding statistical data, including test scores.

Standard Scores

As computed values for understanding data, the mean and standard deviation are surprisingly useful. Their utility is most obvious when it comes to reporting test data as **standard scores**. Standard scores are widely used in standardized testing. SAT scores, for example, are reported as standard scores with a mean of 500 and a standard deviation of 100. IQ test scores are reported on a different scale, however. Standard scores for IQ testing are set with a mean of 100 and a standard deviation of 15. Even though these two scales, SAT and IQ, appear to be different, they are really the same—each places test performance on a normal distribution defined by a mean and a standard deviation. Performance on each scale is translatable to a position on the normal curve.

A handy feature of this system is that performance on any test can be compared to performance on any other test, even if the tested constructs are quite different. The key is to know what values define the means and standard deviations. On the SAT, a score of 600 places it one standard deviation above the mean (mean of 500 plus a standard deviation of 100). An IQ score of 115 is also one standard deviation above the mean (mean of 100 plus a standard deviation of 15). Both values place the score at a known position along the bell curve—namely, at the 84th percentile. If a score lies at one standard deviation above the mean, then we can conclude that it is higher than the scores of 84 percent of the population. This convenience of translation to **percentile rank** holds for any value of mean and standard deviation.

Figure 9.4 shows that the normal curve can be divided into standard deviation units, and that those units work for reporting both IQ scores and SAT scores. The percentile rank scale shows that any value expressed in standard deviation units, both above and below the mean, can be translated to a percentile equivalent. This holds not only for round values of standard deviations, such as +1, +2, and +3, but for also for fractional values. The scale just below the curve is labeled z-score, which is also worth

FIGURE 9.4
Standard Scores *Various scales are translatable to the common language of means and standard deviations.*

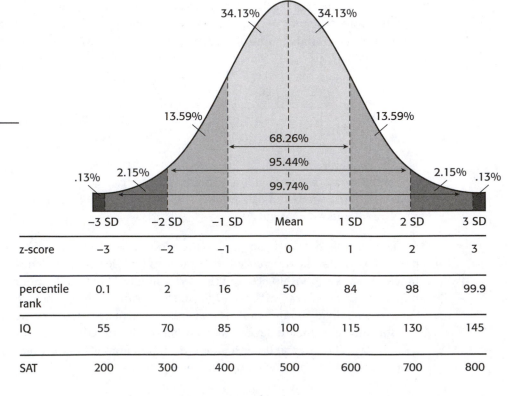

	−3 SD	−2 SD	−1 SD	Mean	1 SD	2 SD	3 SD
z-score	−3	−2	−1	0	1	2	3
percentile rank	0.1	2	16	50	84	98	99.9
IQ	55	70	85	100	115	130	145
SAT	200	300	400	500	600	700	800

understanding. Z-scores are important because they are the simplest of all standard scales, with the mean set at zero and the standard deviation set at one.

By now, you have probably figured out that the specific value for the mean on any scale is not important. A mean can be set at 100, 500, or 5 million—any value will work as long as it is stated clearly. The same is true for the standard deviation. It can be 15 or 100 or 1000; the defined values on scaled scores for the mean and standard deviation are *arbitrary*. What matters is that the values are defined for users of the scale score. Knowing the defined values of mean and standard deviation allows any value to be translated back to the common language of means and standard deviations.

Have another look at the normal distribution. It extends three standard deviations above the mean and three standard deviations below. Why three? The answer is that three standard deviations cover 99.7 percent of the distribution, which is adequate for reporting test performance in nearly every instance. This explains why the SAT scale extends from 200 to 800. This range covers three standard deviations above and below the mean, and therefore can characterize the performance of 99.7 percent of test-takers. Precision beyond three standard deviations is not really required.

The typical range of psychometric scales raises the question of whether performance differences ever extend beyond three standard deviations. The answer is *yes*; Performance on any scale can potentially extend out to four standard deviations, or further to five or six standard deviations. By definition, however, ability or performance at these "distances" from the mean are statistically very rare. Moreover, tests usually are not designed to distinguish extreme levels of performance. For the SAT to be extended to a value of 900 would require additional questions and tasks that would be irrelevant for all but a tiny proportion of students. If such fine differentiation became necessary, a better strategy might be to devise a completely new test specifically designed to make such discriminations. Such tests exist, most notably to measure very low IQ values associated with severe mental retardation. These tests look nothing like typical intelligence tests, but more like functional assessments of behavior. At the high end of the IQ scale, the entire logic for computing IQ is strangely reversed. A judgment is made about the statistical rarity of an intellect, such as Einstein's. Given a justifiable statistical value, say one in a million, that value can be translated back into an astronomically high IQ score.

Norm-Referenced and Criterion-Referenced

Scale scores are tremendously useful for making precise characterizations of test performance and for tying scores to a common metric. But the metric gives meaning to a score entirely by relating it to the performances of other people. It is **norm-referenced** in the sense that all scores are reported on scales defined by the performances (norms) of a group. Scores from norm-referenced tests say nothing about the meaning of a score with reference to the domain of interest—that is, what a person can do skillfully, or what particular knowledge an examinee has mastered.

An alternative way of reporting test scores is making a test criterion-referenced. The basis for reporting on a **criterion-referenced** test is not other examinees, but rather the domain of interest. A mathematics test might yield information about whether a student is competent in factoring algebraic equations or in determining the sine and cosine of a stated angle. As a general pattern, classroom-based tests are loosely criterion-referenced in that they determine whether a student has attained a degree of mastery over a particular content or skill. Classroom tests might have diagnostic value in showing which knowledge and skills were *not* mastered. Standardized tests, as a rule, tend to be norm-referenced when the results are given as standard scores that can make fine discriminations among examinees. In this case, higher priority is given to defining how students differ than to stating precisely what students actually know or don't know.

It is possible for a test to be *both* norm-referenced and criterion-referenced. Many standardized tests now report overall performance, as in reading, along with performance on subscales, such as vocabulary, syntax, and comprehension. When subscale scores are reported along with overall performance, this information on narrower aspects of the larger domain can be seen as linking norm-based reporting to more specific criteria. Likewise, essay scores might be reported on a numeric scale ranging from 1 to 5. Each numeric value, in turn, can be defined by certain qualities of writing. The numeric score might feed into an aggregate scaled score that leads to a norm-referenced scale, but the numeric value of the essay can also be related back to specific qualities of writing, and so is criterion-referenced.

Quantitative Research

This discussion about constructs and measurement leads us to the topic of research in psychology and education. In part, research is an activity designed to define constructs and to relate those constructs to each other. Researchers use a great variety of methods to gather and analyze data. Those methods are sometimes divided broadly into **qualitative research** and **quantitative research**. Qualitative researchers use a wide variety of observational methods that, at least initially, emphasize detailed description rather than numerical measurement. Quantitative research, as the name suggests, emphasizes numerical measurement of constructs, often drawing heavily on the psychometric paradigm featured in this chapter.

In the various chapters of this book, we have considered dozens of constructs. Constructs of interest in education include academic achievement, such as reading ability and science achievement. We could ask many different questions about what leads to differences in student learning. Do those differences arise from genetic causes? Are they related to socioeconomic status and its correlates of wealth and opportunity? To what degree do differences in the quality of education play a role? Do different curricula lead to measurable differences in what students actually learn? Such questions are as endless as they are important. Research can help to answer them.

As research questions are posed, their terms must be defined; that is, the constructs must be **operationalized** to say exactly how they will be measured. We might agree that social class is important, but as a research construct we must specify how to measure it. Here is where the conceptual machinery of the psychometric model can help. If we see the construct as measurable on a continuous scale, we can look to the best current theory to determine how to measure that construct. Theory can inform the research design to ensure that the measurement of the construct is valid from the start. Techniques to assess reliability can also be employed. In other words, the conceptual technologies of assessment can be tremendously useful in measuring constructs that are central to the research.

Descriptive analysis is one form of research where the goal might be simply to state factual information, such as whether girls or boys have higher mathematics scores, or whether they differ in reading ability. The point is to describe—to understand the facts of a situation. A **correlational study** takes the analysis further into quantitative precision, linking variables by computing their degree of association.

Associations between constructs can be presented as correlations that range from -1 to $+1$, with zero indicating no correlation at all. We might expect an intelligence test to predict school grades, for example, but not perfectly. A correlation can pin a number on the degree of relationship between measured intelligence and school grades at, say, $+0.4$.

A different form of research seeks to establish causal relationships between variables. This is important when comparing different teaching methods or curricula to understand which method will produce the best learning outcomes. The ideal way to establish causal connections is to use **experimentation**, which entails **random assignment** of people or groups to one condition or another. In research designed to test the effectiveness of a new drug, patients are randomly assigned to a **treatment group** , which receives the new drug, and a **control group**, which does not. The advantage of random assignment is that, on average, there will be no net differences—such as in cognitive ability, prior knowledge, or health—between treatment and control groups. If a new curriculum produces superior learning in the treatment group as compared to the control group, there is no reason to think that the advantage was caused by anything other than the new curriculum.

By taking advantage of random assignment, experimentation can have compelling benefits. Most importantly, it allows us to infer what caused the eventual differences between groups. This benefit is so compelling that it has led to renewed interest in using experimental methods in educational research. This does not deny potential problems in actually *doing* experimental research on student learning. Parents, teachers, or students might object to randomization on the grounds of unfairness or inconvenience. In some cases, these concerns may make random assignment unfeasible. Under these conditions, the treatment and control groups should be composed as similarly as possible. Nonetheless, randomized experimentation is now considered by some researchers and policymakers in education to be the "gold standard" for research.

When comparing treatment and control groups, the researcher's primary concern is whether there is a significant difference between the two. The concern is not simply whether there is a numeric difference in an outcome of interest, such as learning. Randomization does not guarantee that the groups are precisely equivalent on every variable, but it does bring those differences into some kind of statistical control. Differences in mean scores between treatment and control groups can still arise from random differences in students that compose each group, despite the unbiased technique of randomization. The chief concern is whether the differences are **statistically significant**. Tests of statistical significance can help determine whether the differences between groups are real, rather than simply the result of chance.

We might want to know more than just whether there is a *difference* between groups. We might want to know *how large* that difference is. Statistics permit this kind of analysis, too, in estimates of **effect size**. Effect size tells us the magnitude of benefit provided by the treatment in comparison to the control. It does so by comparing the treatment and control groups as two different distributions. Effect size is calculated in standard deviation units. An effect size of 1, for example, indicates an impressive benefit. It means that the treatment (say, a new curriculum) produced a learning advantage equivalent to one standard deviation above the mean of the control group. Here we see that the language of means and standard deviations extends beyond simply describing the performance of any student and group. It can also be used as a research tool to compare different curricular or instructional approaches in their ability to produce a desirable effect, such as improved student learning.

Education and Individual Differences

The vivid reality of differences between students both complicates teaching and makes it exciting. Students differ along multiple dimensions. Many of those citable differences are relevant to educational decisions and planning. Some dimensions of difference are broadly important: age, level of maturation, background knowledge, English language proficiency, and general intelligence. Other dimensions of difference are relevant to instructional decisions some of the time, but not always. These include gender, ethnicity, and the presence of a disability. Still other differences are *potentially* relevant: socio-economic level, personality, and mood.

In an ideal world, every teacher would know how to respond sensitively and effectively to the unique combination of qualities that each student presents. In a regular classroom, though, this is difficult—or perhaps impossible. Teachers must try to understand and respond to large numbers of students, typically twenty or more. Every teacher must somehow calibrate to the class as a whole, as well as to subgroups, and teach accordingly. Responsiveness to the unique needs of individual students is intermittent, and only if there is no great cost to the class as a whole.

What would happen, however, if each student were tutored one-on-one? Would individualized instruction result in deeper and more extensive learning? Almost certainly, yes. A skillful tutor can respond to the precise pace of the individual learner, posing questions and presenting ideas that respond dynamically to the child. Precision at this level is not possible with a **student-teacher ratio** of 20:1 or 30:1, although somewhat smaller class sizes of about 15:1 can produce superior learning (Resnick, 2003). This oversimplified characterization of group learning ignores the potential for discourse that is absent, or different, in one-on-one instruction (O'Donnell, 2006). Nevertheless, we generally can expect the heightened responsiveness to individual learner characteristics that is possible with skilled tutoring to result in better learning outcomes than occur in classroom-based instruction.

Benjamin Bloom estimated the relative benefit of one-on-one tutoring in comparison to instruction in a typical classroom. Bloom (1984) put the benefit at two sigma, which is an effect size equivalent to two standard deviations above the mean. Bloom called the advantage of tutoring the **two-sigma effect**. This estimate was more than an interesting observation; for Bloom, it was a benchmark representing a pedagogical ideal that produced maximal learning. No other approach, he proposed, could exceed two sigma—only approach it. Even if this is only approximately true, two-sigma is a handy guide. Greater sensitivity to student differences, better instructional quality, better materials, and more effective curricula should be expected produce a measurable effect—an improvement over other alternatives. Those effects can be measured in units of effect size. Do data support Bloom's claim that two-sigma is the maximum we can hope for? The basic answer seems to be *yes*. In educational research, an effect size of 1 is unusually large. More typical effect sizes for improved curricula and teaching approaches hover around +.3, and +.5. These can be statistically significant improvements, yet they are modest compared to the powerful effects expressed in the two-sigma ideal.

Ability Grouping

Knowledge and ability are among the most important qualities for differentiating instruction. Naturally, instruction must take into account what a student already knows. Teachers must respond not only to students' entering knowledge, but also to their pace of learning: Some students learn faster than others do. A teacher's responsiveness to students' prior knowledge and efficiency is the most basic way that student differences are taken into account. Yet variation within a typical classroom means that responsiveness to those student characteristics can only be approximate.

Teachers can respond to variation by establishing groups of students who have similar ability levels. The obvious rationale for **ability grouping** is that teachers can teach more appropriately to the needs of similar groups than to the larger class. Ability grouping is common in education, especially in clustering elementary school students by reading ability. The approach makes sense: Children who already know how to decode can concentrate on higher-level reading skills such as comprehension and interpretation. Less able readers can work on skills not yet mastered. Ability grouping is also common in mathematics, especially during middle school and high school. Indeed, ability grouping proceeds apace during the high school years with the formation of "tracks," which are sometimes rationalized by presumed differences in career goals, in addition to whatever pedagogical benefits might arise from grouping students together homogeneously.

Despite its apparent benefits, ability grouping has been controversial because of concerns about equity. The main concern is that placement in an ability group in the early grades tends to be solidified in subsequent years. In other words, initial placements tend to evolve into durable pathways, which constitute **tracking**. Tracking is troubling because it tends to be very stable. In principle, children can change tracks as their abilities and achievements change relative to peers, but in reality shifting up or down is unlikely. Compounding the concern with tracking is that racial and ethnic groups are often unequally represented within tracks, raising questions of possible bias inherent in tracking as well as the ominous possibility that societal inequalities are reinforced by the educational system.

Besides serious equity concerns, there is a question of whether ability grouping really works. The issue is not simply whether ability grouping conveys educational benefits, but benefits for *whom*. Generally, lower-ability students seem to be harmed somewhat by ability grouping. The optimistic belief that greater consistency of ability leads to more focused instruction, and therefore to greater gains in learning, appears to be unfounded. Instead, lower-ability students learn less when higher-ability students are siphoned off and placed in a group of their own. In heterogeneous groups that include both high- and low-ability students, lower-ability students benefit substantially. Research shows that high-ability students benefit from ability grouping to a modest degree or not at all. Opponents of ability grouping can therefore cite data showing that the practice undermines the learning of the lower-ability students and provides at best modest benefits to students of higher ability.

Special Education

One important instance of adapting instruction to individual differences is special education, which is a programmatic attempt to provide instruction to students for whom regular instruction is not entirely appropriate. Special education students are usually identified by disabilities that are directly related to learning (such as a developmental delay), or indirectly related (such as a sensory impairment), or for whom the physical environment of the school is not optimally structured (often due to a physical disability).

The U.S. federal government provides funding to support special education services in public schools. This funding is contingent on the identification of students' needs by special education category, shown in Table 9.1. In addition to allocating funds

TABLE 9.I Special Education Categories.

Disability	Percentage of students served
Specific learning disabilities	49.2
Speech or language impairments	18.6
Mental retardation	10.3
Emotional disturbance	8.1
Multiple disabilities	2.2
Hearing impairments	1.2
Orthopedic impairments	1.3
Other health impairments	5.8
Visual impairments	0.4
Autism	1.7
Deaf-blindness	0.0
Traumatic brain injury	0.4
Developmental delay	0.8
All disabilities	100.0

[Twenty-Fifth Annual Report to Congress on the Implementation of the Individuals with Disabilities Education Act]: (Figure 1–20)]

and specifying criteria for the identification of special education students, federal laws mandate that all states and local school districts must provide a free and appropriate education for all students. These laws—Public Law 94-142 and its successor, IDEA (Individual with Disabilities Education Act)—place on public schools a legal responsibility to respond appropriately to the educational needs of every child.

The special education category far larger than all the others in the number of children served is **learning disabilities**, sometimes referred to as "specific learning disabilities." Learning disabilities are disorders of basic cognitive processes that interfere with learning, especially the symbol systems of language and mathematics. Traditionally, learning disabilities have been diagnosed by the co-occurrence of two conditions: intelligence in the normal range and lower-than-expected ability in a specific area of cognitive functioning. The most common area of cognitive deficit is in reading, a condition that identifies the learning disability known as **dyslexia**. As a practical matter, dyslexia has been identified by a discrepancy between general cognitive functioning (normal-range IQ) and low functioning in reading. Often that discrepancy must reach a specified magnitude before the classification of learning disability can be made.

Learning disability subcategories besides dyslexia include **dyscalculia**, which is targeted difficulty in mathematics, and **dyspraxia**, a disorder that compromises a person's ability to coordinate bodily movements in an orderly fashion to obtain a goal. As with dyslexia, dyscalculia and dyspraxia are manifested against a backdrop of normal cognitive functioning. This brings us to the presumed cause of learning disabilities, which is a local impairment of brain function. Localized brain abnormalities are thought to produce the specific cognitive processing deficits (Katzir & Paré-Blagoev, 2006). Historically, however, the ascribed origin of learning disabilities as localized brain abnormalities has been mostly a matter of conjecture rather than of conclusions drawn from data.

In addition to learning disabilities, special education categories include mental retardation (developmental delay), behavioral/emotional disorders, hearing impairments, visual impairments, physical disabilities, autism, and "other" health impairments, including chronic diseases. Interestingly, **attention deficit disorder (ADD)**—abnormal difficulty in sustaining attentional focus—and **hyperactivity**—persistent physical activity that interferes with school learning—are not official special education categories as defined by the federal government. Students with ADD or hyperactivity, or their conjunction ADHD, may be classified in the catchall "other" category. Naturally, the most apt teaching approach in special education must attend to the specific disability and the specific child. For this reason, federal requirements include the construction of an **individualized educational program (IEP)** for all special education students. An IEP details annual goals for each student, special education services to be provided, and measures of the progress toward those goals.

Aptitude-Treatment Interactions: ATIs

This chapter is about differences among learners—both the measurement of differences and the adaptation of instruction to those differences so as to optimize learning. This second purpose—adaptation to student differences—is based on the important assumption that different students learn optimally under different conditions. Teachers know that an approach that works well for one student may not work well, or at all, for another. This intuition, that instruction should be adapted to student characteristics, is one that teachers live by as part of their daily professional practice. The purpose of this section is to present that basic pedagogical intuition in more formal terms. The model that formalizes these ideas is known as **aptitude-treatment interactions (ATIs)**.

What Is an Aptitude?

The first concept to clarify in the ATI model is the meaning of **aptitude**. As a starting point, we can think about aptitude as general cognitive ability. Sometimes we say that a student has high aptitude, which is roughly equivalent to intelligence. When the word *aptitude* is used in this way, we expect those with high aptitudes to perform more successfully than those with low aptitudes. But *aptitude* has a secondary meaning, which is closer to *fit*. For example, when a student has a knack for understanding how machines work, that may indicate an aptitude for engineering.

Within the ATI framework, *aptitude* has a very broad meaning (Snow, 1992). It can mean *any* difference that can help predict valued outcomes, including learning. Aptitude can refer to general intelligence, but it can also refer to more focused kinds of cognitive abilities, such as verbal or spatial ability. Personality differences can also be aptitudes. We know, for example, that the **need for achievement** is a good predictor of academic success. Other broad personality qualities, such as extraversion or introversion, may be related to learning outcomes. But those outcomes may also relate to *fit*. Teaching approaches that work well for one kind of person might not be optimal for a different kind of person.

What Is a Treatment?

The definition of **treatment** is any identifiable educational experience. Treatments might be different curricula or different teaching strategies. One goal of educational research is to find out which approaches work best. Comparison of different approaches to education, instructional or curricular, is a basic activity of educational research. When making decisions about whether to adopt a new curriculum—whether a textbook, software, or simply an instructional philosophy or strategy—it is important to proceed on the basis of evidence. We want to know whether data support claims that a prospective new curriculum will be an improvement over the current approach. We also want to know whether the improvement is statistically significant, as well as its effect size.

What Is an Interaction?

The ATI research model questions whether there will be a single best approach for all students. It complicates that logic by asserting the possibility that one treatment might be optimal for one group of students, but that a *different* treatment might be best for another. That complication sets aside the question of which treatment is best for all and substitutes a concern for *matching* treatment to aptitude. When such a matching arrangement can be found, then there is an **interaction**.

The quest to find good matches between aptitudes and treatments is vitally important. But the ATI framework does not regard either aptitudes or treatments as fixed. Ideally, educational treatments improve over time. Different approaches to teaching reading, science, mathematics, history, or music can be tested against each other and evolve over time, especially as those treatments conform progressively to what is known from research about how students learn. Likewise, aptitudes should not be thought of as static or fixed. Most aptitudes, including intelligence, are malleable at least to some extent. In fact, Richard Snow (1997) described education as an aptitude development program. Still, the central concern of ATI research is to understand the ideal match between aptitudes and treatments. The formalism of ATI is a way to gain clarity on a teacher's intuition that different students require different approaches.

Example of an ATI

One ATI has received more verifying evidence than any other. That ATI relates the degree of structure in teaching to general intelligence (Cronbach, 1975; Snow & Lohman, 1984). **Degree of structure** refers to how explicitly teachers provide information to students. A low degree of structure means that teachers omit some connections between ideas, asking instead that students make those connections. Similarly, a low degree of structure may mean that teachers give less explicit direction about how to accomplish a particular task. Particulars about how to proceed are left for students to figure out.

A low degree of structure tends to work best for students with high general ability. The most able students thrive under conditions in which they are permitted, even expected, to fill in conceptual and procedural gaps. In fact, they will learn more under these conditions than in situations where instruction is spelled out in detail. The opposite occurs for students who are lower in academic ability. In low-structure situations, they may have difficulty learning concepts and keeping track of them. Having to infer the missing pieces may make them confused and frustrated. Overall, lower-ability students will have better learning outcomes in a high-structure situation (Kirschner, Sweller, & Clark, 2006). This ATI is depicted in Figure 9.5.

Figure 9.5 shows three trend lines that relate degree of learning (achievement) to intelligence. The dashed line, labeled "typical instruction," shows that school achievement is

FIGURE 9.5
Aptitude-Treatment
Interaction
*An ATI shows
precisely how the
effect of any treat-
ment varies with
differences among
participants.*

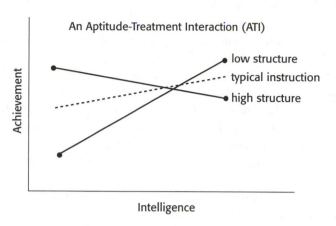

positively related to intelligence. The two solid lines, however, show that the relationship between achievement and intelligence depends on the degree of structure—this is the ATI already noted. The graph shows that for high-intelligence students, low structure produces the best learning outcomes. The most intelligent students do not need explicit instruction; in fact, they learn most effectively when allowed to make connections for themselves. But the opposite is true for less able learners. They learn best when provided with more structure. Somewhere in the middle range of the graph, the two lines cross. For students of roughly average cognitive ability, the two approaches produce comparable results. This particular ATI is relevant to teaching gifted students. Students with high ability tend to thrive in situations that provide relatively low structure. Given sufficient freedom, gifted students can pursue ideas and projects somewhat independently. A more typical student might flounder under such conditions.

ATI theory can clarify what we mean when we say that different students thrive under different learning conditions. This perspective can help us to set aside the simple-minded assumption that there is a single best way to teach. We can also reject the complementary fallacy that a collection of personal qualities together constitutes an ideal learner. Instead, optimal learning is a matter of fit—like a species adapted to a biological niche. In studies of ecosystems, it is pointless to argue about which species is best overall, or what part of the ecosystem is ideal. The pertinent question is what conditions within the ecosystem are best for each species. Each species occupies its optimal niche and thrives there.

The ATI framework allows us to test assumptions about fit that seem plausible, but that may not hold up to scrutiny. One seemingly obvious ATI relates to two major forms of cognitive ability: verbal ability and spatial ability. It is possible to identify learners who are relatively high in spatial ability and others who are relatively high in verbal ability. What happens if we try to match curricula to those differences? On the face of it, it seems that presenting information in verbal form to high-verbal learners would lead to favorable learning outcomes; likewise, presenting information in spatial forms such as diagrams to high-spatial learners would appear to be beneficial. Stated this way, we have hypothesized a testable ATI.

This hypothetical ATI has been tested by several different researchers (Cronbach, 1975). The outcome is a bit surprising: Matching instructional materials to the verbal/spatial profile of students does *not* seem to provide an overall benefit. Cronbach (1975) speculated that high-spatial learners do not need or benefit from actual spatial depictions, such as diagrams, because they are already good at *generating* spatial depictions in their minds. On the other hand, high verbal learners, being relatively weak in spatial ability, might benefit from the diagrams that might be difficult to generate mentally. The point to appreciate from this example is that even highly plausible hypotheses about how to match teaching approaches to student differences might not be correct. They are not always confirmed by ATI data.

The verbal/spatial example illustrates a more general pattern in ATI research. Studies have uncovered far fewer ATIs than were originally believed to exist. In the 1970s, Lee Cronbach and Richard Snow (1977) recognized the potential value of ATIs in education to optimize learning. They wanted to set aside simplistic assumptions about ideal ways to teach and instead explore interactions—to find ways to match instruction to learner characteristics. Nevertheless, the search for stable and confirmable ATIs yielded only a few.

One reason for the difficulty in identifying stable ATIs is the existence of **higher-order interactions**. To understand what this means, consider again the graph in Figure 9.5. Suppose, hypothetically, that the trend lines are different for males and females. In that case, we would have four solid lines rather than two. We would have to conclude that there are two qualities that we must consider—the intelligence of the student as well as the gender of the student. In other words, any conclusion about the relationship of degree of structure to learning outcomes must be qualified by *two* student characteristics: gender and intelligence. This is a higher-order interaction because we must now consider more than one factor when choosing the most fitting treatment. The situation can be even more complex as we consider that still other student characteristics may further moderate the relationship between degree of structure and learning outcomes.

Extend this logic and you will see the difficulty: Interactions are real, but they are far more complex than was originally thought. The effectiveness of any teaching approach may depend on a whole series of student characteristics. That is why Lee Cronbach (1975, p. 119) said, with a note of despair, that when one attends to interactions one enters a "hall of mirrors that extends to infinity." The complexity of learner characteristics relevant to choosing an ideal treatment can be dizzying. The logical endpoint of higher-order interactions is a situation in which forming a generalization is simply not possible because what works for any particular student is unique to that student. If we go this far, then we have given up on a law-like or **nomothetic** approach and have accepted a completely individualistic or **idiographic** approach to understanding how students learn (Allport, 1962).

In the history of ATI research, Cronbach and Snow developed somewhat different conclusions about whether generalizations in the form of ATIs were possible. Cronbach drifted toward a more pessimistic conclusion; he thought that nomothetic statements about social phenomena were so complex that the search for such regularities was fraught with difficulty and possibly misguided. Snow, although surprised by the complexity of higher-order interactions, believed that finding nomothetic generalizations was nonetheless possible, though more difficult than first assumed. He took ATIs to be real and believed that one task of social scientists, including researchers in education, was to find them.

The ATI framework lends precision to the abiding intuition of educators that different students require different teaching approaches to optimize learning—that there is no one best way to teach and to learn. Although we can look to a variety of teaching strategies that are broadly effective (such as cognitive modeling, chunking information, and using praise judiciously), those generalizations need to be tempered by the specifics of a situation, particularly the characteristics of learners. Effective teaching is never a matter of following a formula. The challenge is to adapt teaching to the particular aptitude profile of students. Yet the history of ATIs reminds us to be cautious in assuming that the matching of pedagogical approach to student characteristics is simple.

Diversification of Instruction

Aptitude-treatment interactions show how the characteristics of a learner can align with the teaching approach to produce optimal learning results. This section focuses on one part of the ATI framework: student characteristics. Remember that we can regard student characteristics as aptitudes if those qualities adapt the student more to certain kinds of experience (treatments) than to others. Aptitudes can include cognitive abilities as well as styles.

Cognitive and Learning Styles

Few student characteristics have evoked more interest than cognitive and learning styles. Whenever the word **styles** is used in discussing psychological traits, it refers to personal qualities that are distinguishable from abilities. For that reason, abilities such as intelligence are **value-directional**; in other words, having more is better than having less. Styles are different in that they are **value-differentiated**; the idea of *more* does not really make sense when speaking of styles (Messick, 1996a). Having a particular style is not necessarily beneficial or detrimental; each style conveys an advantage in some situations but not in others. One particular style is, in principle, no better or worse than any other—it is simply different.

The notion of style is attractive because it implies that individual differences are valuable, which is not always the case with abilities. Ability constructs always identify some students as having more and some as having less. Abilities also hint at lingering questions about whether those differences are inborn and perhaps immutable. Style constructs, such as learning styles or cognitive styles, present a more reassuring view of human variation that seems consistent with democratic ideals and human potential, as well as the value of diversity. Many constructs have proliferated under the banner of cognitive styles and learning styles. We will note just a sample of the more important ones.

Cognitive styles are characteristic ways of processing information. The most researched cognitive style construct is **field dependence versus field independence**. This refers to whether individuals perceptually isolate an entity (field independence) or whether they take into account the context of that perception (field dependence). A second style construct is **impulsivity versus reflectivity**. Impulsivity refers to a tendency to process information and make contingent decisions quickly; reflectivity is the tendency to give the decision process more time and consideration before acting (Lajoie & Shore, 1987).

Learning styles are similar to cognitive styles but describe a mode of acquiring knowledge. One learning style characterizes degree of depth in approaches to learning (Messick, 1994). At one end of the continuum are learners who tend to attend to the sensory qualities of information; at the other end are learners who search new information for its underlying meaning. Another model of learning styles presents two dimensions: an active-reflective dimension and a concrete-abstract dimension (Kolb, 1971). Figure 9.6 illustrates how the two dimensions cross to form quadrants: converging (abstract-active), diverging (concrete-reflective), assimilating (abstract-reflective), and accommodating (concrete-active).

FIGURE 9.6
Kolb's Theory of
Learning Styles
*Two dimensions
cross to form four
possible "kinds" of
learners.* [Adapted
with the permission of
Pearson Education, Inc.,
Upper Saddle River, NJ]

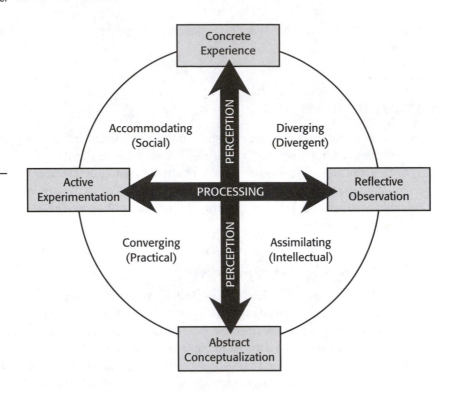

Neither cognitive styles nor learning styles have produced the robust evidence for their validity and usefulness that have been found in ability constructs. Styles seem to be strongly tied to the instrument used, raising questions about their construct validity (Nickerson, 2002). Moreover, the implied ATI of style variables—that style characteristics are useful for designing instruction and for producing superior educational outcomes—has largely been disappointing. This suggests that the field of learning and cognitive styles deserves much greater research attention. On the other hand, research on styles has declined since the 1960s and 1970s, implying that hopes placed on style constructs for improving instruction may have been unrealistic.

Even in the absence of research evidence, style-like differences among students are sometimes assumed to exist. Some educators promote distinctions among "visual" learners, "auditory" learners, and "kinesthetic" learners. This scheme has inherent ambiguities, such as whether "visual" refers to propensities to learn from diagrams, mental images, or printed text. By appealing to a sensory capability (hearing) rather than cognitive representation, the term *auditory learners* is likewise ambiguous about whether the reference is to musical aptitude, speech, or something else. Moreover, differentiating students as categorical types rather than as a differing along continuous dimensions is risky. Although separating students by *kinds* rather than by *degree* is simpler, it assumes membership of category A precludes membership in categories B or C. These distinctions further imply that the qualities that identify these categories cluster together with little overlap. Evidence for discrete student categories in styles is generally weak or absent. Instead of composing neat categories, student variation tends to be continuous—students usually differ by degree rather than by "kind."

Howard Gardner's **multiple intelligences (MI) theory** (1983) has sometimes been cited as supporting a model of student types of the "visual" and "auditory" variety. Gardner proposed a theory of "intelligences" that include logical-mathematical, linguistic, musical, spatial, bodily kinesthetic, interpersonal, intrapersonal, and naturalist. Even a cursory comparison of Gardner's "intelligences," however, shows that they do not map on to the visual-auditory-kinesthetic distinction. Moreover, Gardner's theory is not a theory of types but instead recognizes continuous variation among people. This variation results in characteristic profiles for each individual that may reveal one or more prominent intelligences among the others. Gardner's theory does not claim that every student will evidence high ability in one or more "intelligences." Although Gardner's MI theory seems consistent with democratic values in recognizing a broad range of intelligent functioning, it does not promise that every human being is "smart." Instead, Gardner has advanced a more realistic hope that, consistent with this theory, educational systems will broaden curricular approaches.

Theories of cognitive styles and learning styles, MI theory, and other models that differentiate learners by categories or dimensions of intellectual functioning raise a fundamental question: Do we know enough about the ways in which students vary to apply those theories effectively? In an ideal world, we would have strong theories about dimensions of student difference that interact robustly with different instructional approaches. The mapping of treatment to aptitude would be clear and precise, and the outcomes for student learning would be much more effective than a coarse one-size-fits-all curriculum. But, to this day, the problem of "fit" is still largely unsolved. This conclusion does not minimize the necessity of taking student differences into account in planning instruction. In actual teaching practice, the adaptation of instruction proceeds largely in two ways. First, talented teachers treat student differences *clinically*, with an intuitive sense of what is needed in the moment and for the particular student. Professional insight should not be minimized, even though it may resist explicit law-like nomothetic analysis. A second approach, which follows naturally from Gardner's theory and others, is the *diversification* of instruction. Teaching that promotes a variety of approaches, representations, activities, and assessments will inevitably reach more students than will a single method. Although diversifying instruction does not attain the precision of ATIs, it is a more modest and perhaps more realistic way to consider student differences in the design of learning experiences.

Time and Learning

Time on Task

One important way that students vary in how they learn is on the dimension of *time*. Rate of learning can differ significantly among students. The relationship between time and learning was formulated explicitly in John Carroll's model of school learning (1963). Carroll recognized that learning can vary by degree; some students learn more, or more completely, that others. The degree of learning is a ratio of the time required to learn and the time actually devoted to learning. The normal response to student variation is to hold time constant and allow the degree of learning to vary. But this approach creates problems because it means that, for many students, learning will be only partial. The strategy is ineffective when new concepts and skills build directly on previous ones, such as in mathematics.

An alternative way to treat variation in time and learning is to hold *learning* constant and to allow *time* to vary (Bloom, 1974). If each student has enough time to learn, then presumably fewer students will fall behind because they lack the foundational knowledge needed to move through successive units of the curriculum. When considering the dimension of time, however, there is an important distinction between **seat time**, which is only *nominally* allocated to learning, and time that is actually devoted to advancing learning. Time truly dedicated to thinking and learning has been called **time**

on task or **academically engaged time**. Time on task can vary quite a bit from class-room to classroom, as well as from student to student (Goodlad, 1984).

Mastery Learning

Carroll's theory of time and learning was directly applied in the pedagogical approach known as **mastery learning**. Benjamin Bloom (1971; 1974) developed mastery learning as a teaching strategy designed to provide all students with the time needed for each to learn. Consistent with Carroll's model, degree of learning was held constant—a program feature indicated by the term *mastery*. Students' mastery of each unit was assured by requiring performance on formative tests to some specified criterion, such as 90 percent. If a student was not able to achieve this level of mastery on the first attempt, then he or she received further instruction followed by another test. By insisting on mastery, each student was assured of having the knowledge needed to be successful in the next unit.

Mastery learning, although compelling in some ways, has several inconvenient features. The need to provide supplementary instruction to students who lag can present logistical difficulties. Bloom discovered that the time needed by students initially varied by a ratio of about 3 to 1. Slower learners required *three times* as much time as the fastest learners. To gain the needed time, mastery learning students may have to schedule supplementary instruction after school or on weekends. Additionally, mastery learning tests fall prey to the criticisms that can be leveled at testing broadly. Mastery tests define desired learning outcomes precisely, but this tight coupling can lead to an unwarranted restriction on what learning outcomes ought to be. Learning is multidimensional in ways that are hard to capture on a mastery test (Cronbach, 1971).

Nevertheless, Bloom's research showed that mastery learning led to some desirable outcomes. The approach seemed to work well for most students. At least 90 percent of students could reach the tested criterion given enough time. This produced positive effects on learning: Bloom found that mastery learning led to an achievement effect of one sigma when compared to conventional teaching (Bloom, 1984). He also found that differences between high- and low-achieving students narrowed. Differences in time needed between the faster- and slower-learning students shrunk to a new ratio of about 1.5 to 1. Moreover, the correlation between IQ and time needed to gain mastery dropped to low values. Presumably, students who received supplementary instruction were assured of having foundational skills before proceeding, and this assurance helped narrow the gap. These findings showed that mastery learning could advance a treasured and elusive goal of education—that of promoting more equitable cognitive and learning outcomes (Bloom, 1971).

Group Differences

It seems undeniable that students vary in qualities that affect learning outcomes. Even if such differences are inevitable, various pedagogical approaches can attenuate differences in achievement (as in mastery learning) or can attend to differences and match them to educational experience (ATIs). There is an important difference, however, between the existence of such differences and their association with gender, socioeconomic status, and race. Correlations between cognitive differences and demographic groups raise questions about whether the values and goals of educational equity are being realized for all citizens, or whether some groups of people are unfairly being deprived of the high-quality educational experience that privileged groups enjoy.

Gender Differences

On most tests of cognitive ability, males and females evidence very few differences, and those differences are negligible. With respect to IQ, for example, the overall performance of males and females is essentially indistinguishable. Males and females do differ significantly, however, on one cognitive ability dimension: spatial ability (Halpern, 2006). The spatial ability factor is the cognitive ability that facilitates the manipulation of mental imagery. In spatial ability, males perform significantly higher than females, on average. Naturally, some males are poor performers on spatial ability tests, and some females are high in spatial ability. Nevertheless, the magnitude of average male-female differences in spatial ability tests is not small: Males outperform females by about half a standard deviation or more.

Psychologists have tried to understand the causes of this difference. Some have thought its origins could be entirely experiential (e.g., males are socialized into playing with mechanistic toys) or evolutionary (e.g., males form hunting parties to bring food home for the tribe). As yet, however, there is no completely satisfactory explanation for the higher average performance of males on tests of spatial ability (Newcombe, 2006).

Females and males also differ in some aspects of educational achievement. On the SAT, for example, the average quantitative scores for males are higher than for females. This seems to reflect a developmental progression in which girls are initially more successful than boys in mathematics. At around age 15, however, boys often catch up to and surpass girls when mathematical problem solving begins to be emphasized in coursework. Males are far better represented in advanced coursework in mathematics and in the physical sciences, and especially in doctoral programs in these areas of study. Females are consequently highly underrepresented in careers in mathematics, physics, and computer science.

Females, on the other hand, matriculate to college in much higher numbers than males. In some universities, women compose 60 percent or more of the undergraduate student population. This trend has begun to raise questions about gender equity in education and—perhaps surprisingly to some—whether educational systems somehow disadvantage males. Some writers are beginning to propose that males are an "at risk" population (Miller & Byrnes, 2001).

Socioeconomic Differences

Socioeconomic status (SES) is one demographic variable that is highly correlated to student achievement. SES is a technical term for social class—one defined by a combination of family income, occupational prestige, and parents' education. SES is significantly related to measured cognitive abilities as well as to learning outcomes (Mackintosh, 1998). The large variation in school achievement correlated with SES is one of the major challenges in education. One ideal of recent federal policy in education is to help assure more equitable learning outcomes between rich and poor neighborhoods.

Sociologists have long studied variables associated with socioeconomic status. Differences in wealth, home environments, and parenting practices associated with SES have implications for the experience of children during the preschool years. For example, the amount of mother-child verbal interaction differs between middle-class families and poor families by a factor of about three to one; as does the type and the tone of that verbal interaction also differs (Hart & Risley, 1995). During the school years also, children have different experiences. Schools differ in physical resources, social climate, teacher preparation, and quality of instruction. Additionally, children's extracurricular experiences are relevant to their growing knowledge of science and mathematics, their feelings of interest and curiosity, and the belief that they can understand and solve problems if they persevere.

Promoting educational equity with respect to social class is complicated by the tracking systems that are so characteristic of the practice of education. Separating students by ability or achievement can ostensibly meet the intellectual needs of students, but it can instead have the nefarious effect of reinforcing initial differences. School systems might be accused of preserving social class distinctions rather than promoting social mobility.

Conditions associated with poverty—substandard housing, poor nutrition and health care, and so on—can disadvantage learners. A challenge for education is to offset some of these disadvantages and help reform educational systems so that they can promote opportunity for all. Research can contribute to this enterprise. Some researchers have studied students who are unusually successful despite being "at risk" because of factors associated with poverty. Such **resilience** is itself an object of study, inspiring hope that by understanding how some students rise above unfavorable circumstances, this knowledge can help others to succeed.

Racial-Ethnic Differences: The Achievement Gap

Achievement differences between racial-ethnic groups have long been a difficult fact for educators. The association of school achievement with race and ethnicity has challenged ideals of fairness, opportunity, and equality. Historically, school achievement has lagged for certain racial-ethnic groups: Black, Hispanic, and Native Americans. On both school achievement and cognitive abilities, including measured IQ, these demographic groups have tended to fall below population averages by about a standard deviation. These enduring differences have been referred to broadly as the **achievement gap**.

A difference of one standard deviation is large, and it carries the worrisome implication that differences in the middle of the distribution are magnified at the extremes, or tails. At more than two standard deviations from the mean, the "tails" of a normal curve become quite thin. If two normal curves are offset just a little, the curve with a higher mean will have a thicker "tail" at high values. For the lower-achieving group, a difference between means of one standard deviation will translate to a much lower representation at the high end of the distribution and a much higher representation at the low end. On IQ, for example, the lower-scoring group will be severely underrepresented among people with an IQ of 130 or higher—those whose cognitive abilities are required for admission to the most technical and competitive occupational fields. The lower-scoring group will in turn be more highly represented in the lower-scoring regions of IQ, and may be more frequently classified as slow learners or as developmentally delayed.

Underrepresented minority groups differ from population averages in socioeconomic status, complicating interpretation of the causes of the achievement gap. Minority groups have entered the middle class in increasing numbers in the last two decades, but the incidence of poverty is still much greater among African American and Hispanic families than among White families. Racial and ethnic groups also differ on experiences that affect development. For example, prenatal and perinatal health is compromised in African American babies at about twice the rate of White babies. The incidence of low birth weight, birth complications, poor prenatal care, and similar factors are strongly associated with race and ethnicity. These factors are known to have long-term associations with measured IQ and with school achievement (Martinez, 2000).

Fortunately, data on school learning over time show that the achievement gap has narrowed somewhat since 1970 (Jencks & Phillips, 1998) (Figure 9.7). The partial convergence of trend lines strongly suggests that the gap can close further. If the achieve-

FIGURE 9.7
The Achievement Gap *Convergences over time suggest that the gap could close completely.* [From C. Jencks & M. Phillips (Eds), 1998, Washington DC: Reprinted by permission of The Brookings Institution Press, Washington, DC.]

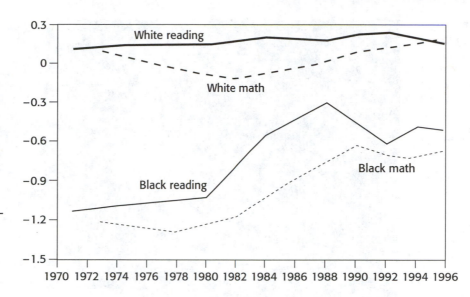

ment gap can close partially, then it seems conceivable that it can close completely. Complete closure—when the association between racial/ethnic grouping and cognitive outcomes becomes zero—would be an extraordinary achievement of a free society and a hard-won fulfillment of social ideals. Of course, closing the achievement gap would not eliminate student differences, only the association of group differences with demographic variables.

Only by reinterpreting *education* as embracing *all* experience will it be possible to close the gap completely. A broadened view of education implies that it is *impossible* to redress the achievement gap with policy changes or admonitions that focus exclusively, or even primarily, on students' classroom experience (Gordon & Bridglall, 2007). Instead, we must take into account the entire breadth of the child's experience, beginning with prenatal experience and extending through the life span. The child's experience relevant to valued achievement, academic and otherwise, extends to all hours of the day, as well as to every social and physical context. Additionally, experience in schools might be adapted to better match the background knowledge and personal interests of students in ways that connect to their cultural backgrounds. This hypothesis, that instruction could be adapted to fit students' cultural background, is sometimes described as **culturally responsive pedagogy** (Gay, 2000).

Test Bias

When we consider the difficult challenge of the achievement gap, a question arises: Are group differences a result of inherent faults of the tests? Perhaps the tests are biased. If so, then the tests unfairly relegate some students to low scores and diminished opportunity, and give advantages to others whose background predisposes them to achieve high scores and to enjoy the resulting benefits.

The first step in addressing these questions is to clarify that group differences by themselves do not necessarily mean that a test is biased. After all, the group differences could be authentic. If so, the test is simply reporting real differences. However, **test bias** does exist. The most infamous example of test bias was an item on an old version of the SAT test:

RUNNER: MARATHON (A) envoy: embassy (B) martyr: massacre (c) oarsman: regatta (D) referee: tournament (E) horse: stable

FIGURE 9.8
A Rowing Regatta
Knowledge about some social practices is more accessible to the middle class than to the poor. [Justin Leighton/DK]

In order to select the correct answer, examinees must know the meaning of the words in the analogy, including the word *regatta* (Herrnstein & Murray, 1994). However, there is a problem here: Students who grow up in wealthy communities set close to waterways are more likely to be exposed to the word *regatta* than are children who grow up inland or in less wealthy neighborhoods. Some students might be advantaged by wealth or by geographical location. These differences, however, do not constitute bias by themselves; one additional factor is required. In the regatta question, knowledge of the word *regatta* does not relate in any meaningful way to the construct being measured. The desired construct is analogical reasoning, not vocabulary. If students are differentiated on this test item by their knowledge of a particular word, *regatta*, then the target construct, analogical reasoning, is thereby contaminated and validity is undermined.

Test bias exists when two conditions are met: Test item content is differentially familiar or meaningful to distinct demographic groups, and that content is unrelated to the target construct. This definition of bias may seem hard to meet, but in fact, it is not. Test questions can be contextualized in a form that requires background knowledge that advantages one group over another. When teachers design their own classroom tests, they must ask whether the background knowledge assumed in the questions is likely to give an advantage based on gender, racial or ethnic group, or socioeconomic level. Those who construct tests, whether professional test designers or classroom teachers, must guard against the unfavorable outcomes that result from test bias.

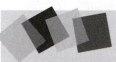

Learning Strategies

This chapter is about the psychometric model, the remarkable conceptualization of knowledge and cognitive abilities that assumes we can measure those traits on a linear quantitative scale. The psychometric way of viewing the world must be considered a specific paradigm, a way of seeing the mind that inter- faces with the cognitive paradigm, yet is distinguishable from it. As we delve into this paradigm, we find many applications to educational practice. This section advances ten strategies that can improve the practice of measurement and addresses how testing can improve learning outcomes.

1 Increase the number of test items.
Test reliability is the degree to which a test score is reproducible. One simple way to improve test reliability is to increase the number of test items. Teachers should be wary of tests that have only a few items. As a test rises in importance, larger numbers of test items help to ensure that the test will have sufficiently high reliability.

2 Use a full representation of the construct.
If tests have any fundamental inadequacy, it is that they seldom convey the full construct that they are intended to measure. Test designers, including classroom teachers, should appreciate the importance of mapping out the meaning of the construct they intend to measure, and of trying to make the test representative of that construct.

3 Widen the process dimension of test design.
Often in test design, the cognitive process dimension is excessively narrow. Tests designed for convenience, especially those that rely on multiple-choice and other discrete item formats only, often fail to capture aspects of complex cognition that tests ought to measure. Sometimes test designers are guided by specific models of higher-order thinking, such as Bloom's taxonomy. Even when not guided by a specific model, however, test design should include aspects of complex cognition, such as problem solving, critical thinking, and creativity. Modes of thought that are valued should be built into the design of the test in order to ensure a fuller representation of the construct, as well as to steer teaching and learning toward complex cognition.

4 Use a variety of testing formats.
Tests that employ a variety of formats, not simply the multiple-choice format, have the advantage that the different formats can encourage different kinds of cognition. Written responses may permit forms of conceptual analysis or synthesis that are difficult or impossible to elicit with multiple-choice questions. Moreover, a variety of formats can help minimize the variance that is format-specific (such as the response-elimination strategy of multiple-choice testing). Minimizing method variance can help safeguard test validity.

5 Use performance assessment but recognize its costs.
Performance assessment offers many advantages, not least of which is its likely contribution to worthy learning goals. Traditional tests often fail to live up to their *de facto* role as models of what students should know and be able to do. The complex cognition and behavior elicited by performance assessments are more sensible targets of learning and instruction. Yet performance assessment is no panacea. It is typically expensive, both monetarily and logistically. Additionally, performance assessment often allows fewer observations than traditional forms of testing, therefore reducing its reliability in comparison to more traditional testing.

6 Be cautious about learning styles.
A clear understanding of learning styles and their application to educational processes has been largely elusive. It has been difficult to establish categories of styles that can reliably characterize students. Teachers should be cautious about seemingly neat theories of learner types. Students typically vary by degree rather than by distinct categories. Ideally, future research will further illuminate the nature of learning styles and their importance to educational decisions.

7 Consider aptitude-treatment interactions.
Every teacher recognizes that different students require different pedagogical approaches. The formal model of aptitude-treatment interactions, also known as ATIs, confirms this. One particular ATI is particularly well established: High-ability learners thrive under instructional approaches that are relatively less structured. Establishing other ATIs has been difficult, however. Teachers might well find that their own clinical judgments offer greater practical value than most attempts at nomothetic, law-like generalizations about the needs of students.

8 Give learning sufficient time.
Carroll's model of time and learning presented instruction in a new light. Education usually works by fixing time and letting learning vary between students. Carroll's alternative approach holds learning outcomes constant and lets time vary so that each student has sufficient time to learn. This model evolved into mastery learning. Teachers adopt this basic approach when they recognize that students learn at different rates. Extra time can provide some students with a stronger foundation on which to build further understanding.

9 **Guard against test bias.**
Test bias is evident whenever tests require background knowledge that is not directly relevant to the measured construct, and when that background knowledge differentiates between demographic groups. Test bias not only implies unfairness, it also undermines the quality of tests, particularly test validity. Teachers need to make sure that test questions do not require incidental knowledge unrelated to the construct that might discriminate against some students.

10 **Close the achievement gap.**
Differences in achievement between demographic groups, particularly those identified by race and ethnicity, have long plagued the U.S. educational system. Yet data from the last few decades have shown that the gap is not fixed in magnitude. Differences in distributions of a standard deviation or so have narrowed considerably. If the achievement gap can narrow, then it seems plausible that it can close completely. Perhaps within our lifetimes we will see the correlation between academic achievement and race/ethnicity reduced to zero.

These ten strategies show that the psychometric paradigm can be used to advance the goals of teaching and learning. Knowledge derived from research can help to ensure that the ubiquitous practice of measurement in education can be improved to make it fairer and more accurate. The potential pitfalls of measurement, including inadequate construct representation and test bias, can be avoided or minimized. Understanding the psychometric paradigm can help educators use measurement to advance, rather than undermine, the goals of education.

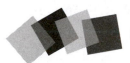

Conclusion

Testing is a remarkable technical achievement—one that is continuously evolving. No test is perfect, and yet virtually every test has value in helping us to understand the construct it is intended to measure. Testing can also promote fairness. Early in the twentieth century, the establishment of the "college boards" (which later became the SAT) helped to overcome the favoritism toward wealthy families that prejudiced decisions about who was allowed to go to college.

The two most important test properties are reliability and validity. Reliability refers to how reproducible the score is; validity refers to whether a test measures what it is intended to measure. No test manifests 100 percent validity and reliability. Test designers can elevate the quality of tests, however, by attending to these two dimensions of test quality. Any widely used standardized test needs to demonstrate satisfactory validity and reliability.

One basic kind of validity is content validity. Test specifications help to ensure that the content is appropriate and that nothing important is left out. The most general form of validity is construct validity. Most tests are built on the assumption that there is an underlying psychological dimension that is important, even if it is imperfectly understood. That underlying psychological dimension is a *construct*. Intelligence is one example of a psychological construct. When the first intelligence test was created by Alfred Binet about a hundred years ago, the idea that intelligence could be quantified made people wonder about the nature of that mental trait. The same question applied to other measurable traits, such as reading comprehension, mathematics achievement, and personality dimensions. Attempts to measure a trait can spur people to wonder what that trait really is. Moreover, the quality of tests is limited by our understanding of the constructs they try to measure. As psychological theories improve, tests can improve along with them.

Despite the utility of traditional forms of testing, they often display deficiencies. In particular, tests composed of multiple-choice and other discrete item formats are often poor at eliciting complex, higher-order cognition. Consequently, they are usually inadequate for measuring the full range of desired educational outcomes. Other assessment formats include performance assessment, such as carrying out a scientific experiment or composing a story. Classroom-based assessment can help teachers to understand what their students know and do not know, and this understanding can inform teaching decisions.

An abiding goal of educational research is to find ways to tailor instruction to the needs, abilities, and styles of individual students so that learning can be optimized. This objective is based on the commonsense notion that students learn in different ways and therefore that different teaching methods work for different students. In the language of educational psychology, this is known as an aptitude-treatment interaction, or ATI. *Aptitude* refers to the ways in which learners differ, and *treatment* refers to a method of instruction. The *interaction* is the connection or fit between the two. Ideally, the treatment (method of instruction) is fitted to the aptitude (characteristics of students), much as a species is adapted to its ecological niche.

Test use raises questions about fairness, especially when test scores are correlated with demographic variables. Bias is indicated when test questions are presented in contexts that are not central to the assessed trait and when that content is more available to some examinees than to others. Although test designers must guard against bias, group differences do not necessarily indicate bias. Often, score differences reveal systemic inequities in society that produce those differences. Challenges remain about how to make testing as fair as possible, and how to use assessment to meet the needs of the individual learner. As tests more validly measure the most important dimensions of cognitive differences, they will advance more effectively the goals of thinking and learning.

References

Allport, G. W. (1962). The general and the unique in psychological science. *Journal of Personality, 30,* 405–422.

Anderson, J. C., & Wall, D. (1993). Does washback exist? *Applied Linguistics, 14,* 115–129.

Black, P., Harrison, C., Lee, C., Marshall, B., & Wiliam, D. (2004). Inside the black box: Assessment for learning in the classroom. *Phi Delta Kappan, 86*(1), 8–21.

Black, P., & Wiliam, D. (1998). Inside the black box. *Phi Delta Kappan, 80*(2), 139–148.

Bloom, B. S. (1971). Mastery learning and its implications for curriculum development. In E. W. Eisner (Ed.), *Confronting curriculum reform* (pp. 17–49). Boston: Little, Brown, and Company.

Bloom, B. S. (1974). Time and learning. *American Psychologist, 29,* 682–688.

Bloom, B. S. (1984). The 2 sigma problem: The search for methods of group instruction as effective as one-to-one tutoring. *Educational Researcher, 13*(6), 4–16.

Burstein, J., Kukich, K., Wolff, S., Lu, C., & Chodorow, M. (2001). *Enriching automated essay scoring using discourse marking* (ERIC Document ED 458267). Washington, DC: Educational Resources Information Clearinghouse.

Cannell, J. J. (1988). Nationally normed elementary achievement testing in America's public schools: How all 50 states are above the national average. *Educational Measurement: Issues and Practice, 7*(2), 5–9.

Carroll, J. B. (1963). A model of school learning. *Teachers College Record, 64,* 723–733.

Chappuls, S., & Stiggins, R. J. (2002). Assessment for learning. *Educational Leadership, 60*(1), 40–43.

Cheng, L., Watanabe, Y., & Curtis, A. (2004) (Eds.), *Washback in language testing: Research and methods.* Mahwah, NJ: Lawrence Erlbaum Associates.

Cronbach, L. J. (1971). Comments on "Mastery learning and its implications for curriculum development." In E. W. Eisner (Ed.), *Confronting curriculum reform* (pp. 49–55). Boston: Little, Brown, and Company.

Cronbach, L. J. (1975). Beyond the two disciplines of scientific psychology. *American Psychologist, 30,* 116–127.

Cronbach, L. J., & Meehl, P. E. (1955). Construct validity in psychological tests. *Psychological Bulletin, 52,* 281–302.

Cronbach, L. J., & Snow, R. E. (1977). *Aptitudes and instructional methods: A handbook for research on interactions.* Oxford: Irvington.

Frederiksen, N. (1984). The real test bias. *American Psychologist, 18*(9), 193–202.

Frederiksen, J. R., & Collins, A. (1989). A systems approach to educational testing. *Educational Researcher, 18*(9), 27–32.

Gardner, H. (1983) *Frames of mind.* New York: Basic Books.

Gay, G. (2000). *Culturally responsive teaching: Theory, research, and practice.* New York: Teachers College Press.

Goodlad, J. I. (1984). *A place called school.* New York: McGraw-Hill.

Gordon, E. W., & Bridglall, B. L. (Eds.) (2007). *The affirmative development of academic ability.* Lanham, MD: Rowman and Littlefield.

Halpern, D. F. (2006). Assessing gender gaps in learning and academic achievement. In P. A. Alexander & P. H. Winne (Eds.), *Handbook of educational psychology* (2nd ed., pp. 635–653). Mahwah, NJ: Lawrence Erlbaum Associates.

Hart, B., & Risley, T. R. (1995). *Meaningful differences in the everyday experiences of young American children.* Baltimore, MD: Paul H. Brookes Publishing Co.

Herrnstein, R. J., & Murray, C. (1994). *The bell curve: Intelligence and class structure in American life.* New York: The Free Press.

Jencks, C., & Phillips, M. (Eds.) (1998). *The black-white test score gap.* Washington, DC: Brookings Institution Press.

Katzir, T., & Paré-Blagoev, J. (2006). Applying cognitive neuroscience research to education: The case of literacy. *Educational Psychologist, 41*(1), 53–74.

Lajoie, S. P., & Shore, B. M. (1987). Impulsivity, reflectivity, and IQ. *Gifted Education International, 4,* 139–141.

Linn, R. L. (2000). Assessments and accountability. *Educational Researcher, 29*(2), 4–16.

Kirschner, P. A., Sweller, J., & Clark, R. E. (2006). Why minimal guidance during instruction does not work: An analysis of the failure of constructivist, discovery, problem-based, experiential, and inquiry-based teaching. *Educational Psychologist, 41*(2), 75–86.

Kolb, D. A. (1971). *Individual learning styles and the learning process.* Cambridge, MA: MIT Press.

Mackintosh, N. J. (1998). *IQ and human intelligence.* New York: Oxford University Press.

Martinez, M. E. (1999). Cognition and the question of test item format. *Educational Psychologist, 34,* 207–218.

Martinez, M. E. (2000). *Education as the cultivation of intelligence.* Mahwah, NJ: Erlbaum.

Messick, S. (1994). Cognitive styles and learning. In T. Husen & T. N. Postlethwaite (Eds.), *International encyclopedia of education* (2nd ed., pp. 868–872). New York: Pergamon.

Messick, S. (1995). Validation of inferences from persons' responses and performances as scientific inquiry into score meaning. *American Psychologist, 50,* 741–749.

Messick, S. (1996a). *Bridging cognition and personality in education: The role of style in performance and development.* Research Report RR-96–22. Princeton, NJ: Educational Testing Service.

Messick, S. (1996b). *Validity and washback in language testing.* Research Report RR-96–17. Princeton, NJ: Educational Testing Service.

Miller, D. C., & Byrnes, J. P. (2001). To achieve or not to achieve: A self-regulation perspective on adolescents' academic decision making. *Journal of Educational Psychology, 93*(4), 677–685.

Newcombe, N. (2006, October). *Are men better visualizers?* Paper presented at the annual meeting of the Geological Society of America. Philadelphia, PA.

Nickerson, R. S. (2002). *Learning styles: What is a learning style? What does it matter?* Notes presented at a workshop of the National Science Foundation.

O'Donnell, A. M. (2006). The role of peers and group learning. In P. A. Alexander & P. H. Winne (Eds.), *Handbook of educational psychology* (2nd ed., pp. 781–802). Mahwah, NJ: Lawrence Erlbaum Associates.

Popham, J. (1987). The merits of measurement-driven instruction. *Phi Delta Kappan, 68,* 679–682.

Popham, W. J. (2003). The seductive allure of data. *Phi Delta Kappan, 60*(5), 48–51.

Powers, D. E., & Leung, S. W. (1995). Answering the new SAT reading comprehension questions without the passages. *Journal of Educational Measurement, 32*(2), 105–129.

Resnick, L. B. (2003). Class size: Counting students can count. *Research Points, 1*(2), 1–4.

Snow, R. E. (1992). Aptitude theory: Yesterday, today, and tomorrow. *Educational Psychologist, 27*(1), 5–32.

Snow, R. E. (1997). Aptitudes and symbol systems in adaptive classroom teaching. *Phi Delta Kappan, 75*(5), 354–360.

Snow, R. E., & Lohman, D. F. (1984). Toward a theory of cognitive aptitude of learning from instruction. *Journal of Educational Psychology, 78*(3), 347–376.

[10] Intelligence

Human intelligence is centrally important to the field of cognitive science and to the practice of education. The importance of intelligence to cognitive science was expressed plainly in the book *Foundations of Cognitive Science*. Authors Simon and Kaplan (1989, p. 2) defined cognitive science as "the study of intelligence and its computational processes." In their view, intelligent behavior is what cognitive science must endeavor to explain. All of cognitive science can be organized around intelligence—its nature and its manifestations.

The centrality of intelligence to education is also direct, although understanding the connection between intelligence and education may require some fresh ways of thinking. To state the connection plainly, the goal of education can be presented as the development of intelligence. Richard Snow (1982, p. 496) put it this way: Intelligence is "education's most important product, as well as its most important raw material."

What Is Intelligence?

One of the strange riddles of intelligence is why it is so hard to define. One reason for the difficulty is that different theories of intelligence lead to different definitions, so a lack of consensus around definitions is symptomatic of the unsettled state of the field. Direct evidence of discrepant definitions of intelligence existed as early as 1921, when intelligence theorists were asked as part of a survey to concisely define the term *intelligence*. The main lesson learned from the survey was that intelligence theorists differed widely in the definitions they gave.

A follow-up survey that was conducted some 65 years later involved 24 intelligence theorists and researchers who were asked to define intelligence. Again, as before, the experts could not agree on the meaning of the word *intelligence*. Moreover, between 1921 and 1986, there was no discernable convergence toward consensus (Sternberg & Detterman, 1986). Definitions seemed to vary as widely in the later study as they did in the earlier one.

These results suggest that disagreement over the meaning of intelligence is one of the primary battles in the history of intelligence research. Yet it would be false to present an impression that the study of intelligence has produced nothing but chaotic disagreement. Many decades of empirical and theoretical work have helped to illuminate just what intelligence is. Though the field is far from complete convergence, we now have a sharper understanding of intelligence than ever before.

A Provisional Definition

Because intelligence is a highly complex entity, or construct, a complete definition of intelligence cannot be presented in a single sentence. It will take some time and effort to create even a faint outline of the meanings of intelligence. The first half of this chapter will therefore be devoted to presenting the different views of intelligence that have evolved over the course of a century or so. Nevertheless, a crisp definition of intelligence can serve as a point of departure to launch into a study of intelligence. A provisional definition of intelligence is as follows:

> Intelligence is a repertoire of learnable cognitive competencies that permit effectiveness in a complex, symbol-rich, and problem-oriented world (Martinez, 2000, p. 7).

In this definition, three words are worth emphasizing: *repertoire*, *learnable*, and *cognitive*. The word *repertoire* recognizes that intelligence is not a single, indivisible entity but instead consists of many capabilities that work together in concert. Like a musical repertoire that can be played or sung, an intelligent mind can select and use its

INTEREST MAGNET 10.1

Evil Intelligence

When the United States dropped successive atomic bombs on Hiroshima and Nagasaki, ending World War II, the great physicist Robert Oppenheimer offered a stunning commentary on this historical turning point. He said, "Science has known sin, and that is a knowledge we dare not lose."

It may be easy to claim that the world can never have enough brilliant minds to cure disease, advance peace, and create great works of art. However, lurking behind that safe and sensible postulate is a disturbing complementary truth: Intelligence can be turned toward hateful and destructive ends. Evil intentions are all the more dangerous when backed by an intelligent mind. The translation of intelligence to horrible outcomes can be unintentional—a possibility explored in Mary Shelley's classic novel *Frankenstein*.

History teaches us that intelligence can be used to advance vile ends (McLaren, 1993). Indeed, one psychologist has recognized that "the brilliant mind can become the most destructive force in the world" (Tannenbaum, 1996, p. 447). For many people, Adolph Hitler is the supreme emblem of evil intelligence. In advancing Nazism, Hitler arguably displayed a skill set that was due not so much to stunted moral development, as it was to a highly developed and skilled immorality. Driven by a twisted idealism, Hitler honed his powers of demagoguery and intimidation to move his nation toward the goal of world domination by a "master race." Of course, Hitler did not act alone. He was able to recruit highly able military, political, and intellectual

leaders to join his cause. Distinguished scholars, many of whom held Ph.D.s, cooperated to formulate a plan to annihilate Jews.

For those considering the ugly spectacle of Nazism from a distance of geography or time, it may strain credulity to believe that the average person can be recruited to the purposes of evil. But psychological experiments by Stanley Milgram (1974) proved that "normal people" could be persuaded to administer electric shocks (or what they *believed* to be real shocks) to an innocent person when an authority figure insisted they must do so. Not only are human beings more susceptible to authority than we would like to believe, we arguably have the potential for finding delight in evil. St. Augustine confessed this ugly self-insight to the world when he recounted that he stole fruit from a neighbor's pear tree not because he was hungry, but only because of the pleasure of doing something wrong.

Einstein said unequivocally that "science can tell us what is, but not what ought to be" (Einstein, 1950, p. 26). To advance good in the world, the power of intelligence must be allied with moral concern. Morality is an aspect of character, and may take different forms, including justice, caring, truth, freedom, and regard for human beings, both collectively and individually. Educators must acknowledge that we cannot know with certainty where developed intellectual talents will lead. The capacity for complex thought seems to contribute to moral reasoning, but it is certainly not sufficient for making moral choices. Moral content must supplement cognitive ability so that the virtues of caring, love, and kindness can turn intelligence into a force for good.

varied capabilities as they fit the occasion or problem. Those competencies are *learnable,* meaning that they are acquired through experience over time. This contrasts with the common assumption that intelligence is innate and unchangeable. Finally, the competencies are *cognitive,* meaning that they are woven into the ways the human mind reasons, solves problems, and thinks critically.

If intelligence is learnable, then it is potentially teachable, and if teachable, it is potentially the province of education. This possibility links the topic of intelligence to the purpose of this book—to further the understanding of the human mind in order to improve thinking and learning.

Intelligence and Achievement

Modern theories of intelligence can be traced back to Francis Galton, a cousin of Charles Darwin. Galton, born into the privileged class of London during the early 1800s, was convinced that British social elite were superior in measurable ways to the working class and the poor. In Galton's view, intelligence was highly heritable, a fact observable in that "eminence" ran in families—typically, father to son. To Galton, the status of Britain's higher social classes was a direct result of their innate biological superiority. Galton therefore focused on rather low-level characteristics, such as visual acuity, grip strength, and reaction time. These were among the physical traits that Galton quantified and tried to relate to differences in social standing. Galton's hypothesis about the constitutional superiority of the British social elite was not borne out in his data. Nonetheless, he is credited with advancing the systematic and precise measurement of human characteristics, an accomplishment for which he has been called the "Father of Mental Measurement."

To Galton, such personal traits as sensory acuity and reaction time reflected an overall level of intelligence that could be used to predict individual achievement. Galton believed that intelligence could be manifest in two major outcomes, academic achievement and occupational success (Mackintosh, 1998). These outcomes—success in school and on the job—have continued to be the main criteria predicted by tests of intelligence. Not long after Galton, however, other scholars began to shift the focus of ability from low-level physical traits to performance on mental tasks.

Alfred Binet's Invention

The next major scholar of intelligence was the French psychologist, Alfred Binet. In 1904, Binet was commissioned by the French government to design a test that could distinguish among failing students. The school system wanted to know which students had the intellectual ability to succeed but were failing for other reasons, such as emotional disturbance or lack of motivation. In response, Binet and his collaborator, Theodore Simon, designed a test that was intended to measure intellectual *ability* as distinct from *achievement.* They saw ability as necessary, but not sufficient, for achievement in schools.

Binet's approach was different from Galton's in that it relied on tasks that were more intellectual rather than physical or sensory. Another difference was that Binet focused on children, whereas Galton was more interested in how adults differed. The tasks on Binet's scale included naming objects, defining words, and repeating sequences of numbers. Binet noted that children differed dramatically in their ability to complete these tasks. Performance also tended to improve as children grew older. But even among children of the same age, Binet found substantial variation. How was Binet to organize such wild cognitive variability and make it sensible to fulfill his commitment to the Paris school system?

Binet's ingenious solution was to establish average performance standards, called **norms**, for each age group. Through field research, Binet was able to determine what the average 8-year-old could do. Similarly, he could specify the average performance of 10-year-olds, 12-year-olds, or children of any other age. Performance on Terman's tasks therefore yielded a **mental age** for each tested child, which was distinct from their actual or **chronological age**. By comparing the two—mental age and chronological age—Binet had a usable metric that could calibrate a child's mental ability, as well as specify whether that ability was above or below average, and how far from average. Binet's problem was solved with the invention of the mental age construct; it was now up to others to build on Binet's breakthrough. The effort now shifted to America, and to the laboratory of Stanford psychologist Lewis Terman.

THE STANFORD-BINET TEST. The history of intelligence testing reached a turning point when Lewis Terman translated Binet's tests to English, lengthened them, and established norms for much larger groups of children. Terman's translation and expansion of the Binet-Simon instrument did much to popularize intelligence testing in the beginning of the twentieth century. Terman's version of the test, called the Stanford-Binet, was highly successful, and its use spread rapidly through North America. The Stanford-Binet has been revised in subsequent decades and is still in use today.

One innovation of the Stanford-Binet is that Lewis Terman adopted the IQ formula of German psychologist William Stern. The **intelligence quotient**, abbreviated IQ, used Binet's construct of mental age, and divided that number by chronological age to form a ratio. The resulting proportion was then multiplied by 100, as follows:

$$IQ = \frac{\text{mental age}}{\text{chronological age}} \times 100$$

The IQ formula adds precision to Binet's comparison of mental age with a child's chronological age. When a child's mental age matches his chronological age, IQ equals 100. Values above 100 indicate above-average performance with respect to age peers; values below 100 indicate that a child's mental age is below his chronological age and falls below the average of his age group.

Academic Success

We know from the work of Binet that intelligence tests were originally designed to predict school success. In Binet's time and in the present, intelligence test scores are good predictors of academic achievement. Correlations of IQ scores with school grades and scores on achievement tests typically range from about 0.5 to 0.6. Remember that correlations can range from -1 to $+1$, with zero indicating no relationship at all. A correlation in the range of 0.5 or 0.6 is moderately positive and noteworthy in social science research. Correlations of this magnitude affirm that IQ tests have fulfilled Binet's hopes of offering good prediction of school success.

Of course, the power of IQ scores to predict subsequent academic achievement is not perfect. A correlation of 0.6 still leaves plenty of unpredicted variation, with some students achieving higher than predicted and others achieving lower than predicted. However, even with these imperfections, the predictive power of IQ scores makes them useful. For the most part, IQ scores figure in educational planning today in the selection of students into some special education or gifted education programs. The use of tests for these purposes is not without controversy—IQ tests have sometimes been judged to be biased against one or another ethnic or cultural group. But their continued use through the decades suggests that they add value to decision-making, or at least are perceived to do so. In addition, IQ-like tests, such as the SAT, have long been used in college admissions because they have some ability to predict first-year college grades.

Job Success

Intelligence scores predict more than school success. A second category of success outcomes predicted by IQ tests is occupational achievement and job success. The manifestations of job success vary widely, from supervisor ratings to salary level. Overall, IQ scores are moderate to good predictors of job success. For example, IQ scores predict supervisors' ratings of employee performance with correlations of about 0.5 or 0.6 (Mackintosh, 1998; Schmidt & Hunter, 1998). There is some evidence that IQ is better at predicting performance on complex work than on simpler work.

Intelligence is an indispensable quality of the modern worker. Economists have noted that, in recent decades, the nature of work has shifted primarily from physical production to mental production. Old divisions of the labor force into blue-collar workers and white-collar workers don't do justice to the rising importance of intellect. Proposing an alternative taxonomy, the economist Robert Reich (1992) recognized three categories of laborers in the contemporary marketplace: symbolic analysts, in-person workers, and routine production laborers. Symbolic analysts are those whose work is essentially intellectual. The raw material for their work consists of ideas and information, and the product of their work is ideas and information as well. In-person workers staff the service industries and interact primarily with people. Routine production laborers correspond largely to old-style assembly line or factory workers.

According to Reich, the modern economy relies heavily on labor performed by symbolic analysts. The work of the mind—whether in generating, transforming, improving, or combining ideas—is the flywheel of the current world economic system. The ability to innovate, to solve problems, and to form and carry out plans, correcting course as necessary, is the work of the intelligent mind—or, more accurately perhaps, the work of intelligent *minds* using intelligently designed *tools* in intelligently designed *environments*. This expansive way of looking at intelligence is described more fully later in this chapter under the heading of "Distributed Intelligence."

Personality traits also contribute to occupational success. Indeed, certain personality traits are known to predict worker effectiveness about as well as IQ scores do. The personality trait of conscientiousness, in particular, correlates highly with supervisors' ratings of workers' competence. Conscientiousness as a personality trait has roughly the same meaning as it has in everyday conversation—attention to detail, persistence in following through on tasks, and concern with the quality of work produced. Interestingly, IQ scores and conscientiousness ratings make independent contributions to the prediction of worker effectiveness. The qualities are non-overlapping, meaning that they are additive in their effects. In other words, the best workers are both conscientious *and* smart!

The relevance of intelligence to work does not necessary follow the rule that *more intelligence is better*. It is possible that complex intellectual work requires no more than a moderately high intelligence corresponding to an IQ of 120 or so. A moderately high IQ may be a threshold that, once crossed, conveys the ability to succeed in any professional field—law, medicine, science, or teaching. If this is so, then helping more learners to acquire the competencies that correspond to a moderately high level of intelligence will help to ensure that as many people as possible have freedom to pursue the fields and careers that most draw them.

If IQ loses some of its predictive force in the higher ranges, a corresponding principle is that its predictive power is greater in the lower IQ bands. Stated differently, as IQ scores rise, their ability to predict success outcomes generally drops off. Low intelligence is a better predictor of failure than high intelligence is of success. Educational goals follow from this finding—it's crucially important to provide educational experiences that help prevent or correct low levels of intelligence. This logic drove many of the early childhood enrichment programs of the 1960s, including Head Start. One important goal of such programs was to prevent or minimize mental retardation associated with poverty.

Life Success

Intelligence tests have been applied mainly to predict two forms of success—academic achievement and occupational success. But why should intelligence predict only these life outcomes? Perhaps they could apply more broadly to other forms of achievement and life satisfaction.

Lewis Terman, translator and popularizer of the original Binet-Simon IQ scale, wanted to know if high IQ could predict valued outcomes through the life span. He posed a fascinating question: "What sort of adult does the typical gifted child become?" (Terman & Oden, 1947, p 2). Starting in 1921, he used the renamed Stanford-Binet Intelligence Scale to identify about 1500 school-age children with IQs in the top 1 percent. The children were selected from first-grade through eighth-grade classrooms in California schools (Terman & Oden, 1959). Terman and his successors followed the lives of these identified students for the next 70-plus years, making the Terman study of "genius" the longest-running longitudinal study of how psychological characteristics shape life pathways.

Terman found that, as a group, his subjects had impressive life achievements. A high percentage completed a college education and earned advanced degrees. A large number wrote books and were elected to high-prestige professional societies. Although they were not immune from personal problems, they tended to become successful, well-adjusted adults (Schoon, 2000). The Terman study showed that IQ measured during childhood could predict life outcomes, including longevity, quality of life, health, and well-being—life outcomes that went far beyond short-term academic and occupational success (Holahan & Sears, 1995). These longer-term and broadly predictive relationships were not particularly strong, but their measurable existence suggests that intelligence plays a role in facilitating life success beyond the narrower range (school and job success) envisioned by Francis Galton and his successors.

One Intelligence or Many?

In the opening pages of this chapter, we surveyed the historical origins of intelligence testing and the early applications of IQ tests. The historical overview temporarily set aside questions about what is measured by an IQ test—or just what *intelligence* means, for that matter. This conceptual question—What is intelligence?—is central to our

INTEREST MAGNET 10.2

The IQs of Eminent People

In 1926, Catherine Cox published an 800-page report entitled "The Early Mental Traits of Three Hundred Geniuses." At the time, Cox was collaborating with Stanford professor Lewis Terman in his longitudinal studies of high-IQ children. As part of Terman's larger study of high intelligence, Cox conducted a historical investigation of 301 eminent men and women—famous historical figures who made great contributions to science, politics, and culture from the Renaissance on. Cox (1926/1992) divided the achievers into groups that included soldiers, artists, musicians, religious leaders, political leaders, writers, scientists, and philosophers. She found that these high achievers typically displayed high intelligence even as children and young adults. Cox reported, for example, that

> Voltaire wrote verses "from his cradle"; Coleridge at 2 could read a chapter from the Bible; Mozart composed a minuet at 5; Goethe, at 8, produced a literary work of adult superiority.

Even if these biographical accounts are exaggerated by popular myth, a common historical pattern seemed to be that eventual geniuses display high cognitive ability early in life. Because of this common pattern, Cox and her collaborators conducted a version of Terman's study, but in reverse. Instead of tracing the life course of contemporary high-IQ children as Lewis Terman did, Cox identified historically eminent people and tried to estimate their IQ. She formed two estimates of the IQs of these individuals: IQ during childhood (birth to 17) and IQ during early adulthood (17 to 26).

For all 301 geniuses considered as a group, Cox estimated that the average IQ was "not below 155 and probably as high as 165." Cox and two other raters formed the IQ estimates based on "their own considerable experience in mental testing" (p. 47).

IQ estimates for the accomplished sample in early adulthood, ages 17 to 26, include the following:

- Jean Jacques Rousseau, 125
- Nicolas Copernicus, 130
- Rembrandt Van Rijn, 135
- Martin Luther, 145
- Charles Darwin, 140
- Abraham Lincoln, 140
- Leonardo da Vinci, 150
- Thomas Jefferson, 150
- Wolfgang Amadeus Mozart, 150
- Charlotte Brontë, 155
- Michelangelo Buonarroti, 160
- Galileo Galilei, 165
- Samuel Taylor Coleridge, 165
- Isaac Newton, 170
- John Stuart Mill, 170
- Gottfried Wilhelm Leibnitz, 190
- Wolfgang Goethe, 200

When Cox averaged the IQs according to group, the soldiers scored lowest, with artists slightly higher. Scientist and writers had middle-range IQs. Philosophers as a group obtained the highest estimated IQ scores.

Based on their research, Cox and her associates were able to generalize: High degrees of accomplishment seemed to require intelligence that was considerably above average. Most of the highly accomplished scientists in Cox's study had estimated IQs in the range of 135 to 180 (Simonton, 1988). Of course, high intelligence did not guarantee eminence. High intelligence functioned as a necessary but not sufficient condition for exceptional creativity and accomplishment. More is not necessarily better, however. Intelligence may have a threshold function as it relates to creative output. Eminent mathematicians, for example, do not have higher IQs than do average Ph.Ds in mathematics (Simonton, 1988). Once a threshold of moderate to high intelligence is met, other personal qualities, such as vision and drive, predict success.

study. Of the many subsidiary questions we could ask about the nature of intelligence, one seems fundamental: Is intelligence one thing or many? Does intelligence have a basic unity, or is it really a multiplicity of capabilities that in aggregate help us to think and act intelligently?

Spearman's g

The British psychologist Charles Spearman took a strong position on the question of whether intelligence is one thing or many. He believed that intelligence is fundamentally unitary and applies to all mental performance. If so, then whatever mental work we engage in requires intelligence to greater or lesser degrees. Spearman's hypothesis was not merely theoretical, however; he found a way to test the idea.

Spearman needed data to test his hypothesis. As raw data, he used performance on a variety of mental tests. Like Binet, Spearman emphasized mental performance rather than sensory acuity or reaction times. But, unlike Binet, Spearman did not aggregate mental performance to determine mental age or IQ. Rather than focusing on individual tests, he shifted attention to the quantitative relationships among the various mental tests. The quantification of those relationships took the form of a correlation coefficient. As we have seen, correlations, symbolized by r, range from $+1$ to -1, with a correlation of zero indicating no relationship at all. Spearman's idea could be put to the test. If intelligence is a general unified trait, it should result in a specific pattern of correlations among mental tests. In particular, correlations should be *positive*.

Among diverse tests of mental ability, Spearman found positive correlations throughout. The size of the correlations varied from low to moderately high. The distinct absence of zero correlations or negative correlations told Spearman that the data were consistent with his hypothesis that a unitary mental capability was relevant to all of the tests. If a person's mental ability were high, then it ought to have a positive influence on every mental test. The pattern of positive correlations, which Spearman called the **positive manifold**, was evidence for the unity of intelligence. Since Spearman's discovery, the positive manifold has been confirmed by dozens of other psychometricians through subsequent decades up to the present. For anyone claiming that intelligence is not a psychological reality, the positive manifold is evidence to the contrary.

Spearman took the analysis further. He invented an early version of **factor analysis** that helped simplify patterns of test correlations. If a single dimension, or **factor**, was influencing patterns of correlations, then the technique could identify that single dimension. With the dimension identified, it became possible to specify the relationships of each test to that general factor. Presumably, some tests were more directly related to that general factor, and other tests were more distantly related.

Mathematically, Spearman was able to extract the dominant dimension, or factor, in the correlation matrix for individual tests. Spearman called that dominant dimension **general mental ability**, which he abbreviated **g**. He also computed the relationship of each test to g. As predicted, some tests had strong relationships to g; others had weaker relationships. But the overall pattern was significant: *all* tests loaded on the general factor. In conformity to Spearman's hypothesis, all tests were influenced by the general factor, g. However, each test also had its own unique variability that was independent of g. This test-unique factor Spearman gave the label, **s**. Spearman summed up these findings in his **two-factor theory**: Performance on each mental test is derived from two sources: g (the factor common to all mental tests) and s (a "factor" specific to each mental test).

Spearman had guesses about what the factor he called g actually was. He conjectured that g was the ability to find connections (to "educe relations") and to apply those relations to find new relationships (to "educe correlates"). Essentially, Spearman believed that g tapped into inductive reasoning ability, which we will see was a very good guess as to the nature of general intelligence, one that corresponds to some well-supported contemporary hypotheses. For our present purposes, it is important to remember that Spearman's research succeeded in finding both a positive manifold of test intercorrelations and a general factor among those correlations. Spearman also developed mathematical techniques, including early versions of the correlation coefficient and factor analysis, which became powerful tools for subsequent generations of psychometric researchers.

Thurstone's Primary Mental Abilities

About 20 years after Spearman's pioneering work on intelligence research, a very different point of view emerged from the work of the American psychometrician, L. L. Thurstone. Using analysis techniques similar to those employed by Spearman, Thurstone arrived at the opposite conclusion—that there was no general factor, g. Thurstone, like Spearman, had obtained test scores on widely divergent mental ability tests, many of which were invented by Thurstone himself. He then computed test intercorrelations, which showed a different pattern than the one identified by Spearman. Thurstone found that the tests did intercorrelate positively, but also that some correlations were much stronger than others. The overall pattern was *not* of a single ability dominating the correlation matrix, but instead of *multiple* abilities influencing clusters of tests.

Factor analysis confirmed the hypothesis. Rather than uncovering a single general ability, Thurstone found multiple independent factors. He called these **primary mental abilities**. The primary mental abilities identified by Thurstone were the following: numerical, verbal comprehension, word fluency, space, reasoning, memory, and perceptual speed. Thurstone's conclusions therefore diverged sharply from Spearman's. Thurstone was direct in making this comparison, declaring: "We have not found the general factor of Spearman" (1938, p. vii).

The dichotomy set up by Spearman's and Thurstone's theoretical positions, each supported by data-based empirical research, influenced the course of intelligence theory for at least the next half century. To some extent, the question of whether there is a single dominant intelligence, or whether instead there are multiple independent intelligences, has endured to the present. For example, Arthur Jensen (1998) has advocated a theory holding to a single dominant g factor; Howard Gardner (1983, 1998) has advanced the well-known contemporary theory of multiple intelligences. Interestingly, neither of these two polar positions is widely accepted by most intelligence theorists today. The truth may lie somewhere in the middle.

Convergence of Viewpoints

Is intelligence one thing or many? Posing the question in this way might limit progress toward gaining a fuller appreciation for the structure of intelligence. This is so because the answer may not be *yes* or *no*, but rather *yes* and *yes*. Human intelligence might have properties of unity (supporting Spearman's g) and properties of diversity (supporting Thurstone's primary mental abilities). Seemingly contradictory statements can be accommodated within a single structural theory of intelligence. That theoretical structure is the *hierarchical* organization of mental abilities. Figure 10.1 depicts the theoretical resolution of Spearman's and Thurstone's theories into a hierarchical structure.

In time, both Spearman and Thurstone came to acknowledge that their theoretical competitor was at least partially correct. As Spearman continued his research, he found

FIGURE 10.1
A Hierarchy of Mental Abilities
The structure combines Spearman's and Thurstone's viewpoints.
[From Martinez, 2000. Reprinted by permission of Copyright Clearance Center on behalf of Lawrence Erlbaum Associates, Inc.]

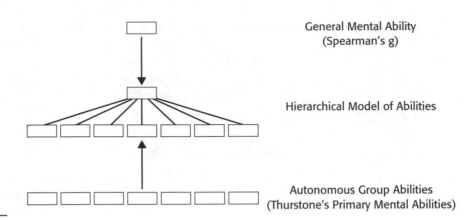

General Mental Ability
(Spearman's g)

Hierarchical Model of Abilities

Autonomous Group Abilities
(Thurstone's Primary Mental Abilities)

clusters of relatively higher correlations among some tests. Eventually, this led Spearman to conclude that there are higher-order factors somewhere between the general factor, g, and factors specific to individual tests, s. Likewise, as Thurstone's research program progressed, especially in the measurement of children's abilities, he found evidence for a general factor that has wide influence over many different ability factors. It is a credit to both men that they were open-minded toward their data, even if it meant moderating or abandoning their original convictions.

Since the time when Spearman and Thurstone each acknowledged both the unity and diversity of mental abilities, hierarchical theories have tended to dominate—at least within the psychometric (test score–based) paradigm. One prominent psychometric researcher summarized the *rapprochement* by noting that the unity and diversity positions on human intelligence were "reconcilable, and with mutual illumination" (Cattell, 1987, p. 30).

Hierarchical Theories of Intelligence

Both Spearman and Thurstone had something important to say about the nature of intelligence. The confluence of their theories led to hierarchical models that accommodated the dual truths that intelligence was both unified (one thing) and diverse (many). Much of the theoretical work of subsequent researchers shifted toward trying to determine the *best possible* hierarchical theory. The question became, what structure best captures the organization of human intelligence?

Carroll's Three-Stratum Model

In the quest to understand the best possible hierarchical model of cognitive ability, there is a short cut. Rather than review the succession of models developed between roughly 1940 and 1990, we can skip directly to the comprehensive model proposed by John B. Carroll (1993). Carroll's approach differed from all preceding research; the difference was the colossal magnitude of the project. Bear in mind that in factor analyses of test data sets, researchers concentrated typically on a *single* data set, usually one of their own construction. Carroll, by contrast, assembled every available data set that could feed into his analysis. The resulting analysis took in 460 data sets, a scale of analysis that exceeded anything previously done by orders of magnitude.

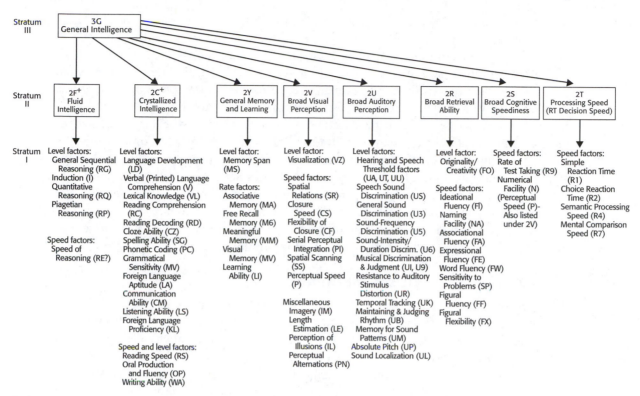

FIGURE 10.2
Carroll's Three-Stratum Model
The hierarchical structure has general intelligence at the top, and includes fluid and crystallized factors. [From Carroll, 1993. Reprinted by permission of Cambridge University Press.]

The summative depiction of Carroll's findings is shown in the diagram above. Note that the basic organization of Carroll's hierarchical model is a three-stratum (three-level) structure. At the pinnacle of the model is general intelligence, or G. (Carroll preferred to use uppercase G, to avoid any unnecessary baggage associated with Spearman's g, but the meaning is largely the same.) We can safely conclude, therefore, that Carroll's analysis vindicated the place and importance of general intelligence at the apex of human cognitive abilities. This general factor contributes in large or small degrees to performance on all other subsidiary factors, which is much the way that Charles Spearman originally thought about intelligence.

However, Carroll's Three-Stratum Model, illustrated in Figure 10.2, tells us much more. At the bottom of the diagram are Stratum I factors, those derived directly from analysis of test score intercorrelations. In fact, you could imagine many thousands of tests in the databases used by Carroll as being situated *below* Stratum I. Listing the actual tests used would make the diagram too unwieldy. Indeed, the large number of factors listed in Stratum I make the diagram almost overly complex. Fortunately, for purposes of this book, Stratum I is not nearly as important as Stratum II or Stratum III.

Stratum II tells us a lot about what constitutes cognitive ability. Relatively few factors are listed, and so we can gain an appreciation for the basic structure of abilities by examining Stratum II. Remember that Stratum II was not produced directly from test intercorrelations, but rather from the correlations among factors listed in Stratum I. In other words, the factor analysis of tests produced the Stratum I factors. The correlated factors in Stratum I were in turn subjected to factor analysis to produce Stratum II. Finally, the Stratum II factors were factor analyzed. This final analysis led to the identification of one additional factor, G, at Stratum III.

One interesting quality of Stratum II is that it bears some resemblance to Thurstone's primary mental abilities. The number of group factors is similar (7 or 8), and some of the factors are comparable between Thurstone's pioneering list and Carroll's near-definitive list. Moreover, Stratum I and Stratum II together depict the essential theoretical struggle between Spearman and Thurstone, a conceptual divide that was eventually bridged by a hierarchical structure of cognitive abilities.

Note an additional structural feature of Carroll's diagram. The Stratum III factor, G, is not positioned centrally over Stratum II. It is offset to the left. Consequently, the lines connecting G to the group factors in Stratum II are unequal in length. The lengths of lines are significant because they show that some Stratum II factors are closer to G than are others. Two factors in particular are strongly associated with general mental ability: crystallized intelligence and fluid intelligence. These two factors are so important to understanding the nature of human intelligence that we will now delve into their meanings as well as their significance to education.

Fluid and Crystallized Intelligence

The discovery of fluid and crystallized intelligence was not a product of Carroll's research. Rather, the identification of these two factors can be traced back to the research of Raymond Cattell in the 1940s. Later, in the 1960s, Cattell collaborated with John Horn to develop further the theory of fluid and crystallized intelligence. Cattell and Horn's exploration of these two ability factors advanced intelligence theory significantly. The verification of the two factors in Carroll's model, and their close empirical connections to G, show just how important fluid and crystallized intelligence are. But *what* are they?

Concise definitions can be given at this point, but these should be considered preliminary:

- **Fluid intelligence** is the ability to deal effectively with novel situations through problem solving.

- **Crystallized intelligence** is the ability to acquire knowledge, often in verbal form.

To get an intuitive feel for fluid and crystallized intelligence, imagine two people who are opposites in these two abilities.

- Floyd is highly adaptable. Put him in an unfamiliar situation and he usually succeeds. He loves practical and intellectual challenges, and is amazingly adept at discovering the key issues and challenges of any problem he faces. Floyd is not a book reader, though, and he has no formal education beyond high school. Even so, everyone who meets Floyd perceives that he is extraordinarily intelligent, and with effort and the right opportunities he could have been successful in any occupation he chose.

- Craig is the consummate student. He loves to learn and he reads voraciously. He is also a very good test-taker, has had considerable success in high school and college, and is currently doing very well in a master's program. But Craig has limitations. Even though his knowledge is impressively broad on many subjects, Craig is not a good problem solver. Put him in an unfamiliar situation and he flounders. If he locks his keys in his car, for example, he's helpless. Everyone agrees that Craig is "book smart," but even given Craig's impressive intellect it's obvious that something is missing—an adaptability to novel problems.

For many people, it's tempting to believe that there is a compensatory principle that people who are smart in one way are not smart in another (e.g., they are good in math, therefore bad in English—or vice versa). But is this really the way things work? Remember the positive manifold, the dominant pattern of positive intercorrelations between tests of mental abilities postulated and confirmed by Spearman a century ago. The dominant reality of mental abilities is that above-average ability on one factor predicts above-average ability in another. Floyd and Craig are conceptual opposites, but in the real world, fluid and crystallized ability tend to go together. This is consistent with the commonsense meaning of intelligence—it applies to all mental abilities. The pattern is quite different from the hypothesis of zero correlations (hypothesized by Thurstone) or of negative correlations (believed by those who think that being smart in one way implies begin non-smart in another).

Let's return to Carroll's diagram. Fluid and crystallized intelligence are the Stratum II factors most strongly connected to G. But the line connecting fluid intelligence to G is shorter, indicating a stronger relationship. The proximity between G and fluid intelligence is important to appreciate. There is such a close association between G and fluid intelligence that some respected investigators have proposed that they are in fact indistinguishable; that is, $G = G_f$ (Gustafsson, 1999). This bold hypothesis is not yet widely accepted, but its very plausibility is provocative. It helps us to see that the nature of general intelligence can be understood partly through appreciating its relationship to fluid intelligence.

TIME COURSE FOR FLUID/CRYSTALLIZED. One purpose of this chapter is to show that intelligence can change. It should not be regarded as a fixed cognitive attribute but instead as a set of cognitive skills that can be developed over time through educative experience. We can identify *typical* patterns of change, and these differ between fluid and crystallized intelligence. The typical trends for fluid and crystallized intelligence over a life span are depicted in Figure 10.3.

Crystallized intelligence, representing the growth of knowledge over time, tends to rise until the age of 60 or so. After then, declines in crystallized intelligence seem to be related to declining health. If good health continues, then crystallized intelligence may continue to grow, or at least to stabilize. The life span trend is not as favorable for fluid intelligence. The ability to deal with novel problems that marks fluid intelligence typically peaks between about age 22 and 30, and declines slowly thereafter. We are most adaptable, apparently, as young adults.

FIGURE 10.3
Fluid and Crystallized Intelligence over the Life Span *Fluid intelligence usually peaks in early adulthood; crystallized intelligence tends to rise indefinitely.* [Copyright © 1967 by Transaction Publishers. Reprinted by permission of the publisher.]

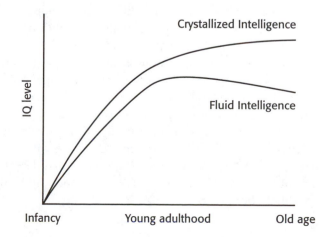

No one knows for sure if the decline of fluid intelligence with age is inevitable. There may be some biological basis for the slow decline. Alternatively, the rise of crystallized intelligence during the decline of fluid intelligence may reflect a natural trade-off that fits changing life circumstances. Early in life, from infancy to young adulthood, there is a great survival need for adaptability. Children learn language and assimilate their native cultures; adolescents engage in abstraction and learn to infer the beliefs and intentions of others. Young adults develop their own identities and independent lives, careers, and relationships. The ferocious pace of change during youth often moderates during the mid-20s when identities and routines stabilize. From then onward, change is still a factor, but personal success also draws significantly from what a person already knows—the fund of crystallized intelligence derived from experience. On the job, also, accumulated crystallized intelligence can equip workers with the indispensable quality of expertise.

If the trend lines for crystallized and fluid intelligence correspond roughly to rising expertise and declining flexibility, it's possible to imagine economic consequences. In countries where the average age of workers is rising, the cost may be a decline in average levels of fluid intelligence. Because the economy depends on rapid innovation, the consequences may be seriously unfavorable. The combination of an aging American workforce and the trend lines for fluid and crystallized intelligence prompted psychologist Earl Hunt (1995) to write a book entitled, *Will We Be Smart Enough*? Not only the United States, but also Germany and Japan face demographic shifts toward older populations due to declining birth rates and lengthening life spans. Those countries, too, might ask whether their workforce will be sufficiently innovative to be optimally competitive in a twenty-first century world economy.

Both fluid intelligence and crystallized intelligence are important for effective work in the decades ahead. Which is more important—fluid or crystallized? Certainly, the flexible and innovative thinking of fluid intelligence is a vital quality for any worker, especially when market success depends on being a step ahead of the competition in idea production. But the dividend of crystallized intelligence from extended experience is also crucial. Crystallized intelligence also predicts school-based learning better than does fluid intelligence (Ackerman, 2006). As knowledge expands, we need people who can learn efficiently and who understand their fields thoroughly. The extensive knowledge that is so central to expertise will be essential in the future workplace. As work becomes more mental, there arise corresponding needs for innovative and flexible cognition (fluid) as well as for deep technical knowledge expressed as expertise (crystallized). Both fluid and crystallized intelligence will become *more* important in the decades ahead.

Fortunately, it is possible to deliberately develop intelligence and so equip people to become more effective in their daily lives, both in the workplace and outside. In fact, schools now are incubators for the development of intelligence, though that particular role of schools is rarely acknowledged. Evidence that schools actually play this role is provided later in the chapter. Assuming that schools develop both fluid intelligence and crystallized intelligence, which one is currently emphasized? The answer seems obvious—schools concentrate heavily on developing crystallized intelligence, perhaps to the neglect of fluid intelligence. There are reasons for this tendency: above all, knowledge (crystallized) is much easier to teach and test than the ability to think innovatively (fluid) (Lohman, 1993). But given the dual importance of fluid and crystallized intelligence now and in the years ahead, this imbalance should be corrected.

Emergent Theories of Intelligence

The field of intelligence theory has been highly productive, but even the best theories have not escaped criticism. One criticism rises above all others in prevalence and importance. Many scholars have felt that traditional intelligence theories can be faulted for being too analytic, meaning that theories focus excessively on mental processes that are convergent, logical, and precise. They emphasize problems that have a definable correct solution. The ability to think analytically is surely an important aspect of intellectual power, but intelligence is more than this.

The informal theories of the layperson reveal that everyday conceptions of who is smart extend beyond narrow analytic abilities. For example, people tend to recognize "street smarts," practical manifestations of intelligence that help people survive and thrive in situations where the rules for success are not necessarily explicit. Informal theories also tend to recognize social intelligence, the ability to work with other people to advance one's own goals and to gain favor. Moreover, there is the mythical intelligence of the creative genius—the unstoppable brilliance of Einstein, Mozart, and Leonardo da Vinci. Their creative transcendence rises far above the mundane variety of intelligence expressed as correct answers on an IQ test.

What then is the next step toward recognizing forms of intelligence that are broader? It's not enough simply to name a form of intelligence and expect it to be valid (e.g., artistic intelligence, technical intelligence, or culinary intelligence). One can plausibly generate a name for any apparent talent and call it "intelligence" but that name does not guarantee a reality. Any proposed theory of intelligence, extending back to Spearman's and Thurstone's, must first appeal to data to determine (or at least help decide) if a hypothetical form of intelligence is the real thing, or if it is just the fanciful creation of a good imagination.

Gardner's Multiple Intelligences Theory

Among the contemporary theories that have challenged the narrow depiction of traditional intelligence, the most widely known is Howard Gardner's (1983, 1998) theory of **multiple intelligences**. In Gardner's theory, the plural–*intelligences*–indicates an implicit rejection of general mental ability in favor of separate, independent intelligences. By rejecting g, Gardner has positioned his theory as distinct from the mainstream of intelligence scholars. Implicitly harking back to Thurstone's theory from the 1930s, Gardner resurrected the idea that there are several intelligences rather than a single overarching intelligence.

One of the truly remarkable features of multiple intelligences (MI) theory is the impressively diverse array of evidence that Gardner advanced to support his theory. Most significantly, Gardner did not rely exclusively or even primarily on psychometric data from mental ability tests. Instead, he drew on such divergent forms of data as clinical impairments caused by brain injuries, studies of savants and prodigies, symbol systems that support intelligent thought, and the tendencies of intelligence to evolve into finely honed expert states. Based on these and other evidence forms, Gardner originally proposed the existence of seven intelligences. These were subsequently expanded to eight intelligences (or perhaps one or two more, on which Gardner was equivocal) presented in Table 10.1.

The list is a mix of the familiar and the innovative. Three of the intelligences—logical-mathematical, linguistic, and spatial—bear some correspondence to traditional

TABLE 10.1 Gardner's Multiple Intelligences

Intelligence	End-States	Core Components
Logical-mathematical	Scientist; Mathematician	Sensitivity to, and capacity to discern, logical or numerical patterns; ability to handle long chains of reasoning.
Linguistic	Poet; Journalist	Sensitivity to the sounds, rhythms, and meanings of words; sensitivity to the different functions of language.
Musical	Composer; Violinist	Abilities to produce and appreciate rhythm, pitch, and timbre; appreciation of forms of musical expressiveness.
Spatial	Navigator; Sculptor	Capacities to perceive the visual-spatial world accurately and to perform transformations of one's initial perceptions.
Bodily-kinesthetic	Dancer; Athlete	Abilities to control one's body movements and to handle objects skillfully.
Interpersonal	Therapist; Salesman	Capacities to discern and respond appropriately to the moods, temperaments, motivations, and desires of other people.
Intrapersonal	Philosopher; Theologian	Access to one's own feelings and the ability to discriminate among them and draw upon them to guide behavior; knowledge of one's own strengths, weaknesses, desires, and intelligences.
Naturalist	Botanist; Geologist; Archaeologist	Ability to distinguish among, classify, and use features of natural and artificial environments.

factors identified within the psychometric tradition. The other intelligences are more innovative, but also more controversial: musical, bodily-kinesthetic, interpersonal, intrapersonal, and naturalist. What seems hard to argue is that they are more than specific talents—that they are broadly applicable abilities, that is, true intelligences. Is there really a bodily-kinesthetic intelligence, for example, that extends broadly to many different manifestations beyond specific forms of dance or sport? Is music an intelligence or instead an area of talent development?

Among the evidences that Gardner marshals to support his theory is the anatomical and functional isolation of each intelligence within the brain. If every intelligence is a separate brain module, as Gardner presumes, then damage to the part of the brain controlling an intelligence should affect that intelligence only, and none of the others. This is the criterion of **selective impairment**—that brain damage in some clinical patients will compromise one intelligence but leave the others intact. Gardner succeeds in presenting clinical evidence to show that the phenomenon of selective impairment holds for most of his identified intelligences—with one major exception. Logical-mathematical intelligence seems not to be localizable to a specific part of the brain but rather corresponds to neural activity over an extensive area of cerebral cortex. Gardner admits that the anatomical spread of logical-mathematical intelligence may suggest that it has a role as a general-purpose intelligence, perhaps coordinating several of the others. Such a role is not far off from the long-held tenets of psychometrically oriented intelligence researchers who see such a general role for g.

Besides citing brain data, Gardner points to the existence of savants and prodigies in whom certain mental capabilities, particularly in music and mathematics, can develop independently to high levels of proficiency. In the case of prodigies, musical talent can be honed to very impressive levels even against a backdrop of rather normal abilities for a child's age. The phenomenon of savants (historically known as *idiot savants*) is similar: Some adults compromised by autism or mental retardation develop very high technical competency—again, often in music or mathematics—that seems preternatural in manifestation.

Gardner's motivation to connect high levels of intelligence to culturally-valued achievements also prompts him to study intelligence manifested as expert states. Gardner sees the many intelligences of his theory as evolving into forms of expertise that are valued and therefore cultivated by societies. The apotheosis of verbal intelligence is the poet, the pinnacle of spatial intelligence is the sculptor or the architect, and so on. In

INTEREST MAGNET 10.3

Savants

The movie *Rain Man* presents the fictional story of Raymond Babbit, an autistic man who has an amazing capacity for numerical memory and calculation. The character of Raymond Babbit was inspired by a real-life savant named Kim Peek. Although not autistic, Peek was born with brain abnormalities that included the absence of a corpus callosum, the nerve bundle that connects the left and right hemispheres. Despite his brain abnormalities, Peek has extraordinary abilities. He is a prodigious reader and is said to have memorized more than 7,600 books (Treffert & Wallace, 2007). He also is extremely facile with mental calculations, a skill he uses in his job as a payroll bookkeeper. Neuroscientists have speculated that Peek's brain compensated for the missing structures by making many other profuse connections.

One musical savant, identified by the initials NP, was an autistic man in his early 20s. After hearing Grieg's "Melodie" only once, NP could reproduce the piano piece almost flawlessly. But when he was exposed to an unusual atonal composition, Bartok's "Whole Tone Scale," NP's repeated attempts to master the piece revealed only slow progress. In trying to reproduce the atonal piece, NP's errors were "structure preserving"—they imposed conventional melodic structure over the composition. NP's expertise was limited in that it could not survive outside the "framework of more conventional tonal structures" (Sloboda, Hermelin, & O'Connor, 1985, p. 165).

In addition to prodigious memory or high degrees of musical or artistic skills, some savants develop highly specialized "splinter skills." These include extraordinary recall of sports statistics, lightning-fast calculation,

precise estimation of distance by sight, and calendrical calculation—the ability to figure the day of the week for any date in a span of thousands of years. Some artistic savants display an amazing ability to reproduce flawless replicas of sculptures or paintings after only brief exposure. One savant named Ellen has a highly accurate internal clock by which she knows the exact time to the second (Treffert & Wallace, 2007).

Savant syndrome is very rare: Only about 100 cases are recognized in the world. Savant syndrome is also much more common in males than in females by a ratio of about 5 to 1. Of the known savants, at least half are autistic; the others have different developmental disabilities, including those caused by brain damage (Treffert & Wallace, 2007). Theories of savant syndrome are still rather primitive. Recent research suggests that the syndrome might arise from damage to the left hemisphere, which is subsequently compensated by a more highly developed right hemisphere.

Savant qualities, especially artistic talent, sometimes appear among people suffering from dementia affecting the brain's language centers (Miller et al., 1998). The sudden appearance of artistic talent suggested an intriguing possibility: Savant qualities might lie dormant in normal minds. This might appear to be only idle speculation, but researchers in Australia have evidence for its truth. Using magnetic pulses, they "switched off" part the left temporal lobes of normal adults and found that savant-like abilities appeared temporarily in some of their subjects (Young, Ridding, & Morrell, 2004; Snyder, Bahramali, Hawker, & Mitchell, 2006). The new abilities, which include enhanced artistic ability and improved accuracy at numerical estimation, lasted only a few hours.

other words, intelligences are not simply abstract mental abilities, ready-made for general purposes by a capable brain. Rather, various intelligences are cultivated and utilized by cultures—and differently from culture to culture. One culture will value bodily-kinesthetic intelligence expressed through dance. Another culture will place great importance on intrapersonal intelligence developed as self-insight or introspective religion. Still another culture will implicitly emphasize yet a different intelligence.

The theory of multiple intelligences has several interesting theoretical and methodological features. However, there is reason to doubt Gardner's claim that his eight or so intelligences are relatively autonomous. Not surprisingly, his theory's more traditional intelligences—logical-mathematical, linguistic, and spatial—are moderately to highly intercorrelated. How, then, are they relatively autonomous? Gardner's other hypothesized intelligences are less intercorrelated as measurable factors, but they are also the intelligences whose validity is most open to question.

INSTRUCTIONAL IMPLICATIONS. Gardner's theory has been applied more directly and broadly to instruction than has any other theory of intelligence. Indeed, the influence of Gardner's theory on the conceptualization of teaching—particularly in the elementary schools—has been profound. The theory of multiple intelligences has in fact been far more widely accepted and promoted among educators than among scholars of human intelligence. Why is this? One possible explanation is the suggestion within Gardner's MI theory that the implicit ordering of human intellectual capability implied by general intelligence is not warranted. If there are different ways of being smart, then the seemingly unfair implications of a single ordering dimension, g, are overturned. For those who prefer a more egalitarian view of talent or who chafe at the thought of a single ordering dimension of intellectual ability, a conceptual shift to multiple intelligences can be liberating.

The egalitarian values that make MI theory appealing have led to misinterpretations of Gardner's theory. For example, educators sometimes mistakenly infer that because multiple intelligences are semi-autonomous they are also compensatory—that being low in one intelligence implies being high in another. A parallel belief is that every child is smart in his or her own way; an imaginary law of fairness prescribes that intelligences are equitably distributed across the population but manifest in different ways. In a perfectly fair world, talent might be distributed in this way, but there is absolutely no evidence that this is true. Nor is there any claim within Gardner's theory that intelligences are equitably distributed. His theory is not a theory of equality but rather of the underappreciated diversity of intelligence.

Gardner's MI theory has been subject to other, related distortions. The tendency to believe in an equitable distribution of intelligences has sometimes prompted educators to identify each child's particular "intelligence." Their assumption is sometimes expressed this way: It's not how smart you are, but *how you are smart*. Used (or misused) in this way, MI theory is transmuted into a theory of learner types—another extrapolation that Gardner never intended. The leap from brain research to theories of learner types is all too common. The misapplication is compounded by a second error: An assumption that if instruction were tailored to these learner types, then learning outcomes would be improved. This is the ATI (aptitude-treatment interaction) hypothesis, presented in the previous chapter. The underlying notion, completely sensible, is that if we really understood learners, we could design instruction tailored to their abilities and preferences. The result would be better learning outcomes. The ATI idea is powerful, but it is not a principle that is incorporated into MI theory. The limited data on the effectiveness of using MI theory in this way has not yielded confirmatory results (Callahan et al., 1995).

Despite citable shortcomings and distortions, we would be wrong to believe that Gardner's theory of intelligence has not had positive effects on education. Above all, the diversification of instructional approaches has enriched pedagogy in elementary schools and among older learners. The belief that there are multiple ways to teach and learn has long been favored by many scholars and teachers, not least of whom were John Dewey and the progressive educators of the early twentieth century. Gardner's theory provides one rationale for instructional experimentation and a heuristic for guiding it. Although an overall benefit is hard to prove, the effect has likely been broadly positive on learning and on learners' attitudes.

Finally, Gardner's theory has prompted educators to rethink the nature of intelligence. MI theory has shown that the construct of intelligence or "intelligences" can be a positive, pro-educational concept. It's not inevitably a dangerous idea for repressive purposes, although it has sometimes been wielded as such in times past (Gould, 1981). Even if MI theory is eventually superseded by a more educationally attractive theory of intelligence, the theory has sensitized educators to the belief that traditional views of intelligence are justifiably criticized as too narrowly analytic. Most intelligence researchers also believe that traditional intelligence theory is excessively narrow, and so many theoretical developments have aimed, as Gardner's has, to extend the conceptualization of intelligence to a broader, more comprehensive understanding of what it means to be smart.

Sternberg's Theory of Successful Intelligence

Only two contemporary comprehensive theories of intelligence have had widespread influence in challenging entrenched conceptions of intelligence as analytical. The one just described, Gardner's MI theory, takes the theoretical stance that the construct of general intelligence should be replaced by a set of relatively autonomous intelligences. A second theory, Robert Sternberg's theory of **successful intelligence**, does not aim to discredit traditional analytic intelligence so much as to maintain that it should be complemented by other forms of intelligence. Moreover, significantly, Sternberg does not use the plural *intelligences* but instead construes his broad model as consisting of different types of intelligence. The theory of successful intelligence recognizes three such forms of intelligence: analytical, practical, and creative.

In Sternberg's theory, analytical intelligence corresponds to intelligence as it has typically been conceptualized through the decades. It is intelligence conceived as convergent, precise, and rational mental operations—the kind of thinking that pays off well on tests of mental ability and on most school-based tests. Sternberg does not question that analytical intelligence is important in the modern world. To be analytically intelligent is to be prepared to engage many life problems that demand rational, convergent thinking. Fields of study and career success often rely heavily on analytical intelligence. Likewise, gatekeeper admissions tests very often require the proficient application of analytical intelligence.

Without denying the importance of analytical intelligence, Sternberg maintains that it must be complemented by two other forms of intelligence, namely, practical and creative intelligence. By practical intelligence, Sternberg refers to the ability to understand and apply the often unwritten or tacit rules for success. Performance in any job requires attention not only to officially recognized knowledge and protocol but also to non-stated rules about expected behavior and what is required to get ahead. The practically intelligent person has the ability to learn the unstated and unofficial, but highly significant, knowledge necessary to succeed. According to the theory, this ability is highly important to success within specific contexts. Among Sternberg's own graduate students, for example, some students who were not as analytically intelligent as their peers made up for their relative deficit by being highly attuned to relevant practical knowledge about how to succeed. Sometimes practical intelligence is more decisive in personal success than is analytical intelligence.

Sternberg has found evidence that measures of practical intelligence sometimes offer superior predictive power over measures of analytic intelligence. Among Kenyan tribespeople, for example, measures of practical intelligence were positively related to a person's ability to specify traditional medicines to treat local diseases (Sternberg et al., 2001). Interestingly, measures of analytical intelligence were *negatively* correlated with the ability to specify folk medicine treatments. Analytical modes of cognition were apparently antagonistic to traditional ways of conceptualizing and solving local problems. In the workplace, also, Sternberg has found positive relationships between employees' practical intelligence and their ability to pick up knowledge about how to be successful in the office or on the job site. These measures in turn predicted workers' occupational success.

The third component of Sternberg's theory is creative intelligence. Creative intelligence directly addresses an obvious shortcoming of intelligence as traditionally construed—that analytical ability succeeds in producing correct answers to well-structured problems but has little to say about how high-quality divergent thinking comes about. Great acts of intelligence through the ages have not been simply analytical; they have also been rich in creative insight. Sternberg's creative intelligence directly identifies flexible idea production as one important kind of intelligent thought. As with measures of practical intelligence, Sternberg has found that measures of creative intelligence predict some aspects of success better than do traditional analytic measures.

Just as Gardner's theory has been subject to criticism, so has Sternberg's theory. Critics have asked whether creative intelligence can justifiably be thought of as a generalized psychological trait. Intuitively, creativity seems bound to specific knowledge domains—people who are highly creative in one area are not necessarily creative in another. In other words, creative intelligence might not have the generalizable utility of analytical intelligence but might instead be highly context- and domain-bound. Much the same criticism applies to practical intelligence; is it really a generalizable intellectual trait broadly useful across many performance contexts? If not, is the word *intelligence* justified?

Questions attending Sternberg's theory are largely the subject of ongoing research. Recent data present the theory of successful intelligence as potentially useful in the prediction of college success (Sternberg, 2006). Measures of analytical ability in the SAT and ACT tests have long been used by college admissions officers because they offer utility for predicting the grades of college freshmen. Indeed, the quantitative prediction of course grades is a major justification for the tests' validity for this purpose. For those wishing to expand admissions testing beyond more traditional measures, an important strategic requirement is to show that alternative tests can offer prediction of academic success *beyond* that offered by traditional SATs and ACTs. Sternberg and his collaborators have found such evidence. Measures of practical and creative intelligence predicted college success in the form of freshman grades. Moreover, their predictive ability was additive to traditional tests. The combined power of analytic, practical, and creative intelligence yielded superior prediction over analytic intelligence alone.

Together, the three forms of intelligence specified in Sternberg's theory are hypothesized to predict success in widely different environments. Prediction is the key. The early intelligence researchers, beginning with Binet, construed intelligence as the mental ability that facilitated success in academic environments. Later, creators of military aptitude tests and industrial psychologists found that measured intelligence likewise had value for predicting workplace performance. Terman's studies of high-IQ children extended this paradigm to test the notion that IQ could predict still broader life outcomes beyond school and workplace success. Sternberg's theory implicitly recognizes a generalized relationship between intelligence and success. The theory also implicitly assumes that conceptualizations of both *intelligence* and *success* must be broader for this dynamic intelligence-success connection to be fully explored. The theory of successful intelligence is the most highly developed attempt to work out the dynamic connections between broadly conceived intelligence and broadly manifested success.

Emotional Intelligence

For many decades, psychologists have sensed that traditional notions of intelligence did not recognize social aspects of intelligence. It seemed obvious that intelligence is often applied—indeed, must be manifested—in social settings. Success or failure is often determined by one's ability to get along with other people, to work toward common goals, to negotiate compromises, and so on. Therefore, an insistence that intelligence should be conceptualized and measured solely as individual performance seemed to neglect an important manifestation of intelligence.

Psychologists hypothesized a form of intelligence called **social intelligence** that describes the ability to interact intelligently with other people (Kihlstrom & Cantor, 2000). The idea seemed sensible. Imagine friends or acquaintances who are fantastically skilled in social contexts, and who use their skills to advance their interests. Is this not intelligence? But while the idea seems obviously believable, social intelligence is not yet fully recognized as a form of intelligence for many of the reasons that Gardner's and Sternberg's proposed constructs have been challenged. It's hard to show that social intelligence is a stable, coherent, and generalized trait that predicts success outcomes broadly. Without such strong evidence, the status of social intelligence has remained equivocal.

Nevertheless, a variant of social intelligence began to gain attention in the 1990s. **Emotional intelligence** shifted the focus of ability to emotions. According to the theory, emotional intelligence is the ability to "read" and respond to the emotions of other people, as well as the ability to understand one's own emotions. Naturally, as with any intelligence, people vary significantly in these abilities and that variability in turn predicts success in various contexts. Once proposed, the construct of emotional intelligence was subject to the same level of scrutiny as other forms of proposed intelligence.

A team of psychologists at Yale University carried out the early research on emotional intelligence (Salovey & Mayer, 1989–90). Drawing on those research efforts, writer and psychologist Daniel Goleman popularized the concept in his bestselling book *Emotional Intelligence* (1995). Since the publication of Goleman's book, psychologists have continued to amass evidence on the validity of emotional intelligence. At this point, emotional intelligence carries much the same status of Gardner's and Sternberg's proposed constructs—it has some credible evidence to back it, but it has not yet risen to the status of a widely accepted theory.

Distributed Intelligence

Traditional intelligence theories have been criticized for their de-emphasis of creative, practical, and other forms of intelligent thought and expression. Another critique has been launched at intelligence theorists' tendency to locate intelligence in the individual human mind rather than in sociocultural systems. Perhaps intelligence has been over-psychologized by insisting on the individual person as the unit of analysis. According to this critique, the strict construal of intelligence as the property of the individual is misguided because it neglects the relationships between intelligence and culture. The form of intelligence that is embedded within and sustains cultures has sometimes been called **distributed intelligence** (Pea, 1993).

Although the theory of distributed intelligence has been developed only sketchily, it occupies a vital theoretical position. The theory claims that intelligence is significantly a function of the patterns of interaction among people. Patterns of social interaction themselves can be intelligent if they advance complex and difficult goals. In addition to social interaction, the artifacts of a culture can have intelligence embedded within them. The inventions of a culture—buildings, furniture, tools, techniques, and crafted products of all kinds—are the continuing residue of intelligent thought. Cultural artifacts embody intelligence in that their existence records and preserves the intelligent insights of the past. Computers contain intelligence, but so does a pencil. Not only tangible artifacts, but also abstract systems of communication (not least of which is language) are elements of culture that "contain" and preserve the advances of intelligent minds.

The theory of distributed intelligence challenges the traditional unit of analysis. Intelligence is not a property of the individual only, or even mostly, but instead is a quality of a dynamic cultural system that includes patterns of social interaction, tangible artifacts, and abstract systems of knowledge representation and communication.

Measuring Intelligence

The early history of intelligence testing shows that, beginning with Binet, intelligence was assessed using individual tests that emphasized mental performance. Binet's original intelligence tests differed in this way from Galton's measurements of physical characteristics, such as sensory acuity and physical strength. With Terman's translation of Binet's test into English, Binet's original conception was popularized widely.

Interestingly, Binet himself was not particularly concerned about the theoretical basis of his intelligence tests. He did speculate about the nature of intelligence, but he primarily regarded his tests as pragmatic tools for estimating children's mental age. Many theorists would agree that he was appropriately cautious about interpreting the theoretical meaning of the Binet scale. Nevertheless, other scholars sought to advance the theory of intelligence more directly. As we have seen, Spearman and Thurstone engaged the pivotal question of whether intelligence is one entity or several. Subsequent decades of research resulted in progress toward consensus views about the nature of human intelligence, as sketched in earlier sections of this chapter, but inquiry into the nature of intelligence remains an unfinished intellectual project. The recent development of emergent theories, such as Gardner's and Sternberg's, and of other alternatives to traditional analytical ability, such as emotional intelligence, attest to the ongoing dynamism of intelligence theory.

As theory building continued, so did the practical technology of intelligence testing. One early technique adopted by Binet was the use of Stern's IQ ratio of mental age divided by chronological age. As intelligence testing began to be applied to adults, however, a new way to calibrate relative ability was needed. Among adults, the notion of mental age made little sense. To make comparisons among adults, it was necessary to adopt a different method of comparison using the normal distribution, otherwise known as the "bell curve," shown in Figure 10.4.

The normal curve is now the basis for computing IQ scores among both children and adults. The method of computation is straightforward: Intelligence is assumed to

FIGURE 10.4
IQ Is No Longer a Quotient *IQ scores are now referenced completely to location on the normal distribution.*

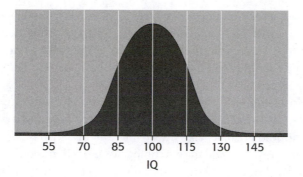

be distributed roughly in the form of the normal curve—most scores are middling, and extreme scores are comparatively rare. The mean score for IQ is arbitrarily set at 100. Half of all IQ scores will by definition be above 100 and half below 100. The entire normal distribution is divided into standard deviation units. Three standard deviation units above and below the mean cover most of the scale—more than 99 percent. In theory, standard deviation units extend beyond three, both above and below the mean, but the curve becomes very thin beyond three standard deviations.

Just as the mean is arbitrarily set at 100, so the value for standard deviation is arbitrarily set at 15. To repeat, the numbers are completely arbitrary. The point to remember is that IQ is measured in standard deviation units. All IQ scores (and all other standard scores for such tests as the SAT) can be converted to a position along the normal curve defined by a mean and standard deviation units. If we consider a mean of 100 and a standard deviation of 15, then an IQ of 145 puts us 3 standard deviation units above the mean. This is higher than 99 percent of the population. Defined by the normal curve, an IQ of 145 is quite high.

IQ Tests

The actual performances that go into computing an IQ score are not uniform. Most current IQ tests require several different kinds of test performance, from verbal responses to solving physical puzzles. The diversity of required performance is consistent with the way that Binet assessed IQ. His goal was not to measure a specific kind of mental activity, but the opposite: Intelligence was believed to be manifest as competent performance on a *diverse* array of tasks. As long as the tasks were mental, the more diverse the array the better, because intelligence was seen as the common element to *all* mental performance. Likewise, in Spearman's theory, g was mathematically computed to be the component of variance common to all cognitive tests.

In the original Stanford-Binet IQ test, and in those that followed, such as the Wechsler Intelligence Scale for Children (WISC), performance was assessed by means of a kit of diverse tests referred to as a **test battery**. The individual examiner administered not a single test but rather a series of tests in the battery. The battery yielded an overall IQ score and often subscores such as verbal IQ or performance (nonverbal) IQ. One benefit of using a battery of tests is that the mental ability common to tests is measured repeatedly and therefore more reliably. At the same time, the variance common to each specific test is diluted over the battery. If a test-taker is particularly good at the specific competencies invoked by one particular test, the contribution of that specific ability to IQ is reduced as other test scores are added to overall performance. The result is a better estimate of general intelligence.

Some individual tests are remarkably good at measuring intelligence, yielding IQ scores that are very similar to those generated from complex batteries. Among those, no single test seems to be more effective than Raven's Progressive Matrices, a nonverbal test that consists of a series of figural analogies. The basic pattern between Raven's test items is shown in Figure 10.5.

Raven's Matrices is the single best predictor of g. Moreover, because there is such a close correspondence between g and fluid intelligence, Raven's Matrices is the single best marker test for fluid intelligence. The explanation for why Raven's offers such good prediction has long been a puzzle for psychologists. Indeed, understanding the cognitive requirements for proficient performance on Raven's Matrices has been viewed as a window into the nature of intelligence from a cognitive perspective. What kinds of cognition does Raven's Matrices require?

Raven's Matrices has two major cognitive demands: inductive reasoning and the ability to manage complex goals in working memory (see Chapter 3). The ability to understand the figural patterns within each matrix is essentially induction. Inductive reasoning is the ability to infer a larger pattern from specifics. Multiple interacting patterns—not just one simple pattern—dictate which response option is the correct one. Among the more difficult Raven's problems, the inductive reasoning required for a correct response is quite complex and difficult. It's easy to detect one pattern but overlook another. Because it relies so heavily on inductive reasoning, it's a very good estimator of fluid intelligence (which is also highly related to induction).

The other aspect of Raven's Matrices that contributes to its effectiveness as a marker test for g is its demands on working memory. Intelligence research has repeatedly confirmed that there is a strong connection between working memory usage and intelligent performance. Working memory, as we have seen, is the central cognitive capability of holding ideas in mind while performing work on them. It is *the* cognitive workspace—and it differs in capacity among not only children, but also adults. When

FIGURE 10.5
Raven's Matrices
Inductive reasoning with figural analogies estimates both g and fluid intelligence. [DK]

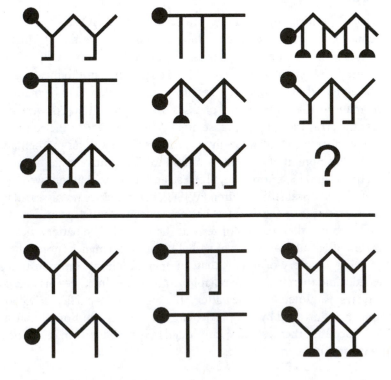

we reach the limits of our working memory capacity, performance breaks down because the information processing demands of the task exceed the ability to keep track of them. At some point, the complexity of Raven's problems stresses the working memory capacity of examinees. Therefore, a crucial ability for high performance on Raven's Matrices is the ability to monitor multiple goals and pieces of information without losing track of any.

The primary cognitive demands of Raven's Matrices—inductive reasoning and an efficient working memory—shed light on the nature of general intelligence from a cognitive point of view. There are applications to education here. It makes sense to include among our educational goals the ability to infer patterns (inductive reasoning) and the ability to manage complex goals (working memory capacity). A sharper definition of intelligence in cognitive terms has at least suggestive power for how teachers could cultivate intelligence as one of the many goals of education.

Raven's Matrices is not the only good estimator of intelligence. Measures of acquired vocabulary also work surprisingly well. Vocabulary test scores are more estimates of verbal intelligence than of fluid intelligence, and they are remarkably good predictors of general ability. They constitute rough-and-ready estimators of overall intelligence, and are much cheaper and easier to administer than a standard IQ battery. The reason appears to be that vocabulary tests are, like Raven's, good measures of inductive reasoning ability. Most vocabulary is acquired through context during reading or listening. Therefore, vocabulary size indirectly estimates inductive reasoning in the verbal realm. Inductive reasoning, in turn, is highly related to g. Both nonverbal (Raven's Matrices) and verbal (vocabulary) tests can predict inductive reasoning ability, and both are good estimators of intelligence.

Can Intelligence Change?

Any claim that intelligence could be enhanced as one goal of education must confront some important questions: Is intelligence inherited? If so, to what degree? To what extent would genetic influences limit attempts to enhance intelligence? The most direct response to these questions is to acknowledge that intelligence is partly heritable. But if intelligence is *partly* heritable, then it is also partly a product of the environment. For many decades, behavioral geneticists have tried to quantify the relative contribution of genetics and experience, of nature and nurture, to intelligence.

The Heritability of Intelligence

As a rough estimate of the heritability of intelligence, behavioral geneticists have converged on a value of about 50 percent. This is depicted as h^2, the symbol for **heritability**, equal to approximately 0.5. The value of h^2 is estimated by comparing IQ scores among groups of people that have known degrees of familial relatedness. Most famously, researchers compare IQ similarities among twins—both identical and fraternal. In addition, the genetic similarities between parents and children, and among non-twin siblings, are known, and so comparisons between these populations can also be used to estimate h^2.

One practical difficulty with trying to estimate heritability among relatives is that they often live together, or have lived together in the past. They share both genes and a common environment, so the two are **confounded**. In the real world, the two overlap. The job of the behavioral geneticist is to separate the two sources of variation, nature

FIGURE 10.6
Genetics influences psychological traits, including intelligence *The heritability of IQ scores is about 0.5.* [DK]

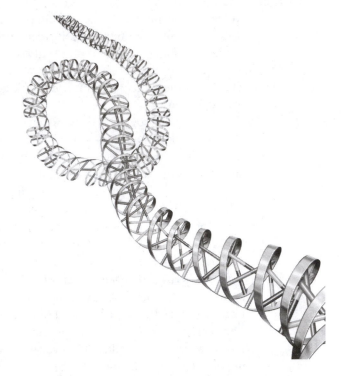

and nurture, even though they tend to co-occur. To attack this problem, the researcher can utilize two exceptions to the confounding of nature and nurture. One exception is the practice of adoption, by which genetically related people experience different home environments, or genetically unrelated people can experience the same (or similar) home environments. The other exception is the existence of identical twins, which are

FIGURE 10.7
Identical twins are genetically equivalent. *Even if twins are raised apart, their IQ scores tend to correlate highly.* [David Mager/Pearson Learning Photo Studio].

genetically equivalent. Because the DNA of identical twins is precisely the same, their variation in IQ or any other characteristic must arise strictly from the environment. By studying combinations of genetic relatedness and adoption, researchers have cleverly disentangled the normally confounded influences of genes and home environment.

Quite understandably, the more genetically related family members are, the higher will be the correlations of their IQ scores. Behavioral geneticists have found, for example, that the IQ scores of identical twins are often highly correlated, much more so than the IQ scores of fraternal twins. But the environment is also important. The IQ scores of fraternal twins are in turn more highly correlated than the IQ scores of non-twin siblings, even though fraternal twins are no more alike genetically than non-twin siblings. The presumed reason for the higher correlation is that fraternal twins tend to be treated more alike than ordinary siblings. This similar treatment contributes to the higher IQ correlation between fraternal twins. In just these ways, behavioral genetics has confirmed the importance of both genes and the environment. Both exert significant, measurable effects on intelligence.

As already mentioned, the many attempts to estimate the heritability of intelligence seem to converge approximately on $h^2 = 0.5$, meaning that about 50 percent of the population variability of intelligence is traceable to genetic variability. The other 50 percent reflects non-genetic sources, namely, environmental variation. The value of $h^2 = 0.5$ applies also to several other psychological characteristics, not only IQ. The heritability of personality and of some psychopathologies also hover around $h^2 = 0.5$. Some traits, of course, have much higher heritabilities. Height, for example, has a heritability value of around $h^2 = 0.9$.

When considering h^2, it's important to realize that the value is not fixed. Heritability values are not set parameters of the human race. They are, instead, descriptive statistics that reflect local conditions and local populations. The value of h^2 estimates the contribution of genetic variation to IQ variation and, indirectly, the environmental contribution to variation in IQ. But populations differ in their genetic diversity. Japan, for example, is relatively genetically homogeneous compared to many other countries, including the United States. Therefore, if genetic variability differs from one location to another, the relative contribution of genetics would also change. The same holds for environmental variability. Residents of countries such as Switzerland enjoy a high standard of living with widespread good-quality education, health care, nutrition, and literacy. Other nations exhibit tremendous internal variability in living conditions; children from rich and poor families may have radically different experiences on the educational, nutritive, and health factors that are relevant to cognitive development. Variability in the environment increases the contribution of the environment to intelligence. In other words, the more unequal the experiences of children, the lower the value for h^2. Conversely, if environmental conditions were standard for all children, then heritabilities would increase. For example, if conditions were maximally favorable—if all children received optimal education, parenting, health care, exposure to books and media, and so on—the contribution of genes to IQ variability would increase, and h^2 would rise.

Another complicating factor is that nature and nurture cannot always be separated into distinct categories. Genes interact with the environment. For example, a child may have a genetic predisposition toward talent in a particular field, such as music or athletics. Parents, seeing signs of this early disposition, might seek opportunities for its development through music lessons or coaching. In such cases, a genetic predisposition is amplified through experiences provided by the surrounding culture. Because parents *react* to the child's propensities, they contribute **reactive covariance** to the child's developing abilities. Later in life, an older child or adult may choose to pursue experiences that are initially prompted by personal qualities that spring from genetics. Active efforts to seek experiences that enhance those traits add **active covariance** to the traits. In both reactive covariance and active covariance, genes interact with the environment, making the initial promptings of genetics even stronger through environmental effects. Are these effects nature or nurture? It's impossible to say for sure. Because nature and nurture commingle, it becomes hard to separate the two.

The important point is that heritability is not a fixed parameter relating genetics to intelligence. Rather, it is a statistic that will fluctuate depending on the particular genetic variability and environmental variability within a population. Behavioral geneticists have observed that the estimated values for h^2 have been somewhat unstable from study to study; they are sometimes higher, sometimes lower. This instability might not reflect imperfect study designs or measurement but instead arise from differing values of h^2 from one population to another (Mackintosh, 1998).

The Flynn Effect

Heritability values for intelligence are important, but they do not impose limitations on how much intelligence can change from generation to generation. Not only intelligence, but also many other traits can change intergenerationally even if that trait is highly heritable. Height is an excellent example of how a highly heritable trait can shift between generations. The heritability of physical stature is quite high, about $h^2 = 0.9$. In other words, 90 percent of the height of a group of people can be traced to genetic influences. It's common knowledge, though, that population heights increased all over the world during the twentieth century. Population height increases of 3 centimeters or more have been documented in North America, Europe, and Japan. How is this possible, given that height has such high heritability? It is possible because the heights of parents are very good predictors of the heights of their children, even if the children are taller. Heritability estimates quantify predictive power based on correlations among data sets, not on the specific values of the data. Imagine a future in which children are twice as tall as their parents. This fantasy could maintain $h^2 = 0.9$ for height, as long as parents' and children's heights were highly correlated. In other words, heritability values impose no limitations on the intergenerational change of any human characteristic, including intelligence.

An intergenerational increase in measured intelligence is not a mere theoretical possibility, but an established fact. During the twentieth century, IQs rose in at least 20 different countries around the world. The worldwide trend of rising IQs, popularized by philosopher James Flynn, became known as the **Flynn effect**, illustrated in Figure 10.8. The effect is no fluke of measurement or artifact of rising test sophistication—the gains in IQ are too large for those explanations. The consensus among psychologists is that the IQ gains—as high as one standard deviation per generation on some tests—are real. The question is, What has caused them?

One likely contributor to rising IQ scores is improved nutrition worldwide. Better nutrition through subsequent generations is certainly a major explanation for the common trend of children surpassing their parents in height. Not only height, but also average head circumference increased during the twentieth century and, along with head size, probably brain volumes. Brain volume, in turn, is very slightly but positively correlated with IQ. A second likely contributor to the Flynn effect is the rising complexity of society, including increases in informational complexity boosted by the introduction of mass media—first print media and radio, then television, then the

FIGURE 10.8
The Flynn Effect
IQ scores rose in the United States and in many other countries through most of the twentieth century. (Y-axis shows a 1998 scale; trendline labels reflect a 1918 scale.) [Copyright © 1995 by Dimitry Schidlovsky. Reprinted by permission of Dimitry Schidlovsky.]

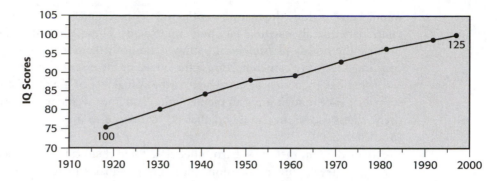

Internet. A group of eminent psychologists summarized the effect this way: "Complexity of life has produced complexity of mind" (Neisser et al., 1996, p.90).

Yet another likely cause of rising IQ scores is the spread of schooling around the world. Since the start of the twentieth century, elementary school education has become nearly universal, leading to higher rates of literacy in wealthy and poor countries alike. In addition, increases in the average duration of schooling up through secondary and university-level education have allowed larger segments of the population to delve into abstract and complex subject matter, including mathematics, science, and literature. The suggested linkage here is between expanding education and increasing intelligence—specifically, that education is one very important mechanism for enhancing intelligence. This connection, vital but seldom appreciated, is one reason why the topic of intelligence is relevant to the goals of education. Further evidence for the education-intelligence connection is explored in the section below. At its heart, this association presumes that the environment exerts important effects on the development of intelligence. The next section develops this theme by presenting evidence that experience can enhance intelligence during every life stage.

Environmental Influences on Intelligence

Experience through the lifespan shapes the developing mind. Intelligence can be amplified or stifled depending on the quality of that experience. Unfortunately, not everyone has access to high-quality experience. An entrenched reality crucial to the mission of education is that there are vast differences in the quality of experience among children. Some children grow up in very favorable conditions, having dependable access to good nutrition and health care, loving and protective home environments, cognitively rich social interactions, and high-quality teachers and schools. Other children face suboptimal experiences in each of these potentially educative contexts.

This section explores some of the variations in experience that lead to differences in cognitive ability as measured by IQ scores. The purpose here is not to present a theory of precisely how experience influences developing intelligence, but to make the more modest point that it does have such influence. If intelligence is susceptible to broad qualities of experience, then such experiential variation can fall within educators' scope of interest. After all, educators are *designers* of experience—experience that has educative value.

Nutrients and Toxins

The quality of a child's experience extends to the rather basic level of nutrients and toxins in the environment. Nutrients are necessary for the promotion of the developing mind. These include the many **essential nutrients** recognized in human physiology—vitamins, minerals, essential fats, and amino acids. These nutrients are called *essential* because the body's physiological pathways cannot manufacture them; they must be consumed. Poverty can compromise the intake of the essential nutrients, just as poor eating habits can, perhaps exacerbated by the availability of junk foods. There is at least some evidence that vitamin supplementation and improvements in the quality of children's diets lead to measurably higher IQ scores and to improved learning outcomes (Martinez, 2000).

Toxins, in contrast, have harmful effects. Toxic chemicals often affect most perniciously the developing fetus. Among the many identifiable toxic poisons, prenatal exposure to alcohol exerts the most widespread and devastating effects on the cognitive development of children. The clinical condition known as **fetal alcohol syndrome** is first apparent in facial abnormalities, such as small eye openings. The cost to the child's developing mind is severe—the syndrome is associated with an IQ decrement of about 35 points. Every year, thousands of children are born with identifiable fetal alcohol syndrome. However, about *ten times* that number of children are exposed to significant quantities of alcohol prenatally but show no outward signs of fetal alcohol syndrome. These much larger populations of children exhibit cognitive deficits, too—approximately 25 IQ points.

Toxins other than alcohol can have negative effects on children's mental development, though the numbers of children affected by these other toxins are probably much fewer. Lead, for example, interferes with the developing neural pathways. Lead exposure is a concomitant of urban poverty, but the pathways by which children intake high quantities of lead, and the blood levels that pose a significant risk, remain poorly understood. Other chemical toxins, including mercury and polychlorinated biphenyls (PCBs), have harmful effects on neural functioning, but their mechanisms of action and extent of their harm in the population are likewise not well understood.

Aside from consuming nutrients and avoiding toxins, eating regular meals is important for the enhancement of cognition. Food can actually help us to think better. Some of us rely on coffee or tea to focus mentally, but a snack might be more effective. Somewhat surprisingly, glucose (simple sugar) is an effective booster of mental performance (Donohoe & Benton, 2000). The body converts all foods to glucose for cell metabolism, and so regular food consumption can promote optimal brain efficiency. Skipping breakfast is not a good idea.

Family and Preschool Experience

The richness of children's social and intellectual experiences varies widely, and this variation exerts potent effects on the developing mind. Children differ broadly, for example, in their sheer volume of language exposure—with some children communicating with adults at many times the rates of other children (Hart & Risley, 1995). Likewise, exposure to books and educational toys, opportunities to visit new people and places, and the availability of positive role models varies greatly from child to child. Moreover, the intellectual richness of a child's early experience is often related to family wealth and social class, and to the parents' education levels (Bradley et al., 1989). Children who live in poverty are at risk for impoverished intellectual environments.

In the 1960s, known associations between early experience and long-term cognitive consequences, including measured intelligence, led to several intervention programs. Experimental preschools were designed to provide intensive exposure to language and social interaction, especially between children and adults. Parent training was sometimes included as a program element. Many programs aimed explicitly to affect children's IQ in order to reduce the rate of mental retardation, operationalized as an IQ of 75 or lower. This goal assumed that large numbers of children falling in the mildly retarded range, just below an IQ of about 75, have no identifying congenital brain or sensory defect. They were at risk for "socio-familial" retardation, a consequence of impoverished circumstances and experience during the preschool years.

Of the many comprehensive preschool programs launched during the War on Poverty in the 1960s, the largest by far was the federal program, Head Start. Head Start is complex partly because it reached huge numbers of children in diverse communities. It aimed to meet a variety of goals, including improving health care, as well as raising children's cognitive status. Federal legislators commissioned evaluations to determine whether Head Start was effective in meeting its stated goals. Program evaluators detected a modest cognitive effect in participating children compared to similar children not enrolled in the program. Unfortunately, the cognitive effects were short-lived, fading just a few years after the children entered school. The rapid "fade out" of program effects is one reason Head Start has been periodically criticized. Though Head Start funding was maintained through subsequent decades and continues to the present, its support by Congress often has been in jeopardy.

Smaller demonstration projects besides Head Start sometimes produced large effects on children's cognitive development, including IQ scores. In some cases, the effects of program participation endured through the elementary grades and even into high school. The Milwaukee Project, for example, claimed IQ gains of up to 25 IQ points by participating children. These huge gains proved to be highly interesting to politicians, some of whom were inspired to introduce legislation for the original funding of Head Start. The Milwaukee Project effects were greeted with skepticism by psychologists, many of whom criticized the researchers for not providing timely and sufficient information about the project. Many years later, one project investigator (Garber, 1988) published a book documenting the details of the project. The follow-up data showed that children who participated in the Milwaukee Project had intellectual and academic benefits that extended into the high school years.

Other intensive preschool programs, such as the Carolina Abecedarian Program, also had detectable positive effects on children's measured intelligence (Ramey, MacPhee, & Yeats, 1982). Though their cognitive effects were not as large as those found in the Milwaukee Project, many other demonstration projects of the 1960s showed that the social and informational richness of a child's experience in the years prior to entering school can influence the child's intelligence upward or downward.

Schooling

When examining the Flynn effect—the worldwide upward trend of IQ scores—we noted that one likely contributing cause was the expansion of formal education during the twentieth century. Education became more prevalent in two ways. One was the expansion of elementary school education, and therefore literacy rates, around the world. Rich and poor nations alike accepted that one basic responsibility of government was to provide universal education. A basic right of children was to receive an education that would guarantee at least fundamental literacy and numeracy. A second dimension of education expansion was in the average duration of schooling. In the United States, the typical duration of schooling rose from an elementary school education to at least some college education. In these ways, the world population became more broadly and deeply educated, all within a hundred years.

History provides more direct evidence of a linkage between degree of education and intelligence. One strand of evidence involves the canal boat children of England, circa 1920 (Gordon, 1970). For a period of ten years or so, the English economy relied on intact families to distribute goods throughout the country using a complex system of canals and locks. Families carried cargo on their barges, distributing it as contracted. The canal boat children suffered in one important sense—their transience precluded regular school attendance. Even though the British government built special schools to serve the children, school attendance averaged only about ten days per year. The effects on developing IQ were measurable. Younger children had near-average IQ levels, but their older siblings had lower measured IQs. As age increased, IQ decreased. Apparently, the lack of exposure to school resulted in children's IQs edging downward each year. Their mental age did not keep up with their advancing chronological age. The IQ ratio shrank in successive years, implying a connection between intelligence and the experience of schooling.

In the United States, rising IQs during the twentieth century were evident in differences between military recruits in World War I and World War II. Soldiers in the later war had measurably higher mental abilities (Humphreys, 1989). These differences reportedly had practical manifestations—soldiers in the later war learned their jobs faster than did their predecessors. The two cohorts differed also in average duration of schooling. World War I soldiers averaged nine years of formal education, whereas World War II soldiers averaged twelve years. Three additional years of schooling may seem like a small amount, but these three years of high school meant significantly more exposure to complex information and abstract thinking.

In still other populations, linkages between degree of formal education and measured IQ were studied more rigorously. The central research question was whether a longer duration of school results in higher measured intelligence. The question is hard to approach because of a well-known and natural connection between IQ and education: People with higher IQs tend to pursue more formal education, whether through personal choice or because of systems that societies use to channel talent. Naturally enough, extent of education and IQ are inevitably correlated. We know that IQ predicts education. The real challenge is to understand the effects of education on IQ. A few studies have been moderately successful at providing an answer.

Studies showing an effect of formal education on IQ have been carried out in the United States and in Sweden. These studies found that when the effects of initial IQ are statistically controlled, there is an independent effect of the extent of formal education on later measured IQ (Husén, 1951; Härnqvist, 1968). More simply, when students are grouped by their initial IQ scores, those in comparable groups who pursue more formal education have higher measured IQs several years later. One telling finding based on U.S. data involved comparing IQs at age 14 and at age 34 to the number of years of schooling (Lorge, 1945). IQ at age 14 did indeed predict years of formal education, as expected, at $r = .36$. But years of education predicted adult IQ at age 34 even more strongly, with a correlation of $r = .67$.

Can Intelligence Be Taught?

Qualities of experience through the life span can have measurable effects on the development of intelligence and can shape the upward or downward trajectories of intelligence within individuals and from one generation to the next. The kinds of experience described in this chapter have not typically been *designed* to raise intelligence. Could experience be structured to enhance intelligence deliberately? Is it possible to design programs specifically to make people smarter?

Head Start and other preschool programs were intended to enhance the cognitive experience of children from poor families. Most of these programs were not specifically intended to enhance intelligence but rather to prevent the slide of intelligence into the low range. A few programs have directly attempted to enhance intelligence. The two programs described below are a subset of a somewhat larger group of interventions that had similar goals (Martinez, 2000).

Project Intelligence was an attempt to raise the intelligence of children in Venezuela (Nickerson, 1986). Organized and implemented in the early 1980s, Project Intelligence was funded by the Venezuelan government but also involved collaboration with American scholars from Harvard and other institutions. Project investigators constructed curricula designed to exercise the thinking skills of young adolescents. The curriculum was implemented for only one year (due to a subsequent change of government in

INTEREST MAGNET 10.4

Are Dolphins Intelligent?

Among nonhuman animals, dolphins have long been associated with a high degree of intelligence. In the 1960s, biologist John Lilly (1967) popularized the idea that dolphins are intelligent, and that human-dolphin communication might even be possible. Lilly recognized that dolphin brains are somewhat larger than human brains (Herman, 2006). Dolphins use some of their brain mass to control the movements of their large bodies, but even when body mass is taken into account, dolphins still compare favorably to other animals. One way to compare animal brains is to use an "encephalization quotient" or EQ, which scales brain size to body size in a way that makes comparisons more fair. An EQ of 1.0 is average for animals. Humans have the highest EQ (7.0), but the value for dolphins is next (4.3). Lower still, but higher than average compared to other animal species, are the EQs for chimpanzees (2.49) and dogs (1.17). Mice fall below average, with an EQ of 0.50.

Biologists have discovered that dolphins are quite good at complex and abstract tasks. Biologist Louis Herman (2006) trained a bottlenose dolphin named Ake in a language system involving nouns and verbs expressed as gestures. Ake learned the "language" and could respond in practical ways. For example, she learned to respond differently to "surfboard swimmer fetch" (bring the swimmer to the surfboard) than to "swimmer surfboard fetch" (bring the surfboard to the swimmer). When the commands indicated new "creative" behavior, Ake could respond appropriately. Sometimes the commands involved physically impossible tasks, in which case Ake

would only "stare" at the trainer. Ake also had knowledge of objects that were absent. When asked questions such as "Is there a ball in your pool?" she could answer correctly by pressing paddles on the side of the pool (right paddle for *yes*; left paddle for *no*).

Dolphins are also known for intelligent behavior in their natural habitats. Like humans, they have long periods of nurturance in which a dolphin calf will stay with its mother. During this period, calves learn complex systems of behavior and social skills. Adult dolphins cooperate in defense. They have a highly developed ability to use sonar, called *echolocation,* in which they emit clicking sounds. By echolocation alone dolphins can distinguish the size, shape, and composition of underwater objects. They can even "eavesdrop" by listening to the sonar clicks of *other* dolphins to make inferences about the location of fish.

Dolphin intelligence is further suggested by their propensity for play. They are known to surf on waves and to ride on the bow waves of ships. They produce "bubble rings" for no apparent reason other than their own entertainment. However, none of these examples definitively answers the question: Are dolphins intelligent? Despite substantial research, strong conclusions about dolphin intelligence have not been reached. Part of the difficulty of understanding the dolphin mind has been the practical challenge of making observations in their natural open-ocean habitats. Another limitation is that their whistle and click communication occurs in frequencies that require special equipment for detection. Perhaps the greatest challenge is to comprehend what the word *intelligence* means for a nonhuman species.

Venezuela), and involved a quite modest intervention of 45 minutes per week of instruction. Nevertheless, the curriculum had measurable, although small, effects on the cognitive abilities of participating children. Participants also showed evidence of superior problem solving abilities compared to a control group of students.

A second project focused on high school students, and in particular students identified as gifted (Stankov, 1986). The students' teacher was a research psychologist in the former Yugoslavia. The approach was distinctive in that it concentrated specifically on creative problem solving. Students' experience consisted of regular exposure to open-ended problems and on finding creative solutions to those problems. The experience had detectable and positive effects on students' cognitive ability scores. Creative problem solving therefore seems to be one possible approach to the enhancement of intelligence.

The dearth of projects designed specifically to enhance intelligence is surprising. Given the centrality of intelligence to the science of mind and to the enterprise of education, we might have guessed that there would be more targeted attempts to enhance intelligence. The scarcity of such projects may be a consequence of commonsensical ideas about intelligence and education. If intelligence is presumed to be a fixed quality of a human being, rather than a malleable trait, then it makes little sense to try to change intelligence. Instead, the system works with the intelligence that is inborn. Likewise, limited views about the nature of education may be a hindrance. If education is perceived as essentially the conveyance of knowledge, then the goal of enhancing cognitive ability may seem to be outside the bounds of its mission. Such assumptions must be challenged.

Education as the Cultivation of Intelligence

What is the purpose of education? There is no single answer to that question, of course. Different stakeholders—parents, educators, community members, and students—have divergent views about the purposes of education. But among the many possible and legitimate goals of education, one is the enhancement of intelligence. This is not a commonly discussed goal, much less a goal that is explicitly adopted and pursued.

To consider the enhancement of intelligence as a legitimate goal of education requires re-thinking the accepted views of both intelligence and education. Perhaps the biggest conceptual step is to see intelligence as a malleable human characteristic, one that is sensitive to the quality of experience. If experience can enhance intelligence, then it becomes conceivable to enhance intelligence deliberately. The goal of intelligence enhancement can be woven into the conceptual structure of education, perhaps as its central organizing goal.

It is not certain that we are ready for such a conceptual shift. If collectively we were to adopt the goal of enhancing the intelligence of all students, the effectiveness of our program would only be as good as our theories of intelligence. Are existing theories up to the challenge? Over the past century and more, from Binet and Galton onward, our understanding of intelligence has grown steadily. But theories of intelligence are not yet mature—at least not *cognitive* theories of intelligence. As our understanding of intelligence deepens, the potential effects of our efforts to enhance intelligence will also grow. Ideally, this vision will take hold and grow in the years ahead. Education should be largely about the cultivation of intelligence.

Learning Strategies

Like the other organizing topics explored in this book, theories of intelligence have practical applicability to teaching and learning. Once we are open to the possibility that intelligence is a product of education, not simply an important raw material, we can tackle the question of *how* to develop intelligence. The ten strategies listed below are starting points for this venture in that they suggest ways in which experience can cultivate intelligence and how theories of intelligence can inform the educational enterprise.

1 Aim to enhance intelligence.

To accept that the development of intelligence is one goal of education is to think of intelligence very differently from the norm. Once this is recognized, the roles of the teacher and parent must shift accordingly. The goals of education expand from conveying knowledge and skill to building more general capabilities of how to engage the world successfully.

2 Build fluid intelligence through problem solving.

General intelligence is strongly related to fluid intelligence, and fluid intelligence connects strongly to problem solving. Teachers should consider problem solving to be an essential educational activity. Whenever students pursue goals that have no obvious solution pathways, they are engaged in problem solving.

3 Enhance crystallized intelligence through knowledge building.

Crystallized intelligence normally increases through most of the life span. But the growth of crystallized intelligence is best pursued actively, not passively. As knowledge expands and society requires more expertise, the pursuit of focused knowledge is one very important goal of education. Rich, interconnected knowledge is a worthy target of the mind.

4 Promote voluntary reading.

Crystallized intelligence grows through diverse experiences, but among the most important is reading. Text often presents material of informational complexity that is rare in spoken discourse. Those who read challenging material regularly grow their crystallized intelligence. Independent reading should be a habit for all.

5 Diversify instruction to reach different intelligence profiles.

Emergent theories, such as Gardner's theory of multiple intelligences, broaden conceptualizations of what it means to be intelligent. We cannot say specifically that tailoring instruction to this or that "intelligence" will result in superior learning. But we can assume that as we diversify the approaches to teaching, more learners will find ways to understand and engage the subject of study. Presenting instruction in different ways is good pedagogical practice.

6 Encourage the management of complex goal structures.

The analyses of Raven's Matrices and other intelligence-demanding tasks have revealed an important aspect of intelligent thought—the ability to manage complex goal structures. When the mind is pressed to pursue complex goals, pushing the capacity limits of working memory, differences in intelligence are revealed. Practicing this sort of mental challenge grows our capacity for managing complex goals.

7 Emphasize inductive reasoning.

Research has revealed that inductive reasoning and intelligence are closely associated, perhaps even identical. Inductive reasoning is the identification of the larger pattern in complex data. When we ask—"What is the general pattern here?"—we engage in inductive reasoning. Practice in inductive reasoning, in discovering the larger pattern, should be woven into the educational experience of every student.

8 Cultivate emotional intelligence.

Emotional intelligence is not yet a widely accepted form of intelligence. But the evidence amassed has made the construct believable as a human capability that predicts broad success. Why not try to develop emotional intelligence in ourselves and in others? As we become more capable of self-insight and of reading the feelings and intentions of others, almost certainly we will become more effective people.

9 Teach students that intelligence is malleable.

Varying conceptions of intellectual ability see intelligence either as fixed or as malleable. We promote personal growth to the extent that we teach learners that their cognitive abilities are not fixed but rather can be improved through effort over time. When students understand that they can become smarter, possibilities emerge that were not previously imagined.

10 Advocate good nutrition.

The mind-brain connection implies that we need to provide the human body with nutrients as well as avoid toxins. Learning processes benefit from the regular consumption of essential nutrients, such as those that the body itself cannot synthesize. Moreover, regular meals will ensure adequate levels of glucose. The availability of glucose for brain metabolism is now known to improve cognitive performance.

These ten strategies are not definitive. Several other practical implications of intelligence theory could be cited. We could ask, for examples: What are the implications of the typical decline of fluid intelligence during adulthood? How can teachers and other professionals keep their own thinking flexible and innovative? Whatever practical steps we take in applying theories of intelligence to education, the best starting point is to understand that intelligence is a mental capability that has unifying qualities as well as diverse elements. We must also appreciate that intelligence is sensitive to the quality of experience through the life span. Once these central ideas are understood, we can then consider the many ways in which intelligence could be enhanced as part of a broader agenda for education.

 ## Conclusion

This completes our survey of intelligence theories. We began by considering how conceptualizations of intelligence have evolved from the days of Galton onward. Theories of intelligence, and the tests used to measure intelligence, were devised to explain variation in human success. Starting with Binet's first intelligence test, the prediction of academic success was strongly associated with the measurement of intelligence. With the development of IQ tests by Terman and others, the use of intelligence testing spread widely. Its applications also spread to the prediction of occupational success and success in other valued life outcomes.

But what is intelligence? What is the nature of g, or general mental ability, that is estimated by IQ tests and related instruments? One answer is that intelligence is composed of all the constituent factors represented in hierarchical models, such as Carroll's (1993). But some factors are more important than others. Among cognitive ability factors, we have seen that inductive reasoning—the ability to find and apply patterns in complex data—is highly related to both fluid intelligence and to g. In addition, the ability to manage complex tasks, including multiple simultaneous tasks, correlates strongly with g (Mackintosh, 1998). As a first approximation, general intel-

ligence is the ability to detect and use patterns in situations that are informationally complex. That ability contributes to success in any endeavor that draws upon the intellect.

The connection between intelligence and success continues to guide the development of intelligence theories up to the present. For example, traditional theories of intelligence that emphasize its analytical aspects are typically perceived as excessively narrow, restricted to a single (though very important) aspect of mental capability. Theoretical development in such emergent theories as Gardner's and Sternberg's press beyond traditional g, as does the theory of emotional intelligence. One practical benefit of these more recent theories is that they can channel efforts to develop mental capabilities beyond the forms of analytical reasoning that are so often prized and rewarded in formal educational settings. Educators can seek to develop intelligence more broadly through the guidance offered by these new theories.

This latter point—that education can cultivate intelligence—is really the central point of this chapter. What is intelligence, after all, but the capabilities that prepare us to be successful in the world? And what is education if not the sum of the experiences that

INTEREST MAGNET 10.5

Extraterrestrial Intelligence

The possibility that we are not alone in the universe has captivated the human imagination for a long time. Contemporary interest in the possibility that nonhuman intelligent life might be found in the universe has arisen partly from the theories of evolutionary biogenesis, which recognizes life as having arisen through natural processes from initially inhospitable conditions. Recent astronomical evidence shows that many stars in our galaxy have planets just as our own sun does. This fact has emboldened some scientists to claim that the universe *must* hold other (perhaps many more) intelligent life forms. Carl Sagan, the famous astronomer, speculated "conservatively" that there are probably a million intelligent civilizations in the galaxy (Lemarchand, 1998). Other scientists have much lower estimates, with many estimating the number at exactly 1—our own!

Even with widespread doubts about whether extraterrestrial intelligence exists, many scientists have searched for it seriously and strategically. This quest goes by the name of Search for Extraterrestrial Intelligence, or SETI. Typically, SETI projects involve monitoring space for signals sent in the microwave band of the electromagnetic spectrum. Why search for microwaves? Microwaves are logical signaling devices because they take little energy to generate, and they are not much affected by planetary atmospheres. Signals from space are analyzed for patterns that are unlikely to be generated from natural processes. Strong and narrow-frequency signals, or patterns that are nonrandom, may be attempts by extraterrestrials

to communicate. Logistically, the search for signals is inefficient owing to the vastness of space. Time is also a factor because human intelligence is known to have existed for only a tiny fraction of the duration of planet earth. If other civilizations are likewise transient, then any signal from space to earth must be detected not only from the right location but also during the period when those civilizations actually exist and are transmitting! By one estimate, this problem is equivalent to searching for a needle in a haystack that is bigger than the entire earth—not exactly a promising strategy. Some SETI workers have tried to quantify the likelihood of making contact with extraterrestrial intelligence through the Drake Equation. The Drake Equation moves toward quantification by estimating, for example, the number of habitable planets in our galaxy, the likelihood of intelligent life arising on those planets, and the expected duration of intelligent civilizations (Drake & Sobel, 1992).

For the most part, SETI has been supported by non-governmental funds, with one exception: In 1992, NASA launched a ten-year, $100 million SETI project. But government funding was cancelled by Congress after its first year. The search for extraterrestrial intelligent life continues with support from private funding. One interesting aspect of SETI is that the search for signals from extraterrestrial civilizations concentrates almost exclusively on our own galaxy, the Milky Way. However, it is only one of about 100 billion known galaxies in the universe (Shostak & Barnett, 2003). It seems ironic that while SETI aims to expand human consciousness by looking beyond our own solar system for intelligent life, it ends up being "local" after all.

develop these capabilities? Ultimately, educators must concern themselves with preparing their students for future success on whatever paths they choose. What do these experiences consist of, and toward what goals? They are not simply learning within knowledge domains such as science or history but also acquiring the capabilities that will outlast the immediate experience of coursework. Dewey pressed for this perspective. He defined education as consisting in only those experiences that have lasting value for the future.

No societal function is more important than education. Yet any nominally educative experience can be either effective or ineffective. Experience can even be *anti*-educational if it reduces a person's ability to learn and thrive in the future. How can we design experiences that are truly educational? To the degree that we can understand the nature and workings of cognition, we are empowered to advance education by arranging experiences according to the mind's design. The perfect outcome is to extend, as far as possible, the power and reach of human intelligence.

References

Ackerman, P. L. (2006, August). *Gf, Gc, non-ability traits and domain knowledge*. Paper presented at the annual meeting of the American Psychological Association. New Orleans, LA.

Bradley, R. H., Caldwell, B. M., Rock, S. L., Ramey, C. T., Barnard, K. E., Gray, C., Hammond, M., Mitchell, S., Gottfried, A. W., Siegel, L., & Johnson, D. L. (1989). Home environment and cognitive development in the first 3 years of life: A collaborative study involving six sites and three ethnic groups in North America. *Developmental Psychology, 25*, 217–235.

Callahan, C. M., Tomlinson, C. A., Moon, T. R., Tomchin, E. M., & Plucker, J. (1995). *Project START: Using a multiple intelligences model in identifying and promoting talent in high-school students* [Research Monograph 95136]. Storrs: University of Connecticut, The National Research Center on the Gifted and Talented.

Carroll, J. B. (1993). *Human cognitive abilities: A survey of factor-analytic studies*. New York: Cambridge University Press.

Cattell, R. B. (1987). *Intelligence: Its structure, growth, and action*. New York: North-Holland.

Cox, C. M. (1926/1992). The early mental traits of 300 geniuses. In R. S. Albert (Ed.), *Genius and eminence* (2nd ed.). Reprinted from C. M. Cox (1926), *The early mental traits of three hundred geniuses*, Volume 2, in L. M. Terman (Ed.), *Genetic studies of genius*. Stanford, CA: Stanford University Press.

Donohoe, R. T., & Benton, D. (2000). Glucose tolerance predicts memory and cognition. *Physiology and Behavior, 71*, 395–401.

Drake, F., & Sobel, D. (1992). *Is anyone out there?* New York: Delacorte Press.

Einstein, A. (1950). *Out of my later years*. New York: Philosophical Library.

Flynn, J. R. (1987). Massive IQ gains in 14 nations: What IQ tests really measure. *Psychological Bulletin, 101*(2), 171–191.

Garber, H. L. (1988). *The Milwaukee Project: Preventing mental retardation in children at risk*. Washington, DC: American Association on Mental Retardation.

Gardner, H. (1983). *Frames of mind*. New York: Basic Books.

Gardner, H. (1998). A multiplicity of intelligences. *Scientific American, 9*(4), 37–41.

Goleman, D. (1995). *Emotional intelligence*. New York: Bantam.

Gordon H. (1970). The intelligence of English canal boat children. In I Al-Issa & W. Dennis (Eds.), *Cross-cultural studies of behavior* (pp. 111–119). New York: Holt, Rinehart, & Winston.

Gould, S. J. (1981). *The mismeasure of man*. New York: Norton.

Gustaffson, J.-E. (1999). Measuring and understanding G: Experimental and correlational approaches. In P. L. Ackerman, P. C. Kyllonnen, & R. D. Roberts (Eds.), *Learning and individual differences: Process, trait, and content determinants* (pp. 275–289). Washington, DC: American Psychological Association.

Härnqvist, K. (1968). Relative changes in intelligence from 13 to 18. *Scandinavian Journal of Psychology, 9*, 50–64 (Part I) & 65–82 (Part II).

Hart, B., & Risley, T. R. (1995). *Meaningful differences in the everyday experience of young American children*. Baltimore, MD: Brookes.

Herman, L. M. (2006). Intelligence and rational behaviour in the bottlenose dolphin. In S. Hurley & M. Nudds (Eds.), *Rational animals?* (pp. 439–467). Oxford: Oxford University Press.

Holahan, C. K., & Sears, R. R. (1995). *The gifted child in later maturity*. Stanford, CA: Stanford University Press.

Humphreys, L. G. (1989). Intelligence: Three kinds of instability and their consequences for policy. In R. L. Linn (Ed.), *Intelligence: Measurement, theory, and public policy* (pp. 193–216). Urbana: University of Illinois Press.

Hunt, E. B. (1995). *Will we be smart enough? A cognitive analysis of the upcoming workforce*. New York: Russell Sage Foundation.

Husén, T. (1951). The influence of schooling upon IQ. *Theoria, 17*, 61–88.

Jensen, A. R. (1998). *The g factor: The science of mental ability*. Westport, CT: Praeger.

Kihlstrom, J. F., & Cantor, N. (2000). Social intelligence. In R. J. Sternberg (Ed.), *Handbook of intelligence* (pp. 359–379). New York: Cambridge University Press.

Lemarchand, G. A. (1998). Is there intelligent life out there? *Scientific American, 9*(4), 96–104.

Lilly, J. C. (1967). *The mind of the dolphin: A nonhuman intelligence*. Garden City, New York: Doubleday & Company.

Lohman, D. F. (1993). Teaching and testing to develop fluid abilities. *Educational Researcher, 22*(7), 12–23.

Lorge, I. (1945). Schooling makes a difference. *Teachers College Record, 46*, 483–492.

Mackintosh, N. J. (1998). *IQ and human intelligence*. Oxford, UK: Oxford University Press.

Martinez, M. E. (2000). *Education as the cultivation of intelligence*. Mahwah, NJ: Lawrence Erlbaum Associates.

McLaren, R. B. (1993). The dark side of creativity. *Creativity Research Journal, 6*(1&2), 137–144.

Milgram, S. (1974). *Obedience to authority: An experimental view*. New York: Harper & Row.

Miller, B. L., Cummings, J., Mishkin, F., Boone, K., Prince, F., Ponton, M., & Cotman, C. (1998). Emergence of artistic talent in frontotemporal dementia. *Neurology, 51*(4), 978–982.

Neisser, U. (1998). Introduction: Rising test scores and what they mean. In U. Neisser (Ed.), *The rising curve: Long-term gains in IQ and related measures* (pp. 3–22). Washington, DC: American Psychological Association.

Neisser, U., Boodoo, B., Bouchard, T. J., Boykin, A. W., Brody, N., Ceci, S. J., Halpern, D. F., Loehlin, J. C., Perloff, R., Sternberg, R. J., & Urbina, S. (1996). Intelligence: Knowns and unknowns. *American Psychologist, 51*(2), 77–101.

Nickerson, R. S. (1986). Project intelligence: An account and some reflections. *Special Services in the Schools 3*(1–2), 83–102.

Pea, R. D. (1993). Practices of distributed intelligence and designs for education. In G. Salomon (Ed.), *Distributed cognitions* (pp. 47–87). New York: Cambridge University Press.

Ramey, C. T., MacPhee, D., & Yeats, K. O. (1982). Preventing developmental retardation: A general systems model. In D. K. Detterman & R. J. Sternberg (Eds.), *How and how much can intelligence be increased* (pp. 67–119). Norwood, NJ: Ablex.

Reich, R. (1992). *The work of nations: Preparing ourselves for 21st-century capitalism*. New York: Vintage.

Salovey, P., & Mayer, J. D. (1989–90). Emotional intelligence. *Imagination, Cognition and Personality, 9*, 185–211.

Schmidt, F. L., & Hunter, J. E. (1998). The validity and utility of selection methods in personnel psychology: Practical and theoretical implications of 85 years of research findings. *Psychological Bulletin, 124*, 262–274.

Schoon, I. (2000). A life span approach to talent development. In K. A. Heller, F. J. Mönks, R. J. Sternberg, & R. F. Sternberg (Eds.), *International handbook of giftedness and talent* (2nd ed., pp. 213–225). New York: Elsevier.

Shostak, S., & Barnett, A. (2003). *The search for life in the universe*. New York: Cambridge University Press.

Simon, H. A., & Kaplan, C. A. (1989). Foundations of cognitive science. In *Foundations of cognitive science* (pp. 1–48). Cambridge, MA: MIT Press.

Simonton, D. K. (1988). *Scientific genius: A psychology of science*. Cambridge, UK: Cambridge University Press.

Slobada, J. A., Hermelin, B., & O'Connor, N. (1985). An exceptional musical memory. *Music Perception, 3,* 155–170.

Snow, R. E. (with Yalow, E.)(1982). Education and intelligence. In R. J. Sternberg (Ed.), *Handbook of human intelligence* (pp. 493–585). New York: Cambridge University Press.

Snyder, A., Bahramali, H., Hawker, T., & Mitchell, D. J. (2006). Savant-like numerosity skills revealed in normal people by magnetic pulses. *Perception, 35,* 837–845.

Stankov, L. (1986). Kvashchev's experiment: Can we boost intelligence? *Intelligence, 10,* 209–230.

Sternberg, R. J. (1996). *Successful intelligence.* New York: Simon & Schuster.

Sternberg, R. J. (2006). The Rainbow Project: Enhancing the SAT through assessments of analytical, practical, and creative skills. *Intelligence, 34,* 321–350.

Sternberg, R. J., & Detterman, D. K. (1986). *What is intelligence?: Contemporary viewpoints on its nature and definition.* Norwood, NJ: Ablex.

Sternberg, R. J., Nokes, K., Geissler, P. W., Prince, R., Okatcha, F., Bundy, D. A., Grigorenko, E. L. (2001). The relationship between academic and practical intelligence. A case study in Kenya. *Intelligence, 29,* 401–418.

Tannenbaum, A. J. (1996). Giftedness: The ultimate instrument for good or evil. In C. P. Benbow & D. Lubinski (Eds.), *Intellectual talent: Psychometric and social issues* (pp. 447–465). Baltimore, MD: The Johns Hopkins University Press.

Terman, L. M., & Oden, M. H. (1947). *Genetic studies of genius, Volume IV: The gifted child grows up.* Stanford, CA: Stanford University Press.

Terman, L. M., & Oden, M. H. (1959). *Genetic studies of genius, Volume V: The gifted child at mid-life.* Stanford, CA: Stanford University Press.

Thurstone, L. L., (1938). Primary mental abilities. *Psychological Monographs, 1.*

Treffert, D. A., & Wallace, G. L. (2007). *Islands of genius.* Scientific American Mind Special Report.

Young, R. L., Ridding, M. C., & Morrell, T. L. (2004). Switching skills on by turning off part of the brain. *Neurocase, 10*(3), 215–222.

GLOSSARY

a posteriori Latin for "after the fact." Refers to knowledge that is based on discovery. Contrasts with *a priori* knowledge.

a priori Latin for "before the fact." Knowledge that is true by necessity or by definition, apart from discovery. Contrasts with *a posteriori* knowledge.

ability grouping The establishment of groups of students who have similar ability levels for the purposes of teaching students in those groups.

abstract goals General goals that guide the formation of specific lesser goals and help determine whether or not more specific goals are worthwhile.

academically engaged time See *time on task*.

accommodation A form of cognitive development that occurs when there is a clash between experience and knowledge-based expectations. As a result, the learner changes knowledge, beliefs, and actions in order to make sense of the new experience. (Contrasts with *assimilation*)

accretion The incremental addition of new knowledge to existing knowledge schemas through experience.

achievement gap The enduring differences in achievement and cognitive ability between demographic groups identified by race, ethnicity, and social class.

achievement motivation The personality trait that creates an ongoing need or desire to use talent to become successful, which then translates ability into achievement. Also known as *need for achievement*.

action control theory A theory of volition that casts the point of goal adoption as a "point of no return" after which goal-focused behavior is inevitable.

action potential (or spike) An electrochemical signal fired in a neuron, often resulting from a sufficient electrical signal received from another neuron or neurons. The action potential travels down the length of the neuron to the *terminal boutons* where the signal may affect other neurons or muscle cells.

active covariance Active efforts by individuals to seek experiences that enhance their own personal traits springing from genetics. Compare with *reactive covariance*.

adaptive expertise A form of expertise shown in an ability to display high levels of technical competence *and* to be truly innovative within that area.

advance organizers A structural preview of a teaching lesson. The preview presents concepts in order to pre-organize the learning experience and prime related knowledge in the learners' minds.

affect Roughly equivalent to emotion; includes temporary feeling states as well as more enduring moods.

alleles Variants of a gene.

alphabetic principle The principle in English and other phonetic languages that letters map onto sounds, even if the mapping is not strictly one to one.

Alzheimer's disease A degenerative condition associated with old age that leads to the progressive deterioration of brain neurons, causing steady declines in memory formation and retrieval.

amusia The inability to discriminate tones, or to appreciate music, caused by damage to the right hemisphere.

analytical scoring A type of test scoring for complex responses that involves evaluating responses in a number of separate dimensions, and then combining the scores of those dimensions to yield an overall score. Contrasts with *holistic scoring*.

analytic statement A definitional statement; it asserts a fact about an object that is already implicit in the definition of the object. For example, "a circle is round."

aphasia A disability caused by damage to *Broca's area* that leads to difficulties in speech.

aptitude Any individual difference—such as a cognitive ability, personality characteristic, or demographic trait—that can predict academic achievement or other valued outcomes.

aptitude complexes Psychological constructs that combine two or more traits or cognitive dimensions in order to provide a more complete description of a student's aptitude than a single aptitude; used to find improved fit of instructional approaches to that student.

aptitude-treatment interactions (ATI) The educational model based on the common intuition that different students learn optimally under different conditions and that instruction should be adapted to student characteristics.

arousal theory A theory of motivation that interprets human and animal behavior as serving to optimize the organism's level of physiological activity by avoiding high or low extremes of arousal.

assessment The broader functions of tests, including asking for complex responses and providing diagnostic feedback.

assessment for learning See *formative assessment*.

assimilation A form of cognitive development that occurs when experiences are interpreted satisfactorily with a previously existing belief system or pool of knowledge. (Contrasts with *accommodation*)

association areas Non-dedicated brain regions, especially in the cerebral cortex, that are used to form connections between dedicated areas of the brain.

attention The process of holding information in conscious awareness (working memory).

attention deficit disorder (ADD) A learning disability characterized by abnormal difficulty in sustaining attentional focus.

attribution theory A theory of motivation that focuses on the explanations people give for their successes and failures.

auditory sensory register The brief sound memory available to be "replayed" for up to a few seconds after it has been heard.

authentic assessment Assessments that have intrinsic value or real-world applications.

automaticity A quality of highly practiced skill that allows performance to be practiced with little conscious attention. The benefit is that the limited cognitive resources of working memory can be spent on higher-level activities, such as comprehension and critique in reading.

axon The cable-like part of the neuron that carries the action potential. Functioning like a wire, its carries signals from one location to another. An axon can be as long as several feet within the human body.

balanced literacy A hybrid approach to teaching reading that combines phonics and whole-language instruction.

Some proponents believe that it is a more effective way of teaching reading than either approach by itself.

behavioral genetics A branch of research that quantifies the contribution of genetic heritability to personal traits, primarily through studying similarities among blood relatives with known degrees of genetic relatedness.

behavioral modification A systematic approach to teaching new behavior that makes use of operant conditioning.

behavioral objectives Specific learning goals set forth by teachers as the desired learning outcomes of a prescribed curriculum.

behaviorism A theory of learning that focuses exclusively on behavior and objective explanations for behavior. Behaviorists are concerned with what can be observed about an organism directly and objectively.

blooming The massive proliferation of synapses during the first three years of life.

bottom-up processing Mental processing that begins with basic sensory information that triggers a known concept in long-term memory.

bounded rationality Each person's limited cognitive ability displayed as an inability to optimize problem solutions; revealed when the environment is too complex to be comprehended fully by an individual mind.

brainstem A primitive unit of the brain's anatomy that connects directly to the spinal cord. It controls life-sustaining functions such as breathing and heart rate as well as regulates sleep and alertness.

Broca's area An area of the brain, typically in the left hemisphere, that assists the articulation of spoken words.

Brodmann area 46 The brain area most strongly associated with working memory; located in the frontal lobe.

cell body (soma) The region of the neuron containing the nucleus.

cells Fundamental building blocks of nearly all life forms, containing DNA, membranes, and the ability to regulate metabolic activity.

central conceptual structures In Case's theory, broad domains in which rising proficiency follows stage-like developmental progressions.

central nervous system (CNS) The neuronal mass composed of the brain and spinal cord.

central sulcus The prominent groove that runs crosswise along the top of the brain, stretching almost from ear to ear and dividing the frontal lobe from the parietal lobe. This area coordinates sensory information and motor control.

cerebellum A major component of the brain located low on the back of the head; controls movement and locomotion.

cerebral cortex (or cortex) A component of the brain that takes up most of the brain's volume. It is the anatomical origin of the higher-order cognitive functions: reasoning, intelligence, creativity, planning, as well as coordination of sensory input and motor control.

child-centered An broad educational philosophy that distrusts repressive tactics of schools and social institutions, and strives to give the student freedom to explore, choose activities, pursue interests, and interact with adults and peers.

chronological age The actual age of a child.

chunk A pattern of meaningful information held in working memory as a single unit.

chunking The grouping of information into meaningful units with the result of cognitive simplification.

cocktail party phenomenon An example of the selective nature of attention in a complex sensory field; refers to the ability to mentally block out noise in order to focus on the immediate conversation.

cognition Rational thought that in some cases is treated as devoid of complicating emotions, wishes, and will. Also, thinking; the mental manipulation of ideas; human information processing.

cognitive dissonance The uncomfortable tension between personal beliefs and contradictory behavior.

cognitive information-processing theory A theory of learning that focuses on mental activity. This model compares the way the human mind processes information to the operation of a digital computer.

cognitive modeling A technique in which the teacher speaks her mental processes aloud when solving a problem so that students can hear her chain of reasoning and internalize her cognitive tools for their own use.

cognitive styles Characteristic individual ways of processing information.

coherence An aspect of truth that evaluates whether ideas are internally consistent or instead contradictory. Compare with *correspondence*.

competence motivation A theory of motivation that recognizes that a basic human motive is to demonstrate control.

complex cognition Multifaceted thinking that includes problem solving, critical thinking, inferential reasoning, and creative thinking.

conation Purposeful striving toward valued goals.

concept Any idea or category commonly identified by a single word; concepts may be concrete, such as "chair," or abstract, such as "justice."

concept maps Diagrams that present ideas in an manner organized by key ideas and their relationships.

concrete operational Piaget's third stage of cognitive development (ages 7–11) in which a new level of sophisticated thinking emerges. The child grasps the concept of conservation in physical qualities. Children learn to make classifications along multiple dimensions, and so make increasingly precise distinctions; they acquire the ability to adopt the perspectives of others.

concurrent validity Evidence that a test measures a distinctive construct within a theoretical system, typically shown by positive correlations with measures of similar constructs.

conditioned reflex A primal response to a stimulus in classical conditioning that is learned by pairing the new stimulus with an old stimulus.

conditioning The term for learning within behaviorist theory.

confidence interval The range of scores within which the true score is located at a known level of probability.

confounded Refers to correlations between two or more potentially causal variables. In behavioral genetics, for example, similarities of lifestyle among relatives that make it difficult to determine the relative contributions of nature and nurture.

consequential validity A form of validity measurement that recognizes that part of a test's meaning is the repercussions it has on learning and its social implications.

conservation The understanding that, in many physical transformations, some qualities of the changing substance remain the same. For example, a liquid being poured into a container of a different shape retains its original volume despite changes in appearance.

construct-irrelevant variance The measurement of variation among people that reflects some trait that is not part of the intended construct.

construct overrepresentation Occurs when a test measures something other than the construct it is intended to measure.

constructs Intangible, abstract traits that are presumed to be enduring properties of people.

construct underrepresentation Occurs when a test falls short of representing the broad construct it is intended to measure.

construct validity The degree to which a test measures the abstract trait it aims to measure.

constructed response A wide range of test item formats in which the examinee generates information as opposed to simply selecting a response from a list, as in multiple-choice questions.

constructivism A philosophy of mind asserting that the mind makes even the simplest perceptions meaningful by filling in information that is not present in the stimulus. At least in part, we construct meaning in order to make sense of our perceptions; a view of learning that sees the learner as active in making sense of the world.

constructivist A view of knowledge that holds that ideas vary in quality, accuracy, and completeness, and are individually created rather than internalized directly from sensory experience.

container model of the mind A misleading assumption that the mind is like a container that holds objects (knowledge) acquired from outside (through learning).

continuing motivation The continued willingness of students to learn as evidenced by the free choices they make.

continuity The idea proposed by John Dewey that in order for an experience to be educational, it must have the potential to be applied broadly to new contexts. To meet this standard, an educational experience must be useful and valuable in future experiences.

continuous reinforcement A behaviorist conditioning method in which an organism is rewarded every time it behaves in the desired way.

contralateral The opposite side of the body. Motor movement is controlled by the contralateral brain hemisphere.

control group The comparison group in an experiment that functions as a baseline in order to determine whether the experimental treatment is effective.

cooperative learning A teaching strategy in which students work in small groups and receive rewards based on group performance rather than individual learning.

corpus callosum The nerve bundle that runs between the two hemispheres; ensures that information is communicated between hemispheres.

correlational A type of study that links variables by stating their degree of association (from −1 to +1) with one another.

correspondence An aspect of truth that evaluates whether or not a claim can be supported by legitimate evidence. Compare with *coherence*.

criterion-referenced A test in which the score is reported on a scale defined by specific competencies within the domain of interest. Contrasts with *norm-referenced*.

critical periods Developmental "windows" that required exposure to certain kinds of environmental stimuli or risk permanent inability to recover.

critical thinking A type of complex cognition that involves evaluating ideas based on their quality and determining their veracity or degree of truth.

crystallized intelligence A form of intelligence entailing knowledge and the ability to acquire knowledge, often in verbal form.

cues Information related to what we are trying to remember; hints that can help evoke knowledge from long-term memory.

culturally responsive pedagogy The hypothesis that instruction can be adapted to fit students' cultural background and so produce superior learning outcomes.

decalage A phenomenon that counters Piaget's stage theory, in which young children reasoned in ways that were characteristic of adolescents or adults on some tasks, but performed in childlike ways in other tasks.

decentrate The capacity to adopt multiple perspectives when making judgments.

declarative knowledge Factual knowledge, such as knowing a phone number; "knowing that."

decoding A sub-process of reading: The translation of written letters, vowels, and consonants into their respective sounds.

deductive reasoning Reasoning from knowledge of established principles to specific conclusions.

deep structure The underlying principles of a domain, such as Newton's Laws in physics, that can help a problem solver to see past the superficial features of a problem and proceed toward an efficient solution.

degree of structure Refers to how explicitly teachers provide information and direction to students.

delay of gratification The decision to put off a reward one could obtain now in order to obtain a more desirable reward later.

deliberate practice In development of expertise, a daily regimen of intense activity designed expressly for improving knowledge and skill in a target domain.

dendrites The branching structures of neurons that receive electrical signals from other neurons. With sufficient depolarization, the dendrites will cause the neuron to "fire."

depolarization A slight reduction in voltage that occurs when a neuron "fires," caused by the rapid influx of sodium into a neuron.

descriptive analysis A form of social research in which the goal is to observe and record the factual information about a situation without attempting to generalize.

determinism A common assumption of behaviorism that present behavior is dictated by past reinforcement. Determinism implies that, because all present behavior is the consequence of previous behavior, there is no true moral responsibility.

discovery A type of inductive reasoning that proceeds from specific data, often about the natural world, to an understanding of a larger pattern or principle.

discovery learning The application of inductive reasoning to an instructional method in which the primary goal is the student's inference of broad explanatory principles from direct experience and personal analysis of data.

discrete item A test item that calls for a brief, simple response. A typical example is a multiple-choice question.

disequilibrium A sense of unsettledness in the mind of an individual based on a conflict between knowledge-based expectations and actual experience. Disequilibrium can lead to *accommodation*.

distal goals Long-term and typically ambitious goals that are less likely to be accomplished than are proximal goals. (Contrasts with *proximal goals*)

distributed intelligence A form of intelligence that is embedded within and sustains cultures; recognizes that social interactions, tools, and other artifacts all contribute to intelligent thought and action.

distributed practice A pattern of practice that spreads learning or study time into numerous sessions; contrasts with *massed practice*.

divergent production The generation of new ideas, such as new uses of common objects or possible connections that extend beyond traditional associations.

dopamine An important brain neurotransmitter that regulates the brain's ability to exercise motor control; underlies the brain's "pleasure system" and reward anticipation.

drive theory A theory that specifies that behavior is motivated by physiological needs such as food, sleep, and sex.

dual coding theory Paivio's theory that recognizes language and mental imagery as two dominant forms of knowledge representation.

dualism A philosophy of being that asserts that reality is both material and nonmaterial.

dyscalculia A learning disability that is identified by a discrepancy between a normal-range IQ and unusual difficulty in learning mathematics.

dyslexia A learning disability that is identified by a discrepancy between a normal-range IQ and low functioning in reading.

dyspraxia A learning disability that is identified by a discrepancy between a normal-range IQ and a person's low ability to coordinate bodily movements in an orderly fashion to obtain a goal.

effect size The magnitude of the benefit, measured in standard deviation units, provided by the treatment in comparison to the control.

ego involvement A framework for judging personal competence by comparing it to the performance of others. (Contrasts with *task involvement*)

egocentrism The inability to take another person's point of view in a given situation, leading to actions that may seem selfish but are simply a reflection of an inability to perform the cognitive task of seeing another's perspective.

elaboration The formation of connections between new knowledge and existing knowledge.

emergent New properties that arise in a complex system that go beyond the features of its compenents; in cognitive psychology, mental qualities that cannot be explained from a reductionist approach.

emotional intelligence A proposed form of intelligence encompassing the ability to "read" and respond to the emotions of other people, as well as the ability to understand one's own emotions.

empiricism A philosophy of knowing (*epistemology*) established by Locke, Berkeley, and Hume; the theory assumes that knowledge always begins with the senses, and that we know with the most certainty that which can be tied directly to sense experience.

encoding specificity The finding that knowledge is best recalled in the same environmental, emotional, or semantic context in which it was learned.

engram Hypothetical construct by which new knowledge changes the brain to form an enduring memory trace.

entity theory A theory of ability that holds that intellectual abilities are fixed and stable throughout life, and that intelligence cannot be increased or decreased. (Contrasts with *incremental theory*)

epiphenomena Incidental byproducts of a more fundamental and real process.

episodic memory A form of memory that that can be accessed to relive a personal experience; such memories can often be "replayed" in a movie-like fashion.

epistemology A branch of philosophy concerned with the nature of knowledge and knowing. It asks, "How do we know what we know?"

equal-odds principle The idea that the probability of producing a highly recognized work product is roughly the same for all contributors, whether eminent achievers or more common experts; implies that eminence is a function of prolific output.

equilibration The mind's tendency toward regaining the mental balance between knowledge and the world as experienced.

essential nutrients Vitamins, minerals, essential fats, and amino acids; molecules that cannot be synthesized in the body but rather must be consumed.

expectancy-value theory A theory of motivation based on the kinds of mental calculations a person makes when facing decisions, and on the nature of information that feeds into those calculations.

experience-dependant development Occurs when specific experience gives rise to the particular synaptic structure of the organism, and leads to abilities that are not necessarily common to the species.

experience-expectant development Occurs when experiences that are typical of a species give rise to normal competencies, such as speech in humans.

experimentation A research method that in pure form entails random assignment to treatment groups, thereby controlling extrinsic variables to ensure an unbiased estimate of an effect.

explicit knowledge Knowledge that can be understood with self-awareness and communicated. to others. (Contrasts with *tacit knowledge*)

external memory Memory that lies outside the brain; for example, a note written to oneself originates from information in personal memory but exists in a physical (external) rather than mental (internal) environment.

extinction The reduction of a learned behavior. Occurs when a lack of reinforcement causes a behavior to diminish in regularity and intensity, or to cease altogether.

extrinsic motivation External motivations that lead a person to engage in an activity for the sake of outside reward or approval, rather than for its own sake.

extrinsic rewards The external rewards a person receives upon completing an activity or executing an activity well, which motivates further engagement in that activity.

factor A single dimension influencing patterns of correlation.

factor analysis A mathematical technique that permits identifying factors that contribute to correlations among variables.

far transfer The application of knowledge to problems and situations that are much different from the original learning context; often difficult or impossible to accomplish.

fear of failure An aversion to negative consequences that can either debilitate or energize a person facing a challenge.

feedback The responses elicited from expert coaches, internalized standards of excellence, or textbooks during practice sessions.

fetal alcohol syndrome A clinical condition among infants born to women who consume large amounts of alcohol during pregnancy; it is characterized by facial abnormalities, and an IQ decrement averaging about 35 points.

field dependence versus field independence A cognitive style construct that refers to whether individuals perceptually isolate an entity (field independence) or whether they take into account the context of that perception (field dependence).

fight or flight response A fear-induced physiological state in which the heart pounds quickly in order to move blood to the outer limbs. This aroused state allows either an aggressive (fight) or protective (flight) response to the fear stimulus.

figure A perceived object as distinguished from its surroundings.

fixed interval reinforcement schedules A reinforcement pattern in which behavior is rewarded when an organism engages in a target behavior after a predetermined period of time.

fixed ratio schedules A reinforcement pattern in which behavior is rewarded after a fixed number of displays of behavior.

flow The zen-like state of consciousness in which subjective feelings of intense concentration on a focal activity can be highly pleasurable.

fluid intelligence A form of intelligence entailing the ability to deal effectively with novel situations through problem solving.

Flynn effect The worldwide trend of rising IQs.

fMRI (functional magnetic resonance imaging) Imaging technique that uses a very large, strong magnet to cause an alignment and disturbance in the body's protons. It records the changes in the levels and forms of hemoglobin that signal changes in blood flow and metabolism, and helps locate fleeting or rapidly changing cognitive activity.

formal operational Piaget's fourth and final stage of cognitive development that can begin as early as 11 and stretch through adulthood. Individuals in this stage can think flexibly about abstract concepts, comprehend multiple causal forces, complete complex classifications, and engage in sophisticated scientific reasoning.

formative assessment A test that is designed to provide feedback to teachers and students during the flow of teaching and learning. (Contrasts with *summative assessment*)

frontal lobe The most distinguishing lobe for complex cognition and metacognition, includes the prefrontal cortex.

fuzzy logic A logic of ideas that allows for degrees of truth or partial category membership.

fuzzy sets Concepts that are not sharply defined, but rather approximate the truth. For example, "the earth is round" is only roughly true because the earth is not perfectly spherical.

general mental ability (g) The dominant dimension of intelligence expressed in the correlation matrices for all tests of cognitive ability. (Contrasts with *s*)

generation effect Occurs in *Type II elaboration*, in which the production or manipulation of new information with existing information produces meaningful, highly memorable connections.

genius An individual who makes outstanding contributions to a field and ultimately leaves a permanent mark on that field.

Gestalt psychology A movement in the early 20th century in which psychologists studied in detail the cognitive act of distinguishing a single object from its surroundings. They asserted that because our senses only have access to incomplete data, our minds must search for patterns in the sensory field to understand it. In essence, we perceive objects as having a form that is more "whole" (or "Gestalt," in German) than it actually is.

glial cells "Support cells" for neurons, making up about 90% of the brain. These cells form the myelin sheath, remove dead tissue, and support neurotransmitters.

globalist hypothesis The belief that the brain as a whole participates in cognition. (Contrasts with *localist hypothesis*)

going underground In Vygotskian theory, the progression from reasoning as social discourse to individual thought spoken aloud to unvocalized thought.

ground The unperceived objects that surround a perceived object (*figure*).

gyrus (gyri) A ridge or protrusion in the cerebral cortex.

habit strength The strength of stimulus-response associations in behaviorism.

Hebbian model The theory that *neurons that fire together, wire together*. Neurons that frequently interact or fire simultaneously experience increased connectivity to one another.

hemispheres The two symmetrical halves of the brain, which play somewhat different roles in cognition.

heritability The extent to which genetics contributes to intelligence or other personal traits. Behavioral geneticists estimate the heritability of intelligence to be roughly 0.5.

heuristics Rules of thumb that increase one's likelihood of success in problem-solving without guaranteeing an effective solution.

high-stakes tests Tests in which the consequences of test scores are highly important, often determining academic or career choices

higher-order interactions Any situation in which multiple factors must be considered in order to choose the most fitting treatment for a student.

hippocampus A small pair of structures located deep within the brain, which has an essential function in long-term memory.

holistic scoring A type of scoring for complex responses that involves separating performances into levels with descriptions for each level. (Contrasts with *analytic scoring*)

horizontal transfer The application of knowledge across situations and contexts, in which knowledge in one area can assist learning or performance in another area.

humanistic psychology A branch of psychology that focuses on psychologically healthy people in order to understand them, and on the application of that understanding to help others realize their potential for psychological health and fulfillment.

hyperactivity A clinical condition characterized by persistent physical activity that interferes with school learning.

idiographic An individualistic approach to understanding human thought and behavior. (Contrasts with *nomothetic*)

ill-structured problems Problems in which the goals and rules for proceeding are fuzzy and require elucidation as problem solving proceeds.

illusion of knowing A learner's misplaced confidence that he or she understands new information, when in fact comprehension is poor.

impulsivity versus reflectivity A cognitive style construct that refers to whether an individual has a tendency to process information and make contingent decisions quickly, or whether he or she has a tendency to give the decision processes more time and consideration before acting.

incremental theory A theory of ability that states that intellectual abilities are highly modifiable through effort and experience. (Contrasts with *entity theory*)

individualized educational program (IEP) A specialized program for special education students that details annual goals for each student, the special education services to be provided, and how progress toward goals is to be measured.

inductive reasoning Reasoning from a specific instance or observation to a general principle.

inert knowledge Knowledge that has no real usefulness, relevance, or meaning.

inference The cognitive act of using available data to draw a new conclusion. Going beyond the data given.

information-processing model A cognitive model that uses computers as a metaphor for how the human mind is structured and how it functions.

insight A type of inductive reasoning in which a meaningful pattern emerges suddenly.

intelligence quotient (IQ) A measure of intelligence that initially used the ratio of a child's mental age to his or her chronological age, and multiplied that ratio by 100 to obtain an IQ. Now computed by position along the normal distribution.

interaction A matching arrangement in which the optimal educational treatment depends on the characteristics of the student.

interference The disruption of new learning by exposure to previous information (proactive interference) or subsequent information (retroactive interference).

interneurons Neurons in the spinal cord that connect sensory neurons to motor neurons; they permit a motor response to sensory stimuli. Interneurons also compose brain neural tissue.

interpretant In Peirce's semiotic theory, the multifaceted meaning or signification behind a specific sign; the chain reaction of ideas and mental images presented upon hearing a word or nonlinguistic signifier.

intrinsic motivation An organism's internal drive to perform a behavior, without exterior prompting or reinforcement. Also, emotional associations that lead a person to engage in an activity for its own sake, rather than for rewards that lie outside the activity.

intrinsic rewards The inherent pleasures of an activity that motivate a person to engage in that activity.

ions Electrically charged molecules.

knowing Holding information, or knowledge, in long-term memory.

la langue In Saussure's semiotic theory, a stable system of signs, especially the web of meanings and relationships composing a language system.

language acquisition device Linguist Noam Chomsky's idea that linguistic capacity is inborn; an expression of nativism.

lateral sulcus A prominent groove in the brain that sits directly above the temporal lobe.

Law of Effect E. L. Thorndike's idea that behavior followed by rewards is more likely to be repeated than behavior that is not followed by rewards.

learned helplessness An attribute of people who, through experience, become extremely passive toward the circumstances of their lives; people who are so oriented feel that they can do nothing that will lead to their own success.

learning The acquisition of knowledge; the cognitive act of moving information from temporary working memory to enduring long-term memory.

learning disabilities Disorders of basic cognitive processes involved in understanding or using language or mathematics among students of normal intelligence.

learning goals Goals established to increase personal competence. (Contrasts with *performance goals*)

learning styles Characteristic, individual modes of acquiring knowledge.

left-brain thinkers A faulty categorization that certain individuals favor their "left brain," meaning that they prefer to think analytically and are detail-oriented.

linguistic turn A philosophical shift away from attempts to anchor epistemologies in the physical world or in rational thought as means to establish certain knowledge. Instead, sees meaning as negotiable and bound to language and culture.

lobes The four major areas of the cerebral cortex: the frontal, parietal, temporal, and occipital lobes.

local independence A test quality in which each item is independent of all others; exposure to one test item should not help or hinder performance on another item.

localist hypothesis The belief that cognition is identifiable with specific areas of the brain. (Contrasts with *globalist hypothesis*)

locus of control A motivational orientation in which people place the blame or credit for events either within or outside themselves.

logical positivism An intellectual movement to build a philosophy with strong epistemological foundations by reducing knowledge to its most simple (and presumably factual) components.

long-term memory The huge mental storehouse of knowledge, including knowledge of people, places, things, skills, behavior patterns, and personal experiences.

long-term potentiation Significant structural changes to neurons involving the durable strengthening of synapses or the formation of new synapses.

massed and distributed practice (law of) A general principles that summarizes the relationship between learning and time; asserts the advantages of multiple learning sessions (*distributed practice*) over a single learning session (*massed practice*), when time is held constant.

massed practice A pattern of practice that combines all study or learning time into a single session or small number of sessions; less effective than *distributed practice*.

mastery learning A teaching approach designed to provide all students with the time needed for each to learn. Students are required to achieve mastery (to a certain performance criterion) on a formative test before they are allowed to move on to the next unit or instruction period.

mean The mathematical average of all measured values.

means-ends analysis A problem-solving heuristic in which the goal is not to solve a problem in a single step, but rather to make progress toward the eventual goal. Normally, this heuristic is applied repeatedly.

measurement contamination Occurs when the intended construct is inaccurately measured due to the measurement tapping traits that are incidental, rather than central, to the construct.

measurement-driven instruction A model in which testing is openly recognized as a major driving force behind teaching and learning, and the washback effects of testing on teaching and learning are intentional.

measurement error The effect of various contributors to a test's unreliability.

mental age The age assigned to a child based on performance on certain tasks or items.

mental discipline hypothesis The idea that, through training the mind in one subject, such as Latin or chess, the knowledge gained can improve performance in other, distantly related subjects.

mental model Dynamic mental imagery; a moving picture "seen" in the mind"s eye, such as planets revolving at different speeds and distances from the sun. Synonymous with *runnable mental model*.

metacognition The monitoring and control of one's own thought; "thinking about thinking." This form of complex cognition occurs when a person monitors and controls cognition—including comprehension and problem-solving—to make it more effective.

metamemory A person's ability to accurately appraise what she does and does not know.

method variance The contribution of format-specific test skill to test scores.

mind-body problem Attempts to describe the connection between the body (a material reality) and the mind (sometimes presumed a nonmaterial reality).

mindfulness Thinking through situations by asking whether ideas or actions are working, whether they make sense, and whether they are consistence with available knowledge and evidence. (Contrasts with *mindlessness*)

mindlessness The ridiculously foolish or absurd ways in which people sometimes act, often within prescribed "social scripts." (Contrasts with *mindfulness*)

minimal competency testing A form of measurement-driven instruction that intends to guarantee that students have at least basic skills, especially in literacy and numeracy.

mode The value that is most frequent within a distribution of data.

modular Brain functions that are innate (unlearned), and stored in brain areas dedicated to specific information processes.

monism A philosophy of being that asserts that the only reality is the material world.

mood-congruent processing A particular form of encoding specificity; states that knowledge is recalled more effectively when the emotional context of remembering matches the emotional context of initial learning.

morphemes Word and word parts, such as prefixes and suffixes, that are basic units of meaning in language.

motivation All factors and processes that lead to a decision about a course of action or goal. (Contrasts with *volition*)

motivational equity A broad societal goal that all students should have the motivational resources to be successful learners.

motor neurons Neurons whose function is to relay signals from the central nervous system to muscle groups throughout the body.

multiple-choice A type of test item that poses a question and presents a limited number of response options, from which the examinee must choose the correct answer.

multiple intelligences (MI) theory Howard Gardner's theory that there is not a general mental ability but rather separate, independent intelligences: logical-mathematical, linguistic, spatial, musical, bodily-kinesthetic, interpersonal, intrapersonal, and naturalist.

multitasking Occurs when attention is divided among multiple competing goals.

myelin The fatty insulation covering an axon, which speeds up the signal in a neuron.

naive realism The simplistic assumption that knowledge is strictly an uncomplicated internalization of the material world—that what the mind knows is an accurate version of external truth.

naive theories Semi-coherent systems of explanation in which people fabricate their own (incorrect) theories in an attempt to make sense of the world.

nativism The theory that the brain is pre-wired to perform certain cognitive tasks. Through native brain modules, organisms can display unmodeled behaviors of their species from infancy.

near transfer The application of knowledge to situations that are similar to the original learning context, often without much difficulty.

need for achievement A personality trait reflected in the ongoing desire to use talent to become successful. Also known as *achievement motivation*.

need for cognition Variation among people in their tendency to engage in and enjoy cognition.

negative punishment Punishes an organism's behavior by removing a desirable stimulus (e.g., taking away a rebellious teenager's privilege driving the family car).

negative reinforcement Rewards an organism's behavior by removing an unpleasant stimulus (e.g., reducing a well-behaved inmate's prison time).

negative transfer A maladaptive form of transfer in which knowledge or skill in one area hinders knowledge acquisition or skilled performance in a different area. (Contrasts with *positive transfer*)

neobehaviorists Behaviorists who refuse to accept that behavior is based *only* on stimulus and response and who factor an organism's enduring characteristics into the behaviorist model. Neobehaviorism can be roughly reduced to the model: stimulus → organism → response.

neo-Piagetian Theories built on Piaget's original ideas; they reject the all-embracing logic of Piaget's theory, but retain a stage-like progression in modeling the intellectual advancement of the child.

neural circuits Multiple brain sites that coordinate to produce complex cognitive performance.

neural network A computer architecture in which specific information is not locatable to a single spot in the computer, but rather is spread across many pieces of the hardware. Compare with *von Neumann machine*

neurogenesis The formation of new neurons.

neurons Individual nerve cells that make up the nervous system and allow the mind to operate, including coordination of sensory and motor functions. Neurons are often quite long and can communicate with one another through electro-chemical impulses.

neuroscience The study of neural structure and function. Cognitive neuroscientists seek connections between thought processes and brain structure.

neurotransmitters Chemicals released at the end of an axon that move across the synapse and are taken up by the dendrites of a second neuron, possibly causing the next neuron to fire.

neurotrophins Locally acting hormones that induce the proliferation of neurons as well as stimulate vascularization. They are released through both cognition and exercise and can enhance brain function.

noble savage Rousseau's idea that the innocent state of a child is corrupted by the surrounding society, but that given sufficient freedom from these corrupting agents, a child could retain his original goodness or nobility.

node-link structures A way of representing knowledge in long-term memory as a network of concepts (as nodes) and relationships (as links). Also known as *semantic networks*.

nomothetic An approach to understanding human thought and behavior intended to result in law-like general statements. (Contrasts with *idiographic*)

norm-referenced A kind of test in which the score is reported on a scale defined by the group performance or norm; a score derives its meaning from its position relative to other scores. (Contrasts with *criterion-referenced*)

normal distribution (normal curve) The "bell curve" that represents the natural variation, such as in test scores, in which medium values are common and both high and low values are comparatively rare.

norms Average performance standards for a certain age group.

objective items Test formats, such as multiple-choice, in which the scoring is made with high reliability based on clearly stated correct answers.

object permanence The ability to understand that though an object is hidden from view, it still exists.

observed score An actual test score that estimates a student's ability, but also reflects some measurement error. (Contrasts with *true score*)

occipital lobe The area of the brain that is set just above the cerebellum at the back of the brain, known for its role in processing visual information. Also known as the *visual cortex*.

Ockham's razor The principle that if a simple explanation can take the place of a more complex one, the simpler one is preferable.

ontology A branch of philosophy concerned with the nature of reality or being; poses the question, "What is real in the universe?"

operant A random behavior that is generated by an organism.

operant conditioning A behaviorist version of learning, advanced by B. F. Skinner, that is composed of three stages: stimulus, response, and reinforcement. It differs from classical conditioning in that it takes into account how the consequences of a behavior affect its repetition (the principle of reinforcement).

operation A physical change in an environment.

operationalized The manner in which theoretical constructs are measured.

origin A person with an internal locus of control who tends to see himself or herself as responsible for events, whether good or bad. (Contrasts with *pawn*)

overjustification A mental calculation that occurs when either extrinsic or intrinsic rewards are sufficient to motivate a person to engage in an activity. Often occurs when extrinsic rewards are so plentiful that the person loses intrinsic motivation because it is no longer necessary to explain the motivation for the behavior.

parallel data processor Synonym of *neural network*.

parietal lobe The area of the brain that extends backward over the top of the head and processes somatosensory input.

parole In Saussure's semiotics theory, refers to specific uses of language such as a spoken sentence; demonstrates the freshness and creative potential within the stable structure of language (*la langue*).

parsing Dividing and connecting a continuous sound stream into a meaningful organization of words, phrases, and larger units of discourse.

pattern recognition A function of a *neural network* in which the machine learns to connect information inputs and category outputs by means of a complex system of feedback loops.

pawn A person with an external locus of control who sees other people or circumstances as responsible for personal events. (Contrasts with *origin*)

peer-assessment An assessment involving students evaluating the work of their peers, providing feedback about the quality of work, and giving insight into how the work can be improved.

percentile rank Any test value translated into a percentile equivalent to facilitate comparison to other examinees.

perception The cognitive act of imposing order on sensory data as it enters working memory. Perception follows sensation; perceptual processes interpret sensory data in order to make sense of it.

performance assessment Tests that allow students to demonstrate their proficiency through constructive activity that typically has some intrinsic value.

performance goals Goals established with the ultimate purpose of gaining the positive judgments of other people. (Contrasts with *learning goals*)

perseveration The continuation of action despite its ineffectiveness or inefficiency.

PET (positron emission tomography) A brain imaging technique that requires the injection of a small dose of radioactive glucose tracer that is taken up by cells proportional to how active they are. The image records differential glucose uptake, which reflects varying levels of heightened neuron activity.

phi phenomenon An illusion in which two alternating lights are interpreted to be a single oscillating light; illustrates the perceptual tendencies by the mind to "fill in" missing details to make the pattern intelligible.

phonemic awareness The understanding that spoken words can be broken down into their constituent sounds (phonemes), and that phonemes can be blended together to form words; skill in this process.

phonics An approach to teaching reading that emphasizes learning letter-sound correspondences.

positive manifold The common pattern of positive correlations among tests of mental ability.

positive psychology A movement of psychology that focuses on the study and advancement of health, well-being, success, and happiness. Similar to the older movement of humanistic psychology.

positive punishment Punishes an organism's behavior by administering an unpleasant stimulus (e.g., corporal punishment).

positive reinforcement Rewards an organism's behavior by administering a desirable stimulus (e.g., the tip a waitress receives for good service).

positive transfer A useful form of transfer in which knowledge learned in one knowledge or skill domain assists learning or skill performance in a different domain. (Contrasts with *negative transfer*)

posteriorization The shifting of brain activity away from the frontal cortex toward the parietal, temporal, and occipital lobes. This signifies increasing automaticity in the novice-expert progression.

postsynaptic neuron The neuron that receives neurotransmitters crossing the synapse; maintains signal that originates from the presynaptic neuron.

pragmatic A category of linguistic analysis; use of language to accomplish practical goals.

pre-frontal cortex The area within the frontal lobe that controls attention, planning, decision making, goal-setting, strategic reasoning, and self-monitoring.

predictive validity The degree to which a test predicts a student's success or failure in school or similar educational environment, or that predicts other future performance connected to the measured trait.

preoperational Piaget's second stage of cognitive development (ages 2–7) in which a child's mind is increasingly independent of the immediate environment. The child grasps object permanence and begins to use language and explore abstract concepts, but still is limited by his egocentrism.

presynaptic neuron The neuron that releases the neurotransmitters into the synapse in order to relay a signal to another neuron.

primacy effect A memory effect in which ideas presented toward the beginning of a learning experience are more memorable than those in the middle of a series.

primary mental abilities In Thurstone's historical theory of intelligence, the independent cognitive abilities that countered Spearman's view that intelligence is unified around a common factor. These abilities include: numerical skill, verbal comprehension, word fluency, space, reasoning, memory, and perceptual speed.

primary motor cortex Region of the cortex at the posterior edge of the frontal lobe; controls motor responses especially as they relate to somatosensory input.

priming A cognitive process in which concepts are partially activated so as to be more easily accessible, while at the same time being not quite activated enough to bring them to conscious awareness.

prior knowledge Information that an individual already knows; the "foundation" to which new knowledge can connect and be made meaningful during learning.

problem finding The task of imagining potential problems, and determining which problems are worthy of efforts to solve them.

problem solving A type of complex thinking that involves pursuing a goal when the path to that goal is unclear.

problem space In problem solving, includes all possible options connecting an initial state to a goal state; all acceptable ways to solve a problem.

procedural knowledge Knowing *how* to do things, such as make a sandwich or ride a bicycle.

process-product research A research orientation concerned with finding optimal teaching methods by identifying teaching processes that produce measurable student learning.

prodigies Children who exhibit very high levels of proficiency in a certain area, such as music, mathematics, or art.

productions If-then statements in computer programs or models of cognition.

production system A series of if-then rules (productions) that can model thought or behavior.

programmed instruction A behaviorist curriculum that breaks down learning into discrete units in order to help students reach specific educational objectives.

progressive education An educational movement developed in the early 20th century movement that sparked experimentation with a student-centered, activity-oriented curriculum.

projective test A highly subjective test that presents ambiguous stimuli and asks the examinee to say what each stimulus means to them. The significances they attribute to the stimuli are analyzed in order to gain insight into the personality of the examinee.

proximal goals Near-term goals that are typically within reach; such goals inspire perceptions of competence, and intrinsically motivate practical action. (Contrasts with *distal goals*)

pruning A long-term reduction in the number of brain synapses; a normal mechanism of cognitive development.

psychometric model The paradigm that complex personal traits, including knowledge and cognitive abilities, can be measured in a way that parallels the measurement of physical qualities, such as weight and distance.

psychometric theory A theoretical perspective that assumes that properties of the mind can be measured along particular dimensions, such as intelligence or knowledge in particular subject areas.

punisher In operant conditioning, any consequence that makes a behavior less likely. It is the counterpart to a reinforcer in operant conditioning.

punishment A learning process that makes a displayed behavior less likely to re-occur. Two forms are positive punishment and negative punishment.

purposive behaviorism The theoretical branch of behaviorism that holds that an organism's behavior can be purposeful, as if guided by a goal.

qualitative research A variety of observational methods that emphasize detailed description and analysis.

quantitative research A variety of methods that emphasize numerical measurement of constructs and quantification of relationships among constructs.

radical doubt Descartes' method of doubting all knowledge in order to build certain knowledge from the ground up. He found that only one truth was absolutely certain: his own existence, which in turn provided the basis for deducing other realities.

random assignment The random placement of subjects in experimental and groups; designed to minimize differences between groups in cognitive ability, prior knowledge, or health and ensure an unbiased estimate of treatment effects.

rationalism A philosophy of knowledge (epistemology) that counters *empiricism* by asserting that the senses cannot be completely trusted, and that rational thought is the most trustworthy basis of knowledge.

raw score The most basic measure of test performance; the point value of a particular examinee on a particular test.

reactive covariance The phenomenon in which a child's genetic predisposition toward a certain skill is recognized and supported by his parents or others, causing the genetic predisposition to be amplified by experiences provided by the surrounding culture. Compare with *active covariance*

realm theory Perkins' theory that we can become so comfortable and familiar with a body of knowledge that we feel at home in it. In this way, the knowledge domain becomes our "realm."

recall The ability to generate information from long-term memory. (Contrasts with *recognition*)

recency effect A memory effect in which ideas presented toward the end of a learning experience are usually more memorable than those in the middle of a series.

reciprocal teaching A teaching method that aims to improve reading comprehension in which the students and teacher study a common text. Using this method, each student has occasion to lead the group as a teacher, and the teacher becomes a participant in the group.

recognition The ability to recognize familiar information when presented externally rather than internally generated. (Contrasts with *recall*)

reductionism A philosophy of knowledge that assumes the best possible explanations for phenomena require analyzing processes into their smallest components.

reference What a word indicates in the physical world.

reflection The act of deeply considering the ideas that one engages, the evidence for those ideas, and their implications.

reflex arc The three-neuron relay spanning a sensory neuron, interneuron, and motor neuron; allows adaptive reflex behavior without having to first involve the brain in conscious decision making.

rehearsal A basic strategy of repetition used to remember information; repeating the new information mentally or audibly keeps it active in working memory, assisting the formation of a long-term memory trace.

reinforcement A consequence to a behavior that leads to the repetition of that behavior. Two forms are positive reinforcement and negative reinforcement.

reinforcement schedules Refers to different ways of administering reinforcement, including continuous reinforcement, fixed ratio schedules, variable ratio schedules, fixed interval schedules, and variable interval schedules.

reinforcer In operant conditioning, any action that increases the likelihood of a behavior.

reliability A test quality that gauges how accurate and dependable a test is based on the replicability of the score it yields.

remembering The movement of information stored in long-term memory into working memory for conscious processing and use.

repolarization An increase in voltage across a neuron membrane that readies a neuron to "fire" again, caused by the outflow of potassium ions from the neuron.

resilience The quality of being unusually successful despite being "at risk" because of unfavorable circumstances associated with poverty.

response The behavioral effect of a stimulus. In Pavlov's experiment, for example, the response (salivation) was brought on by the stimulus (the sound of footsteps).

response-elimination strategy The test-taking strategy that involves eliminating implausible response options and therefore improving the chances for a correct response on multiple-choice questions.

restructuring The major overhaul of a schema; a complete rethinking of the order and logic of one's beliefs or understanding about a topic.

retrieval A cognitive process involving access to information stored in long-term memory. Synonymous with *remembering*.

retrograde amnesia A loss of memory for past events.

reverse engineering Similar to "working backward," a design process that starts with the finished product and proceeds to take something apart or ask what steps went into its construction, with the ultimate goal of re-creating that product.

reversibility Mental undoing or reversal of a change in the environment that permits separation of what changes from what is conserved.

right-brain thinkers A faulty categorization that certain individuals favor their "right-brain," meaning that they prefer to think holistically and in mental images.

rubric A scoring guide used to evaluate and score complex responses in a test.

runnable mental model Dynamic mental imagery that displays a cause-and-effect pattern, useful for reasoning through or making predictions about problems.

s In Spearman's historical theory of intelligence, the factor of unique variability inherent in each intelligence test. [Contrasts with *general mental ability (g)*.]

sampling The representative selection of test items intended measure a student's capability on a certain construct; "sampled" test items reflect hypothetical performance on a larger set of items within that domain.

Sapir-Whorf hypothesis The perspective that language shapes and constrains thought, and so different languages offer different categories for framing knowledge.

scaffolding The skilled assistance lent to learners by teachers, parents, or other adults.

schema A cluster of knowledge about a concept or object.

scientific reasoning The study of natural phenomena that combines systematic isolation, independent manipulation, and control of variables to make inferences about causal relations.

scoring reliability The degree to which test scoring is consistent; the replicability of scoring accuracy. Higher scoring reliability contributes to higher overall test reliability.

scoring rubric A scoring guide used for constructed response test items that communicates the valued characteristics of a response and permits reliable scoring. Same as *rubric*.

script A procedure-oriented schema that guides actions in familiar situations, such as restaurants.

search The amount of time and the level of cognitive engagement given to any conclusion or decision.

seat time The amount of time nominally allocated to learning, but not necessarily reflective of the time the student is actually learning.

selective impairment Clinical effects in which localized brain damage will compromise one "intelligence," while leaving the others intact. Used in the rationale of Gardner's multiple intelligences theory.

self-actualization In humanistic psychology, the rare state of personal development reached when a person attains his or her highest potential as a human being—when a person is the best possible version of himself or herself.

self-assessment An assessment in which a learner appraises his or her own success in learning and adjusts his or her learning habits accordingly.

self-efficacy A person's sense of his or her own capability in a specific performance or skill domain. Estimates that people make about their ability to perform specific actions in specific cognitive or performance domains.

self-fulfilling prophecy The hypothesis that other peoples' positive or negative beliefs about an individual's ability strongly affect his or her performance.

self-regulation strategies Strategies people employ in order to be more cognitively effective, including goal setting, planning, seeking information, monitoring progress, and reducing distractions.

self-worth theory Explores peoples' motives to act in ways that elevate other peoples' opinions of them or that shield them from low opinions.

semantic networks A way of modeling knowledge in long-term memory as a collection of concepts related by meaning. Also known as *node-link structures*.

semantic universe All the semiotic signs within a given culture.

semiotics The study of signs that, by convention, constitute the webs of meaning in any society. Language is an important subset of semiotic signs.

sensation The brief preconscious recording of environmental stimuli in the sensory register that occurs when data impinges on our eyes, ears, and other senses.

sense The intellectual meaning of a word, or what it symbolizes, as distinct from what it actually means in the physical world (*reference*)

sensorimotor Piaget's first stage of cognitive development in which understanding is rooted in present action. Children ages 0–2 learn primarily through movement in and manipulation of their physical world and by gaining information about it through their senses.

sensorium The total sensory system of the human body.

sensory neurons Neurons whose function is to receive signals and transmit them to the central nervous system.

sensory register The first stop in the mind after information reaches the sensory organs; holds information very briefly (a few seconds or less) in high-fidelity form.

serial position curve A U-shaped curve showing that ideas presented at the beginning and the end of a learning experience (e.g., a lecture or conversation) are usually the most memorable.

seriation The ordering of objects along a single dimension, such as size, height, or weight.

serotonin An important brain neurotransmitter that regulates memory, emotions, wakefulness, sleep, temperature, and blood pressure.

shaping The process by which a teacher or trainer rewards behavior in order to gradually evoke a more ideal behavior pattern in an organism. Synonymous with *successive approximations*.

short-term memory The memory structure holding one's current thoughts; the locus of consciousness; roughly synonymous with *working memory*.

short-term potentiation A form of learning that involves temporary changes in efficiency of communication across existing synapses.

signified Part of any sign: the meaning and concept triggered by a signifier

signifier Part of any sign: the stimulus that triggers meaning, such as a spoken word.

sign Any semiotic entity that conveys meaning, including language, symbols, and gestures.

situated cognition The perspective that knowledge is not simply mental content, but is expressed in and constituted by the goals, practices, people, language, and tools in a culture.

social construction of knowledge The idea that knowledge about the world is largely a product of the human mind's efforts to find order in the world and to share that order with others.

social intelligence A proposed form of intelligence encompassing the ability to interact intelligently with other people.

social learning theory A theory put forth by Albert Bandura that recognizes that social observation and imitation play a large role in human learning.

socioeconomic status (SES) The social class of a family as understood through such categories as wealthy, middle-class, working class, and poor.

soma The portion of a neuron that contains the nucleus; the cell body.

somatosensory cortex Area of the cerebral cortex at the front edge of the parietal lobe, just behind the central sulcus; processes sensory input from the body, including touch, temperature, pain, and posture.

specific goals Precisely stated goals with clear criteria used to determine whether or not they have been achieved. (Contrasts with *abstract goals*)

speech acts A linguistic theory that language often accomplishes goals that have little or nothing to do with naming things.

spinal cord The bundle of nerves that runs directly in front of the spine and is attached to the brainstem. It relays sensory information to the brain and, conversely, brain signals that control muscles.

split-brain Individuals who have had their corpus collosum surgically severed, resulting in no communication between the left and right hemispheres of the brain.

spreading activation model Within a semantic network, the process in which thinking about one idea can lead to thoughts about related ideas.

stages Discrete periods of human development marked by stability within stages and rather large changes between stages.

standard deviation The measurement of how far a particular value deviates from the mean.

standard error of measurement Expresses the likely difference between a true score and an observed score.

standard score(s) The raw score converted to numeric values that place test performance on a normal distribution defined by a mean and a standard deviation. Standard scores are informative about a student's performance relative to other test-takers.

standardized testing A form of assessment in which the conditions are kept as uniform as possible to permit fair comparisons among scores; instructions and time allotment are consistent among test-takers.

statistically significant Describes whether differences between groups are real, rather than simply the result of chance (sampling error) differences between groups.

stimulus Any sensory experience. A stimulus may cause a behavioral response. In Pavlov's experiment, the stimulus (the sound of footsteps) caused the dog's response (salivation).

stimulus discrimination Perception of a discrepancy between two stimuli that produces a learned response to one but not the other.

stimulus generalization An expansion of an original stimulus to include similar stimuli. The similar stimuli evoke the same response in an organism as the original stimulus.

student-teacher ratio The proportion of students relative to teachers in an educational setting.

styles Personal qualities that are distinguishable from abilities; a particular style is not necessarily beneficial or detrimental, but simply different.

subgoaling The act of breaking down large goals into smaller, more manageable subgoals.

subordinate concepts A lower-order, more specific concept (e.g., *Mars* is subordinate to *planet*).

successful intelligence Robert Sternberg's theory that intelligence is a broad personal quality consisting of three different types of intelligence: analytical, practical, and creative.

successive approximations The process by which a teacher or trainer rewards behavior as it progresses toward its ideal complex form. Synonymous with *shaping*.

sulcus (sulci) A groove in the cerebral cortex.

summative assessment A test that estimates the total effect of an educational experience on learning. (Contrasts with *formative assessment*)

superficial learning A quality of learning that entails relatively meaningless connections between new knowledge and existing knowledge; does not produce significant or long-term understanding of the new knowledge. Can be a product of *Type I* elaboration.

superordinate concepts A higher-order, more general concept (e.g., *planet* is superordinate to *Mars*).

surface features The particular objects or terms given in the description of problems that may distract novices from attending to *deep structure*.

syllogism The most basic reasoning form in traditional logic, including two premises that naturally lead to a conclusion.

synapse The gap between two neurons through which neurotransmitters pass in order to relay signals from one neuron to another.

synaptogenesis The massive proliferation of synapses during the first three years of life. Synonymous with *blooming*.

syntax Rules of language use; grammar.

synthetic a priori Synthetic (discoverable) knowledge that is known before an actual experience of that thing.

synthetic statement A statement that is true by discovery, not simply by definition. For example, the synthetic statement "the earth is round" is true, but not implicit in the definition of earth (i.e., the earth could have been a different shape).

tacit knowledge Unconscious, incommunicable knowledge, such as often characterizes a skill—we know how to do something, but cannot explain it. (Contrasts with *explicit knowledge*)

task involvement A framework for judging personal competence in which people judge their competence at a task based on their own past performance. (Contrasts with *ego involvement*)

teacher-centered An educational approach in which the teacher is the focal point of learners' attention and the presumed authority and source of knowledge. Typically, obedience and order are highly valued; group work, discussion, and creative expression may be avoided.

teaching machines A precursor to computer-based learning, teaching machines immediately rewarded correct answers and punished incorrect answers in order to optimize operant conditioning–based learning.

teaching to the test A washback effect in which educators feel pressured to adjust their teaching and curriculum to the content and format of the test in order to boost their students' test scores.

temporal lobe Sits along both sides of the brain just under the lateral sulcus; processes complex auditory information, especially language, and assists in speech production.

ten-year rule The general rule that the acquisition of expert knowledge and skill requires a time investment on the order of ten years of concentrated study and practice.

terminal boutons Knob-like structures at the end of the fibers at the end of a neuron's axon that release signaling chemicals called *neurotransmitters*.

test anxiety An individual trait manifest as worry or fear in a test situation; can be highly debilitating to test performance and can contaminate construct validity.

test battery A kit of diverse tests that yield an overall IQ score, typically giving a better estimate of general intelligence than one test alone.

test bias A detrimental quality of assessment in which a test unfairly relegates some students to low scores and diminished opportunity and advantages others. A biased test predisposes some examinees to achieve high scores based on knowledge or experience that it not directly relevant to the measured construct.

test items Individual test questions or tasks that ask for a response.

testwiseness The student's knowledge of test-taking skills that can assist performance on the test, and that contributes to construct overrepresentation.

thinking dispositions The ability and propensity to think in productive ways, including the tendency to think clearly, critically, and creatively, in appropriate contexts.

time on task The amount of time that is dedicated to thinking and learning.

tip of the tongue phenomenon The experience of knowledge at the edge of one's awareness, without quite being able to retrieve it.

token economy A teaching approach that reinforces behavioral learning with nonvaluable objects (i.e. poker chips) that can be later exchanged for desirable items of the learner's choice.

top-down processing Mental processing that begins with a concept and uses known information about that concept to prompt the search for confirmatory details in a sensory experience. Uses the concept to fill in missing details to complete a sensory perception.

tracking The separation of students into independent curricular streams that vary in academic rigor; a one-time academic placement tends to be repeated and made more robust in subsequent years.

transfer The application of knowledge learned in one context to a new context, such as the use of an abstract principle in real-life problems. Transfer occurs, for example, when academic knowledge takes on meaning, significance, or utility outside the classroom.

transformational grammars The (usually implicit) rules we use when changing sentences from questions to statements, and vice versa, involving shifts in word order and in the tones used.

treatment In educational research, especially experiments, any identifiable educational experience, such as a new curriculum.

treatment group A group that receives an experimental treatment in an attempt to determine whether that treatment is preferable to the experience of a control group.

triadic reciprocality Bandura's model that recognizes three components that exhibit mutual influence: the person, the environment, and behavior.

trial and error A simple heuristic that relies on trying each possible option within a problem space until one achieves the desired outcome or state.

trilogy of mind The ancient understanding of the human psyche as composed of cognition, affect, and conation.

true score The hypothetical score of a perfect test, one free from measurement error (if such a test existed). (Contrasts with *observed score*)

tuning The correction of knowledge within a schema.

two-factor theory In Spearman's historical theory of intelligence, the proposal that performance on each mental test is derived from two sources: *g* (the factor common to all mental tests), and *s* (a "factor" specific to each mental test).

two-sigma effect A theoretical maximum of benefit from instructional innovations; quantifies the benefits of one-on-one tutoring in comparison to instruction in a typical classroom; refers to a learning increase with an effect size equivalent to two standard deviations (two sigma) above the mean.

Type I elaboration Describes learning in which connecting new knowledge to prior knowledge requires little real understanding of the new knowledge. For example, memorizing a definition solely by repetition, without understanding it in a meaningful way.

Type II elaboration Meaningful connection of new knowledge with existing knowledge in a way that produces greater understanding of both, and that makes the new information more memorable.

understanding The meaningful comprehension of information, entailing an ability to extend what is already known in order to gain new insights, and to find new implications and applications of knowledge.

unlimited semiosis The idea that a sign carries infinite potential to signify chains of meaning. A sign can spark an idea, which sparks another, and so on, *ad infinitum*.

validity The most important test quality; refers to whether and to what degree a test measures what it is intended to measure.

value-differentiated A quality of cognitive and learning styles, in which having more or less of a particular style is not better or worse, but simply different.

value-directional A quality of abilities in which having more is better than having less.

variable interval schedules A reinforcement pattern in which the desired behavior is reinforced after random time intervals.

variable ratio schedules A reinforcement pattern in which the target behavior is reinforced after a randomly fluctuating number of behavior displays.

variance A quantified measurement of variation; mathematically, the square of the standard deviation.

vertical transfer Transfer of knowledge within a complex skill, in which simpler skills combine to permit a more complex performance or understanding.

visual cortex See *occipital lobe*.

visual sensory register The brief visual memory available to be "replayed" for about a half-second after it has been seen.

volition Processes following a decision that guide action toward a particular goal. (Contrasts with *motivation*)

von Neumann machine A computer architecture that is the basis for almost all existing digital computers. In such a machine, content is fixed to a single location in the computer's memory and computation is done serially.

washback effect The phenomenon in which the anticipation of the effects of a test can feed back to influence the processes of learning and teaching that lead up to the test.

Wernicke's area An area of the left hemisphere that allows individuals to comprehend language and to produce coherent speech.

whole-language A method of teaching reading that asserts that learning to read should be a natural process in which reading skills are acquired as children are immersed into literature and writing.

whole-word method An instructional method that involves concentrating on words as the units of learning. A precursor of the *whole-language* approach.

working backward A heuristic that begins with the desired goal, and asks, "What would be the step just prior to achieving this goal?" By proceeding backward the problems solver can construct a path from distal goals to more proximal, reachable goals.

working forward A heuristic characteristic of experts that relies on recognizing familiar elements within a problem situation and taking appropriate steps based on such familiar patterns.

working memory Similar to *short-term memory*, but also suggests the function of mental work or transformation in addition to temporary storage.

Yerkes-Dodson Law A psychological principle that recognizes optimal performance is associated with moderate states of arousal, and that for any given activity, performance will suffer if the level of arousal is too low or too high.

zone of proximal development A Vygotskian concept that sees each learner as having an ideal learning "zone" defined by the difference between the competence of a person acting alone and what that person can achieve with the skilled assistance of others.

AUTHOR INDEX

SUBJECT INDEX